Lecture Notes in Computer Science 7976

Commenced Publication in 1973
Founding and Former Series Editors:
Gerhard Goos, Juris Hartmanis, and Jan van Leeuwen

Ezio Bartocci   C.R. Ramakrishnan (Eds.)

Model Checking Software

20th International Symposium, SPIN 2013
Stony Brook, NY, USA, July 8-9, 2013
Proceedings

 Springer

Volume Editors

Ezio Bartocci
TU Wien
Faculty of Informatics
Favoritenstr. 9-11, 1084 Vienna, Austria
E-mail: ezio.bartocci@gmail.com

C.R. Ramakrishnan
Stony Brook University
Computer Science Department
Stony Brook, NY 11794-4400, USA
E-mail: cram@cs.stonybrook.edu

ISSN 0302-9743   e-ISSN 1611-3349
ISBN 978-3-642-39175-0   e-ISBN 978-3-642-39176-7
DOI 10.1007/978-3-642-39176-7
Springer Heidelberg Dordrecht London New York

Library of Congress Control Number: 2013941132

CR Subject Classification (1998): D.2.4-5, D.2, D.3, F.3

LNCS Sublibrary: SL 1 – Theoretical Computer Science and General Issues

Typesetting: Camera-ready by author, data conversion by Scientific Publishing Services, Chennai, India

Printed on acid-free paper

Springer is part of Springer Science+Business Media (www.springer.com)

Preface

This volume contains the proceedings of the International SPIN Symposium on Model Checking of Software (SPIN 2013), which was held at Stony Brook University during July 8–9, 2013. SPIN 2013 marked the 20th anniversary of the SPIN workshop series.

The SPIN series is an annual forum for researchers and practitioners interested in verification of software systems. The traditional focus of SPIN has been on explicit-state model-checking techniques, as implemented in SPIN and other related tools. While such techniques are still of key interest to the workshop, its scope has broadened over recent years to include techniques for the verification and formal testing of software systems in general.

SPIN 2013 featured an invited lecture by Dirk Beyer (University of Passau) on "Reuse of Verification Results," and an invited tutorial by Gerard Holzmann (NASA/JPL) on "Proving Properties of Concurrent Programs." In his lecture, Dirk Beyer showed how the resources used in verification can be reduced by making the results of verification runs reusable. In particular, he focused on using conditional model checking, precision reuse, and verification witnesses to guide future verification runs. In his tutorial, Gerard Holzmann cited the increasing use of static analyzers in industrial software development, even though static analyzers yield false negatives as well as false positives. He then showed how SPIN can be used for analyzing multi-threaded programs, without false positives, while retaining some of the usability and speed of static analyzers.

SPIN 2013 received 40 submissions, from which the Program Committee accepted 18 regular papers and two tool demonstration papers. All papers received at least three reviews. The paper selection process involved extensive discussion among the members of the Program Committee and external reviewers. The status of the papers was decided once a consensus was reached in the committee.

We are extremely grateful to the members of the Program Committee and their sub-reviewers for their insightful reviews and discussion. The editors are also grateful to the authors of the accepted papers for revising the papers according to the suggestions of the Program Committee and for their responsiveness on providing the camera-ready copies within a tight deadline.

We would also like to thank Scott Smolka for serving as the General Chair, and the members of the SPIN Steering Committee and the Program Chairs of SPIN 2012, Alastair Donaldson and David Parker, for their advice on organizing and running the symposium. Special thanks go to Scott Stoller for his handling of all publicity-related matters while serving as the SPIN 2013 Publicity Chair. We thank Stony Brook University, and in particular, Ann Brody and Kathy Germana, for their valuable assistance with local organization. The EasyChair conference management system was used in the submission, review, and revision processes, as well as for the assembly of the symposium proceedings. We thank the developers of EasyChair for this invaluable service. Finally, we thank IBM, Microsoft Research, NEC, and Nvidia for providing generous financial support to SPIN 2013.

May 2013   Ezio Bartocci
                                                            C.R. Ramakrishnan

Organization

Steering Committee

Dragan Bosnacki   Eindhoven University of Technology,
                              The Netherlands
Susanne Graf   CNRS VERIMAG, France
Gerard Holzmann   NASA JPL, USA
Stefan Leue   University of Konstanz, Germany
Willem Visser   University of Stellenbosch, South Africa

General Chair

Scott A. Smolka   Stony Brook University, USA

Publicity Chair

Scott D. Stoller   Stony Brook University, USA

Program Committee

Gogul Balakrishnan   NEC Labs, USA
Paolo Ballarini   Ecole Centrale Paris, France
Ezio Bartocci   TU Wien, Austria
Armin Biere   Johannes Kepler University, Austria
Marsha Chechik   University of Toronto, Canada
Hana Chockler   IBM, Israel
Giorgio Delzanno   Università di Genova, Italy
Alastair Donaldson   Imperial College London, UK
Dimitra Giannakopoulou   NASA Ames, USA
Patrice Godefroid   Microsoft Research, USA
Radu Grosu   TU Wien, Austria
Klaus Havelund   NASA JPL, USA
Gerard J. Holzman   NASA JPL, USA
Stefan Leue   University of Konstanz, Germany
Madanlal Musuvathi   Microsoft Research, USA
David Parker   University of Birmingham, UK
C.R. Ramakrishnan   Stony Brook University, USA
S. Ramesh   General Motors Global R&D, India
Stefan Schwoon   ENS Cachan, France
Scott A. Smolka   Stony Brook University, USA
Oleg Sokolsky   University of Pennsylvania, USA
Scott D. Stoller   Stony Brook University, USA
Stavros Tripakis   UC Berkeley, USA

Helmut Veith   TU Wien, Austria
Farn Wang   National Taiwan University, Taiwan
Lenore Zuck   University of Illinois at Chicago, USA

Additional Reviewers

Aleksandrowicz, Gadi   Margalit, Oded
Beer, Adrian   Rossetti, Daniele
Bey, Alina   Satpathy, Manoranjan
Bogomolov, Sergiy   Seidl, Martina
Donzé, Alexandre   Traverso, Riccardo
Elshuber, Martin   Von Essen, Christian
Gotsman, Alexey   Wang, Shaohui
Kahsai, Temesghen   Wasicek, Armin
Katsaros, Panagiotis   Widder, Josef
Ketema, Jeroen   Yorav, Karen
Leitner-Fischer, Florian

Table of Contents

Reuse of Verification Results

Conditional Model Checking, Precision Reuse, and Verification Witnesses

Dirk Beyer and Philipp Wendler

University of Passau, Germany

Abstract. Verification is a complex algorithmic task, requiring large amounts of computing resources. One approach to reduce the resource consumption is to reuse information from previous verification runs. This paper gives an overview of three techniques for such information reuse. Conditional model checking outputs a condition that describes the state space that was successfully verified, and accepts as input a condition that instructs the model checker which parts of the system should be verified; thus, later verification runs can use the output condition of previous runs in order to not verify again parts of the state space that were already verified. Precision reuse is a technique to use intermediate results from previous verification runs to accelerate further verification runs of the system; information about the level of abstraction in the abstract model can be reused in later verification runs. Typical model checkers provide an error path through the system as witness for having proved that a system violates a property, and a few model checkers provide some kind of proof certificate as a witness for the correctness of the system; these witnesses should be such that the verifiers can read them and —with less computational effort— (re-) verify that the witness is valid.

1 Introduction

Algorithms for automatic verification require large amounts of computing resources [2, 18]. Furthermore, one verification run of a single verification tool is often not sufficient to completely solve practical verification problems. The verifier might fail to give an answer for various reasons, for example due to the lack of resources (time and memory), an architectural weakness or a missing feature, or simply due to a bug in the verifier. In such cases, the verification process would often be continued on a more powerful engine or using a different verification approach. Sometimes automatic verifiers report wrong answers, and thus, in safety-critical applications it might be desired to rely not only on a single tool, but instead repeat the verification using several other verifiers in order to increase the confidence in the result. A verification run might also be repeated because it was run by an untrusted third party, and the result needs to be re-checked. Some systems consist of many connected components that are verified independently (compositional verification), or of a series of similar products that differ in the set of features that they contain (product-line verification) [1].

E. Bartocci and C.R. Ramakrishnan (Eds.): SPIN 2013, LNCS 7976, pp. 1–17, 2013.

When a system is developed, it is desired to detect specification violations soon after they are introduced in order to support early bug fixing; thus, verification should be applied on each new version of the system (regression verification) [21, 30], and even after each single change. This requires a large number of verification runs and enormous computing resources. Regression checking is state-of-the-art in testing, and regression test selection is a well-known and established technique to reduce the number of tests [27]. Verification tools themselves are also under development, and a regression-checking test suite consisting of many verification tasks with known verification result [4] can be used to detect new bugs in current versions of the verifier.

In all of the above-mentioned verification tasks it would be possible and beneficial to store information from previous verification runs to reduce the computational effort, or to increase the quality of the verification result. More research projects are necessary to provide solutions for more reuse of (intermediate) verification results, and for making the existing verification technology more successful in industrial applications.

We identified three categories in which information from a previous verification run should be used in order to spare computational effort that would otherwise be necessary: (1) the use of partial results of verification runs that were not able to completely verify the system; (2) the reuse of auxiliary information that was computed during previous verification runs in order to speed up later verification runs; (3) the use of witnesses for verifying the correctness of previous results.

For each of these categories we present one example from software verification and illustrate the effectiveness of the approach by some experimental evaluation. First, conditional model checking [8] is an approach in which a verifier takes as input a condition that specifies which parts of the program should be verified, and produces an output condition that specifies which parts of the state space were successfully verified. The output condition of one verification run can be used as the input condition of a subsequent run such that the latter can skip the already-verified parts of the state space and focus on the remaining state space. Second, many approaches that are based on CEGAR [17] use some form of *precision* that specifies the level of abstraction of the abstract model that gets constructed for the analysis of the system (e.g., predicate abstraction [3,7,19,20]). This information about the precision can be dumped after a verification run and read in before starting another run (e.g., [13]), reducing the verification time of the latter run because the precision is already computed and many refinement steps are automatically omitted. Third, model checkers typically provide a counterexample (an error path) if a violation of the specification is found in the system, in order to help the user identifying and eliminating the bug. Such counterexamples can also be used —if exported in a machine-readable format— for (re-)verifying if the result of the model checker is (still) correct.

Related Work. We restrict our discussion of related work to automated software verification. Conditional model checking [8] allows to start the overall verification process using one verifier (depending on the abilities of the verifier, the result might be partial), and later use another verifier to further increase the verification coverage, i.e., check the remaining state space. For example, if model checkers are not able to verify certain properties of the system, (guided) testing tools can be used in a second step to increase confidence of correctness for the remaining, not yet verified parts of the state space [16].

Reusing information from a successful verification run for previous versions of a modified system is the basis of many approaches for regression verification [30]. Different forms of information have been proposed for reuse: state-space graphs [23,24,33], constraint-solving results [31,34], function summaries [29], and abstraction precisions [13]. Some of the data can become quite large compared to the system under investigation, and in most cases there needs to be a validation check on whether it is sound to reuse the information (i.e., whether the information still applies to a new version of the system). Precisions are concise and can be reused by the same algorithm that produces them, without a separate validation step.

Most state-of-the-art model checkers produce a counterexample for inspection by the user if the system violates the property, in order to guide the user in the defect-identification process. However, only a few verifiers support witnesses for verification runs showing that the property holds: more verifiers should provide witnesses for correctness. Well-known forms of witnesses for the correctness of a program are proof-carrying code [26], program invariants [22], and abstract reachability graphs [23]. A program for which a safety proof has been found can also be transformed into a new program that is substantially easier to re-verify [32], although verifying the transformed program does not guarantee that the original program is correct.

Experimental Setup. In order to show that reusing verification results is beneficial in many cases, we perform a series of experiments using the open-source software-verification framework CPACHECKER[1]. We use revision 7952 from the trunk of the project's SVN repository. CPACHECKER integrates many successful verification approaches. In particular, we use its predicate analysis [11] and its explicit-value analysis [12]. Both are based on CEGAR and lazy abstraction.

The benchmark set that we use in this paper consists of the C programs from the 2nd Competition on Software Verification[2] [5], except for the categories "Concurrency" and "Memory Safety", for which CPACHECKER has no support. Thus, our benchmark set contains a total of 2250 C programs, 480 of which contain a known specification violation.

We use machines with an Intel Core i7-2600 3.4 GHz quad-core CPU and 32 GB of RAM, allowing the verifier to use two cores (plus two hyper-threading cores) and 15 GB of RAM. The time limit is set to 15 minutes of CPU time. We run two independent instances of the verifier in parallel on each machine, in order to speed up the benchmarking. The operating system of the machines is Ubuntu 12.04 with Linux 3.2 as kernel and OpenJDK 1.7 as Java virtual machine.

---

[1] http://cpachecker.sosy-lab.org
[2] http://sv-comp.sosy-lab.org

The CPU time is measured and reported in seconds with two significant digits. The memory consumption is measured including the Java VM that CPACHECKER uses as well as the memory that all other components of the verification process (e.g., the SMT solver) need and is given in megabyte with two significant digits.

We present our results using scatter plots that compare a configuration without information reuse versus a configuration with information reuse. Each data point in such a plot represents the performance results of one verification task, where the x-value reports the verification time that is needed in the initial run, and the y-value reports the verification time that is needed in the second run, in which some information from the first run was reused. Thus, data points in the lower-right triangle (with the x-value greater than the y-value) show a speedup through information reuse, with the performance benefit increasing with the distance of the data point from the diagonal. Instances that cannot be verified due to a timeout of the verifier are shown with a time of 900 s and are drawn at the right or top of the plots.

2   Conditional Model Checking

In traditional model checking, the outcome of a verification run is either "safe" or "unsafe". However, it may also happen that a model checker fails and produces no result at all, for example due to resource exhaustion. In such cases, the computational effort that was invested is lost. Conditional model checking [8] redefines model checking in order to solve this problem. A conditional model checker gives as output a *condition* Ψ that states under which condition the analyzed program satisfies the given specification. This condition is produced even in case of a failure, and thus, the consumed resources are not wasted because every run produces some useful result. The previous outcome "safe" translates to $\Psi = true$, and the outcome "unsafe" translates to $\Psi = false$, however, the condition allows for more flexible outcomes. For example, in case of a timeout, a conditional model checker would summarize the already verified part of the state space in the condition, stating that the program is safe, as long as its execution stays within this part. In case of an unsound analysis like bounded model checking with a fixed loop bound, or an algorithm with an incomplete pointer-alias analysis, these assumptions for program safety would also be explicitly given in the output condition, e.g., the program is safe under the assumption "pointers p and q are not aliased".

Furthermore, a conditional model checker also takes as input a condition that specifies parts of the state space that are already verified, i.e., which the model checker can omit and should not verify again. This can be used to restrict the analysis, e.g., to at most k loop unrollings (well-known as bounded model checking [14]), to paths not longer than n states, or to some maximum amount of time or memory.

Conditional model checking makes it possible to combine two (or more) verifiers and leverage the power of both. Figure 2 illustrates two example combinations, sequential combination with information passing and combination by

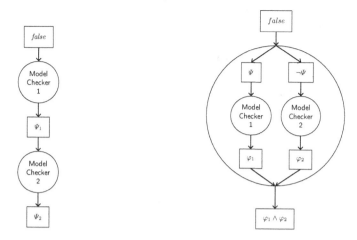

Fig. 1. Combination strategies using conditional model checkers; left: sequential combination with information passing; right: combination by partitioning (compositional verification)

partitioning; for more application examples, we refer the reader to the full article [8]. In contrast to previous combinations of different techniques (e.g., reduced product for combining different abstract domains [9, 15]), the techniques that are combined using conditional model checking can be implemented in different tools, can run on different platforms, even at different locations, or in the cloud, because the interaction and information exchange is realized via implementation-independent conditions.

Sequential Combination with Information Passing. Conditional model checking supports a sequential combination of two verifiers, such that the output condition of the first verifier (describing the successfully verified state space) can be used as input condition for the second verifier. This way, the second verifier will not attempt to verify the state space that was already proven safe by the first verifier. The left part of Fig. 2 illustrates how information can be passed from the first to the second model checker through condition Ψ_1; per default, the first model checker starts with *false* as input condition, i.e., nothing is already verified. The condition Ψ_1 represents the state space that the first model checker was able to verify. The second model checker starts with Ψ_1 as input and tries to verify the state space outside of Ψ_1, i.e., tries to weaken the condition. If the second model checker terminates with output condition $\Psi_2 = true$, then the sequential combination was successful in completely solving the verification problem. If already the first model checker returns $\Psi_1 = true$, then the second model checker has nothing to do; otherwise, the sequential combination is reusing information from the first verification run in the second verification run, making the analysis more powerful than any of them alone.

It is well known that different verification techniques have different strengths and weaknesses on different kinds of programs; the same applies to program parts.

For example, consider a program that contains loops with many iterations as well as non-linear arithmetic. An explicit-state analysis might fail on the loops due to resource exhaustion, whereas a predicate-based analysis might not be able to reason about non-linear arithmetic, and thus, none of the two techniques is able to verify the program on its own. Given an implementation of each analysis as conditional model checker, and a setup that reuses the output condition of one as the input condition for the other, verification of such a program becomes possible. One could run the (conditional) explicit-value analysis first, specifying a maximum path length as input condition. Thus the analysis would not waste all available resources on endlessly unwinding loops, but instead verify the rest of the program, and summarize the results in the output condition. If the subsequent run of the predicate analysis gets this information as input condition, it can focus on the still-missing parts of the state space (the loops), and skip the rest (which in this case, the predicate analysis would not be able to verify due to the non-linear arithmetic). Thus, the complete analysis might prove the program safe, although the same sequential combination without information reuse would not be able to verify the program.

Combination by Partitioning. Conditional model checking also supports compositional verification, which can be set up as a combination where the state space is partitioned into two partitions and two verifiers are started each with an input condition that represents its (negation of the) partition. This way, each verifier concentrates on different aspects of the verification task. If both verifiers succeed to relax the condition to *true*, then the verification task is completely solved. Otherwise, the output condition $\phi_1 \wedge \phi_2$ represents the state space that was successfully verified. This concept allows a convenient construction of compositional verification strategies. In this paper, in which we focus on reuse of verification results, we now concentrate on experiments with the sequential composition.

Experimental Evaluation. We refer to previous experimental results from 2012 [8] to give evidence that conditional model checking, and the combination of verifiers that it makes possible, can verify more programs in less time. For those experiments, we used a benchmark set that consists of 81 programs created from the programs in the categories "SystemC" and "DeviceDrivers64" (two categories that were considered particularly hard) of the Competition on Software Verification 2012 (SVCOMP'12) [4].

As an example for conditional model checking we show the results for a configuration that combines two verifiers sequentially with information passing between the verifiers. The first verifier that is used is an explicit-value analysis that is quite fast for some programs but inefficient for other, more complex programs due to state-space explosion. This analysis is configured to stop itself after at most 100 s. If it terminates without a complete result "safe" or "unsafe" (due to the timeout, or due to imprecision), it dumps a summary of the successfully verified state space as an output condition. The second verifier, which uses a powerful predicate analysis based on CEGAR, lazy abstraction, and adjustable-block encoding [11], continues the verification for the remaining time up to the

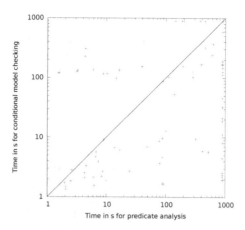

Fig. 2. Scatter plot comparing the verification time of a predicate analysis with the verification time of a conditional-model-checking configuration that uses both an explicit-value analysis and a predicate analysis

global time limit of 900 s. This analysis takes the output condition that was produced by the first verifier as input condition such that it will ignore the already verified state space and focus on the remaining parts. We compare this instance of conditional model checking against a stand-alone predicate analysis, in the configuration that was submitted to SVCOMP'12 [25].

The stand-alone predicate analysis is able to solve 58 of the 81 verification tasks in 31 000 s. The configuration based on conditional model checking instead verified 75 programs in only 14 000 s. Figure 2 presents the verification times for both configurations for 78 out of the 81 benchmark verification tasks (excluding 3 cases where one verifier ran out of memory and aborted prematurely). The majority of the data points is positioned in the lower-right triangle, which shows the performance advantage of conditional model checking. In some cases, the verification time for conditional model checking is just over 100 s and the predicate analysis alone needs only a few seconds. These are verification tasks for which the explicit-value analysis, which is started first in our setup of conditional model checking, is not able to solve the program in its time limit of 100 s, and the predicate analysis that is started subsequently verifies the programs in a short time. Note that there is a significant amount of data points to the right-most area of the plot: these are the verification tasks on which the predicate analysis alone times out. Some of these programs even take more than 100 s when verified with conditional model checking, which means that they were successfully verified by the predicate analysis after the explicit-value analysis terminated, although the predicate analysis alone could not successfully verify them. The verification of these programs is only possible by information reuse, that is, by restricting the predicate analysis to the state space that the explicit-value analysis could not successfully verify. A simple sequential combination of both analyses without information passing would not have been able to verify those programs.

3 Precision Reuse

There are many applications for re-verifying a program that was already verified. Common to all these cases is the fact that information from previous verification runs for the same program would in principle be available, and could be used to speedup subsequent verification runs. Thus, it seems worthwhile to save such information in a machine-readable way after each verification run for the program, for later reuse.

Several successful software-verifiers are based on CEGAR, and continuously refine an abstract model of the program to be analyzed, until the model is strong enough to prove safety or find a violation of the property. The *precision* (level of abstraction) that is used for constructing and verifying the abstract model is crucial information for the success of such CEGAR-based analyses, and discovering an appropriate precision is usually one of the most expensive tasks of the verifier (possibly involving a large number of refinement steps). However, given the precision as input, the verifier can immediately construct an appropriate abstract model and verify the abstract model without further refinements. Thus, such precisions are suited for being reused in subsequent verification runs, as was shown in previous work for the application of this concept to regression verification [13]. For example, predicate analysis with CEGAR and lazy abstraction (e.g., [7]) is a well-known analysis that uses precisions. In this case, the precision contains the set of predicates over program variables that are tracked by the analysis, and (in case of lazy abstraction) the program locations at which the predicates are relevant. A precision can also be used for explicit-value model checking [12], in which case the precision stores the program variables that are relevant for the verification; all other program variables should be abstracted away by the verifier. Similar precisions can be used for analyses based on other abstract domains, such as intervals or octagons. Precisions are usually much smaller than the program itself, and can be easily dumped after the verification run.

If a precision for a given program is present from a previous verification run, it can easily be used as the initial precision of a subsequent verification run, instead of the usual (coarse) initial precision. Thus, no refinements are necessary anymore (given that the program was not changed). In contrast to other approaches like proof checking, where a separate algorithm is needed for verifying the proof, precision reuse does not require a new algorithmic setup: the same analysis and algorithm that produce the precision in a first verification run are the components that use the precision in a subsequent verification run. Furthermore, if the provided precision does not fit to the program (for example because the program was changed, or the user provided a wrong input file), there is no risk of incorrect verification results. Instead, the verifier will simply detect that the abstract model is not strong enough to verify the given property by finding spurious counterexamples, and will use refinements to strengthen the abstract model as it would in a verification run without a given input precision.

Experimental Evaluation. Both the predicate analysis and the explicit-value analysis of CPACHECKER are based on CEGAR and use a precision to define the

Table 1. Results for precision reuse

Analysis	Programs	Without precision reuse				With precision reuse			
		Solved Tasks	CPU Time	Memory Avg.	Max.	Solved Tasks	CPU Time	Memory Avg.	Max.
Explicit-Value	Safe	1529	13000	270	9600	1529	6100	170	8200
	Unsafe	298	23000	1400	8100	298	2000	320	3200
Predicate	Safe	1518	27000	280	13000	1516	13000	210	12500
	Unsafe	422	16000	480	8700	420	11000	360	8600

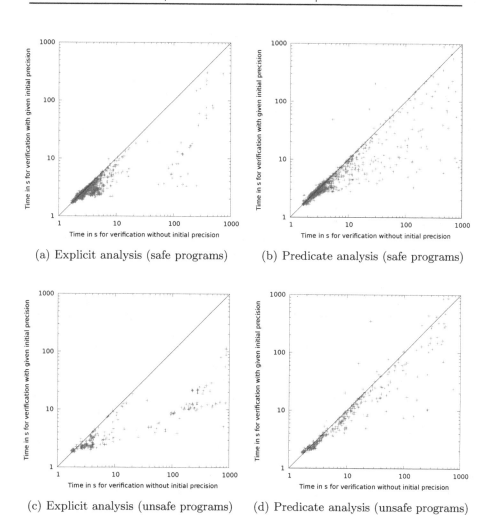

(a) Explicit analysis (safe programs)   (b) Predicate analysis (safe programs)

(c) Explicit analysis (unsafe programs)   (d) Predicate analysis (unsafe programs)

Fig. 3. Scatter plots comparing the verification time without input precision versus with precision reuse

level of abstraction. We used the existing implementation for writing precisions to disk after each verification run and for reading an initial precision from disk before the verification. We experimented with precision reuse for all 2 250 programs of the benchmark set described in Sect. 1. A summary of all results can be found in Table 1. Detailed results are provided on the supplementary web page [3].

Out of the 1 770 programs that are known to be safe, the explicit-value analysis of CPACHECKER successfully verified 1 529 instances in 13 000 s, using 270 MB of memory on average. Out of the 480 unsafe programs, 298 were verified in 23 000 s, using 1 400 MB of memory on average. If we reuse the precisions that were produced in these runs as initial precision in a second run, the verification takes only 6 100 s, i.e., less than half of the time for the safe programs, and 2 000 s, i.e., less than 10 %, for the unsafe programs. The memory consumption is also considerably lower if reusing a given precision, dropping (for the unsafe programs) from 1400 MB on average to 320 MB.

The predicate analysis could successfully verify 1 518 out of 1 770 safe programs in 27 000 s. With the precisions reused, 1 516 programs can be verified in only 13 000 s. There are two programs that were verified in the initial run in 480 s and 680 s, respectively, but CPACHECKER reached the timeout of 900 s when the precision was given as input. Also there are three programs for which the verification with precision reuse needs significantly more time (factor 3 to 10). For all five programs mentioned above, there was only a small number of refinements (1 to 7) in the initial run, and only less than 4 s was spent on these refinements per program (mostly even around only 0.5 s). This means that the potential benefit was already small for these programs. Furthermore, CPACHECKER uses lazy abstraction and thus may have used different precisions on different paths of the programs. Our implementation of precision reuse, however, assigns the same precision on all paths of the program, leading to a possibly stronger and thus more expensive abstract model. This is not a general drawback of precision reuse.

The results for the unsafe programs are similar. The predicate analysis finds a counterexample for 422 out of 480 unsafe programs in 16 000 s, and using the generated precisions as input it finds 420 counterexamples in 11 000 s. Again, two programs cannot be verified when a precision is reused, and there are a few cases for which the necessary verification time is higher. For unsafe programs, there are also other factors that influence the results. For example, depending on the order in which the control-flow automaton is traversed, the analysis might find the first counterexample sooner or later, and with more or less refinements, thus with a different potential performance advantage by precision reuse.

Figure 3 illustrates the results using four scatter plots, one for each CPACHECKER configuration, and for the safe and the unsafe programs. Cases in which the verifier timed out in the initial run and thus produced no reusable precision are omitted. The graphs show that precision reuse is beneficial, because the vast majority of data points are located in the lower-right triangle. For the explicit-value analysis, there is no verification task for which the run time is significantly increased by precision reuse.

---

[3] http://www.sosy-lab.org/~dbeyer/cpa-reuse-gen/

4   Verification Witnesses and Their Re-verification

It is common that model checkers produce a counterexample if the system violated the property, as witness of the verification result. The main purpose of the counterexample is to convince the user of the verification result and to guide the user in the defect-identification process. Below we argue that it is necessary to (1) produce a counterexample in a machine-readable format, such that the counterexample can be re-verified later, and to (2) analyze the counterexample for feasibility not in isolation, but in relation to the program to be analyzed.

It would also be desirable to produce witnesses for verification runs that prove that the property holds. It seems to be an open research question to achieve this, perhaps because a witness for correctness can have a size exponential in the size of the input program. There are important research results available on witnesses for the correctness of a program, for example, proof-carrying code [26], program invariants [22], and abstract reachability graphs [23]. Unfortunately, it did not yet become state-of-the-art to support those techniques in verification tools. Hopefully, since tools for software verification became more mature in the last years, as witnessed by the competition on software verification [5], there will be a need for certification of verification claims. That is, in the future, it will not be sufficient to report a verification answer ("safe" or "unsafe"), but one has to support the claim by a verification witness (proof certificate).

Re-verification of Counterexamples. The re-verification of previous verification results can be supported by intermediate results, as outlined in the previous sections, but also by providing witnesses for the verification result. We now consider the re-verification of verification results where a violation of the property is reported and a counterexample is produced. It seems obvious that verifying if only a single given path out of the program violates the specification is more efficient than verifying the complete program and finding a specification-violating path in it. Our experiments support this claim with encouraging numbers, showing that the benefit is indeed present, even if the counterexample is re-verified against the original program. There are two important properties that the witness-based re-verification has to fulfill: the use of machine-readable counterexamples and the re-verification against the original program.

Machine-readable counterexamples. First, we need the verifier to dump information about the found counterexample of an unsafe program in a *machine-readable* format, which can later be reused in a re-verification run to restrict the verification process to this single path (e.g., by giving the negation of the counterexample as input to a conditional model checker). One possibility would be to dump the source code of a new program that corresponds to a single counterexample of the original program. This new program would be free of loops and branches, and thus hopefully easy to verify. However, in the case where the goal of re-verifying a counterexample is increased confidence, this is not a good idea. If the verifier that is used in the first verification run is imprecise and reports an infeasible counterexample, it might generate a witness program that does contain a specification violation, but does not correspond to an actual path of the original

```
CONTROL AUTOMATON PathGuidingAutomaton

INITIAL STATE s0;

STATE USEFIRST s0:
  // match declaration statement of program and goto state s1
  MATCH "int x;" -> GOTO s1;
  // match all other statements and stop exploration of path
  TRUE           -> STOP;

STATE USEFIRST s1:
  // match assume statement of program and signal specification violation
  MATCH "[x==0]" -> ERROR;
  // match all other statements and stop exploration of path
  TRUE           -> STOP;

END AUTOMATON
```

Fig. 4. Example automaton for guiding the verifier along a certain path (written in CPACHECKER's specification language), which can be used for re-playing a previously reported counterexample on the original program

program. In this case, the second verifier would correctly claim that the witness program is indeed unsafe, leading the user to an incorrect conclusion about the correctness of the original program.

"Re-playing" Counterexamples. Second, counterexamples should be re-verified against the original program, not in isolation. This strategy is motivated by verification results delivered from untrusted verification engines, the need to re-verify slightly changed programs (regression verification), and excluding spurious counterexamples that were reported by imprecise verification tools. For the implementation of this strategy —using the original program as input for the re-verification run— we propose to use a simple language for automata that guide the verifier along a certain path, in order to have the verifier exactly re-play the previously found counterexample. The automaton needs to be able to match operations of the program (possibly by textual matching, or by line numbers), to guide the verification, preventing the exploration of unrelated paths, and to specify a certain state of the program as a target state whose reachability should be checked by the verifier. Previous work on specification languages based on automata can be used to implement this strategy (e.g., [6, 10, 28]).

We can use the automaton language that the verifier CPACHECKER accepts as specification format for counterexamples without any changes. An example for such an automaton is given in Fig. 4. An automaton for guiding the verifier along a single path in a program consists of a set of states, where each state has exactly one edge that matches a single program operation and leads to the successor state. For all other program operations that cannot be matched, the automaton instructs the verifier to stop exploring the path along that program operation. At the end of this chain of states, the automaton switches to a special

Table 2. Results for re-verification of counterexamples

Analysis	Initial verification				Re-verification			
	Solved Tasks	CPU Time	Memory Avg.	Max.	Solved Tasks	CPU Time	Memory Avg.	Max.
Explicit-Value	299	24000	1400	8400	299	870	140	890
Predicate	422	18000	490	8900	422	1300	120	590

error state, which informs the verifier that the corresponding program state is a specification violation. If the verifier reaches this state, then it reports the program as unsafe.

Such an automaton that matches program operations along a counterexample path is easy to produce for all kinds of analyses that are able to reproduce a single finite path through the control-flow of the verified program as a representation of a counterexample. This includes analysis approaches based on creating abstract reachability graphs (which are unrollings of the control flow), but also other analyses like bounded model checking, if some information about the structure of the control flow is encoded in the generated formula and a path is reconstructed using the information from a model for the program formula.

The automaton is also easy to use as input for the re-verification step, if the verifier is based on traversing the control-flow of the program. In this case, whenever the verifier follows a control-flow edge, it would also execute one edge of the automaton and act accordingly (i.e., continue or stop exploring this path). Again, this strategy is applicable to verifiers based on abstract reachability graphs, but also to others. For bounded model checking, this can be implemented in the first phase where the program is unrolled and a single formula is created representing the program. With such an automaton, the unrolling would be restricted and the generated formula represents only that single path, which could then be verified by checking the formula for satisfiability as usual. The complexity of both generating and using the automaton is linear in the length of the counterexample.

Experimental Evaluation. To support experiments with re-verification of counterexamples, we implemented the export of a counterexample as automaton in CPACHECKER's specification language. Our implementation in the CPACHECKER framework can be used with all available configurable program analyses that are based on abstract reachability graphs and is available via the project's SVN repository.

We experimented again with the explicit-value analysis and the predicate analysis. A summary of the results is presented in Table 2. Detailed results are provided on the supplementary web page[4]. The explicit-value analysis of CPACHECKER finds the bug in 299 out of the 480 unsafe programs from our benchmark set (for the remainder, it fails or runs into a timeout). The produced counterexample automaton can be used as verification witness, e.g., in a second

---

[4] http://www.sosy-lab.org/~dbeyer/cpa-reuse-gen/

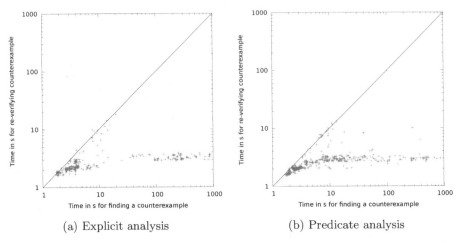

(a) Explicit analysis   (b) Predicate analysis

Fig. 5. Scatter plots comparing the run time for finding a counterexample in the complete program vs. re-verifying a given counterexample

verification run of the original program in order to explicitly verify only this single path. The re-verification confirms the counterexample for all verification tasks. The run time for finding the counterexamples in the first run was 24 000 s for the 299 programs. The run time for re-verifying the produced counterexamples was only 870 s, i.e., less than 4 %. The average memory consumption was 1 400 MB for the initial runs, and 140 MB for the re-verification runs.

CPACHECKER's predicate analysis could find a counterexample for 422 programs in 18 000 s. The re-verification of these counterexamples took only 1 300 s. There was only one verification task for which the re-verification took longer than 13 s. For 40 verification tasks, the initial verification run to identify a counterexample took longer than 100 s.

The maximum memory consumption per analyzed program, i.e., the amount of memory that the machine needs to have available, is also lower for re-verification. For the initial verification runs, the maximum memory consumption was 8 400 MB (explicit-value analysis) and 8 900 MB (predicate analysis). During the re-verification of the counterexamples, the maximum memory consumption was 890 MB and 590 MB, respectively. This means the following: while for finding the bugs in the complete programs, the machine needs to be powerful (more than 8 GB of RAM are still not common for developer machines), the re-verification can be performed on practically any available machine (even machines older than 8 years and small netbooks tend to have at least 1 GB).

Scatter plots for the results of all successfully verified programs are shown in Fig. 5. The results are interesting: the verification time for re-verifying a counterexample is less than 4 s for most of the programs, regardless of the verification time that was needed for finding the counterexample in the original program. There are no verification tasks for which the verification time for re-verification significantly exceeds the run time for the initial verification run.

It is an important insight to have confirmed that the re-verification can be performed on a much less powerful verification engine, and thus, is significantly less expensive overall. This justifies the use of untrusted computing engines for the verification process: it is reasonably inexpensive to confirm the correctness of verification results that arrived with status "unreliable".

5 Conclusion

We have shown that the reuse of verification results from previous verification runs can save significant amounts of resources (time and memory). As example applications, we explained three different strategies for reusing verification results: conditional model checking, precision reuse, and verification witnesses. We illustrated the benefits of reusing verification results by reporting on experimental results. Reusing verification results from previous verification attempts does not only improve the performance, but sometimes also the effectiveness, i.e., more verification tasks can be solved. Systems that are currently still too complex to be verified by one single verifier could be verified by combination and information passing between verification runs. More such techniques need to be developed and used in the future, in order to apply automatic verification to large-scale industrial systems.

Important future work, in order to make information reuse practically applicable, includes research on defining standardized formats. Such standard formats are the key for combining different verification tools and for reusing (partial) verification results across different verification approaches. For example, a common format for verification witnesses (proof certificates as well as counterexamples) would increase the adoption of verification technology by verification engineers in practice, by providing an easy way for re-verifying results and integrating verification within development tool chains. Besides the conditions of conditional model checking and the witnesses, we demonstrated that intermediate results such as precisions have a lot of potential for reuse. More research is necessary to investigate which information is to be saved and reused.

References

1. Apel, S., von Rhein, A., Wendler, P., Größlinger, A., Beyer, D.: Strategies for product-line verification: Case studies and experiments. In: ICSE 2013. IEEE (2013)
2. Baier, C., Katoen, J.-P.: Principles of Model Checking. MIT Press (2008)
3. Ball, T., Rajamani, S.K.: The SLAM project: Debugging system software via static analysis. In: POPL 2002, pp. 1–3. ACM (2002)
4. Beyer, D.: Competition on software verification (SV-COMP). In: Flanagan, C., König, B. (eds.) TACAS 2012. LNCS, vol. 7214, pp. 504–524. Springer, Heidelberg (2012)
5. Beyer, D.: Second competition on software verification. In: Piterman, N., Smolka, S.A. (eds.) TACAS 2013. LNCS, vol. 7795, pp. 594–609. Springer, Heidelberg (2013)

6. Beyer, D., Chlipala, A.J., Henzinger, T.A., Jhala, R., Majumdar, R.: The BLAST query language for software verification. In: Giacobazzi, R. (ed.) SAS 2004. LNCS, vol. 3148, pp. 2–18. Springer, Heidelberg (2004)
7. Beyer, D., Henzinger, T.A., Jhala, R., Majumdar, R.: The software model checker BLAST. Int. J. Softw. Tools Technol. Transfer 9(5-6), 505–525 (2007)
8. Beyer, D., Henzinger, T.A., Keremoglu, M.E., Wendler, P.: Conditional model checking: A technique to pass information between verifiers. In: FSE 2012. ACM (2012)
9. Beyer, D., Henzinger, T.A., Théoduloz, G.: Configurable software verification: Concretizing the convergence of model checking and program analysis. In: Damm, W., Hermanns, H. (eds.) CAV 2007. LNCS, vol. 4590, pp. 504–518. Springer, Heidelberg (2007)
10. Beyer, D., Holzer, A., Tautschnig, M., Veith, H.: Information reuse for multi-goal reachability analyses. In: Felleisen, M., Gardner, P. (eds.) ESOP 2013. LNCS, vol. 7792, pp. 472–491. Springer, Heidelberg (2013)
11. Beyer, D., Keremoglu, M.E., Wendler, P.: Predicate abstraction with adjustable-block encoding. In: FMCAD 2010, pp. 189–197. FMCAD (2010)
12. Beyer, D., Löwe, S.: Explicit-state software model checking based on CEGAR and interpolation. In: Cortellessa, V., Varró, D. (eds.) FASE 2013. LNCS, vol. 7793, pp. 146–162. Springer, Heidelberg (2013)
13. Beyer, D., Löwe, S., Novikov, E., Stahlbauer, A., Wendler, P.: Reusing precisions for efficient regression verification. Technical Report MIP-1302, University of Passau (2013)
14. Biere, A., Cimatti, A., Clarke, E.M., Zhu, Y.: Symbolic model checking without BDDs. In: Cleaveland, W.R. (ed.) TACAS 1999. LNCS, vol. 1579, pp. 193–207. Springer, Heidelberg (1999)
15. Blanchet, B., Cousot, P., Cousot, R., Feret, J., Mauborgne, L., Miné, A., Monniaux, D., Rival, X.: A static analyzer for large safety-critical software. In: PLDI 2003, pp. 196–207. ACM (2003)
16. Christakis, M., Müller, P., Wüstholz, V.: Collaborative verification and testing with explicit assumptions. In: Giannakopoulou, D., Méry, D. (eds.) FM 2012. LNCS, vol. 7436, pp. 132–146. Springer, Heidelberg (2012)
17. Clarke, E.M., Grumberg, O., Jha, S., Lu, Y., Veith, H.: Counterexample-guided abstraction refinement for symbolic model checking. J. ACM 50(5), 752–794 (2003)
18. Clarke, E.M., Grumberg, O., Peled, D.A.: Model Checking. MIT (1999)
19. Clarke, E.M., Kröning, D., Sharygina, N., Yorav, K.: SATABS: SAT-based predicate abstraction for ANSI-C. In: Halbwachs, N., Zuck, L.D. (eds.) TACAS 2005. LNCS, vol. 3440, pp. 570–574. Springer, Heidelberg (2005)
20. Graf, S., Saïdi, H.: Construction of abstract state graphs with Pvs. In: Grumberg, O. (ed.) CAV 1997. LNCS, vol. 1254, pp. 72–83. Springer, Heidelberg (1997)
21. Hardin, R.H., Kurshan, R.P., McMillan, K.L., Reeds, J.A., Sloane, N.J.A.: Efficient regression verification. In: WODES 1996, pp. 147–150 (1996)
22. Henzinger, T.A., Jhala, R., Majumdar, R., Necula, G.C., Sutre, G., Weimer, W.: Temporal-safety proofs for systems code. In: Brinksma, E., Larsen, K.G. (eds.) CAV 2002. LNCS, vol. 2404, pp. 526–538. Springer, Heidelberg (2002)
23. Henzinger, T.A., Jhala, R., Majumdar, R., Sanvido, M.A.A.: Extreme model checking. In: Dershowitz, N. (ed.) Verification: Theory and Practice. LNCS, vol. 2772, pp. 332–358. Springer, Heidelberg (2004)
24. Lauterburg, S., Sobeih, A., Marinov, D., Viswanathan, M.: Incremental state-space exploration for programs with dynamically allocated data. In: ICSE 2008, pp. 291–300. ACM (2008)

25. Löwe, S., Wendler, P.: CPACHECKER with adjustable predicate analysis (competition contribution). In: Flanagan, C., König, B. (eds.) TACAS 2012. LNCS, vol. 7214, pp. 528–530. Springer, Heidelberg (2012)
26. Necula, G.C.: Proof carrying code. In: POPL 1997, pp. 106–119. ACM (1997)
27. Rothermel, G., Harrold, M.J.: Analyzing regression test selection techniques. IEEE Trans. Softw. Eng. 22(8), 529–551 (1996)
28. Šerý, O.: Enhanced property specification and verification in BLAST. In: Chechik, M., Wirsing, M. (eds.) FASE 2009. LNCS, vol. 5503, pp. 456–469. Springer, Heidelberg (2009)
29. Šerý, O., Fedyukovich, G., Sharygina, N.: Incremental upgrade checking by means of interpolation-based function summaries. In: FMCAD 2012, pp. 114–121. FMCAD (2012)
30. Sokolsky, O.V., Smolka, S.A.: Incremental model checking in the modal μ-calculus. In: Dill, D.L. (ed.) CAV 1994. LNCS, vol. 818, pp. 351–363. Springer, Heidelberg (1994)
31. Visser, W., Geldenhuys, J., Dwyer, M.B.: Green: Reducing, reusing, and recycling constraints in program analysis. In: FSE 2012. ACM (2012)
32. Wonisch, D., Schremmer, A., Wehrheim, H.: Programs from proofs: A PCC alternative. In: CAV 2013, LNCS. Springer (2013)
33. Yang, G., Dwyer, M.B., Rothermel, G.: Regression model checking. In: ICSM 2009, pp. 115–124. IEEE (2009)
34. Yang, G., Păsăreanu, C.S., Khurshid, S.: Memoized symbolic execution. In: ISSTA 2012, pp. 144–154. ACM (2012)

Proving Properties of Concurrent Programs
(Extended Abstract)

Gerard J. Holzmann*

Jet Propulsion Laboratory, California Institute of Technology
gholzmann@acm.org

Abstract. How do you prove the correctness of multi-threaded code? This question has been asked since at least the mid-sixties, and it has inspired researchers ever since. Many approaches have been tried, based on mathematical theories, the use of annotations, or the construction of abstractions. An ideal solution would be a tool that one can point at an arbitrary piece of concurrent code, and that can resolve correctness queries in real-time. We describe one possible method for achieving this capability with a logic model checker.

Keywords: software verification, logic model checking, statistical model checking, model extraction, bitstate hashing, swarm verification, multi-core, cloud computing.

Spin is a logic model checking tool that is designed to help the user find concurrency related defects in software systems.[6] Originally the tool was designed to analyze models of concurrent, or multi-threaded, software systems, but today it is increasingly used to analyze implementation level code directly, without the need to construct a design model first. The benefit of this approach is an increase in convenience, but the penalty can be a notable increase in computational complexity.

Formal methods tools are generally designed to produce reliable results: they should be able to reveal true defects without omissions, and they should not report non-defects, i.e., they should not allow either *false negatives* or *false positives*. Ideally, they should also be fast and easy to use.

This sets three requirements for the design of an effective verification tool: reliability, ease-of-use, and efficiency. There are many software development tools that satisfy all three, and that developers rely on daily. A good example is a language compiler. Most modern compilers harness sound theory, yet they are easy to use, fast, and reliable.

Although formal methods tools are generally *reliable*, they are rarely accused of being fast or easy to use. On the contrary, a frequent complaint about these tools is that they can require extensive training, and consume excessive, and

---

* This research was carried out at the Jet Propulsion Laboratory, California Institute of Technology, under a contract with the National Aeronautics and Space Administration. The work was supported by NSF Grant CCF-0926190.

E. Bartocci and C.R. Ramakrishnan (Eds.): SPIN 2013, LNCS 7976, pp. 18–23, 2013.

often unpredictable, amounts of time. Although there have been many successes in the application of formal methods, the impact of formal methods tools on general software development practice remains very limited.

Against this background it is interesting to note that in the last five to ten years at least one verification technology did successfully emerge from relative obscurity to evolve into a significant new force in industrial software development. This technology is static source code analysis. After a long period of development, static source code analysis tools have become very successful commercial products, and they are now used broadly. The tools in this class require little or no explanation to use well, and can execute reasonably quickly. But curiously, they make no claim to be *reliable* as described above. The tools can, and do, miss reporting true defects (false negatives), and they can, and so, mis-report non-defects (false positives). Yet, it is clear that these tools have reached more users, and have a greater impact on software development practice, than the technically far more *reliable* formal methods tools.

In some cases then, ease of use and speed can outrank precision and reliability. After all, perfect knowledge that is inaccessible has less practical value to the end-user than partial knowledge that is easy to obtain. Phrased differently, it can be better to get *some* results from a partial method that is easy to use, than *no* results from a complete method that is too difficult to use.

We will describe how we can use the Spin model checker in a way that allows it to replicate some of the speed and usability of static analyzers. When used in the way we will describe, the model checker will be fast and easy to use, while still retaining its accuracy by never reporting non-defects. We can call this mode of allowing only false negatives but not false positives *robustness*, to distinguish it from the informal definition of *reliability* we gave earlier. In return for increased speed and ease of use, we must yield only the certainty of complete coverage. No new algorithms are needed to deploy the model checker in this way. All that is needed is to leverage the availability of already existing multi-core or cloud computing networks. When used in this way, the model checker can return robust and actionable results in seconds, even for large applications.

An Example. In 1999 we used the Spin model checker for the formal verification of the call processing code from a new commercial switching system that was marketed by Lucent Technologies, called the PathStar access server [5]. The target of this work was to automate as much as possible of the logic verification process, and to maximize its performance by parallelizing the verification tasks. The system we developed consisted of 16 small networked computers, each running at 500 MHz.

A few hundred correctness requirements were captured as part of this project, and a first model extraction technique was developed that allowed us to mechanically extract Spin verification models from the implementation level code, which was written in C. Once the requirements were formalized, the entire verification process could then be automated, and executed as part of a regression test suite without user intervention. At the time, the verification process took roughly 40 minutes to verify all requirements, running independent verification tasks on all computers in parallel.[1]

Today, integrated multi-core desktop systems larger and faster than the network of standalone computers from 1999 have become ubiquitous. In an experiment we repeated the same verification task from before on a single desktop system with 32 cores (i.e., well below what is currently available), with each core running at 2.5 GHz.

Generating the model checking code for all properties with Spin is virtually instantaneous. A straight compilation of the generated code, without optimization, takes a little under 5 seconds. With -O1 optimization that increases to 10 seconds, with -O2 it becomes 16 seconds, and with -O3 it reaches 45 seconds. The use of compiler optimization affects how fast the model checking runs can be executed, but there is of course a tradeoff that can be made between preparation time and execution time.

The verification process itself is based on bitstate hashing with iterative search refinement, to optimize the chances of finding errors fast [5]. This works remarkably well on the multi-core system. The first 11 counter-examples are generated in just 1 second, and after 7 seconds a total of 38 counter-examples have been generated.[2]

At this point the verification could be stopped, having yielded enough evidence for developers to act on. If we allow the search process to continue, though, it can find another 38 counter-examples in the next 11 minutes, with the number of errors found per minute quickly decreasing. The total number of issues reported is slightly larger than what was obtained in 1999. Using more cores, or faster CPUs, could trivially increase the performance further. More specifically, a total of 234 different properties were verified in this experiment, with each property checked up to 5 times with the iterative search refinement method that we discuss in more detail below. This means that up to 1,170 verification runs are performed on 32 cores in parallel. If 1,170 CPUs were available, for instance with brief access to the capacity of a cloud-computing platform, the performance could trivially improve still further.

The minimum time that is required to locate the first counter-examples in this experiment is measured in seconds, with the time dominated by compilation, and not verification. It is also interesting to note that in this experiment we achieve performance that is on par with, if not better than that of static analysis.

As we discuss in more detail below, the set of counter-examples that is generated with this system is not necessarily complete: there is no guarantee that *all* errors are found, or even can be found. But this is also not necessary. The speed and ease with which counter-examples are generated can add significant practical value especially in the early phases of software development.

---

[1] http://cm.bell-labs.com/cm/cs/what/feaver/

[2] For this example we compiled the verifiers with -O3. The verification times can double at lower optimization settings.

Key Enablers. There is a relatively small number of enabling technologies that we used in this example, and we believe that each of these is essential to the success of the method. They are:

- Model extraction [3],
- Bitstate hashing [2],
- Iterative search refinement [5], and
- Swarm verification [8].

Below we briefly discuss each of these, already existing, techniques, and consider the potential of their combined use.

Model Extraction. The mechanical extraction of verification models directly from implementation level source code would be fairly straightforward if it wasn't for one single complicating factor: the need to define and apply sound logical abstractions. The abstractions can help to render complex verification tasks computationally tractable, which is needed to secure logical soundness. If we yield on soundness, though, the burden of finding strong abstractions is lessened, and sometimes removed. The Modex[3] tool, for instance, that can be used as a front-end to the Spin model checker to extract verification models from C source code, allows the user to define abstractions, but it can also operate without it.

The problem is that if we try to use model checking to exhaustively solve a complex verification task without the benefit of prior abstraction, the tool can take an unpredictable amount of time, and will likely eventually exhaust available memory and abandon the search without completing the task. We then get a partial answer to the verification task: the tool renders an incomplete result. But the result is not just incomplete, it is also highly biased by the search algorithm to fully explore only one part of the search space and ignore all of the remainder. This type of incompleteness[4] is not comparable to the incompleteness that is inherent in static source code analyzers, precisely because it is systematically biased. There is literally zero chance that an error in the unexplored part of the search space can be reported.

All types of software analyses do of course face the same intractability issues as logic model checkers do, but they handle it differently. A tool that performs an incomplete analysis but provides a meaningful sampling of the *complete search space* can still provide useful feedback to the user, as illustrated by the success of static source code analyzers. So if we could modify the model checker to make it work in a fixed amount of memory and provide a true *sampling* of the entire search space, instead of a detailed search of one small unknown portion of it we should be able to make a similar improvement in the practical value of model checking of complex applications. This, though, is precisely the type of behavior that is available through the use of bitstate hashing algorithms.

---

[3] http://spinroot.com/modex/

[4] For completeness: we mean the incompleteness of the set of results that could in principle be provided, not the *logical incompleteness* that is shared by all program analysis systems. Logical incompleteness refers to the impossibility to design a program that could prove all true properties (e.g., halting) for any program.

Bitstate Hashing. The bitstate hashing technique was introduced in 1987 [2], and as we later discovered, can be theoretically founded in the still older theory of Bloom filters from 1970.[1] Since the basic algorithms have in the last two decades been described in detail in many sources, the method itself will need no detailed explanation here. The key characteristics of the method are, though, that it (1) allows us to define a fixed upper-bound on the amount of memory that the model checking algorithm will use, and (2) that it allows us to predict with some accuracy what the maximum runtime of a verification will be. (After a fixed period of time all bits in the hash-array must have flipped from zero to one, which limits the maximum search time.) The algorithm further has the desirable feature that any counter-examples that are generated are necessarily accurate (i.e., the algorithm permits no false positives). The fundamental properties of the hashing method that is used further guarantees that in an incomplete search the part of the search space that is verified will be a random sampling of the entire search space: the search is not systematically biased. This means that all parts of a large search space will be considered, though not necessarily exhaustively. By selecting the size of the bitstate hash-array we can control both the accuracy of the search and its speed. The two are always correlated, with accuracy increasing as speed decreases.

Iterative Search Refinement. As noted, there is an inverse relation between precision (or coverage of the search space) and speed. The size of the bitstate hash array determines the maximum runtime for a bitstate hashing run. We can now increase the probability of locating errors early by performing a series of bitstate runs, starting with very small bitstate hash array sizes, and repeating as necessary with larger sizes. The first runs performed will typically complete in a fraction of a second. If they succeed in generating a counter-example, the search has been successful and can stop. If not, we double the size of the hash array to sample a larger part of the search space, and repeat. Each time the hash array size is increased, the probability of locating defects also increases. In the process we adopted in [5] the doubling of the hash array size continues until a physical memory limit is reached, or a preset upperbound on the runtime that can be used is reached. It would also be possible to terminate the search process once the the time between new error reports drops below a given limit.

A series of bitstate searches can of course be executed purely sequentially on a single CPU, but it would then consume more time than necessary. Since all runs are in principle independent, we can also perform all these runs in parallel. For the last key enabling technology we will now look at methods that further leverage available parallelism by increasing the coverage of the sampling method still further. We can achieve this effects with a swarm verification method.

Swarm Verification. If we have access to large numbers of CPU-cores, or a cloud network of computers with potentially hundreds or thousands of compute engines available, we can deploy large numbers of independent verification tasks that jointly can solve a single large problem. Each task can, for instance, be defined by a small bitstate hashing run of the model checker. To increase the quality of the statistical sampling of the search space, we can now configure each of the verifiers to perform a slightly different type of search. We can achieve this search diversity with the Swarm[5] tool, a front-end to Spin, by:

- Using different types hash functions for each search,
- Using different numbers of hash functions for each search,
- Using different search orders in each search,
- Using randomized search methods, with different seed values.
- Using different search algorithms in each search (e.g., breadth-first, depth-first, context-bounded search [7], depth-bounded search, different types of heuristic search methods, etc.)

The variety thus added gives us the search diversity we need. It is not difficult to define as many different search variants as there are CPUs available to perform the search on, even for very large numbers.

All independent searches can be executed in parallel, using a fixed and pre-determined amount of memory per CPU and completing in a known amount of time, which can now be limited to a few seconds. As we saw in the example application, the joint effectiveness of all these independent, small, and individually incomplete searches can be impressive, and can contribute true practical value.

Based on the above, we believe to be near a tipping point in the application of software model checking techniques that may be comparable in its effects on multi-threaded software development to the introduction of static source code analyzers in the last decade.

References

1. Bloom, B.H.: Spacetime trade-offs in hash coding with allowable errors. Comm. ACM 13(7), 422–426 (1970)
2. Holzmann, G.J.: On limits and possibilities of automated protocol analysis. In: Rudin, H., West, C. (eds.) Proc. 6th Int. Conf. on Protocol Specification Testing and Verification, INWG IFIP, Zurich Switzerland (June 1987)
3. Holzmann, G.J., Smith, M.H.: Software model checking – extracting verification models from source code. In: Formal Methods for Protocol Engineering and Distributed Systems, pp. 481–497. Kluwer Academic Publ. (October 1999), also in: Software Testing Verification and Reliability 11(2), 65–79 (June 2001)
4. Holzmann, G.J.: Logic Verification of ANSI-C Code with Spin. In: Havelund, K., Penix, J., Visser, W. (eds.) SPIN 2000. LNCS, vol. 1885, pp. 131–147. Springer, Heidelberg (2000)
5. Holzmann, G.J., Smith, M.H.: Automating software feature verification. Bell Labs Technical Journal 5(2), 72–87 (2000)
6. Holzmann, G.J.: The Spin Model Checker: Primer and Reference Manual. Addison-Wesley (2004)
7. Holzmann, G.J., Florian, M.: Model checking with bounded context switching. Formal Aspects of Computing 23(3), 365–389 (2011)
8. Holzmann, G.J., Joshi, R., Groce, A.: Swarm verification techniques. IEEE Trans. on Software Eng. 37(6), 845–857 (2011)

---

[5] http://spinroot.com/swarm/

Verifying a Quantitative Relaxation of Linearizability via Refinement*

Kiran Adhikari[1], James Street[1], Chao Wang[1], Yang Liu[2], and ShaoJie Zhang[3]

[1] Virginia Tech, Blacksburg, Virginia, USA
[2] Nanyang Technological University, Singapore
[3] Singapore University of Technology and Design, Singapore

Abstract. Concurrent data structures have found increasingly widespread use in both multi-core and distributed computing environments, thereby escalating the priority for verifying their correctness. *Quasi linearizability* is a relaxation of *linearizability* to allow more implementation freedom for performance optimization. However, ensuring the quantitative aspects of this correctness condition is an arduous task. We propose a new method for formally verifying quasi linearizability of the implementation model of a concurrent data structure. The method is based on checking the refinement relation between the implementation and a specification model via explicit state model checking. It can directly handle concurrent programs where each thread can make infinitely many method calls, and it does not require the user to write annotations for the linearization points. We have implemented and evaluated our method in the PAT verification framework. Our experiments show that the method is effective in verifying quasi linearizability or detecting its violations.

1 Introduction

Linearizability [10,9] is a widely used correctness condition for concurrent data structures. A concurrent data structure is linearizable if each of its operations (method calls) appears to take effect instantaneously at some point in time between its invocation and response. Although being linearizable does not necessarily ensure the full-fledged correctness, linearizability violations are clear indicators that the implementation is buggy. In this sense, linearizability serves as a useful correctness condition for implementing concurrent data structures. However, ensuring linearizability of highly concurrent data structures is a difficult task, due to the subtle interactions of concurrent operations and the often astronomically many interleavings.

Quasi linearizability [1] is a quantitative relaxation of linearizability [12,17] to allow for more flexibility in how the data structures are implemented. While preserving the basic intuition of linearizability, quasi linearizability relaxes the semantics of the data structures to achieve increased runtime performance. For example, when implementing a queue for task schedulers in a thread pool, it is often the case that we do not need the strict first-in-first-out semantics; instead, we may allow the dequeue operations to be overtaken occasionally to improve the runtime performance. The only requirement is that such out-of-order execution should be bounded by a fixed number of steps.

---

* This work is supported in part by the National Science Foundation under Grant CCF-1149454.

E. Bartocci and C.R. Ramakrishnan (Eds.): SPIN 2013, LNCS 7976, pp. 24–42, 2013.

Despite the advantages of quasi linearizability and its rising popularity (e.g., [12,17]), such relaxed consistency property is difficult for testing and validation. Although there is a large body of work on formally verifying linearizability, for example, the methods based on model checking [15,14,23,5], runtime verification [4], and mechanical proofs [22], they cannot directly verify quasi linearizability. Quasi linearizability is harder to verify because, in addition to the requirement of covering all possible interleavings of concurrent events, one needs to accurately analyze the quantitative aspects of these interleavings.

In this paper, we propose the first automated method for formally verifying quasi linearizability in the implementation models of concurrent data structures. There are several technical challenges. First, since the number of concurrent operations in each thread is unbounded, the execution trace may be infinitely long. This precludes the use of existing methods such as LineUp [4] because they are based on checking permutations of finite histories. Second, since the method needs to be fully automated, we do not assume that the user will find and annotate the linearization points of each method. This precludes the use of existing methods that are based on either user guidance (e.g., [22]) or annotated linearization points (e.g., [23]).

To overcome these challenges, we rely on explicit state model checking. That is, given an implementation model M_{impl} and a specification model M_{spec}, we check whether the set of execution traces of M_{impl} is a subset of the execution traces of M_{spec}. Toward this end, we extend a classic refinement checking algorithm so that it can check for the newly defined *quantitative relaxation* of standard refinement relation. Consider a quasi linearizable queue as an example. Starting from the pair of initial states of a FIFO queue specification model and its quasi linearizable implementation model, we check whether all subsequent *state transitions* of the implementation model can match some subsequent *state transitions* of the specification model. To make sure that the verification problem remains decidable, we bound the capacity of the data structure in the model, to ensure that the number of states of the program is finite.

We have implemented the new method in the PAT verification framework [20]. PAT provides the infrastructure for parsing and analyzing the specification and implementation models written in a process algebra that resembles CSP [11]. Our new method is implemented as a module in PAT, and is compared against the existing module for checking standard refinement relation. Our experiments show that the new method is effective in detecting subtle violations of quasi linearizability. When the implementation model is indeed correct, our method can also generate the formal proof quickly.

Paper Organization. We establish notations and review the existing refinement checking algorithm in Section 2. We present the overall flow of our method in Section 3. In Section 4, we present a manual approach for verifying quasi linearizability based on the existing refinement checking algorithm, which is labor intensive and error prone. We present our fully automated method in Section 5, based on our new algorithm for checking the relaxed refinement relation. We present our experimental results in Sections 6. We review related work in Section 7 and conclude in Section 8.

2 Preliminaries

We define standard and quasi linearizability in this section, and review an existing algorithm for checking the refinement relation between two labeled transition systems.

2.1 Linearizability

Linearizability [10] is a safety property of concurrent systems, over sequences of actions corresponding to the invocations and responses of the operations on shared objects. We begin by formally defining the shared memory model.

Definition 1 (System Models). *A shared memory model* $\mathcal{M}$ *is a 3-tuple structure* $(O, init_O, P)$, *where* O *is a finite set of shared objects,* $init_O$ *is the initial valuation of* O, *and* P *is a finite set of processes accessing the objects.* □

Every shared object has a set of states. Each object supports a set of *operations*, which are pairs of invocations and matching responses. These operations are the only means of accessing the state of the object. A shared object is *deterministic* if, given the current state and an invocation of an operation, the next state of the object and the return value of the operation are unique. Otherwise, the shared object is *non-deterministic*. A *sequential specification*[1] of a deterministic (resp. non-deterministic) shared object is a function that maps every pair of invocation and object state to a pair (resp. a set of pairs) of response and a new object state. response and a new object state).

An execution of the shared memory model $\mathcal{M} = (O, init_O, P)$ is modeled by a history, which is a sequence of operation invocations and response actions that can be performed on O by processes in P. The behavior of $\mathcal{M}$ is defined as the set, H, of all possible histories together. A history $\sigma \in H$ induces an irreflexive partial order $<_\sigma$ on operations such that $op_1 <_\sigma op_2$ if the response of operation op_1 occurs in σ before the invocation of operation op_2. Operations in σ that are not related by $<_\sigma$ are concurrent. A history σ is *sequential* iff $<_\sigma$ is a strict total order.

Let $\sigma|_i$ be the projection of σ on process p_i, which is the subsequence of σ consisting of all invocations and responses that are performed by p_i in P. Let $\sigma|_{o_i}$ be the projection of σ on object o_i in O, which is the subsequence of σ consisting of all invocations and responses of operations that are performed on object o_i. Every history σ of a shared memory model $\mathcal{M} = (O, init_O, P)$ must satisfy the following basic properties:

- **Correct interaction:** For each process $p_i \in P$, $\sigma|_i$ consists of alternating invocations and matching responses, starting with an invocation. This property prevents *pipelining*[2] operations.
- **Closedness**[3]: Every invocation has a matching response. This property prevents *pending* operations.

---

[1] More rigorously, the sequential specification is for a *type* of shared objects. For simplicity, however, we refer to both actual shared objects and their types interchangeably in this paper.

[2] Pipelining operations mean that after invoking an operation, a process invokes another (same or different) operation before the response of the first operation.

[3] This property is not required in the original definition of linearizability in [10]. However adding it will not affect the correctness of our result because by Theorem 2 in [10], for a pending invocation in a linearizable history, we can always extend the history to a complete one and preserve linearizability. We include this property to obviate the discussion for pending invocations.

A sequential history σ is *legal* if it respects the sequential specifications of the objects. More specifically, for each object o_i, there exists a sequence of states $s_0, s_1, s_2, \ldots$ of object o_i, such that s_0 is the initial valuation of o_i, and for all $j = 1, 2, \ldots$ according to the sequential specification (the function), the j-th invocation in $\sigma|_{o_i}$ together with state s_{j-1} will generate the j-th response in $\sigma|_{o_i}$ and state s_j. For example, a sequence of read and write operations of an object is *legal* if each read returns the value of the preceding write if there is one, and otherwise it returns the initial value.

Given a history σ, a *sequential permutation* π of σ is a sequential history in which the set of operations as well as the initial states of the objects are the same as in σ.

Definition 2 (Linearizability). *Given a model* $\mathcal{M} = (O = \{o_1, \ldots, o_k\}, init_O, P = \{p_1, \ldots, p_n\})$. *Let H be the behavior of $\mathcal{M}$. $\mathcal{M}$ is linearizable if for any history σ in H, there exists a sequential permutation π of σ such that*

1. *for each object o_i ($1 \leq i \leq k$), $\pi|_{o_i}$ is a legal sequential history (i.e., π respects the sequential specification of the objects), and*
2. *for every op_1 and op_2 in σ, if $op_1 <_\sigma op_2$, then $op_1 <_\pi op_2$ (i.e., π respects the run-time ordering of operations).* □

Linearizability can be equivalently defined as follows. In every history σ, if we assign increasing time values to all invocations and responses, then every operation can be shrunk to a single time point between its invocation time and response time such that the operation appears to be completed instantaneously at this time point [16,3]. This time point is called its *linearization point*.

2.2 Quasi Linearizability

For two histories σ and σ' such that one is the permutation of the other, we define their distance as follows. Let $\sigma = e_1, e_2, e_3, \ldots, e_n$ and $\sigma' = e'_1, e'_2, e'_3, \ldots, e'_n$. Let $\sigma[e]$ and $\sigma'[e]$ be the indices of the event e in histories σ and σ', respectively. The distance between the two histories, denoted $\Delta(\sigma, \sigma')$, is defined as follows:

$$\Delta(\sigma, \sigma') = max_{e \in \sigma}\{|\sigma'[e] - \sigma[e]|\} .$$

In other words, the distance between σ and σ' is the maximum distance that an event in σ has to move to arrive at its position in σ'.

While measuring the distance between two histories, we often care about only a subset of method calls. For example, in a concurrent queue, we may care about the ordering of enqueue and dequeue operations while ignoring calls to size operation. In the remaining of this work, we use words enq and deq for the interests of space. Furthermore, we may allow deq operations to be executed out of order, but keep enq operations in order. In such case, we need a way to add ordering constraints on a subset of the methods of the shared object.

Let $Domain(o)$ be the set of all operations of a shared object o. Let $d \subset Domain(o)$ be a subset of operations. Let $Powerset(Domain(o))$ be the set of all subsets of $Domain(o)$. Let $D \subset Powerset(Domain(o))$ be a subset of the powerset.

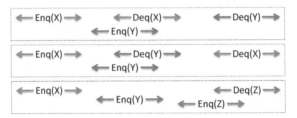

Fig. 1. Execution traces of a queue. Only the first trace (at the top) is linearizable. The second trace is not linearizable, but is 1-quasi linearizable. The third trace is only 2-quasi linearizable.

Definition 3 (Quasi Linearization Factor). *A* quasi-linearization factor *is a function* $Q_O : D \to \mathbb{N}$, *where D is a subset of the powerset and $\mathbb{N}$ is the set of natural numbers.*

Example 1. For a bounded queue that stores a set X of non-zero data items, we have $Domain(\texttt{queue}) = \{enq.x, deq.x, deq.0 \mid x \in X\}$, where $enq.x$ denotes the enqueue operation for data x, $deq.x$ denotes the dequeue operation for data x, and $deq.0$ indicates that the queue is empty. We may define two subsets of $Domain(\texttt{queue})$:

$$d_1 = \{enq.y \mid y \in Y\}, d_2 = \{deq.y \mid y \in Y\}.$$

Let $D = \{d_1, d_2\}$, where d_1 is the subset of deq events and d_2 is the subset of enq events. The distance between σ and σ', after being projected to subsets d_1 and d_2, is defined as $\Delta(\sigma|_{d_1}, \sigma'|_{d_2})$. If we require that the enq calls follow the FIFO order and the deq calls be out-of-order by at most K steps, the quasi-linearization factor $Q_{\{queue\}} : D \to \mathbb{N}$ is defined as $Q_{\{queue\}}(d_1) = 0, Q_{\{queue\}}(d_2) = K$.

Definition 4 (Quasi Linearizability). *Given a model $\mathcal{M} = (O = \{o_1, \ldots, o_k\}, init_O, P = \{p_1, \ldots, p_n\})$. Let H be the behavior of $\mathcal{M}$. $\mathcal{M}$ is quasi linearizable under the quasi factor $Q_O : D \to \mathbb{N}$ if for any history σ in H, there exists a sequential permutation π of σ such that*

- *for every op_1 and op_2 in σ, if $op_1 <_\sigma op_2$, then $op_1 <_\pi op_2$ (i.e., π respects the run-time ordering of operations), and*
- *for each object o_i ($1 \leq i \leq k$), there exists another sequential permutation π' of π such that*
    1. *$\pi'|_{o_i}$ is a legal sequential history (i.e., π' respects the sequential specification of the objects) and*
    2. *$\Delta((\pi|_{o_i})|_d, (\pi'|_{o_i})|_d) \leq Q_O(d)$ for all $d \in D$.*

This definition subsumes the definition for linearizability because, if the quasi factor is $Q_O(d) = 0$ for all $d \in D$, then the objects behave as a standard linearizable data structure, e.g., a FIFO queue.

Example 2. Consider the concurrent execution of a queue as shown in Fig. 1. In the first part, it is clear that the execution is linearizable, because it is a valid permutation of the sequential history where Enq(Y) takes effect before Deq(X). The second part is not linearizable, because the first dequeue operation is Deq(Y) but the first enqueue operation is Enq(X). However, it is interesting to note that the second history is not far from a linearizable history, since swapping the order of the two dequeue events would make it linearizable. Therefore, flexibility is provided in dequeue events to allow them to be reordered. Similarly, for the third part, if the quasi factor is 0 (no out-of-order execution) or 1 (out-of-order by at most 1 step), then the history is not quasi linearizable. However, if the quasi factor is 2 (out-of-order by at most 2 steps), then the third history in Fig.1 is considered as quasi linearizable.

2.3 Linearizability as Refinement

Linearizability is defined in terms of the invocations and responses of high-level operations. In a real concurrent program, the high-level operations are implemented by algorithms on concrete shared data structures, e.g., a linked list that implements a shared stack object [21]. Therefore, the execution of high-level operations may have complicated interleaving of low-level actions. Linearizability of a concrete concurrent algorithm requires that, despite low-level interleaving, the history of high-level invocation and response actions still has a sequential permutation that respects both the run-time ordering among operations and the sequential specification of the objects.

For verifying standard (but not quasi) linearizability, an existing method [15,14] can be used to check whether a real concurrent algorithm (we refer as *implementation* in this work) refines the high-level linearizable requirement (we refer as *specification* in this work). In this case, the behaviors of the implementation and the specification are modeled as labeled transition systems (LTSs), and the refinement checking is accomplished by using explicit state model checking.

Definition 5 (Labeled Transition System). *A Labeled Transition System (LTS) is a tuple $L = (S, init, Act, \rightarrow)$ where S is a finite set of states; $init \in S$ is an initial state; Act is a finite set of actions; and $\rightarrow \subseteq S \times Act \times S$ is a labeled transition relation.*

For simplicity, we write $s \xrightarrow{\alpha} s'$ to denote $(s, \alpha, s') \in \rightarrow$. The set of enabled actions at s is $enabled(s) = \{\alpha \in Act \mid \exists s' \in S.\ s \xrightarrow{\alpha} s'\}$. A path π of L is a sequence of alternating states and actions, starting and ending with states $\pi = \langle s_0, \alpha_1, s_1, \alpha_2, \cdots \rangle$ such that $s_0 = init$ and $s_i \xrightarrow{\alpha_{i+1}} s_{i+1}$ for all i. If π is finite, then $|\pi|$ denotes the number of transitions in π. A path can also be infinite, i.e., containing infinite number of actions. Since the number of states are finite, infinite paths are paths containing loops. The set of all possible paths for L is written as $paths(L)$.

A transition label can be either a visible action or an invisible one. Given an LTS L, the set of visible actions in L is denoted by vis_L and the set of invisible actions is denoted by $invis_L$. A τ-transition is a transition labeled with an invisible action. A state s' is *reachable* from state s if there exists a path that starts from s and ends with s', denoted by $s \xRightarrow{*} s'$. The set of τ-successors is $\tau(s) = \{s' \in S \mid s \xrightarrow{\alpha} s' \wedge \alpha \in invis_L\}$. The set of states reachable from s by performing zero or more τ transitions, denoted as $\tau^*(s)$, can be obtained by repeatedly computing the τ-successors starting from s until a fixed point is reached. We write $s \xRightarrow{\tau*} s'$ iff s' is reachable from s via only τ-transitions, i.e., there exists a path $\langle s_0, \alpha_1, s_1, \alpha_2, \cdots, s_n \rangle$ such that $s_0 = s$, $s_n = s'$ and $s_i \xrightarrow{\alpha_{i+1}} s_{i+1} \wedge \alpha_{i+1} \in invis_L$ for all i. Given a path π, we can obtain a sequence of visible actions by omitting states and invisible actions. The sequence,

---

Algorithm 1. Standard Refinement Checking

```
 1: Procedure Check-Refinement(impl, spec)
 2: checked := ∅
 3: pending.push((init_impl, init_spec))
 4: while pending ≠ ∅ do
 5:    (impl, spec) := pending.pop()
 6:    if enabled(impl) ⊄ enabled(spec) then
 7:       return false
 8:    end if
 9:    checked := checked ∪ {(impl, spec)}
10:    for all (impl', spec') ∈ next(impl, spec) do
11:       if (impl', spec') ∉ checked then
12:          pending.push((impl', spec'))
13:       end if
14:    end for
15: end while
16: return true
```

---

denoted as $trace(\pi)$, is a trace of L. The set of all traces of L, is written as $traces(L)$ = $\{trace(\pi) \mid \pi \in paths(L)\}$.

Definition 6 (Refinement). *Let L_1 and L_2 be two LTSs. L_1 refines L_2, written as $L_1 \sqsupseteq_T L_2$ iff $traces(L_1) \subseteq traces(L_2)$.*   □

In [15], we have shown that if L_{impl} is an implementation LTS and L_{spec} is the LTS of the linearizable specification, then L_{impl} is linearizable iff $L_{impl} \sqsupseteq_T L_{spec}$.

Algorithm 1 shows the pseudo code of the refinement checking procedure in [15,14]. Assume that L_{impl} refines M_{spec}, then for each reachable transition in M_{impl}, denoted as $impl \xrightarrow{e} impl'$, there must exist a reachable transition in L_{spec}, denoted as $spec \xrightarrow{e} spec'$. Therefore, the procedure starts with the pair of initial states of the two models, and repeatedly checks whether their have matching successor states. If the answer is no, the check at lines 6-8 would fail, meaning that L_{impl} is not linearizable. Otherwise, for each pair of immediate successor states $(impl', spec')$, we add the pair to the *pending* list. The entire procedure continues until either (1) a non-matching transition in L_{impl} is found at lines 6-8, or (2) all pairs of reachable states are checked, in which case L_{impl} is proved to be linearizable.

In Algorithm 1, the subroutine $next(impl, spec)$ is crucially important. It takes the current states of L_{impl} and L_{spec} as input, and returns a set of state pairs of the form $(impl', spec')$. Here each pair $(impl', spec')$ is one of the immediate successor state pairs of $(impl, spec)$. They are defined as follows:

1. if $impl \xrightarrow{\tau} impl'$, where τ is an internal event, then let $spec' = spec$;
2. if $impl \xrightarrow{e} impl'$, where e is a method call event, then $spec \xrightarrow{e} spec'$;

We have assumed, without loss of generality, that the specification model L_{spec} is deterministic. If the original specification model is nondeterministic, we can always apply standard *subset construction* (of DFAs) to make it deterministic.

3   Verifying Quasi Linearizability: The Overview

Our verification problem is defined as follows: Given an implementation model M_{impl}, a specification model M_{spec}, and a quasi factor Q_O, decide whether M_{impl} is quasi linearizable with respect to M_{spec} under the quasi factor Q_O.

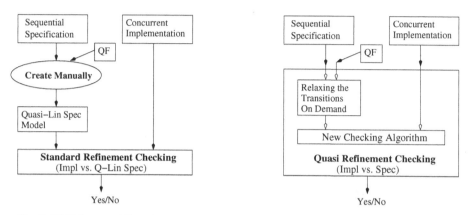

Fig. 2. Verifying quasi linearizability: manual approach (left) and automated approach (right)

The straightforward approach for solving the problem is to leverage the procedure in Algorithm 1. However, since the procedure checks for standard refinement relation, not quasi refinement relation, the user has to manually construct a relaxed specification model, denoted M'_{spec}, based on the given specification model M_{spec} and the quasi factor Q_O. This so-called *manual approach* is illustrated by Fig. 2 (left). The relaxed specification model M'_{spec} must be able to produce all histories that can be produced by M_{spec}, as well as the new histories that are allowed under the relaxed consistency condition in Definition 4.

Unfortunately, there is no systematic method, or general guideline, on constructing such relaxed specification models. Each M'_{spec} may be different depending on the type of data structures to be checked. And there is significant amount of creativity required during the process, to make sure that the new specification model is both simple enough and permissive enough. For example, to verify that a K-segmented queue [1] is quasi linearizable, we can create a relaxed specification model whose dequeue method randomly removes one of the first K data items from the otherwise standard FIFO queue. This new model M'_{spec} will be more complex than M_{spec}, but can still be significantly simpler than the full-fledged implementation model M_{impl}, which requires the use of a complex segmented linked list.

Since the focus of this paper is on designing a fully automated verification method, we shall briefly illustrate the manual approach in Section 4, and then focus on developing an automated approach in the subsequent sections.

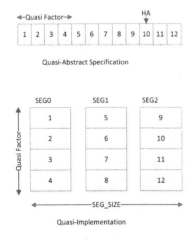

Quasi-Abstract Specification

Quasi-Implementation

Fig. 3. Implementations of a 4-quasi queue

H1-a	H1-b	H1-a	H1-b
enq(1)	enq(1)	enq(1)	enq(1)
enq(2)	enq(2)	enq(2)	enq(2)
enq(3)	enq(3)	enq(3)	enq(3)
enq(4)	enq(4)	enq(4)	enq(4)
deq()=1	deq()=1	deq()=2	deq()=2
deq()=2	deq()=2	deq()=1	deq()=1
deq()=3	deq()=4	deq()=3	deq()=4
deq()=4	deq()=3	deq()=4	deq()=3

Fig. 4. Valid histories of a *1-quasi linearizable* queue, meaning that deq can be out-of-order by 1. The first deq randomly returns a value from the set $\{1, 2\}$ and the second deq returns the remaining one. Then the third deq randomly returns a value from the set $\{3, 4\}$ and the forth deq returns the remaining one.

Our automated approach is shown in Fig. 2 (right). It is based on designing a new refinement checking algorithm that, in contrast to Algorithm 1, can directly check a *relaxed version* of the standard refinement relation between M_{impl} and M_{spec}. Therefore, the user does not need to manually construct the relaxed specification model M''_{spec}. Instead, inside the new refinement checking procedure, we systematically extend states and transitions of the specification model M_{spec} so that the new states and transitions as required by M'_{spec} are added on the fly. This would lead to the inclusion of a bounded degree of out-of-order execution on the relevant subset of operations as defined by the quasi factor Q_O. A main advantage of our new method is that the procedure is fully automated, thereby avoiding the user intervention, as well as the potential errors that may be introduced during the user's manual modeling process. Furthermore, by exploring the relaxed transitions on a *need-to* basis, rather than upfront as in the manual approach, we can reduce the number of states that need to be checked.

4   Verifying Quasi Linearizability via Refinement Checking

In this section, we will briefly describe the manual approach and then focus on presenting the automated approach in the subsequent sections. Although we do not intend to promote the manual approach – since it is labor-intensive and error prone – this section will illustrate the intuitions behind our fully automated verification method.

Given the specification model M_{spec} and the quasi factor Q_O, we show how to manually construct the relaxed specification model M'_{spec} in this section. We use the standard FIFO queue and two versions of quasi linearizable queues as examples. The construction needs to be tailored case by case for the different types of data structures.

Specification Model M_{spec}: The standard FIFO queue with a bounded capacity can be implemented by using a linked list, where deq operation removes a data item at one end of the list called the *head* node, and enq operation adds a data item at the other end of the list called the *tail* node. When the queue is full, enq does not have any impact. When the queue is empty, deq returns NULL. As an example, consider a sequence of four enqueue events enq(1), enq(2), enq(3), enq(4), the subsequent dequeue events would be deq.1, deq.2, deq.3, deq.4, which obey the FIFO semantics. This is illustrated by the first history H1-a in Fig. 4. In PAT verification framework, the specification model M_{spec} is written in a process algebra language, named CSP# [19].

Implementation Model M_{impl}: The bounded quasi linearizable queue can be implemented using a segmented linked list. This is the original algorithm proposed by Afek *et al.* [1]. A segmented linked list is a linked list where each list node can hold K data items, as opposed to a single data item in the standard linked list. As shown in Fig. 3 (lower half), these K data items form a *segment*, in which the data slots are numbered as 1, 2, ..., K. In general, the segment size needs to be set to $(QF + 1)$, where QF is the maximum number of out-of-order execution steps. The example in Fig. 3 has the quasi factor set to 3, meaning that a deq operation can be executed out of order by at most 3 steps. Consequently, the size of each segment is set to $(3+1)=4$. Since $Q_{\{queue\}}(D_{enq}) = 0$, meaning that the enq operations cannot be reordered, the data items are enqueued regularly in the empty slots of one segment, before the *head* points to the next segment. But for deq operations, we randomly remove one existing data item from the current segment.

Relaxed Specification Model M'_{spec}: Not all execution traces of M_{impl} are traces of M_{spec}. In Fig. 4, histories other than H1-a are not linearizable. However, they are all quasi linearizable under the quasi factor 1. They may be produced by a segmented queue where the segment size is $(1+1)=2$. To verify that M_{impl} is quasi linearizable, we construct a new model M'_{spec}, which includes not only all histories of M_{spec}, but also the histories that are allowed only under the relaxed consistency condition. In this example, we choose to construct the new model by slightly modifying the standard FIFO queue. This is illustrated in Fig. 3 (upper half), where the first K data items are grouped into a cluster. Within the cluster, the deq operation may remove any of the k data items based on randomization. Only after the first k data items in the cluster are retrieved, will the deq move to the next k data items (a new cluster). The external behavior of this model is expected to match that of the segmented queue in M_{impl}: both are *1-quasi linearizable*.

Checking Refinement Relation: Once M'_{spec} is available, checking whether M_{impl} refines M'_{spec} is straightforward by using Algorithm 1. For the segmented queue implementation [1], we have manually constructed M'_{spec} and checked the refinement relation in PAT. Our experimental results are summarized in Table 1. Column 1 shows the different quasi factors. Column 2 shows the number of segments – the capacity of the queue is $(QF + 1) \times Seg$. Column 3 shows the refinement checking time in seconds. Column 4 shows the total number of visited states during refinement checking. Column 5 shows the total number of state transitions activated during refinement checking. The experiments are conducted on a computer with an Intel Core-i7, 2.5 GHz processor and 8GB RAM running Ubuntu 10.04.

Table 1. Experimental results for standard refinement checking. MOut means memory-out.

Quasi Factor	#. Segment	Verification Time (s)	#. Visited State	#. Transition
1	1	0.1	423	778
1	2	0.1	2310	4458
1	3	0.1	8002	15213
1	4	0.4	22327	41660
1	5	0.9	55173	101443
1	6	2.0	126547	230259
1	10	55.9	2488052	4421583
1	15	MOut	-	-
2	1	0.6	26605	58281
2	2	12.6	456397	970960
2	3	130.7	4484213	8742485
2	4	MOut	-	-
3	1	8.8	284484	638684
3	2	MOut	-	-
4	1	124.4	3432702	7906856
4	2	MOut	-	-

The experimental results in Table 1 show an exponential increment in the verification time when we increase the size of the queue or the quasi factor. This is inevitable since the size of the state space grows exponentially. However, this method requires the user to manually construct M'_{spec}, which is a severe limitation.

For example, consider the seemingly simple random dequeued model in Fig. 3. A subtle error would be introduced if we do not use the *cluster* to restrict the set of data items that can be removed by deq operation. Assume that deq always returns one of the first k data items in the current queue. Although it appears to be correct, such implementation will not be k-quasi linearizable, because it is possible for some data item to be over-taken indefinitely. For example, if every time deq chooses *the second data item in the list*, we will have the following deq sequence: deq.2, deq.3, deq.4, ..., deq.1, where the dequeue of value 1 can be delayed by an arbitrarily long time. This is no longer a *1-quasi linearizable* queue. In other words, if the user constructed M'_{spec} incorrectly, the verification result becomes invalid.

Therefore, we need to design a fully automated method to directly verify quasi linearizability of M_{impl} against M_{spec} under the given quasi factor QF.

5   New Algorithm for Checking the Quasi Refinement Relation

We shall start with the standard refinement checking procedure in Algorithm 1 and extend it to directly check a relaxed version of the refinement relation between M_{impl} and M_{spec} under the given quasi factor. The idea is to establish the simulation relationship from specification to implementation while allowing relaxation of the specification.

5.1   Linearizability Checking via Quasi Refinement

The new procedure, shown in Algorithm 2, is different from Algorithm 1 as follows:

1. We customize *pending* to make the state exploration follow a breadth-first search (BFS). In Algorithm 1, it can be either BFS or DFS based on whether *pending* is a queue or stack.

Algorithm 2. Quasi Refinement Checking

```
 1: Procedure Check-Quasi-Refinement(impl, spec, QF)
 2: checked := ∅
 3: pending.enqueue((init_impl, init_spec))
 4: while pending ≠ ∅ do
 5:    (impl, spec) := pending.dequeue()
 6:    if enabled(impl) ⊄ enabled_relaxed(spec, QF) then
 7:       return false
 8:    end if
 9:    checked := checked ∪ {(impl, spec)}
10:    for all (impl', spec') ∈ next_relaxed(impl, spec, QF) do
11:       if (impl', spec') ∉ checked then
12:          pending.enqueue((impl', spec'))
13:       end if
14:    end for
15: end while
16: return true
```

---

2. We replace *enabled(spec)* with *enabled_relaxed(spec,QF)*. It will return not only the events enabled at current *spec* state in M_{spec}, but also the additional events allowed under the relaxed consistency condition.

3. We replace *next(impl,spec)* with *next_relaxed(impl,spec,QF)*. It will return not only the successor state pairs in the original models, but also the additional pairs allowed under the relaxed consistency condition.

Conceptually, it is equivalent to first constructing a relaxed specification model M'_{spec} from (M_{spec}, QF) and then computing the *enabled(spec)* and *next(impl,spec)* on this new model. However, in this case, we are constructing M'_{spec} automatically, without the user's intervention. Furthermore, the additional states and edges that need to be added to M'_{spec} are processed incrementally, on a *need-to* basis.

At the high level, the new procedure performs a BFS exploration for the state pair $(impl, spec)$, where *impl* is the state of implementation and *spec* is a state of specification. The initial implementation and specification events are enqueued into *pending* and each time we go through the while-loop, we dequeue from *pending* a state pair, and check if all events enabled at state *impl* match with some events enabled at state *spec* under the relaxed consistency condition (line 6). If there is any mismatch, the check fails and we can return a counterexample showing how the violation happens. Otherwise, we continue until *pending* is empty. Lines 10-14 explore the new successor state pairs, by invoking *next_relaxed* and add to *pending* if they have not been checked.

Subroutine enabled_relaxed(spec,QF): It takes the current state *spec* of model M_{spec}, along with the quasi factor QF, and generates all events that are enabled at state *spec*.

Consider the graph in Fig. 5 as M_{spec}. Without relaxation, $enabled(s_1)=\{e_1\}$. This is equivalent to $enabled\_relaxed(s_1, 0)$. However, when $QF = 1$, according to the dotted edges in Fig. 6, the set $enabled\_relaxed(s_1, 1)=\{e_1, e_2, e_3\}$.

The reason why e_2 and e_3 become enabled is as follows: before relaxation, starting at state s_1, there are two length-3 $(2QF + 1)$ event sequences $\sigma_1 = e_1, e_2, e_5$ and

$\sigma_2 = e_1, e_3, e_4$. When $QF = 1$, it means an event can be out-of-order by at most 1 step. Therefore, the possilbe valid permutations of σ_1 is $\pi_1 = e_2, e_1, e_5$ and $\pi_2 = e_1, e_5, e_2$, and the possible valid permutations of σ_2 is $\pi_3 = e_3, e_1, e_4$ and $\pi_4 = e_1, e_4, e_3$ for $QF = 1$. In other words, at state s_1, events e_2, e_3 can also be executed. We will discuss the generation of valid permutation sequences in Section 5.2.

Subroutine next_relaxed(impl, spec, QF): It takes the current state $impl$ of M_{impl} and the current state $spec$ of M_{spec} as input, and returns a set of state pairs of the form $(impl', spec')$. Similar to the definition of $next(impl, spec)$ in Section 2, we define each pair $(impl', spec')$ as follows:

1. if $impl \xrightarrow{\tau} impl'$, where τ is an internal event, then let $spec' = spec$;
2. if $impl \xrightarrow{e} impl'$, where e is a method call event, then $spec \xrightarrow{e} spec'$ where event $e \in enabled\_relaxed(spec, QF)$ is enabled at $spec$ after relaxation.

For example, when $spec = s_1$ in Fig. 5, and the quasi factor is set to 1 – meaning that the event at state s_1 can be out-of-order by at most one step – the procedure *next_relaxed(impl, s_1, 1)* would return not only $(impl', s_2)$, but also $(impl', s_6)$ and $(impl', s_9)$, as indicated by the dotted edges in Fig. 6. The detailed algorithm for generation of the relaxed next states in specification is described in Section 5.2.

5.2   Generation of Relaxed Specification

In this subsection, we show how to relax the specification M_{spec} by adding new states and transitions – those that are allowed under the condition of quasi linearizability – to form a new specification model. Notice that we accomplish this automatically, and incrementally, on a *need-to* basis.

For each state $spec$ in M_{spec}, we compute all the event sequences starting at $spec$ with the length $(2QF + 1)$. These event sequences can be computed by using a simple graph traversal algorithm, e.g., a breadth first search.

Fig. 5 shows an example for the computation of these event sequences. The specification model M_{spec} has the following set of states $\{s_1, s_2, s_3, s_4, s_5\}$. Suppose that the current state is s_1 (in *step* 0), then the current frontier state set is $\{s_1\}$, and the current event sequence is $\langle s_1 \rangle$. The results of each BFS step are shown in Table 2. In *step* 1, the frontier state set is $\{s_2\}$, and the event sequence becomes $\langle s_1 \xrightarrow{e_1} s_2 \rangle$. In *step* 2, the frontier state set is $\{s_3, s_4\}$, and the event sequence is split into two sequences. One is $\langle s_1 \xrightarrow{e_1} s_2 \xrightarrow{e_2} s_3 \rangle$ and the other is $\langle s_1 \xrightarrow{e_1} s_2 \xrightarrow{e_3} s_4 \rangle$. The traversal continues until the BFS depth reaches $(2QF + 1)$.

After completing the $(2QF+1)$ steps of BFS starting at state $spec$, as above, we have to generate possible valid permutations first and then we will be able to evaluate the two subroutines: $enabled\_relaxed(spec, QF)$ and $next\_relaxed(impl, spec, QF)$.

We transform the original specification model in Fig. 5 to the relaxed specification model in Fig. 6 for $QF = 1$. The dotted states and edges are newly added to reflect the relaxation. More specifically, for $QF = 1$, we will reach $(2QF + 1) = 3$ steps during the BFS. At *step* 3, there are two existing sequences $\{e_1, e_2, e_5\}$ and $\{e_1, e_3, e_4\}$. For each existing sequence, we compute all possible valid permutation sequences.

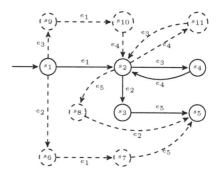

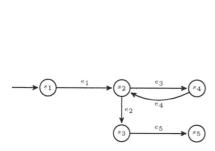

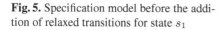

Fig. 5. Specification model before the addition of relaxed transitions for state s_1

Fig. 6. Specification model after adding relaxed edges for state s_1 and quasi factor 1

Table 2. Specification Sequence Generation at State s_1

BFS Steps	(Frontier)	EventSequences
step 0	$\{s_1\}$	$\langle s_1 \rangle$
step 1	$\{s_2\}$	$\langle s_1 \xrightarrow{e_1} s_2 \rangle$
step 2	$\{s_3, s_4\}$	$\langle s_1 \xrightarrow{e_1} s_2 \xrightarrow{e_2} s_3 \rangle \langle s_1 \xrightarrow{e_1} s_2 \xrightarrow{e_3} s_4 \rangle$
step 3	$\{s_5, s_2\}$	$\langle s_1 \xrightarrow{e_1} s_2 \xrightarrow{e_2} s_3 \xrightarrow{e_5} s_5 \rangle \langle s_1 \xrightarrow{e_1} s_2 \xrightarrow{e_3} s_4 \xrightarrow{e_4} s_2 \rangle$

In this case, the valid permutation sequences are $\{e_2, e_1, e_5\}, \{e_1, e_5, e_2\}$ and $\{e_3, e_1, e_6\}$, $\{e_1, e_3, e_6\}$. For each newly generated permutation sequence, we add new edges and states to the specification model. From an initial state s_1, if we follow the new permutation $\{e_2, e_1, e_5\}$, as shown in Fig. 6, the transition e_2 will lead to newly formed pseudo state s_6, the transition e_1 will lead to s_7 from state s_6 and from this state it is reconnected back to the original state s_5 via transition e_5. Similarly, if we follow the new permutation $\{e_3, e_1, e_4\}$, the transition e_3 will lead to newly formed pseudo state s_9, the transition e_1 will lead to s_{10} from state s_9 and from this state it is reconnected back to state s_2 via transition e_4. We continue this process of state expansion for all the valid permutation sequences. This relaxation process needs to be conducted by using every existing state of M_{spec} as the starting point (for BFS up to $2QF + 1$ steps) and then adding the new states and edges. Note that this process is conducted on the fly.

Algorithm 3 explains the high level pseudo-code for expanding the state space for the current specification state under the check. Let $SEQ = \{seq_1, seq_2, ..., seq_k\}$ be the sequences which are reachable from the state s_0 in M_{spec} such that each sequence has less than or equal to $2QF + 1$ events. Each sequence $seq \in SEQ$ calls a *genValidPermut(seq,QF)* (line 4) to generate all the possible valid permutation paths for that trace. A new state is formed with a new transition for each event in the permuted sequences, hence allowing the relaxed refinement checking of the implementation trace.

The valid permutations for a given sequence is generated using an Algorithm 4 which is based on the cost associated with the event. Initially, for each events e_i where $1 \leq i < n$ associated with the *seq*, the cost is initialized to QF (line 2). We generate all possible permutations and update cost with respect to the relative ordering of the events for each reshuffled sequences. This cost attribute of an event stores the information on

---

Algorithm 3. Pseudo-code for Expanding Specification Under Check

---

1: Let s_0 be a specification state and QF be the quasi factor
2: Let $SEQ = \{seq_1, seq_2, seq_3, \cdots, seq_k\}$ be the set of all possible event sequences reachable from s_0 in M_{spec} such that for $1 \leq i \leq k$, each seq_i has less than or equal to $2QF + 1$
   relaxed events
3: **for all** *seq* in *SEQ* **do**
4:    *PERMUT_VALID* = $genValidPermut(seq, QF)$
5:    **for all** *perm* in *PERMUT_VALID* **do**
6:       Let *perm* = $\langle e_1, e_2, \cdots, e_n \rangle$
7:       Let s_n be the specification state reached from s_0 via *seq*
8:       **if** *perm* is not equal to *seq* **then**
9:          **for all** e_i where $1 \leq i < n$ **do**
10:            Create a new state s_i and a new transition from s_{i-1} to s_i via event e_i
11:         **end for**
12:         Create a new transition from s_{n-1} to s_n via e_n
13:      **end if**
14:   **end for**
15: **end for**

Algorithm 4. $genValidPermut(seq, QF)$

1: *PERMUT_VALID* := $\emptyset$
2: Initialize cost associated with each event in *seq* to QF
3: Generate possible permutations *PERMUT_SEQ* and update cost
4: **for all** p in *PERMUT_SEQ* **do**
5:    isValid = *true*
6:    Let $p = \langle e_1, e_2, \cdots, e_n \rangle$
7:    **for all** e_i where $1 \leq i < n$ **do**
8:       **if** $e_i.cost \geq 2QF \lor e_i.cost \leq 0$ **then**
9:          isValid = *false*
10:         break
11:      **end if**
12:   **end for**
13:   **if** isValid **then**
14:      *PERMUT_VALID* = *PERMUT_VALID* $\bigcup p$
15:   **end if**
16: **end for**
17: return *PERMUT_VALID*

---

how many more steps an event may be postponed. Each time an event is postponed, the cost associated with this event is decremented by 1. On the contrary, the event can also be chosen upto QF steps ahead and for each step, the cost is increased by 1. So, the cost attribute of the event that is allowed for relaxation is $2QF \leq cost \leq 0$. We check the validity of each of these sequences using this cost attribute (line 8). Finally, only the valid permutations are appended in *PERMUT_VALID* after each check and once the check is completed for all permuted sequences, the function returns the valid traces.

Consider the event sequence $\{e_1, e_2, e_5\}$ from state s_1 be *seq* as shown in Fig. 5. If $QF = 1$, the cost for each of these events is initialized to 1. We generate all possible permutations by reshuffling the events and updating the cost based on the relative positioning of the event with respect to the initial sequence. There are as many as 6 possible permutations including the original sequence in this case. If we consider reordering be the sequence $\{e_2, e_1, e_5\}$, then the cost associated with event e_2 is 2 as it is chosen one step earlier. For the event e_1, it is postponed for one step meaning its cost is decreased by 1 which makes the cost associated with it be 0. Event e_3 is not reordered and hence its cost is unchanged and is 1. This sequence is valid because cost associated with each of the events in this sequence lies within the allowable range. Similarly, if we consider another permuted sequence $\{e_3, e_1, e_2\}$, then the cost associated with each of these events is $\{3, 0, 0\}$ which exceeds the allowable range. So, this permutation sequence is not valid. We do this for all the permuted sequences to generate the valid traces.

6   Experiments

We have implemented and evaluated the quasi linearizability checking method in the PAT verification framework [20]. Our new algorithm can directly check a relaxed version of the refinement relation. This new algorithm subsumes the standard refinement checking procedure that has already been implemented in PAT. In particular, when $QF = 0$, our new procedure degenerates to the standard refinement checking procedure. When $QF > 0$, our new procedure has the added capability of checking for the quantitatively relaxed refinement relation. Our algorithm can directly handle the implementation model M_{impl}, the standard (not quasi) specification model M_{spec}, and the quasi factor QF, thereby completely avoiding the user's intervention.

We have evaluated our new algorithm on a set of models of standard and quasi linearizable concurrent data structures [1,12,17], including queues, stacks, quasi queues, quasi stacks, and quasi priority queues. For each data structure, there can be several variants, each of which has a slightly different implementation. In addition to the implementations that are known to be linearizable and quasi linearizable, we also have versions which initially were thought to be correct, but were subsequently proved to be buggy by our verification tool. The characteristics of all benchmark examples are shown in Table 3. The first two columns list the name of the concurrent data structures and a short description of the implementation. The next two columns show whether the implementation is linearizable and quasi linearizable.

Table 4 shows the results of the experiments. The experiments are conducted on a computer with an Intel Core-i7, 2.5 GHz processor and 8 GB RAM running Windows 7. The first column shows the statistics of the test program, including the name and the size of benchmark. The second column is the quasi factor showing the relaxation bound allowed for the model. The next three columns show the runtime performance, consisting of the verification time in seconds, the total number of visited states, and the total number of transitions made. The number of states and the running time for each of the models increase with the data size.

For 3 segmented quasi queue with quasi factor 2, the verification completes in 7.2 seconds. It is much faster than the first approach presented in Section 4, where the same setting requires 130.7 seconds for the verification. Subsequently, as the size increases, the time to verify the quasi queue increases. For queue with size 6 and 9, verification

Table 3. Statistics of Benchmark Examples

Class	Description	Linearizable	Quasi Lin.
Quasi Queue (3)	Segmented linked list implementation (size=3)	No	Yes
Quasi Queue (6)	Segmented linked list implementation (size=6)	No	Yes
Quasi Queue (9)	Segmented linked list implementation (size=9)	No	Yes
Queue buggy1	Segmented queue with a bug (Dequeue on the empty queue may erroneously change current segment)	No	No
Queue buggy2	Segmented queue with a bug (Dequeue may get value from a wrong segment)	No	No
Lin. Queue	A linearizable (hence quasi) implementation	Yes	Yes
Q. Priority Queue (6)	Segmented linked list implementation (size=6)	No	Yes
Q. Priority Queue (9)	Segmented linked list implementation (size=9)	No	Yes
Priority Queue buggy	Segmented priority queue (Dequeue on the empty priority queue may change current segment)	No	No
Lin. Stack	A linearizable (hence quasi) implementation	Yes	Yes

Table 4. Results for Checking Quasi Linearizability with 2 threads

Class	QF	Verification Time (s)	Number of Visited States	Number of Visited Transitions
Quasi Queue (3)	2	7.2	126,810	248,122
Quasi Queue (6)	2	21.2	237,760	468,461
Quasi Queue (9)	2	114.5	1,741,921	3,424,280
Quasi Queue (4)	3	131.6	442,558	869,129
Quasi Queue (8)	3	1517.1	1,986,924	3,754,489
Queue buggy1	2	0.4	1,204	809
Queue buggy2	2	0.1	345	345
Lin. Queue	2	5.5	240,583	121,548
Q. Priority Queue (6)	2	34.3	472,981	918,530
Q. Priority Queue (9)	2	198.4	1,478,045	2,905,016
Q. Priority Queue (4)	3	343.1	1,408,763	2,566,427
Priority Queue buggy	2	5.4	894	894
Lin. Stack	2	0.2	2,690	6,896

is completed in 21.2 seconds and 114.5 seconds, respectively. As the quasi factor is increased to 3, the verification time for quasi queue with size 4 and 8 is increased to 131.6 seconds 1517.1 seconds respectively, which is much higher in comparison to the time for quasi factor 2. This is basically because of the significant increment in state expansion for the higher quasi factor. For the priority queues where enqueue and dequeue operations are performed based on the priority, the verification time is higher than the regular quasi queue. Also, it is important to note that the counterexample is produced with exploration of only part of the state space for the buggy models. The verification time is much faster for the buggy queue, which shows that our approach is effective if the quasi linearizability is not satisfied. In all test cases, our method was able to correctly verify quasi linearizability or detect the violations.

7 Related Work

In the literature, although there exists a large body of work on formally verifying linearizability in models of data structure implementations, none of them can verify quasi linearizability. For example, Liu et al. [15,14] use a process algebra based tool to verify that an implementation model refines a specification model – the refinement relation implies linearizability. Vechev et al. [23] use SPIN to verify linearizability. Cerný et al. [5] use automated abstractions together with model checking to verify linearizability properties. There also exists some work on proving linearizability by constructing mechanical proofs, often with significant manual intervention (e.g., [22]).

There are also runtime verification algorithms such as Line-Up [4], which can directly check the actual source code implementation but for violations on bounded executions and deterministic linearizability. However, quasi linearizable data structures are inherently nondeterministic. For example, the deq operation in a quasi queue implementation may choose to return any of the first k items in a queue. To the best of our knowledge, no existing method can directly verify quasi linearizability for execution traces of unbounded length.

Besides (quasi) linearizability, there also exist many other consistency conditions for concurrent computations, including sequential consistency [13], quiescent consistency [2], and eventual consistency [24]. Some of these consistency conditions in principle may be used for checking the correctness of data structure implementations, although so far, none of them is as widely used as (quasi) linearizability. These consistency conditions do not involve quantitative aspects of the properties. We believe that it is possible to extend our refinement algorithm to verify some of these properties. work.

Outside the domain of concurrent data structures, *serializability* and *atomicity* are two popular correctness properties for concurrent programs, especially at the application level. There exists a large body of work on both static and dynamic analysis for detecting violations of such properties (e.g., [8,6] and [26,7,18,25]). These existing methods are different from ours because they are checking different properties. Although atomicity and serializability are fairly general correctness conditions, they have been applied mostly to the correctness of shared memory accesses at the load/store instruction level. Linearizability, in contrast, defines correctness condition at the method call level. Furthermore, existing methods for checking atomicity and serializability do not deal with the quantitative aspects of the properties.

8 Conclusions

We have presented a new method for formally verifying quasi linearizability of the implementation models of concurrent data structures. We have explored two approaches, one of which is based on manual construction of the relaxed specification model, whereas the other is fully automated, and is based on checking a relaxed version of the refinement relation between the implementation model and the specification model. For future work, we plan to incorporate advanced state space reduction techniques such as symmetry reduction and partial order reduction.

References

1. Afek, Y., Korland, G., Yanovsky, E.: Quasi-Linearizability: Relaxed consistency for improved concurrency. In: Lu, C., Masuzawa, T., Mosbah, M. (eds.) OPODIS 2010. LNCS, vol. 6490, pp. 395–410. Springer, Heidelberg (2010)
2. Aspnes, J., Herlihy, M., Shavit, N.: Counting networks. J. ACM 41(5), 1020–1048 (1994)

3. Attiya, H., Welch, J.: Distributed Computing: Fundamentals, Simulations, and Advanced Topics, 2nd edn. John Wiley & Sons, Inc., Publication (2004)
4. Burckhardt, S., Dern, C., Musuvathi, M., Tan, R.: Line-up: a complete and automatic linearizability checker. In: PLDI, pp. 330–340 (2010)
5. Černý, P., Radhakrishna, A., Zufferey, D., Chaudhuri, S., Alur, R.: Model checking of linearizability of concurrent list implementations. In: Touili, T., Cook, B., Jackson, P. (eds.) CAV 2010. LNCS, vol. 6174, pp. 465–479. Springer, Heidelberg (2010)
6. Farzan, A., Madhusudan, P.: Causal atomicity. In: Ball, T., Jones, R.B. (eds.) CAV 2006. LNCS, vol. 4144, pp. 315–328. Springer, Heidelberg (2006)
7. Farzan, A., Madhusudan, P.: Monitoring atomicity in concurrent programs. In: Gupta, A., Malik, S. (eds.) CAV 2008. LNCS, vol. 5123, pp. 52–65. Springer, Heidelberg (2008)
8. Flanagan, C., Qadeer, S.: A type and effect system for atomicity. In: PLDI, pp. 338–349 (2003)
9. Herlihy, M., Shavit, N.: The art of multiprocessor programming. Morgan Kaufmann (2008)
10. Herlihy, M., Wing, J.M.: Linearizability: A correctness condition for concurrent objects. ACM Trans. Program. Lang. Syst. 12(3), 463–492 (1990)
11. Hoare, C.A.R.: Communicating Sequential Processes. Prentice Hall, Englewood Cliffs (1985)
12. Kirsch, C.M., Payer, H., Röck, H., Sokolova, A.: Performance, scalability, and semantics of concurrent FIFO queues. In: Xiang, Y., Stojmenovic, I., Apduhan, B.O., Wang, G., Nakano, K., Zomaya, A. (eds.) ICA3PP 2012, Part I. LNCS, vol. 7439, pp. 273–287. Springer, Heidelberg (2012)
13. Lamport, L.: How to make a multiprocessor computer that correctly executes multiprocess programs. IEEE Trans. Computers 28(9), 690–691 (1979)
14. Liu, Y., Chen, W., Liu, Y., Zhang, S., Sun, J., Dong, J.S.: Verifying linearizability via optimized refinement checking. IEEE Transactions on Software Engineering (2013)
15. Liu, Y., Chen, W., Liu, Y.A., Sun, J.: Model checking linearizability via refinement. In: Cavalcanti, A., Dams, D.R. (eds.) FM 2009. LNCS, vol. 5850, pp. 321–337. Springer, Heidelberg (2009)
16. Lynch, N.: Distributed Algorithms. Morgan Kaufmann (1997)
17. Payer, H., Röck, H., Kirsch, C.M., Sokolova, A.: Scalability versus semantics of concurrent fifo queues. In: PODC, pp. 331–332 (2011)
18. Sadowski, C., Freund, S.N., Flanagan, C.: Singletrack: A dynamic determinism checker for multithreaded programs. In: Castagna, G. (ed.) ESOP 2009. LNCS, vol. 5502, pp. 394–409. Springer, Heidelberg (2009)
19. Sun, J., Liu, Y., Dong, J.S., Chen, C.: Integrating specification and programs for system modeling and verification. In: TASE, pp. 127–135 (2009)
20. Sun, J., Liu, Y., Dong, J.S., Pang, J.: PAT: Towards Flexible Verification under Fairness. In: Bouajjani, A., Maler, O. (eds.) CAV 2009. LNCS, vol. 5643, pp. 709–714. Springer, Heidelberg (2009)
21. Treiber, R.K.: Systems Programming: Coping with Parallelism. Technical Report RJ 5118, IBM Almaden Research Center (1986)
22. Vafeiadis, V.: Shape-value abstraction for verifying linearizability. In: Jones, N.D., Müller-Olm, M. (eds.) VMCAI 2009. LNCS, vol. 5403, pp. 335–348. Springer, Heidelberg (2009)
23. Vechev, M., Yahav, E., Yorsh, G.: Experience with model checking linearizability. In: Păsăreanu, C.S. (ed.) SPIN 2009. LNCS, vol. 5578, pp. 261–278. Springer, Heidelberg (2009)
24. Vogels, W.: Eventually consistent. Commun. ACM 52(1), 40–44 (2009)
25. Wang, C., Limaye, R., Ganai, M., Gupta, A.: Trace-based symbolic analysis for atomicity violations. In: Esparza, J., Majumdar, R. (eds.) TACAS 2010. LNCS, vol. 6015, pp. 328–342. Springer, Heidelberg (2010)
26. Wang, L., Stoller, S.D.: Runtime analysis of atomicity for multithreaded programs. IEEE Trans. Software Eng. 32(2), 93–110 (2006)

A Map-Reduce Parallel Approach to Automatic Synthesis of Control Software

Vadim Alimguzhin[1,2], Federico Mari[1], Igor Melatti[1],
Ivano Salvo[1], and Enrico Tronci[1]

[1] Computer Science Department, Sapienza University of Rome, Italy
{alimguzhin,mari,melatti,salvo,tronci}@di.uniroma1.it
[2] Department of Computer Science and Robotics, Ufa State Aviation Technical University,
Russian Federation

Abstract. Many Control Systems are indeed Software Based Control Systems,
i.e. control systems whose controller consists of control software running on a
microcontroller device. This motivates investigation on Formal Model Based Design approaches for automatic synthesis of control software.

Available algorithms and tools (e.g., *QKS*) may require weeks or even months
of computation to synthesize control software for large-size systems. This motivates search for parallel algorithms for control software synthesis.

In this paper, we present a Map-Reduce style parallel algorithm for control
software synthesis when the controlled system (*plant*) is modeled as a discrete
time linear hybrid system. Furthermore we present an MPI-based implementation
PQKS of our algorithm. To the best of our knowledge, this is the first parallel
approach for control software synthesis.

We experimentally show effectiveness of *PQKS* on two classical control synthesis problems: the inverted pendulum and the multi-input buck DC/DC converter. Experiments show that *PQKS* efficiency is above 60%. As an example,
PQKS requires about 16 hours to complete the synthesis of control software for
the pendulum on a cluster with 60 processors, instead of the 25 days needed by
the sequential algorithm implemented in *QKS*.

1 Introduction

Many Embedded Systems are indeed Software Based Control Systems (SBCSs). An
SBCS consists of two main subsystems: the controller and the plant. Typically, the
plant is a physical system consisting, for example, of mechanical or electrical devices
whereas the controller consists of control software running on a microcontroller. In an
endless loop, at discrete time instants (*sampling*), the controller reads plant sensor outputs from the plant and computes commands to be sent back to plant actuators. Being
the control software discrete and the physical system typically continuous, sensor outputs go through an Analog-to-Digital (AD) conversion (*quantization*) before being read
from the control software. Analogously, controller commands need a Digital-to-Analog
(DA) conversion before being sent to plant actuators. The controller selects commands
in order to guarantee that the closed-loop system (that is, the system consisting of both
plant and controller) meets given safety and liveness specifications (System Level Formal Specifications).

E. Bartocci and C.R. Ramakrishnan (Eds.): SPIN 2013, LNCS 7976, pp. 43–60, 2013.
© Springer-Verlag Berlin Heidelberg 2013

Software generation from models and formal specifications forms the core of Model Based Design of embedded software [1]. This approach is particularly interesting for SBCSs since in such a case system level (formal) specifications are much easier to define than the control software behavior itself.

1.1 Motivations

In this paper we focus on the algorithm presented in [2,3,4], which returns correct-by-construction control software starting from system level formal specifications. This algorithm is implemented in *QKS* (*Quantized Kontroller Synthesizer*), which takes as input: i) a formal model of the controlled system, modeled as a Discrete Time Linear Hybrid System (DTLHS), ii) safety and liveness requirements (goal region) and iii) b and b_u as the number of bits for, respectively, AD and DA conversions. Given this, *QKS* outputs a correct-by-construction control software together with the controlled region on which the software is guaranteed to work.

To this aim, *QKS* first computes a suitable finite state abstraction (*control abstraction* [4]) $\hat{\mathcal{H}}$ of the DTLHS plant model $\mathcal{H}$, where $\hat{\mathcal{H}}$ depends on the quantization schema (i.e. number of bits b, b_u needed for AD/DA conversions) and it is the plant as it can be seen from the control software after AD conversion and before DA conversion. Then, given an abstraction $\hat{G}$ of the goal states G, it is computed a controller $\hat{K}$ that, starting from any initial abstract state, drives $\hat{\mathcal{H}}$ to $\hat{G}$ regardless of possible nondeterminism. Control abstraction properties ensure that $\hat{K}$ is indeed a (quantized representation of a) controller for the original plant $\mathcal{H}$. Finally, $\hat{K}$ is translated into control software (C code).

While effective on moderate-size systems, *QKS* requires a huge amount of computational resources when applied to larger systems. In fact, the most critical step of *QKS* is the control abstraction $\hat{\mathcal{H}}$ generation (which is responsible for more than 95% of the overall computation, see [3]). This stems from the fact that $\hat{\mathcal{H}}$ is computed explicitly, by solving a Mixed Integer Linear Programming (MILP) problem for each triple $(\hat{x}, \hat{u}, \hat{x}')$, where $\hat{x}, \hat{x}'$ are abstract states of $\hat{\mathcal{H}}$ and $\hat{u}$ is an abstract action of $\hat{\mathcal{H}}$. Thus *QKS* is based on an *hybrid* approach, being both *explicit* in the abstract state space enumeration and *symbolic* in the usage of MILP solvers. Since the number of abstract states is 2^b, being b the number of bits needed for AD conversion of all variables describing the plant, and since the number of abstract actions is 2^{b_u}, we have that *QKS* computation time is exponential in $2b + b_u$. In *QKS*, suitable optimizations reduce the complexity to be exponential in $b + b_u$, and thus in b since $b_u \ll b$. However, in large-size systems b may be large for two typical reasons. First, since each plant state variable needs to be quantized (if a state variable v is discrete, then the number of bits for v is not an input, since $\lfloor \log_2 |\text{dom}(v)| \rfloor + 1$ bits are needed), the number of bits is necessarily high when the plant model consists of many variables. As an example, the plane collision avoidance control system in [5] is described by 4 continuous variables and 7 discrete variables. Second, controllers synthesized by considering a finer quantization schema (i.e., with an higher value of b) usually have a better behavior with respect to non-functional requirements, such as *ripple* and *set-up time*. Therefore, when a high precision is required, a large number of quantization bits must be considered.

As an example, experimental results show that *QKS* takes nearly one month (25 days) of CPU time to synthesize the controller for a 26 bits quantized inverted pendulum (which is described by only two continuous state variables, see Sect. 5.1). Moreover, 99% of those 25 days of computation is due to control abstraction generation. This may result in a loss in terms of time-to-market in control software design when *QKS* is used.

This motivates search of parallel versions of *QKS* synthesis algorithm.

1.2 Main Contributions

To overcome the computation time bottleneck in *QKS*, we present a *Map-Reduce* style parallel algorithm for control abstraction generation in control software synthesis.

Map-Reduce [6] is a (LISP inspired) programming paradigm advocating a form of embarrassing parallelism for effective massive parallel processing. An implementation of such an approach is in Hadoop (e.g., see [7]). The effectiveness of the Map-Reduce approach stems from the minimal communication overhead of embarrassing parallelism. This motivates our goal of looking for a Map-Reduce style parallel algorithm for control software synthesis from system level formal specifications.

To this aim, we design a parallel version of *QKS*, that is inspired to the Map-Reduce programming style and that we call *Parallel QKS* (*PQKS* in the following). *PQKS* is actually implemented using MPI (Message Passing Interface [8]) in order to exploit the computational power available in modern computer clusters (distributed memory model). Such an algorithm will be presented in Sect. 4, after a discussion of the basic notions needed to understand our approach (Sect. 2) and the description of the standalone (i.e. serial) algorithm of *QKS* (Sect. 3).

We show the effectiveness of *PQKS* by using it to synthesize control software for two widely used embedded systems, namely the multi-input buck DC-DC converter [9] and the inverted pendulum [10] benchmarks. These are challenging examples for the automatic synthesis of correct-by-construction control software. Experimental results on the above described benchmarks will be discussed in Sect. 5. Such results show that we achieve a nearly linear speedup w.r.t. *QKS*, with efficiency above 60%. As an example, *PQKS* requires about 16 hours to complete the above mentioned synthesis of the 26-bits pendulum on a cluster with 60 processors, instead of the 25 days of *QKS*.

2 Background on Control Abstraction for DTLHSs

To make this paper self-contained, in this section we briefly summarize the notions necessary to understand our parallel approach to control software synthesis. For more details, we refer the reader to [4].

Guarded Constraints. We denote with $[n]$ an initial segment $\{1, \ldots, n\}$ of the natural numbers. We denote with $X = [x_1, \ldots, x_n]$ a finite sequence of variables that we may regard, when convenient, as a set. Each variable x ranges on a known (bounded or unbounded) interval $\mathcal{D}_x$ either of the reals (continuous variables) or of the integers (discrete variables). We denote with $\mathcal{D}_X$ the set $\prod_{x \in X} \mathcal{D}_x$. Boolean variables are discrete variables ranging on the set $\mathbb{B} = \{0, 1\}$. If x is a boolean variable, we write $\bar{x}$

for $(1 - x)$. A *linear expression* over a list of variables X is a linear combination of variables in X with rational coefficients. A *linear constraint* over X (or simply a *constraint*) is an expression of the form $L(X) \leq b$, where $L(X)$ is a linear expression over X and b is a rational constant. Given a constraint $C(X)$ and a fresh boolean variable (*guard*) $y \notin X$, a *guarded constraint* has either the form $y \rightarrow C(X)$ (if y then $C(X)$) or $\bar{y} \rightarrow C(X)$ (if not y then $C(X)$). A *guarded predicate* is a conjunction of either constraints or guarded constraints.

Labeled Transition Systems. A *Labeled Transition System* (LTS) is a tuple $\mathcal{S} = (S, \mathcal{A}, T)$ where S is a (possibly infinite) set of states, $\mathcal{A}$ is a (possibly infinite) set of *actions*, and $T : S \times \mathcal{A} \times S \rightarrow \mathbb{B}$ is the *transition relation* of $\mathcal{S}$. Let $s \in S$ and $a \in \mathcal{A}$. We call *self loop* a transition of the form (s, a, s). A *run* or *path* for an LTS $\mathcal{S}$ is a sequence $\pi = s_0, a_0, s_1, a_1, s_2, a_2, \ldots$ of states s_t and actions a_t such that $\forall t \geq 0$ $T(s_t, a_t, s_{t+1})$. The length $|\pi|$ of a finite run π is the number of actions in π.

Discrete Time Linear Hybrid Systems. A *Discrete Time Linear Hybrid System* is a tuple $\mathcal{H} = (X, U, Y, N)$ where:

- $X = X^r \cup X^d$ is a finite sequence of real (X^r) and discrete (X^d) *present state* variables. We denote with X' the sequence of *next state* variables obtained by decorating with $'$ all variables in X.
- $U = U^r \cup U^d$ is a finite sequence of *input* variables.
- $Y = Y^r \cup Y^d$ is a finite sequence of *auxiliary* variables that are typically used to model *modes* (e.g., from switching elements such as diodes) or "local" variables.
- $N(X, U, Y, X')$ is a guarded predicate over $X \cup U \cup Y \cup X'$ defining the *transition relation* (*next state*).

The semantics of a DTLHS $\mathcal{H}$ is an LTS $\text{LTS}(\mathcal{H}) = (\mathcal{D}_X, \mathcal{D}_U, \tilde{N})$ where $\tilde{N} : \mathcal{D}_X \times \mathcal{D}_U \times \mathcal{D}_X \rightarrow \mathbb{B}$ is a function s.t. $\tilde{N}(x, u, x') \equiv \exists \, y \in \mathcal{D}_Y \, N(x, u, y, x')$.

Quantizations for DTLHSs. A *quantization function* γ for a real interval $I = [a, b]$ is a non-decreasing function $\gamma : I \mapsto \mathbb{Z}$ s.t. $\gamma(I)$ is a bounded integer interval. In the following we will only consider quantization functions γ s.t.: i) $\gamma(I) = \{0, \ldots, 2^b - 1\}$ for some $b \in \mathbb{N}$ (number of bits); ii) γ divides the interval $[a, b]$ into 2^b equal subintervals, so that $\gamma(x) = i - 1$ iff x is in the i-th subinterval. Thus we will specify quantizations by only defining the number of bits b. Finally, if I is a discrete set $I \subseteq \mathbb{Z}$, then $\gamma(x) = x - \min I$.

Let $\mathcal{H} = (X, U, Y, N)$ be a DTLHS, and $W = X \cup U \cup Y$. A *quantization* $\mathcal{Q}$ for $\mathcal{H}$ is a pair (A, Γ), where:

- A explicitly bounds each variable in W (i.e., $A = \bigwedge_{w \in W} \alpha_w \leq w \leq \beta_w$, with $\alpha_w, \beta_w \in \mathcal{D}_W$). For each $w \in W$, we denote with $A_w = [\alpha_w, \beta_w]$ its *admissible region* and with $A_W = \prod_{w \in W} A_w$.
- Γ is a set of maps $\Gamma = \{\gamma_w \mid w \in W$ and γ_w is a quantization function for $A_w\}$.

Let $W = [w_1, \ldots, w_k]$ and $v = [v_1, \ldots, v_k] \in A_V$, with $V \subseteq W$. We write $\Gamma(v)$ for the tuple $[\gamma_{w_1}(v_1), \ldots, \gamma_{w_k}(v_k)]$, $\Gamma^{-1}(\hat{v})$ for the set $\{v \in A_V \mid \Gamma(v) = \hat{v}\}$, and $\Gamma(A_W) = \{\Gamma(v) \mid v \in A_W\}$. Finally, we call *abstract states (resp., actions)* the elements in the finite set $\Gamma(A_X)$ (resp., $\Gamma(A_U)$).

3 Control Abstraction Computation

As explained in Sect. 1.1, the heaviest computation step for *QKS* is the computation of the control abstraction. In this section, we recall the definition of control abstraction, as well as how it is computed by *QKS*.

In the following, let $\mathcal{H} = (X, U, Y, N)$ and $\mathcal{Q} = (A, \Gamma)$ be, respectively, a DTLHS and a quantization for $\mathcal{H}$. We say that an abstract action $\hat{u} \in \Gamma(A_U)$ is $\mathcal{Q}$-admissible in an abstract state $\hat{x} \in \Gamma(A_X)$ iff actions in $\hat{u}$ always maintain the plant inside its admissible region when starting from states in $\hat{x}$ (i.e., for all plant states $x \in \Gamma^{-1}(\hat{x})$, plant actions $u \in \Gamma^{-1}(\hat{u})$, and plant states x', if (x, u, x') is a transition in LTS($\mathcal{H}$) then $x' \in A_X$).

Definition 1. *The $\mathcal{Q}$ control abstraction of a DTLHS $\mathcal{H}$ is an LTS $\hat{\mathcal{H}} = (\Gamma(A_X), \Gamma(A_U), \hat{N})$, where for $\hat{N}$ the following holds:*

1. *each abstract transition in $\hat{N}$ stems from a concrete transition in N;*
2. *each concrete transition (x, u, x') in N is faithfully represented by an abstract transition $(\Gamma(x), \Gamma(u), \Gamma(x'))$ in $\hat{N}$, provided that $\Gamma(x) \neq \Gamma(x')$ and $\Gamma(u)$ is $\mathcal{Q}$-admissible in $\Gamma(x)$;*
3. *if there is no upper bound to the length of concrete paths in LTS($\mathcal{H}$) s.t. all states are inside the counter-image of an abstract state $\hat{x}$ and all actions are inside the counter-image of an abstract action $\hat{u}$, then there is an abstract self loop $(\hat{x}, \hat{u}, \hat{x})$ in $\hat{N}$.*

Algorithm 1. Building a control abstraction

Input: DTLHS $\mathcal{H} = (X, U, Y, N)$, quantization $\mathcal{Q} = (A, \Gamma)$.
function *ctrAbs* $(\mathcal{H}, \mathcal{Q})$
  1. $\hat{N} \leftarrow \varnothing$
  2. **for all** $\hat{x} \in \Gamma(A_X)$ **do**
  3. $\hat{N} \leftarrow$ *ctrAbsAux*$(\mathcal{H}, \mathcal{Q}, \hat{x}, \hat{N})$
  4. **return** $(\Gamma(A_X), \Gamma(A_U), \hat{N})$

Given a quantization $\mathcal{Q} = (A, \Gamma)$ for a DTLHS $\mathcal{H} = (X, U, Y, N)$, Function *ctrAbs* in Alg. 1 computes a $\mathcal{Q}$-control abstraction $(\Gamma(A_X), \Gamma(A_U), \hat{N})$ of $\mathcal{H}$ following Def. 1. Namely, the control abstraction transition relation $\hat{N}$ is incrementally computed by starting with the empty relation (line 1) and then adding, for all abstract states $\hat{x}$ (line 2), all transitions which starts from $\hat{x}$ and fulfills Def. 1 (line 3). This is done by calling the auxiliary function *ctrAbsAux*, which is detailed in Alg. 2. Namely, function *ctrAbsAux* checks, for all abstract actions $\hat{u}$ (line 1) and all possible next abstract states $\hat{x}' \in \mathcal{O}$ (line 5), if $(\hat{x}, \hat{u}, \hat{x}')$ may be added to the current $\hat{N}$. Self loops are separately handled in line 3. Note that the checks in lines 2, 3 and 6, and the computation in line 4 are performed by properly defining MILP problems, which are solved using known algorithms (available in the GLPK package).

Algorithm 2. Building a control abstraction: transitions from a given abstract state

---

Input: DTLHS $\mathcal{H}$, quantization $\mathcal{Q}$, abstract state $\hat{x}$, partial control abstraction $\hat{N}$.
function $ctrAbsAux$ $(\mathcal{H}, \mathcal{Q}, \hat{x}, \hat{N})$
  1. **for all** $\hat{u} \in \Gamma(A_U)$ **do**
  2.   **if** $\neg$ $\mathcal{Q}$-admissible$(\mathcal{H}, \mathcal{Q}, \hat{x}, \hat{u})$ **then**
  3.   **if** $selfLoop(\mathcal{H}, \mathcal{Q}, \hat{x}, \hat{u})$ **then** $\hat{N} \leftarrow \hat{N} \cup \{(\hat{x}, \hat{u}, \hat{x})\}$
  4. $\mathcal{O} \leftarrow overImg(\mathcal{H}, \mathcal{Q}, \hat{x}, \hat{u})$
  5.   **for all** $\hat{x}' \in \Gamma(\mathcal{O})$ **do**
  6.   **if** $\hat{x} \neq \hat{x}' \wedge existsTrans(\mathcal{H}, \mathcal{Q}, \hat{x}, \hat{u}, \hat{x}')$ **then**
  7. $\hat{N} \leftarrow \hat{N} \cup \{(\hat{x}, \hat{u}, \hat{x}')\}$
  8. **return** $\hat{N}$

---

4   Parallel Synthesis of Control Software

In this section we present our novel parallel algorithm for the control abstraction generation of a given DTLHS. Such algorithm is a parallel version of the standalone Alg. 1. In this way we significantly improve the performance on the control abstraction generation (which is the bottleneck of *QKS*), thus obtaining a huge speedup for the whole approach to the synthesis of control software for DTLHSs.

In the following, let $\mathcal{H} = (X, U, Y, N)$, $\mathcal{Q} = (A, \Gamma)$ be, respectively, the DTLHS and the quantization in input to our algorithm for control abstraction generation. Moreover, let b be the overall number of bits needed in $\mathcal{Q}$ to quantize plant states (i.e., $b = \sum_{x \in X} b_x$, where b_x is the number of bits for $\gamma_x \in \Gamma$). Finally, let p be the number of processors available for parallel computation.

Our parallel algorithm rests on the observation that all calls to function *ctrAbsAux* (see Alg. 2) are independent of each other, thus they may be performed by independent processes without communication overhead. This observation allows us to use parallel methods targeting *embarrassingly parallel* problems in order to obtain a significant speedup on the control abstraction generation phase. To this aim, we use a Map-Reduce based parallelization technique to design a parallel version of Alg. 1. Namely, our parallel computation is designed as follows (see Fig. 1 for an example).

1. A *master* process assigns (*maps*) the computations needed for an abstract state $\hat{x}$ (i.e., the execution of a call to function *ctrAbsAux* of Alg. 2) to one of p computing processes (*workers*, enumerated from 1 to p). This is done in a way so that each worker approximately handles $\frac{|\Gamma(A_X)|}{p}$ abstract states, thus balancing the parallel workload. Namely, abstract states are enumerated from 1 to 2^b, and abstract state i is assigned to worker $1 + ((i - 1) \bmod p)$. We denote with $\Gamma^{(i,p)}(A_X) \subseteq \Gamma(A_X)$ the set of abstract states mapped to worker i out of p available workers. Note that worker i may locally decide which abstract states are in $\Gamma^{(i,p)}(A_X)$ by only knowing i and p (together with the overall input $\mathcal{H}$ and $\mathcal{Q}$). This allows us to avoid sending to each worker the explicit list of abstract states it has to work on, since it is sufficient that the master sends i and p (plus $\mathcal{H}$ and $\mathcal{Q}$) to worker i.

2. Each worker *works* on its abstract states partition $\Gamma^{(i,p)}(A_X)$, by calling *ctrAbsAux* for each abstract state in such partition. Once worker i has completed its task (i.e., all abstract states in $\Gamma^{(i,p)}(A_X)$ have been considered), a local (partial) control abstraction $\hat{N}_i$ is obtained, which is sent back to the master.

3. The master collects the local control abstractions coming from the workers and composes (*reduces*) them in order to obtain the desired complete control abstraction for $\mathcal{H}$. Note that, as in embarrassingly parallel tasks, communication only takes place at the beginning and at the end of local computations.

Algorithm 3. Building a control abstraction in parallel: master process

---

Input: DTLHS $\mathcal{H}$, quantization $\mathcal{Q}$, workers number p
function *ctrAbsMaster* $(\mathcal{H}, \mathcal{Q}, p)$
1. **for all** $i \in \{1, \ldots, p\}$ **do**
2.   create a worker and send $\mathcal{H}, \mathcal{Q}, i$ and p to it
3. wait to get $\hat{N}_1, \ldots, \hat{N}_p$ from workers
4. **return** $(\Gamma(A_X), \Gamma(A_U), \cup_{j=1}^{p} \hat{N}_j)$

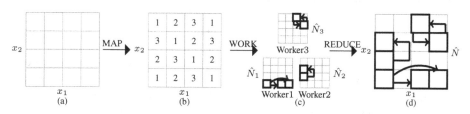

Fig. 1. Example of execution of the parallel algorithm using 3 workers on a DTLHS $\mathcal{H} = (X, U, Y, N)$ and a quantization $\mathcal{Q}$ for $\mathcal{H}$ s.t. $X = [x_1, x_2]$ and $\mathcal{Q}$ discretizes both x_1, x_2 with two bits. In (a) the starting point is shown, where each cell corresponds to an abstract state. In (b), function *ctrAbsMaster* maps the workload among the 3 workers (abstract states labeled with $i \in [3]$ are handled by worker i). In (c) each worker i computes its local control abstraction $\hat{N}_i$, which is assumed to have the shown transitions only. Finally, in (d) the master rejoins the local control abstractions in order to get the final one, i.e. $\hat{N}$.

Our parallel algorithm is described in Algs. 3 (for the master) and 4 (for workers).

4.1   Implementation with MPI

We actually implemented Algs. 3 and 4 in *PQKS* by using MPI (Message Passing Interface, see [8]). Since MPI is widely used, this allows us to run *PQKS* on nearly all computer clusters. Note that in MPI all computing processes execute the same program, each one knowing its rank i and the overall number of computing processes p (Single Program Multiple Data paradigm). Thus lines 1–2 of Alg. 3 are directly implemented by the MPI framework. Moreover, in our implementation the master is not a separate node, but it actually performs as worker with id 1 while waiting for local control abstractions from other workers. Local control abstraction from other workers are collected once the

---

Algorithm 4. Building a control abstraction in parallel: worker processes

---

Input: DTLHS $\mathcal{H} = (X, U, Y, N)$, quantization $\mathcal{Q} = (A, \Gamma)$, index i, workers number p

function *parCtrAbs* $(\mathcal{H}, \mathcal{Q}, i, p)$

1. $\hat{N}_i \leftarrow \varnothing$
2. **for all** $\hat{x} \in \Gamma^{(i,p)}(A_X)$ **do**
3. $\hat{N}_i \leftarrow ctrAbsAux(\mathcal{H}, \mathcal{Q}, \hat{x}, \hat{N}_i)$
4. send $\hat{N}_i$ to the master

---

master local control abstraction (i.e., $\hat{N}_1$) has been completed. This allows us to use p nodes instead of $p + 1$, as well as to save communication time ($\hat{N}_1$ is already available to the master node, thus it needs not to be sent).

Note that lines 3 and 4 of, respectively, Algs. 3 and 4 require workers to send their local control abstraction to the master. Being control abstractions represented as OB-DDs (*Ordered Binary Decision Diagrams* [11]), which are sparse data structures, this step may be inefficient if implemented with a call to MPI_Send (as it is usually done in MPI programs), which is designed for contiguous data. In order to make *PQKS* efficient, MPI_Send is not used. Instead, workers use known algorithms (implemented in the CUDD package) to efficiently dump the OBDD representing their local control abstraction on the shared filesystem. Since current MPI implementations are typically based on a shared filesystem, this is not a limitation for *PQKS*. Then each computing process calls MPI_Barrier, in order to synchronize all workers with the master. After this, the master node collects local control abstraction from workers, by reloading them from the shared filesystem, in order to build the final global one. Consequently, when presenting experimental results in Sect. 5, we include I/O time in communication time. Note that communication based on shared filesystem is very common also in Map-Reduce native implementations like Hadoop [7].

Finally, we note that Algs. 3 and 4 may conceptually be implemented on multi-threaded systems with shared memory. However, in our implementation we use GLPK as external library to solve MILP problems required in computations inside function *ctrAbsAux* (see Alg. 2). Since GLPK is not thread-safe, we may not implement Algs. 3 and 4 on multithreaded shared memory systems.

5 Experimental Results

We implement functions *ctrAbsMaster* and *parCtrAbs* of Algs. 3 and 4 in C programming language using the CUDD package for OBDD based computations and the GLPK package for MILP problems solving, and MPI for the parallel setting and communication. The resulting tool, *PQKS (Parallel QKS)*, extends the tool *QKS* [3] by replacing function *ctrAbs* of Alg. 1 with function *ctrAbsMaster* of Alg. 3.

In this section we present experimental results obtained by using *PQKS* on two meaningful and challenging examples for the automatic synthesis of correct-by-construction control software, namely the inverted pendulum and multi-input buck DC-DC converter. In such experiments, we show the gain of the parallel approach with respect to the serial algorithm, also providing standard measures such as communication and I/O time.

This section is organized as follows. In Sects. 5.1 and 5.2 we will present the inverted pendulum and the multi-input buck DC-DC converter, on which our experiments focus. In Sect. 5.3 we give the details of the experimental setting, and finally, in Sect. 5.4, we discuss experimental results.

5.1 The Inverted Pendulum Case Study

The inverted pendulum [10] (see Fig. 2) is modeled by taking the angle θ and the angular velocity $\dot\theta$ as state variables. The input of the system is the torquing force $u \cdot F$, that can influence the velocity in both directions. Here, the variable u models the direction and the constant F models the intensity of the force. Differently from [10], we consider the problem of finding a discrete controller, whose decisions may be only "apply the force clockwise" ($u = 1$), "apply the force counterclockwise" ($u = -1$)", or "do nothing" ($u = 0$). The behavior of the system depends on the pendulum mass m, the length of the pendulum l, and the gravitational acceleration g. Given such parameters, the motion of the system is described by the differential equation $\ddot\theta = \frac{g}{l}\sin\theta + \frac{1}{ml^2}uF$, which may be normalized and discretized in the following transition relation (being T the sampling time constant, $x_1 = \theta$ and $x_2 = \dot\theta$): $N(x_1, x_2, u, x_1', x_2') \equiv (x_1' = x_1 + Tx_2) \wedge (x_2' = x_2 + T\frac{g}{l}\sin x_1 + T\frac{1}{ml^2}uF)$. Such transition relation is not linear, as it contains the function $\sin x_1$. A linear model can be found by under- and over-approximating the non-linear function $\sin x$ on different intervals for x. Namely, we may proceed as follows [12]. First of all, in order to exploit sinus periodicity, we consider the equation $x_1 = 2\pi y_k + y_\alpha$, where y_k represents the period in which x_1 lies and $y_\alpha \in [-\pi, \pi]^1$ represents the actual x_1 inside a given period. Then, we partition the interval $[-\pi, \pi]$ in four intervals: $I_1 = \left[-\pi, -\frac{\pi}{2}\right]$, $I_2 = \left[-\frac{\pi}{2}, 0\right]$, $I_3 = \left[0, \frac{\pi}{2}\right]$, $I_4 = \left[\frac{\pi}{2}, \pi\right]$. In each interval I_i ($i \in [4]$), we consider two linear functions $f_i^+(x)$ and and $f_i^-(x)$, such that for all $x \in I_i$, we have that $f_i^-(x) \leq \sin x \leq f_i^+(x)$. As an example, $f_1^+(y_\alpha) = -0.637y_\alpha - 2$ and $f_1^-(y_\alpha) = -0.707y_\alpha - 2.373$.

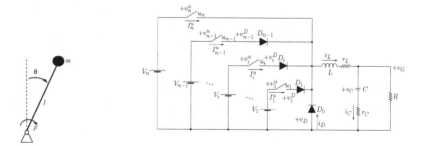

Fig. 2. Inverted Pendulum with Stationary Pivot Point   **Fig. 3.** Multi-input Buck DC-DC converter

---

[1] In this section we write π for a rational approximation of it.

Let us consider the set of fresh continuous variables $Y^r = \{y_\alpha, y_{\sin}\}$ and the set of fresh discrete variables $Y^d = \{y_k, y_q, y_1, y_2, y_3, y_4\}$, being $y_1, \ldots, y_4$ boolean variables. The DTLHS model $\mathcal{I}_F$ for the inverted pendulum is the tuple (X, U, Y, N), where $X = \{x_1, x_2\}$ is the set of continuous state variables, $U = \{u\}$ is the set of input variables, $Y = Y^r \cup Y^d$ is the set of auxiliary variables, and the transition relation $N(X, U, Y, X')$ is the following guarded predicate:

$$(x_1' = x_1 + 2\pi y_q + T x_2) \wedge (x_2' = x_2 + T\frac{g}{l}y_{\sin} + T\frac{1}{ml^2}uF)$$

$$\wedge \bigwedge_{i\in[4]} y_i \to f_i^-(y_\alpha) \le y_{\sin} \le f_i^+(y_\alpha)$$

$$\wedge \bigwedge_{i\in[4]} y_i \to y_\alpha \in I_i \wedge \sum_{i\in[4]} y_i \ge 1$$

$$\wedge x_1 = 2\pi y_k + y_\alpha \wedge -\pi \le x_1' \le \pi$$

Overapproximations of the system behaviour increase system nondeterminism. Since $\mathcal{I}_F$ dynamics overapproximates the dynamics of the non-linear model, the controllers that we synthesize are inherently *robust*, that is they meet the given closed loop requirements *notwithstanding* nondeterministic small *disturbances* such as variations in the plant parameters. Tighter overapproximations of non-linear functions makes finding a controller easier, whereas coarser overapproximations makes controllers more robust.

The typical goal for the inverted pendulum is to turn the pendulum steady to the upright position, starting from any possible initial position, within a given speed interval.

5.2   The Multi-input Buck DC-DC Converter Case Study

The *multi-input* buck DC-DC converter [9] in Fig. 3 is a mixed-mode analog circuit converting the DC input voltage (V_i in Fig. 3) to a desired DC output voltage (v_O in Fig. 3). As an example, buck DC-DC converters are used off-chip to scale down the typical laptop battery voltage (12-24) to the just few volts needed by the laptop processor (e.g. [13]) as well as on-chip to support *Dynamic Voltage and Frequency Scaling* (DVFS) in multicore processors (e.g. [14]). Because of its widespread use, control schemas for buck DC-DC converters have been widely studied (e.g. see [14,13]). The typical software based approach (e.g. see [13]) is to control the switches $u_1, \ldots, u_n$ in Fig. 3 (typically implemented with a MOSFET) with a microcontroller.

In such a converter (Fig. 3), there are n power supplies with voltage values $V_1, \ldots, V_n$, n switches with voltage values $v_1^u, \ldots, v_n^u$ and current values $I_1^u, \ldots, I_n^u$, and n input diodes $D_0, \ldots, D_{n-1}$ with voltage values $v_0^D, \ldots, v_{n-1}^D$ and current $i_0^D, \ldots, i_{n-1}^D$ (in the following, we will write v_D for v_0^D and i_D for i_0^D).

The circuit state variables are i_L and v_C. However we can also use the pair i_L, v_O as state variables in the DTLHS model since there is a linear relationship between i_L, v_C and v_O, namely: $v_O = \frac{r_C R}{r_C + R}i_L + \frac{R}{r_C + R}v_C$. We model the n-input buck DC-DC converter with the DTLHS $\mathcal{B}_n = (X, U, Y, N)$, with $X = [i_L, v_O]$, $U = [u_1, \ldots, u_n]$, $Y = [v_D, v_1^D, \ldots, v_{n-1}^D, i_D, I_1^u, \ldots, I_n^u, v_1^u, \ldots, v_n^u, q_0, \ldots, q_{n-1}]$.

Finally, the transition relation N, depending on variables in X, U and Y (as well as on circuit parameters $V_i, R, R_{on}, R_{off}, r_L, r_C, L$ and C), may be derived from simple circuit analysis [15]. Namely, we have the following equations:

$$\dot{i}_L = a_{1,1}i_L + a_{1,2}v_O + a_{1,3}v_D, \qquad \dot{v}_O = a_{2,1}i_L + a_{2,2}v_O + a_{2,3}v_D$$

where the coefficients $a_{i,j}$ depend on the circuit parameters R, r_L, r_C, L and C in the following way: $a_{1,1} = -\frac{r_L}{L}$, $a_{1,2} = -\frac{1}{L}$, $a_{1,3} = -\frac{1}{L}$, $a_{2,1} = \frac{R}{r_c+R}[-\frac{r_c r_L}{L} + \frac{1}{C}]$, $a_{2,2} = \frac{-1}{r_c+R}[\frac{r_c R}{L} + \frac{1}{C}]$, $a_{2,3} = -\frac{1}{L}\frac{r_c R}{r_c+R}$. Using a discrete time model with sampling time T (writing x' for $x(t+1)$) we have:

$$i'_L = (1 + Ta_{1,1})i_L + Ta_{1,2}v_O + Ta_{1,3}v_D$$
$$v'_O = Ta_{2,1}i_L + (1 + Ta_{2,2})v_O + Ta_{2,3}v_D.$$

The algebraic constraints stemming from the constitutive equations of the switching elements are the following:

$$q_0 \to v_D = R_{on}i_D$$
$$q_0 \to i_D \geq 0$$
$$\bigwedge_{i=1}^{n-1} q_i \to v_i^D = R_{on}I_i^u$$
$$\bigwedge_{i=1}^{n-1} q_i \to I_i^u \geq 0$$
$$\bigwedge_{j=1}^{n} u_j \to v_j^u = R_{on}I_j^u$$
$$i_L = i_D + \sum_{i=1}^{n} I_i^u$$

$$\bar{q}_0 \to v_D = R_{off}i_D$$
$$\bar{q}_0 \to v_D \leq 0$$
$$\bigwedge_{i=1}^{n-1} \bar{q}_i \to v_i^D = R_{off}I_i^u$$
$$\bigwedge_{i=1}^{n-1} \bar{q}_i \to v_i^D \leq 0$$
$$\bigwedge_{j=1}^{n} \bar{u}_j \to v_j^u = R_{off}I_j^u$$
$$\bigwedge_{i=1}^{n-1} v_D = v_i^u + v_i^D - V_i$$
$$v_D = v_n^u - V_n$$

The typical goal for a multi-input buck is to drive i_L and v_O within given goal intervals.

5.3 Experimental Setting

All experiments have been carried out on a cluster with 4 nodes and Open MPI implementation of MPI. Each node contains 4 quad-core 2.83 GHz Intel Xeon E5440 processors with 25 GB of RAM. This allows us to run fully parallel experiments by configuring the MPI computation to use up to 16 processes per node. However, in order not to overload each node, we run maximum 15 processes per node, thus our upper bound for the number of processes is 60.

In the inverted pendulum $\mathcal{I}_F$ with force intensity F, as in [10], we set pendulum parameters l and m in such a way that $\frac{g}{l} = 1$ (i.e. $l = g$) $\frac{1}{ml^2} = 1$ (i.e. $m = \frac{1}{l^2}$). As for the admissible region, we set $A_{x_1} = [-1.1\pi, 1.1\pi]$ (we write π for a rational approximation of it) and $A_{x_2} = [-4, 4]$.

In the multi-input buck DC-DC converter with n inputs $\mathcal{B}_n$, we set constant parameters as follows: $L = 2 \cdot 10^{-4}$ H, $r_L = 0.1$ Ω, $r_C = 0.1$ Ω, $R = 5$ Ω, $R_{on} = 0$ Ω, $R_{off} = 10^4$ Ω, $C = 5 \cdot 10^{-5}$ F, and $V_i = 10i$ V for $i \in [n]$. As for the admissible region, we set $A_{i_L} = [-4, 4]$ and $A_{v_O} = [-1, 7]$.

As for quantization, we will use an even number of bits b, so that each state variable of each case study is quantized with $\frac{b}{2}$ bits. We recall that the number of abstract states is exactly 2^b.

We run *QKS* and *PQKS* on the inverted pendulum model $\mathcal{I}_F$ with $F = 0.5N$ (force intensity), and on the multi-input buck DC-DC model $\mathcal{B}_n$, with $n = 5$ (number of inputs). For the inverted pendulum, we use sampling time $T = 0.01$ seconds. For the multi-input buck, we set $T = 10^{-6}$ seconds. For both systems, we run experiments varying the number of bits $b = 18, 20$ (also 22 for the inverted pendulum) and the number of processors (workers) $p = 1, 10, 20, 30, 40, 50, 60$. Furthermore, each single experiment (corresponding to a (b, p) pair) is repeated 10 times, and all experimental measures are obtained by averaging among the 10 different runs.

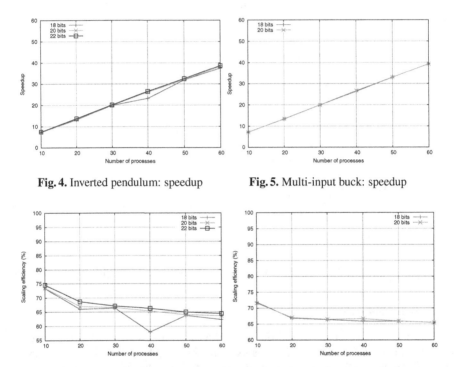

Fig. 4. Inverted pendulum: speedup   **Fig. 5.** Multi-input buck: speedup

Fig. 6. Inverted pendulum: scaling efficiency **Fig. 7.** Multi-input buck: scaling efficiency

In order to evaluate effectiveness of our approach, we use the following standard measures: speedup, efficiency, communication time (in seconds) and I/O time (in seconds). The *speedup* of our approach is given by the percentage ratio between the serial CPU time and the parallel CPU time, i.e. Speedup $= \frac{\text{serial CPU}}{\text{parallel CPU}}\%$. To evaluate scalability of our approach, we define the *scaling efficiency* (or simply *efficiency*) as the percentage ratio between speedup and number of processors p, i.e. Efficiency $= \frac{\text{Speedup}}{p}\%$. W.r.t. Algs. 3 and 4, the *communication time* is given by $\sum_{i=2}^{p} t_i$, being t_i the time needed by worker i to communicate with the master (we recall that worker 1 coincides with the master). Essentially, each t_i includes the time for MPI_Barrier synchronization (see Sect. 4.1) and local control abstraction $\hat{N}_i$ sending. In agreement with Sect. 4.1, the communication time is increased by the I/O time, that is the overall time spent by processors in input/output activities. The I/O time measure will also be shown separately in our experimental results.

Figs. 4, 6, 8 and 10 show, respectively, the speedup, the scaling efficiency, the communication time and the I/O time of Algs. 3 and 4 as a function of p, for the inverted pendulum with $b = 18, 20, 22$. Analogously, Figs. 5, 7, 9 and 11 show the same measures for the multi-input buck with $b = 18, 20$.

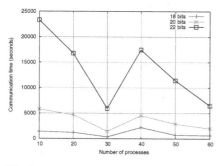

Fig. 8. Inverted pendulum: communication time

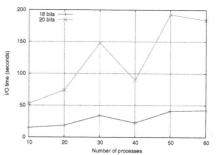

Fig. 9. Multi-input buck: communication time

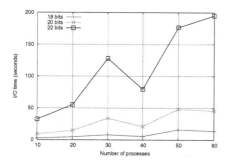

Fig. 10. Inverted pendulum: I/O time

Fig. 11. Multi-input buck: I/O time

We also show the absolute values for such experiments in Tabs. 1 (for the pendulum) and 2 (for the buck). Tabs. 1 and 2 have common columns. The meaning of such common columns is as follows. Column **b** is the number of bits used for quantization. Column **QKS** reports the execution time in seconds (averaged on 10 runs, with maximum standard deviation 0.9%) needed by *QKS* to compute the control abstraction (i.e. Alg. 1). Columns **PQKS** report experimental values for *PQKS*. Namely, column **p** shows the number of processors, column **CPU** reports the execution time in seconds (averaged on 10 runs, with maximum standard deviation 4.2%) for Alg. 3 (i.e., the master execution time, since it wraps the overall parallel computation), column **CT** shows the communication time (averaged on 10 runs, with maximum standard deviation 21%; we recall that I/O time is included in this measure), column **IO** shows the I/O time only (averaged on 10 runs, with maximum standard deviation 31%), column **Speedup** reports the speedup and column **Efficiency** reports the scaling efficiency. Finally, column **CPU K** shows the execution time in seconds for the control software generation (i.e., the remaining computation of *QKS*, after the control abstraction generation).

Table 1. Experimental Results for inverted pendulum

	QKS		PQKS					
b	CPU	p	CPU	CT	IO	Speedup	Efficiency	CPU K
18	6.141e+03	10	8.378e+02	1.395e+03	2.545e+00	7.330	73.297	2.000e+01
18	6.141e+03	20	4.650e+02	1.195e+03	4.500e+00	13.206	66.032	2.000e+01
18	6.141e+03	30	3.083e+02	3.477e+02	7.900e+00	19.919	66.396	2.000e+01
18	6.141e+03	40	2.646e+02	2.176e+03	5.400e+00	23.209	58.022	2.000e+01
18	6.141e+03	50	1.926e+02	7.065e+02	1.600e+01	31.885	63.770	2.000e+01
18	6.141e+03	60	1.642e+02	6.254e+02	1.380e+01	37.400	62.333	2.000e+01
20	2.608e+04	10	3.551e+03	5.800e+03	9.222e+00	7.346	73.456	8.500e+01
20	2.608e+04	20	1.946e+03	4.680e+03	1.460e+01	13.402	67.008	8.500e+01
20	2.608e+04	30	1.306e+03	1.425e+03	3.390e+01	19.978	66.593	8.500e+01
20	2.608e+04	40	9.981e+02	4.511e+03	2.100e+01	26.135	65.337	8.500e+01
20	2.608e+04	50	8.145e+02	2.889e+03	4.840e+01	32.026	64.052	8.500e+01
20	2.608e+04	60	6.828e+02	1.991e+03	4.590e+01	38.203	63.672	8.500e+01
22	1.106e+05	10	1.484e+04	2.331e+04	3.240e+01	7.457	74.566	3.520e+02
22	1.106e+05	20	8.055e+03	1.675e+04	5.530e+01	13.736	68.681	3.520e+02
22	1.106e+05	30	5.494e+03	5.923e+03	1.279e+02	20.141	67.136	3.520e+02
22	1.106e+05	40	4.171e+03	1.742e+04	7.960e+01	26.526	66.314	3.520e+02
22	1.106e+05	50	3.404e+03	1.142e+04	1.767e+02	32.503	65.005	3.520e+02
22	1.106e+05	60	2.861e+03	6.491e+03	1.952e+02	38.672	64.453	3.520e+02

5.4   Experiments Discussion

From Figs. 4 and 5 we note that the speedup is almost linear, with a $\frac{3}{5}$ slope. From Figs. 6 and 7 we note that scaling efficiency remains high when increasing the number of processors p. For example, for $b = 22$ bits, our approach efficiency is in a range from 74% (10 processors) to 64% (60 processors). In any case, efficiency is almost always above 60%, especially for bigger values of b.

Figs. 8 and 9 show that communication time almost always decreases when p increases. This is motivated by the fact that, in our MPI implementation, communication among nodes takes place mostly when workers send their local control abstractions to the master via the shared filesystem. Since in our implementation this happens only after an MPI_Barrier (i.e., the parallel computation may proceed only when all nodes have reached an MPI_Barrier statement), the communication time also includes waiting time for workers which finishes their local computation before the other ones. Thus, if all workers need about the same time to complete the local computation, then the communication time is low. Note that this explains also the discontinuity when passing from 30 to 40 nodes which may be observed in the figures above. In fact, each worker has (almost) the same workload in terms of abstract states number, but some abstract states may need more computation time than others (i.e., computation time of function *minCtrAbsAux* in Alg. 2 may have significant variations on different abstract states). If such "hard" abstract states are well distributed among workers, communication time is low (with higher efficiency), otherwise it is high. Figs. 12 and 13 show such phenomenon on the inverted pendulum quantized with 18 bits, when the parallel algorithm is executed by 30 and 40 workers, respectively. In such figures, the x-axis represents computation time, the y-axis the workers, and hard abstract states are represented in red. Indeed, in Fig. 12 hard abstract states are well distributed among workers, which corresponds to a low communication time in Fig. 8 (and high speedup and efficiency in Figs. 4 and 6). On the other hand, in Fig. 13 hard abstract states are mainly distributed on only a dozen of the 40 workers (thus, about 30% of the workers performs the most part of the total workload), which corresponds to a high communication time in Fig. 8 (and low speedup and efficiency in Figs. 4 and 6). Note that I/O time is nearly always at least 2 orders of magnitude less than communication time, thus hard abstract states distribution is indeed the cause of the above described phenomenon.

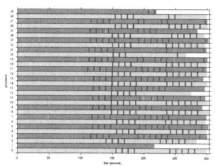

Fig. 12. Details about pendulum computation time (30 nodes, 18 bits)

Fig. 13. Details about pendulum computation time (40 nodes, 18 bits)

Finally, in order to show feasibility of our approach also on DTLHSs requiring a huge computation time to generate the control abstraction, we run *PQKS* on the inverted pendulum with $b = 26$. We estimate the computation time for control abstraction generation for $p = 1$ to be 25 days. On the other hand, with $p = 60$, we are able to compute the control abstraction generation in only 16 hours.

Table 2. Experimental Results for multi-input buck DC-DC converter

	QKS	PQKS					
b	CPU	p	CPU	CT	IO	Speedup	Efficiency	CPU K
18	6.484e+04	10	9.024e+03	1.666e+04	1.490e+01	7.185	71.847	2.600e+01
18	6.484e+04	20	4.849e+03	1.095e+04	1.850e+01	13.371	66.854	2.600e+01
18	6.484e+04	30	3.256e+03	3.721e+03	3.410e+01	19.914	66.381	2.600e+01
18	6.484e+04	40	2.460e+03	9.710e+03	2.260e+01	26.358	65.895	2.600e+01
18	6.484e+04	50	1.968e+03	6.677e+03	4.090e+01	32.945	65.889	2.600e+01
18	6.484e+04	60	1.650e+03	4.001e+03	4.240e+01	39.287	65.478	2.600e+01
20	2.629e+05	10	3.673e+04	6.938e+04	5.300e+01	7.159	71.590	8.000e+01
20	2.629e+05	20	1.962e+04	4.439e+04	7.400e+01	13.401	67.007	8.000e+01
20	2.629e+05	30	1.318e+04	1.484e+04	1.480e+02	19.945	66.484	8.000e+01
20	2.629e+05	40	9.862e+03	3.513e+04	9.000e+01	26.662	66.654	8.000e+01
20	2.629e+05	50	7.976e+03	2.645e+04	1.930e+02	32.966	65.932	8.000e+01
20	2.629e+05	60	6.697e+03	1.603e+04	1.840e+02	39.262	65.436	8.000e+01

6   Related Work

Algorithms (and tools) for the automatic synthesis of control software under different assumptions (e.g., discrete or continuous time, linear or non-linear systems, hybrid or discrete systems, etc.) have been widely investigated in the last decades. As an example, see [16,17,18,10,19,20,21,22] and citations thereof. However, no one of such approaches has a parallel version of any type, our focus here. On the other hand, parallel algorithms have been widely investigated for formal verification (e.g., see [23,24,25]).

A parallel algorithm for control software synthesis has been presented in [26], where however non-hybrid systems are addressed, control is obtained by Monte Carlo simulation and quantization is not taken into account. Moreover, note that in literature "parallel controller synthesis" often refers to synthesizing parallel controllers (e.g., see [27] and [28] and citations thereof), while here we parallelize the (offline) computation required to synthesize a standalone controller. Summing up, to the best of our knowledge, no previous parallel algorithm for control software synthesis from formal specifications has been published.

As discussed in Sect. 1.1, the present paper builds mainly upon the tool *QKS* presented in [2,3]. Other works about *QKS* comprise the following ones. In [29] it is shown that expressing the input system as a linear predicate over a set of continuous as well as discrete variables (as it is done in *QKS*) is not a limitation on the modeling power. In [12] it is shown how non-linear systems may be modeled by using suitable linearization techniques. The paper in [15] addresses model based synthesis of control software by trading system level non-functional requirements (such us optimal set-up time, ripple) with software non-functional requirements (its footprint, i.e. size). The procedure which generates the actual control software (C code) starting from a finite states automaton of a control law is described in [30]. In [31] it is shown how to automatically generate a picture illustrating control software coverage. Finally, in [32] it is shown that the quantized control synthesis problem underlying *QKS* approach is undecidable. As a consequence, *QKS* is based on a correct but non-complete algorithm. Namely, *QKS* output is one of the following: i) SOL, in which case a correct-by-construction control software is returned; ii) NOSOL, in which case no controller exists for the given specifications; iii) UNK, in which case *QKS* was not able to compute a controller (but a controller may exist).

7   Conclusions and Future Work

In this paper we presented a Map-Reduce style parallel algorithm (and its MPI implementation for computer clusters, *PQKS*) for automatic synthesis of correct-by-construction control software for discrete time linear hybrid systems, starting from a formal model of the controlled system, safety and liveness requirements and number of bits for analog-to-digital conversion. Such an algorithm significantly improves performance of an existing standalone approach (implemented in the tool *QKS*), which may require weeks or even months of computation when applied to large-sized hybrid systems.

Experimental results on two classical control synthesis problems (the inverted pendulum and the multi-input buck DC/DC converter) show that our parallel approach efficiency is above 60%. As an example, with 60 processors *PQKS* outputs the control software for the 26-bits quantized inverted pendulum in about 16 hours, while *QKS* needs about 25 days of computation.

Future work consists in further improving the communication among processors by making the mapping phase aware of "hard" abstract states (see Sect. 5.4), as well as designing a parallel version for other architectures than computer clusters, such as GPGPU architectures. Finally, future work also includes extending the presented approach so as to provide a general parallelization framework for abstraction procedures (of a suitable type).

Acknowledgments. We are grateful to our anonymous referees for their helpful comments. Our work has been partially supported by: i) MIUR project DM24283 (TRAMP); ii) EC FP7 project GA600773 (PAEON); iii) EC FP7 project GA317761 (SmartHG); and iv) Erasmus Mundus MULTIC scholarship from the European Commission (EMA 2 MULTIC 10-837).

References

1. Henzinger, T.A., Sifakis, J.: The embedded systems design challenge. In: Misra, J., Nipkow, T., Sekerinski, E. (eds.) FM 2006. LNCS, vol. 4085, pp. 1–15. Springer, Heidelberg (2006)
2. Mari, F., Melatti, I., Salvo, I., Tronci, E.: Synthesis of quantized feedback control software for discrete time linear hybrid systems. In: Touili, T., Cook, B., Jackson, P. (eds.) CAV 2010. LNCS, vol. 6174, pp. 180–195. Springer, Heidelberg (2010)
3. Mari, F., Melatti, I., Salvo, I., Tronci, E.: Model based synthesis of control software from system level formal specifications. ACM Trans. on Soft. Eng. and Meth. (to appear)
4. Mari, F., Melatti, I., Salvo, I., Tronci, E.: Quantized feedback control software synthesis from system level formal specifications. CoRR abs/1107.5638v1 (2011)
5. Tomlin, C.J., Lygeros, J., Sastry, S.S.: Computing controllers for nonlinear hybrid systems. In: Vaandrager, F.W., van Schuppen, J.H. (eds.) HSCC 1999. LNCS, vol. 1569, pp. 238–255. Springer, Heidelberg (1999)
6. Dean, J., Ghemawat, S.: Mapreduce: Simplified data processing on large clusters. In: OSDI, pp. 137–150 (2004)
7. Lin, J., Dyer, C.: Data-Intensive Text Processing with MapReduce. Synthesis Lectures on Human Language Technologies. Morgan & Claypool Publishers (2010)
8. Pacheco, P.: Parallel Programming with MPI. Morgan Kaufmann (1997)
9. Rodriguez, M., Fernandez-Miaja, P., Rodriguez, A., Sebastian, J.: A multiple-input digitally controlled buck converter for envelope tracking applications in radiofrequency power amplifiers. IEEE Trans. on Pow. El. 25(2), 369–381 (2010)
10. Kreisselmeier, G., Birkhölzer, T.: Numerical nonlinear regulator design. IEEE Trans. on Automatic Control 39(1), 33–46 (1994)
11. Bryant, R.: Graph-based algorithms for boolean function manipulation. IEEE Trans. on Computers C-35(8), 677–691 (1986)
12. Alimguzhin, V., Mari, F., Melatti, I., Salvo, I., Tronci, E.: Automatic control software synthesis for quantized discrete time hybrid systems. In: CDC, pp. 6120–6125. IEEE (2012)
13. So, W.C., Tse, C., Lee, Y.S.: Development of a fuzzy logic controller for dc/dc converters: design, computer simulation, and experimental evaluation. IEEE Trans. on Power Electronics 11(1), 24–32 (1996)
14. Kim, W., Gupta, M.S., Wei, G.Y., Brooks, D.M.: Enabling on-chip switching regulators for multi-core processors using current staggering. In: ASGI (2007)

15. Alimguzhin, V., Mari, F., Melatti, I., Salvo, I., Tronci, E.: On model based synthesis of embedded control software. In: EMSOFT (2012)
16. Bemporad, A., Giorgetti, N.: A SAT-based hybrid solver for optimal control of hybrid systems. In: Alur, R., Pappas, G.J. (eds.) HSCC 2004. LNCS, vol. 2993, pp. 126–141. Springer, Heidelberg (2004)
17. Della Penna, G., Magazzeni, D., Tofani, A., Intrigila, B., Melatti, I., Tronci, E.: Automated Generation of Optimal Controllers through Model Checking Techniques. In: Cetto, J.A., Ferrier, J.-L., Costa dias Pereira, J.M., Filipe, J. (eds.) Informatics in Control Automation and Robotics. LNEE, vol. 15, pp. 107–119. Springer, Heidelberg (2008)
18. Della Penna, G., Magazzeni, D., Mercorio, F., Intrigila, B.: UPMurphi: A tool for universal planning on pddl+ problems. In: ICAPS (2009)
19. Mazo, M.J., Tabuada, P.: Symbolic approximate time-optimal control. Systems & Control Letters 60(4), 256–263 (2011)
20. Jha, S., Seshia, S.A., Tiwari, A.: Synthesis of optimal switching logic for hybrid systems. In: EMSOFT, pp. 107–116. ACM (2011)
21. Larsen, K.G., Pettersson, P., Yi, W.: UPPAAL: Status & developments. In: Grumberg, O. (ed.) CAV 1997. LNCS, vol. 1254, pp. 456–459. Springer, Heidelberg (1997)
22. Cassez, F., Jessen, J.J., Larsen, K.G., Raskin, J.-F., Reynier, P.-A.: Automatic synthesis of robust and optimal controllers – an industrial case study. In: Majumdar, R., Tabuada, P. (eds.) HSCC 2009. LNCS, vol. 5469, pp. 90–104. Springer, Heidelberg (2009)
23. Melatti, I., Palmer, R., Sawaya, G., Yang, Y., Kirby, R.M., Gopalakrishnan, G.: Parallel and distributed model checking in eddy. Int. J. Softw. Tools Technol. Transf. 11(1), 13–25 (2009)
24. Bulychev, P.E., David, A., Larsen, K.G., Mikucionis, M., Legay, A.: Distributed parametric and statistical model checking. In: PDMC, pp. 30–42 (2011)
25. Barnat, J., Brim, L., Ceska, M., Rockai, P.: Divine: Parallel distributed model checker. In: PDMC. PDMC-HIBI 2010, pp. 4–7. IEEE Computer Society, Washington, DC (2010)
26. Schubert, W., Stengel, R.: Parallel synthesis of robust control systems. IEEE Trans. on Contr. Sys. Techn. 6(6), 701–706 (1998)
27. Jurikovič, M., Čičák, P., Jelemenská, K.: Parallel controller design and synthesis. In: Proceedings of the 7th FPGAworld Conference, FPGAworld 2010, pp. 35–40. ACM, New York (2010)
28. Pardey, J., Amroun, A., Bolton, M., Adamski, M.: Parallel controller synthesis for programmable logic devices. Microprocessors and Microsystems 18(8), 451–457 (1994)
29. Mari, F., Melatti, I., Salvo, I., Tronci, E.: Linear constraints as a modeling language for discrete time hybrid systems. In: ICSEA. IARIA (2012)
30. Mari, F., Melatti, I., Salvo, I., Tronci, E.: Synthesizing control software from boolean relations. Int. J. on Advances in SW 5(3&4), 212–223 (2012)
31. Mari, F., Melatti, I., Salvo, I., Tronci, E.: Control software visualization. In: INFOCOMP. IARIA (2012)
32. Mari, F., Melatti, I., Salvo, I., Tronci, E.: Undecidability of quantized state feedback control for discrete time linear hybrid systems. In: Roychoudhury, A., D'Souza, M. (eds.) ICTAC 2012. LNCS, vol. 7521, pp. 243–258. Springer, Heidelberg (2012)

On-the-Fly Control Software Synthesis[*]

Vadim Alimguzhin[1,2], Federico Mari[1], Igor Melatti[1],
Ivano Salvo[1], and Enrico Tronci[1]

[1] Dip. di Informatica Sapienza Università di Roma,
Via Salaria 113, 00198 Roma, Italy
[2] Department of Computer Science and Robotics Ufa State Aviation Technical
University 12 Karl Marx Street, Ufa, 450000, Russian Federation

Abstract. The Model Based Design approach for Hybrid Systems control software synthesis is particularly appealing since Formal System Level Specifications are usually much easier to define than the control software itself. In this setting, *Design Space Exploration* has the goal to find a suitable (with respect to *costs* and *performance*) choice for system *design parameters*. Unfortunately, a substantial part of the time devoted to design space exploration is spent trying to solve control software synthesis problems that do not have a solution. We present an *on-the-fly* algorithm to control software synthesis that enables effective design space exploration by speeding-up termination when no controller is found. Our experimental results show the effectiveness of our approach and how it can support a concrete realizability and schedulability analysis.

1 Introduction

A *Software Based Control System* (SBCS) consists of two main subsystems, the *controller* and the *plant* that together form the *closed loop system*. In an endless loop, every T seconds (*sampling time*), output y from plant sensors go through an *analog-to-digital* (AD) conversion, yielding a *quantized* value $\ddot{y}$ to the control software implementing the *control law*. The control software then computes the command $\hat{u}$ to be sent (after a *digital-to-analog* (DA) conversion) to plant actuators in order to guarantee that the closed loop system satisfies given *safety* and *liveness* specifications (*System Level Formal Specifications*).

Traditionally, the control software is designed using a *separation-of-concerns* approach. That is, *Control Engineering* techniques (e.g., see [10]) are used to design functional specifications (control law) from the closed loop system level specifications, whereas *Software Engineering* techniques are used to design control software implementing functional specifications.

Motivations. In SBCS design the interface between Control Engineering and Software Engineering activities is basically summarized by the choice of: 1) control law, 2) number of quantization bits b, 3) sampling time T. Taking into

[*] This work has been partially supported by the the EC FP7 projects GA317761 (SmartHG), GA600773 (PAEON), by MIUR project DM24283 (TRAMP), and by Erasmus Mundus MULTIC scholarship from the European Commission (EMA 2 MULTIC 10-837).

E. Bartocci and C.R. Ramakrishnan (Eds.): SPIN 2013, LNCS 7976, pp. 61–80, 2013.
© Springer-Verlag Berlin Heidelberg 2013

account that a SBCS is a real-time system, the control software *Worst Case Execution Time* (WCET) must be less than or equal to T. As a result we have contrasting requirements on the choice of *design parameters* b and T. Namely, typically performance (e.g., set-up time and ripple) of the closed loop system improves as b increases or T decreases. On the other hand, hardware/software costs decrease when b decreases or T increases (e.g., a faster processor is needed in order to guarantee that the control software WCET is less than T).

In our context, one of the main goals of *Design Space Exploration* is to find a suitable (with respect to costs and performance) choice for *design parameters* b and T. The current approach is to define (using Control Engineering techniques) a control law along with values for b and T and then to devise (using Software Engineering techniques) a software implementation for it. Once the software is implemented, its *realizability* and its *schedulability* must be evaluated. Namely, the software is realizable if it fits in the microcontroller flash memory. Moreover, it is schedulable if its WCET is smaller of the sampling time and small enough to make feasible the schedulability of other periodic processes (as reading quantized values from plant sensors) that run on the same microcontroller (see e.g. [15] for a more-in-depth discussion). Performance of the closed loop system is then evaluated using *Hardware In the Loop Simulation* (e.g., nicely supported by *Model Based* tools like Simulink [20] or Reactis [34]).

One may wish to partially automate design space exploration by using tools like QKS [25] that from the plant model, system level formal specifications for the closed loop system and implementation parameters (namely, number of quantization bits), automatically synthesize correct-by-construction control software meeting the given requirements and with a guaranteed WCET. We note that, for many choices of the design parameters b and T, QKS fails to find control software solving the synthesis problem. As a result, a substantial part of the time devoted to design space exploration will be spent trying to solve control software synthesis problems that do not have a solution. Unfortunately the control software synthesis algorithm presented in [25] takes about the same time both when it finds a solution and when it cannot find one.

This paper investigates control software synthesis algorithms that can support design space exploration by detecting *as soon as possible* when a solution to the synthesis problem cannot be found.

Our Contributions. We model the plant as a *Discrete Time Linear Hybrid System* (DTLHS), that is a (discrete time) hybrid system whose dynamics is modeled with linear constraints over a set of continuous as well as discrete variables. Safety and liveness specifications for the closed loop system are defined as linear constraints on state variables. A DTLHS $\mathcal{H}$ approximates a continuous time system dynamics by *sampling* it only at discrete time points multiple of a *time step* τ chosen on the base of physical considerations. Building on this, we can approximate the dynamics of a system *sampled* each $T = n\tau$ seconds by iterating n times the dynamics of $\mathcal{H}$. Using such an approach we can investigate in our DTLHS framework existence of a controller for $\mathcal{H}$ for different configurations of b and $T = n\tau$. Our main contributions can be summarized as follows.

On-the-fly control software synthesis algorithm. We present an *on-the-fly* algorithm for DTLHS control software synthesis, in the same spirit of on-the-fly Model Checking [19]. Such an approach enables effective design space exploration by speeding-up termination of the control software synthesis algorithm in the typical case occurring in the design space exploration phase, namely when no controller is found for the given configuration parameters (b, T).

Experimental results. We implemented our algorithm within the *QKS* tool [25]. To assess the effectiveness of our approach, we present results on its usage for design space exploration of control software for the inverted pendulum, a challenging and widely studied example (e.g., see [22]). We carry out such a design space exploration using both the on-the-fly algorithm presented here and the synthesis algorithm presented in [25]. We have considered 18 choices for the design parameters b and T, 10 of which return a control software. Our experimental results (Sect. 6) show that, using our on-the-fly algorithm we have a time saving of nearly 80%. Finally, we show how our Model Based Design approach can effectively support a concrete realizability and schedulability analysis on a specific family of microcontrollers.

Related Work. *Model based* design space exploration for embedded systems (typically modeled as *Hybrid Systems* [5]) has been widely studied in the last decades. Many tools and paradigms have been proposed to support designers in this phase. For example, see [6] and citations thereof for a *formal* (using UP-PAAL [17]) model based tool and a survey on available tools. In this respect we note that all proposed methods focus on designing the software/hardware system once the control law is given and, in particular, once b (number of quantization bits) and T (sampling time) are given. To the best of our knowledge none of them supports *trading* between Control Engineering *wishes* (large b and small T) and System/Software Engineering *wishes* (small b and large T) *before* the control law is designed. In such a framework our contribution complements the available approaches by enabling trade-offs between the control law, b and T before the control law is designed.

The sampling time T is one of the main requirements to take into account for schedulability analysis. In [24] is proposed a scheduling algorithm that cleverly trades, at run time, T (by delaying execution of control software) and closed loop performances. The main difference with our contribution is that in [24] the control law and b are both given whereas our approach enables exploring (*offline*) the possibility of changing any of them in order to increase T. It is worth noticing that indeed the approach in [24] could be used to further increase (at run time) the T resulting from our control software synthesis method.

We check performance of the closed loop system after control software synthesis. Methods to synthesize control laws satisfying given performance indexes on the closed loop system have been investigated, for example, in [21]. We differ from such work since our plant model is a DTLHS rather than a multi-modal system for [21].

Automatic synthesis of software from models has also been widely studied. For example, see [23] and citations thereof. We differ from such approaches since our starting point is the plant model and closed loop specifications for the closed loop system whereas model based software generation (e.g., as the one also available in tools like Simulink) starts from a model based definition (e.g., using Stateflow/Simulink diagrams) of the control law and then generates a software implementation for such a control law model.

Control software synthesis from formal system level specifications for Discrete Time (possibly non Linear) Hybrid Systems has been investigated in [25,26,3,2]. The *on-the-fly* algorithm presented here improves on the one in [25,26] by reducing of about 99% the time to terminate when it cannot find a controller, possibly at a price of a 25% time penalty when it can find one. This, in turn, enables, formal model based design space (i.e.: *control law*, b, T) exploration.

On-the-fly algorithms for the analysis of Timed Games has been proposed in [12]. Our backward algorithm has to handle linear constraints where both continuous and discrete state variables may appear. In fact, we need to solve many MILP problems to back-propagate a state region. This is quite different from the class of Timed Automata considered in [12], where constraints have the form $x \sim k$, where x is a clock and $\sim$ is one of $<, \leq, \geq, >, =$.

In [31] it is presented a semi-automatic method that, taking as input a continuous time linear system and a goal specification, produces a control law (represented as an OBDD) through PESSOA [30,35]. Such an approach differs from ours as follows. First, our method is fully automatic whereas the one in [31] is not, since it relies on a user provided Lyapunov function, much in the spirit of [22]. Second, [31] does not provide any guarantee on the WCET of the generated software, thus it cannot be used for design space exploration in our context.

Verification and control law synthesis for *Linear Hybrid Automata* (LHA) [4] has been investigated, e.g., in [18,38,16,9]. Control law synthesis for *Piecewise Affine Discrete Time Hybrid Systems* (PWA-DTHS) has been investigated in [7,8]. All such approaches, when dealing with control synthesis, do not account for state feedback quantization since they all assume *exact* (i.e. real valued) state measures and do not generate control software with a guaranteed WCET. As a result they cannot be used for design space exploration in our context, where the number of AD bits b and the software WCET play a crucial role.

2   Background

We denote with $[n]$ an initial segment $\{1, \ldots, n\}$ of the natural numbers. We denote with $X = [x_1, \ldots, x_n]$ a finite sequence of variables. We may regard X as a set when convenient. Each variable x ranges over a bounded or unbounded interval Γ_x, being either $\Gamma_x \subseteq \mathbb{R}$ or $\Gamma_x \subseteq \mathbb{Z}$. We say that Γ_x is a *typing* for x and $\Gamma_X = \prod_{x \in X} \Gamma_x$ is a typing for X. If, for all $x \in X$, Γ_x is a bounded interval, we say that Γ_X is a *bounded* typing for X.

Predicates. A *linear expression* $L(X)$ over a list of variables X is a linear combination of variables in X with rational coefficients, $\sum_{x_i \in X} a_i x_i$. A *linear constraint* over X (or simply a *constraint*) is an expression of the form

$L(X) \leq b$, where b is a rational constant. *Predicates* are inductively defined as follows. A constraint $C(X)$ is a predicate. If $A(X)$ and $B(X)$ are predicates then $(A(X) \wedge B(X))$ and $(A(X) \vee B(X))$ are predicates. Parentheses may be omitted, assuming usual associativity and precedence rules of logical operators. A *conjunctive predicate* is a conjunction of constraints. For conjunctive predicates we will also write: $L(X) \geq b$ for $-L(X) \leq -b$, $L(X) = b$ for $((L(X) \leq b) \wedge (L(X) \geq b))$, and $a \leq x \leq b$ for $x \geq a \wedge x \leq b$, where $x \in X$.

A *valuation* over a list of variables X is a function v that maps each variable $x \in X$ to a value $v(x) \in \Gamma_x$. Given a valuation v, we denote with $X^* \in \Gamma_X$ the sequence of values $[v(x_1), \ldots, v(x_n)]$. By abuse of language, we call valuation also the sequence of values X^*. A *satisfying assignment* to a predicate P over X is a valuation X^* such that $P(X^*)$ holds. If a satisfying assignment to a predicate P over X exists, we say that P is *feasible*. Abusing notation, we may denote with P the set of satisfying assignments to the predicate $P(X)$. A variable $x \in X$ is said to be *bounded* in P if there exist $a, b \in \Gamma_x$ such that $P(X)$ implies $a \leq x \leq b$. A predicate P is bounded if all its variables are bounded.

Given a constraint $C(X)$ and a fresh boolean variable (*guard*) $y \notin X$, the *guarded constraint* $y \to C(X)$ (if y then $C(X)$) denotes the predicate $((y = 0) \vee C(X))$. Similarly, we use $\bar{y} \to C(X)$ (if not y then $C(X)$) to denote the predicate $((y = 1) \vee C(X))$. A *guarded predicate* is a conjunction of either constraints or guarded constraints. If a guarded predicate P is bounded, then P can be transformed into a (bounded) conjunctive predicate [27].

A *linear predicate* $P(X)$ is a (guarded) predicate or an expression of form $\exists Z \in \Gamma_Z \ \tilde{P}(X, Z)$, where $\tilde{P}(X, Z)$ is a (guarded) predicate and Z is set of *auxiliary variables*. Note that, if $\tilde{P}(X, Z)$ is bounded, then $P(X)$ is also bounded.

Mixed Integer Linear Programming. A MILP problem with *decision variables* X is a tuple (max, $J(X)$, $A(X)$) where: X is a list of variables, $J(X)$ (*objective function*) is a linear expression on X, and $A(X)$ (*constraints*) is a conjunctive predicate on X. A *solution* to (max, $J(X)$, $A(X)$) is a valuation X^* such that $A(X^*)$ and $\forall Z \ (A(Z) \to (J(Z) \leq J(X^*)))$. $J(X^*)$ is the *optimal value* of the MILP problem. A *feasibility* problem is a MILP problem of the form (max, 0, $A(X)$). We write also $A(X)$ for (max, 0, $A(X)$). We write (min, $J(X)$, $A(X)$) for (max, $-J(X)$, $A(X)$).

Moore Automata. A *Nondeterministic Moore Automaton* (NMA) [13] is a tuple $\mathcal{M} = (S, A, O, T, \Omega)$ where: S is a set of states, A is a set of *actions*, O is a set of *outputs*, $T : S \times A \times S \to \mathbb{B}$ is the *transition relation* of $\mathcal{M}$, and $\Omega : S \times O \to \mathbb{B}$ is the *output predicate*, such that $\forall s \in S \ \exists o \in O \ \Omega(s, o)$ (there is an output for each state). We call a NMA $\mathcal{M} = (S, A, O, T, \Omega)$ a *Labelled Transition System* (LTS) whenever $S = O$ and for all s_1, s_2 if $\Omega(s_1, s_2)$ holds then $s_1 = s_2$. In such a case we may write simply $\mathcal{M} = (S, A, T)$. In the following, let $s \in S$, $a \in A$ and $o \in O$.

The set of actions *enabled* in s is denoted by $\text{En}(\mathcal{M}, s) = \{a \in A \mid \exists s' T(s, a, s')\}$. An action a is *enabled* in $o \in O$, notation $\text{En}(\mathcal{M}, o)$ if there exists a state s such that $\Omega(s, o)$ holds and $a \in \text{En}(\mathcal{M}, s)$. An action is *admissible* in o, notation $\text{Adm}(\mathcal{M}, o, a)$ if it is enabled in o and for all s such that $\Omega(s, o)$

holds a is enabled in s. The *image* of s through a is denoted by $\text{Img}(\mathcal{M}, s, a) = \{s' \in S \mid T(s, a, s')\}$. We call *transition* of $\mathcal{M}$ a tuple (s, a, s') s.t. $T(s, a, s')$ and *self–loop* a transition (s, a, s') s.t. $T(s, a, s') \land \exists o[\Omega(s, o) \land \Omega(s', o)]$.

A *run* or *path* for an NMA $\mathcal{M}$ is a sequence $\pi = s_0, a_0, s_1, a_1, s_2, a_2, \ldots$ of states s_t and actions a_t such that $\forall t \geq 0 \ T(s_t, a_t, s_{t+1})$. The length $|\pi|$ of a finite run π is the number of actions in π. We denote with $\pi^{(S)}(t)$ the t-th state element of π, and with $\pi^{(A)}(t)$ the t-th action element of π. That is $\pi^{(S)}(t) = s_t$, and $\pi^{(A)}(t) = a_t$.

Given two NMAs $\mathcal{M}_1 = (S, A, O, T_1, \Omega)$ and $\mathcal{M}_2 = (S, A, O, T_2, \Omega)$, we write $\mathcal{M}_1 \sqsubseteq \mathcal{M}_2$ iff $T_1(s, a, s')$ implies $T_2(s, a, s')$ for each state $s, s' \in S$ and action $a \in A$.

3   Output Feedback Control Problem

A *controller* restricts the dynamics of a system, so that all paths starting in a initial state, eventually reach a state in a goal region (*liveness specifications*), while keeping the system in the safe region (*safety specifications*). In this section, we formally define the notion of output feedback control problem and its solutions, by extending to possibly infinite NMAs the definitions in [37,14] for finite LTSs. With respect to [25], the output feedback control problem slightly generalize the notion of quantized feedback control problem in order to provide a natural framework for modelling control problems where plant state is not fully observable. In what follows, let $\mathcal{M} = (S, A, O, T, \Omega)$ be an NMA, and $I, \Sigma, G \subseteq S$ be, respectively, the initial, the safe, and the goal region.

An *output feedback controller* for $\mathcal{M}$ is a function $K : O \times A \to \mathbb{B}$ such that $\forall o \in O, \forall a \in A$, if $K(o, a)$ then $\text{Adm}(\mathcal{M}, o, a)$. We denote with $\text{dom}(K)$ the set of states for which a control action is defined. Formally, $\text{dom}(K) = \{s \in S \mid \exists a \exists o \ \Omega(s, o) \land K(o, a)\}$. $\mathcal{M}^{(K)}$ denotes the *closed loop system*, that is the NMA $(S, A, O, T^{(K)}, \Omega)$, where $T^{(K)}(s, a, s') = T(s, a, s') \land \exists o[\Omega(s, o) \land K(o, a)]$. $\mathcal{M}_\Sigma$ denotes the *safe system*, that is the NMA $(S, A, O, T_\Sigma, \Omega)$, where $T_\Sigma(s, a, s') = T(s, a, s') \land \Sigma(s')$.

We call a path π *fullpath* if either it is infinite or its last state $\pi^{(S)}(|\pi|)$ has no successors. We denote with $\text{Path}(s, a)$ the set of fullpaths starting in state s with action a, i.e. the set of fullpaths π such that $\pi^{(S)}(0) = s$ and $\pi^{(A)}(0) = a$. Given a path π in $\mathcal{M}$, we define the measure $j(\mathcal{M}, G, \pi)$ on paths as the distance of $\pi^{(S)}(0)$ to the goal on π. That is, if there exists $n > 0$ s.t. $\pi^{(S)}(n) \in G$, then $j(\mathcal{M}, G, \pi) = \min\{n \mid n > 0 \land \pi^{(S)}(n) \in G\}$. Otherwise, $j(\mathcal{M}, G, \pi) = +\infty$. We require $n > 0$ since our systems are nonterminating and each controllable state (including a goal state) must have a path of positive length to a goal state. Taking $\sup \varnothing = +\infty$, the *worst case distance* of a state s from the goal region G is $J(\mathcal{M}, G, s) = \sup\{j(\mathcal{M}, G, \pi) \mid \pi \in \text{Path}(s, a), a \in \text{Adm}(\mathcal{M}, s)\}$.

Definition 1. *An NMA output feedback control problem $\mathcal{P}$ is a tuple $(\mathcal{M}, I, \Sigma, G)$. An LTS control problem is an NMA output feedback control problem where $\mathcal{M}$ is an LTS and $\Sigma = S$, thus it is a triple $(\mathcal{M}, I, G)$.*

A strong solution *(or simply, a solution) to $\mathcal{P}$ is a controller K for $\mathcal{M}_\Sigma$ such that $I \subseteq \mathrm{dom}(K)$, and for all $s \in \mathrm{dom}(K)$, $J(\mathcal{M}_\Sigma^{(K)}, G, s)$ is finite.*

An optimal *solution to $\mathcal{P}$ is a solution K^* to $\mathcal{P}$ such that for all solutions K to $\mathcal{P}$, for all $s \in S$, we have $J(\mathcal{M}_\Sigma^{(K^*)}, G, s) \le J(\mathcal{M}_\Sigma^{(K)}, G, s)$.*

The most general optimal (mgo) *solution to $\mathcal{P}$ is an optimal solution $\tilde{K}$ to $\mathcal{P}$ such that for all other optimal solutions K to $\mathcal{P}$, for all $o \in O$, for all $a \in A$ we have that $K(o, a) \to \tilde{K}(o, a)$.*

Intuitively, a strong solution takes a *pessimistic* view by requiring that for each initial state, *all* runs in the closed loop system reach the goal, no matter nondeterminism outcomes.

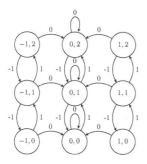   

Fig. 1. Transition relation of NMAs $\mathcal{M}_1$ and $\mathcal{M}_2$ in Example 1

Fig. 2. Inverted Pendulum with Stationary Pivot Point

Example 1. Let $S = \{-1, 0, 1\} \times \{0, 1, 2\}$, $A = \{-1, 0, 1\}$, and $T : S \times A \times S \to \mathbb{B}$ be defined by all arrows in Fig. 1. Let us consider the set of outputs $O_1 = \{-1, 0, 1\}$, the output relation $\Omega_1 = \{((s_1, s_2), s_1) \mid (s_1, s_2) \in S\}$, and the NMA $\mathcal{M}_1 = (S, A, O_1, T, \Omega_1)$. Let $I = \Sigma = S$ and $G = \{(0, 1)\}$. The NMA output feedback control problem $\mathcal{P}_1 = (\mathcal{M}_1, I, \Sigma, G)$ has no solution, because on output 0 it is not possible to determine if the correct action to enable is 0 (as it is in state $(0, 1)$), 1 (as it is in state $(0, 0)$), or -1 (as it is in state $(0, 2)$).

Let us now consider the set of outputs $O_2 = \{0, 1, 2\}$ and the output relation $\Omega_2 = \{((s_1, s_2), s_2) \mid (s_1, s_2) \in S\}$, and the NMA $\mathcal{M}_2 = (S, A, O_2, T, \Omega_2)$. The NMA output feedback control problem $\mathcal{P}_2 = (\mathcal{M}_2, I, \Sigma, G)$ has the mgo solution $K(o, a) = ((o = 0) \to (a = 1)) \wedge ((o = 1) \to (a = 0)) \wedge ((o = 2) \to (a = -1))$.

4   Discrete Time Linear Hybrid Systems

Discrete Time Linear Hybrid Systems (DTLHSs) provide a uniform framework to model both the plant and the closed loop system. In this section, we extend the definition of DTLHSs in [25] by considering *outputs* in order to model measurements of system state (as usual in Control Theory [36]).

Definition 2. *A* Discrete Time Linear Hybrid Systems *(DTLHS) $\mathcal{H}$ is a tuple (X, U, Y, N, W, Γ) such that:*
1. *X is a finite set of real and discrete present state variables. The set X' of next state variables is obtained by decorating with $'$ all variables in X.*

2. U is a finite set of discrete input (controllable) variables.
3. Y is a finite set of discrete output variables.
4. $\Gamma = \Gamma_X \cup \Gamma_U \cup \Gamma_Y$ is a typing for all variables. Moreover, $\Gamma_{X'} = \Gamma_X$.
5. $N(X, U, X')$ is a bounded linear predicate defining the transition relation of $\mathcal{H}$.
6. $W(X, Y)$ is a linear predicate defining the output relation of $\mathcal{H}$. We require that there is always an output associated to any state, formally: $\forall x \in \Gamma_X$ $\exists y \in \Gamma_Y \ W(x, y)$. We write $W^{-1}(y)$ the set of states that has output y. Formally, $W^{-1}(y) = \{x \in \Gamma_X \mid W(x, y)\}$.

Observe that Γ_U and Γ_Y are bounded discrete typings for U and Y. This models the fact that software controllers can only read a finite set of discrete values and can only choose one among a finite set of actions. For this reason we only have discrete outputs. Moreover, our DTLHSs also include the model of the AD conversion (always present in our SBCS setting) via predicate W.

Definition 3. Let $\mathcal{H} = (X, U, Y, N, W, \Gamma)$ be a DTLHS. The dynamics of $\mathcal{H}$ is defined by the Nondetermistic Moore Automata NMA($\mathcal{H}$) = (S, A, O, T, Ω), where: $S = \Gamma_X$, $A = \Gamma_U$, $O = \Gamma_Y$, $T(s, a, s')$ holds if and only if $N(s, a, s')$ holds, and $\Omega(s, o)$ holds if and only if $W(s, o)$ holds. A state x for $\mathcal{H}$ is a state x for NMA($\mathcal{H}$) and a run (or path) for $\mathcal{H}$ is a run for NMA($\mathcal{H}$).

Example 2. Let T be a positive constant (time step). We define the DTLHS $\mathcal{H} = ([x_1, x_2], [u], [y_1, y_2], N, \Gamma, W)$, where $\Gamma_{x_1} = [-1, 1]$, $\Gamma_{x_2} = [0, 2]$, $\Gamma_u = \Gamma_{y_1} = \{-1, 0, 1\}$, $\Gamma_{y_1} = \{0, 1, 2\}$, and the transition relation $N(x_1, x_2, u, x_1', x_2')$ is defined by $((u = 0) \to x_1' = \frac{x_1}{2}) \wedge ((u \neq 0) \to x_1' = x_1) \wedge (x_2' = x_2 + uT)$. Finally, let the output predicate W be the rounding of the continuous variables x_1 and x_2. Formally, $W(x_1, x_2, y_1, y_2)$ is defined by $(x_1 - \frac{1}{2} \leq y_1 \leq x_1 + \frac{1}{2}) \wedge (x_2 - \frac{1}{2} \leq y_2 \leq x_2 + \frac{1}{2})$.

An output feedback control problem for a DTLHS $\mathcal{H}$ is the NMA output feedback control problem induced by the dynamics of $\mathcal{H}$.

Definition 4. Given a DTLHS $\mathcal{H} = (X, U, Y, N, W, \Gamma)$ and linear predicates $I(X)$, $\Sigma(X)$, $G(X)$ the DTLHS output feedback control problem ($\mathcal{H}$, I, Σ, G) is the NMA output feedback control problem (NMA($\mathcal{H}$), I, Σ, G). Thus, a controller $K : \Gamma_Y \times \Gamma_U \to \mathbb{B}$ is a solution to ($\mathcal{H}$, I, Σ, G) iff it is a solution to (NMA($\mathcal{H}$), I, Σ, G).

Example 3. Let $\mathcal{H}$ be the DTLHS in Ex. 2 and $X = [x_1, x_2]$. Let $I(X) = \Sigma(X) = \Gamma_X$ and $G(X) = (-\frac{1}{2} \leq x_1 \leq -\frac{1}{2}) \wedge (-\frac{1}{2} \leq x_2 \leq \frac{1}{2})$. The DTLHS output control problem ($\mathcal{H}, I, \Sigma, G$) has the solution $K(y_1, y_2, u) = ((y_2 = 1) \to (u = 0)) \wedge ((y_2 = 2) \to (u = -1)) \wedge ((y_2 = 0) \to (u = 1))$. Observe, that this solution depends on the output variable y_2 only. As a consequence, if we consider the DTLHS $\mathcal{H}' = ([x_1, x_2], [u], [y_2], \Gamma, W')$ with the output predicate W' defined by $W(x_1, x_2, y_1, y_2) = (x_2 - \frac{1}{2} \leq y_2) \wedge (y_2 \leq x_2 + \frac{1}{2})$ (rounding of the variable x_2), we have that K is a solution also to the control problem ($\mathcal{H}', I, \Sigma, G$).

4.1   A DTLHS Model for the Inverted Pendulum Case Study

In this section, we present the DTLHS model of the inverted pendulum, on which our experiments focus. The inverted pendulum (see Fig. 2) is a classical, hard control problem [22] whose DTLHS formulation is far from trivial [2]. The inverted pendulum is modeled by taking the angle θ and the angular velocity $\dot{\theta}$ as state variables and the torquing force $u \cdot F$ as the system input. The variable u models the direction and the constant F models the intensity of the force. Differently from [22], we consider the problem of finding a discrete controller, whose decisions can be only "apply the force clockwise" ($u = 1$), "apply the force counterclockwise" ($u = -1$)", or "do nothing" ($u = 0$). A linear model can be found by under- and over-approximating the non linear function $\sin x$ with piecewise linear functions f_i^- and f_i^+ (see [2] for details). The resulting model is the DTLHS $\mathcal{I}^b = (X, U, Y, N, W^b, \Gamma)$ discretized with b bits, where $X = \{x_1, x_2\}$ is the set of continuous state variables with $\Gamma_X = \times_{i=1}^2 [c_{x_i}, d_{x_i}]$ (being c_{x_i}, d_{x_i} the lower and upper bound constants for variable x_i), $U = \{u\}$ is the set of input variables with $\Gamma_u = \{-1, 0, 1\}$, $Y = \{y_1, y_2\}$ is the set of output variables (where y_1 is a discretization for x_1 and y_2 for x_2) with $\Gamma_{y_1} = \Gamma_{y_2} = \{0, \ldots, 2^b - 1\}$, and the transition relation $N(X, U, X')$ is the following linear predicate (m is the pendulum mass, l is the pendulum length, and g is the gravitational acceleration):

$$\exists Z \in \Gamma_Z (x_1' = x_1 + 2\pi z_q + \tau x_2) \wedge (x_2' = x_2 + \tau \frac{g}{l} z_{\sin} + \tau \frac{1}{ml^2} uF)$$

$$\wedge \bigwedge_{i \in [4]} z_i \to f_i^-(z_\alpha) \leq z_{\sin} \leq f_i^+(z_\alpha)$$

$$\wedge \bigwedge_{i \in [4]} z_i \to z_\alpha \in I_i \wedge \sum_{i \in [4]} z_i \geq 1$$

$$\wedge x_1 = 2\pi z_k + z_\alpha \wedge -\pi \leq x_1' \leq \pi \wedge X \in \Gamma_X \wedge U \in \Gamma_U$$

Finally, the output predicate is $W^b(x_1, x_2, y_1, y_2) \equiv \bigwedge_{i=1}^2 c_{x_i} + \frac{d_{x_i} - c_{x_i}}{2^b} y_i \leq x_i \leq c_{x_i} + \left(\frac{d_{x_i} - c_{x_i}}{2^b} + 1 \right) y_i \wedge y_i \in \Gamma_{y_i}$.

5   On-the-Fly Control Software Synthesis

Given a DTLHS output control problem $\mathcal{P} = (\mathcal{H}, I, \Sigma, G)$, a typical approach to the automatic synthesis of controllers consists of building a suitable finite state representation $\hat{\mathcal{H}}_\Sigma$ of the plant $\mathcal{H}$, computing an abstraction $\hat{I}$ (resp. $\hat{G}$) of the initial (resp. goal) region I (resp. G) so that any solution to the control problem $(\hat{\mathcal{H}}_\Sigma, \hat{I}, \hat{G})$ is a finite representation of a solution to $\mathcal{P}$. For example, this can be done by giving conditions ensuring that the abstract system satisfies some equivalence relation with respect to the concrete system (e.g. see [33,1,25]).

To avoid useless computation, our on-the-fly control synthesis algorithm (Sect. 5.2) simultaneously computes the finite abstraction $\hat{\mathcal{H}}_\Sigma$ and the solution to the control problem $(\hat{\mathcal{H}}_\Sigma, \hat{I}, \hat{G})$. To make the algorithm description clear, we first present in Sect. 5.1 the notion of *output abstraction* that adapts the notion of control abstraction [25] to the output model considered in this paper.

5.1   Output Abstraction

In our setting [25], the finite state representation induced by the output relation of a DTLHS is a design constraint rather than a methodological tool, since it models the finite precision of sensor measurements.

Definition 5. *Let* $\mathcal{H} = (X, U, Y, N, W, \Gamma)$ *be a DTLHS and* $(\mathcal{H}, I, \Sigma, G)$ *be a DTLHS control problem. The output abstraction of* $\mathcal{H}$ *is the LTS* $\hat{\mathcal{H}}_\Sigma = (S, A, T_\Sigma)$ *such that* $S = \Gamma_Y$, $A = \Gamma_U$, *and for all* $s, s' \in S$, $a \in A$ *we have* $T_\Sigma(y, a, y')$ *iff* a *is an admissible transition in* y *and there exists* $x, x' \in \Gamma_X$ *such that* $W(x, y) \wedge W(x', y') \wedge N(x, a, x')$.

The output abstraction could be a highly non-deterministic LTS, thus making problematic the existence of a strong solution to the output feedback control problem. In particular, for small values of the sampling time, the output abstraction may contain a large number of self-loops: for any output y that is not in the goal region, a self-loop (y, a, y) of $\hat{\mathcal{H}}_\Sigma$ prevents the action a to be enabled in y in any strong solution to the output control problem. On the other hand, if by repeatedly performing an action a in an abstract state y, it is guaranteed that the system will leave the region $W^{-1}(y)$ represented by the output y after a finite number of steps, a self-loop (y, a, y) of $\hat{\mathcal{H}}_\Sigma$ can be eliminated and the action a can be enabled by a strong controller in the state y.

Definition 6. *Let* $\mathcal{H} = (X, U, Y, N, W, \Gamma)$ *be a DTLHS,* $(\mathcal{H}, I, \Sigma, G)$ *be a DTLHS control problem and let* $\hat{\mathcal{H}}_\Sigma = (S, A, T_\Sigma)$ *be its output abstraction.*

A self-loop (y, a, y) *of* $\hat{\mathcal{H}}_\Sigma$ *is non-eliminable if there exists at least an infinite run* $\pi = x_0 a x_1 a x_2 \ldots$ *in* $\mathcal{H}$ *such that* $\forall t \in \mathbb{N}$ $x_t \in W^{-1}(y)$. *Otherwise, a self-loop* (y, a, y) *of* $\hat{\mathcal{H}}_\Sigma$ *is said to be an* eliminable *self-loop.*

We call adequate output abstraction *any LTS* $\hat{\mathcal{H}}' \sqsubseteq \hat{\mathcal{H}}_\Sigma$ *that omits some eliminable self-loops.*

Example 4. Let $\mathcal{P} = (\mathcal{H}, I, \Sigma, G)$ be the control problem in Ex. 3. An adequate output abstraction of $\mathcal{H}$ is the automaton considered in Ex. 1. Observe that, for all $z \in \Gamma_{y_2}$, the self-loops $((0, z), 0, (0, z))$ are non-eliminable self-loops. In fact, $N((0, z), 0, (0, z))$ holds, and hence there are runs of $\mathcal{H}$ which infinitely cycle on $(0, z)$ with action 0. Thus self-loops $((0, z), 0, (0, z))$ belong to the output abstraction and to all adequate output abstractions. On the contrary, the output abstraction contains, for all $(z_1, z_2) \in \Gamma_Y$, self-loops $((z_1, z_2), 1, (z_1, z_2))$ and $((z_1, z_2), -1, (z_1, z_2))$, as well as self-loops $((z_1, z_2), 0, (z_1, z_2))$ where $z_1 \neq 0$. It is easy to see that all such self-loops are eliminable, thus adequate output abstractions (as the one in Ex. 1) may not contain them. Finally, observe that, for all $z_1 \in \Gamma_{y_1}$, action 1 is not admissible in $(z_1, 2)$, since for example $N((z_1, 2), 1, (z_1, 2 + T))$ holds and $\Sigma((z_1, 2 + T))$ does not hold. Similarly, for all $z_1 \in \Gamma_{y_1}$, action -1 is not admissible in $(z_1, 0)$.

The following theorem [25] states that it is correct to consider output adequate abstractions when looking for a strong solution to a output feedback DTLHS control problem.

Theorem 1. *Let $\mathcal{H} = (X, U, Y, N, W, \Gamma)$ be a DTLHS, let $(\mathcal{H}, I, \Sigma, G)$ be an output feedback DTLHS control problem, and let $\hat{\mathcal{H}}_\Sigma$ be an adequate abstraction of $\mathcal{H}$. If $\hat{I}, \hat{G} \subseteq \Gamma_Y$ are such that $I \subseteq W^{-1}(\hat{I})$ and $G \supseteq W^{-1}(\hat{G})$, then a strong solution $\hat{K}$ to the LTS control problem $(\hat{\mathcal{H}}_\Sigma, \hat{I}, \hat{G})$ is a strong solution to the output feedback control problem $(\mathcal{H}, I, \Sigma, G)$.*

5.2   On-the-Fly Computation of Output Abstraction

Stemming from Theorem 1, the solution of an output control problem $(\mathcal{H}, I, \Sigma, G)$ can be found as the solution to the finite LTS control problem $(\hat{\mathcal{H}}_\Sigma, \hat{I}, \hat{G})$. In [25], we presented a MILP-based approach to the computation of the output abstraction $\hat{\mathcal{H}}_\Sigma$. The solution to the finite LTS control problem is computed by adapting the symbolic algorithm in [14]. Starting from goal states, the most general optimal controller is found looping backward, adding at each step to the set of states D controlled so far, the *strong preimage* of D, i.e. the set of states for which there exists at least an action a that drives the system to D, regardless of possible nondeterminism.

In order to determine as soon as possible if a solution to a given output control problem cannot be found, and actually compute the solution otherwise, Alg. 1 implements an incremental approach to control software synthesis, in the same spirit of *on-the-fly Model Checking* [19]. Instead of first fully computing $\hat{\mathcal{H}}_\Sigma$, and then solving the finite LTS control problem $(\hat{\mathcal{H}}_\Sigma, \hat{I}, \hat{G})$, function *strongCtrInc* incrementally and simultaneously computes the abstraction $\hat{\mathcal{H}}_\Sigma$ and the solution $\hat{K}$ to the control problem $(\hat{\mathcal{H}}_\Sigma, \hat{I}, \hat{G})$ in such a way that, at the i-th iteration, the computed abstraction $\hat{\mathcal{H}}_i$ is large enough to correctly determine the set of states that can be driven to the goal in at most i steps.

Function *strongCtrIncr* in Alg. 1. uses *Ordered Binary Decision Diagrams* (OBDD) to represent sets and relations over sets. In Alg. 1, variable $\hat{K}$ is the OBDD representing the computed controller so far, $\hat{D}$ is the domain of $\hat{K}$, $\hat{F} \subseteq \hat{D} \cup \hat{G}$ is the set of outputs which have been added to $\hat{D}$ in the last iteration, and $\hat{N}$ is the transition relation of $\hat{\mathcal{H}}_\Sigma$ computed so far. To save useless computation, the OBDD $\hat{E}$ stores the set of pairs $(y, u) \in \Gamma_Y \times \Gamma_U$ already considered in the construction of $\hat{N}$.

Function *strongCtrIncr* first computes a finite underapproximation $\hat{G}$ of the goal region G (line 1), and a finite overapproximation $\hat{I}$ of the initial region I (line 2). Then, in line 3, the controller $\hat{K}$, the controllable region $\hat{D}$, the set $\hat{E}$, and the transition relation $\hat{N}$ are initialized to the empty set (i.e. the empty OBDD) and $\hat{F}$ is initialized to the set of abstract goal states $\hat{G}$.

After this initialization phase, function *strongCtrIncr* enters a loop (lines 4–18) in which, at iteration i, all states which may be strongly controlled in at most i steps are added to $\hat{K}$. To this aim, a nested loop (lines 5–15) is performed where, at each iteration, the algorithm computes the part of the transition relation $\hat{N}$ that is necessary to find all states that a controller can drive in one step to the controllable region $\hat{D}$ computed so far. To this end, for any output $y \in \hat{F}$ and for any action u, it is computed an overapproximation $\hat{P}$ of the set of outputs that can reach y in one step by performing action u (line 6). The overapproximation

Algorithm 1. Incremental Controller Synthesis

Input: A DTLHS $\mathcal{H} = (X, U, Y, N, W, \Gamma)$, a control problem $(\mathcal{H}, I, \Sigma, G)$.
function $strongCtrInc(\mathcal{H}, I, \Sigma, G)$
1. $\hat{G} \leftarrow \{y \in \Gamma_Y \,|\, \neg \exists x \in \Gamma_X . W(x, y) \wedge \neg G(x)\}$
2. $\hat{I} \leftarrow \{y \in \Gamma_Y \,|\, \exists x \in \Gamma_X . W(x, y) \wedge I(x)\}$
3. $\hat{K} \leftarrow \varnothing;\ \hat{D} \leftarrow \varnothing;\ \hat{N} \leftarrow \varnothing;\ \hat{F} \leftarrow \hat{G};\ \hat{E} \leftarrow \varnothing$
4. **repeat**
5.   **for all** $y \in \hat{F}$, $u \in \Gamma_U$ **do**
6. $\hat{P} \leftarrow overCounterImage(y, u)$
7.   **for all** $\tilde{y} \in \hat{P}$ **do**
8.   **if** $(\tilde{y}, u) \notin \hat{E}$ **then**
9. $\hat{E} \leftarrow \hat{E} \cup \{(\tilde{y}, u)\}$ {mark $(\tilde{y}, u)$ as "examined"}
10.   **if** $admissible(\Sigma, \tilde{y}, u)$ **then**
11.   **if** $selfLoop(\tilde{y}, u)$ **then** $\hat{N} \leftarrow \hat{N} \cup \{(\tilde{y}, u, \tilde{y})\}$
12. $\hat{O} \leftarrow overImg(\tilde{y}, u)$
13.   **for all** $\tilde{y}' \in \hat{O}$ **do**
14.   **if** $\tilde{y} \neq \tilde{y}' \wedge existsTrans(\tilde{y}, u, \tilde{y}')$ **then**
15. $\hat{N} \leftarrow \hat{N} \cup \{(\tilde{y}, u, \tilde{y}')\}$
16. $\hat{C}_{new} \leftarrow \{(y, u) \,|\, y \notin \hat{D}, \exists s'\, \hat{N}(y, u, y') \wedge \forall y'\, \hat{N}(y, u, y') \Rightarrow y' \in \hat{D} \cup \hat{G}\}$
17. $\hat{K} \leftarrow \hat{K} \cup \hat{C}_{new};\ \hat{F} \leftarrow \{y \,|\, (y, u) \in \hat{C}_{new}\};\ \hat{D} \leftarrow \hat{D} \cup \hat{F}$
18. **until** $C_{new} = \varnothing$
19. **if** $\hat{I} \subseteq \hat{D}$ **then return** $\langle \text{TRUE}, \hat{D}, \hat{K} \rangle$
20. **else return** $\langle \text{FALSE}, \hat{D}, \hat{K} \rangle$

$\hat{P}$ is computed by function $overCounterImg$ which, for each variable $y_i \in Y$, computes the minimum and maximum value that y_i can assume in a satisfying assignment of $N(x, a, x') \wedge W(x, y) \wedge W(x', y')$ (thus $2|Y|$ MILP problems are set up and solved). Since the set $\hat{E}$ contains all the output-action pairs already considered in the construction of $\hat{N}$ so far, to avoid the same part of $\hat{N}$ to be recomputed, only state-action pairs not in $\hat{E}$ will be considered (line 8).

As prescribed by the definition of adequate output abstraction, a transition (y, u, y'), with $y \neq y'$, is added to $\hat{N}$ whenever u is an admissible action in y and there exist $x \in W^{-1}(y), x' \in W^{-1}(y')$ such that $N(x, u, x')$ (lines 10–15). As for self-loops (y, u, y), we want to add them to $\hat{N}$ only if they are non-eliminable (line 11). Since self-loop elimination is an undecidable problem [29], we employ function $selfLoop$ [25] to check a sufficient gradient based condition for self-loop elimination that in practice turns out to be very effective. Namely, for each variable x_i, $selfLoop$ tries to establish if x_i is either always increasing or always decreasing inside $W^{-1}(y)$ by performing action u. If this is the case, we have that, being $W^{-1}(y)$ a compact set, no Zeno-phenomena may arise, thus executing action u it is guaranteed that $\hat{\mathcal{H}}_\Sigma$ will eventually leave the region $W^{-1}(y)$.

Lines 16–17 update the controller $\hat{K}$ (and its domain $\hat{D}$) computed so far. The set $\hat{F}$ is updated with the set of new controlled states. Finally, the outermost **repeat-until** loop (lines 4–18) is performed until no more new controlled states have been found.

Theorem 2. *Let* $\mathcal{P} = (\mathcal{H}, I, \Sigma, G)$ *be a DTLHS output feedback control problem. If function strongCtrInc returns* $\langle \text{TRUE}, \hat{D}, \hat{K} \rangle$ *then* $\hat{K}$ *is a strong solution to* $\mathcal{P}$.

Finally, the actual control software (i.e., C code) for the DTLHS is synthesized by translating $\hat{K}$ as it is described in [28]. The *guaranteed WCET* (worst case execution time) $T_{\hat{K}}$ of the synthesized control software is also computed.

6   Experimental Results

In this section we present our experiments that aim at evaluating the effectiveness of our control software synthesis technique. We implemented *strongCtrInc* in the C programming language using the CUDD package for OBDD based computations and GLPK for solving MILP problems. The resulting tool, QKS^{otf}, extends the tool QKS by adding the possibility of using the on-the-fly approach described in Alg. 1.

The objective of our experiments is threefold. First, in Sect. 6.1 and 6.2 we evaluate, on a meaningful case study, the speedup obtained with the on-the-fly algorithm with respect to the exhaustive method presented in [25] in the context of design space exploration. Second, in Sect. 6.3 we show how our on-the-fly algorithm can be used for realizability and schedulability analysis issues [11] for control software in design space exploration. Finally, in Sect. 6.4 we assess the quality of our controllers, by evaluating their system level performances, such as ripple and set-up time.

6.1   Experimental Setting: Design Space Exploration

In our experiments, we consider the inverted pendulum case study introduced in Sect. 4.1. To this aim, we model the inverted pendulum with the DTLHS $\mathcal{I}^b = (X, U, Y, N, W^b, \Gamma)$ defined in Sect. 4.1, where the state variables bounds are fixed as follows: $c_{x_1} = -1.1\pi$ radiants, $d_{x_1} = 1.1\pi$ radiants, $c_{x_2} = -4$ radiants per second, $d_{x_2} = 4$ radiants per second. As for pendulum parameters, we set $F = 0.5$ N and, as in [22,2,3], we set l and m in such a way that $\frac{g}{l} = 1$ (i.e. $l = g$) and $\frac{1}{ml^2} = 1$ (i.e. $m = \frac{1}{l^2}$). Finally, the DTLHS control problem is $(\mathcal{I}^b, \Sigma, I, G)$, where $I(x_1, x_2) \equiv \bigwedge_{i=1}^{2} 0.9c_{x_i} \leq x_i \leq 0.9d_{x_i}$, $G(x_1, x_2) \equiv \bigwedge_{i=1}^{2} 0.1 \leq x_i \leq 0.1$, and $\Sigma(x_1, x_2) \equiv \bigwedge_{i=1}^{2} x_i \in \Gamma_{x_i}$. That is, the goal is to turn the pendulum nearly steady to the upright position, starting from nearly any possible initial position and without going out of the state variables bounds.

Our aim here is to carry out experiments for different values of the number of quantization bits b and of the *sampling time* T, i.e., the time between two samples of the system state in the closed loop system. On the other hand, the DTLHS $\mathcal{I}^b$ approximates the continuous time pendulum dynamics by discretizing the corresponding differential equations with a time step τ ($\tau = 0.05$ seconds in our experiments). T is typically greater than τ. If we directly set $\tau = T$ in $\mathcal{I}^b$, we would obtain a not accurate model, since τ depends on physical considerations [36] (such considerations are not our focus here). Building on this, we approximate the dynamics of the pendulum with sampling time T by iterating $n = \lceil \frac{T}{\tau} \rceil$ times the transition relation N of $\mathcal{I}^b$. Namely, we consider the transition relation $N_n(X, U, X') \equiv \exists \tilde{X}^{(0)}, \ldots, \tilde{X}^{(n)} \bigwedge_{i=0}^{n-1} N(\tilde{X}^{(i)}, U, \tilde{X}^{(i+1)}) \wedge X = \tilde{X}^{(0)} \wedge X' = \tilde{X}^{(n)}$, being $\tilde{X}^{(0)}, \ldots, \tilde{X}^{(n)}$ sets of variables not occurring in N (note that N_n is a linear predicate). Namely, $N_n(x, u, x')$ holds if, by holding action u for n transitions of step τ, the systems goes from x to x'. This allows us to have a sampling time (at least) T, while retaining model accuracy. In the following, we will use n instead of T, with the understanding that $T = n\tau$. Thus, the DTLHS reference model for our experiments is $\mathcal{I}_n^b = (X, U, Y, N_n, W^b, \Gamma)$, and the DTLHS control problem is $(\mathcal{I}_n^b, I, \Sigma, G)$.

In order to experimentally show that function *strongCtrInc* of Alg. 1 effectively supports design space exploration, we will run both QKS^{otf} and QKS on $\mathcal{I}_n^b$ for $(b, n) \in \{8, 9, 10\} \times \{10, 8, 6, 4, 2, 1\}$, and then compare the corresponding computation times.

6.2   Experimental Results for Design Space Exploration

All experiments have been carried out on an Intel(R) Xeon(R) CPU @ 2.27GHz, with 23GiB of RAM, Kernel: Linux 2.6.32-5-686-bigmem, distribution Debian GNU/Linux 6.0.3 (squeeze).

Results of QKS and QKS^{otf} are in Table 1. Columns meaning in Table 1 are as follows. Columns b and n have the same meaning as in Sect. 6.1. Columns CPU^{exh} (resp., CPU^{otf}) shows the computation time in seconds of QKS (resp.,

Table 1. Experimental results for pendulum

b	n	CPU^{exh}	RAM^{exh}	CPU^{otf}	RAM^{otf}	$|\hat{K}|$	%	Speedup	Result
8	10	9.90e+04	1.70e+08	4.58e+02	3.03e+07	1.25e+02	99.54	216.16	FAIL
8	8	4.41e+04	1.68e+08	3.06e+02	3.05e+07	2.06e+02	99.31	144.12	FAIL
8	6	2.28e+04	1.65e+08	2.77e+04	9.12e+07	6.40e+03	-21.49	0.82	PASS
8	4	1.17e+04	1.63e+08	1.47e+04	8.68e+07	7.53e+03	-25.64	0.80	PASS
8	2	4.91e+03	1.63e+08	1.35e+01	2.98e+07	1.63e+02	99.73	363.70	FAIL
8	1	2.69e+03	1.53e+08	4.72e+00	2.98e+07	1.61e+02	99.82	569.92	FAIL
9	10	4.95e+05	2.39e+08	2.70e+03	3.16e+07	1.88e+02	99.45	183.33	FAIL
9	8	2.31e+05	2.31e+08	2.40e+05	2.70e+08	1.08e+04	-3.90	0.96	PASS
9	6	1.20e+05	2.18e+08	1.19e+05	2.71e+08	1.25e+04	0.83	1.01	PASS
9	4	5.66e+04	1.98e+08	5.34e+04	2.50e+08	1.55e+04	5.65	1.06	PASS
9	2	2.18e+04	1.91e+08	2.29e+04	2.43e+08	2.16e+04	-5.05	0.95	PASS
9	1	1.16e+04	1.78e+08	1.97e+01	3.02e+07	2.11e+02	99.83	588.83	FAIL
10	10	3.82e+06	6.08e+08	1.45e+04	3.65e+07	2.87e+02	99.62	263.45	FAIL
10	8	1.71e+06	5.40e+08	6.74e+03	3.83e+07	6.01e+02	99.61	253.71	FAIL
10	6	7.45e+05	4.72e+08	6.67e+05	8.81e+08	2.45e+04	10.47	1.12	PASS
10	4	3.05e+05	4.13e+08	2.77e+05	8.31e+08	2.99e+04	9.18	1.10	PASS
10	2	1.05e+05	3.29e+08	9.96e+04	8.12e+08	4.52e+04	5.14	1.05	PASS
10	1	5.29e+04	2.64e+08	5.09e+04	8.07e+08	6.31e+04	3.78	1.04	PASS
Overall		7.85e+06	6.08e+08	1.60e+06	8.81e+08		79.62	4.91	

QKS^{otf}). Columns RAM^{exh} (resp., RAM^{otf}) shows the RAM memory usage peak in bytes for QKS (resp., QKS^{otf}). Column $|\hat{K}|$ shows the generated controller size, i.e. the number of nodes in the OBDD representing $\hat{K}$. Column **Speedup** shows the speedup obtained by using QKS^{otf} instead of QKS, that is $\frac{\text{CPU}^{exh}}{\text{CPU}^{otf}}$. Column % shows the gain (in terms of computation time) obtained by using QKS^{otf} instead of QKS, that is $\% = 100(1 - \frac{\text{CPU}^{exh} - \text{CPU}^{otf}}{\text{CPU}^{exh}})$. Column **Result** is PASS if a controller for $\mathcal{I}_n^b$ exist (i.e., if function *strongCtrInc* returns TRUE), FAIL otherwise. Finally, the last row in Table 1 shows the sum of all computation times for QKS and QKS^{otf}, the maximum RAM memory usage peak for QKS and QKS^{otf}, and the overall computation time gain of QKS^{otf} w.r.t QKS.

From Table 1 we note that, as expected, QKS^{otf} obtain a huge speedup (near to 100%) for the cases in which a control software is not found, while it requires approximately the same time of QKS otherwise. This is due to the fact that the on-the-fly algorithm introduces both an overhead (mainly due to counterimages computations at line 6 of Alg. 1 and OBDD $\hat{E}$ management) and a speedup (even when the control software is found, the adequate output abstraction $\hat{N}$ may be not fully computed). Summing up, our approach obtain an overall gain of nearly 80% when performing design space exploration, with an acceptable memory usage overhead. This shows effectiveness of QKS^{otf} for design space exploration.

6.3 Control Software Realizability and Schedulability

In order to verify if the control software works properly on a given microcontroller, two issues must be taken into account: *realizability* and *schedulability*.

A control software is *realizable* on a given microcontroller if the whole control software fits in the microcontroller flash memory. Since our approach directly outputs the C code for the control software, it is sufficient to compile the C code on the given microcontroller architecture, obtain the hex file to be copied on the microcontroller flash, and check if its size fits in the microcontroller flash.

As for *schedulability*, we note that the real-time requirement $T_W \leq T = n\tau$ must hold, being T_W an upper bound for the control software WCET. Since our approach also outputs the synthesized control software guaranteed WCET, we are able to directly check if this requirement is fulfilled. Namely, since $2b$ (resp. 2) bits are needed to encode pendulum states (resp. actions), in all our experiments the WCET is $T_W \leq 4bT_B$, being T_B an upper bound for the time needed to compute an `if-then-else` C block of a given known structure [28]. More in detail, by directly looking at the assembly code generated for such an `if-then-else` C block on a candidate microcontroller (an example is shown in Fig. 3), and by considering the number of clock cycles needed for each assembly instruction, we obtain the upper bound for the number of microcontroller clock cycles A needed to compute such a block. Thus, given the microcontroller frequency $F = \frac{1}{T_C}$, we have that $T_B \leq AT_C$.

The schedulability analysis of the control software has to consider that other *processes* need to run with given periods together with the controller itself. Namely, the controller computation (which in this setting is a process with period $n\tau$) must be preceded by processes reading quantized values from plant sensors (one process per plant state variable) and must be followed by a process sending the computed action to plant actuators. Moreover, other processes may be needed, e.g. to accept keyboard input for debugging. In the following, we will assume each of such processes to require at most 100 clock cycles, and to have a period of 10^{-3} seconds (which is less than $n\tau$ for all n). We consider the schedulability test for the *Rate-Monotonic Scheduling* (RMS, see e.g. [11]), that is $\sum_{i=1}^{k+1} \frac{C_i}{T_i} \leq (k+1)(2^{1/(k+1)} - 1)$, being C_i the WCET and T_i the period for process i and k the number of processes running together with the controller. Supposing the controller to be the process with index $(k+1)$, we have that the schedulability test is implied by $\frac{4b\bar{A}T_C}{n\tau} + k\frac{100T_C}{10^{-3}} < 0.69$. Again, being all the required measures either known or computed by our model-based approach, we are able to determine beforehand (i.e., without having to actually copy the control software in the microcontroller and test it) if the control software is schedulable in the given microcontroller.

Table 2. Experimental results for realizability and schedulability

b	n	$|\hat{K}_{hex}|$	Arch	WCET	α	k
8	10	5.00e+03	atmega8	3.20e-04	6.40e-04	27
8	8	7.39e+03	atmega8	2.56e-04	6.40e-04	27
8	6	1.45e+05	atmega16	1.92e-04	6.40e-04	27
8	4	1.74e+05	atmega16	1.28e-04	6.40e-04	27
8	2	4.85e+03	atmega8	6.40e-05	6.40e-04	27
8	1	4.31e+03	atmega8	3.20e-05	6.40e-04	27
9	10	7.66e+03	atmega8	3.60e-04	7.20e-04	27
9	8	2.37e+05	atmega16	2.88e-04	7.20e-04	27
9	6	2.80e+05	atmega16	2.16e-04	7.20e-04	27
9	4	3.37e+05	atmega16	1.44e-04	7.20e-04	27
9	2	9.50e+05	ARM	4.32e-06	4.32e-05	344
9	1	5.98e+03	atmega8	3.60e-05	7.20e-04	27
10	10	1.20e+04	atmega8	4.00e-04	8.00e-04	27
10	8	2.18e+04	atmega8	3.20e-04	8.00e-04	27
10	6	1.06e+06	ARM	1.44e-05	4.80e-05	344
10	4	1.31e+06	ARM	9.60e-06	4.80e-05	344
10	2	1.96e+06	ARM	4.80e-06	4.80e-05	344
10	1	2.63e+06	ARM	2.40e-06	4.80e-05	344

```
.L398:
    ldd r24,Z+10
    cpi r24,lo8(1)
    brne .L17
.L37:
    ld r24,Z
    cpi r24,lo8(1)
    breq .L17
    ldi r24,lo8(0)
    ldi r25,hi8(0)
    or r18,r19
    brne .L38
    ldi r24,lo8(1)
    ldi r25,hi8(1)
.L38:
    movw r18,r24
.L39:
    ldd r24,Z+9
    rjmp .L440
.L35:
    ldi r18,lo8(0)
    ldi r19,hi8(0)
```

Fig. 3. Snapshot of Atmel atmega16 assembly control software

Our experimental results on control software schedulability and realizability are shown in Table 2. Columns meaning in Table 2 are as follows. Columns b and n have the same meaning as in Sect. 6.1. Column $|\hat{K}_{hex}|$ shows the generated controller size, as the number of bytes to be written in the target microcontroller flash memory. Column **Arch** shows the microcontroller having the smallest fit flash memory for $|\hat{K}_{hex}|$. We consider the following microcontrollers of the Atmel family [32]: atmega8 (8K of flash), atmega16 (16K) and at91sam (1MB). For both atmega8 and atmega16, the clock frequency F is 4MHz (i.e., each clock tick needs $T_C = 250$ nanoseconds), and the upper bound of the number of clock cycles needed to compute the greatest `if-then-else` C block in the software implementing $\hat{K}$ is $A = 16$. For at91sam, which, being ARM-based, is shown as ARM in Table 2, $F = 50$ MHz, $T_C = 250$ nanoseconds and $A = 12$. Column **WCET** shows an upper bound for the control software WCET, i.e., $4bAT_C$. Column α shows the ratio between the WCET and the period of the controller process (note that this is part of the schedulability test for RMS), i.e., $\alpha = \frac{\text{WCET}}{n\tau}$. Let β be an upper bound for the ratio between WCET and period for all other possible processes as computed in our strengthened RMS schedulability test, i.e., $\beta = 0.69 - \alpha$ ($\beta \approx 0.69$ in all cases of Table 2). Column k shows a lower bound for the maximum number of processes which may be run together with the controller on the given microcontroller, under the hypothesis that each process requires 100 clock cycles and has a period of 10^{-3} seconds. Namely, following again the RMS schedulability test, $k = \lfloor \frac{10^{-3}\beta}{100T_C} \rfloor$. Note that k must be at least 3 for the inverted pendulum case study, since 2 processes are required to read the quantized value plant state from sensors and a third process is needed to send the computed action to the actuators. Indeed, in all cases we have $k \geq 27$.

Summing up, our on-the-fly approach allows us to directly obtain the final microcontroller implementation, by using a *model-based* methodology.

6.4 Control Software Performances

For the sake of completeness, though it is not the scope of our paper, we evaluate performances of the generated control software for different values of b and n. Namely, we simulate $\mathcal{I}_n^{b\,(\hat{K})}$, that is the pendulum closed loop system. In order to show impact of parameter n, in Figs. 4 and 5, we show simulations (on setup time and ripple) for a fixed value of b (namely, $b = 10$) and for $n \in \{1, 6\}$. Finally, in order to show impact of parameter b, in Figs. 6 and 7, we show simulations (on setup time and ripple) for a fixed value of n (namely, $n = 6$) and for $b \in \{8, 10\}$.

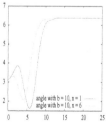 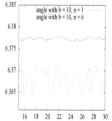 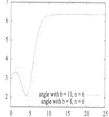 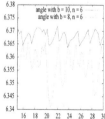

Fig. 4. Pendulum setup for $b = 10$, $n \in \{1, 6\}$ (angle x_1 is shown, time is in seconds)

Fig. 5. Pendulum ripple for $b = 10$, $n \in \{1, 6\}$ (angle x_1 is shown, time is in seconds)

Fig. 6. Pendulum setup for $n = 6$, $b \in \{8, 10\}$ (angle x_1 is shown, time is in seconds)

Fig. 7. Pendulum ripple for $n = 6$, $b \in \{8, 10\}$ (angle x_1 is shown, time is in seconds)

7   Conclusion

In this paper, we address correct-by-construction control software synthesis from Formal System Level Specifications for Discrete Time Linear Hybrid Systems. Since in our approach the control software has a WCET known in advance, a concrete schedulability analysis can be easily carried out. We present an on-the-fly algorithm for control software synthesis that detects as soon as possible if it can not find a solution to a given control problem. This property turns out to be very useful in design space exploration. Looking for an optimal choice of design parameter, it is typical to try to solve control software synthesis problems that do not have a solution. As confirmed by our experimental results, our algorithm effectively supports design space exploration. On the inverted pendulum benchmark, using our on-the-fly algorithm we get a time saving of about 80% with respect to an exhaustive approach.

References

1. Agrawal, M., Thiagarajan, P.S.: The discrete time behavior of lazy linear hybrid automata. In: Morari, M., Thiele, L. (eds.) HSCC 2005. LNCS, vol. 3414, pp. 55–69. Springer, Heidelberg (2005)
2. Alimguzhin, V., Mari, F., Melatti, I., Salvo, I., Tronci, E.: Automatic control software synthesis for quantized discrete time hybrid systems. In: CDC (2012)
3. Alimguzhin, V., Mari, F., Melatti, I., Salvo, I., Tronci, E.: On model based synthesis of embedded control software. In: EMSOFT, pp. 227–236 (2012)
4. Alur, R., Courcoubetis, C., Halbwachs, N., Henzinger, T.A., Ho, P.H., Nicollin, X., Olivero, A., Sifakis, J., Yovine, S.: The algorithmic analysis of hybrid systems. TCS 138(1), 3–34 (1995)
5. Alur, R.: Formal verification of hybrid systems. In: EMSOFT, pp. 273–278 (2011)
6. Basten, T., et al.: Model-driven design-space exploration for embedded systems: The octopus toolset. In: Margaria, T., Steffen, B. (eds.) ISoLA 2010, Part I. LNCS, vol. 6415, pp. 90–105. Springer, Heidelberg (2010)
7. Bemporad, A.: Hybrid Toolbox (2004),
   http://cse.lab.imtlucca.it/~bemporad/hybrid/toolbox/
8. Bemporad, A., Giorgetti, N.: A SAT-based hybrid solver for optimal control of hybrid systems. In: Alur, R., Pappas, G.J. (eds.) HSCC 2004. LNCS, vol. 2993, pp. 126–141. Springer, Heidelberg (2004)
9. Benerecetti, M., Faella, M., Minopoli, S.: Revisiting synthesis of switching controllers for linear hybrid systems. In: CDC-ECC, pp. 4753–4758 (2011)
10. Brogan, W.L.: Modern control theory, 3rd edn. Prentice-Hall, Inc., Upper Saddle River (1991)
11. Buttazzo, G.C.: Hard Real-Time Computing Systems, 3rd edn. Springer (2011)
12. Cassez, F., David, A., Fleury, E., Larsen, K.G., Lime, D.: Efficient on-the-fly algorithms for the analysis of timed games. In: Abadi, M., de Alfaro, L. (eds.) CONCUR 2005. LNCS, vol. 3653, pp. 66–80. Springer, Heidelberg (2005)
13. Castiglione, G., Restivo, A., Sciortino, M.: Nondeterministic moore automata and brzozowski's algorithm. In: Bouchou-Markhoff, B., Caron, P., Champarnaud, J.-M., Maurel, D. (eds.) CIAA 2011. LNCS, vol. 6807, pp. 88–99. Springer, Heidelberg (2011)

14. Cimatti, A., Roveri, M., Traverso, P.: Strong planning in non-deterministic domains via model checking. In: AIPS, pp. 36–43 (1998)
15. Easwaran, A., Lee, I., Shin, I., Sokolsky, O.: Compositional schedulability analysis of hierarchical real-time systems. In: ISORC, pp. 274–281 (2007)
16. Frehse, G.: Phaver: algorithmic verification of hybrid systems past hytech. Int. J. Softw. Tools Technol. Transf. 10(3), 263–279 (2008)
17. Larsen, K.G., Pettersson, P., Yi, W.: UPPAAL: Status & Developments. In: Grumberg, O. (ed.) CAV 1997. LNCS, vol. 1254, pp. 456–459. Springer, Heidelberg (1997)
18. Henzinger, T.A., Kopke, P.W.: Discrete-time control for rectangular hybrid automata. In: Degano, P., Gorrieri, R., Marchetti-Spaccamela, A. (eds.) ICALP 1997. LNCS, vol. 1256, pp. 582–593. Springer, Heidelberg (1997)
19. Holzmann, G.J.: The spin model checker. IEEE Trans. on Software Engineering 23(5), 279–295 (1997)
20. Simulink by mathworks, http://www.mathworks.com
21. Jha, S., Seshia, S.A., Tiwari, A.: Synthesis of optimal switching logic for hybrid systems. In: EMSOFT, pp. 107–116. ACM (2011)
22. Kreisselmeier, G., Birkhölzer, T.: Numerical nonlinear regulator design. IEEE Trans. on on Automatic Control 39(1), 33–46 (1994)
23. Lublinerman, R., Szegedy, C., Tripakis, S.: Modular code generation from synchronous block diagrams: modularity vs. code size. In: POPL, pp. 78–89 (2009)
24. Majumdar, R., Saha, I., Zamani, M.: Performance-aware scheduler synthesis for control systems. In: EMSOFT 2011, pp. 299–308 (2011)
25. Mari, F., Melatti, I., Salvo, I., Tronci, E.: Model based synthesis of control software from system level formal specifications. ACM Trans. Softw. Eng. Methodol. (to appear, 2013), A preliminary version is available at http://arxiv.org/pdf/1107.5638v2
26. Mari, F., Melatti, I., Salvo, I., Tronci, E.: Synthesis of quantized feedback control software for discrete time linear hybrid systems. In: Touili, T., Cook, B., Jackson, P. (eds.) CAV 2010. LNCS, vol. 6174, pp. 180–195. Springer, Heidelberg (2010)
27. Mari, F., Melatti, I., Salvo, I., Tronci, E.: Linear constraints as a modeling language for discrete time hybrid systems. In: ICSEA 2012, pp. 664–671 (2012)
28. Mari, F., Melatti, I., Salvo, I., Tronci, E.: Synthesizing control software from boolean relations. Int. J. on Advances in SW 5(3&4), 212–223 (2012)
29. Mari, F., Melatti, I., Salvo, I., Tronci, E.: Undecidability of quantized state feedback control for discrete time linear hybrid systems. In: Roychoudhury, A., D'Souza, M. (eds.) ICTAC 2012. LNCS, vol. 7521, pp. 243–258. Springer, Heidelberg (2012)
30. Mazo Jr., M., Davitian, A., Tabuada, P.: PESSOA: A tool for embedded controller synthesis. In: Touili, T., Cook, B., Jackson, P. (eds.) CAV 2010. LNCS, vol. 6174, pp. 566–569. Springer, Heidelberg (2010)
31. Mazo, M., Tabuada, P.: Symbolic approximate time-optimal control. Systems & Control Letters 60(4), 256–263 (2011)
32. Atmel megaAVR Microcontroller (2013), http://www.atmel.com/products/microcontrollers/avr/megaavr.aspx
33. Pola, G., Girard, A., Tabuada, P.: Approximately bisimilar symbolic models for nonlinear control systems. Automatica 44(10), 2508–2516 (2008)
34. Reactis White Paper (2013), http://www.reactive-systems.com/simulink-testing-validation.html

35. Roy, P., Tabuada, P., Majumdar, R.: Pessoa 2.0: a controller synthesis tool for cyber-physical systems. In: HSCC 2011, pp. 315–316 (2011)
36. Sontag, E.D.: Mathematical Control Theory: Deterministic Finite Dimensional Systems, 2nd edn. Springer, New York (1998)
37. Tronci, E.: Automatic synthesis of controllers from formal specifications. In: ICFEM, pp. 134–143. IEEE (1998)
38. Wong-Toi, H.: The synthesis of controllers for linear hybrid automata. In: CDC, vol. 5, pp. 4607–4612. IEEE (1997)

Compositional Approach to Suspension and Other Improvements to LTL Translation

Tomáš Babiak[2], Thomas Badie[1], Alexandre Duret-Lutz[1],
Mojmír Křetínský[2], and Jan Strejček[2]

[1] LRDE, EPITA, Le Kremlin-Bicêtre, France
{badie,adl}@lrde.epita.fr
[2] Faculty of Informatics, Masaryk University, Brno, Czech Republic
{xbabiak, kretinsky, strejcek}@fi.muni.cz

Abstract. Recently, there was defined a fragment of LTL (containing fairness properties among other interesting formulae) whose validity over a given infinite word depends only on an arbitrary suffix of the word. Building upon an existing translation from LTL to Büchi automata, we introduce a compositional approach where subformulae of this fragment are translated separately from the rest of an input formula and the produced automata are composed in a way that the subformulae are checked only in relevant accepting strongly connected components of the final automaton. Further, we suggest improvements over some procedures commonly applied to generalized Büchi automata, namely over generalized acceptance simplification and over degeneralization. Finally we show how existing simulation-based reductions can be implemented in a signature-based framework in a way that improves the determinism of the automaton.

1 Introduction

Linear Temporal Logic (LTL) is a standard formalism for description of temporal properties of systems. LTL is mainly used as a specification formalism, typically in the context of model checking or control synthesis. Algorithms taking an LTL formula as input usually translate the formula (or its negation) to an equivalent *Büchi automaton* (BA) and subsequently work with that automaton.

Since the publication of the first algorithm translating LTL to Büchi automata [18], 30 years ago, dozens of papers presenting different translation algorithms and their optimizations have been published [e.g., 3, 11, 2, 12, 15, 10]. The quality of automata produced by current translators is much higher than before: automata are substantially smaller and are more often deterministic. In spite of this, we present several ideas to further improve the produced automata.

First, we introduce a *compositional approach to suspension* (or simply *compositional suspension*). It elaborates on the notion of suspension introduced recently [1]. The idea is based on the observation that validity of many interesting formulae (including fairness formulae) over an infinite word depends only on an arbitrary suffix of the word. We say that these formulae are *suspendable*. The original suspension technique, implemented in LTL3BA [1], was closely bound to the translation of LTL to BA of Gastin and Oddoux [11]. The compositional

E. Bartocci and C.R. Ramakrishnan (Eds.): SPIN 2013, LNCS 7976, pp. 81–98, 2013.
© Springer-Verlag Berlin Heidelberg 2013

suspension technique presented in this paper is more effective and more general as it can work on top of an arbitrary translation using *generalized Büchi automata* (GBAs) or *transition-based generalized Büchi automata* (TGBAs) as an intermediate (or a target) formalism. Note that nearly all LTL to BA translation algorithms use either a GBA or a TGBA in some form. (A notable exception is the translation of Fritz [10].) We present our techniques using the TGBA formalism as it encompasses GBAs, and it has been used by translators such as LTL2BA [11], Spot [6, 5], and LTL3BA [1] with a great success.

We also improve some post-processings used in LTL translators:

SCC-based simplifications of acceptance conditions reduce the number of acceptance sets in a TGBA by studying the relation between acceptance sets in each accepting *strongly connected component* (SCC) separately. The implementation of this technique requires careful fine-tuning, as it may greatly affect final Büchi automata produced by the next two procedures.

Transition-based simulation reductions We show how to implement *direct* and *reverse* simulation reductions of TGBAs in a signature-based framework, and show how to adjust these to improve determinism as a side-effect.

SCC-based degeneralization We suggest some improvements to the standard transformation of a TGBA into an equivalent BA.

The rest of the paper is organized as follows. The next section recalls the definition of LTL and several kinds of automata. Section 3 introduces the compositional suspension technique. Section 4 successively describes the other improvements. Experimental results are presented in Section 5.

2   Preliminaries

Let AP be a finite set of (atomic) propositions, and let $\mathbb{B} = \{\texttt{ff}, \texttt{tt}\}$ represent Boolean values. An assignment is a function $\ell : AP \to \mathbb{B}$ that valuates each proposition. $\mathbb{B}^{AP}$ is the set of all assignments of AP. X^* (resp. X^ω) denotes the set of finite (resp. infinite) sequences over a set X. In a sequence $\pi = \pi_1 \pi_2 \pi_3 \ldots \in X^\omega$, π_i denotes the ith element and $\pi_{i..} = \pi_i \pi_{i+1} \pi_{i+2} \ldots$. A *word* $w \in (\mathbb{B}^{AP})^\omega$ is an infinite sequence of assignments. For $\ell \in \mathbb{B}^{AP}$, let $\ell|_{AP'}$ denote the restriction of ℓ to $AP' \subseteq AP$; we extend this notation to words $(w|_{AP'})$ as well.

2.1   Linear Temporal Logic (LTL)

We define LTL with $\varphi ::= \texttt{tt} \mid \texttt{ff} \mid a \mid \bar{a} \mid \varphi \wedge \varphi \mid \varphi \vee \varphi \mid \mathsf{X}\varphi \mid \mathsf{F}\varphi \mid \mathsf{G}\varphi \mid \varphi \mathbin{\mathsf{U}} \varphi \mid \varphi \mathbin{\mathsf{R}} \varphi$ where $a \in AP$ and $\bar{a}$ denotes negation of a. We omit $\wedge$ in conjunctions of atomic propositions (e.g., $a\bar{b} \equiv a \wedge \bar{b}$). We allow negation only in front of atomic propositions as it is well known that any LTL formula can be rewritten into this form. The *validity* of a formula φ over a word $w \in (\mathbb{B}^{AP})^\omega$, written $w \models \varphi$, is defined by a structural induction on φ in the standard way. For example:

$$w \models a \qquad \text{iff} \quad w_1(a) = \texttt{tt};$$
$$w \models \varphi \mathbin{\mathsf{U}} \psi \quad \text{iff} \quad \exists i \geq 1, (w_{i..} \models \psi \text{ and } \forall j \in \{1, \ldots, i-1\}, w_{j..} \models \varphi).$$

We say that φ *holds at position* i of w iff $w_{i..} \models \varphi$.

2.2   Automata

A *labeled transition system* (LTS) is a tuple $\mathcal{S} = \langle AP, Q, q_0, \delta \rangle$ where AP is a finite set of atomic propositions, Q is a finite set of states, $q_0 \in Q$ is the initial state, $\delta \subseteq Q \times \mathbb{B}^{AP} \times Q$ is the transition relation, labeling each transition by an assignment. As an implementation optimization, and to simplify illustrations, it is practical to use *edges* labeled by Boolean formulae to group *transitions* with same sources and destinations: for instance two *transitions* $(s_1, a\bar{b}, s_2)$ and (s_1, ab, s_2) will be represented by an *edge* from s_1 to s_2 and labeled by the Boolean formula a. We use the terms *transition* and *edge* to distinguish between these two representations.

An infinite sequence $\pi = (s_1, \ell_1, d_1)(s_2, \ell_2, d_2) \ldots \in \delta^\omega$ is a run of $\mathcal{S}$ if $s_1 = q_0$ and $\forall i \geq 1$, $d_i = s_{i+1}$. Run($\mathcal{S}$) denotes the set of all runs of $\mathcal{S}$. Let $\mathrm{Inf}_Q(\pi)$ (resp. $\mathrm{Inf}_\delta(\pi)$) denote the set of states (resp. transitions) that appear infinitely often in π, and let $\mathrm{Labels}(\pi) = \ell_1 \ell_2 \ldots \in (\mathbb{B}^{AP})^\omega$ be the word evaluated by π.

A *Büchi automaton* is a pair $\mathcal{B} = \langle \mathcal{S}, F \rangle$ where $\mathcal{S} = \langle AP, Q, q_0, \delta \rangle$ is an LTS and $F \subseteq Q$ is a set of accepting states. Let $\mathrm{Acc}(\mathcal{B}) = \{\pi \in \mathrm{Run}(\mathcal{S}) \mid \mathrm{Inf}_Q(\pi) \cap F \neq \emptyset\}$ denote the accepting runs of $\mathcal{B}$. The language of $\mathcal{B}$ is the set of words evaluated by accepting runs: $\mathscr{L}(\mathcal{B}) = \{\mathrm{Labels}(\pi) \mid \pi \in \mathrm{Acc}(\mathcal{B})\}$.

A *Transition-based Generalized Büchi automaton* (TGBA) is a pair $\mathcal{T} = \langle \mathcal{S}, F \rangle$ where $\mathcal{S} = \langle AP, Q, q_0, \delta \rangle$ is an LTS and $F \subseteq 2^\delta$ is a set of *acceptance sets* of transitions. Let $\mathrm{Acc}(\mathcal{T}) = \{\pi \in \mathrm{Run}(\mathcal{S}) \mid \forall Z \in F, \mathrm{Inf}_\delta(\pi) \cap Z \neq \emptyset\}$ denote the accepting runs of $\mathcal{B}$, i.e., runs of $\mathcal{S}$ whose transitions visit each acceptance set infinitely often. The language of $\mathcal{T}$ is the set of words evaluated by accepting runs: $\mathscr{L}(\mathcal{T}) = \{\mathrm{Labels}(\pi) \mid \pi \in \mathrm{Acc}(\mathcal{T})\}$. On figures, membership of transitions to acceptance sets is indicated using one colored marker ($\bullet, \circ, \blacksquare, \ldots$) per set.

A Büchi automaton $\mathcal{B} = \langle \mathcal{S}, F_\mathcal{B} \rangle$ can easily be converted into a TGBA $\mathcal{T} = \langle \mathcal{S}, F_\mathcal{T} \rangle$ such that $\mathscr{L}(\mathcal{B}) = \mathscr{L}(\mathcal{T})$ by setting $F_\mathcal{T} = \{\{(s, \ell, d) \in \delta \mid s \in F_\mathcal{B}\}\}$. A similar view can be used to interpret state-based generalized Büchi automata (which we do not define) as TGBAs. Although we describe our improvements on TGBAs, they adapt easily to these classes of Büchi automata with such views.

The reverse operation, *degeneralizing* a TGBA with multiple acceptance sets into a Büchi automaton, is discussed in Sec. 4.3.

A *promise automaton* is again a pair $\mathcal{P} = \langle \mathcal{S}, F \rangle$ where $F \subseteq 2^\delta$ is a set of *promise sets* of transitions. The runs accepted by a promise automaton are those which have no suffix that stays continuously in any promise set: $\mathrm{Acc}(\mathcal{P}) = \{\pi \in \mathrm{Run}(\mathcal{S}) \mid \forall Z \in F, \forall i \geq 1, \pi_{i..} \notin Z^\omega\}$. As expected, the language of $\mathcal{P}$ is $\mathscr{L}(\mathcal{P}) = \{\mathrm{Labels}(\pi) \mid \pi \in \mathrm{Acc}(\mathcal{P})\}$.

Because a run that does not visit infinitely often a set of transitions Z will have a suffix that stays continuously in the set $\delta \smallsetminus Z$, $\mathcal{T} = \langle \mathcal{S}, F_\mathcal{T} \rangle$ can be converted into a promise automaton $\mathcal{P} = \langle \mathcal{S}, F_\mathcal{P} \rangle$ such that $\mathscr{L}(\mathcal{T}) = \mathscr{L}(\mathcal{P})$ by complementing the acceptance sets: $F_\mathcal{P} = \{\delta \smallsetminus Z \mid Z \in F_\mathcal{T}\}$. The converse holds as well. The name of *promise automaton* comes from an interpretation of the elements of $F_\mathcal{P} = \{Z_1, \ldots, Z_n\}$ as promises: a transition in the set Z_i can be seen as *making* the promise Z_i. A promise Z_i is *fulfilled* by a run that does not stay in Z_i continuously, and a run is accepting if it fulfills all promises.

A strongly connected component (SCC) $C \subseteq Q$ is a non-empty set of states such that any ordered pair of states of C can be connected by a sequence of transitions. Let $C_\delta = \{(s, \ell, d) \in \delta \mid s \in C, d \in C\}$ denote the set of transitions induced by C. An SCC C is said to be *accepting* if: $C \cap F \neq \emptyset$ on a Büchi automaton, $\forall Z \in F, C_\delta \cap Z \neq \emptyset$ on a TGBA, $\forall Z \in F, C_\delta \cap Z \neq C_\delta$ on a promise automaton. With these definitions, any accepting run π is necessarily ultimately contained by some accepting SCC C, i.e., $\mathrm{Inf}_\delta(\pi) \subseteq C_\delta$.

3   Compositional Approach to Suspension

3.1   Suspendable Formulae

A *suspendable* formula, originally called *alternating* formula [1][1], has at least one F and at least one G operator on each branch of its syntax tree. The formal definition is given by the following abstract syntax equations, where φ ranges over general LTL formulae. Besides suspendable formulae ξ, these equations also define *pure eventuality* formulae μ and *pure universality* formulae ν introduced by Etessami and Holzmann [8].

$$\mu ::= \mathsf{F}\varphi \mid \mu \vee \mu \mid \mu \wedge \mu \mid \mathsf{X}\mu \mid \varphi \mathsf{U} \mu \mid \mu \mathsf{R} \mu \mid \mathsf{G}\mu$$
$$\nu ::= \mathsf{G}\varphi \mid \nu \vee \nu \mid \nu \wedge \nu \mid \mathsf{X}\nu \mid \nu \mathsf{U} \nu \mid \varphi \mathsf{R} \nu \mid \mathsf{F}\nu$$
$$\xi ::= \mathsf{G}\mu \mid \mathsf{F}\nu \mid \xi \vee \xi \mid \xi \wedge \xi \mid \mathsf{X}\xi \mid \varphi \mathsf{U} \xi \mid \varphi \mathsf{R} \xi \mid \mathsf{F}\xi \mid \mathsf{G}\xi$$

The class of suspendable formulae contains many specification patterns frequently used in practical applications of LTL like model checking. For example, unconditional fairness $\mathsf{GF}\varphi$, weak fairness $\mathsf{FG}\varphi \rightarrow \mathsf{GF}\rho$ ($\equiv \mathsf{GF}(\varphi \rightarrow \rho)$), strong fairness $\mathsf{GF}\varphi \rightarrow \mathsf{GF}\rho$, and their negation can be easily transformed into suspendable formulae (our definition of LTL does not allow $\rightarrow$).

The following lemma states that a suspendable formula either holds at each position of a word or at none of them.

Lemma 1 ([1]). *Let ξ be a suspendable formula. For all $u \in (\mathbb{B}^{AP})^*$, $w \in (\mathbb{B}^{AP})^\omega$, we have $uw \models \xi \iff w \models \xi$.*

Consequently, every suspendable formula ξ satisfies $\xi \equiv \mathsf{X}\xi$. This property provides a theoretical base for the *suspension* technique [1] that was used to improve the translation of Gastin and Oddoux [11]. This translation uses a *very weak alternating automaton* (VWAA) and a TGBA as intermediate formalisms. States of the VWAA are identified with subformulae of the input formula. States of the TGBA are sets of VWAA states. Transitions leaving from a TGBA state M are computed as combinations of transitions leaving from the VWAA states in M. If M contains a suspendable subformula ξ, the corresponding VWAA state can be temporarily suspended: during the computation step, ξ is treated as $\mathsf{X}\xi$ and hence it has only one transition leading back to ξ. As a result, the number of transition combinations is reduced and a smaller automaton is produced.

---

[1] We change the terminology here as the original name seems to be ambiguous.

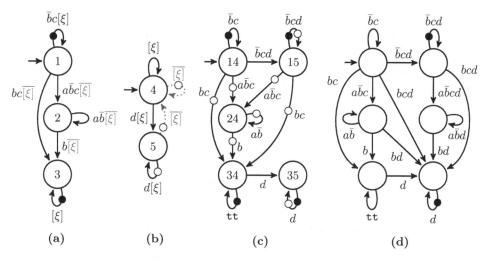

Fig. 1. (a) Skeleton TGBA for $((a \cup b) R c) \wedge \xi$. (b) Suspendable TGBA for $\xi = FGd$ (equipped with suspending arcs). (c) Composition of the previous two automata. (d) Traditional translation of $((a \cup b) R c) \wedge FGd$.

For correctness, ξ should not be suspended forever during any accepting run of the TGBA, we therefore enable suspension only in TGBA states that are not on any accepting cycle. Because the detection of such a cycle is complicated as the TGBA is only under construction, a heuristic was used to detect some of the TGBA states not lying on any accepting cycle [1].

3.2 Translation with Compositional Suspension

We now present a new version of the suspension technique that has two advantages over the original one: it can be combined with all LTL translation algorithms producing a TGBA or GBA and it is more effective as it uses a more precise detection of TGBA states not lying on any accepting cycle.

To explain the general idea, consider an LTL formulae of the form $\varphi \wedge \xi$ where ξ is a suspendable formula. If $\mathcal{T}_\varphi$ and $\mathcal{T}_\xi$ are TGBAs for φ and ξ, we can construct an automaton for $\varphi \wedge \xi$ by composing $\mathcal{T}_\varphi$ and $\mathcal{T}_\xi$ using a synchronous product. However, ξ is suspendable, so by Lemma 1 we can suspend its verification by any finite prefix. In our composition we could delay the verification of ξ until $\mathcal{T}_\varphi$ has entered an accepting SCC. This remark calls for the implementation of a new synchronous product, that synchronizes $\mathcal{T}_\xi$ only in the accepting SCCs of $\mathcal{T}_\varphi$.

One way to describe this product is to introduce a new atomic proposition $[\xi]$ and its negation $\overline{[\xi]}$ to mark where the two automata should be synchronized. Figure 1(a) shows a TGBA for $\varphi = (a \cup b) R c$ equipped with these new properties and ready to be composed: transitions induced by accepting SCCs $\{1\}$ and $\{3\}$ carry the additional label $[\xi]$, while all other transitions have $\overline{[\xi]}$. We call such an automaton a *skeleton automaton* for $\varphi \wedge \xi$ because it indicates the places where the suspended ξ should be composed. Figure 1(b) shows a TGBA $\mathcal{T}_\xi$ for $\xi =$ FGd also equipped with the same labels: transitions from the original translation of ξ carry the $[\xi]$ label, and additional "suspending transitions" (the dotted arcs) have been added to reset the automaton to its initial state when $\mathcal{T}_\xi$ leaves an accepting SCC (and thus suspend checking ξ by another step). We call this a *suspendable automaton* for ξ. The synchronous product of both automata can then be stripped of all occurrences of the auxiliary proposition $[\xi]$ and its negation, and $[\xi]$ is removed from its set of atomic propositions. The resulting Fig. 1(c), should be compared to the automaton of Fig 1(d) that we would get by a traditional translation. The superfluous acceptance set we obtain can be easily removed, as explained in Sec. 4.1.

We now focus on constructing a skeleton automaton for an arbitrary formula φ that contains suspendable subformulae (not necessarily at the top level). We first replace every maximal suspendable subformula ξ of φ by the subformula G$[\xi]$ with fresh auxiliary propositions $[\xi]$. The resulting formula, denoted φ' is translated into a TGBA $\mathcal{T}_{\varphi'}$. This automaton can directly be used as a skeleton for φ: whenever G$[\xi]$ holds at some positions of a word accepted by this automaton, the product with a suspendable TGBA for ξ will check the validity of ξ on this word. Note that we do not say that validity of ξ will be checked exactly at the positions where G$[\xi]$ holds. Indeed, this is not needed as ξ is a suspendable formula and thus it either holds at each position of a word or at none of them.

Even if $\mathcal{T}_{\varphi'}$ is a correct skeleton for φ, it is not what we typically use in the synchronous product with a suspendable TGBA for ξ. To avoid checking ξ whenever possible, we want to reduce the set of words w' accepted by the skeleton and such that G$[\xi]$ holds at some positions of w'. We use two reductions:

- We replace $[\xi]$ with $\overline{[\xi]}$ on transitions that are not induced by any accepting SCC. (This is what we did in Fig 1(a).) The reduction is correct as for every word w' accepted by the original skeleton, there is a word w'' accepted by the reduced skeleton such that $w'|_{AP} = w''|_{AP}$ and G$[\xi]$ holds at some positions of w' if and only if it holds at some position of w''. The last equivalence holds because we do not change transition labels in accepting SCCs.

- We remove transitions labeled with $[\xi]$ from the skeleton if they are not needed, i.e. there are analogous transitions that differ only in validity of $[\xi]$. Formally, we remove each transition (s, ℓ, d) such that $\ell([\xi]) = $ tt if there exists a transition (s, ℓ', d) where $\ell'|_{AP} = \ell|_{AP}$, $\ell'([\xi]) = $ ff, and the two transitions belong to the same acceptance sets. This reduction is correct as for each w' accepted before this reduction and such that G$[\xi]$ holds at some position of w', there is another word w'' accepted by the reduced skeleton and satisfying $w'|_{AP} = w''|_{AP}$. (Note that either G$[\xi]$ holds at some positions of w'' too and then the product with suspendable automaton for ξ checks validity of ξ on $w'|_{AP}$ anyway, or G$[\xi]$ does not hold at any positions of w'' and $w'|_{AP}$ satisfies φ regardless validity of ξ.)

We call $\mathsf{susp}(\varphi)$ the function that transforms φ into φ', $\mathsf{make\_suspendable}(\mathcal{T}, [\xi])$ the function that transforms a TGBA $\mathcal{T}$ for

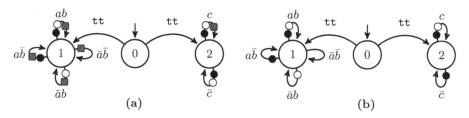

Fig. 2. (a) TGBA for $(\mathsf{GF}(a) \wedge \mathsf{GF}(b)) \vee \mathsf{GF}(c)$, with three acceptance sets denoted by ●, ○, and ■. (b) Same automaton after SCC-based acceptance simplification.

a suspendable subformula ξ into a suspendable automaton for ξ, and `reduce_skel(` $\mathcal{T}, \{\xi_1, ..., \xi_n\}$ `)` the function that reduces a skeleton automaton for a set of suspendable subformulae. They will be used in Fig. 6.

4 Other Improvements

4.1 SCC-Based Simplifications of Acceptance Conditions

While simplifying the acceptance sets of an automaton does not immediately change the size of the underlying LTS, it can lead to smaller automata as it eases the job of simulation-based reductions (Sec. 4.2) and degeneralization (Sec. 4.3).

Let $\mathcal{T} = \langle \mathcal{S}, F \rangle$ be a TGBA with n acceptance sets: $F = \{Z_1, Z_2, \ldots, Z_n\}$. Let $\{A_1, \ldots, A_m\}$ denote the set of all accepting SCCs of $\mathcal{T}$ and let $A_\delta = A_{1\delta} \cup \ldots \cup A_{m\delta}$ be the set of all transitions induced by these accepting SCCs.

Because any accepting run will ultimately be contained in some accepting SCC, any transition outside of A_δ can be removed from the acceptance sets without changing the language. A typical simplification is therefore to restrict all Z_i to A_δ: we have $\mathcal{L}(\langle \mathcal{S}, F \rangle) = \mathcal{L}(\langle \mathcal{S}, \{Z_1 \cap A_\delta, \ldots, Z_n \cap A_\delta\} \rangle)$.

If there exists $i \neq j$ such that $Z_i \subseteq Z_j$, then any run that visits Z_i infinitely often will necessarily visit Z_j infinitely often. In other words, Z_j can be removed from F without changing the language: $\mathcal{L}(\langle \mathcal{S}, F \rangle) = \mathcal{L}(\langle \mathcal{S}, F \smallsetminus \{Z_j\} \rangle)$.

If we define $U = \{Z_j \in F \mid \exists Z_i \in F, (Z_i \subsetneq Z_j) \vee (Z_i = Z_j \wedge j > i)\}$ to be the set of useless acceptance sets, we have $\mathcal{L}(\langle \mathcal{S}, F \rangle) = \mathcal{L}(\langle \mathcal{S}, F \smallsetminus U \rangle)$. Note that the definition of U carefully keeps one copy when two sets are equal. We view this simplification as the standard way to diminish the number of acceptance sets in an automaton [16]. For instance after restricting the acceptance sets of Fig. 1c to the accepting SCCs $\{15\}_\delta \cup \{35\}_\delta$, one of ○ or ● can be removed (not both).

Detecting inclusion between acceptance sets at the automaton level fails to simplify the TGBA from Fig. 2(a): in this automaton there is no inclusion between acceptance sets. However, by considering such inclusions in each accepting SCC, we can notice that ■ is useless in SCC $A_1 = \{1\}$ (because ■ includes either ● or ○), while ● and ○ are both useless in SCC $A_2 = \{2\}$. We can therefore reorganize the acceptance sets of the automaton to use only two acceptance sets: Fig. 2(b) shows one possibility.

More formally, for an accepting SCC A_k, let $U_k = \{j \in \{1, \ldots, n\} \mid \exists i \in \{1, \ldots, n\}, (Z_i \cap A_{k\delta} \subsetneq Z_j \cap A_{k\delta}) \vee (Z_i \cap A_{k\delta} = Z_j \cap A_{k\delta} \wedge j > i)\}$ be the set of *indices* of useless acceptance sets in the sub-automaton induced by A_k, and let $N_k = \{1, \ldots, n\} \smallsetminus U_k$ be the set of *needed* acceptance sets. Because acceptance sets are defined for the whole automaton, we may not use a different number of acceptance sets for each SCC: $n' = \max_{k \in \{1, \ldots, n\}} |N_k|$ acceptance sets are required to hold all *needed* acceptance sets. Let N'_k be a copy of N_k in which we have added $n' - |N_k|$ items from U_k. Then for each accepting SCC A_k, $|N'_k| = n'$ and let $\alpha_k : \{1, \ldots, n'\} \to N'_k$ be any bijection. We can define the new acceptance sets $F' = \{Z'_1, \ldots, Z'_{n'}\}$ as:

$$Z'_i = \bigcup_{k \in \{1, \ldots, m\}} (Z_{\alpha_k(i)} \cap A_{k\delta}) \tag{1}$$

Then we have $\mathscr{L}(\langle \mathcal{S}, F \rangle) = \mathscr{L}(\langle \mathcal{S}, F' \rangle)$. In the example of Fig. 2(a), with $A_1 = \{1\}$ and $A_2 = \{2\}$, let us assume that ●, ○, and ▣ respectively denote the acceptance sets Z_1, Z_2, and Z_3. We have $U_1 = \{3\}$, $N_1 = \{1,2\}$, $U_2 = \{1,2\}$, $N_2 = \{3\}$, $n' = 2$, and we define $N'_1 = N_1$, $N'_2 = N_2 \cup \{1\}$, $\alpha_1(1) = 1$, $\alpha_1(2) = 2$, $\alpha_2(1) = 1$, $\alpha_2(2) = 3$ to get the TGBA of Fig. 2(b).

Note that there is a lot of freedom in the definition of the bijective function α_k for each accepting SCC. In our implementation we make sure α_k is monotonic so that the order of the acceptance sets are preserved: we have found that this usually helps the degeneralization algorithm that is run afterwards. Furthermore, in accepting SCCs that require less than n' acceptance sets, the $n' - |N_k|$ extra sets that are added could be defined in many different ways: instead of reusing some of the *useless* acceptance sets, we could duplicate some of the *needed* ones (making $\alpha_k : \{1, \ldots, n'\} \to N_k$ a surjection), or adding all transitions of $A_{k\delta}$ into the extra sets (at the price of more complex definitions). Our attempts at implementing these alternative definitions had a negative effect on the simulation-based reductions described in the next section.

Note that Somenzi and Bloem [16, Theorem 4] proposed another SCC-based acceptance simplification, that simplifies Fig. 2(a) differently. If we have $Z_i \cap A_{k\delta} \subseteq Z_j \cap A_{k\delta}$ for some i, j, k, they remove the transitions $A_{k\delta} \smallsetminus Z_i$ from Z_j. While this reduces the size of Z_i, it does not yet change the number of acceptance sets. On Fig. 2(a), this would remove the bottom right loop from the sets ● and ○, after which it would be possible to detect that ▣ includes all sets, and remove it.

4.2   Transition-Based Simulation Reductions

Spot has an implementation of simulation-based reductions described by Somenzi and Bloem [16], but adapted to work on promise automata (easily converted to and from TGBAs, see Sec. 2.2) instead of BAs. Intuitively, *direct* simulation can merge states or remove transitions based on the inclusion of the sets of infinite runs *starting from* these states, while *reverse* simulation is based on the inclusion between sets of (finite or infinite) runs *leading to* these states.

Our implementation is a signature-based implementation of Moore's classic partition refinement algorithm: initially all states belong to the same class, and the partition is iteratively refined until fixpoint. Depending on the definition of the signature, we compute a bisimulation or simulation relation, direct or reverse.

Direct Bisimulation: We first explain how to perform a signature-based, direct bisimulation of a promise automaton $\langle S, F \rangle$, using a setup inspired from Wimmer et al. [17]. The signature $\text{sig}^i(q)$ of a state q is a Boolean function that describes the outgoing transitions of q, their membership to acceptance sets, and the class of their destination at iteration i.

If the acceptance sets are $F = \{Z_1, \ldots, Z_n\}$, and the partition of Q at iteration i is $P^i = \{C_1^i, \ldots, C_m^i\}$, we use Boolean variables $\hat{Z}_k$ and $\hat{C}_k$ to denote membership to the sets Z_k and C_k^i, and we define $\text{sig}^i(s)$ as:

$$\text{sig}^i(q) = \bigvee_{\substack{(s,\ell,d)\in\delta \\ q=s}} \ell \wedge \text{Acc}(s, \ell, d) \wedge \text{Class}^i(d);$$

$$\text{where} \quad \text{Acc}(s, \ell, d) = \bigwedge_{\substack{Z_k \in F \\ (s,\ell,d)\in Z_k}} \hat{Z}_k \quad \text{and} \quad \text{Class}^i(d) = \hat{C}_k \iff d \in C_k^i.$$

With this encoding, two states that have the same outgoing transitions (same labels, membership to acceptance sets, and destination class) will have the same signature. Also if a state q has two outgoing transitions $t_1 = (q, a, d_1)$ and $t_2 = (q, a, d_2)$ such that $t_1 \in Z_1$ is in a promise set but $t_2 \notin Z_1$ we have $\text{sig}^i(q) = a \wedge ((\hat{Z}_1 \wedge \text{Class}^i(d_1)) \vee \text{Class}^i(d_2))$. If the two classes are the same, the signature simplifies to $\text{sig}^i(q) = a \wedge \text{Class}^i(d_2)$, as if t_1 had been merged into t_2. This simplification, correct on promise automata, would be incorrect on TGBAs.

To compute a direct bisimulation relation we start with the partition $P^0 = \{Q\}$ that considers all states as equivalent, and then split the partition according to the signatures of the states: $P^{i+1} = \{\{s \in Q \mid \text{sig}^i(s) \equiv \text{sig}^i(q)\} \mid q \in Q\}$. Once a fixpoint has been reached (i.e., $P^j = P^{j+1}$ for some j), the partition provides the set of states that are (direct) bisimilar and can therefore be merged. It should be noted that the signature associated to each class can also be used to reconstruct the quotient automaton. By extension, let $\text{sig}^{i-1}(C)$ denote the signature common to all states of the class $C \in P^i$.

Direct Simulation: To perform the (direct) simulation of a promise automaton, we alter sig to include all the classes implied by the destination class:

$$\text{sig}^i(q) = \bigvee_{\substack{(s,\ell,d)\in\delta \\ q=s}} \ell \wedge \text{Acc}(s, \ell, d) \wedge \text{Implied}^i(d) \quad \text{where} \quad \text{Implied}^i(d) = \bigwedge_{\substack{C_k^i \in P^i \\ \text{sig}^{i-1}(d)\rightarrow\text{sig}^{i-1}(C_k^i)}} \hat{C}_k$$

We fix $\text{Implied}^0(q) = \hat{C}_1$ for all $q \in Q$ initially, as there is only one class. Then partition refinement can be iterated until both $P^k = P^{k+1}$ and $\text{Implied}^k = \text{Implied}^{k+1}$. The implication $\text{sig}^{i-1}(d) \rightarrow \text{sig}^{i-1}(C_k^i)$ can be tested easily since signatures are encoded as BDDs.

Figure 3 illustrates this reduction on an example. Although all states start in the same class, computing sig^0 is enough to separate all states into four

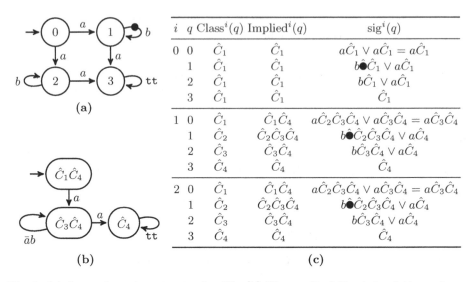

Fig. 3. (a) A promise automaton to simplify. (b) The result of direct simulation reduction. (c) Detailed steps for the signature-based direct simulation.

classes. The refinement stops at iteration $i = 2$ because $\text{Class}^2 = \text{Class}^1$ and $\text{Implied}^2 = \text{Implied}^1$. The signatures computed at the last iteration can be used to reconstruct the automaton. Especially, the edge $(0, a, 1)$ in the original automaton is dominated by edge $(0, a, 2)$ in the computation of $\text{sig}^2(0)$ (intuitively, the suffixes accepted via $(0, a, 1)$ are included in those accepted via $(0, a, 2)$), so only the latter edge appears in the resulting signature and in the final automaton.

An additional trick can be used to improve the determinism of the constructed automaton. Because $\text{sig}^2(2) = b\hat{C}_3\hat{C}_4 \vee a\hat{C}_4$ is equivalent to $\bar{a}b\hat{C}_3\hat{C}_4 \vee a\hat{C}_4$, the self-loop to state 2 (represented by $\hat{C}_3\hat{C}_4$ in the signature) can be labeled by $\bar{a}b$ instead of just b. In practice, for each state q we iterate over all assignments $f \in \mathbb{B}^{AP}$, and compute the possible destinations by rewriting $\text{sig}^i(q) \wedge f$ as an irredundant sum of products.

Reverse Simulation: A reverse simulation can be built and used similarly by computing a signature using the incoming transitions:

$$\text{sig}^i(q) = \text{Init}(q) \vee \bigvee_{\substack{(s,\ell,d)\in\delta \\ q=d}} \ell \wedge \text{Acc}(s, \ell, d) \wedge \text{Implied}^i(d) \quad \text{with} \quad \text{Init}(q) = \begin{cases} \hat{I} \text{ if } q = q_0; \\ \texttt{ff} \text{ else.} \end{cases}$$

Because the reverse simulation has to distinguish finite prefixes from infinite prefixes we use an extra Boolean variable $\hat{I}$ to distinguish the initial state.

In practice we alternate direct and reverse simulations until the automaton is no longer reduced. Most of the time only one iteration is needed (meaning that we do the second iteration just to discover that the produced automaton has the same size). As an optimization, we abort this loop when the automaton produced

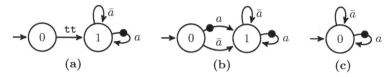

Fig. 4. Three equivalent TGBAs. (a) is obtained from (b) with the acceptance simplifications of Sec. 4.1. (c) is obtained from (b) using the simulation reductions of Sec. 4.2, however the latter reductions are unable to reduce (a) into (c).

by the direct simulation is deterministic: the reverse simulation cannot improve a deterministic automaton since all prefixes leading to a state are unique.

Other simulations have been suggested, such as *fair* or *delayed* simulation [9], both relaxing the handling of acceptance conditions, and these have also been extended to (state-based) generalized Büchi automata [13]. All of these are presented in a game-theoretic framework that is not straightforward to implement, especially in the generalized Streett game version required for generalized Büchi automata. Conversely, our implementation of direct and reverse simulation easily deals with TGBAs (when first converted as promise automata), augments the determinism as a side-effect, and was simple to implement because it uses the same BDD framework that Spot is already using for the LTL translation.

Although the operations described in Section 4.1 simplify the SCC-based acceptance conditions of a TGBA, there are situations where it worsens the results of the simulation-based reductions. A typical example is given by Fig. 4.

Since Couvreur's translation can produce automata with a configuration similar to Fig. 4(b), we use an alternative acceptance simplification that preserves the acceptance of all transitions entering an accepting SCC. This corresponds to replacing $A_{k\delta}$ by $\{(s, \ell, d) \in \delta \mid d \in A_k\}$ in equation (1). In our tests, this is always favorable to the simulation.

Unfortunately, the situation depicted by Fig. 4(a) also occurs in the output of some translations, even before acceptance simplification. This is even more frequent with the compositional approach to suspension presented in Sec. 3.

4.3 SCC-Based Degeneralization

While any Büchi automaton can be converted into a TGBA without altering the underlying LTS (see Sec. 2.2), the reverse is not generally true.

A TGBA $\mathcal{T} = \langle \mathcal{S}, F \rangle$ with $\mathcal{S} = \langle AP, Q, q_0, \delta \rangle$ and $F = \{Z_1, \ldots, Z_n\}$ can be degeneralized into a BA $\mathcal{B} = \langle \mathcal{S}', F' \rangle$ with $\mathcal{S}' = \langle AP, Q', q'_0, \delta' \rangle$ as follows [11, 12]:

- $Q' = Q \times \{0, \ldots, n\}$, i.e., the original automaton is cloned in $n + 1$ levels,
- $F' = Q \times \{n\}$, i.e., states from the last level are accepting,
- $\delta' = \{((s, j), \ell, (d, L_j((s, \ell, d)))) \mid (s, \ell, d) \in \delta, j \in \{0, \ldots, n\}\}$ where

$$L_j(t) = \begin{cases} 0 & \text{if } j = n; \\ j + 1 & \text{if } t \in Z_{j+1}; \\ j & \text{otherwise.} \end{cases}$$

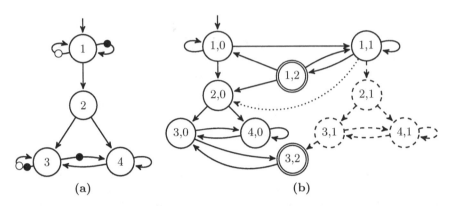

Fig. 5. Example of degeneralization of the TGBA (a) with $F = \{\bullet, \circ\}$ taken in this order. Transition labels are omitted for clarity. The automaton (b) with the dashed part is obtained by the classical degeneralization (with jumping of levels). Our redefinition replaces the dashed part by the dotted transition.

i.e., for each level $j < n$ the outgoing transitions that belong to Z_{j+1} are redirected to the next level and all outgoing transitions from the last level are redirected to the first one.

- $q'_0 = q_0 \times \{0\}$, i.e., the initial state is on the first level (any level works).

This leveled setup guarantees that any accepting path in $\mathcal{B}$ correspond to an infinite path that sees all acceptance conditions infinitely often in $\mathcal{T}$. If $\mathcal{T}[q]$ denotes the automaton $\mathcal{T}$ in which the initial state has been changed to q, we have $\mathcal{L}(\mathcal{T}[q]) = \mathcal{L}(\mathcal{B}[(q,j)])$ for all states $q \in Q$ and all levels $j \in \{0, \ldots, n\}$.

The classical optimization is to "jump levels", i.e., when a transition from level $j < n$ belongs to acceptance sets Z_{j+1}, Z_{j+2}, and Z_{j+3}, it can be redirected to the level $j + 3$. This corresponds to the following redefinition of L_j:

$$L_j(t) = \begin{cases} \max\{k \in \{j, \ldots, n\} \mid t \in Z_{j+1} \cap \ldots \cap Z_k\} & \text{if } j < n; \\ \max\{k \in \{0, \ldots, n\} \mid t \in Z_1 \cap \ldots \cap Z_k\} & \text{if } j = n. \end{cases}$$

Of course only the reachable part of $\mathcal{B}$ is constructed, so it is not frequent to construct the maximum number of $(n+1) \times |Q|$ states. Fig. 5 applies the above definition to an example. The transition from $(3,0)$ to $(3,2)$ jumps level 1.

This construction offers several degrees of freedom: for instance there are $n!$ possible orderings of the acceptance sets, and $n+1$ possible levels for the initial state. Giannakopoulou and Lerda [12] perform two degeneralizations starting respectively at level 0 and n, then they keep the best. We are not aware on any work on the selection of a suitable ordering. Empirical evidence shows that the order in which these sets are created during translation is often favorable to the degeneralization (the reverse order, at least, is catastrophic), this is why Sec. 4.1 defines α in a way that preserves the ordering.

Staying away from these combinatorial possibilities, we suggest two ideas to improve degeneralization procedures: *level reset* and *level caching*. Both require knowledge of the set $\{A_1, \ldots, A_m\}$ of accepting SCCs of $\mathcal{T}$.

Level Reset: Since non-accepting SCCs of $\mathcal{T}$ do not contain accepting cycles (by definition), they do not need to be cloned on different levels. Therefore all transitions that are not induced by any accepting SCC, are directed to level 0.

Level Caching: Consider a transition (s, ℓ, d) that enters an accepting SCC ($\exists i, s \notin A_i \wedge d \in A_i$): as with the initial state, the level associated to d can be set to any arbitrary value. If a copy of d already exists on some level, we should start on that level to avoid creating a new one. This optimization is of course affected by the order chosen to construct the degeneralized automaton (we do a simple DFS but there could be room for improvement).

These two optimizations can be implemented with $L_j((s, \ell, d)) =$

$$
\begin{cases}
\max\{k \in \{j, \ldots, n\} \mid (s, \ell, d) \in Z_{j+1} \cap \ldots \cap Z_k\} & \text{if } j < n \wedge \exists i, (s, d) \in A_i^2; \\
\max\{k \in \{0, \ldots, n\} \mid (s, \ell, d) \in Z_1 \cap \ldots \cap Z_k\} & \text{if } j = n \wedge \exists i, (s, d) \in A_i^2; \\
0 & \text{if } \nexists i, d \in A_i; \\
x & \text{if } \exists i, s \notin A_i \wedge d \in A_i.
\end{cases}
$$

Where x is any level such that the state (d, x) already exists, or 0 otherwise.

On the example of Fig. 5, the *level reset* alone is enough to replace transition $((1,1), \ell, (2,1))$ by transition $((1,1), \ell, (2,0))$, therefore avoiding state $(2,1)$ and all its descendants. Using *level caching* without *level reset*, and assuming the descendants of $(2,0)$ have been built before those of $(2,1)$, then state $(2,1)$ would be connected to states $(3,0)$ and $(4,0)$ instead of states $(3,1)$ and $(4,1)$. It is hard to find a small example to illustrate that both optimizations are useful together: the smallest such occurrence in our benchmarks has 20 states.

5   Experimental Results

5.1   Translation Scenarios

All of the above improvements are implemented in Spot 1.1[2] on top of Couvreur's LTL to BA translation algorithm [2] (denoted by $\texttt{Cou99}(\varphi)$ in the sequel although it has been regularly improved over the past years [5]). Besides the techniques discussed in this paper, Spot implements the WDBA-minimization algorithm of Dax et al. [4] that converts any TGBA representing an *obligation property* [14] into a minimal Weak Deterministic Büchi Automaton. The corresponding function $\texttt{WDBA\_minimize}(\mathcal{T}, \varphi)$ requires the formula φ represented by automaton $\mathcal{T}$ to check the validity of the minimized automaton.

There are cases where the deterministic BA produced by WDBA-minimization is bigger than the nondeterministic automaton obtained via simulation and

---

[2] http://spot.lip6.fr/. After download and installation, see the man pages of ltl2tgba(1) and spot-x(7) for the options to enable the algorithms discussed here, and see also bench/spin13/README.

	"small size" scenario	"determinism" scenario
composition	$\varphi', \{\xi_1, ..., \xi_n\} \leftarrow \texttt{susp}(\varphi)$ $\mathcal{T} \leftarrow \texttt{Cou99}(\varphi')$ (S) $\mathcal{T} \leftarrow \texttt{iter\_simulations}(\mathcal{T})$ $\mathcal{T} \leftarrow \texttt{reduce\_skel}(\mathcal{T}, \{\xi_1, ..., \xi_n\})$ for $\xi \in \{\xi_1, ..., \xi_n\}$ do: $\quad \mathcal{T}_\xi \leftarrow \texttt{Cou99}(\xi)$ (S) $\quad \mathcal{T}_\xi \leftarrow \texttt{iter\_simulations}(\mathcal{T}_\xi)$ $\quad \mathcal{T}_\xi \leftarrow \texttt{make\_suspendable}(\mathcal{T}_\xi, [\xi])$ $\quad \mathcal{T} \leftarrow \texttt{product}(\mathcal{T}, \mathcal{T}_\xi)$	$\varphi', \{\xi_1, ..., \xi_n\} \leftarrow \texttt{susp}(\varphi)$ $\mathcal{T}' \leftarrow \texttt{Cou99}(\varphi')$ $\mathcal{T} \leftarrow \texttt{WDBA\_minimize}(\mathcal{T}', \varphi')$ if $\mathcal{T}$ could not be built: (S) $\quad \mathcal{T} \leftarrow \texttt{iter\_simulations}(\mathcal{T}')$ $\quad \mathcal{T} \leftarrow \texttt{reduce\_skel}(\mathcal{T}, \{\xi_1, ..., \xi_n\})$ $\quad$for $\xi \in \{\xi_1, ..., \xi_n\}$ do: $\quad\quad \mathcal{T}_\xi \leftarrow \texttt{Cou99}(\xi)$ $\quad\quad \mathcal{T}_\xi \leftarrow \texttt{iter\_simulations}(\mathcal{T}_\xi)$ $\quad\quad \mathcal{T}_\xi \leftarrow \texttt{make\_suspendable}(\mathcal{T}_\xi, [\xi])$ $\quad\quad \mathcal{T} \leftarrow \texttt{product}(\mathcal{T}, \mathcal{T}_\xi)$
post-processing	$\mathcal{T} \leftarrow \texttt{prune\_dead\_SCCs}(\mathcal{T})$ (A) $\mathcal{T} \leftarrow \texttt{acc\_simplify}(\mathcal{T})$ $\mathcal{T}_1 \leftarrow \texttt{WDBA\_minimize}(\mathcal{T}, \varphi)$ (S) $\mathcal{T} \leftarrow \texttt{iter\_simulations}(\mathcal{T})$ (D) $\mathcal{T} \leftarrow \texttt{degeneralize}(\mathcal{T})$ (B) $\mathcal{T} \leftarrow \texttt{iter\_simulations}(\mathcal{T})$ if $\mathcal{T}_1$ could be built: $\quad$return $\texttt{smallest}(\mathcal{T}, \mathcal{T}_1)$ return $\mathcal{T}$	$\mathcal{T} \leftarrow \texttt{prune\_dead\_SCCs}(\mathcal{T})$ (A) $\mathcal{T} \leftarrow \texttt{acc\_simplify}(\mathcal{T})$ $\mathcal{T}_1 \leftarrow \texttt{WDBA\_minimize}(\mathcal{T}, \varphi)$ if $\mathcal{T}_1$ could be built: $\quad$return $\mathcal{T}_1$ (S) $\mathcal{T} \leftarrow \texttt{iter\_simulations}(\mathcal{T})$ (D) $\mathcal{T} \leftarrow \texttt{degeneralize}(\mathcal{T})$ (B) $\mathcal{T} \leftarrow \texttt{iter\_simulations}(\mathcal{T})$ return $\mathcal{T}$

Fig. 6. Two translation scenarios that use compositional suspension (denoted "Comp" in the sequel) to produce a BA. Automata are stored as TGBAs even when they represent BAs. The scenarios without compositional suspension (denoted as "Cou99") arise by replacing all the composition lines by $\mathcal{T} \leftarrow \texttt{Cou99}(\varphi)$. To produce a TGBA instead of a BA, we omit lines (D) and (B).

degeneralization. In the context of model checking, it is not clear when a deterministic automaton should be favored over a small one. For instance, Sebastiani and Tonetta [15] have shown that their larger and more deterministic automata yield smaller synchronized products with a model than the smaller automata produced by Gastin and Oddoux [11]. Spot implements two translation scenarios: the "small size" scenario tries to reduces the size of the automaton, while the "determinism" scenario tries to reduces the number of nondeterministic states. According to our experience with Spot, automata produced by our "small size" scenario tends to give smaller synchronized products.

Fig. 6 shows how the different techniques we have presented are chained in these two scenarios. The function $\texttt{prune\_dead\_SCCs}$ is a classical optimization that removes states that may not reach an accepting SCC. $\texttt{susp}$, $\texttt{reduce\_skel}$, $\texttt{make\_suspendable}$ correspond to operations defined in Sec. 3.2. We will use keys (S),(A),(D),(B) to denote lines that are enabled or disabled in our experiments. For acceptance simplification (A) and degeneralization (D), we write (a) and (d) to indicate that old definitions are used. For instance "Cou99 (a)" means that Spot's implementation of Couvreur's translation was used to translate the formulae, and that the only post-processings performed were $\texttt{prune\_dead\_SCCs}$,

Table 1. Results for selected combinations of the presented techniques. Numbers are accumulated over all translated formulae. Smaller numbers are better everywhere. Keys A/a,S,D/d,B indicate when the corresponding lines of Fig. 6 have been enabled a/d respectively denote the original acceptance simplification and degeneralization while A/D apply the definitions from this paper. Compositional suspension is only enabled on "**Comp**" lines.

			"small size" scenario					"determinism" scenario				
		$|Q|$	$|\delta|$	$|F|$	ns	nA	time	$|Q|$	$|\delta|$	$|F|$	ns	nA	time

known.ltl: 184 formulae

TGBA
1	Cou99 (a)	672	10921	198	113	49	7.09	676	10805	198	105	45	7.13
2	Cou99 (A)	672	10921	195	113	49	7.24	676	10805	195	105	45	7.38
3	Cou99 (AS)	636	9848	195	88	50	7.50	641	9958	195	82	45	7.34
4	**Comp** (AS)	636	9838	195	85	50	7.63	644	9968	195	79	45	7.53

BA
5	Cou99 (ad)	717	11653	184	124	49	6.93	721	11537	184	116	45	6.84
6	Cou99 (Ad)	717	11653	184	124	49	6.94	721	11537	184	116	45	6.97
7	Cou99 (ASd)	678	10511	184	97	50	7.28	683	10621	184	91	45	7.02
8	Cou99 (ASD)	675	10463	184	97	50	7.35	680	10573	184	91	45	7.08
9	Cou99 (ASDB)	673	10362	184	95	49	7.50	678	10472	184	89	44	7.14
10	**Comp** (ASDB)	673	10352	184	92	49	7.56	687	10530	184	86	44	7.32

weak3.ltl: 100 formulae

TGBA
1	Cou99 (a)	749	116312	361	324	92	6.81	749	116312	361	324	92	6.83
2	Cou99 (A)	743	115104	357	319	90	8.89	743	115104	357	319	90	8.94
3	Cou99 (AS)	618	84603	355	237	86	10.42	618	84603	355	237	86	10.36
4	**Comp** (AS)	617	83875	355	225	87	7.51	647	90771	355	195	69	7.84

BA
5	Cou99 (ad)	2030	299376	100	776	92	7.75	2030	299376	100	776	92	7.76
6	Cou99 (Ad)	2018	296904	100	765	90	8.50	2018	296904	100	765	90	8.55
7	Cou99 (ASd)	1700	212984	100	549	86	10.04	1700	212984	100	549	86	9.92
8	Cou99 (ASD)	1565	193157	100	493	86	9.99	1565	193157	100	493	86	9.90
9	Cou99 (ASDB)	1525	188873	100	435	86	11.32	1525	188873	100	435	86	11.41
10	**Comp** (ASDB)	1530	188939	100	424	87	8.48	1588	201611	100	387	69	8.51

strong2.ltl: 100 formulae

TGBA
1	Cou99 (a)	6237	3524004	261	4633	100	82.32	6237	3524004	261	4633	100	82.65
2	Cou99 (A)	6183	3485348	257	4583	100	151.17	6183	3485348	257	4583	100	151.49
3	Cou99 (AS)	1900	508972	255	879	100	178.43	1900	508972	255	879	100	178.68
4	**Comp** (AS)	1731	434812	255	703	100	50.41	1801	464412	255	675	100	46.80

BA
5	Cou99 (ad)	8207	3928868	100	5379	100	114.24	8207	3928868	100	5379	100	114.38
6	Cou99 (Ad)	8083	3876308	100	5290	100	151.76	8083	3876308	100	5290	100	151.57
7	Cou99 (ASd)	3488	782324	100	1368	100	178.83	3488	782324	100	1368	100	178.73
8	Cou99 (ASD)	3330	745280	100	1292	100	177.44	3330	745280	100	1292	100	178.14
9	Cou99 (ASDB)	3259	727416	100	1211	100	181.43	3259	727416	100	1211	100	182.34
10	**Comp** (ASDB)	3091	668768	100	1039	100	53.92	3201	713152	100	991	100	49.98
11	ltl3ba	5389	2473408	100	5041	100	2.38	8660	2281988	100	4515	100	4.77
12	ltl3ba susp.	5298	2458372	100	4950	100	2.38	5418	1424964	100	2409	100	2.56

the old version of `acc_simplify`, and WDBA-minimization when applicable; especially, no simulation-based reduction or degeneralization was performed.

We note that suspendable formulae are not obligation properties, so the presence of a suspendable subformulae prevents the application of WDBA-minimization except in pathological cases.

5.2   Experiments

Table 1 presents results of selected combinations of the presented techniques applied according to the two scenarios to three different sets of formulae.[3] For each configuration, scenario, and set of formulae we show the cumulative size

---

[3] More measures and details at http://www.lrde.epita.fr/~adl/spin13/.

of the automata produced for formulae in the set, namely numbers of states, transitions, acceptance sets, nondeterministic states (ns.), and nondeterministic automata (nd.). We also provide total translation time. Grey rectangles mark the best results: smallest automata for the "small size" scenario and automata with the least nondeterminism for the "determinism" scenario.

known.ltl contains 92 formulae and their negation, collected from the literature [7, 16, 8]. 122 of these 184 formulae describe obligation properties, for which WDBA minimization computes a minimal deterministic automaton during the post-processing. Only 14 formulae of the set require more than one acceptance set for the translation. The potential for improvement on this set is very thin.

weak3.ltl contains 100 formulae combined with a weak fairness hypothesis. Formulae have the form $\varphi_i \wedge \mathsf{GF}a \wedge \mathsf{GF}b \wedge \mathsf{GF}c$ where φ_i is a random LTL formula with a syntax tree of 15..20 nodes, using up to 6 atomic propositions. The fairness hypothesis $\mathsf{GF}a \wedge \mathsf{GF}b \wedge \mathsf{GF}c$ is a single suspendable subformula which can be translated to a one-state deterministic TGBA.

strong2.ltl contains 100 formulae combined with a strong fairness hypothesis. Formulae have the form $\varphi_i \wedge (\mathsf{GF}a \rightarrow \mathsf{GF}b) \wedge (\mathsf{GF}c \rightarrow \mathsf{GF}d)$ where φ_i are the same as in the previous set.

For each formula set, the table can be read vertically to see the incremental effect of improvements presented in Sec. 4 on translations "Cou99". The difference between lines 1 and 2 shows that our acceptance simplification improvement is rather small: situations such as the one depicted by Fig. 2 are rare. Applying simulations to move from line 2 to 3 shows a much greater improvement, both in term of states and determinism. Analogous conclusions can be made by comparing lines 5, 6, and 7 where the original degeneralization is additionally applied to get BAs. The effect of the new degeneralization (line 8) defined in Sec. 4.3 is very limited on known.ltl because most BAs come directly out of the WDBA minimization function. It is much clearer in the other two sets of formulae. Application of a final simulation on the BA (line 9) saves a few more states.

The table also includes a compositional suspension with all other improvements (line 10). Its results on known.ltl are not very relevant as only 18 formulae of this set contain at least some suspendable subformula. The results are more interesting on the other two sets. As suspendable subformula $\mathsf{GF}a \wedge \mathsf{GF}b \wedge \mathsf{GF}c$ of each formula in weak3.ltl translates only to a one-state TGBA, one cannot expect improvements in automata size. The improvement here comes from the fact that the one-state TGBA is deterministic and the compositional approach allows to apply WDBA minimization to skeletons (note that it cannot be applied to the full formulae as fairness breaks obligation property). In many cases, we get a deterministic skeleton and composition with a deterministic TGBA results into a deterministic TGBA. To sum up, compositional suspension used in "deterministic" scenario produces substantially more deterministic automata (both TGBAs and BAs) than any other translation. The situation regarding automata size is different for strong2.ltl as $(\mathsf{GF}a \rightarrow \mathsf{GF}b) \wedge (\mathsf{GF}c \rightarrow \mathsf{GF}d)$ is a suspendable formulae that translates into a nondeterministic TGBA with 5 states. As the suspended TGBA is relatively big, compositional suspension brings a nice reduction of automata size and also an interesting speedup (again, for both TGBAs and BAs).

The table finally presents the results of ltl3ba [1] on strong2.ltl. ltl3ba improves ltl2ba [11] in several ways including the original suspension technique (see Sec. 3.1) and application of direct simulation on the final BA (but not before). We run ltl3ba with options -S -A to enable the direct simulation and disable the suspension and with option -S to enable both. Moreover, in the "deterministic" scenario we add the option -M leading to more deterministic automata. The lines 11 and 12 illustrate the gain that could be expected from the on-the-fly suspension [1] implemented in ltl3ba. It can be compared to the gain of compositional suspension from Sec. 3: the reduction between lines 11 and 12 should be compared to the reduction between lines 9 and 10.

6 Conclusion

We have presented four techniques to improve LTL-to-Büchi translators.

The compositional suspension improves the translations of *suspendable* subformulae (such as fairness constraints) and is especially effective in the case where the suspendable subformulae are expressed with automata of more than one state: in that case we avoid synchronizing the suspendable subformulae in non-accepting SCCs of the resulting automaton. The technique can accommodate any translator, by replacing the suspendable subformulae by fresh atomic propositions.

The other three contributions are improvements to the post-processings performed on the translated automaton. The SCC-based acceptance simplifications is an improvement over the transitional acceptance simplifications used in GBA. Its effect is limited as the forms of automata it attempts to simplify are not frequent in our benchmarks. Our simulation-based reductions build upon the existing *direct* and *reverse* simulations, but have been adapted to generalized acceptance sets, and implemented in a way that can be used to improve the determinism of the reduced automaton. Finally, we have shown that the degeneralization procedure could also benefit from the knowledge of the accepting SCCs.

In our experiments, we managed to reduce automata by a few states even on set of simple formulae (known.ltl) where years of developments have left only a little room for improvement. The bigger reduction were clearly achieved on formulae using strong fairness hypotheses (strong2.ltl).

Along the way, we pointed a couple of opportunities for further improvements. For instance in the degeneralization, and as far as we know, nobody has ever studied the selection of a suitable ordering (maybe SCC-based), or the selection of the best initial level. Our simulation currently suffers from the fact that Fig. 4(a) cannot be reduced to Fig. 4(c). Since suspendable subformulae are best translated separately, maybe we could consider other class of subformulae to translate separately (e.g., obligation properties are appealing since we already know how to construct a minimal WDBA from them).

Acknowledgments. T. Babiak, M. Křetínský, and J. Strejček have been supported by The Czech Science Foundation, grant No. P202/12/G061.

References

1. Babiak, T., Křetínský, M., Řehák, V., Strejček, J.: LTL to Büchi automata translation: Fast and more deterministic. In: Flanagan, C., König, B. (eds.) TACAS 2012. LNCS, vol. 7214, pp. 95–109. Springer, Heidelberg (2012)
2. Couvreur, J.-M.: On-the-fly verification of linear temporal logic. In: Wing, J.M., Woodcock, J. (eds.) FM 1999. LNCS, vol. 1708, pp. 253–271. Springer, Heidelberg (1999)
3. Daniele, M., Giunchiglia, F., Vardi, M.Y.: Improved automata generation for linear temporal logic. In: Halbwachs, N., Peled, D.A. (eds.) CAV 1999. LNCS, vol. 1633, pp. 249–260. Springer, Heidelberg (1999)
4. Dax, C., Eisinger, J., Klaedtke, F.: Mechanizing the powerset construction for restricted classes of ω-automata. In: Namjoshi, K.S., Yoneda, T., Higashino, T., Okamura, Y. (eds.) ATVA 2007. LNCS, vol. 4762, pp. 223–236. Springer, Heidelberg (2007)
5. Duret-Lutz, A.: LTL translation improvements in Spot. In: VECoS 2011, Electronic Workshops in Computing. British Computer Society (2011)
6. Duret-Lutz, A., Poitrenaud, D.: SPOT: An extensible model checking library using transition-based generalized Büchi automata. In: MASCOTS 2004, pp. 76–83. IEEE (2004)
7. Dwyer, M.B., Avrunin, G.S., Corbett, J.C.: Property specification patterns for finite-state verification. In: FMSP 1998, pp. 7–15. ACM Press, New York (1998)
8. Etessami, K., Holzmann, G.J.: Optimizing Büchi Automata. In: Palamidessi, C. (ed.) CONCUR 2000. LNCS, vol. 1877, pp. 153–167. Springer, Heidelberg (2000)
9. Etessami, K., Wilke, T., Schuller, R.A.: Fair simulation relations, parity games, and state space reduction for Büchi automata. In: Orejas, F., Spirakis, P.G., van Leeuwen, J. (eds.) ICALP 2001. LNCS, vol. 2076, pp. 694–707. Springer, Heidelberg (2001)
10. Fritz, C.: Constructing Büchi automata from linear temporal logic using simulation relations for alternating Büchi automata. In: Ibarra, O.H., Dang, Z. (eds.) CIAA 2003. LNCS, vol. 2759, pp. 35–48. Springer, Heidelberg (2003)
11. Gastin, P., Oddoux, D.: Fast LTL to Büchi Automata Translation. In: Berry, G., Comon, H., Finkel, A. (eds.) CAV 2001. LNCS, vol. 2102, pp. 53–65. Springer, Heidelberg (2001)
12. Giannakopoulou, D., Lerda, F.: From states to transitions: Improving translation of LTL formulae to Büchi automata. In: Peled, D.A., Vardi, M.Y. (eds.) FORTE 2002. LNCS, vol. 2529, pp. 308–326. Springer, Heidelberg (2002)
13. Juvekar, S., Piterman, N.: Minimizing generalized Büchi automata. In: Ball, T., Jones, R.B. (eds.) CAV 2006. LNCS, vol. 4144, pp. 45–58. Springer, Heidelberg (2006)
14. Manna, Z., Pnueli, A.: A hierarchy of temporal properties. In: PODC 1990, pp. 377–410. ACM Press (1990)
15. Sebastiani, R., Tonetta, S.: "More Deterministic" vs. "Smaller" Büchi Automata for Efficient LTL Model Checking. In: Geist, D., Tronci, E. (eds.) CHARME 2003. LNCS, vol. 2860, pp. 126–140. Springer, Heidelberg (2003)
16. Somenzi, F., Bloem, R.: Efficient Büchi Automata from LTL Formulae. In: Emerson, E.A., Sistla, A.P. (eds.) CAV 2000. LNCS, vol. 1855, pp. 248–263. Springer, Heidelberg (2000)
17. Wimmer, R., Herbstritt, M., Hermanns, H., Strampp, K., Becker, B.: SIGREF — a symbolic bisimulation tool box. In: Graf, S., Zhang, W. (eds.) ATVA 2006. LNCS, vol. 4218, pp. 477–492. Springer, Heidelberg (2006)
18. Wolper, P., Vardi, M.Y., Sistla, A.P.: Reasoning about infinite computation paths. In: FOCS 1983, pp. 185–194. IEEE (1983)

Regression Verification Using Impact Summaries

John Backes[1], Suzette Person[2], Neha Rungta[3], and Oksana Tkachuk[3]

[1] University of Minnesota
back0145@umn.edu
[2] NASA Langley Research Center
suzette.person@nasa.gov
[3] NASA Ames Research Center
{neha.s.rungta,oksana.tkachuk}@nasa.gov

Abstract. Regression verification techniques are used to prove equivalence of closely related program versions. Existing regression verification techniques leverage the similarities between program versions to help improve analysis scalability by using abstraction and decomposition techniques. These techniques are sound but not complete. In this work, we propose an alternative technique to improve scalability of regression verification that leverages change impact information to partition program execution behaviors. Program behaviors in each version are partitioned into (a) behaviors impacted by the changes and (b) behaviors not impacted (unimpacted) by the changes. Our approach uses a combination of static analysis and symbolic execution to generate summaries of program behaviors impacted by the differences. We show in this work that checking equivalence of behaviors in two program versions reduces to checking equivalence of just the impacted behaviors. We prove that our approach is both sound and complete for sequential programs, with respect to the depth bound of symbolic execution; furthermore, our approach can be used with existing approaches to better leverage the similarities between program versions and improve analysis scalability. We evaluate our technique on a set of sequential C artifacts and present preliminary results.

1 Introduction

Various reduction, abstraction, and compositional techniques have been developed to help scale software verification techniques to industrial-sized systems. Although such techniques have greatly increased the size and complexity of systems that can be checked, analysis of large software systems remains costly. Regression analysis techniques, e.g., regression testing [16], regression model checking [22], and regression verification [19], restrict the scope of the analysis by leveraging the differences between program versions. These techniques are based on the idea that if code is checked early in development, then subsequent versions can be checked against a prior (checked) version, leveraging the results of the previous analysis to reduce analysis cost of the current version.

Regression verification addresses the problem of proving equivalence of closely related program versions [19]. These techniques compare two programs with a

E. Bartocci and C.R. Ramakrishnan (Eds.): SPIN 2013, LNCS 7976, pp. 99–116, 2013.

large degree of syntactic similarity to prove that portions of one program version are equivalent to the other. Regression verification can be used for guaranteeing backward compatibility, and for showing behavioral equivalence in programs with syntactic differences, e.g., when a program is refactored to improve its performance, maintainability, or readability.

Existing regression verification techniques leverage similarities between program versions by using abstraction and decomposition techniques to improve scalability of the analysis [10,12,19]. The abstraction- and decomposition-based techniques, e.g., summaries of unchanged code [12] or semantically equivalent methods [19], compute an over-approximation of the program behaviors. The equivalence checking results of these techniques are sound but not complete—they may characterize programs as not functionally equivalent when, in fact, they are equivalent.

In this work we describe a novel approach that leverages the impact of the differences between two programs for scaling regression verification. We partition program behaviors of each version into (a) behaviors impacted by the changes and (b) behaviors not impacted (unimpacted) by the changes. Only the impacted program behaviors are used during equivalence checking. We then prove that checking equivalence of the impacted program behaviors is equivalent to checking equivalence of all program behaviors for a given depth bound. In this work we use symbolic execution to generate the program behaviors and leverage control- and data-dependence information to facilitate the partitioning of program behaviors. The impacted program behaviors are termed as *impact summaries*. The dependence analyses that facilitate the generation of the impact summaries, we believe, could be used in conjunction with other abstraction and decomposition based approaches, [10,12], as a complementary reduction technique. An evaluation of our regression verification technique shows that our approach is capable of leveraging similarities between program versions to reduce the size of the queries and the time required to check for logical equivalence.

The main contributions of this work are:

- A regression verification technique to generate impact summaries that can be checked for functional equivalence using an off-the-shelf decision procedure.
- A proof that our approach is sound and complete with respect to the depth bound of symbolic execution.
- An implementation of our technique using the LLVM compiler infrastructure, the KLEE Symbolic Virtual Machine [4], and a variety of Satisfiability Modulo Theory (SMT) solvers, e.g., STP [7] and Z3 [6].
- An empirical evaluation on a set of C artifacts which shows that the use of impact summaries can reduce the cost of regression verification.

2   Motivation and Background

2.1   Checking Functional Equivalence

In this work, we focus on functional equivalence [12]. Two programs, P_0 and P_1, are functionally equivalent iff for all possible input values to the programs, they

```
1: int func(unsigned int val) {
2:   if((val & 0x03) == 0) { //divisible by 4
3:       val = val + 4; // change to val = val + 2;
4:       return mod2(val)
5:   } else return 0;
6: }
7: int mod2(unsigned int x) {
8:   return ((x & 0x01) == 0); // divisible by 2
9: }
```

Fig. 1. Program behavior is unchanged when the constant value in line 3 is even

both produce the same output, i.e., they return the same value and result in the same global state. In general, proving functional equivalence is undecidable, so we prove functional equivalence with respect to a user-specified depth-bound for loops and recursive functions. Note that this notion of equivalence is similar to the k-equivalence defined in [19].

Equivalence checking techniques that use uninterpreted functions as a mechanism for abstraction and decomposition [10,12,19] produce sound but not complete results. The example in Figure 1 demonstrates how the use of uninterpreted functions can lead to false negatives. The input to methods func and mod2 is an unsigned integer. If the input to func, val, is divisible by four, then in version V_0 of func, four is added to val and method mod2 is invoked with the updated variable, val. Next, mod2 returns true if its input, x, is divisible by two; otherwise it returns false. Suppose, a change is made to line 3 in V_1 of fun and two is added to val in lieu of four. Both versions of func are functionally equivalent, i.e., for all possible inputs to func, the output is the same in both versions.

Symdiff is a technique which uses uninterpreted functions during equivalence checking [10]. It modularly checks equivalence of each pair of procedures in two versions of the program. To check the equivalence of the func method, it replaces the call to mod2 at line 4 with an uninterpreted function. The inputs to the uninterpreted function are parameters and global values read by the method. In V_0 of func the uninterpreted function for the call to mod2 is $f\_mod2(val + 4)$ while in V_1 it is $f\_mod2(val + 2)$. The procedures are then transformed to a single logical formula whose validity is checked using verification condition generation. Symdiff will report V_0 and V_1 of func as not equivalent due to the different input values to the uninterpreted function: f_mod2. The use of uninterpreted functions results in an over-approximation because equality logic with uninterpreted functions (EUF) relies on functional congruence (consistency) —a conservative approach to judging functional equivalence which assumes that instances of the same function return the same value if given equal arguments [9]. Other equivalence checking techniques that rely on uninterpreted functions will report similar false negatives.

2.2 Symbolic Execution

Symbolic execution uses symbolic values in lieu of concrete values for program inputs and builds a path condition for each execution path it explores. A path

```
1: int a, b;
2: void test(int x, int y){
3: if(x > 0) a = a + 1; else a = a + 2; //change x <= 0
4: if(y > 0) b = b + 1; else b = b + 2;
5: }
```

Fig. 2. An example where equivalence cannot be naively checked using DiSE

condition contains (a) a conjunction of constraints over the symbolic input values and constants such that they represent the semantics of the statements executed on a given path p and (b) the conjunction of constraints that represent the effects of executing p—the return value and the final global state. The disjunction of all the path conditions generated during symbolic execution is a symbolic summary of the program behaviors. Version V_0 of the `test` method in Figure 2 has two integer inputs x and y whose values determine the updates made to the global variables a and b. There are four path conditions for V_0 generated by symbolic execution:

1. $x > 0 \land y > 0 \land a_0 = a + 1 \land b_0 = b + 1$
2. $\neg(x > 0) \land y > 0 \land a_1 = a + 2 \land b_0 = b + 1$
3. $x > 0 \land \neg(y > 0) \land a_0 = a + 1 \land b_1 = b + 2$
4. $\neg(x > 0) \land \neg(y > 0) \land a_1 = a + 2 \land b_1 = b + 2.$

Each path condition has constraints on the inputs x and y that lead to the update of global variables a and b. The variables a_0, a_1, b_0, and b_1 are temporary variables that represent the final assignments to global variables a and b.

2.3   Change Impact Analysis

The DiSE framework, in our previous work, implements a symbolic execution based change impact analysis for a given software maintenance task [13,17]. DiSE uses the results of static change impact analyses to direct symbolic execution toward the parts of the code that may be impacted by the changes. The output of DiSE is a set of impacted path conditions, i.e., path conditions along program locations impacted by differences in programs.

The inputs to DiSE are two program versions and a target client analysis. DiSE first computes a syntactic diff of the program versions to identify locations in the source code that are modified. Then DiSE uses program slicing-based techniques to detect impacted program locations, i.e., locations that have control- and data-dependencies on the modified program locations. The set of impacted program locations is used to direct symbolic execution to explore execution paths containing impacted locations. In the parts of the program composed of locations not impacted by the change, DiSE explores a subset of the feasible paths through that section.

The dependence analyses and pruning within the DiSE framework are configurable based on the needs of the client analysis. To illustrate how DiSE computes path conditions for generating test inputs to cover impacted branch statements, consider the example in Figure 2. Suppose a change is made to line 3 where the condition $x > 0$ in V_0 of test is changed to $x <= 0$ in V_1. Due to this change, the conditional statement and assignments to global variable a on line 3 are marked as impacted in both versions. The goal of the symbolic execution in DiSE is to generate path conditions that cover both *true* and *false* branches of the conditional branch statement, $x <= 0$, and explore *any one* of the branches of the conditional branch statement, $y > 0$. The path conditions for program version, V_0, that may be generated by DiSE are:

1. $x > 0 \wedge y > 0 \wedge a_0 = a + 1 \wedge b_0 = b + 1$
2. $\neg(x > 0) \wedge y > 0 \wedge a_1 = a + 2 \wedge b_0 = b + 1$;

Here both branches of the $x \leq 0$ are explored while the *true* branch of the $y > 0$ is explored. Similarly the path conditions for version V_1 that may be generated by DiSE are:

1. $x \leq 0 \wedge \neg(y > 0) \wedge a_0 = a + 1 \wedge b_1 = b + 2$
2. $\neg(x \leq 0) \wedge \neg(y > 0) \wedge a_1 = a + 2 \wedge b_1 = b + 2$.

In version, V_1 both branches of $x \leq 0$ are still explored but the *false* branch of the $y > 0$ is explored. Note this is because DiSE does not enforce a specific branch to be explored for an unimpacted conditional statement. These path conditions can be solved to generate test inputs that drive execution along the paths that contain impacted locations.

The path conditions generated for regression testing, related to impacted branch coverage, in the DiSE framework under-approximate the program behaviors. The constraints on the variable y in the path conditions generated by DiSE, shown above, can be different in V_0 from those generated in V_1—the path conditions represent different under-approximations of the program behaviors. This under-approximation does not allow the path conditions to be used for equivalence checking. Furthermore the dependence analysis is also tailored to suit the needs of the client analyses. The client analyses that are currently supported in DiSE are related to regression testing (test inputs to satisfy different coverage criteria) and improving DARWIN based delta debugging.

In this work we add support for performing equivalence checking within the DiSE framework. For this we define a set of static change impact rules that allow us to precisely characterize the program statements as impacted or unimpacted such that checking equivalence of behaviors of two programs reduces to the problem of checking equivalence of the behaviors encoded by the impacted statements.

3   Regression Verification Using Impact Summaries

An overview of our regression verification technique is shown in Figure 3. Steps 1–3 in Figure 3 represent a static change impact analysis that is performed on V_0 and V_1. The change impact analysis marks the program statements that are

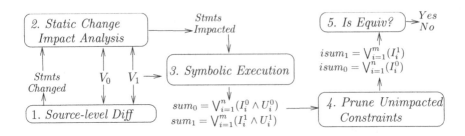

Fig. 3. Overview of regression verification using impact summaries

impacted by the differences between V_0 and V_1. The outputs from Step 3 are the program behavior summaries (full summaries) for program versions V_0 and V_1. Each symbolic summary consists of the path conditions representing the program execution behaviors.

In order to facilitate the characterization of the program behaviors as impacted or unimpacted, we first define a mechanism to distinguish between different behaviors encoded within a given path condition. For the example shown in Figure 2 each path condition encodes two program behaviors; the first program behavior is related to the input variable x and global variable a; while the second program behavior is related to the input variable y and global variable b. We can make this distinction because the operations on variables x and a are completely disjoint from the operations on variables y and b. The constraints on x and a represent one set of program behaviors for the example in Figure 2 while the constraints on y and b represent another set of behaviors. Based on this distinction a path condition can contain num behaviors such that the set of constraints encoding each behavior are completely disjoint from the constraints encoding the other behaviors.

In this work, we partition the constraints in each path condition generated by the change impact analysis as either *impacted* or *unimpacted*. An impacted (unimpacted) constraint I_i (U_i) is a constraint that is added to the path condition as a result of executing an impacted (unimpacted) program statement during symbolic execution. The conjunction of the impacted constraints, I_i, in a path condition represents impacted program behaviors, while the conjunction of the unimpacted constraints, U_i in a path condition, represents unimpacted program behaviors.

Definition 1. *A **full summary** is a disjunction of the impacted constraints I_i and the unimpacted constraints U_i for a program with n paths: $sum = \bigvee_{i=1}^{n}(I_i \wedge U_i)$.*

For example, the full summary for V_0 containing n paths is given by $sum_0 = \bigvee_{i=1}^{n}(I_i^0 \wedge U_i^0)$. The full summaries are post-processed in Step 4, as shown in Figure 3 to remove the unimpacted constraints and generate *impact summaries*.

Table 1. Control and data dependence rules for computing impacted statements

---

(1) if $S_i \in \mathbb{I}$ and S_j is *control dependent* on S_i then $\mathbb{I} \cup \{S_j\}$

(2) if $S_i \in \mathbb{I}$ and S_j *uses* (reads) the value of a variable *defined* (written) at S_i
    then $\mathbb{I} \cup \{S_j\}$

---

(3) if $S_i \in \mathbb{I}$ an S_i is *control dependent* on S_j then $\mathbb{I} \cup \{S_j\}$

(4) if $S_i \in \mathbb{I}$ and S_j defines (writes) a variable whose value is *used* (read) at S_i
    then $\mathbb{I} \cup \{S_j\}$

Definition 2. *An **impact summary** consists of a disjunction of the impacted constraints I_i for a program with n paths: $isum = \bigvee_{i=1}^{n}(I_i)$.*

The resulting impact summaries are then checked for functional equivalence [12] in Step 5, by using an off-the-shelf SMT solver, e.g., STP [7] or Z3 [6] to check for logical equivalence. In Section 4 we prove that the full summaries for two programs are functionally equivalent iff their impact summaries are functionally equivalent. Formally, we demonstrate that for a program V_0 with n paths and a program V_1 with m paths, Formula 1 is a tautology.

$$[(\bigvee_{i=1}^{n} I_i^0) \leftrightarrow (\bigvee_{i=1}^{m} I_i^1)] \leftrightarrow [\bigvee_{i=1}^{n} (I_i^0 \wedge U_i^0) \leftrightarrow \bigvee_{i=1}^{m} (I_i^1 \wedge U_i^1)] \tag{1}$$

3.1 Computing Impacted Program Statements and Behaviors

In this section we present the set of rules that are necessary to conservatively compute, for sequential programs, the set of program statements that may be *impacted* by added or deleted program statements. We then briefly discuss how the set of impacted statements can be used to compute impacted program behaviors. The static analysis in this work uses standard control- and data-flow analysis to compute the set of impacted statements. The rules for the forward and backward flow analysis are shown in Table 1. Given the conservative nature of the analysis, it may mark certain unimpacted statements as impacted. The analysis, however, is guaranteed to find all impacted statements. We present a high-level description of how the rules are applied in the steps below:

Step 1. A source-level syntactic diff is performed to generate the change sets for the related program versions V_0 and V_1. The change set for V_0 is $\mathbb{C}_0$. It contains the set of statements in V_0 that are removed in V_1. The change set for V_1 is $\mathbb{C}_1$ which contains statements in V_1 that are added with respect to V_0. Note that all edited statements can be treated as removed in one version and added in another.

Step 2. The impact set for program version V_0 is initialized with statements in the change set of V_0: $\mathbb{I}_0 := \mathbb{C}_0$.

Step 3. To account for forward control- and data-flow dependence, rules (1) and (2) in Table 1 are iteratively applied to $\mathbb{I}_0$ until they reach a fixpoint.

Step 4. The impact set for program version V_1 is initialized to the change set of V_1: $\mathbb{I}_1 := \mathbb{C}_1$.

Step 5. For all statements in the impact set of V_0, $\forall S_i \in \mathbb{I}_0$, if there exists a corresponding statement $S_i' \in V_1$ such that $S_i \sim S_i'$—then it is added to the impact set of V_1, $\mathbb{I}_1 := \mathbb{I}_1 \cup \{S_i'\}$. This step is performed to account for the impact of the statements *removed* in V_0.

Step 6. To compute the impact of the changes using forward control- and data-flow dependences, rules (1) and (2) in Table 1 are iteratively applied to $\mathbb{I}_1$ until a fixpoint is reached. Rule (3) is applied once to $\mathbb{I}_1$ to account for backward control-flow dependence. Finally, Rule (4) is applied to $\mathbb{I}_1$ transitively to compute the reaching definitions.

Step 7. Statements from the impact set of V_1 are mapped to the impact set of V_0: $\forall S_i \in \mathbb{I}_1$, if there exists a corresponding statement in $S_i' \in V_0$, $S_i \sim S_i'$—then it is added to the impact set of V_0, $\mathbb{I}_0 := \mathbb{I}_0 \cup \{S_i'\}$. This step accounts for the impact of statements *added* to V_1.

The constraints generated by symbolic execution at impacted program statements on path i are added to the impact summary, I_i while the unimpacted constraints are added to U_i. We can check functional equivalence of two programs using their impact summaries.

The static analysis rules presented in this section compute the set of impacted program statements within a method, i.e., the analysis is intraprocedural. In [17] we present an interprocedural change impact analysis. The algorithm in [17] statically computes the impacted program statements (impact set) for all the methods disregarding the flow of impact through different method invocations. During symbolic execution these impact sets are then dynamically refined based on the calling context, propagating the impact of changes between methods through method arguments, global variables and method return values. Due to space limitations we present only the intraprocedural version of the impact analysis in this paper. Our empirical evaluation of regression verification, however, is performed using the interprocedural version of the algorithm. Next we present an example to illustrate how impact summaries are computed for an interprocedural program.

3.2 Example

Figure 4 shows two versions of the C function Init_Data that invoke the same function Set_Struct (shown in Figure 4 (c)). Note that even though the analysis is performed on the single static assignment form of the program, to enable better readability we describe it in terms of the source. The Init_Data function first initializes two arrays, Data0 and Data1, and the pointer to a data structure, StructA. Then, if the value of capacity is greater than the constant length defined for arrays Data0 or Data1, the function returns zero; otherwise, it returns one. V_1 is a refactored version of V_0. In V_1, a single value specifies the length of both arrays, Data0 and Data1. The refactoring also moves the initialization of

```
 1: #define Len0 512
 2: #define Len1 512
 3: int Data0[Len0], Data1[Len1];
 4: struct_A* StructA;
 5: int Init_Data(int capacity)
 6:   for(int i = 0; i < capacity∧i < Len0; i++)

 7:     Data0[i] = 0;
 8:   for(int i = 0; i < capacity∧i < Len1; i++)

 9:     Data1[i] = 0;
10:   StructA = Set_Struct(StructA)
11:   if(capacity > Len0)
12:     return 0;
13:   if(capacity > Len1)
14:     return 0;
15:   return 1;
```

(a) V_0

```
 1: #define Len0 512
 2: int Data0[Len0], Data1[Len0];
 3: struct_A* StructA;
 4: int Init_Data(int capacity)
 5:   for(int i = 0; i < capacity∧i < Len0; i++)

 6:     Data0[i] = 0;
 7:     Data1[i] = 0;
 8:   StructA = Set_Struct(StructA)
 9:   if(capacity > Len0)
10:     return 0;
11:   return 1;
```

(b) V_1

```
 1: struct_A * Set_Struct(struct_A * st)
 2:   if(st == NULL)
 3:     return newStructA();
 4:   else
 5:     return ClearContents(st);
```

(c) the Set_Struct function

Fig. 4. Two related versions of Init_Data that are functionally equivalent

Data1 into the upper for loop. The two versions of Init_Data in Figure 4 are functionally equivalent; given same value of capacity, both implementations produce the same output, i.e., return the same value, and Data0, Data1, and StructA will point to the same initialized memory[1].

The edits to the refactored program version in Figure 4 are related to statements that access and edit the array Data1 and the constant Len1. These edits, however, do not impact the program statements that reference the data structure StructA and Data0. First, let us consider the accesses to StructA (via st in function Set_Struct); these are completely disjoint from the operations related to Data1 and Len1. Hence, the program behaviors related to the operations on st in this context are not impacted by the changes. The constraints related to StructA and st generated at line 10 in V_0 and line 8 in V_1 of function Init_Data and at lines 2 − 5 in function Set_Struct are unimpacted and can safely be discarded from the full summaries before checking equivalence. Now, consider the accesses to Data0 and its interactions with accesses to Data1. Although the assignments to both Data0 and Data1 are control dependent on the for loop at line 6, in the context of V_0, the assignment to Data0 is not impacted by the changes. Consequently, the constraints on Data0 at line 7 can also be discarded before checking equivalence. Moreover, functional equivalence of V_0 and V_1 in Figure 4 can be proven using impact summaries that do not contain constraints over Data0, StructA, or st.

The arrays Data0 and Data1, the pointer to StructA, and the input variable capacity are defined as symbolic in this example. In Figure 5(a) we show a

---

[1] We make no claims about the initialized memory's location (the value of the pointers), only the contents of the memory.

$(i_0 = 0) \wedge (i_0 < capacity) \wedge (i_0 < 512) \wedge (Data0\,[i_0] = 0) \wedge (Data1\,[i_0] = 0) \wedge$
$(i_1 = 1) \wedge (i_1 < capacity) \wedge (i_1 < 512) \wedge (Data0\,[i_1] = 0) \wedge (Data1\,[i_1] = 0) \wedge$

$\ldots$

$(i_{511} = 511) \wedge (i_{511} < capacity) \wedge (i_{511} < 512) \wedge (Data0\,[i_{511}] = 0) \wedge (Data1\,[i_{511}] = 0) \wedge$
$st = 0 \wedge st = objRef \wedge$
$StructA = st \wedge capacity <= 512 \wedge ret = 1$

(a)

$(i_0 = 0) \wedge (i_0 < capacity) \wedge (i_0 < 512) \wedge (Data1\,[i_0] = 0) \wedge$
$(i_1 = 1) \wedge (i_1 < capacity) \wedge (i_1 < 512) \wedge (Data1\,[i_1] = 0) \wedge$

$\ldots$

$(i_{511} = 511) \wedge (i_{511} < capacity) \wedge (i_{511} < 512) \wedge (Data1\,[i_{511}] = 0) \wedge$
$capacity <= 512 \wedge ret = 1$

(b)

Fig. 5. (a) A conjunction of an unimpacted and impacted constraints along path i in V_1: $I_i^1 \bigwedge U_i^1$. (b) An impacted constraint along path i in V_1: I_i^1.

summary for the path in program V_1 shown in Figure 4(b) that contains both impacted and unimpacted constraints. There are 512 iterations of the for loop that are encoded in the path using the loop index i, and there are constraints over StructA, st, and capacity as well. In contrast, Figure 5(b) contains only the set of impacted constraints from the same path. From this example, we can see that discarding unimpacted constraints can dramatically reduce the size of the summaries used in regression verification.

4   Correctness Proofs

In this section we compare two program versions V_0 and V_1. We eventually show that the equivalence of their respective summaries, sum_0 and sum_1, can be implied by proving the equivalence of $isum_0$ and $isum_1$. Likewise, we show that if $isum_0$ and $isum_1$ are not equivalent, then sum_0 and sum_1 are not equivalent.

To simplify the presentation of our work, we discuss the correctness of the equivalence checking using the intraprocedural change impact analysis. The same correctness argument holds for an interprocedural analysis that dynamically tracks the flow of impact through method parameters and global variables. The change impact analysis described in Section 3 is conservative for sequential programs; it adds every statement that *may* be impacted by a change to the impact sets $\mathbb{I}_0$ and $\mathbb{I}_1$. We argue that the statements that are considered unimpacted by the analysis are not relevant to a proof of equivalence of the program versions.

Lemma 1. *Given closely related program versions V_0 and V_1, if a program statement is common to both versions, then it is either impacted in both versions or unimpacted in both versions.*

Proof. This follows from Steps 5 and 7 of the static impact analysis shown in Table 1 (Section 3). Step 5 assigns $\mathbb{I}_1$ to be equal to $\mathbb{I}_0$ after performing the data- and control-flow analysis on V_0 (except for statements that are removed in V_1 or added in V_0). Then Step 7 adds statements from $\mathbb{I}_1$ to $\mathbb{I}_0$ after performing the data-flow, control-flow, backward control-flow, and reaching definition analysis on V_1 (except for statements added to V_1 or removed from V_0). Therefore, the only statements that differ between $\mathbb{I}_0$ and $\mathbb{I}_1$ are those that have been added or removed.

Next we argue that for every path i in V_0, there exists a path j in V_1 such that i and j contain the same set of unimpacted statements and, similarly, for every path j in V_1, there exists a path i in V_0 such that i and j contain the same set of unimpacted statements.

Lemma 2. *Given closely related program versions V_0 and V_1, for every path $(I_i^0 \wedge U_i^0)$ there exists a path $(I_j^1 \wedge U_j^1)$ such that $U_i^0 \equiv U_j^1$. Likewise, for every path $(I_j^1 \wedge U_j^1)$ there exists a path $(I_i^0 \wedge U_i^0)$ such that $U_j^1 \equiv U_i^0$*

Proof. By contradiction. Assume there is some path containing a certain sequence of unimpacted instructions in one program version but not the other. This implies that the result of some conditional statement S_c differs between the two versions and that the set of unimpacted instructions is control dependent on S_c. Clearly the predicate in S_c uses the result of an impacted write statement or S_c is control dependent on another impacted conditional statement. According to Rules (1) – (4) in Table 1, S_c is impacted. Furthermore, because the unimpacted statements are control dependent on S_c, they are also impacted.

Corollary 1. *The set of* unique *unimpacted constraints in V_0 is the same as the set of* unique *unimpacted constraints in V_1. This implies Formula 2*

$$(\bigvee_{i=1}^{n} U_i^0) \leftrightarrow (\bigvee_{i=1}^{m} U_i^1) \tag{2}$$

As defined in Section 3, a program's symbolic summary consists of the disjunction of the constraints along each possible execution path in the program. Each path consists of a set of impacted and unimpacted constraints. In Theorem 1 we show that the unimpacted and impacted constraints can be effectively *de-coupled* from each other in a program's summary.

Theorem 1. *Given a program version V_0 with n paths, Formula 3 is valid.*

$$\bigvee_{i=1}^{n} (I_i^0 \wedge U_i^0) \leftrightarrow [(\bigvee_{i=1}^{n} I_i^0) \wedge (\bigvee_{i=1}^{n} U_i^0)] \tag{3}$$

Proof. See extended technical report for this proof [1].

In Theorem 2 we consider the overlap between the space of assignments to program variables that satisfy impacted constraints and the space of assignments to program variables that satisfy unimpacted constraints. Specifically, we claim that for some path in a program summary, if there is some concrete assignment to the program variables that satisfies the impacted constraints, then there is a concrete assignment to the remaining variables (those only present in the unimpacted constraints) that satisfies the unimpacted constraints.

Theorem 2. *Consider a program version V_0 with n paths and a closely related program version V_1 with m paths. Let $u_1, u_2, \ldots u_k$ be program variables present in the unimpacted statements of V_0 (V_1). Let AU be the set of possible concrete assignments to these variables. Let AI_0 (AI_1) be the set of possible concrete assignments to all other variables in V_0 (V_1). For any assignment $x \in AI_0$ ($x \in AI_1$) that satisfies the impacted constraints, there exists an assignment $y \in AU$ that satisfies the unimpacted constraints. Formally, Formulas 4 and 5 are valid.*

$$\forall_{x \in AI_0} \exists_{y \in AU} (I_i^0[x] \rightarrow U_i^0[y]) \tag{4}$$

$$\forall_{x \in AI_1} \exists_{y \in AU} (I_i^1[x] \rightarrow U_i^1[y]) \tag{5}$$

Proof. Rule (4) in Table 1 dictates that the statements defining the value of every variable used in an impacted statement are also impacted. Accordingly, the variables that are common to the impacted and unimpacted statements are *not constrained* by the unimpacted statements. I.e., the result of an unimpacted statement cannot affect the result of an impacted statement. Therefore, if it is possible to satisfy the constraints of I_i^0 (I_j^1), then it is possible to satisfy the constraints of U_i^0 (U_j^1).

Now we show that the impact summaries for two programs versions V_0 and V_1 are equivalent if and only if the summaries for V_0 and V_1 are equivalent. We use the result of Theorem 1 to prove the forward direction (if the impact summaries are equivalent, then the summaries are equivalent). Then we use the result of Theorem 2 to prove the reverse direction (if the summaries are equivalent, then the impact summaries are equivalent).

Theorem 3. *Given program version V_0 with n paths and a closely related program version V_1 with m paths. $isum_0$ and $isum_1$ are equivalent if and only if sum_0 and sum_1 are equivalent. This is formally stated in Formula 1 and is also shown below.*

$$[(\bigvee_{i=1}^{n} I_i^0) \leftrightarrow (\bigvee_{i=1}^{m} I_i^1)] \leftrightarrow [\bigvee_{i=1}^{n} (I_i^0 \wedge U_i^0) \leftrightarrow \bigvee_{i=1}^{m} (I_i^1 \wedge U_i^1)]$$

Proof. ($\Rightarrow$)We begin by assuming Formula 6 is valid

$$(\bigvee_{i=1}^{n} I_i^0) \leftrightarrow (\bigvee_{i=1}^{m} I_i^1) \tag{6}$$

Conjoining the term representing the disjunction of unimpacted constraints of V_0 to the left and right side of Formula 6 yields Formula 7.

$$(\bigvee_{i=1}^{n} I_i^0) \wedge (\bigvee_{i=1}^{n} U_i^0) \leftrightarrow (\bigvee_{i=1}^{m} I_i^1) \wedge (\bigvee_{i=1}^{n} U_i^0) \tag{7}$$

Applying Formula 2 yields Formula 8.

$$(\bigvee_{i=1}^{n} I_i^0) \wedge (\bigvee_{i=1}^{n} U_i^0) \leftrightarrow (\bigvee_{i=1}^{m} I_i^1) \wedge (\bigvee_{i=1}^{m} U_i^1) \tag{8}$$

Applying Formula 3 yields Formula 9.

$$\bigvee_{i=1}^{n} (I_i^0 \wedge U_i^0) \leftrightarrow \bigvee_{i=1}^{m} (I_i^1 \wedge U_i^1) \tag{9}$$

This proves the forward direction, i.e., $(isum_0 \leftrightarrow isum_1) \rightarrow (sum_0 \leftrightarrow sum_1)$. The latter half of the proof, $(sum_0 \leftrightarrow sum_1) \rightarrow (isum_0 \leftrightarrow isum_1)$, is more complex than the first half and is available in the technical report [1].

5   Evaluation

To empirically evaluate the regression verification technique described in this work, we implemented a DiSE framework, Proteus, for analyzing C programs. Note that the earlier DiSE framework implementation was an extension of the Java PathFinder, [21], toolkit to analyze Java programs [13,17]. A large number of safety critical systems are developed in C; Proteus was developed at NASA to assist in the analysis of these systems.

In Proteus, we use the GNU DiffUtils[2] to compute the initial change set containing the actual source level differences between program versions. The static analysis is implemented as a customized LLVM optimization pass [11]. The output of the static analysis is the set of impacted program statements. The partitioning of constraints during symbolic execution is implemented as an extension to the KLEE symbolic execution engine [4]. As an optimization for discarding unimpacted constraints, we employ the directed search in the DiSE algorithm to prune execution of paths that *differ only* in unimpacted constraints [13,17]. The final post-processing of the symbolic summaries is performed using a custom application that iterates over the impacted path conditions, removing constraints that are not impacted by the differences. We use the Z3 constraint solver to check for logical equivalence of impact summaries [6].

We present the results for the different versions of the six artifacts in Table 2. The details of the artifacts and their versions are described in further detail in the technical report [1]. The experiments are run on a 64-bit Linux machine, with a 2.4GHz processor, and 64GB memory. The Example column lists the

---

[2] http://www.gnu.org/software/diffutils

Table 2. Equivalence Checking Results

Example	Versions	Equiv	Paths		Constraints			Time Symbc (s)		Time Solver (s)		
			Full	iDiSE	Full	iDiSE	iSum	Full	iDiSE	Full	iDiSE	iSum
Init_Data	V0V1	yes	400	400	103400	103400	82800	51.87	50.67	1.94	1.94	0.76
tcas1	V0V1	yes	118	12	4748	524	332	1.62	0.60	0.09	0.04	0.04
	V1V2	yes	118	118	4772	4772	3956	1.64	1.92	0.09	0.09	0.06
	V2V3	yes	118	118	4796	4796	2908	1.62	1.91	0.08	0.08	0.05
tcas2	V0V1	no	150	12	6052	520	328	2.21	0.63	0.12	0.06	0.05
replace1	V0V1	yes	18	8	98	68	48	0.31	0.25	0.01	0.03	0.03
	V1V2	yes	18	10	98	98	78	0.31	0.32	0.01	0.04	0.04
	V2V3	no	18	2	98	8	4	0.31	0.18	0.01	0.03	0.03
replace2	V1V2	yes	604	604	23736	23736	20980	1.14	1.35	0.11	0.11	0.10
wbs1	V0V1	yes	336	190	13416	11478	9158	1.18	1.63	0.10	0.10	0.08
	V1V2	yes	336	336	13416	13416	10784	1.25	1.42	0.10	0.10	0.09
	V2V3	yes	336	190	13416	11478	10784	1.19	1.34	0.11	0.09	0.08
wbs2	V0V1	no	336	134	13388	5601	4551	1.18	0.83	0.11	0.06	0.06
cornell1	V0V1	yes	10	8	62	48	24	0.10	0.11	0.03	0.03	0.03
cornell2	V0V1	yes	18	10	1864	810	663	0.27	0.29	0.01	0.01	0.01
kernel1	V0V1	yes	-	4	-	282	226	-	21.09	-	218	200
	V1V2	yes	-	4	-	282	226	-	21.32	-	211	208
kernel2	V0V1	yes	4	2	130	114	88	1.56	1.92	0.20	0.13	0.04
kernel3	V0V1	no	4	2	118	58	48	0.67	0.78	0.19	0.12	0.12

name of the artifact and the `Versions` column lists the version numbers of the
artifacts compared. The `Equiv` column shows whether the versions are equivalent or not. The results contain data from three different configurations: (1)
`Full` symbolic execution explores all paths, (2) `iDiSE` prunes paths that only
differ in unimpacted constraints (iDiSE refers to the interprcoedural extension
of the DiSE framework as defined in [17]), and (3) `iSum` represents the final impact summaries. The `Paths` column lists the number of paths, the `Constraints`
column presents the number of constraints in the summaries, and `Time Symbc`
column lists the time in seconds. The time reported for iDiSE includes the time
to perform the static analysis and incremental symbolic execution. Finally, the
`Time Solver` column lists the time taken by Z3 to solve the equivalence queries
generated by full symbolic execution, iDiSE, and iSum. The rows marked with
'-' indicate that the analysis does not finish within the time bound of one hour.

Overall, the results in Table 2 indicate that reducing the size of the queries
reduces the time to check equivalence. In the `tcas2` example, full symbolic execution generates 150 paths while iDiSE only generates 12 paths and we can
see corresponding reductions in the number of constraints and time taken to
check equivalence. The iDiSE overhead for the set of artifacts is quite small,
and the total analysis time (Symbc + Solver) can be considerably less for iDiSE
combined with constraint pruning over full symbolic execution. In the two versions of the `kernel1` example, full symbolic execution is unable to complete the
analysis within the time bound of one hour, while only four paths are generated by iDiSE. There is a loop in `kernel1` that does not contain any impacted

Table 3. Evaulation of artifacts using SymDiff

Example	Modular (s)	Non-modular (s)	Example	Modular (s)	Non-modular (s)
tcas1V0V1	12.9	17.4	tcas1V2V3	13.6	15
tcas1V1V2	13.6	15	tcas2V0V1	14.3	18.2
wbs1V0V1	13.8	13.8	wbs1V2V3	13.7	14.1
wbs1V0V2	13.8	13.8	wbs2V0V1	14.6	14.4
replace2 V1V2	31.9	29:53.2			

statements; iDiSE is able to ignore paths through the loop and quickly generate the impact summaries. For this example, we can see how leveraging program similarities can dramatically improve the performance of regression verification. Although the time taken for equivalence checking for the other examples is relatively small – just a few seconds – the artifacts themselves are relatively small. We believe that the reductions will be applicable to larger examples as well. For the **replace** example, the solver time for the summaries without pruning is much faster than those with pruning. The tool we used to translate the CVC formula generated by KLEE into SMTLIB format (to be interpreted by Z3) parsed the CVC query into a trivial SMTLIB query for these examples. It is unclear to us why this occurred with the full summaries but not the impact summaries.

Limitations. The regression verification technique presented in this work currently supports checking equivalence between two sequential programs without exceptional flow. The equivalence checking reports generated by Proteus are sound and complete for programs that do not have runtime errors or make calls to unsupported libraries. For examples that have runtime errors or make calls to unsupported libraries, the tool reports warnings and continues execution; the equivalence result are reported as inconclusive in the presence of such warnings. The sound and complete reasoning about the equivalence is with respect to a loop bound. It is possible to leverage automatic loop invariant generation and loop summarization techniques in the context of symbolic execution to reason about equivalent programs without a depth bound.

6   Discussion

Revisiting Table 2, the data in the **Full** columns can be considered representative of results in UC-KLEE [15]. The results demonstrate that UC-KLEE can benefit from using our reduction techniques, when analyzing related program versions.

In order to evaluate how other tools perform equivalence checking, we ran SymDiff [10]. We set up the experiments for SymDiff and ran them on a Windows 7 machine with a 1.8 GHz processor and 6 GB of RAM. We experimented with two SymDiff configurations (a) modular, where the methods are summarized as uninterpreted functions, and (b) non-modular, where the invocations to the different methods are inlined. The non-modular approach is sound and complete with respect to a depth-bound as well. The **kernel** and the **cornell** examples contain constructs that are not currently supported by the C front-end in the current version of SymDiff, so we report on experiments for the rest of the examples. Table 3 shows the total wall clock time in seconds. In the modular approach, SymDiff does not report any false negatives for the examples shown in Table 3. We used a loop bound of four for the `replace` example, the same as the one used in Table 2. We also used the flag in Symdiff to analyze only callers and callees that are reachable from the changed methods to ensure that the set of methods analyzed by SymDiff and Proteus is the same. SymDiff runs on a Windows platform while Proteus runs on a Unix-based platform; we had to run the experiments on different machines and it is not possible to make empirical comparative claims between the two in terms of time. Furthermore, SymDiff and Proteus encode the program behaviors differently, therefore, it is not possible to compare the approaches in terms of the size of the generated formulas. SymDiff does not use any slicing techniques based on change impact analysis, and we believe that it can be beneficial to add such a reduction technique to SymDiff.

Abstract Syntax Tree. To calculate the precise initial change sets we can use standard algorithms to match Abstract Syntax Trees (ASTs), [14], and discard differences due to variable renaming and simple re-ordering before we perform the data and control flow analysis. The syntatic differences based on the ASTs are more precise compared to those generated by the GNU DiffUtils. We have support for the AST based syntatic diff in the Java implementation of the DiSE framework and we are currently working on adding it to Proteus.

Static Encoding vs. Bounded Unrolled Program Encoding. The correctness of Eq. (1) does not rely on any specific encoding of constraints. We choose, however, to encode the program behaviors generated by symbolic execution (bounded unrolled programs) as constraints rather than use a static encoding for the constraints because (a) the static constraints on heap and array operations are often harder to solve than those generated by symbolic execution and (b) scalable static slicing techniques for interprocedural programs often ignore calling context and are imprecise; we leverage work in [17] to dynamically compute impact information for interprocedural programs.

7   Related Work

Several techniques have been developed for checking equivalence. Differential Symbolic Execution (DSE) uses uninterpreted functions to represent unchanged blocks of code [12]. SymDiff [10] summarizes methods as uninterpreted functions, and uses verification conditions to summarize observable behavioral differences. Regression verification techniques by Strichman et al. [8,19] use the Context-Bounded Model Checker (CBMC) to check equivalence of closely related C programs. It establishes partial equivalence of functions using a bottom-up decomposition algorithm. Another approach [18] performs an increment upgrade checking in a bottom-up manner similar to regression verification, using function summaries computed by means of Craig interpolation. These techniques are sound but not complete. Techniques from [18] are used in the PINCETTE project [5]. To curb over-approximations, the PINCETTE project also employs dynamic techniques (e.g., concolic testing) to generate regression tests for system upgrades. There is also ongoing work to support program slicing based on the program differences in CBMC.

Similar to our work, UC-KLEE [15] is built on top of KLEE. UC-KLEE is designed to run two functions under test with the same input values and check if they produce the same outputs. As an optimization, UC-KLEE is able to skip unchanged instructions. However, it neither produces nor leverages the impacted behavior information. Partition-based regression verification, [3], computes partitions on-the-fly using concolic execution and dynamic slicing techniques. Each partition contains behaviors generated from a subset of the input space common to two program versions. The goal of the technique is to find test cases that depict semantic differences rather than prove equivalence.

Approaches that cache or reuse constraints to speed up performance (e.g., Green [20]) are orthogonal to our reduction technique. Such techniques are complementary to this work and can be leveraged to achieve higher reduction factors.

8   Conclusions and Future Work

In this work on regression verification we leverage control- and data-flow information to partition the program behavior summaries as either impacted or unimpacted based on the differences between two program versions. We then prove that the impacted constraints of two closely related programs are functionally equivalent iff their entire program behavior summarizations are functionally equivalent. An empirical evaluation on a set of sequential C artifacts shows that reducing the size of the summaries helps reduce the cost of equivalence checking.

In future work, we plan to study the effects of other more compact program summarization encoding schemes such as large-block encoding [2] in combination with the work proposed here. Another avenue of future work is to develop an abstraction-refinement technique using uninterpreted functions to abstract large parts of the program as done in [12,19], but, use the information about the impacted parts of the code to refine the abstraction when required. We believe such techniques can further improve checking equivalence of large programs.

Acknowlegements. We thank Shuvendu Lahiri at Microsoft Research for his help with SymDiff.

References

1. Backes, J., Person, S., Rungta, N., Tkachuk, O.: Regression verification using impact summaries (2013), Extended version available online
   http://ti.arc.nasa.gov/profile/nrungta/pubs/
2. Beyer, D., Cimatti, A., Griggio, A., Keremoglu, M., Sebastiani, R.: Software model checking via large-block encoding. In: FMCAD, pp. 25–32 (November 2009)

3. Boehme, M., Oliveira, B.C.d.S., Roychoudhury, A.: Partition-based regression verification. In: ICSE (2013)
4. Cadar, C., Dunbar, D., Engler, D.R.: Klee: Unassisted and automatic generation of high-coverage tests for complex systems programs. In: OSDI, pp. 209–224 (2008)
5. Chockler, H., Denaro, G., Ling, M., Fedyukovich, G., Hyvrinen, A.E.J., Mariani, L., Muhammad, A., Oriol, M., Rajan, A., Sery, O., Sharygina, N., Tautschnig, M.: Pincette – validating changes and upgrades in networked software. In: CSMR (2013)
6. de Moura, L., Bjørner, N.: Z3: An efficient SMT solver. In: Ramakrishnan, C.R., Rehof, J. (eds.) TACAS 2008. LNCS, vol. 4963, pp. 337–340. Springer, Heidelberg (2008)
7. Ganesh, V., Dill, D.L.: A decision procedure for bit-vectors and arrays. In: Damm, W., Hermanns, H. (eds.) CAV 2007. LNCS, vol. 4590, pp. 519–531. Springer, Heidelberg (2007)
8. Godlin, B., Strichman, O.: Regression verification. In: DAC (2009)
9. Kroening, D., Strichman, O.: Decision Procedures: An Algorithmic Point of View. Springer Publishing Company, Incorporated (2008)
10. Lahiri, S.K., Hawblitzel, C., Kawaguchi, M., Rebêlo, H.: SYMDIFF: A language-agnostic semantic diff tool for imperative programs. In: Madhusudan, P., Seshia, S.A. (eds.) CAV 2012. LNCS, vol. 7358, pp. 712–717. Springer, Heidelberg (2012)
11. Lattner, C., Adve, V.: LLVM: A Compilation Framework for Lifelong Program Analysis & Transformation. In: CGO (2004)
12. Person, S., Dwyer, M.B., Elbaum, S., Păsăreanu, C.S.: Differential symbolic execution. In: FSE, pp. 226–237 (2008)
13. Person, S., Yang, G., Rungta, N., Khurshid, S.: Directed incremental symbolic execution. In: PLDI, pp. 504–515 (2011)
14. Raghavan, S., Rohana, R., Leon, D., Podgurski, A., Augustine, V.: Dex: a semantic-graph differencing tool for studying changes in large code bases. In: ICSM, pp. 188–197 (2004)
15. Ramos, D.A., Engler, D.R.: Practical, low-effort equivalence verification of real code. In: Gopalakrishnan, G., Qadeer, S. (eds.) CAV 2011. LNCS, vol. 6806, pp. 669–685. Springer, Heidelberg (2011)
16. Rothermel, G., Harrold, M.J.: A safe, efficient regression test selection technique. ACM TOSEM, 173–210 (1997)
17. Rungta, N., Person, S., Branchaud, J.: A change impact analysis to characterize evolving program behaviors. In: ICSM (2012)
18. Sery, O., Fedyukovich, G., Sharygina, N.: Incremental upgrade checking by means of interpolation-based function summaries. In: FMCAD, UK (2012)
19. Strichman, O., Godlin, B.: Regression Verification - A Practical Way to Verify Programs. In: Meyer, B., Woodcock, J. (eds.) VSTTE 2005. LNCS, vol. 4171, pp. 496–501. Springer, Heidelberg (2008)
20. Visser, W., Geldenhuys, J., Dwyer, M.B.: Green: reducing, reusing and recycling constraints in program analysis. In: SIGSOFT FSE, p. 58 (2012)
21. Visser, W., Havelund, K., Brat, G.P., Park, S., Lerda, F.: Model checking programs. ASE 10(2), 203–232 (2003)
22. Yang, G., Dwyer, M.B., Rothermel, G.: Regression model checking. In: ICSM, pp. 115–124 (2009)

Abstraction-Based Guided Search
for Hybrid Systems

Sergiy Bogomolov[1], Alexandre Donzé[2], Goran Frehse[3], Radu Grosu[4],
Taylor T. Johnson[5], Hamed Ladan[1], Andreas Podelski[1], and Martin Wehrle[6]

[1] University of Freiburg, Germany
{bogom,ladanh,podelski}@informatik.uni-freiburg.de
[2] University of California, Berkeley, USA
donze@eecs.berkeley.edu
[3] Université Joseph Fourier Grenoble 1 – Verimag, France
goran.frehse@imag.fr
[4] Vienna University of Technology, Austria
radu.grosu@tuwien.ac.at
[5] University of Illinois at Urbana-Champaign, USA
taylor.johnson@gmail.com
[6] University of Basel, Switzerland
martin.wehrle@unibas.ch

Abstract. Hybrid systems represent an important and powerful formalism for modeling real-world applications such as embedded systems. A verification tool like SpaceEx is based on the exploration of a symbolic search space (the *region space*). As a verification tool, it is typically optimized towards proving the absence of errors. In some settings, e.g., when the verification tool is employed in a feedback-directed design cycle, one would like to have the option to call a version that is optimized towards finding an error path in the region space. A recent approach in this direction is based on *guided search*. Guided search relies on a cost function that indicates which states are promising to be explored, and preferably explores more promising states first. In this paper, an abstraction-based cost function based on *pattern databases* for guiding the reachability analysis is proposed. For this purpose, a suitable abstraction technique that exploits the flexible granularity of modern reachability analysis algorithms is introduced. The new cost function is an effective extension of pattern database approaches that have been successfully applied in other areas. The approach has been implemented in the SpaceEx model checker. The evaluation shows its practical potential.

1 Introduction

Hybrid systems are extended finite automata whose discrete states correspond to the various modes of continuous dynamics a system may exhibit, and whose transitions express the switching logic between these modes [1]. Hybrid systems have been used to model and to analyze various types of embedded systems [23,28,13,7,14,4,24].

E. Bartocci and C.R. Ramakrishnan (Eds.): SPIN 2013, LNCS 7976, pp. 117–134, 2013.
© Springer-Verlag Berlin Heidelberg 2013

A hybrid system is considered safe if a given set of bad states cannot be reached from the initial states. Hence, reachability analysis is a main concern for hybrid systems. Since the reachability analysis of hybrid systems is in general undecidable [1], modern reachability-analysis tools such as SpaceEx [16] resort to semi-decision procedures based on over-approximation techniques [10,16]. In this paper, we explore the utility of guided search in order to improve the efficiency of such techniques.

Guided search is an approach that has recently found much attention for finding errors in large systems [21,9]. As suggested by the name, guided search performs a search in the state space of a given system. In contrast to standard search methods like breadth-first or depth-first search, the search is guided by a cost function that estimates the search effort to reach an error state from the current state. This information is exploited by preferably exploring states with lower estimated costs. If accurate cost functions are applied, the search effort can significantly be reduced compared to uninformed search. Obviously, the cost function therefore plays a key role within the setting of guided search, as it should be as accurate as possible on the one hand, and as cheap to compute as possible on the other. Cost functions that have been proposed in the literature are mostly based on *abstractions* of the original system. An important class of abstraction-based cost functions is based on *pattern databases (PDBs)*. PDBs have originally been proposed in the area of Artificial Intelligence [11] and also have successfully been applied to model checking discrete and timed systems [26]. Roughly speaking, a PDB is a data structure that contains abstract states together with abstract cost values based on an abstraction of the original system. During the concrete search, concrete states s are mapped to corresponding abstract states in the PDB, and the corresponding abstract cost values are used to estimate the costs of s. Overall, PDBs have demonstrated to be powerful for finding errors in different formalisms. The open question is if guided search can be applied equally successfully to finding errors in hybrid systems.

A first approach in this direction [9] is to estimate the cost of a symbolic state based on the Euclidean distance from its continuous part to a given set of error states. This approach appears to be best suited for systems which behavior is strongly influenced by the (continuous) differential equations. However, it suffers from the fact that discrete information like mode switches is completely ignored, which can lead to arbitrary degeneration of the search. To see this, consider the example presented in Fig. 1. It shows a simple hybrid system with one continuous variable which obeys the differential equation $\dot{x} = 1$ in every location (differential equations are omitted in the figure). The error states are given by the locations $l_{e1}, \ldots, l_{en}$ and invariants $0 \leq x \leq 8$. In this example, the box-based distance heuristic wrongly explores the whole lower branch first (where no error state is reachable) because it only relies on the continuous information given by the invariants. More precisely, for the box-based distance heuristic, the invariants suggest that the costs of the "lower" states are equal to 0, whereas the costs of the "upper" states are estimated to be equal to 4 (i.e., equal to the distance of the centers of the bounding boxes of the invariants).

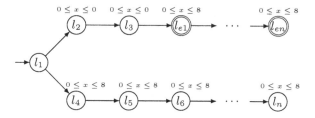

Fig. 1. A motivating example

In this paper, we introduce a PDB-based cost function for hybrid systems to overcome these limitations. In contrast to the box-based approach based on Euclidean distances, this cost function is also able to properly reflect the discrete part of the system. However, compared to the "classical" discrete setting, the investigation of PDBs for hybrid systems becomes more difficult for several reasons. First, hybrid systems typically feature both discrete and continuous variables with complex dependencies and interactions. Therefore, the question arises how to compute a suitable (accurate) abstraction of the original system. Second, computations for symbolic successors and inclusion checks become more expensive than for discrete or timed systems – can these computations be performed or approximated efficiently to get an overall efficient PDB approach as well? In this paper, we provide answers to these questions, leading to an efficient guided search approach for hybrid systems. In particular, we introduce a technique leveraging properties of the set representations used in modern reachability algorithms. By simply using much coarser parameters for the explicit representation, we obtain suitable and cheap abstractions for the behaviors of a given hybrid system. Furthermore, we adapt the idea of *partial* PDBs, which has been originally proposed for solving discrete search problems [5], to the setting of hybrid systems in order to reduce the size and computation time of "classical" PDBs. Our implementation in the SpaceEx tool [16] shows the practical potential.

The remainder of the paper is organized as follows. After introducing the necessary background for this work in Sec. 2, we present our PDB approach for hybrid systems in Sec. 3. This is followed by a discussion about related work in Sec. 4. Afterwards, we present our experimental evaluation in Sec. 5. Finally, we conclude the paper in Sec. 6.

2   Preliminaries

In this section, we introduce the preliminaries that are needed for this work.

2.1   Notations

We consider models that can be represented by hybrid systems. A hybrid system is formally defined as follows.

Definition 1 (Hybrid System). *A* hybrid system *is a tuple* $\mathcal{H}$ = (*Loc, Var, Init, Flow, Trans, Inv*) *defining*

- *the finite set of locations Loc,*
- *the set of continuous variables* $Var = \{x_1, \ldots, x_n\}$ *from* $\mathbb{R}^n$,
- *the initial condition, given by the constraint* $Init(\ell) \subset \mathbb{R}^n$ *for each location* ℓ,
- *for each location* ℓ, *a relation called* $Flow(\ell)$ *over the variables and their derivatives. We assume* $Flow(\ell)$ *to be of the form*

$$\dot{x}(t) = Ax(t) + u(t), u(t) \in \mathcal{U},$$

  where $x(t) \in \mathbb{R}^n$, *A is a real-valued* $n \times n$ *matrix and* $\mathcal{U} \subseteq \mathbb{R}^n$ *is a closed and bounded convex set,*
- *the discrete transition relation, given by a set Trans of discrete transitions; a discrete transition is formally defined as a tuple* (ℓ, g, ξ, ℓ') *defining*
  - *the source location* ℓ *and the target location* ℓ',
  - *the guard, given by a linear constraint g,*
  - *the update, given by an affine mapping* ξ, *and*
- *the invariant* $Inv(\ell) \subset \mathbb{R}^n$ *for each location* ℓ.

The semantics of a hybrid system $\mathcal{H}$ is defined as follows. A *state* of $\mathcal{H}$ is a tuple $(\ell, \mathbf{x})$, which consists of a location $\ell \in Loc$ and a point $\mathbf{x} \in \mathbb{R}^n$. More formally, $\mathbf{x}$ is a valuation of the continuous variables in *Var*. For the following definitions, let $\mathcal{T} = [0, \Delta]$ be an interval for some $\Delta \geq 0$. A *trajectory* of $\mathcal{H}$ from state $s = (\ell, \mathbf{x})$ to state $s' = (\ell', \mathbf{x}')$ is defined by a tuple $\rho = (L, \mathbf{X})$, where $L : \mathcal{T} \rightarrow Loc$ and $\mathbf{X} : \mathcal{T} \rightarrow \mathbb{R}^n$ are functions that define for each time point in $\mathcal{T}$ the location and values of the continuous variables, respectively. Furthermore, we will use the following terminology for a given trajectory ρ. A sequence of time points where location switches happen in ρ is denoted by $(\tau_i)_{i=0\ldots k} \in \mathcal{T}^{k+1}$. In this case, we define the *length* of ρ as $|\tau| = k$. Trajectories $\rho = (L, \mathbf{X})$ (and the corresponding sequence $(\tau_i)_{i=0\ldots k}$) have to satisfy the following conditions:

- $\tau_0 = 0$, $\tau_i < \tau_{i+1}$, and $\tau_k = \Delta$ – the sequence of switching points increases, starts with 0 and ends with Δ
- $L(0) = \ell$, $\mathbf{X}(0) = \mathbf{x}$, $L(\Delta) = \ell'$, $\mathbf{X}(\Delta) = \mathbf{x}'$ – the trajectory starts in $s = (\ell, \mathbf{x})$ and ends in $s' = (\ell', \mathbf{x}')$
- $\forall i \; \forall t \in [\tau_i, \tau_{i+1}) : L(t) = L(\tau_i)$ – the location is not changed during the continuous evolution
- $\forall i \; \forall t \in [\tau_i, \tau_{i+1}) : (\mathbf{X}(t), \dot{\mathbf{X}}(t)) \in Flow(L(\tau_i))$, i.e. $\dot{\mathbf{X}}(t) = A\mathbf{X}(t) + u(t)$ holds and thus the continuous evolution is consistent with the differential equations of the corresponding location
- $\forall i \; \forall t \in [\tau_i, \tau_{i+1}) : \mathbf{X}(t) \in Inv(L(\tau_i))$ – the continuous evolution is consistent with the corresponding invariants
- $\forall i \; \exists (L(\tau_i), g, \xi, L(\tau_{i+1})) \in Trans : \mathbf{X}_{end}(i) = \lim_{\tau \to \tau_{i+1}^-} \mathbf{X}(\tau) \wedge \mathbf{X}_{end}(i) \in g \wedge \mathbf{X}(\tau_{i+1}) = \xi(\mathbf{X}_{end}(i))$ – every continuous transition is followed by a discrete

one, $\mathbf{X}_{end}(i)$ defines the values of continuous variables right before the discrete transition at the time moment τ_{i+1} whereas $\mathbf{X}_{start}(i) = \mathbf{X}(\tau_i)$ denotes the values of continuous variables right after the switch at the time moment τ_i.

A state s' is *reachable* from state s if there exists a trajectory from s to s'.

In the following, we mostly refer to *symbolic states*. A symbolic state $s = (\ell, R)$ is defined as a tuple, where $\ell \in Loc$, and R is a convex and bounded set consisting of points $\mathbf{x} \in \mathbb{R}^n$. The continuous part R of a symbolic state is also called *region*. The symbolic state space of $\mathcal{H}$ is called the *region space*. The initial set of states S_{init} of $\mathcal{H}$ is defined as $\bigcup_\ell (\ell, Init(\ell))$. The reachable state space $\mathcal{R}(\mathcal{H})$ of $\mathcal{H}$ is defined as the set of symbolic states that are reachable from an initial state in S_{init}, where the definition of reachability is extended accordingly for symbolic states.

In this paper, we assume there is a given set of symbolic bad states S_{bad} that violate a given property. Our goal is to find a sequence of symbolic states which contains a trajectory from S_{init} to a symbolic *error state*, where a symbolic error state s_e has the property that there is a symbolic bad state in S_{bad} that agrees with s_e on the discrete part, and that has a non-empty intersection with s_e on the continuous part. A trajectory that starts in a symbolic state s and leads to a symbolic error state is called an *error trajectory* $\rho_e(s)$.

2.2 Guided Search

In this section, we introduce a guided search algorithm (Algorithm 1) along the lines of the reachability algorithm used by the current version of SpaceEx [16]. It works on the region space of a given hybrid system. The algorithm checks if a symbolic error state is reachable from a given set of initial symbolic states S_{init}. As outlined above, we define a symbolic state s_e in the region space of $\mathcal{H}$ to be a symbolic error state if there is a symbolic state $s \in S_{bad}$ such that s and s_e agree on their discrete part, and the intersection of the regions of s and s_e is not empty (in other words, the error states are defined with respect to the given set of bad states). Starting with the set of initial symbolic states from S_{init}, the algorithm explores the region space of a given hybrid system by iteratively computing symbolic successor states until an error state is found, no more states remain to be considered, or a (given) maximum number of iterations i_{max} is reached. The exploration of the region space is guided by the *cost* function such that symbolic states with lower cost values are considered first.

In the following, we provide a conceptual description of the algorithm using the following terminology. A symbolic state s' is called a symbolic *successor state* of a symbolic state s if s' is obtained from s by first computing the continuous successor of s, and then by computing a discrete successor state of the resulting (intermediate) state. Therefore, for a given symbolic state s_{curr}, the function CONTINUOUSSUCCESSOR (line 7) returns the symbolic state which is reachable from s_{curr} within the given time horizon according to the continuous evolution

---

Algorithm 1. A guided reachability algorithm

Input: Set of initial symbolic states S_{init}, set of symbolic bad states S_{bad}, cost function
    $cost$
Output: Can a symbolic error state be reached from a symbolic state in S_{init} ?
1: compute $cost(s)$ for all $s \in S_{init}$
2: PUSH $(\mathcal{L}_{waiting}, \{(s, cost(s)) \mid s \in S_{init}\})$
3: $i := 0$
4: **while** $(\mathcal{L}_{waiting} \neq \emptyset \wedge i < i_{max})$ **do**
5:    $s_{curr} :=$ GETNEXT $(\mathcal{L}_{waiting})$
6:    $i := i + 1$
7:    $s'_{curr} :=$ CONTINUOUSSUCCESSOR(s_{curr})
8:    **if** s'_{curr} is a symbolic error state **then**
9:       return "Error state reached"
10:   **end if**
11:   PUSH $(\mathcal{L}_{passed}, s'_{curr})$
12:   $S' :=$ DISCRETESUCCESSORS(s'_{curr})
13:   **for all** $s' \in S'$ **do**
14:     **if** $s' \notin \mathcal{L}_{passed}$ **then**
15:       compute $cost(s')$
16:       PUSH $(\mathcal{L}_{waiting}, (s', cost(s')))$
17:     **end if**
18:   **end for**
19: **end while**
20: **if** $i = i_{max}$ **then**
21:   return "Maximal number of iterations reached"
22: **else**
23:   return "Error state not reachable"
24: **end if**

---

described by the differential equations. Accordingly, the function DISCRETESUC-CESSOR (line 12) returns the symbolic state that is reachable due to the outgoing discrete transitions.

A symbolic state s is called *explored* if its symbolic successor states have been computed. A symbolic state s is called *visited* if s has been computed but not yet necessarily explored. To handle encountered states, the algorithm maintains the data structures $\mathcal{L}_{passed}$ and $\mathcal{L}_{waiting}$. $\mathcal{L}_{passed}$ is a list containing symbolic states that are already explored; this list is used to avoid exploring cycles in the region space. $\mathcal{L}_{waiting}$ is a priority queue that contains visited symbolic states together with their cost values that are candidates to be explored next. The algorithm is initialized by computing the cost values for the initial symbolic states and pushing them accordingly into $\mathcal{L}_{waiting}$ (lines 1 – 2). The main loop iteratively considers a best symbolic state s_{curr} from $\mathcal{L}_{waiting}$ according to the cost function (line 5), computes its symbolic continuous successor state s'_{curr} (line 7), and checks if s'_{curr} is a symbolic error state (lines 8 – 10). (Recall that s'_{curr} is defined as a symbolic error state if there is a symbolic bad state $s \in S_{bad}$ such that s and s'_{curr} agree on their discrete part, and the intersection of the regions of s and s'_{curr} is not empty.) If this is the case, the algorithm terminates. If this is not the case, then s'_{curr} is pushed into $\mathcal{L}_{passed}$ (line 11). Finally, for the resulting symbolic state s'_{curr}, the symbolic discrete successor states are computed, prioritized and pushed into $\mathcal{L}_{waiting}$ if they have not been considered before (lines 12 – 18). Obviously, the search behavior of Algorithm 1 is crucially determined by the cost function that is applied. In the next section, we give a generic description of *pattern database* cost functions.

2.3   General Framework of Pattern Databases

For a given system $\mathcal{S}$, a pattern database (PDB) in the classical sense (i. e., in the sense PDBs have been considered for discrete and timed systems) is represented as a table-like data structure that contains abstract states together with abstract cost values. The PDB is used as a cost estimation function by mapping concrete states s to corresponding abstract states $s^{\#}$ in the PDB, and using the abstract cost value of $s^{\#}$ as an estimation of the cost value of s. The computation of a classical PDB is performed in three steps. First, a subset $\mathcal{P}$ of variables and automata of the original system $\mathcal{S}$ is selected. Such subsets $\mathcal{P}$ are called *pattern*. Second, based on $\mathcal{P}$, an abstraction $\mathcal{S}^{\#}$ is computed that only keeps the variables occurring in $\mathcal{P}$. Third, the entire state space of $\mathcal{S}^{\#}$ is computed and stored in the PDB. More precisely, all reachable abstract states together with their abstract cost values are enumerated and stored. The abstract cost value for an abstract state is defined as the shortest length of a path from that state to an abstract error state. The resulting PDB of these three steps is used as the *cost* function during the execution of Algorithm 1; in other words, the PDB is computed *prior* to the actual model checking process, where the resulting PDB is used as an input for Algorithm 1. In the next section, we will consider this PDB approach as a basis for a cost function for hybrid systems.

3   Pattern Databases for Hybrid Systems

In Sec. 2.3, we have described the general approach for computing and using a PDB for guiding the search. However, for hybrid systems, there are several problems using the classical PDB approach. First, it is not clear how to effectively compute suitable abstractions for hybrid systems with complex variable dependencies. In Sec. 3.1, we address this problem with an abstraction technique based on varying the granularity of the reachability analysis. Second, in Sec. 3.2, we address the general problem that the precomputation of a PDB is often quite expensive. Moreover, in many cases, only a small fraction of the PDB is actually needed for the search [18]. This is undesirable in general, and specifically becomes problematic in the context of hybrid systems because reachability analysis in hybrid systems is typically much more expensive than, e. g., for discrete systems. In Sec. 3.2, we introduce a variant of *partial* PDBs for hybrid systems to address these problems.

3.1 Abstractions Based on Coarse-Grained Space Exploration

A general question in the context of PDBs is how to compute suitable abstractions of a given system. For hybrid systems, one could apply one of the abstraction techniques that have been proposed based on simplifying the dynamics [17,6]. In this paper, we propose a simpler yet elegant way to obtain a coarse grained and fast analysis: For the computation of the PDB, we observe that the LeGuernic-Girard (LGG) algorithm implemented in SpaceEx [16] uses support function representation (based on the chosen set of template directions) to compute and store over-approximations of the reachable states. Therefore, a reduced number of *template directions* and an increased *time step* results in an abstraction of the original region space in the sense that the dependency graph of the reachable abstract symbolic states is a discrete abstraction of the system. The granularity of the resulting abstraction is directly correlated with the parameter selection: Choosing coarser parameters in the reachability algorithm makes this abstraction coarser, whereas finer parameters lead to finer abstractions as well. This is a significant difference compared to the classical approaches that have been proposed in the literature for pattern databases (see Sec. 2.3): Instead of computing a (projection) abstraction based on a *subset* of all variables, we *keep* all variables (and hence, the original system), and instead choose a coarser exploration of the region space.

3.2 Partial Pattern Databases

A classical PDB for a hybrid system $\mathcal{H}$ is represented by a data structure that contains abstract states together with corresponding abstract cost values of a suitable abstraction $\mathcal{H}^{\#}$ of $\mathcal{H}$ (according to Sec. 3.1). The abstract states and corresponding cost values are obtained by a region space exploration of $\mathcal{H}^{\#}$. The abstract cost value of an abstract state $s^{\#}$ is defined as the length of the shortest found trajectory in $\mathcal{H}^{\#}$ from $s^{\#}$ to an abstract error state. The PDB computes the cost function

$$cost^{P}(s) := cost^{\#}(s^{\#}),$$

where s is a symbolic state, $s^{\#}$ is a corresponding abstract state to s in the PDB (see below for a more detailed description of *corresponding abstract state*), and $cost^{\#}$ is the length of the corresponding trajectory from $s^{\#}$ to an abstract error state as defined above. In this context, an abstract state $s^{\#}$ is called a *corresponding* state to s if s and $s^{\#}$ agree on their discrete part, the symbolic part of s is included in the symbolic part of $s^{\#}$, and $s^{\#}$ is an abstract state with minimal abstract costs that satisfies these requirements.

   As already outlined, a general drawback of classical PDBs is the fact that their precomputation might become quite expensive. Even worse, in many cases, most of this precomputation time is often unnecessary because only a small fraction of the PDB is actually needed during the symbolic search in the region space [18]. One way that has been proposed in the literature to overcome this problem is to compute the PDB on demand: So-called *switchback search* maintains a family of abstractions with increasing granularity; these abstractions are used to compute the PDB to guide the search in the next-finer level [22]. In the following, we apply a variant of *partial* PDBs for hybrid systems to address this problem: Instead of computing the whole abstract region space for a given abstraction, we restrict the abstract search to explore only a fraction of the abstract region space while focusing on those abstract states that are likely to be sufficient for the concrete search.

Definition 2 (Partial Pattern Database). *Let $\mathcal{H}$ be a hybrid system. A partial pattern database for $\mathcal{H}$ is a pattern database for $\mathcal{H}$ that contains only abstract state/cost value pairs for abstract states that are part of some trajectory of shortest length from an initial state to an abstract error state. The partial pattern database computes the function*

$$cost^{PP}(s) := \begin{cases} cost^{\#}(s^{\#}) & \text{if there is corresponding } s^{\#} \text{ to } s \\ +\infty & \text{otherwise} \end{cases}$$

where s, $s^{\#}$, and $cost^{\#}$ are defined as above, and $+\infty$ is a default value indicating that no corresponding abstract state to s exists.

Informally, a partial PDB for a hybrid system $\mathcal{H}$ only contains those abstract states of $\mathcal{H}^{\#}$ that are explored on some *shortest* trajectory (instead of containing *all* abstract states of a complete abstract region space exploration to *all* abstract error states as it would be the case for a classical PDB). In other words, partial PDBs are incomplete in the sense that there might exist concrete states with no corresponding abstract state in the PDB. In such cases, the default value $+\infty$ is returned with the intention that corresponding concrete states are only explored if no other states are available. Obviously, this might worsen the overall search guidance compared to the fully computed PDB. However, in special cases, a partial PDB is sufficient to obtain the same cost function as obtained with the original PDB. For example, this is the case when only abstract states are excluded from which no abstract error state is reachable anyway. More generally, a partial PDB suffices to deliver the same *search behavior* as the original PDB if at least one abstract error trace is feasible in the original, i. e., in the concrete region space. The search behavior is defined as the sequence of symbolic states the search algorithm explores.

Proposition 1. *Let $\mathcal{H}$ be a hybrid system. If there is a symbolic abstract error state $s_p = (l, \mathbf{R})$ in the partial PDB such that there is an error state $s = (l, \mathbf{x})$ with $\mathbf{x} \in \mathbf{R}$, where s is reachable in $\mathcal{H}$ from some initial state of $\mathcal{H}$, and the length of a shortest trajectory in $\mathcal{H}$ to reach s is equal to the length of a shortest abstract trajectory to reach s in the partial PDB, then the search behavior of Algorithm 1 with $cost^{PP}$ is equal to the search behavior of Algorithm 1 with $cost^{P}$, i.e., with respect to the fully computed PDB.*

Intuitively, if the preconditions of Prop. 1 are satisfied, then the abstract states in the partial PDB suffice to guide the search in the same way as the fully computed PDB would do (because we never "leave" the partial PDB). If the requirements are not satisfied, we can end up with less accurate cost functions. However, in practice, partial PDBs turn out to be powerful because even if Prop. 1 does not apply, they can often be computed significantly faster than full PDBs, and still contain enough abstract states to accurately guide the search. Overall, although in case the requirements of Prop. 1 are not fulfilled, partial PDBs can still be a good heuristic choice that lead to cost functions that are efficiently computable on the one hand, and that accurately guide the concrete search on the other hand. We will come back to this point in the evaluation section.

3.3   Discussion

Abstraction techniques for verification of hybrid systems have been studied intensively. Our pattern database approach for finding error states is based on a similar idea, but exploits abstractions in a different way than in common approaches for verification. Most notably, the main focus of our abstraction is to provide the basis for the cost function to guide the search, rather than to prove correctness (although, under certain circumstances, it can be efficiently used for verification as well – we will come back to this point in the experiments section). As a short summary of the overall approach, we first compute a symbolic abstract region space (as described in Sec. 3.1), where the encountered symbolic abstract states $s^{\#} = (L^{\#}, R^{\#})$ are stored in a table together with the corresponding abstract cost values of $s^{\#}$. To avoid the (costly) computation of an *entire* PDB, we only compute the PDB partially (as described in Sec. 3.2). This partial PDB is then used as the cost function of our guided reachability algorithm. As in many other approaches that apply abstraction techniques to reason about hybrid systems, the abstraction that is used for the PDB is supposed to accurately reflect the "important" behavior of the system, which results in accurate search guidance of the resulting cost function and hence, of our guided reachability algorithm.

An essential feature of the PDB-based cost function is the ability to reflect the continuous *and* the discrete part of the system. To make this more clear, consider again the motivating example from the introduction (Fig. 1). As we have discussed already, the box-based distance function first wrongly explores the whole lower branch of this system because no discrete information is used to guide the search. In contrast, a partial PDB is also able to reflect the discrete behavior of the system. In this example, the partial PDB consists of an abstract trajectory to the first reachable error state, which is already sufficient to guide the (concrete) region space exploration towards to first reachable error state as well. In particular, this example clearly shows the advantage of partial PDBs compared to fully computed PDBs (recall that fully computed PDBs would include *all* error states, whereas the partial PDB only contains the trajectory to the shortest one). In general, our PDB-approach is well suited for hybrid systems with a non-trivial amount of discrete behavior. However, the continuous behavior is still considered according to our abstraction technique as introduced in Sec. 3.1. Overall, partial PDBs appear to be an accurate approach for guided search because they accurately balance the computation time for the cost function on the one hand, and lead to efficient and still accurately informed cost functions on the other hand.

Finally, let us discuss the relationship of PDBs to counterexample-guided abstraction refinement (CEGAR) [3,2]. Our approach shares with CEGAR the general idea of using an abstraction to analyze a concrete system. However, in contrast to CEGAR, where abstract counterexamples have to be validated and possibly used in further abstraction refinement, abstractions for PDBs are never refined and only used as a heuristic to *guide* the search within the concrete automaton. In other words, in contrast to CEGAR, the accuracy of the abstraction influences the *order* in which concrete states are explored and therefore the *performance* of the resulting model checking algorithm. Therefore, a crucial difference lies in the fact that CEGAR does the search in the abstract space, replays the counterexample in the concrete space, and stops if the error path cannot be followed. In contrast, our approach does the search in the concrete space and uses the PDBs for guidance, only. If an abstract path cannot be followed, the search does not stop, but tries other branches until either a counterexample is found, or all paths have been exhausted.

4   Related Work

Techniques to efficiently find error states in faulty hybrid systems have recently found increasing attention in the hybrid systems community. Bhatia and Frazzoli [8] propose using rapidly exploring random trees (RRTs). In the context of hybrid systems, the objective of a basic RRTs approach is to efficiently cover the region space in an "equidistant" way in order to avoid getting stuck in some part of the region space. Recently, RRTs were extended by adding guidance of the input stimulus generation [12]. However, in contrast to our approach, RRTs approaches are based on numeric simulations, rather than symbolic executions. Applying PDBs to RRTs would be an interesting direction for future work. In a further approach, Plaku, Kavraki and Vardi [25] propose to combine motion planning with discrete search for falsification of hybrid systems. The discrete search and continuous search components are intertwined in such a way that the discrete search extracts a high-level plan that is then used to guide the motion planning component. In a slightly different setting, Ratschan and Smaus [27] apply search to finding error states in hybrid systems that are deterministic. Hence, the search reduces to the problem of finding an accurate initial state. SpaceEx [16] is a recently developed, yet already prominent model checker for hybrid systems. As suggested by the name, it explores the region space by applying search. The most related approach to this paper has recently been presented by Bogomolov et al. [9], who propose a cost function based on Euclidean distances of the regions of the current state and error states. The resulting guided search algorithm is implemented in SpaceEx and has demonstrated to achieve significant guidance and performance improvements compared to the uninformed search of SpaceEx.

Table 1. Experimental results for the navigation benchmarks. Abbreviations: Uninformed DFS: Uninformed depth-first search, Box-heuristic: box-based distance heuristic, PDB: our PDB cost function $cost^{PP}$, #loc: number of locations, #it: number of iterations, length: length of the found error trajectory, time: total time in seconds including any preprocessing. For our PDB approach, the fraction of the total time that is needed for the PDB computation is additionally reported in parenthesis.

Inst.	#loc	Uninformed DFS			Box-heuristic			PDB		
		#it	length	time	#it	length	time	#it	length	time (time abs.)
1	400	122	15	145.756	62	15	70.548	16	15	**20.04** (1.984)
2	400	183	33	186.93	86	33	120.428	34	33	**53.998** (7.553)
3	625	75	33	70.717	34	33	**36.609**	34	33	44.718 (7.472)
4	625	268	158	261.86	231	158	209.637	159	158	**127.458** (10.458)
5	625	85	79	118.8	26	25	**37.775**	26	25	42.117 (3.728)
6	625	96	53	110.816	101	53	104.938	54	53	**76.296** (9.849)
7	625	227	34	198.95	105	34	96.978	35	34	**47.612** (9.385)
8	625	178	25	266.142	86	25	137.291	26	25	**43.541** (7.09)
9	625	297	17	356.042	102	17	131.965	18	17	**30.789** (7.595)
10	625	440	30	534.041	136	30	201.843	31	30	**60.91** (13.64)
11	900	234	72	269.314	129	21	149.086	22	21	**32.744** (8.107)
12	900	317	43	339.093	174	61	198.326	44	43	**62.829** (15.764)
13	900	367	37	421.902	148	37	190.355	38	37	**70.748** (20.132)
14	900	411	32	434.555	278	32	297.89	33	32	**57.692** (10.934)
15	900	379	44	445.863	107	44	137.757	45	44	**69.912** (9.011)

Moreover, guided search has been intensively and successfully applied to finding error states in a subclass of hybrid systems, namely to *timed* systems. In particular, PDBs have been investigated in this context [20,21]. In contrast to this paper, the PDB approaches for timed systems are "classical" PDB approaches, i.e., a subset of the available automata and variables are selected to compute a projection abstraction. To select this subset, Kupferschmid et al. [20] compute an abstract error trace and select the automata and variables that occur in transitions in this abstract trace. In contrast, Kupferschmid and Wehrle [21] start with the set of all automata and variables (i.e., with the complete system), and iteratively remove variables as long as the resulting projection abstraction is "precise enough" according to a certain quality measure. In both approaches, the entire PDB is computed, which is more expensive than the partial PDB approach proposed in this paper.

5   Evaluation

We have implemented $cost^{PP}$ in the SpaceEx tool [16] and evaluated it on a number of challenging benchmarks. The implementation and the benchmarks are available at http://www.informatik.uni-freiburg.de/~bogom/spin2013.

Table 2. Experimental results for the satellite benchmarks. Abbreviations: Uninformed DFS: Uninformed depth-first search, Box-heuristic: box-based distance heuristic, PDB: our PDB cost function $cost^{PP}$, #loc: number of locations, #it: number of iterations, length: length of the found error trajectory, time: total time in seconds including any preprocessing, OOM: out of memory. For our PDB approach, the fraction of the total time that is needed for the PDB computation is additionally reported in parenthesis.

Inst.	#loc	Uninformed DFS			Box-heuristic			PDB		
		#it	length	time	#it	length	time	#it	length	time (time abs.)
1	36	116	32	27.112	75	10	13.44	16	10	**10.317** (7.413)
2	36	464	24	101.252	473	13	116.991	30	13	**16.306** (12.24)
3	64	718	87	31.514	278	87	**11.04**	263	121	20.362 (9.543)
4	100	111	107	38.085	44	15	21.073	23	14	**14.802** (6.029)
5	100	109	104	262.944	45	15	178.617	23	14	**62.985** (5.893)
6	159	2170	∞	78.95	1352	∞	49.853	0	∞	**15.587** (15.587)
7	324	323	102	105.589	1289	106	457.702	25	24	**32.102** (8.767)
8	557	1637	42	45.76	936	42	**26.297**	156	42	44.147 (39.674)
9	574	7113	41	223.648	561	10	17.45	14	10	**6.607** (6.224)
10	575	9092	4	284.783	387	5	12.315	15	4	**2.439** (2.032)
11	576	5693	3769	816.596	257	13	36.479	15	13	**9.937** (5.866)
12	576	32966	13	7059.52	826	13	118.947	15	13	**10.012** (5.813)
13	576	n/a	n/a	OOM	579	52	579.738	58	52	**163.206** (82.013)
14	1293	13691	∞	436.164	7719	∞	249.554	0	∞	**135.507** (135.507)
15	1296	n/a	n/a	OOM	1806	142	1869.72	206	139	**617.423** (434.675)

5.1 Benchmarks

We consider benchmark problems with problem spaces with a large discrete part, with a large branching factor and paths with dead-ends where search involves heavy backtracking.

As a first set of benchmarks, we consider a variant of the well-known navigation benchmark [15]. This benchmark models an object moving on the plane which is divided into a grid of cells. The dynamics of the object's planar position in each cell is governed by the differential equations $\dot{x} = v$, $\dot{v} = A(v - v_d)$ where v_d stands for the targeted velocity in this location. Compared to the originally proposed navigation benchmark problem, we address a slightly more complex version with the following additional constraints. First, we add inputs allowing perturbation of object coordinates, i.e., the system of differential equations is extended to: $\dot{x} = v + u$, $\dot{v} = A(v - v_d)$, $u_{min} \leq u \leq u_{max}$. Second, to make the search task even harder, the benchmark problems also feature obstacles between certain grid elements. This is particularly challenging because, in contrast to the original benchmark system, one can get stuck in a cell where no further transitions can be taken, and consequently, backtracking might become necessary. The size of the problem instances varies from 400 to 900 locations, and all instances feature 4 variables.

Second, we consider benchmarks that result from *hybridization*. For a hybrid system $\mathcal{H}$ with nonlinear continuous dynamics, hybridization is a technique for generating a hybridized hybrid automaton from $\mathcal{H}$. The hybridized automaton has simpler continuous dynamics (usually affine or rectangular) that over-approximate the behavior of $\mathcal{H}$ [6], and can be analyzed by SpaceEx. For our evaluation, we consider benchmarks from this hybridization technique applied to nonlinear *satellite orbital dynamics* [19], where two satellites orbit the earth with nonlinear dynamics described by Kepler's laws. The orbits in three-dimensional space lie in a two-dimensional plane and may in general be any conic section, but we assume the orbits are periodic, and hence circular or elliptical. Fixing some orbital parameters (e.g., the orientations of the orbits in three-space), the states of the satellites in three-dimensional space $x_1, x_2 \in \mathbb{R}^3$ can be completely described in terms of their true anomalies (angular positions). Likewise, one can transform between the three-dimensional state description and the angular position state description. The nonlinear dynamics for the angular position are $\dot{\nu}_i = \sqrt{\mu/p_i^3}(1 + e_i \cos \nu_i)^2$ for each satellite $i \in \{1, 2\}$, where μ is a gravitational parameter, $p_i = a_i(1 - e_i^2)$ is the semi-latus rectum of the ellipse, a_i is the length of the semi-major axis of the ellipse, and $0 \le e_i < 1$ is the eccentricity of the ellipse (if $e_i = 0$, then the orbit is circular and p_i simplifies to the radius of the circle). These dynamics are periodic with a period of 2π, so we consider the bounded subset $[0, 2\pi]^2$ of the state-space $\mathbb{R}^2$, and add invariants and transitions to create a hybrid automaton ensuring $\nu_i \in [0, 2\pi]$. For the benchmark cases evaluated, we fixed $\mu = 1$ and varied p_i and e_i for several scenarios. For more details, we refer to the work of Johnson et al. [19]. The size of the problem instances varies from 36 to 1296 locations, and all instances feature 4 variables.

The verification problem is *conjunction avoidance*, i.e., to determine whether there exists a trajectory where the satellites come too close to one another and may collide. Some of the benchmark instances considered are particularly challenging because they feature several sources of non-determinism, including several initial states and several bad states. As an additional source of nondeterminism, some benchmarks model thrusting. A change in a satellite's orbit is usually accomplished by firing thrusters. This is usually modeled as an instantaneous change in the orbital parameters e_i and a_i. However, the angular position ν_i in this new orbit does not, in general, equal the angular position in the original orbit, and a change of variables is necessary, which can be modeled by a reset of the ν_i values when the thrusters are fired. The transitions introduced for thrusting add additional discrete nondeterminism to the system.

5.2   Experiments

The experiments have been performed on a machine running under Ubuntu 11.10 with a four-core Intel Core i3 2.4GHz processor and 4GB memory. In the following, we report results for our PDB implementation of $cost^{PP}$ in SpaceEx. For the navigation benchmarks, while conducting search in the concrete state space, we use octagonal template directions and sampling time equals to 0.05. In the abstract run, we use box template directions and sampling time equals to 0.5. For different satellite benchmark instances, we used different choices of the directions and sampling times for the concrete and abstract runs, based on

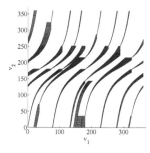 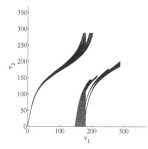 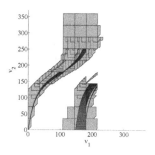

Fig. 2. Uninformed search error trajectory

Fig. 3. Box-based heuristic search error trajectory

Fig. 4. PDB search error trajectories (abstract: light gray, concrete: dark gray)

the choice of the e_i and p_i parameters in the nonlinear dynamics prior to hybridization, since higher values of e_i result in greater overapproximation error from hybridization. We compared $cost^{PP}$ with uninformed depth-first search as implemented in SpaceEx, and with the recently proposed box-based distance function [9]. We compare the number of iterations of SpaceEx, the length of the error trajectory found as well as the overall search time (including the computation of the PDB for $cost^{PP}$) in seconds. For the PDB approach, we also report the fraction of the total time to compute the PDB in parenthesis. The results are reported in Table 1 and Table 2. Considering the overall run-time, the best results are given in bold fonts.

Our results in Table 1 and Table 2 show that the precomputation time for the PDB mostly pays off in terms of guidance accuracy and overall run-time. Specifically, the overall run-time could (sometimes significantly) be reduced compared to uninformed search and also compared to the box-based heuristic. For example, in satellite instance 5, the precomputation for the PDB only needs around 6 seconds, leading to an overall run-time of around 60 seconds, compared to around 178 seconds with the box-based heuristic and about 263 seconds with uninformed search. This search behavior for instance 5 is also visualized in Fig. 2, Fig. 3, and Fig. 4, where we observe that the part of the covered search space with our PDB approach is lower compared to the box-based heuristic and uninformed search. Fig. 4 particularly shows the part of the search space that is covered by the abstract run (which can be performed efficiently due to our abstraction as described in Sec. 3.1), showing that our partial PDB approach finds an accurate balance between the computation time and the accuracy of the resulting cost function. Generally, in our benchmarks, we observed a large range of computation time savings when using partial PDBs compared to full PDBs (approximately, up to a factor of 1.5 in the navigation benchmarks, and up to a factor of 350 in the satellite benchmarks).

Looking at the results in more detail, we first observe that the number of iterations of SpaceEx and also the length of the found error trajectories are mostly at most as high with PDB as with uninformed search and the box-based heuristic. In particular, our PDB approach could solve instances from the satellite problem where uninformed search ran out of memory. In some cases, the precomputation of the PDB does not pay off compared to the box-based heuristic (recall that the box-based heuristic does not have any precomputation time at all), however, in these cases, the pure search time is still similar to the pure search time of the box-based approach. Second, we observe that the length of the trajectories found by the box-based heuristic and the PDB heuristic is often similar or even equal, while the number of iterations is mostly decreased. This again shows that the search with the PDB approach is more focused than with the box-based heuristic in such cases, and less backtracking is needed. In particular, the box-based heuristic always tries to find a direct path to an error state, while ignoring possible obstacles. Therefore, the search can get stuck in a dead-end state if there is an obstacle, and as a consequence, backtracking becomes necessary. Furthermore, the box-based heuristic can perform worse than the PDB if several bad states are present. In such cases, the box-based heuristic might "switch" between several bad states, whereas the better accuracy of the PDB heuristic better focuses the search towards one particular bad state. In contrast, in problems that are structured more easily (e. g., where no "obstacles" exist and error states are reachable "straight ahead"), the box-based heuristic might yield better performance because the precomputation of the PDB does not pay off.

Finally, we remark that our approach is also able to effectively and efficiently *verify* systems where no bad states exist – this is the case in the satellite instances 6 and 14. In these instances, the *abstract* run (which is supposed to build the PDB) does not reveal any reachable error state. As our abstraction is an over-approximation, we can safely conclude that no reachable error state in the concrete system exists either, and do not need to start the concrete search at all. Being able to efficiently verify hybrid systems with PDBs (that are rather supposed to *guide* the search) is a significant advantage compared to the box-based heuristic.

6   Conclusion

We have explored the application of pattern databases (PDBs) for hybrid systems. For a given safety property and hybrid system with linear dynamics in each location, we compute an abstraction by coarsening the over-approximation SpaceEx computes in its reachability analysis. The abstraction is used to construct a PDB, by associating to each abstract symbolic state the distance in number of transitions to the symbolic error state. This distance is then used in guiding SpaceEx in the concrete search. Given a concrete symbolic state, the guiding heuristics returns the smallest distance to the error state of an enclosing abstract symbolic state. This distance is used to choose the most promising concrete symbolic successor. In our implementation, we have taken advantage of the SpaceEx parametrization support, and were able to report a significant speedup in counterexample detection and even for verification. Our new PDB support for

SpaceEx can be seen as a nontrivial extension of our previous work on guided reachability analysis for hybrid systems where the discrete system structure was ignored completely [9]. For the future, it will be interesting to further refine and extend our approach by, e.g., considering even more fine grained abstraction techniques, or by combinations of *several* abstraction techniques and therefore, by combining several PDBs. We expect that this will lead to even more accurate cost functions and better model checking performance.

Acknowledgments. This work was partly supported by the German Research Foundation (DFG) as part of the Transregional Collaborative Research Center "Automatic Verification and Analysis of Complex Systems" (SFB/TR 14 AVACS, http://www.avacs.org/), by the Swiss National Science Foundation (SNSF) as part of the project "Abstraction Heuristics for Planning and Combinatorial Search" (AHPACS) and by STARnet, a Semiconductor Research Corporation program sponsored by MARCO and DARPA.

References

1. Alur, R., Courcoubetis, C., Halbwachs, N., Henzinger, T., Ho, P., Nicolin, X., Olivero, A., Sifakis, J., Yovine, S.: The algorithmic analysis of hybrid systems. Theoretical Computer Science 138, 3–34 (1995)
2. Alur, R., Dang, T., Ivančić, F.: Counter-example guided predicate abstraction of hybrid systems. In: Garavel, H., Hatcliff, J. (eds.) TACAS 2003. LNCS, vol. 2619, pp. 208–223. Springer, Heidelberg (2003)
3. Alur, R., Dang, T., Ivančić, F.: Progress on reachability analysis of hybrid systems using predicate abstraction. In: Maler, O., Pnueli, A. (eds.) HSCC 2003. LNCS, vol. 2623, pp. 4–19. Springer, Heidelberg (2003)
4. Alur, R., Grosu, R., Hur, Y., Kumar, V., Lee, I.: Modular specifications of hybrid systems in CHARON. In: Lynch, N.A., Krogh, B.H. (eds.) HSCC 2000. LNCS, vol. 1790, pp. 6–19. Springer, Heidelberg (2000)
5. Anderson, K., Holte, R., Schaeffer, J.: Partial pattern databases. In: Miguel, I., Ruml, W. (eds.) SARA 2007. LNCS (LNAI), vol. 4612, pp. 20–34. Springer, Heidelberg (2007)
6. Asarin, E., Dang, T., Girard, A.: Hybridization methods for the analysis of nonlinear systems. Acta Informatica 43(7), 451–476 (2007)
7. Balluchi, A., Benvenuti, L., Benedetto, M.D.D., Pinello, C., Sangiovanni-Vincentelli, A.L.: Automotive engine control and hybrid systems: challenges and opportunities. Proceedings of the IEEE 88(7), 888–912 (2000)
8. Bhatia, A., Frazzoli, E.: Incremental search methods for reachability analysis of continuous and hybrid systems. In: Alur, R., Pappas, G.J. (eds.) HSCC 2004. LNCS, vol. 2993, pp. 142–156. Springer, Heidelberg (2004)
9. Bogomolov, S., Frehse, G., Grosu, R., Ladan, H., Podelski, A., Wehrle, M.: A box-based distance between regions for guiding the reachability analysis of SpaceEx. In: Madhusudan, P., Seshia, S.A. (eds.) CAV 2012. LNCS, vol. 7358, pp. 479–494. Springer, Heidelberg (2012)
10. Chutinan, C., Krogh, B.: Computational techniques for hybrid system verification. IEEE Transactions on Automatic Control 48(1), 64–75 (2003)

11. Culberson, J.C., Schaeffer, J.: Pattern databases. Computational Intelligence 14(3), 318–334 (1998)
12. Dang, T., Nahhal, T.: Coverage-guided test generation for continuous and hybrid systems. Formal Methods in System Design 34(2), 183–213 (2009)
13. Deshpande, A., Godbole, D., Göllü, A., Varaiya, P.: Design and evaluation of tools for automated highway systems. In: Alur, R., Sontag, E.D., Henzinger, T.A. (eds.) HS 1995. LNCS, vol. 1066, pp. 138–148. Springer, Heidelberg (1996)
14. Egerstedt, M.: Behavior based robotics using hybrid automata. In: Lynch, N.A., Krogh, B.H. (eds.) HSCC 2000. LNCS, vol. 1790, pp. 103–116. Springer, Heidelberg (2000)
15. Fehnker, A., Ivančić, F.: Benchmarks for hybrid systems verification. In: Alur, R., Pappas, G.J. (eds.) HSCC 2004. LNCS, vol. 2993, pp. 326–341. Springer, Heidelberg (2004)
16. Frehse, G., et al.: SpaceEx: Scalable verification of hybrid systems. In: Gopalakrishnan, G., Qadeer, S. (eds.) CAV 2011. LNCS, vol. 6806, pp. 379–395. Springer, Heidelberg (2011)
17. Henzinger, T., Wong-Toi, H.: Linear phase-portrait approximations for nonlinear hybrid systems. In: Alur, R., Sontag, E.D., Henzinger, T.A. (eds.) HS 1995. LNCS, vol. 1066, pp. 377–388. Springer, Heidelberg (1996)
18. Holte, R.C., Grajkowski, J., Tanner, B.: Hierarchical heuristic search revisited. In: Zucker, J.-D., Saitta, L. (eds.) SARA 2005. LNCS (LNAI), vol. 3607, pp. 121–133. Springer, Heidelberg (2005)
19. Johnson, T.T., Green, J., Mitra, S., Dudley, R., Erwin, R.S.: Satellite rendezvous and conjunction avoidance: Case studies in verification of nonlinear hybrid systems. In: Giannakopoulou, D., Méry, D. (eds.) FM 2012. LNCS, vol. 7436, pp. 252–266. Springer, Heidelberg (2012)
20. Kupferschmid, S., Hoffmann, J., Larsen, K.G.: Fast directed model checking via russian doll abstraction. In: Ramakrishnan, C.R., Rehof, J. (eds.) TACAS 2008. LNCS, vol. 4963, pp. 203–217. Springer, Heidelberg (2008)
21. Kupferschmid, S., Wehrle, M.: Abstractions and pattern databases: The quest for succinctness and accuracy. In: Abdulla, P.A., Leino, K.R.M. (eds.) TACAS 2011. LNCS, vol. 6605, pp. 276–290. Springer, Heidelberg (2011)
22. Larsen, B.J., Burns, E., Ruml, W., Holte, R.: Searching without a heuristic: Efficient use of abstraction. In: AAAI Conference on Artificial Intelligence (2010)
23. Livadas, C., Lygeros, J., Lynch, N.A.: High-level modelling and analysis of tcas. In: IEEE Real-Time Systems Symposium, pp. 115–125 (1999)
24. Lygeros, J., Pappas, G.J., Sastry, S.: An approach to the verification of the center-tracon automation system. In: Henzinger, T.A., Sastry, S.S. (eds.) HSCC 1998. LNCS, vol. 1386, pp. 289–304. Springer, Heidelberg (1998)
25. Plaku, E., Kavraki, L.E., Vardi, M.Y.: Hybrid systems: From verification to falsification. In: Damm, W., Hermanns, H. (eds.) CAV 2007. LNCS, vol. 4590, pp. 463–476. Springer, Heidelberg (2007)
26. Qian, K., Nymeyer, A.: Guided invariant model checking based on abstraction and symbolic pattern databases. In: Jensen, K., Podelski, A. (eds.) TACAS 2004. LNCS, vol. 2988, pp. 497–511. Springer, Heidelberg (2004)
27. Ratschan, S., Smaus, J.-G.: Finding errors of hybrid systems by optimising an abstraction-based quality estimate. In: Dubois, C. (ed.) TAP 2009. LNCS, vol. 5668, pp. 153–168. Springer, Heidelberg (2009)
28. Varaiya, P.: Smart cars on smart roads: problems of control. IEEE Trans. Automatic Control 38(2) (1993)

Probabilistic Verification of Coordinated Multi-robot Missions

Sagar Chaki and Joseph Andrew Giampapa

Carnegie Mellon Software Engineering Institute
{chaki,garof}@sei.cmu.edu

Abstract. Robots are increasingly used to perform a wide variety of tasks, especially those involving dangerous or inaccessible locations. As the complexity of such tasks grow, robots are being deployed in teams, with complex coordination schemes aimed at maximizing the chance of mission success. Such teams operate under inherently uncertain conditions – the robots themselves fail, and have to continuously adapt to changing environmental conditions. A key challenge facing robotic mission designers is therefore to construct a mission – i.e., specify number and type of robots, number and size of teams, coordination and planning mechanisms etc. – so as to maximize some overall utility, such as the probability of mission success. In this paper, we advocate, formalize, and empirically justify an approach to compute quantitative utility of robotic missions using probabilistic model checking. We show how to express a robotic demining mission as a restricted type of discrete time Markov chain (called $\alpha\mathbf{PA}$), and its utility as either a linear temporal logic formula or a reward. We prove a set of compositionality theorems that enable us to compute the utility of a system composed of several $\alpha\mathbf{PA}s$ by combining the utilities of each $\alpha\mathbf{PA}$ in isolation. This ameliorates the statespace explosion problem, even when the system being verified is composed of a large number of robots. We validate our approach empirically, using the probabilistic model checker PRISM.

1   Introduction

Robots are increasingly used to perform a wide variety of tasks. Examples include situations where the task is dangerous (e.g., demining) or involves physically inaccessible localities (e.g., a disaster area). They are often deployed in teams to provide fault tolerance, and to accommodate a wider variety of plans. The tasks consist of both unpredictable and known parts. For example, the operating conditions change unpredictably, and robots might malfunction, become indisposed, or be unable to complete its task due to the lack of capability. These are unknown. On the other hand, there are known parameters, e.g., the number of robots, the capabilities of each robot, the set of plans available to each robot, and the coordination algorithms used by the robots, that are within the control of the mission designer. The goal of the designer is to select these parameters so as to increase overall mission utility.

E. Bartocci and C.R. Ramakrishnan (Eds.): SPIN 2013, LNCS 7976, pp. 135–153, 2013.

We focus on missions that involve foraging-and-reacting (FAR), where robots have to explore an arena, look for specific objects, and react to them in specific ways. Examples of such missions are demining a minefield [16] where robots attempt to defuse detected mines, and search-and-rescue of a disaster area where robots report the location and status of discovered survivors to authorities.

Designing FAR missions requires assessing two aspects: (a) *success*: estimate the probability of mission success within a certain deadline; and (b) *coverage*: compute the expected amount of terrain covered within a given deadline. Currently, designers rely on their prior knowledge as well as field tests and simulations to solve these two problems. Both have limitations. Relying on prior knowledge is an ad-hoc approach, limited, and typically does not cover unknown and unforeseen situations. Full scale field tests are expensive, time-consuming, and may not be conducted in a way that permits a generalization of the relative impacts of certain parameter settings to similar missions in other contexts.

In this paper, we propose a more systematic, repeatable, and analytic method, based on probabilistic model checking, to solve both success and coverage problems. Specifically, we show how to model a robotic demining mission as a probabilistic automaton (PA). In addition, we show how to express success as a probabilistic LTL [1] formula, and coverage as a cumulative reward over the PA. This is our first contribution. Further details are presented in Section 5.

Our second contribution is tackling the statespace explosion problem during probabilistic model checking of FAR missions. We leverage two types of restrictions commonly found in such missions. First, robots are divided into teams, and each team operates independently on a separate portion of the arena. We call this property independence (**IND**). Second, the PAs for the teams "synchronize" over a common action corresponding to a clock tick since the robot teams operate under the same global clock. We call this property synchronization (**SYNC**). In our approach, these two restrictions are incorporated by modeling each team as a α**PA**, i.e., a PA with a singleton alphabet $\{\alpha\}$. When α**PA**s are composed, they synchronize over the common action α. The result is also a α**PA**.

Our requirement of synchronization between robotic teams is a purely modeling construct. The teams do not have to possess physically synchronized clocks. However, the time taken by a team for an action must respect the timing constraint on the action used in the model. For example, if the model assumes that sensing a mine requires 40 units of time, and 1 unit equals 1 second, then each team must complete the mine sensing activity within 40 seconds. Otherwise, the predictions made by the model checker will be invalid. Therefore, the model must be constructed based on realistic values for timing constraints and probabilities.

The restricted nature of α**PA**s enables us to obtain two compositionality results: (a) probability of satisfying an LTL formula accumulates multiplicatively over α**PA**s (cf. Theorem 1 and 2); and (b) expected reward accumulates additively over α**PA** (cf. Theorem 3 and 4). Our compositionality theorems hold for an arbitrary (but finite) number of α**PA**s. Further details are presented in Section 4. These theorems enable us to solve success and coverage for our demining case study in a completely compositional manner by model checking the α**PA** for each team individually. Note that these compositionality results do not hold if we remove the restriction to singleton (and identical) alphabets.

Our third and final contribution is an empirical validation of our results by using the state-of-the-art probabilistic model checker PRISM [11] to compute the values of success and coverage for our demining case study using both the compositional approach and the direct non-compositional approach. We show how the non-compositional model checking runs out of resources even for two robotic teams, while the compositional approach scales easily to even thirty teams. Further details are presented in Section 6.

The rest of the paper is structures as follows. In Section 2 we survey related work. In Section 3, we present basic definitions. In Section 4 we present our compositionality theorems. In Section 5, we present our robotic demining scenario and its α**PA** model, as well as the properties we want to verify. In Section 6, we present experimental results, and in Section 7, we conclude.

2   Related Work

This paper builds on a wide body of work in modeling and verifying probabilistic systems [14]. In particular, probabilistic model checking has been used to verify systems ranging from pacemakers [3], root contention protocols [13] and biological pathways [8]. Our work explores the application of probabilistic model checking to yet another domain – coordinated multi-robot missions.

The connection between probabilistic systems and compositionality has been studied by a number of researchers. For example, de Alfaro et al. [4] provide a semantic notion of compositionality in the context of probabilistic reactive modules. Our notion of probabilistic automata and parallel composition is borrowed from that proposed by Stoelinga [15] and others. In essence, α**PA** are a restricted, yet useful, version of probabilistic automata that admit to strong compositionality results.

A number of projects on compositional verification of probabilistic systems [12] use automated assume-guarantee algorithms that are based on learning [6,7]. There is also work on learning-based assume-guarantee reasoning for synchronous probabilistic systems [5], assume-guarantee and abstraction refinement for probabilistic systems [9], and on compositional reasoning for probabilistic model checking of hardware designs [10]. Our approach is also compositional, but does not involve assume-guarantee reasoning.

A preliminary version of the demining scenario presented here, its probabilistic model, and experimental results were reported in our previous work [2]. The model was less elaborate, e.g., it did not include uncertainty when moving from cell to cell. Also, it was a DTMC, not α**PA**, and hence not amenable to the compositionality theorems presented here. Indeed, our prior work [2] did not include any compositionality theorems, nor empirical results showing their effectiveness.

3   Preliminaries

We adopt the formalism of probabilistic automata [15], modifying it in two ways: (a) extending it by labeling states with atomic propositions; and (b) restricting the alphabet to be a singleton. The result is a class of automata we call α**PA**. Let $Dist(X)$ be the set of all probability distributions over any set X.

Definition 1 (αPA). *A αPA is a 6-tuple $(S, Init, \Sigma, \delta, AP, \mathcal{L})$ where: (i) S is a countable set of states; (ii) $Init \in S$ is the initial state; (iii) $\Sigma = \{\alpha\}$ is the singleton alphabet; (iv) $\delta : S \mapsto Dist(S)$ is the transition relation; (v) AP is a set of atomic propositions; and (vi) $\mathcal{L} : S \mapsto 2^{AP}$ is a mapping from states to sets of atomic propositions, such that $\mathcal{L}(s)$ is the set of propositions true in s.*

If $M = (S, Init, \Sigma, \delta, AP, \mathcal{L})$ is a α**PA**, we write $S(M)$, $Init(M)$, $\Sigma(M)$, $\delta(M)$, $AP(M)$, and $\mathcal{L}(M)$ to mean S, $Init$, Σ, δ, AP and $\mathcal{L}$, respectively.

Definition 2 (Execution). *Let M be a αPA. An execution π is a (finite or infinite) sequence of states $s_0, s_1, \ldots$ such that:*

$$\forall i \geq 0 \text{ . } \delta(M)(s_i)(s_{i+1}) > 0$$

The execution π starts from s_0. The set of all executions starting from s is denoted by $Ex(s, M)$, and $Ex(M)$ means $Ex(Init(M), M)$. The set of all finite executions starting from s is denoted by $\widehat{Ex}(s, M)$ and $\widehat{Ex}(M)$ means $\widehat{Ex}(Init(M), M)$. We omit M from $Ex(s, M)$ and $\widehat{Ex}(s, M)$ when it is clear from the context.

Given two probability distributions $\mu_1 \in Dist(X_1)$ and $\mu_2 \in Dist(X_2)$, the distribution $(\mu_1 \times \mu_2) \in Dist(X_1 \times X_2)$ is defined as follows:

$$\forall (x_1, x_2) \in X_1 \times X_2 \text{ . } (\mu_1 \times \mu_2)(x_1, x_2) = \mu_1(x_1) \times \mu_2(x_2)$$

For any set X and an element $x \in X$, the Dirac distribution $\Delta(x) \in Dist(X)$ maps x to 1 and every other element of X to 0. α**PA**s synchronize via the common action α. Let M_1 and M_2 be two α**PA**s. We write $M_1 \diamond M_2$ to mean $AP(M_1) \cap AP(M_2) = \emptyset$. Formally, the composition of α**PA** is defined as follows.

Definition 3. *Let M_1 and M_2 be αPAs such that $M_1 \diamond M_2$. Their parallel composition $M_1 \parallel M_2$ is the αPA $(S, Init, \Sigma, \delta, AP, \mathcal{L})$ where:*

$$S = S(M_1) \times S(M_2) \qquad Init = (Init(M_1), Init(M_2))$$
$$\Sigma = \{\alpha\} \qquad \delta(s_1, s_2) = \delta(M_1)(s_1) \times \delta(M_2)(s_2)$$
$$AP = AP(M_1) \cup AP(M_2) \qquad \mathcal{L}(s_1, s_2) = \mathcal{L}(M_1)(s_1) \cup \mathcal{L}(M_2)(s_2)$$

Properties. We assume that properties are specified as LTL [1] formulas. The syntax of a LTL formula Ψ over the set of atomic propositions AP is given by:

$$\Psi := \text{TRUE} \mid a \mid \neg\Psi \mid \Psi \wedge \Psi \mid \mathsf{X}\Psi \mid \Psi\mathsf{U}\Psi$$

where $a \in AP$ is an atomic proposition. We write $\pi \models \Psi$ to mean that the infinite execution π satisfies the formula Ψ. Consider a PA M. We write $Ex(s, \Psi)$ to mean the infinite executions starting from s that satisfy Ψ, i.e.,

$$Ex(s, \Psi) = \{\pi \in Ex(s) \mid \pi \models \Psi\}$$

Cylinders. Every finite execution $\widehat{\pi}$ induces a set of infinite executions for which $\widehat{\pi}$ is a prefix. This is known as the cylinder of $\widehat{\pi}$, or $\mathsf{Cyl}(\widehat{\pi})$. A finite execution $\widehat{\pi}$ satisfies Ψ, denoted $\widehat{\pi} \models \Psi$, if $\forall \pi \in \mathsf{Cyl}(\widehat{\pi}) \,.\, \pi \models \Psi$. We write $\widehat{\pi_1} \sqsubseteq \widehat{\pi_2}$ to mean that $\widehat{\pi_1}$ is a prefix of $\widehat{\pi_2}$. A set of finite executions E is *minimal* if it has no two distinct elements $\widehat{\pi_1}$ and $\widehat{\pi_2}$ such that $\widehat{\pi_1} \sqsubseteq \widehat{\pi_2}$. For every LTL formula Ψ and state s, there is a unique minimal subset [17] of $\widehat{Ex}(s)$, denoted $\mathcal{B}(s, \Psi)$, such that:

$$Ex(s, \Psi) = \bigcup_{\widehat{\pi} \in \mathcal{B}(s, \Psi)} \mathsf{Cyl}(\widehat{\pi})$$

Informally, $\mathcal{B}(s, \Psi)$ is a "finite basis" of Ψ whose cylinders generate all (and exactly all) executions from s that satisfy Ψ. Let $\widehat{Ex}(s, k)$ be the subset of $\widehat{Ex}(s)$ containing only executions with $k+1$ states. Let $\widehat{\pi} = s_0, \ldots, s_n \in \widehat{Ex}(s_0, n)$. Let us define $\mathbf{p}(\widehat{\pi})$ as follows:

$$\mathbf{p}(\widehat{\pi}) = 1 \text{ if } n = 0 \text{ and } \mathbf{p}(\widehat{\pi}) = \prod_{0 \le i < n} \delta(M)(s_i)(s_{i+1}) \text{ otherwise}$$

Definition 4. *Given a state s and a LTL formula Ψ, $\mathsf{P}(s, \Psi)$ is the probability that s satisfies Ψ, and is defined as:*

$$\mathsf{P}(s, \Psi) = \sum_{\widehat{\pi} \in \mathcal{B}(s, \Psi)} \mathbf{p}(\widehat{\pi})$$

Rewards. We write $\mathsf{P}(M, \Psi)$ to mean $\mathsf{P}(Init(M), \Psi)$. A reward structure on a $\alpha\mathbf{PA}$ M is a pair (ρ, ι) such that $\rho : S(M) \mapsto \mathbb{R}$ and $\iota : S(M) \times S(M) \mapsto \mathbb{R}$ map states and transitions of M, respectively, to real-valued rewards. Each transition of M corresponds to a discrete unit of time.

Definition 5. *The cumulative reward due to a reward structure $R = (\rho, \iota)$ from state s up to time k (i.e., up to k transitions of M from s), denoted by $C_{\le k}(s, R)$ is defined recursively as follows:*

$$C_{\le 0}(s, R) = 0$$
$$\forall k > 0 \,.\, C_{\le k}(s, R) = \rho(s) + \sum_{s' \in S(M)} \delta(M)(s)(s') \times (\iota(s, s') + C_{\le (k-1)}(s', R))$$

4   Compositional Verification

In this section, we present our compositionality theorems. We begin by defining the "product" of two executions. Let $M_1 \in \alpha\mathbf{PA}$ and $M_2 \in \alpha\mathbf{PA}$. Let $\widehat{\pi_1} = s_0, \ldots, s_n \in \widehat{Ex}(M_1, n)$ and $\widehat{\pi_2} = s'_0, \ldots, s'_n \in \widehat{Ex}(M_2, n)$ be two finite executions.

Then, $\widehat{\pi_1} \times \widehat{\pi_2} \in \widehat{Ex}(M_1 \parallel M_2, n)$ is the execution $(s_0, s_0'), \ldots, (s_n, s_n')$. If $\widehat{\pi} = \widehat{\pi_1} \times \widehat{\pi_2}$, then we write $\pi \downharpoonright 1$ and $\pi \downharpoonright 2$ to mean $\widehat{\pi_1}$ and $\widehat{\pi_2}$, respectively.

This extends to executions of different length as follows. Given a finite execution $\widehat{\pi} = s_0, \ldots, s_m$, and $n \geq m$, the set of n-extensions of $\widehat{\pi}$, denoted by $\widehat{\pi}^{+n}$, is defined as follows:

$$\widehat{\pi}^{+n} = \{\widehat{\pi'} \in \widehat{Ex}(s_0, n) \mid \widehat{\pi} \sqsubseteq \widehat{\pi'}\}$$

$$\widehat{\pi_1} \times \widehat{\pi_2} = \{\widehat{\pi'}_1 \times \widehat{\pi'}_2 \mid \widehat{\pi'}_1 \in \widehat{\pi_1}^{+n} \wedge \widehat{\pi'}_2 \in \widehat{\pi_2}^{+n} \wedge n = \max(|\widehat{\pi_1}|, |\widehat{\pi_2}|)\}$$

$$E_1 \times E_2 = \bigcup_{(\widehat{\pi_1}, \widehat{\pi_2}) \in E_1 \times E_2} \widehat{\pi_1} \times \widehat{\pi_2}$$

Note that if $\widehat{\pi} \in \widehat{\pi_1} \times \widehat{\pi_2}$, then $\widehat{\pi_1} \sqsubseteq \widehat{\pi} \downharpoonright 1$ and $\widehat{\pi_2} \sqsubseteq \widehat{\pi} \downharpoonright 2$. Next we present two lemmas (proofs in extended version: http://works.bepress.com/chaki/24).

Lemma 1. *Let $M_1 \in \alpha\mathbf{PA}$, $M_2 \in \alpha\mathbf{PA}$ be $\alpha\mathbf{PA}$s such that $M_1 \diamond M_2$. Let $s_1 \in S(M_1)$, $s_2 \in S(M_2)$, and Ψ_1 and Ψ_2 be LTL formulas over $AP(M_1)$ and $AP(M_2)$, respectively. Then:*

$$\mathcal{B}((s_1, s_2), \Psi_1 \wedge \Psi_2) = \mathcal{B}(s_1, \Psi_1) \times \mathcal{B}(s_2, \Psi_2)$$

Lemma 2. *Let E_1 and E_2 be two minimal sets of finite executions. Then:*

$$\sum_{\widehat{\pi} \in E_1 \times E_2} \mathbf{p}(\widehat{\pi}) = \left(\sum_{\widehat{\pi_1} \in E_1} \mathbf{p}(\widehat{\pi_1})\right) \times \left(\sum_{\widehat{\pi_2} \in E_2} \mathbf{p}(\widehat{\pi_2})\right)$$

Now we present and prove our first compositionality theorem.

Theorem 1. *Let $M_1 \in \alpha\mathbf{PA}$, $M_2 \in \alpha\mathbf{PA}$ be $\alpha\mathbf{PA}$s such that $M_1 \diamond M_2$. Let Ψ_1 and Ψ_2 be LTL formulas over $AP(M_1)$ and $AP(M_2)$, respectively. Then:*

$$\mathsf{P}(M_1 \parallel M_2, \Psi_1 \wedge \Psi_2) = \mathsf{P}(M_1, \Psi_1) \times \mathsf{P}(M_2, \Psi_2)$$

Proof. The proof proceeds as follows:

▷ using Definition 4

$$\mathsf{P}(M_1 \parallel M_2, \Psi_1 \wedge \Psi_2) = \sum_{\widehat{\pi} \in \mathcal{B}((Init_1, Init_2), \Psi_1 \wedge \Psi_2)} \mathbf{p}(\widehat{\pi})$$

▷ using Lemma 1

$$= \sum_{\widehat{\pi} \in \mathcal{B}(Init_1, \Psi_1) \times \mathcal{B}(Init_2, \Psi_2)} \mathbf{p}(\widehat{\pi})$$

▷ using Lemma 2

$$= \left(\sum_{\widehat{\pi_1} \in \mathcal{B}(Init_1, \Psi_1)} \mathbf{p}(\widehat{\pi_1})\right) \times \left(\sum_{\widehat{\pi_2} \in \mathcal{B}(Init_2, \Psi_2)} \mathbf{p}(\widehat{\pi_2})\right)$$

▷ again using Definition 4

$$= \mathsf{P}(M_1, \Psi_1) \times \mathsf{P}(M_2, \Psi_2)$$

$\square$

Theorem 1 generalizes from 2 to n α**PA**s as follows.

Theorem 2. *Let* $M_1, \ldots, M_n$ *be* α**PA**s *such that* $\forall 1 \leq i < j \leq n$. $M_i \diamond M_j$. *Let* $\Psi_1, \ldots, \Psi_n$ *be LTL formulas over* $AP(M_1), \ldots, AP(M_n)$, *respectively. Then:*

$$\mathsf{P}(M_1 \parallel \cdots \parallel M_n, \Psi_1 \wedge \cdots \wedge \Psi_n) = \prod_{i=1}^{n} \mathsf{P}(M_i, \Psi_i)$$

We omit the proof of Theorem 2 for brevity, and turn our attention to rewards. Let M_1 and M_2 be α**PA**s and let $R_1 = (\rho_1, \iota_1)$ and $R_2 = (\rho_2, \iota_2)$ be reward structures defined on them. The composition of R_1 and R_2, denoted by $R_1 \oplus R_2$, is the reward structure (ρ, ι) on $M_1 \parallel M_2$ defined as follows:

$$\rho(s_1, s_2) = \rho_1(s_1) + \rho_2(s_2) \qquad \iota((s_1, s_2), (s_1', s_2')) = \iota_1(s_1, s_1') + \iota_2(s_2, s_2')$$

Our second compositionality theorem relates to rewards, as stated next.

Theorem 3. *Let* $M_1 \in \alpha$**PA**, $M_2 \in \alpha$**PA** *be* α**PA**s *such that* $M_1 \diamond M_2$. *Let* R_1 *and* R_2 *be reward structures* M_1 *and* M_2, *respectively. Then:*

$$\forall k \, . \, C_{\leq k}((s_1, s_2), R_1 \oplus R_2) = C_{\leq k}(s_1, R_1) + C_{\leq k}(s_2, R_2)$$

Proof. The proof is by induction on k. If $k = 0$, then it follows from Definition 5. Let $R_1 \oplus R_2 = (\rho, \iota)$, $\delta(M_1) = \delta_1$, $\delta(M_2) = \delta_2$, $\delta(M_1 \parallel M_2) = \delta$. If $k > 0$, then:

▷ using Definition 5
$$C_{\leq k}((s_1, s_2), R_1 \oplus R_2) = \rho(s_1, s_2) +$$
$$\sum_{(s_1', s_2')} \delta(s_1, s_2)(s_1', s_2') \times (\iota((s_1, s_2), (s_1', s_2')) + C_{\leq(k-1)}((s_1', s_2'), R_1 \oplus R_2))$$

▷ expanding ρ and ι and applying inductive hypothesis
$$= \rho_1(s_1) + \rho_2(s_2) +$$
$$\left(\sum_{s_1' \in S(M_1)} \sum_{s_2' \in S(M_2)} \delta_1(s_1, s_1') \times \delta_2(s_2, s_2') \times (\iota_1(s_1, s_1') + C_{\leq(k-1)}(s_1', R_1)) \right) +$$
$$\left(\sum_{s_1' \in S(M_1)} \sum_{s_2' \in S(M_2)} \delta_1(s_1, s_1') \times \delta_2(s_2, s_2') \times (\iota_2(s_2, s_2')) + C_{\leq(k-1)}(s_2', R_2)) \right)$$

$\triangleright$ rewriting

$= \rho_1(s_1) + \rho_2(s_2) +$

$$\underbrace{\left(\sum_{s_2' \in S(M_2)} \delta_2(s_2, s_2') \right)}_{=1} \times \left(\sum_{s_1' \in S(M_1)} \delta_1(s_1, s_1') \times (\iota_1(s_1, s_1') + C_{\leq(k-1)}(s_1', R_1)) \right) +$$

$$\underbrace{\left(\sum_{s_1' \in S(M_1)} \delta_1(s_1, s_1') \right)}_{=1} \times \left(\sum_{s_2' \in S(M_2)} \delta_2(s_2, s_2') \times (\iota_2(s_2, s_2')) + C_{\leq(k-1)}(s_2', R_2)) \right)$$

$$= \rho_1(s_1) + \left(\sum_{s_1' \in S(M_1)} \delta_1(s_1, s_1') \times (\iota_1(s_1, s_1') + C_{\leq(k-1)}(s_1', R_1)) \right) +$$

$$\rho_2(s_2) + \left(\sum_{s_2' \in S(M_2)} \delta_2(s_2, s_2') \times (\iota_2(s_2, s_2')) + C_{\leq(k-1)}(s_2', R_2)) \right)$$

$\triangleright$ using Definition 5

$$= C_{\leq k}(s_1, R_1) + C_{\leq k}(s_2, R_2)$$

$\square$

Theorem 3 generalizes from 2 to n α**PA**s as follows.

Theorem 4. *Let $M_1, \ldots, M_n$ be α**PA**s such that $\forall 1 \leq i < j \leq n \,.\, M_i \diamond M_j$. Let $R_1, \ldots, R_n$ be reward structures over $M_1, \ldots, M_n$, respectively. Then:*

$$\forall k \,.\, C_{\leq k}(M_1 \parallel \cdots \parallel M_n, R_1 \oplus \ldots \oplus R_n) = \sum_{1 \leq i \leq n} C_{\leq k}(M_i, R_i)$$

We omit the proof of Theorem 4 for brevity. The power of Theorems 2 and 4 is that they enable compositional verification of α**PA**s. Specifically, Theorem 2 enables us to compute probabilities satisfying a conjunctive LTL formula on the composition of several α**PA**s from the probabilities of satisfying individual conjuncts on each component α**PA**. Similarly, Theorem 4 enables us to compute rewards on the composition of several α**PA**s from the individual rewards on each component α**PA**. This avoids having to computes the reachable statespace of the composed α**PA**, and therefore the statespace explosion.

In the next section, we present an example that is compositionally verifiable using Theorem 2 and Theorem 4. After that, in Section 6, we present empirical evidence about the improvement in verification due to the compositionality enabled by Theorem 2 and Theorem 4.

5   The Scenario: Robotic Demining

We consider a two-dimensional area (modeled as a grid of cells with Row rows and Col columns) randomly seeded with mines. Robots are organized into T teams, each comprising of N robots. The teams sweep the area, detect each mine, and either defuse it or (failing which) mark it. The mission succeeds if all mines are detected and defused (or marked) within a specified deadline D. The mission is parameterized not only by Row, Col, T, N, and D, but also the capabilities of each robot, the terrain, and coordination algorithm used by the robots. We first describe how each team is modeled as a α**PA**.

5.1   Modeling a Team

Each team has a pre-defined initial cell *cInit*, final cell *cFinal*, and a path plan P that dictates how to move cell-to-cell from *cInit* to *cFinal*. At any point, the team has a leader, and zero or more followers. In each cell, the team (specifically, the leader) first attempts to sense a mine. If a mine is detected, the leader attempts to defuse it. On successfully defusing, the team moves on to the next cell according to its path plan P. If defusing fails, then the cell is first marked as being mined, and then the team moves on to the next cell according to its path plan P. If the mine explodes (thereby destroying the leader) the followers elect a new leader using a pre-defined leader election algorithm. We are concerned with several sources of uncertainty in this scenario:

1. Due to the terrain and the quality of the leader's sensing capability, it fails to detect a mine.
2. Due to the terrain, the time required to defuse a mine varies.
3. Due to the quality of the leader's defusing capability, the mine explodes while it is being defused.
4. Due to the quality of the leader's marking capability, the mine explodes while the cell is being marked.
5. Due to communication problems, the leader election algorithm fails.
6. Due to the terrain and the team's locomotion capability, the team fails to move to the next cell in its path plan.

To express these uncertainties as part of the team's behavior, we model each team as a α**PA**. The α**PA** is composed of two sub-α**PA**s – M_{cell} corresponding to the team's behavior within a cell, and M_{step} corresponding to the team's locomotion from the current cell to the next. Figure 1(a) shows the overall α**PA** for a team, and its decomposition into the two sub-α**PA**s M_{cell} and M_{step}. The initial state is INIT, and the α**PA** ends up in one of three possible end-states – DONE indicates that the team has covered all cells; STUCK indicates that the team is unable to move to its next cell; BLOWNUP indicates that the team has been destroyed by exploding mines.

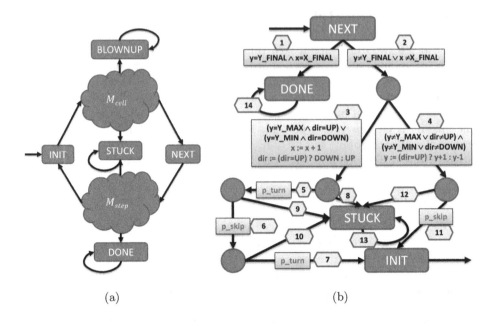

(a)   (b)

Fig. 1. (a) α**PA** for a team, and its decomposition into sub-α**PA**s M_{cell} and M_{step}; (b) α**PA** M_{step}; transitions are numbered for ease of reference, and labeled by associated probabilities (green), guards (black) and commands (red); t_k = transition number k; TRUE guards and implied probabilities are omitted for brevity, e.g., the probability of t_1 is 1.0, the guard of t_5 is TRUE, and the probability of t_{12} is $(1 - \mathsf{p\_skip})$. Note that Y_MIN=0 and Y_MAX=Row-1. All transitions are labeled by action tick, i.e., α = tick.

α**PA** M_{step}. We assume that the teams follow a pre-determined path through the grid. Specifically, if there is a single team (i.e., $T = 1$), then it follows the path shown in Fig. 2(a). If $T > 1$, then each team operates independently on a distinct fragment of the path that is pre-allocated to it. For example, if $T = 4$, the starting and ending cells, and the path of each team is shown in Fig. 2(b).

Figure 1(b) shows the α**PA** M_{step}. The team maintains: (a) its current position in the grid – using variables x and y which are initialized to values (X_INIT and Y_INIT, respectively) corresponding to $cInit$; and (b) the direction of movement – using variable dir which is initialized according to P and takes two possible values UP and DOWN. All transitions are labeled by the action tick.

Let t_k mean transition number k in Figure 1(b). From the initial state NEXT, the team first checks if it has reached $cFinal$. In this case (t_1), the team moves to state DONE and stutters (t_{14}). Otherwise, the team attempts to move to the next cell (t_2). This involves two cases: (a) the team moves to the next column (t_3) which involves two turns (t_5, t_7), a skip (t_6), and a change in direction; or (b) the team moves to the next row (t_4) which involves just a skip (t_{11}). Skips and turns succeed with probability p_skip and p_turn, respectively.

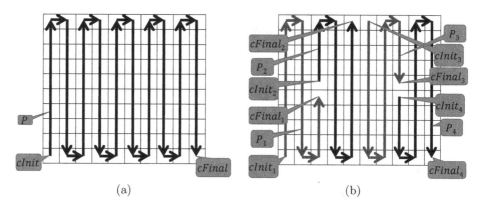

(a)   (b)

Fig. 2. Path followed by the teams: (a) path with one team; (b) path with four teams; $cInit_i$, $cFinal_i$, and P_i are the starting cell, ending cell, and path plan for i-th team.

These probabilities are determined by the terrain and the team's locomotion capability, as discussed later. If a skip or a turn fails, the team moves to a STUCK state (t_8, t_9, t_{10}, t_{12}) and stutters (t_{13}).

α**PA** M_{cell}. The α**PA** M_{cell} is shown in Fig. 3. We model whether a mine was missed using variable failed, initialized to FALSE. We also model the number of remaining robots in the team using variable sz, initialized to N. In the following, t_k means the transition labeled k in Fig. 3. The teams begins in state INIT and the leader attempts to detect a mine. The result of mine detection is either an explosion with probability p_explode_detect (t_2), a mine found with probability p_detect_mine (t_1), or no mine found (t_3).

If no mine was detected (state NOT_DETECTED), then we assume that with probability p_false_neg, there is actually a mine. In this case, with equal likelihood, the leader either explodes (t_4) or the team moves to the next cell (t_5). In the latter case, we indicate mission failure (since a mine has been missed) by setting failed to TRUE. Finally, with probability (1 - p_false_neg), the team moves to the next cell (t_6), continuing with its mission. The probability p_false_neg is a function of the leader's detecting capability and the terrain, as discussed later.

If a mine was detected, the leader attempts to defuse it. We assume that the leader is in one of three defusing situations with increasing difficulty – easy, medium and hard. Initially (DEFUSE1), the leader assumes that it is in the easy defusing situation. The result is either an explosion with probability (p_d1 $\times$ p_ed1) (t_8), successful defusing of the mine with probability (p_d1 $\times$ (1 $-$ p_ed1)) (t_7), or a decision to move on to the medium defusing scenario (t_9). Here, p_d1 is the probability that the leader is actually in an easy defusing situation, and p_ed1 is the probability that there is an explosion given that the leader is trying to defuse in an easy situation. As discussed later, while p_d1 is a function of the terrain, p_ed1 is a function of the leader's defusing capability.

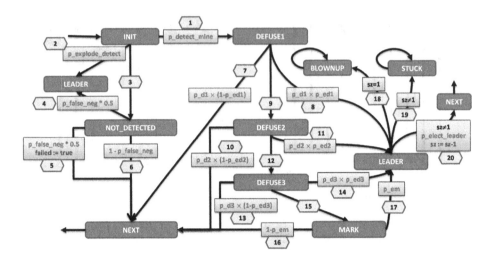

Fig. 3. α**PA** M_{cell}; transitions are numbered and labeled, and guards and probabilities are omitted as in Figure 1(b); states **LEADER** and **NEXT** are repeated to reduce clutter; all transitions are labeled by action tick, i.e., $\alpha = $ tick.

In the medium defusing scenario (**DEFUSE2**), the leader either blows up (t_{11}), successfully defuses the mine (t_{10}), or moves to the hard defusing scenario (t_{12}). The probabilities involved in this step are: p_d2 – the terrain-dependent probability that the leader is actually in a medium defusing situation, and p_ed2 – the probability (dependent on the leader's defusing capability) that there is an explosion given that it is trying to defuse in a medium situation.

In the hard defusing scenario (**DEFUSE3**), the leader either blows up (t_{14}), successfully defuses the mine (t_{13}), or attempts to mark the cell (t_{15}) as being mined. The probabilities involved in this step are: p_d3 – the terrain-dependent probability that the leader is actually in a hard defusing situation, and p_ed3 – the probability (dependent on the leader's defusing capability) that there is an explosion given that it is trying to defuse in a hard situation.

Finally, when the leader attempts to mark the cell, it either blows up (t_{17}) with probability p_em, or succeeds (t_{16}) and the team continues to the next cell. The probability p_em of an explosion during the marking operation is a function of the leader's defusing capability, as discussed later.

If the leader blows up, the team elects a new leader from state **LEADER**. If there are no remaining robots in the team (i.e., sz=0), the team moves to **BLOWNUP** (t_{18}) and stutters. Otherwise, with probability p_elect_leader, a new leader is elected successfully and the team moves on to the next cell (t_{20}), and with probability (1 - p_elect_leader) leader election fails and the team moves to **STUCK** (t_{19}) and stutters.

5.2   Team αPA Parameters

The α**PA** for a team is parameterized by the following:

1. The number of robots N, and the coordinates for *cInit* and *cFinal*.
2. The probability (p_detect_mine) of detecting a mine in a cell.
3. The probability (p_elect_leader) of successful leader election.
4. The remaining probabilities were computed from the terrain and the robot's capabilities as discussed next.

Modeling Terrain and Robot Capabilities. The robot's mine detection capability was modeled by a parameter DET with three possible values – LOW, MEDIUM and HIGH. The robot's mine defusing capability was modeled by a parameter DEF with three possible values – LOW, MEDIUM and HIGH. The robot's locomotion capability was modeled by a parameter LOC with three possible values – LOW, MEDIUM and HIGH. The terrain was modeled by eighteen independent parameters: (i) p_fn_dc0, p_fn_dc1 and p_fn_dc2 are the probabilities of a false negative (i.e., mine present but not detected) given that DET = LOW, MEDIUM and HIGH, respectively; (ii) p_d1, p_d2 and p_d3 are the probabilities of being in an easy, medium, or hard defusing situation, respectively; (iii) p_edet_dc0, p_edet_dc1 and p_edet_dc2 are the probabilities of an explosion during mine detection given that DET = LOW, MEDIUM and HIGH, respectively; (iv) p_edef_dc0, p_edef_dc1 and p_edef_dc2 are the probabilities of an explosion during mine defusing given that DEF = LOW, MEDIUM and HIGH, respectively; (v) p_skip_lc0, p_skip_lc1 and p_skip_lc2 are the probabilities of successful skip given that LOC = LOW, MEDIUM and HIGH, respectively; and (vi) p_turn_lc0, p_turn_lc1 and p_turn_lc2 are the probabilities of successful turn given that LOC = LOW, MEDIUM and HIGH, respectively. For our experiments, all terrain parameters were assigned constant values, but in practice we expect that these atomistic probabilities will be obtained empirically.

Remaining Probabilities. The probability of a false negative in Fig. 3 are computed as follows:

$$\text{p\_false\_neg} = \begin{cases} \text{p\_fn\_dc0 if DET} = \text{LOW,} \\ \text{p\_fn\_dc1 if DET} = \text{MEDIUM,} \\ \text{p\_fn\_dc2 if DET} = \text{HIGH.} \end{cases}$$

The probability of an explosion while detecting a mine is computed as follows:

$$\text{p\_explode\_detect} = \begin{cases} \text{p\_edet\_dc0 if DET} = \text{LOW,} \\ \text{p\_edet\_dc1 if DET} = \text{MEDIUM,} \\ \text{p\_edet\_dc2 if DET} = \text{HIGH.} \end{cases}$$

The probabilities of an explosion while defusing or marking a cell are computed as follows:

$$\text{p\_ed1} = \text{p\_ed2} = \text{p\_ed3} = \text{p\_em} = \begin{cases} \text{p\_edef\_dc0 if DEF} = \text{LOW,} \\ \text{p\_edef\_dc1 if DEF} = \text{MEDIUM,} \\ \text{p\_edef\_dc2 if DEF} = \text{HIGH.} \end{cases}$$

The probability of successful skip is computed as follows:

$$\text{p\_skip} = \begin{cases} \text{p\_skip\_lc0 if LOC} = \text{LOW}, \\ \text{p\_skip\_lc1 if LOC} = \text{MEDIUM}, \\ \text{p\_skip\_lc2 if LOC} = \text{HIGH}. \end{cases}$$

Finally, the probability of successful turn is computed as follows:

$$\text{p\_turn} = \begin{cases} \text{p\_turn\_lc0 if LOC} = \text{LOW}, \\ \text{p\_turn\_lc1 if LOC} = \text{MEDIUM}, \\ \text{p\_turn\_lc2 if LOC} = \text{HIGH}. \end{cases}$$

5.3 Multiple Teams and Properties

Let $M_i = (S_i, Init_i, \Sigma_i, \delta_i, AP_i, \mathcal{L}_i)$ be the α**PA** for the i-th team. Recall that all transitions in the α**PA** for a team are labeled by the action tick, i.e., $\Sigma_i = \{\text{tick}\}$. A state of M_i is a valuation to the variables x, y, dir, failed, sz and pc, where pc is the *program counter* whose value indicates the position of the α**PA** w.r.t. the state machines in Figure 1(b) and Figure 3. For example, pc = LEADER means that the team is about to elect a new leader. Note that all variables have a finite domain, hence S_i is finite as well. In addition, M_i has three atomic propositions: (i) $done_i$ which is true in all states where pc = DONE; (ii) $succ_i$ which is true in all states where failed = FALSE; and (iii) $init_i$ which is true in all states where pc = INIT. Now consider a scenario with T teams. Clearly, the α**PA**s $M_1, \ldots, M_T$ satisfy the conditions of Theorem 2.

Success. The first property we consider is true for all executions where all teams cover all their cells without missing a single mine within a deadline D. Let us write $\mathsf{F}^{\leq k}\Psi$ to mean $\Psi \vee \mathsf{X}\Psi \vee \mathsf{XX}\Psi \vee \cdots \vee \underbrace{\mathsf{XX}\ldots\mathsf{X}}_{k \text{ times}}\Psi$. Then our first property is expressed by the following path formula:

$$success_D \equiv (\mathsf{F}^{\leq D}(done_1 \wedge succ_1)) \wedge \cdots \wedge (\mathsf{F}^{\leq D}(done_T \wedge succ_T))$$

Note that $success_D$ satisfies the conditions of Theorem 2.

Coverage. The second property we consider is coverage. Informally, this is the number of cells processed by all the teams within a deadline D. Formally, it is expressed as the cumulative reward:

$$coverage_D \equiv C_{\leq D}((Init_1, \ldots, Init_T), R_1 \oplus \ldots \oplus R_T)$$

where, for $1 \leq i \leq T$, $R_i = (\rho_i, \iota_i)$ is the reward structure such that:

$$\forall s \in S_i \bullet \rho_i(s) = 1 \text{ if } Init_i \in \mathcal{L}_i(s) \text{ and } \rho_i(s) = 0 \text{ otherwise}$$
$$\forall (s, s') \in S_i \times S_i \bullet \iota_i(s, s') = 0$$

In other words, R_i assigns a reward 1 whenever the i-th team enters a new cell.

6 Experiments

We performed a set of experiments using the α**PA** model of the robotic demining scenario presented in Section 5. The goal was to demonstrate the suitability of our approach to make appropriate tradeoff decisions when designing robotic missions, and to demonstrate the effectiveness of our compositionality theorem in improving scalability. All our experiments were performed on an Intel Core i7 machine with four cores (each running at 2.7GHz) and 8GB of RAM. We used a timeout of 1800s, and fixed certain parameters as follows:

$$
\begin{array}{lll}
\mathsf{p\_fn\_dc0} = 0.05 & \mathsf{p\_fn\_dc1} = 0.01 & \mathsf{p\_fn\_dc2} = 0.005 \\
\mathsf{p\_d1} = 0.25 & \mathsf{p\_d2} = 0.33 & \mathsf{p\_d3} = 0.5 \\
\mathsf{p\_edet\_dc0} = 0.05 & \mathsf{p\_edet\_dc1} = 0.04 & \mathsf{p\_edet\_dc2} = 0.03 \\
\mathsf{p\_edef\_dc0} = 0.05 & \mathsf{p\_edef\_dc1} = 0.04 & \mathsf{p\_edef\_dc2} = 0.03 \\
\mathsf{p\_skip\_lc0} = 0.9999 & \mathsf{p\_skip\_lc1} = 0.99999 & \mathsf{p\_skip\_lc2} = 0.999999 \\
\mathsf{p\_turn\_lc0} = 0.9999 & \mathsf{p\_turn\_lc1} = 0.99999 & \mathsf{p\_turn\_lc2} = 0.999999 \\
\mathsf{p\_detect\_mine} = 0.5 & D = 250 & \mathsf{p\_elect\_leader} = 0.9
\end{array}
$$

We also set Row=10, and Col=12. Other parameters were varied based on the experiment. We used PRISM version 4.0.3, which was the latest version available at the start of this project. We modeled α**PA**s in PRISM as DTMCs with every transition labeled by an action called tick. Thus, the default synchronization semantics for DTMCs used by PRISM coincided with the semantics of composition of α**PA**s. All our PRISM models, results, as well as instructions to reproduce them are available at www.contrib.andrew.cmu.edu/ schaki/ discover/spin13.tgz.

Experiments about success. The first set of experiments were designed to evaluate the impact of DET, DEF, LOC, T and N on $success_D$. The results are summarized in Table 1. We consider eight possible combinations of DET, DEF, and LOC.

The first five rows are the values of $success_D$ for each of these eight combinations using $T = 2$ and different values of N. We observe that changing DET from LOW to HIGH has a much bigger impact on the value of $success_D$ compared to changing DEF or LOC. This suggests that using robots with good mine detection capability should be of high priority during mission design.

The next five rows show the value of $success_D$ with different values of T and N such that $T \times N = 30$, i.e., different team configurations with 30 robots. They indicate that three teams with ten robots each provide optimal values of $success_D$. Note that $success_D$ drops off sharply for $N < 5$ since small teams have a high chance of being blown up completely before mission completion.

The final column shows the average time required to compute $success_D$ over all eight combinations of DET, DEF, and LOC considered. The average is a good

Table 1. Results for $success_D$ with different T, N, DET, DEF and LOC; second row entries indicate values of DET, DEF and LOC; e.g., LLL = (DET=LOW, DEF=LOW, LOC=LOW); LHL = (DET=LOW, DEF=HIGH, LOC=LOW), etc.; Time = average time to compute $success_D$ over all combinations of DET, DEF and LOC.

T	N	$success_D$								Time
		LLL	LLH	LHL	LHH	HLL	HLH	HHL	HHH	seconds
2	2	0.000	0.000	0.000	0.000	0.013	0.014	0.035	0.035	21
2	3	0.001	0.001	0.003	0.004	0.065	0.066	0.129	0.131	26
2	5	0.018	0.018	0.030	0.031	0.256	0.259	0.355	0.359	38
2	10	0.073	0.074	0.086	0.087	0.386	0.391	0.443	0.449	62
2	15	0.076	0.077	0.087	0.089	0.386	0.391	0.443	0.449	87
3	10	0.088	0.090	0.100	0.101	0.435	0.441	0.491	0.498	46
6	5	0.080	0.081	0.094	0.095	0.429	0.434	0.488	0.494	29
10	3	0.046	0.047	0.062	0.063	0.354	0.359	0.435	0.441	35
15	2	0.011	0.012	0.020	0.020	0.175	0.177	0.261	0.264	48
30	1	0.000	0.000	0.000	0.000	0.001	0.001	0.003	0.003	100

Table 2. Results for $coverage_D$ with different T, N, DET, DEF and LOC; second row entries indicate values of DET, DEF and LOC; e.g., LLL = (DET=LOW, DEF=LOW, LOC=LOW); LHL = (DET=LOW, DEF=HIGH, LOC=LOW), etc.; Time = average time to compute $coverage_D$ over all combinations of DET, DEF and LOC.

T	N	DET:DEF:LOC								Time
		LLL	LLH	LHL	LHH	HLL	HLH	HHL	HHH	seconds
2	2	43.3	43.3	48.3	48.4	61.8	62.0	70.6	70.8	7
2	3	60.1	60.2	66.2	66.4	80.8	81.0	89.1	89.3	7
2	5	82.1	82.4	87.5	87.7	97.8	98.1	102.5	102.8	7
2	10	93.5	93.8	96.2	96.5	101.7	102.0	104.6	105.0	7
2	15	93.6	93.9	96.2	96.5	101.7	102.0	104.6	105.0	7
3	10	101.6	101.8	103.5	103.8	107.5	107.7	109.6	109.8	9
6	5	110.3	110.4	111.4	111.5	113.6	113.8	114.7	114.9	16
10	3	112.9	113.0	113.9	114.0	115.8	115.9	116.6	116.7	25
15	2	112.4	112.4	113.6	113.6	115.8	115.8	116.7	116.8	37
30	1	105.3	105.3	106.9	107.0	110.2	110.3	111.9	111.9	84

indicator since the standard deviation was quite low. These times were measured when we performed our experiments *compositionally*, i.e., computing $success_D$ for each team individually, and multiplying the results (in accordance with Theorem 2). When we used the monolithic approach, i.e., all teams composed in the same model, PRISM timed out at 1800 seconds in all cases.

Experiments about coverage. The next set of experiments were designed to evaluate the impact of DET, DEF, LOC, T and N on $coverage_D$. The results are summarized in Table 2. Each cell of the table corresponds to the same values of DET, DEF, LOC, T and N as in the corresponding cell in Table 1.

Not surprisingly, we again observe that changing DET from LOW to HIGH has a much bigger impact on the value of $coverage_D$ compared to changing DEF or LOC. This suggests that using robots with good mine detection capability is a good tradeoff for not only $success_D$, but $coverage_D$ as well.

The results for different values of T (last five rows of Table 1) are somewhat different. The optimal $coverage_D$ is observed for ten teams with three robots each. This reflects a subtle difference between $coverage_D$ and $success_D$ – a cell is covered as soon as the team reaches it, but that does not contribute to success unless the team avoids being blown up as well. In general, the benefit of smaller teams extends further for $coverage_D$ simply because more teams are able to "reach" more cells even if they get blown up. However, for $T > 15$, even $coverage_D$ falls off.

The final column shows the average time required to compute $coverage_D$ over all eight combinations of DET, DEF, and LOC considered. Once again, these times arc for the compositional approach, i.e., computing $coverage_D$ for each team individually, and adding the results (in accordance with Theorem 4). For the monolithic approach, PRISM timed out at 1800 seconds in all cases.

7   Conclusion

We present an approach to compute quantitative utility of robotic missions using probabilistic model checking. We show how to express a robotic demining mission as a $\alpha\mathbf{PA}$, its success as a LTL formula, and its coverage as a reward. We prove a set of compositionality theorems that enable us to compute the success probability (or, coverage) of a system composed of several $\alpha\mathbf{PA}s$ by combining the success probability (or, coverage) of each $\alpha\mathbf{PA}$ in isolation. This ameliorates the statespace explosion problem, even when the system being verified is composed of many $\alpha\mathbf{PA}s$. We validate our approach empirically, using the probabilistic model checker PRISM for our experiments.

We envision building on this work in several directions. One issue is that our model for the demining mission is based on several atomistic probabilities (e.g., p_fn_dc0). We assume that these probabilities are available with sufficient accuracy. Otherwise, the predictions made via probabilistic model checking will be correspondingly inaccurate. As part of our ongoing work, we are developing ways to estimate these probabilities via field experiments. Another direction is to adapt probabilistic model checking to create a more generative approach – one that constructs an optimal mission – that can handle an expressive range of mission configurations and constraints.

Acknowledgements. We thank Anvesh Komuravelli and Arie Gurfinkel for many helpful discussions and comments that helped shape this work[1].

References

1. Baier, C.: On algorithmic verification methods for probabilistic systems. PhD thesis, University of Mannheim, Habilitation thesis (1998)
2. Chaki, S., Dolan, J.M., Giampapa, J.A.: Toward A Quantitative Method for Assuring Coordinated Autonomy. In: Proc. of ARMS Workshop (to appear, 2013)
3. Chen, T., Diciolla, M., Kwiatkowska, M.Z., Mereacre, A.: Quantitative Verification of Implantable Cardiac Pacemakers. In: Proc. of RTSS (2012)
4. de Alfaro, L., Henzinger, T.A., Jhala, R.: Compositional Methods for Probabilistic Systems. In: Larsen, K.G., Nielsen, M. (eds.) CONCUR 2001. LNCS, vol. 2154, pp. 351–365. Springer, Heidelberg (2001)
5. Feng, L., Han, T., Kwiatkowska, M., Parker, D.: Learning-Based Compositional Verification for Synchronous Probabilistic Systems. In: Bultan, T., Hsiung, P.-A. (eds.) ATVA 2011. LNCS, vol. 6996, pp. 511–521. Springer, Heidelberg (2011)
6. Feng, L., Kwiatkowska, M.Z., Parker, D.: Compositional Verification of Probabilistic Systems Using Learning. In: Proc. of QEST (2010)
7. Feng, L., Kwiatkowska, M., Parker, D.: Automated Learning of Probabilistic Assumptions for Compositional Reasoning. In: Giannakopoulou, D., Orejas, F. (eds.) FASE 2011. LNCS, vol. 6603, pp. 2–17. Springer, Heidelberg (2011)
8. Heath, J., Kwiatkowska, M.Z., Norman, G., Parker, D., Tymchyshyn, O.: Probabilistic model checking of complex biological pathways. Theoretical Computer Science (TCS) 391(3) (2008)
9. Komuravelli, A., Păsăreanu, C.S., Clarke, E.M.: Assume-Guarantee Abstraction Refinement for Probabilistic Systems. In: Madhusudan, P., Seshia, S.A. (eds.) CAV 2012. LNCS, vol. 7358, pp. 310–326. Springer, Heidelberg (2012)
10. Kumar, J.A., Vasudevan, S.: Automatic Compositional Reasoning for Probabilistic Model Checking of Hardware Designs. In: Proc. of QEST (2010)
11. Kwiatkowska, M., Norman, G., Parker, D.: PRISM 4.0: Verification of Probabilistic Real-Time Systems. In: Gopalakrishnan, G., Qadeer, S. (eds.) CAV 2011. LNCS, vol. 6806, pp. 585–591. Springer, Heidelberg (2011)

[1] This material is based upon work funded and supported by the Department of Defense under Contract No. FA8721-05-C-0003 with Carnegie Mellon University for the operation of the Software Engineering Institute, a federally funded research and development center. NO WARRANTY. THIS CARNEGIE MELLON UNIVERSITY AND SOFTWARE ENGINEERING INSTITUTE MATERIAL IS FURNISHED ON AN AS-IS BASIS. CARNEGIE MELLON UNIVERSITY MAKES NO WARRANTIES OF ANY KIND, EITHER EXPRESSED OR IMPLIED, AS TO ANY MATTER INCLUDING, BUT NOT LIMITED TO, WARRANTY OF FITNESS FOR PURPOSE OR MERCHANTABILITY, EXCLUSIVITY, OR RESULTS OBTAINED FROM USE OF THE MATERIAL. CARNEGIE MELLON UNIVERSITY DOES NOT MAKE ANY WARRANTY OF ANY KIND WITH RESPECT TO FREEDOM FROM PATENT, TRADEMARK, OR COPYRIGHT INFRINGEMENT.This material has been approved for public release and unlimited distribution. Carnegie Mellon is registered in the U.S. Patent and Trademark Office by Carnegie Mellon University. DM-0000246.

12. Kwiatkowska, M., Norman, G., Parker, D., Qu, H.: Assume-Guarantee Verification for Probabilistic Systems. In: Esparza, J., Majumdar, R. (eds.) TACAS 2010. LNCS, vol. 6015, pp. 23–37. Springer, Heidelberg (2010)
13. Kwiatkowska, M.Z., Norman, G., Sproston, J.: Probabilistic Model Checking of Deadline Properties in the IEEE 1394 FireWire Root Contention Protocol. Formal Aspects of Computing (FACJ) 14(3) (2003)
14. Segala, R.: Modeling and Verification of Randomized Distributed Real-Time Systems. PhD thesis, Massachusetts Institute of Technology. Available as Technical Report MIT/LCS/TR-676 (1995)
15. Stoelinga, M.: Alea jacta est: verification of probabilistic, real-time and parametric systems. PhD thesis, University of Nijmegen (2002), Available via http://www.soe.ucsc.edu/~marielle
16. Sukthankar, G., Sycara, K.: Team-aware Robotic Demining Agents for Military Simulation, http://www.cs.cmu.edu/~softagents/iaai00/iaai00.html
17. Vardi, M.Y.: Automatic Verification of Probabilistic Concurrent Finite-State Programs. In: Proc. of FOCS (1985)

Synthesizing Controllers for Automation Tasks with Performance Guarantees

Chih-Hong Cheng, Michael Geisinger, and Christian Buckl

fortiss GmbH, Guerickestr. 25, 80805 München, Germany
http://mgsyn.fortiss.org/

Abstract. We present an extension of the MGSyn toolbox that allows synthesizing parallelized controller programs for industrial automation with performance guarantees. We explain the underlying design, outline its algorithmic optimizations, and exemplify its usage with examples for controlling production systems.

1 Introduction

Game-based synthesis is a technique that automatically generates controllers implementing high-level specifications. A controller in the game-based setting corresponds to the finite representation of a winning strategy of a suitable game. Recent algorithmic improvements allow synthesis to be applied in research domains such as programming languages, hardware design and robotics. Within the domain of industrial automation, we created the MGSyn toolbox [3] to synthesize centralized controller programs for industrial automation that orchestrate multiple processing stations. Uncertainties from sensor readings are modeled as uncontrollable (but fully specified) environment moves, thereby creating a game. The use of game-based modeling even allows the automation plant to be dependable with respect to the introduction of faults. Although the initial experiment is encouraging, the road to a solid methodology applicable to useful industrial settings is still long. One crucial requirement is to generate efficient controllers, where efficiency can be referred to several measures in production such as processing time, throughput or consumed power.

In this paper, we present an extension of MGSyn that allows synthesis of programs that not only win the corresponding game (i.e., successfully accomplish production tasks), but also provide explicit guarantees concerning specified quantitative measures. Admittedly, efforts within the research community target to synthesize optimal controllers [1,7,2,4]. Nevertheless, we argue that finding optimal controllers can be difficult in practice – apart from complexity considerations, the optimality criteria are often multiple yet independent measures and no global optimum exists in general. Creating engines that synthesize controllers and guarantee performance is a reasonable alternative to the typical approach of listing performance criteria as secondary specifications that need to be *guaranteed*.

The extensions of MGSyn presented in this paper target the following aspects:

- Enable an intuitive method to select *performance measures* in a cost-annotated model. For every type of performance measure, provide a corresponding synthesis engine.

E. Bartocci and C.R. Ramakrishnan (Eds.): SPIN 2013, LNCS 7976, pp. 154–159, 2013.

Table 1. Semantics of sequential ($\odot$) and parallel ($\otimes$) composition (WC = worst case, ET = execution time).

cost ≈ ET	$\odot := \mathsf{max}$	$\odot := \mathsf{sum}$	cost ≈ power	$\odot := \mathsf{max}$	$\odot := \mathsf{sum}$
$\otimes := \mathsf{max}$	WCET of any single action	Total WCET	$\otimes := \mathsf{max}$	Peak power consumption of any single action	–
$\otimes := \mathsf{sum}$	–	Total ET of all actions	$\otimes := \mathsf{sum}$	WC peak power consumption	WC total power consumption

- Identify sets of actions that may be *executed in parallel*, as efficient execution of production tasks requires the exploitation of parallelization.
- Synthesize controllers that guarantee performance under *non-cooperative scenarios*. For many problems, completing the task is only possible when the environment cooperates. Our approach allows a synthesized controller to loop as long as the environment does not cooperate. The control task is achieved when the environment (e.g., a human operator) turns cooperative.

2 Approach

Cost annotation. For quantitative synthesis, the common model of computation is based on weighted automata [5], where costs of actions are annotated on edges. The quantitative extension of MGSyn allows specifying costs as a performance metric with the following restrictions: (1) Cost is annotated on a parameterized action as an upper bound and every concretized action (i.e., action instance with concrete parameter values) inherits that cost. (2) All costs are non-negative integers. (3) Uncontrollable actions (i.e., environment moves) have zero cost. The first restriction is due to the syntactic format of the PDDL language [6]. The second restriction is used for symbolic encoding in *binary decision diagrams* (BDD).

MGSyn allows selecting a *sequential composition operator* $\odot$ that calculates a new value from the value of the existing trace and the current cost associated with the selected edge. Two common operators are max and sum. For example, if cost annotation in the weighted automaton corresponds to power consumption, then a sequential composition based on the max operator models peak power consumption, whereas the sum operator models total power consumption.

Parallel execution. MGSyn by default generates a *sequence* of control actions that achieve the specified task. However, executing independent actions *in parallel* can be of advantage, for example by reducing the overall execution time. MGSyn assumes that two or more actions can in principle be executed in parallel when the workspaces affected by the actions are disjoint and the actions have disjoint parameters (i.e., no "resource sharing"). When parallel execution of degree d is used, MGSyn generates combinations of d actions with syntactic guards to prevent dependent actions from being executed in parallel[1]. Consider conveyor belt action belt-move(dev, wp, p_a, p_b) which allows to use device dev to move a work piece wp from position p_a to position p_b.

---

[1] We currently do not consider executing multiple sequential actions in parallel with another action.

For $d = 2$, MGSyn automatically derives action PAR_belt-move_belt-move(dev_1, wp_1, $p_{1a}, p_{1b}, dev_2, wp_2, p_{2a}, p_{2b}$) for moving two different work pieces on two different conveyor belts at the same time. In the precondition of this action, the constraints $dev_1 \neq dev_2$, $wp_1 \neq wp_2$, $p_{1a} \neq p_{2a}, p_{2b}$ and $p_{1b} \neq p_{2a}, p_{2b}$ are automatically added to ensure that parameter values are different[2].

To use quantitative synthesis, we provide parallel composition operators orthogonal to sequential composition operators. Table 1 lists some examples for cost semantics with respect to execution time and power consumption and the two operators sequential composition ($\odot$) and parallel composition ($\otimes$), where "−" indicates that no meaningful semantics was found. The effects of parallel composition operators are statically created in MGSyn and are independent of the synthesis algorithm. For example, if action belt-move has cost 3, MGSyn creates parallel action PAR_belt-move_belt-move with cost 6 if $\otimes := $ sum and cost 3 if $\otimes := $ max.

Synthesis engine. We outline how the synthesis engine supports sequential operators.

- For max, given a performance (i.e., cost) bound k, the engine statically removes every parameterized control action whose cost is greater than k. Notice that as the cost of any environment action is always zero (cf. restriction 3), we never restrict the ability of the environment. Then the game is created as if no cost is used. Therefore, max can be used in all game types.
- For sum, the support of quantitative synthesis is mainly within reachability games where a synthesized strategy does not contain a loop, since any loop with nonzero cost implies the overall cost to be infinite. Given a performance bound k, the synthesis engine starts with the set of goal states whose cost equals k and computes the reachability attractor. Let the state be (q, α), where q is the state of the non-quantitative reachability game and α is the cost. During the attractor computation, if (q, α) is in the attractor, one can reach the goal state from q with cost $k - \alpha$, because the environment has no control over the cost (cf. restriction 3). This allows reusing our existing game engine with reachability winning conditions. The controller wins the game if the attractor contains the initial state whose cost is greater than zero.

Non-cooperative environment. Lastly, MGSyn allows the backend solver to find strategies for *goal-or-loop* specifications. This extension focuses on specifying non-cooperative scenarios as a looping invariant. Whenever a run of the game leaves the invariant, the goal (i.e. the accomplishment of the task) should eventually be reached. This concept can also be applied to synthesize low-level controllers realizing parameterized actions. For example, consider the action belt-move of the conveyor belt. Realizing such a controller requires a specification which checks when the work piece has appeared at the start of the belt, and the synthesized program should allow to loop as long as the work piece is not detected.

It is undesirable that an automation system behaves arbitrarily during the looping process (although still conforming to the specification), because this would consume excessive energy. This problem can be handled by a game reduction that sets the cost

---

[2] MGSyn does not generate constraints such as $dev_1 \neq p_{2a}$, because dev_1 and p_{2a} are of different types.

of idle or sensor-triggering actions to be zero and all other actions greater than zero. When specifying an upper bound on the total accumulated cost, the synthesis engine will ensure that the cost accumulation is zero during the looping process, because this is the only way to ensure that the accumulated cost does not exceed the threshold.

Given a looping condition *Loop* and a goal condition *Goal*, where both are sets of states, the synthesis algorithm is based on an approach that solves reachability and safety games in sequence: first apply reachability game solving and compute the control attractor $A := \mathsf{Attr}_0(Goal)$ where states within A can eventually enter the goal regardless of choices made by the environment. Then use safety game to compute the environment attractor $B := \mathsf{Attr}_1(\neg Loop \wedge \neg A)$ where the environment can guarantee to reach $\neg Loop \wedge \neg A$ for every state $s \in B$ regardless of choices made by the controller. If a state is within A, a strategy to reach the goal exists. Otherwise, if a controllable state s is not within B, it has a strategy to stay outside $\neg Loop \wedge \neg A$, i.e., to stay within $Loop \vee A$. As s is not within A, it is within $Loop$.

Therefore, with the above computation, a feasible strategy can guarantee to loop within *Loop*, or reach a state that is within A. From that state, the reachability strategy is used to guide the run towards the goal. The complexity of solving goal-or-loop specifications is linear to the size of the arena, making it feasible to be applied in larger scenarios. By annotating actions with cost, MGSyn allows to synthesize controllers that guarantees efficiency in looping (i.e., looping cannot increase cost).

3   Using MGSyn for Quantitative Synthesis

In the following, we demonstrate how quantitative synthesis is achieved in MGSyn in a simplified scenario. The FESTO Modular Production System (MPS)[3] is a modular system of mechatronic devices that model industrial automation tasks by processing simple work pieces. Our demonstration comprises two FESTO MPS units that form a circular processing chain, namely *storage* and *processing* (compare Figure 1). The formal model derived from this setup consists of:

- A list of formal predicates that describe the system state space, for example at(?work-piece ?position), drilled(?work-piece) and color(?work-piece ?value).
- A list of devices (instances of the predefined device types robot arm storage RAS, conveyor belt CB, lever Lever, rotary plate RP, height sensor HS, drill Drill) with operating positions.
- Behavioral interfaces (actions) associated with each device type (e.g., belt-move, plate-rotate, trigger-color-sensor) with annotated individual *costs*. Formally, a behavioral interface specifies preconditions and effects on the system state space.
- Quantitative properties (i.e., goal conditions over the system state space) with annotated *cost bounds* as well as sequential and parallel *composition operators*. Composition operators can be either sum or max as presented in Section 1.

We formulate a formal specification in PDDL which resembles the following informal specification: initially, work pieces wp1 and wp2 are located at CB01-mid and CB02-mid, respectively. The goal is to drill wp1 if it is facing up (which means the work

---

[3] http://www.festo-didactic.com/int-en/learning-systems/
mps-the-modular-production-system/

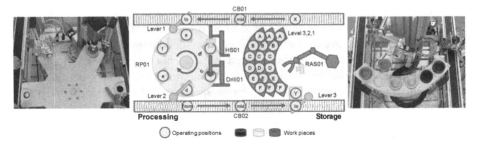

Fig. 1. FESTO MPS automation system and its simplified abstract model

Table 2. Results of synthesis from quantitative specifications. For comparison, results for experiments without cost model are provided. Times refer to a 3 GHz system with 4 GB of RAM (single-threaded algorithm).

Experiment	Max. degree of parallelization d	Cost bound	$\odot$	$\oplus$	WC moves	WC cost	Synthesis time (sec)
1. WCET optimization	2	28	sum	max	inf.[1]	inf.[1]	18.7
	2	29	sum	max	15	29	19.4
	2	30^2	sum	max	14	29	22.1
2. WC total power consumption optimization	2	41	sum	sum	inf.[1]	inf.[1]	20.8
	2	42	sum	sum	15	42	21.0
	2	43^2	sum	sum	14	42	21.1
3. WC peak power consumption optimization	2	2	max	sum	inf.[1]	inf.[1]	14.9[3]
	2	3	max	sum	18	3	16.3
	2	4^2	max	sum	15	4	19.2
Parallelization disabled	1	41	sum	N/A	inf.[1]	inf.[1]	6.5
	1	42	sum	N/A	22	42	7.1
	1	43^2	sum	N/A	21	42	7.6
	1	2	max	N/A	inf.[1]	inf.[1]	5.4
	1	3^2	max	N/A	21	3	6.3
Non-quantitative (no consideration of cost)	1	∞	N/A	N/A	21	N/A	6.4
	2	∞	N/A	N/A	14	N/A	19.0

[1] Infeasible (i.e., no solution) due to cost bound being too restrictive.

[2] The same strategy is generated also for higher cost bounds, only synthesis time differs.

[3] Since it is not obvious whether behavioral interfaces with cost 3 are actually used in the generated strategy, the infeasibility of this scenario cannot be directly decided from the cost annotation/bound.

piece's orientation is correct) and to move it to CB02-mid. wp2 should be stored in the storage rack level that corresponds to its color (red work pieces go to upper level and silver work pieces to middle level), but when the rack is already occupied, it should be moved to CB01-mid. Costs are annotated as follows: behavioral interfaces robot-move (for RAS01) and belt-move (for CB01 and CB02) have cost 3, plate-rotate for RP-01 has cost 2 and all other behavioral interfaces (including sensor triggerings) have cost 1. Furthermore, we formulate the following optimization goals:

1. *WCET optimization:* Synthesize a strategy that does not exceed a specified maximal execution time. Cost corresponds to execution time with $\odot := \mathsf{sum}$, $\otimes := \mathsf{max}$.

2. *WC total power consumption optimization:* Synthesize a strategy not exceeding a given WC total power consumption. Cost represents power consumption with $\odot := \mathsf{sum}, \otimes := \mathsf{sum}$.

3. *WC peak power consumption optimization:* Synthesize a strategy not exceeding a given WC peak power consumption. Cost represents power consumption with $\odot := \mathsf{max}, \otimes := \mathsf{sum}$.

Table 2 summarizes the results. In case of feasibility, synthesis times also include C code generation for execution on real hardware or simulation. Worst case (WC) numbers of moves were directly extracted from the generated strategy. Worst case costs were derived by inspecting all possible paths in the generated strategy using simulation.

The results show that about one third of the control moves can be parallelized and that parallelization requires about three times the synthesis time of the non-parallel case for the given specification. Higher cost bounds require a slightly higher synthesis time. When the cost bound is very tight, the tool synthesizes a strategy with more, but cheaper moves (e.g., 15 instead of 14). The generated strategy for experiment 3 significantly differs from the strategy for 1 and 2.

4   Conclusion

In this paper, we report how MGSyn is extended to synthesize controllers with performance guarantees. The key factors are (1) flexible interpretation of cost as a performance bound using sequential and parallel composition operators as well as (2) suitable integration into the symbolic synthesis engine. Experiments show that the resulting controllers are quantitatively better than controllers being synthesized without cost analysis. The extra synthesis time can be tolerated when controllers are generated offline.

References

1. Bloem, R., Chatterjee, K., Henzinger, T.A., Jobstmann, B.: Better quality in synthesis through quantitative objectives. In: Bouajjani, A., Maler, O. (eds.) CAV 2009. LNCS, vol. 5643, pp. 140–156. Springer, Heidelberg (2009)
2. Chatterjee, K., Henzinger, T.A., Jobstmann, B., Singh, R.: Measuring and synthesizing systems in probabilistic environments. In: Touili, T., Cook, B., Jackson, P. (eds.) CAV 2010. LNCS, vol. 6174, pp. 380–395. Springer, Heidelberg (2010)
3. Cheng, C.-H., Geisinger, M., Ruess, H., Buckl, C., Knoll, A.: MGSyn: Automatic synthesis for industrial automation. In: Madhusudan, P., Seshia, S.A. (eds.) CAV 2012. LNCS, vol. 7358, pp. 658–664. Springer, Heidelberg (2012)
4. Desharnais, J., Gupta, V., Jagadeesan, R., Panangaden, P.: Metrics for labelled Markov processes. Theoretical Computer Science 318(3), 323–354 (2004)
5. Droste, M., Kuich, W., Vogler, H.: Handbook of weighted automata. Springer (2009)
6. Ghallab, M., Howe, A., Krobnock, C., McDermott, D., Ram, A., Veloso, M., Weld, D., Wilkins, D.: PDDL-the planning domain definition language. Technical Report CVC TR-98003/DCS TR-1165, Yale Center for Computer Vision and Control (October 1998)
7. Černý, P., Chatterjee, K., Henzinger, T.A., Radhakrishna, A., Singh, R.: Quantitative synthesis for concurrent programs. In: Gopalakrishnan, G., Qadeer, S. (eds.) CAV 2011. LNCS, vol. 6806, pp. 243–259. Springer, Heidelberg (2011)

Specification and Validation of Link Reversal Routing via Graph Transformations

Giorgio Delzanno and Riccardo Traverso

DIBRIS, Università di Genova, Italy

Abstract. We apply executable Graph Transformation Systems for the formal specification of the Gafni-Bertsekas algorithm, a Link Reversal Routing algorithm for Mobile Ad Hoc Networks. The considered case-study and the corresponding correctness properties require the combination of graph production rules with operations on data fields, control strategies and temporal properties defined over graph patterns. The model is automatically validated via the GROOVE model checker.

1 Introduction

Following a recently established connection between graph grammars and verification (see e.g. [14,2,16,15,18]), we propose to apply Graph Transformation Systems (GTS) as an automated validation method for distributed algorithms. As a case-study we consider here the Gafni-Bertsekas algorithm [11], an instance of the more general class of Link Reversal Routing (LRR) algorithms used for route maintenance in Mobile Ad Hoc Networks [22]. In this version of the protocol heights (tuples of integers) are associated to individual nodes. The lexicographic order of heights specifies the direction of an overlay network that points towards a fixed destination node. A virtual link between two nodes is well-defined only if they are connected in the underlying communication topology, made of undirected links. The main feature of the protocol is that link reversal steps maintain the virtual network in form of a DAG.

In our approach we specify the protocol via executable graph production rules as provided by the GROOVE tool [12]. GROOVE has been developed as an automated support for object-oriented program transformations. Its specification language however can easily be adapted to model dynamically changing networks [15]. We exploit this feature to express link updates that describe unexpected network modifications (link deletion and addition) as well as route maintenance phases. Conditions and updates on data fields are combined with graph production rules in order to reason on a height-based version of the protocol. All specifications are given by exploiting symmetries induced by the use of transformations that work modulo graph isomorphism. To validate our model, we use the GROOVE model checker for a CTL temporal logic on transitions. The model checker operates on the labelled transition system (LTS) induced by a set of graph productions. CTL propositions are defined on top of transition names. This way it is possible to state properties on graph patterns that define the

E. Bartocci and C.R. Ramakrishnan (Eds.): SPIN 2013, LNCS 7976, pp. 160–177, 2013.

enabling of a rule. This is particularly useful when considering enabling conditions defined via regular expressions on edge labels. E.g., they can be used to formally specify reachability of partitioned configurations. Strategies for generating the LTS can be defined by associating priorities to production rules and by using control programs. The combination of priorities, rich patterns expressing bad configurations, and temporal properties allows to specify all the correctness requirements of the Gafni-Bertsekas algorithm.

In the paper we report on experimental results obtained with the model checker by varying both the size of the initial configuration and the number of dynamic link modifications. Starting from fully connected topologies and admitting dynamic modifications, we manage to handle networks with up to six nodes. Our study can be viewed as a preliminary step towards the application of GROOVE as a model checker for Link Reversal Routing and, more in general, of distributed fault-tolerant algorithms.

Outline. In Section 2 we introduce the main concepts underlying the GROOVE tool. In Section 3 we describe Link Reversal Routing and the Gafni-Bertsekas protocol. In Section 4 we describe in detail the specification of the protocol in GROOVE, and, in Section 5, the results of our analysis. In Section 6 we compare our work with other approaches for the specific classes of protocol considered here.

2   Graph Grammars as Executable Specifications

GROOVE is based on a graph representation of system states and on a representation of state updates via graph transformations. Graph production rules specify both matching patterns and negative application conditions (NAC). Graph matching is used to select the pattern in the host graph that has to be rewritten into a new graph (obtained by deleting/adding/merging nodes and edges). A NAC specifies a sub-pattern that must be absent in the host graph in order for the rule to be applicable (e.g. they specify global conditions).

2.1   Graph Transformation Systems (GTS)

To define a GTS, we follow the style of [7,13]. A graph $G = \langle N, E, L \rangle$ consists of a finite set N of nodes, a finite set $E \subseteq N \times N$ of edges, and a labelling function L of nodes and edges. We use $\mathcal{G}$ to denote the set of all graphs, ranged over by $G, H, \ldots$. A graph matching $m : \mathcal{G} \to \mathcal{G}$ is a graph morphism that preserves node and edge labels, i.e., for $G = \langle N, E, L \rangle$ and $G' = \langle N', E', L' \rangle$, if $e = \langle n, n' \rangle \in E$, then $e' = \langle m(n), m(n') \rangle \in E'$, $L(n) = L'(m(n))$, $L(n') = L'(m(n'))$, and $L(e) = L'(e')$. A graph transformation rule $p \in R$ specifies how the system evolves when going from one state to another: it is identified by its name ($Np \in \mathcal{N}$, where $\mathcal{N}$ is a global set of rule names) and consists of a left-hand side graph (L_p), a right-hand side graph (R_p), and a set of so-called negative application conditions (NAC$_p$, which are super-graphs of L_p).

Definition 1. *A Graph Production System (GPS)* $P = \langle I, R \rangle$ *consists of a graph* I *(the initial state), and a set of graph transformation rules* R.

The application of a graph transformation rule p transforms a graph G, the source graph, into a graph H, the target graph, by looking for an occurrence of L_p in G (specified by a graph matching m that cannot be extended to an occurrence of any graph in NAC_p) and then by replacing that occurrence with R_p, resulting in H. Such a rule application is denoted as $G \to_{p,m} H$. Each GPS $P = \langle R, I \rangle$ specifies a (possibly infinite) state space which can be generated by repeatedly applying the graph transformation rules on the states, starting from the initial state I.

Definition 2. *A GTS* $T = \langle S, \to, I \rangle$ *generated by* $P = \langle R, I \rangle$ *consists of a set* $S \subseteq \mathcal{G}$ *of graphs representing states, an initial state* $I \in S$, *and a transition relation* $\to \in S \times R \times [\mathcal{G} \to \mathcal{G}] \times S$, *such that* $\langle G, p, m, H \rangle \in \to$ *iff there is a rule application* $G \to_{p,m} H'$ *with* H' *isomorphic to* H.

2.2   The GROOVE Simulator and Model Checker

GROOVE [12] consists of a GUI that allows editing of rules and graphs and animated simulations of a specification. The state space is stored as an LTS. The strategy according to which the state space is explored can be set as a parameter. In the latest versions of GROOVE there are several specification facilities. We will hereafter refer to the latest version to date, version 4.8.6. Node labels can either be node types or flags. A flag is used to model a boolean condition which is true for a node if and only if the flag is present. To specify data fields ranging over basic types like booleans, integers, and strings, we can use node attributes. Attributes are treated as special edges that do not point to a standard node, but to a node that corresponds to a data value. The type of a node specifies the set of allowed flags and edge labels and and the type of its data fields. Operations over data fields are specified as node relations (evaluated automatically in data fields corresponding to the results) or as typed expressions with constructs for both updates (e.g. let) and nested expressions.

   Universal quantification is another interesting feature of the input language. A universally quantified (sub)rule is a rule that is applied to all subgraphs that satisfy the relevant application conditions, rather than just a single one as in the standard case. The use of universally quantified rules allows to naturally define parametric transformations (thus saving space in both the input model and in the state space). Universal quantification can be nested within existential quantifiers to define shared patterns between multiple applications of the same production (e.g. to rewrite all nodes that have a field/data in common with a specific node). The documentation of the feature is not very detailed, so we will use it in a restricted way.

   GROOVE provides different means for controlling the rewriting process. The first method is based on priorities. Low-priority rules may only be applied if no higher-priority rule is applicable. Another method is via control programs, which can be used to restrict the system to specific sequences of rule applications.

A control program can be viewed as an automata whose language specifies admissible sequences of transition applications.

Finally, another interesting feature is the use of regular expressions to define nested conditions on configurations. They extend graph matching with parametric pattern conditions such as the existence of a path between two nodes. For instance, an edge with label $a+$ between two nodes matches any (non null) path in which edges have only labels in a. Such a pattern can then be used to update the host graph.

2.3   An Example: Linked List

To illustrate how graph productions are specified in the GROOVE visual language we consider an example in which graphs represent dynamically created linked lists with tail insertion (put) and head removal (get). In the initial configuration we use two nodes as sentinels to denote the empty list. The first node has two forward pointers (h=head, t=tail) both pointing to the second node.

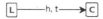

The *put* operation inserts a new node pointed by the tail pointer. The GROOVE visual language adopts coloured nodes and edges to denote deletion and addition of edges, nodes, and label updates. Indeed, the rule is specified as follows.

The dashed line denotes the deletion of the old t-edge. A deletion acts both as a guard (the edge being removed has to exist) and as a postcondition (the edge is removed from the graph). The thick lines denote the addition of two new edges. This notation can be expanded into a graph production containing a graph L_p with two nodes L and C connected via a t-edge in the left-hand side, and a graph R_p with three nodes L, C and C, with an n-edge connecting the last two nodes and a t-edge connecting the first and last node. The L_p graph is removed and the nodes and edges of R_p are created at its place. The nodes of R_p are linked to the nodes of L_p via a further graph morphism (usually denoted by using extra numerical labels to put in relation nodes in the left- and right-hand side).

Deletion of a cell is specified via the following rule.

Dashed lines denote removal of old h- and n-edges. The thick line denotes the addition of a new h-edge. Clearly, the two productions assume that in the transformed graph there exists only one h-edge and only one t-edge (this property is invariant under applications of the productions). Starting from the initial configuration, the firing of *put* produces the following sequence of configurations.

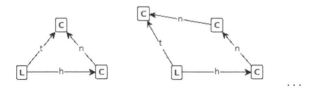

The transformation can continue either back to the previous states, or to a list with an additional cell. Therefore, the considered graph production system generates lists of arbitrary length.

GROOVE provides a GUI with a Simulator for the step-by-step visualization of the behaviour of a system, in which it is possible to highlight the matching pattern for a specific rule. Rules are partitioned in accord to the associated priorities. The simulator guides the execution via the corresponding rule ordering.

The built-in verifier generates the LTS of a given graph production system in form of a reachability graph. Based on this representation of the state-space, the model checker supports verification of CTL/LTL specifications that can be defined over graph patterns. This is achieved by using rule names as propositions. Specifically, the left-hand side of a formula (and the corresponding NAC) is used to check for the presence of a given sub-pattern in the current configuration. Consider a rule with name *bad*, whose left-hand side denotes a bad pattern (e.g. a cycle in a graph). Then, the firing of *bad* denotes the occurrence of the bad pattern in the reachability graph. Formulas are built over predicates defined over rule names, temporal operators like A, E (for CTL only), F, G, X (for CTL/LTL), and of their Boolean combinations (and/or/negation). A CTL formula like AG !*bad* can then be used to specify the safety property "the bad pattern can never be reached". In our linked list example we could specify bad patterns like self-loops with regular expressions on h- and t-edges (unreachable in our model). If a property does not hold, the model checker returns a counter-example.

3   Link Reversal Routing Algorithms

Link Reversal Routing (LRR) [22] algorithms are designed for large, dynamically changing networks, in which topology changes are too frequent to make flooding of routing informations a viable solution. The main goal is to quickly repair a corrupted route with a new valid, but not necessarily optimal, one. The adaptivity and scalability of LRR algorithms make them suitable for Ad Hoc Networks. We assume here to work on networks in which nodes are connected via bidirectional channels (i.e. the communication layer is an undirected graph). LRR works with an overlay network used to identify routes to a specific destination node. The overlay network is defined via a Directed Acyclic Graph (DAG) with exactly one destination node (a node with only incoming links). Other nodes have either incoming and outgoing links or just outgoing links. When the last outgoing link of a node breaks, the node becomes a sink for the network and it starts route maintenance. One possible strategy, called full reversal, is to reverse all incoming edges. After link reversal, the maintenance procedure is recursively applied to the surrounding nodes. The algorithm stabilizes after finitely many steps if the graph is not partitioned.

3.1 The Gafni-Bertsekas Algorithm

We consider here the partial reversal version of the Gafni-Bertsekas algorithm [11]. In this setting a node that becomes a sink tries to minimize the number of links to be reversed. The partial reversal method can be implemented using heights. More in detail, every node u has a tuple of values $\langle \alpha_u, \beta_u, id_u \rangle$, where α_u is a non negative integer, β_u is an integer, and id_u is an integer that denotes a unique identifier for the node. Initially, α_u is 0 for every node u. Furthermore, heights are totally ordered using the lexicographic ordering, namely

$$\langle \alpha_u, \beta_u, u \rangle < \langle \alpha_v, \beta_v, v \rangle$$

if and only if $\alpha_u < \alpha_v$ or ($\alpha_u = \alpha_v$ and $\beta_u < \beta_v$) or ($\alpha_u = \alpha_v$ and $\beta_u = \beta_v$ and $id_u < id_v$). The latter condition is used to break the tie whenever the other values cannot be used to order a pair of nodes. For every pair u and v of adjacent nodes, v points to u in the overlay network via a virtual edge if and only if $\langle \alpha_u, \beta_u, u \rangle < \langle \alpha_v, \beta_v, v \rangle$. The destination node is always considered as a global minimum, i.e., its height is $\langle 0, 0, 0 \rangle$ and it has only incoming virtual edges that must never be reversed. Route maintenance is triggered when a node u has no more incoming edges, i.e., the node is a local minimum w.r.t. $<$. Let N_u be the set of neighbours of node u. The node tries to repair the configuration by updating the value of α_u with a value that is larger than the minimum value of the α's for nodes in N_u,

$$\alpha'_u = (min_{v \in N_u} \alpha_v) + 1$$

After the update, all edges directed to nodes with smaller α will be reversed. To minimize the number of reversals for nodes with the same value for α we operate on β. Namely, we set the new value of β_u to be strictly less than the minimum value of the β's for those nodes in N_u with a value for α equal to α'_u, i.e.,

$$\beta'_u = (min_{v \in \{v' \in N_u | \alpha_{v'} = \alpha'_u\}} \beta_v) - 1$$

If the graph is connected, the algorithm is guaranteed to terminate and to produce a new DAG pointing to the destination node (Propositions 1 and 2 in [11]). As in the scenario considered in the original algorithm, we assume here that route maintenance is performed after the failure of a single link and terminated before the subsequent link failure (the algorithm is designed for networks with such a relation between the frequency of the two types of events). We show an example of reversal steps in Figure 1.

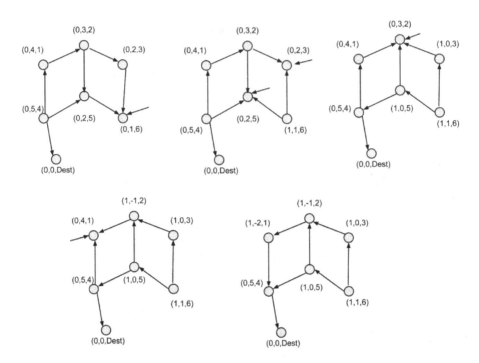

Fig. 1. Execution of Height-based Reversal

We remark that the full reversal algorithm can be obtained by ignoring β and changing the updates of α as follows:

$$\alpha'_u = (max_{v \in N_u} \alpha_v) + 1$$

This way all incoming edges of a sink node are reversed into outgoing edges. Only when passing from informal specifications to formal ones, we can uncover details that must be taken into account in a real implementation of the protocol. Since the informal specification of the LRR algorithm is based on graph transformations, it seems a natural case-study for a tool like GROOVE in order to fully exploit symmetries and compactness of graph production rules.

4   Formal Specification using GROOVE

In this section we describe a formal specification of the Gafni-Bertsekas algorithm using the GROOVE input language. The model has a type system which defines three types of nodes, together with the flags and edges which they support: **Node** is the type for nodes which execute the LRR protocol, **Counter** is used for the unique node keeping a global counter for generating fresh node identifiers, and, finally, **Lock** is the type of a control node used to serialize application of a specific set of rules.

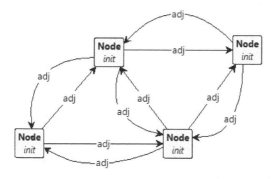

Fig. 2. Initial configuration with four nodes

4.1   Network Initialization

An initial configuration for the protocol consists of a graph where *adj* edges represent communication links between adjacent nodes. All nodes are initially labelled with the *init* flag. In Figure 2 we show a initial configuration with four nodes. To model undirected edges we use pairs of directed edges connecting the same nodes. We will discuss in Section 5 how to specify rules that can dynamically rearrange the connection topology of the network (add and delete edges). On top of the communication topology, the protocol builds a virtual DAG, that we will represent via *next* edges, with a single destination node. One of the properties that we will have to ensure is that, after dynamic modifications that do not partition the network and after route maintenance, every node maintains a path of *next*-edges leading to the destination node.

To define an initial consistent DAG w.r.t. *next*-edges, we first select a destination node and then initialize the heights of all other nodes by choosing increasing identifiers. For this purpose, we use the rules in Figure 3, 4, and 5. They are all given the maximum priority level, in order to ensure no other rule will be fired before the initialization of the system is complete. For clarity, we remark that flags and attributes added or removed as a postcondition of a rule are respectively preceded by a plus or a minus sign, whereas nodes [resp. edges] with thick green borders [resp. green lines] are created as a side effect of the rule.

Fig. 3. INIT-DEST: Non-deterministic choice of destination node and counter initialization

Fig. 4. INIT-LRR: Initialization of active LRR nodes

Rule INIT-DEST of Fig. 3 introduces a new **Counter** node with fields *deleteOnly* and *edits* used in the validation phase (see Section 5), and *nextId* used for the generation of fresh identifiers. In addition it non-deterministically selects a destination node. INIT-DEST may fire only if the system is still uninitialized, i.e., both the **Counter** and a destination node are missing. This negative conditions (NAC) are expressed through nodes with thick red dashed borders. The rule INIT-LRR (Figure 4) fires once for each **Node** still labelled by *init*. It introduces the integer fields *alpha* and *beta* initialized to 0, and it assigns a unique identifier *id*. The flag of the node is changed to *lrr* to mark it as ready, and the *nextId* field of **Counter** is increased by one. When INIT-LRR is done (i.e.

Fig. 5. INIT-DONE: Removal of *nextId* field

there are no more *init* nodes), INIT-DONE (Figure 5) marks the end of the initialization phase and the beginning of the simulation of the Gafni-Bertsekas LRR protocol.

4.2   Virtual DAG of *next*-edges

At first no virtual edges (labelled by *next*) towards the destination exist, as the nodes did not interact with each other, yet. In such a case the preconditions to fire NEW-LINKS (Figure 6) are satisfied. NEW-LINKS creates *next*-edges between pairs of adjacent nodes in accord to their relative heights (a *next*-edge goes from higher to lower heights). The special syntax a : **Node** fixes an identifier a for the node of type **Node**. Such identifier can be used in expressions, e.g., $a.alpha$, to concisely access fields of node a. Thick, dashed edges are treated as negative preconditions. The rule selects each pair of adjacent nodes a and b without any *next* edge connecting them (negative condition specified by a dashed edges with label *next*) and creates an *next* edge from a to b iff a has an height lexicographically greater than b. The comparison of triples is specified as a *test* label inside node a. Since nodes a and b are universally quantified,

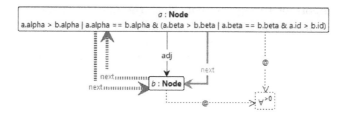

Fig. 6. NEW-LINKS: Creation of *next*-edges

the considered pattern is applied to all matching subgraphs of the host graph at the same time. In other words, with just one firing of the rule every missing next edge is added. When the network is initialized and all of the *next* edges are ready,

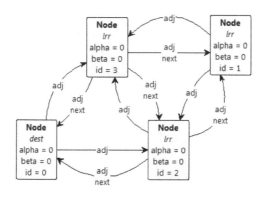

Fig. 7. Fully-initialized network with four nodes and *next* edges

a configuration with four nodes may look like that of Figure 7. This configuration contains an example of a sink node (with $id = 1$), i.e., a node other than the destination without outgoing *next* edges. The considered graph is a DAG w.r.t. the *next* relation. We remark that even though *next* edges are redundant w.r.t. the information on heights, they are useful for several reasons. Indeed, they represent an abstraction of data maintained in local tables as specified by the protocol, with the purpose of minimizing the number of height comparisons. This is useful also in our model, because by looking at *next* edges rather than at the heights many rules can be significantly simplified. Furthermore, the heights cannot be exploited when checking properties like, e.g., the existence of a route of arbitrary length to the destination. Instead, the presence of edges encoding the same information enables us to write such properties as regular expressions on paths, like *next+* (we will discuss this point in Section 5).

It is also important to remark that, since the initialization of the heights is done non-deterministically, even for a fixed initial topology, the creation of *next*-edges can generate several different DAGs that depend on the order in which identifiers are assigned to nodes. During state-exploration GROOVE applies symmetry reduction to avoid generation of isomorphic (w.r.t. both *adj*- and *next*-links) graphs.

4.3   Sink Detection

Sink nodes (e.g. the node with $id = 1$ in Fig. 7) trigger the route maintenance phase. The rules in Figures 8 and 9 have a decreasing priority in order to execute

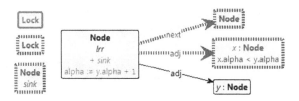

Fig. 8. SINK-ALPHA: Detection of a sink node and update of *alpha*

Fig. 9. SINK-BETA: Update of *beta*

them in the correct order. We also use a **Lock** node in order to ensure that each rule is applied at most once, depending on the cases.

In a situation such as in Figure 7, a new *sink* can be detected through rule SINK-ALPHA. The preconditions require that **Lock** is not present, there are no *sink* nodes, and that the node has no outgoing *next* edges. All these negative conditions are marked with dashed lines. The chosen *lrr* node n is marked with the *sink* label, and a fresh **Lock** node is generated to enable SINK-BETA (and forbid other applications of SINK-ALPHA). To update the value of the *alpha* attribute of n, say $n.alpha$, we first select a neighbour node y with minimum value v for *alpha* and then we assign $v + 1$ to $n.alpha$. Note that to select the node y with minimum *alpha*, we reason by contraposition and require that no other neighbour x has a value strictly smaller than $y.alpha$ (NAC that combines edges and conditions on fields).

Once *alpha* is updated, the LRR protocol can proceed with the update of *beta*, which is performed via the rule SINK-BETA of Figure 9. SINK-BETA requires the presence of a **Lock** node without the *beta* flag, which is added as a post-condition in order to let the rule fire at most once. Differently from *alpha*, *beta* has only to be compared w.r.t. the neighbours sharing the same *alpha* as the *sink*. Since it is not always the case that there are such neighbours, this rule may be skipped. The rule exploits again negative conditions and *test* labels to select the neighbour node with adequate values for *alpha* and *beta*.

4.4   Link Reversal

At this point both *alpha* and *beta* in the *sink* have been updated, so we can proceed with the reversal of all incoming *next* edges in the *sink* which originate from neighbours with a smaller height. Rule REVERSAL of Figure 10 works

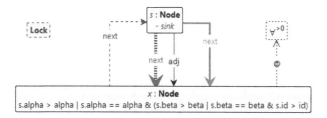

Fig. 10. REVERSAL: Reversal of virtual edges according to the new height

lexicographically w.r.t. the heights of the *sink*'s neighbours, exactly as NEW-LINK, except that it changes the orientation of all incoming *next* edges instead of adding new ones. The dashed blue edge *next* is used to remove an existing *next* edge. The dashed thick red edge *next* is used to test the absence of a reversed *next* edge, while the green edge specifies the addition of the reversed *next* edge. Via universal quantification, we specify that the same updates must be applied to all subgraphs of the host graph that match the specified pattern. The rule must be read as existentially quantified on *s* (to fix a *sink* node) and universally quantified on *x* (to specify reversal of edges from *x* to *s* for every neighbour of *x* of *s*). The rule also deletes the *sink* label from the selected node *s*, and removes the **Lock** node to terminate the reversal phase of the selected sink. New sink nodes may appear as a result of the first series of reversals. This would trigger another sequence of rule applications to propagate the height update, starting again from SINK-ALPHA. In the case of the example configuration in Figure 7, a complete run of link reversal in the sink node with $id = 1$ would result in the configuration of Figure 11. Its *alpha* has been updated from 0 to 1, *beta* is still 0 (since there is no neighbour with $alpha = 1$), and all of its *next* edges have been reversed.

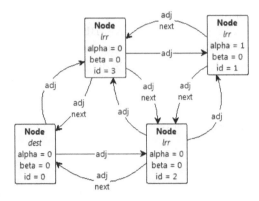

Fig. 11. Example network without sinks

In the next section we will discuss how to apply GROOVE to validate our model.

5   Bounded Model Checking

Based on our model, we have performed different types of analysis using the GROOVE model checker for configurations of fixed size.

The analysis starts from a fixed initial topology, i.e., we fix the number of nodes and the *adj*-edges as in the four nodes example in Fig. 2. Since the protocol addresses route maintenance in wireless networks, in order to test our implementation we have to introduce rules to model dynamic changes to the underlying connectivity network. Such changes will trigger the link reversal phases. Since updates non-deterministic, the initial topology can change in arbitrary ways.

The rules LINK-ADD (Figure 12) and LINK-DEL (Figure 13) have the lowest possible priority. In this way changes to the network will occur only when the protocol is stable, i.e., when there are no more sinks.

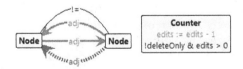

Fig. 12. LINK-ADD: Addition of a new link between two nodes

We put an upper bound to the number of dynamic changes to the network in the following way. The boolean field *deleteOnly* of the **Counter** node is used to distinguish between two variants of bounded model checking. When it is set to

Fig. 13. LINK-DEL: Deletion of a link between two adjacent nodes

true, rule LINK-ADD is disabled while LINK-DEL may fire without restrictions. When *deleteOnly* is set to *false*, both rules are enabled, but just for a limited number of times decided by the *edits* field of the **Counter**.

Link deletions may lead to partitionings, i.e., configurations where subsets of *lrr* nodes do not have a path of *adj* edges to the destination. In such cases the Gafni-Bertsekas protocol is known to diverge, as there is no mechanism to detect partitions. With rule BOUND-PARTITION (Figure 14) we filter out every such divergent execution. This means also that we do not need a bound for the heights

Fig. 14. BOUND-PARTITION: Detection of a partitioning

of the nodes, because only terminating executions are left. The rule has a rather high priority and no side effects because we want to block the computation as soon as a partitioning arises (matching configurations become final states). Thanks to a NAC expressed as a regular expression, the rule matches as soon as the current configuration contains an *lrr* node without a path to the destination.

The objective of our analysis is to check loop-freedom and ensure that, when the protocol is stable, every *lrr* node has at least a route to the destination. The rule LOOP (Figure 15) has high priority and, provided the network is sink-free, matches as soon as a node exposes a loop of any length of *next* edges. The rule

Fig. 15. LOOP: Loop detection in routes

DISCONNECTED (Figure 16) has the lowest possible priority and it is very similar to BOUND-PARTITION, except that the regular expression on paths to the destination uses *next* instead of *adj*.

Fig. 16. DISCONNECTED: Bad routes detection

5.1 Correctness Requirements

We formally specify the correctness of the algorithm via the following CTL formula.

$$AG \ !(\text{DISCONNECTED} \ || \ \text{LOOP})$$

For a fixed initial configuration, the formula requires that in every derivation π of the LTS associated to our model (temporal connective A), and in every configurations G occurring in π (temporal connective G), it is never possible to fire the transitions DISCONNECTED and LOOP (! [resp. ||] denotes negation [resp. disjunction]).

Following from the order induced by the priorities associated to the rules, the formula is true only if after each route maintenance phase that does not partition the topology, the protocol repairs the routes for every sink node. Thus the combination of execution strategies and CTL property can be used to formalize the correctness of the Gafni-Bertsekas algorithm.

5.2 Experiments and Evaluation

We checked the CTL property for a number of different bounds on the number of nodes and edits (link modifications). The tests were conducted on a common laptop with an Intel i5 CPU @ 2.53GHz and 4GB of RAM. The results of state-space exploration are listed in Table 1. For each number n of nodes considered, with *deleteOnly* equal to *true* we started the exploration from the fully connected configuration with n nodes (dynamic modifications are used then to generate arbitrary topologies). On the other hand, when *deleteOnly* is equal to *false*, we fix an initial configuration with n nodes and some missing edges. This is to ensure both LINK-ADD and LINK-DEL have different options to edit the connectivity graph right from the start.

The CTL correctness specification holds in every considered test-case. As expected, by removing the detection of partitionings the algorithm does not terminate (heights grows unboundedly).

The analysis scales up to 6 nodes with only deletions or at most 3 edits. With 4 [resp. 5] nodes we managed to consider at most 16 [resp. 8] edits. The low number of nodes considered in initial configurations is due to the fast growing of the state space (e.g. more than 750000 graphs with 7 nodes). The high number of combinations is also due to the presence of heights and, in particular, identifiers. On one hand they are a basic feature of the height-based version of the protocol. The consistency between these information and the virtual DAG is part of the correctness requirements of the algorithm. On the other hand they

Table 1. Experimental results

#nodes	deleteOnly	edits	#states	time (s)
4	true	-	143	1
	false	7	4503	4
		8	7642	5
		9	13040	6
		10	20963	8
		11	34028	11
		12	52120	16
		13	80690	22
		14	118060	32
		15	174644	48
		16	244769	78
5	true	-	3556	4
	false	3	4416	4
		4	10732	7
		5	24541	10
		6	55487	19
		7	124001	35
		8	279591	109
6	true	-	172166	67
	false	2	65936	22
		3	271035	99

reduce the application of symmetry reduction (graph isomorphism) during state exploration. The use of symmetry reductions guided by user-defined observations (e.g. restricting isomorphisms to *adj*- and *next*-edges) could be useful here as an heuristics to reduce state-space.

6   Conclusions and Related Work

In this paper we have proposed a non-standard application of GROOVE and Graph Transformation Systems to the validation of a distributed algorithm taken from the class of Link Reversal Routing algorithms [22].

Specification and verification of routing protocols dates back to the seminal work on HOL/SPIN for AODV in [3]. More recently, model checking tools (e.g. SPIN [9] and Uppaal[8]) and constraint-based engines [19,20,21] have been applied to verification of Ad Hoc and wireless protocols. In these approaches executions of a fixed number of agents are explored via enumerative or symbolic methods [9,8], or by generating positive/negative constraints on links in a lazy manner [19,20,21]. Parameterized verification of models of broadcast communication has been studied from a theoretical point of view in [5,6,4], where decidability and complexity frontiers have been given for problems like control state reachability (reachability of a state in which a node has a certain state). Applications of the invisible invariant method to distributed algorithms has been considered in [1]. Cut-off properties for link reversal routing has been considered in [10]. The manifesto on automated verification of distributed algorithms is presented in [17].

The use of graph transformation systems for automated validation of dynamic systems has been proposed in [15] using GROOVE. In [18] symbolic backward exploration with subgraph relation as termination test has been applied to parameterized verification of routing protocols like LUNAR. In the same line of thoughts, in [14] the graph minor ordering is used as termination test for symbolic analysis of ring protocols. Decidability of reachability problems for Graph Transformation Systems are studied in [2]. A comparison of the performance of GROOVE, used as a verification tool for dynamical systems, and SPIN is considered in [15].

Acknowledgements. The authors would like to thank Prof. Arend Rensink for precious suggestions on the use of GROOVE.

References

1. Balaban, I., Pnueli, A., Zuck, L.D.: Invisible safety of distributed protocols. In: Bugliesi, M., Preneel, B., Sassone, V., Wegener, I. (eds.) ICALP 2006, Part II. LNCS, vol. 4052, pp. 528–539. Springer, Heidelberg (2006)
2. Bertrand, N., Delzanno, G., König, B., Sangnier, A., Stückrath, J.: On the decidability status of reachability and coverability in graph transformation systems. In: RTA, pp. 101–116 (2012)
3. Bhargavan, K., Obradovic, D., Gunter, C.A.: Formal verification of standards for distance vector routing protocols. J. ACM 49(4), 538–576 (2002)
4. Delzanno, G., Sangnier, A., Traverso, R., Zavattaro, G.: On the complexity of parameterized reachability in reconfigurable broadcast networks. In: FSTTCS, pp. 289–300 (2012)
5. Delzanno, G., Sangnier, A., Zavattaro, G.: Parameterized verification of ad hoc networks. In: Gastin, P., Laroussinie, F. (eds.) CONCUR 2010. LNCS, vol. 6269, pp. 313–327. Springer, Heidelberg (2010)
6. Delzanno, G., Sangnier, A., Zavattaro, G.: On the power of cliques in the parameterized verification of ad hoc networks. In: Hofmann, M. (ed.) FOSSACS 2011. LNCS, vol. 6604, pp. 441–455. Springer, Heidelberg (2011)
7. Ehrig, H., Rozenberg, G.: Handbook of Graph Grammars and Computing by Graph Transformations, vol. 1-3. World Scientific Publishing (1997)
8. Fehnker, A., van Glabbeek, R., Höfner, P., McIver, A., Portmann, M., Tan, W.L.: Automated analysis of AODV using UPPAAL. In: Flanagan, C., König, B. (eds.) TACAS 2012. LNCS, vol. 7214, pp. 173–187. Springer, Heidelberg (2012)
9. Fehnker, A., van Hoesel, L., Mader, A.: Modelling and verification of the LMAC protocol for wireless sensor networks. In: Davies, J., Gibbons, J. (eds.) IFM 2007. LNCS, vol. 4591, pp. 253–272. Springer, Heidelberg (2007)
10. Függer, M., Widder, J.: Efficient checking of link-reversal-based concurrent systems. In: Koutny, M., Ulidowski, I. (eds.) CONCUR 2012. LNCS, vol. 7454, pp. 486–499. Springer, Heidelberg (2012)

11. Gafni, E., Bertsekas, D.: Distributed algorithms for generating loop-free routes in networks with frequently changing topology. IEEE Transactions on Communications 29, 11–18 (1981)
12. Ghamarian, A.H., de Mol, M., Rensink, A., Zambon, E., Zimakova, M.: Modelling and analysis using groove. STTT 14(1), 15–40 (2012)
13. Heckel, R.: Graph transformation in a nutshell. Electronic Notes in Theoretical Computer Science 148(1), 187–198 (2006)
14. Joshi, S., König, B.: Applying the graph minor theorem to the verification of graph transformation systems. In: Gupta, A., Malik, S. (eds.) CAV 2008. LNCS, vol. 5123, pp. 214–226. Springer, Heidelberg (2008)
15. Kastenberg, H., Rensink, A.: Model checking dynamic states in GROOVE. In: Valmari, A. (ed.) SPIN 2006. LNCS, vol. 3925, pp. 299–305. Springer, Heidelberg (2006)
16. König, B.: Analysis and verification of systems with dynamically evolving structure. PhD thesis, Universität Stuttgart (2004)
17. Konnov, I., Veith, H., Widder, J.: Who is afraid of model checking distributed algorithms? Unpublished contribution to: CAV Workshop $(EC)^2$ (2012)
18. Saksena, M., Wibling, O., Jonsson, B.: Graph grammar modeling and verification of ad hoc routing protocols. In: Ramakrishnan, C.R., Rehof, J. (eds.) TACAS 2008. LNCS, vol. 4963, pp. 18–32. Springer, Heidelberg (2008)
19. Singh, A., Ramakrishnan, C.R., Smolka, S.A.: A process calculus for mobile ad hoc networks. In: Lea, D., Zavattaro, G. (eds.) COORDINATION 2008. LNCS, vol. 5052, pp. 296–314. Springer, Heidelberg (2008)
20. Singh, A., Ramakrishnan, C.R., Smolka, S.A.: Query-based model checking of ad hoc network protocols. In: Bravetti, M., Zavattaro, G. (eds.) CONCUR 2009. LNCS, vol. 5710, pp. 603–619. Springer, Heidelberg (2009)
21. Singh, A., Ramakrishnan, C.R., Smolka, S.A.: A process calculus for mobile ad hoc networks. Sci. Comput. Program. 75(6), 440–469 (2010)
22. Welch, J.L., Walter, J.E.: Link Reversal Algorithms. Synthesis Lectures on Distributed Computing Theory. Morgan & Claypool Publishers (2011)

Local Model Checking of Weighted CTL with Upper-Bound Constraints

Jonas Finnemann Jensen, Kim Guldstrand Larsen,
Jiří Srba, and Lars Kaerlund Oestergaard

Department of Computer Science, Aalborg University
Selma Lagerlöfs Vej 300, 9220 Aalborg, Denmark
{jopsen,larsko}@gmail.com, {kgl,srba}@cs.aau.dk

Abstract. We present a symbolic extension of dependency graphs by
Liu and Smolka in order to model-check weighted Kripke structures
against the logic CTL with upper-bound weight constraints. Our extension introduces a new type of edges into dependency graphs and lifts
the computation of fixed-points from boolean domain to nonnegative
integers in order to cope with the weights. We present both global and
local algorithms for the fixed-point computation on symbolic dependency
graphs and argue for the advantages of our approach compared to the
direct encoding of the model checking problem into dependency graphs.
We implement all algorithms in a publicly available tool prototype and
evaluate them on several experiments. The principal conclusion is that
our local algorithm is the most efficient one with an order of magnitude improvement for model checking problems with a high number of
"witnesses".

1 Introduction

Model-driven development is finding its way into industrial practice within the
area of embedded systems. Here a key challenge is how to handle the growing
complexity of systems, while meeting requirements on correctness, predictabil-
ity, performance and not least time- and cost-to-market. In this respect model-
driven development is seen as a valuable and promising approach, as it allows
early design-space exploration and verification and may be used as the basis for
systematic and unambiguous testing of a final product. However, for embedded
systems, verification should not only address functional properties but also a
number of non-functional properties related to timing and resource constraints.

Within the area of model checking a number of state-machine based modeling
formalisms has emerged, allowing for such quantitative aspects to be expressed.
In particular, timed automata (TA) [1], and the extensions to weighted timed
automata (WTA) [6,2] are popular and tool-supported formalisms that allow for
such constraints to be modeled.

Interesting behavioural properties of TAs and WTAs may be expressed in
natural weight-extended versions of classical temporal logics such as CTL for

E. Bartocci and C.R. Ramakrishnan (Eds.): SPIN 2013, LNCS 7976, pp. 178–195, 2013.

branching-time and LTL for linear-time. Just as TCTL and MTL provide extensions of CTL and LTL with time-constrained modalities, WCTL and WMTL are extensions with weight-constrained modalities interpreted with respect to WTAs. Unfortunately, the addition of weight now turns out to come with a price: whereas the model-checking problems for TAs with respect to TCTL and MTL are decidable, it has been shown that model-checking WTAs with respect to WCTL is undecidable [9].

In this paper we reconsider this model checking problem in the setting of *untimed* models, i.e. essentially weighted Kripke structures, and negation-free WCTL formula with only upper bound constraints on weights. As main contributions, we show that in this setting the model-checking problem is in PTIME, and we provide an efficient symbolic, local (on-the-fly) model checking algorithm.

Our results are based on a novel symbolic extension of the dependency graph framework of Liu and Smolka [16] where they encode boolean equation systems and offer global and local algorithms for computing minimal and maximal fixed points in linear time. Whereas a direct encoding of our model checking problem into dependency graphs leads to a pseudo-polynomial algorithm[1], the novel symbolic dependency graphs allow for a polynomial encoding and a polynomial time fixed-point computation. Most importantly, the symbolic dependency graph encoding enables us to perform a symbolic local fixed-point evaluation. Experiments with the various approaches (direct versus symbolic encoding, global versus local algorithm) have been conducted on a large number of cases, demonstrating that the combined symbolic and local approach is the most efficient one. For model-checking problems with affirmative outcome, this combination is often one order or magnitude faster than the other approaches.

Related Work

Laroussinie, Markey and Oreiby [14] consider the problem of model checking durational concurrent game structures with respect to timed ATL properties, offering a PTIME result in the case of non-punctual constraints in the formula. Restricting the game structures to a single player gives a setting similar to ours, as timed ATL is essentially WCTL. However, in contrast to [14], we do allow transitions with zero weight in the model, making a fixed-point computation necessary. As a result, the corresponding CTL model checking (with no weight constraints) is a special instance of our approach, which is not the case for [14]. Most importantly, the work in [14] does not provide any local algorithm, which our experiments show is crucial for the performance. No implementation is provided in [14].

Buchholz and Kemper [10] propose a valued computation tree logic (CTL$) interpreted over a general set of weighted automata that includes CTL in the logic as a special case over the boolean semiring. For model checking CTL$ formulae they describe a matrix-based algorithm. Their logic is more expressive than the one proposed here, since they support negation and all the comparison

---

[1] Exponential in the encoding of the weights in the model and the formula.

operators. In addition, they permit nested CTL formulae and can operate on max/plus semirings in $O(\min(log(t) \cdot mm, t \cdot nz))$ time, where t is the number of vector matrix products, mm is the complexity of multiplying two matrices of order n and nz is the number of non-zero elements in special matrix used for checking "until" formulae up to some bound t. However, they do not provide any on-the-fly technique for verification.

Another related work [8] shows that the model-checking problem with respect to WCTL is PSPACE-complete for one-clock WTAs and for TCTL (the only cost variable is the time elapsed).

Several approaches to on-the-fly/local algorithms for model checking the modal mu-calculus have been proposed. Andersen [3] describes a local algorithm for model checking the modal mu-calculus for alternation depth one running in $O(n \cdot log(n))$ (where n is the product of the size of the assertion and the labeled transition system). Liu and Smolka[16] improve on the complexity of this approach with a local algorithm running in $O(n)$ (where n is the size of the input graph) for evaluating alternation-free fixed points. This is also the algorithm that we apply for WCTL model checking and the one we extend for symbolic dependency graphs. Cassez et. al. [11] present another symbolic extension of the algorithm by Liu and Smolka; a zone-based forward, local algorithm for solving timed reachability games. Later Liu, Ramakrishnan and Smolka [15] also introduce a local algorithm for the evaluation of alternating fixed points with the complexity $O(n + (\frac{n+ad}{ad})^{ad})$, where ad is the alternation depth of the graph. We do not consider the evaluation of alternating fixed points in the weighted setting and this is left for the future work.

Outline. Weighted Kripke structures and weighted CTL (WCTL) are presented in Section 2. Section 3 then introduces dependency graphs. Model checking WCTL with this framework is discussed in Section 4. In Section 5 we propose symbolic dependency graphs and demonstrate how they can be used for WCTL model checking in Section 6. Experimental results are presented in Section 7 and Section 8 concludes the paper.

2   Basic Definitions

Let $\mathbb{N}_0$ be the set of nonnegative integers. A *Weighted Kripke Structure* (WKS) is a quadruple $\mathcal{K} = (S, \mathcal{AP}, L, \rightarrow)$, where S is a finite set of states, $\mathcal{AP}$ is a finite set of atomic propositions, $L : S \rightarrow \mathcal{P}(\mathcal{AP})$ is a mapping from states to sets of atomic propositions, and $\rightarrow \subseteq S \times \mathbb{N}_0 \times S$ is a transition relation.

Instead of $(s, w, s') \in \rightarrow$, meaning that from the state s, under the weight w, we can move to the state s', we often write $s \xrightarrow{w} s'$. A WKS is *nonblocking* if for every $s \in S$ there is an s' such that $s \xrightarrow{w} s'$ for some weight w. From now on we consider only nonblocking WKS[2].

---

[2] A blocking WKS can be turned into a nonblocking one by introducing a new state with no atomic propositions, zero-weight self-loop and with zero-weight transitions from all blocking states into this newly introduced state.

A *run* in an WKS $\mathcal{K} = (S, \mathcal{AP}, L, \rightarrow)$ is an infinite computation

$$\sigma = s_0 \xrightarrow{w_0} s_1 \xrightarrow{w_1} s_2 \xrightarrow{w_2} s_3 \ldots$$

where $s_i \in S$ and $(s_i, w_i, s_{i+1}) \in \rightarrow$ for all $i \geq 0$. Given a *position* $p \in \mathbb{N}_0$ in the run σ, let $\sigma(p) = s_p$. The *accumulated weight* of σ at position $p \in \mathbb{N}_0$ is then defined as $W_\sigma(p) = \Sigma_{i=0}^{p-1} w_i$.

We can now define negation-free Weighted Computation Tree Logic (WCTL) with weight upper-bounds. The set of WCTL formulae over the set of atomic propositions $\mathcal{AP}$ is given by the abstract syntax

$$\varphi ::= \textbf{true} \mid \textbf{false} \mid a \mid \varphi_1 \wedge \varphi_2 \mid \varphi_1 \vee \varphi_2 \mid$$
$$EX_{\leq k} \varphi \mid AX_{\leq k} \varphi \mid E \varphi_1 U_{\leq k} \varphi_2 \mid A \varphi_1 U_{\leq k} \varphi_2$$

where $k \in \mathbb{N}_0 \cup \{\infty\}$ and $a \in \mathcal{AP}$. We assume that the ∞ element added to $\mathbb{N}_0$ is larger than any other natural number and that $\infty + k = \infty - k = \infty$ for all $k \in \mathbb{N}_0$. We now inductively define the satisfaction triple $s \models \varphi$, meaning that a state s in an implicitly given WKS satisfies a formula φ.

$s \models \textbf{true}$

$s \models a$ if $a \in L(s)$

$s \models \varphi_1 \wedge \varphi_2$ if $s \models \varphi_1$ and $s \models \varphi_2$

$s \models \varphi_1 \vee \varphi_2$ if $s \models \varphi_1$ or $s \models \varphi_2$

$s \models E \varphi_1 U_{\leq k} \varphi_2$ if there exists a run σ starting from s and a position $p \geq 0$
                               s.t. $\sigma(p) \models \varphi_2, W_\sigma(p) \leq k$ and $\sigma(p') \models \varphi_1$ for all $p' < p$

$s \models A \varphi_1 U_{\leq k} \varphi_2$ if for any run σ starting from s, there is a position $p \geq 0$
                               s.t. $\sigma(p) \models \varphi_2, W_\sigma(p) \leq k$ and $\sigma(p') \models \varphi_1$ for all $p' < p$

$s \models EX_{\leq k} \varphi$ if $\exists s'$ s.t. $s \xrightarrow{w} s', s' \models \varphi$ and $w \leq k$

$s \models AX_{\leq k} \varphi$ if $\forall s'$ s.t. $s \xrightarrow{w} s'$ where $w \leq k$ it holds that $s' \models \varphi$

3 Dependency Graph

In this section we present the dependency graph framework and a local algorithm for minimal fixed-point computation as originally introduced by Liu and Smolka [16]. This framework can be applied to model checking of the alternation-free modal mu-calculus, including the CTL logic. Later, in Section 4, we demonstrate how to extend the framework from CTL to WCTL.

Definition 1 (Dependency Graph). *A dependency graph is a pair* $G = (V, E)$ *where* V *is a finite set of* configurations, *and* $E \subseteq V \times \mathcal{P}(V)$ *is a finite set of* hyper-edges.

Let $G = (V, E)$ be a dependency graph. For a hyper-edge $e = (v, T)$, we call v the source configuration and T the target (configuration) set of e. For a configuration v, the set of its successors is given by $succ(v) = \{(v, T) \in E\}$.

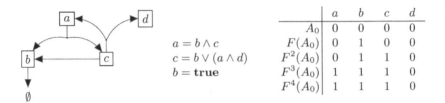

	a	b	c	d
A_0	0	0	0	0
$F(A_0)$	0	1	0	0
$F^2(A_0)$	0	1	1	0
$F^3(A_0)$	1	1	1	0
$F^4(A_0)$	1	1	1	0

$a = b \wedge c$
$c = b \vee (a \wedge d)$
$b = \textbf{true}$

Fig. 1. A dependency graph, function F, and four iterations of the global algorithm

An *assignment* $A : V \rightarrow \{0,1\}$ is a function that assigns boolean values to configurations of G. A *pre fixed-point assignment* of G is an assignment A where, for every configuration $v \in V$, holds that if $(v,T) \in E$ and $A(u) = 1$ for all $u \in T$ then also $A(v) = 1$.

By taking the standard component-wise ordering $\sqsubseteq$ on assignments, where $A \sqsubseteq A'$ if and only if $A(v) \leq A'(v)$ for all $v \in V$ (assuming that $0 < 1$), we get by Knaster-Tarski fixed-point theorem that there exists a unique minimum pre fixed-point assignment, denoted by A_{min}.

The minimum pre fixed-point assignment A_{min} of G can be computed by repeated applications of the monotonic function F from assignments to assignments, starting from A_0 where $A_0(v) = 0$ for all $v \in V$, and where

$$F(A)(v) = \bigvee_{(v,T) \in E} \left(\bigwedge_{u \in T} A(u) \right)$$

for all $v \in V$. We are guaranteed to reach a fixed point after a finite number of applications of F due to the finiteness of the complete lattice of assignments ordered by $\sqsubseteq$. Hence there exists an $m \in \mathbb{N}_0$ such that $F^m(A_0) = F^{m+1}(A_0)$, in which case we have $F^m(A_0) = A_{min}$. We will refer to this algorithm as the *global* one.

Example 1. Figure 1 shows a dependency graph, its corresponding function F given as a boolean equation system, and four iterations of the global algorithm (sufficient to compute the minimum pre fixed-point assignment). Configurations in the dependency graph are illustrated as labeled squares and hyper-edges are drawn as a span of lines to every configuration in the respective target set.

In model checking we are often only interested in the minimum pre-fixed point assignment $A_{min}(v)$ for a specific configuration $v \in V$. For this purpose, Liu and Smolka [16] suggest a local algorithm presented with minor modifications[3] in Algorithm 1. The algorithm maintains three data-structures throughout its execution: an assignment A, a dependency set D for every configuration and a set of hyper-edges W. The dependency set $D(v)$ for a configuration v maintains

---

[3] At line 12 we added the current hyper-edge e to the dependency set $D(u)$ of the successor configuration u, i.e. $D(u) = \{e\}$. The original algorithm sets the dependency set to empty here, leading to an incorrect propagation.

Algorithm 1. Liu-Smolka Local Algorithm

   Input: Dependency graph $G = (V, E)$ and a configuration $v_0 \in V$
   Output: Minimum pre fixed-point assignment $A_{min}(v_0)$ for v_0
1 Let $A(v) = \bot$ for all $v \in V$
2 $A(v_0) = 0;\ D(v_0) = \emptyset$
3 $W = succ(v_0)$
4 **while** $W \neq \emptyset$ **do**
5   let $e = (v, T) \in W$
6 $W = W \setminus \{e\}$
7   **if** $A(u) = 1$ *for all* $u \in T$ **then**
8 $\mid$ $A(v) = 1;\ W = W \cup D(v)$
9   **else if** *there is* $u \in T$ *such that* $A(u) = 0$ **then**
10 $\mid$ $D(u) = D(u) \cup \{e\}$
11   **else if** *there is* $u \in T$ *such that* $A(u) = \bot$ **then**
12 $\lfloor$ $A(u) = 0;\ D(u) = \{e\};\ W = W \cup succ(u)$

13 **return** $A(v_0)$

---

a list of hyper-edges that were processed under the assumption that $A(v) = 0$. Whenever the value of $A(v)$ changes to 1, the hyper-edges from $D(v)$ must be reprocessed in order to propagate this change to the respective sources of the hyper-edges.

Theorem 1 (Correctness of Local Algorithm [16]). *Given a dependency graph $G = (V, E)$ and a configuration $v_0 \in V$, Algorithm 1 computes the minimum pre-fixed point assignment $A_{min}(v_0)$ for the configuration v_0.*

As argued in [16], both the local and global model checking algorithms run in linear time.

4   Model Checking with Dependency Graphs

In this section we suggest a reduction from the model checking problem of WCTL (on WKS) to the computation of minimum pre fixed-point assignment on a dependency graph.

    Given a WKS $\mathcal{K}$, a state s of $\mathcal{K}$, and a WCTL formula φ, we construct a dependency graph where every configuration is a pair of a state and a formula. Starting from the initial pair $\langle s, \varphi \rangle$, the dependency graph is constructed according to the rules given in Figure 2.

Theorem 2 (Encoding Correctness). *Let $\mathcal{K} = (S, \mathcal{AP}, L, \rightarrow)$ be a WKS, $s \in S$ a state, and φ a WCTL formula. Let G be the constructed dependency graph rooted with $\langle s, \varphi \rangle$. Then $s \models \varphi$ if and only if $A_{min}(\langle s, \varphi \rangle) = 1$.*

Proof. By structural induction on the formula φ. $\square$

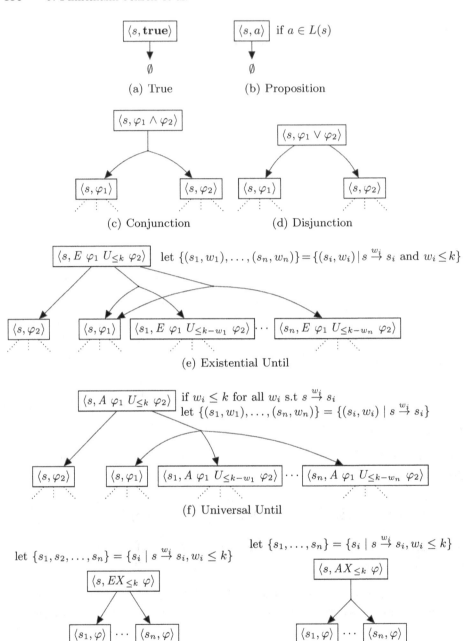

Fig. 2. Dependency graph encoding of state-formula pairs

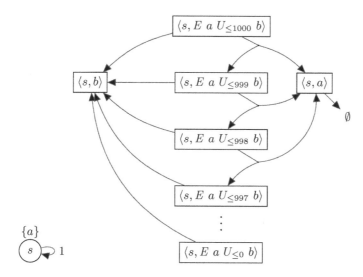

Fig. 3. A WKS and its dependency graph for the formula $E \; a \; U_{\leq 1000} \; b$

Clearly, to profit from the local algorithm by Liu and Smolka [16] presented in the previous section, we construct the dependency graph on-the-fly whenever successor configurations are requested by the algorithm. Such an exploration gives us often more efficient local model checking algorithm compared to the global one (see Section 7).

However, the drawback of this approach is that we may need to construct exponentially large dependency graphs. This is demonstrated in Figure 3 where a single-state WKS on the left gives rise to a large dependency graph on the right where its size depends on the bound in the formula. Hence this method gives us only a pseudo-polynomial algorithm for model checking WCTL.

5   Symbolic Dependency Graph

We have seen in previous section that the use of dependency graphs for WCTL model checking suffers from the exponential explosion as the graph grows in proportion to the bounds in the given formula (due to the unfolding of the until operators). We can, however, observe that the validity of $s \models E \; a \; U_{\leq k} \; b$ implies $s \models E \; a \; U_{\leq k+1} \; b$. In what follows we suggest a novel extension of dependency graphs, called *symbolic dependency graphs*, that use the implication above in order to reduce the size of the constructed graphs. Then in Section 6 we shall use symbolic dependency graphs for efficient (polynomial time) model checking of WCTL.

Definition 2 (Symbolic Dependency Graph). *A symbolic dependency graph (SDG) is a triple $G = (V, H, C)$, where V is a finite set of configurations, $H \subseteq V \times \mathcal{P}(\mathbb{N}_0 \times V)$ is a finite set of hyper-edges, and $C \subseteq V \times \mathbb{N}_0 \times V$ is a finite set of cover-edges.*

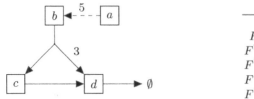

i	a	b	c	d
A_0	∞	∞	∞	∞
$F(A_0)$	∞	∞	∞	0
$F^2(A_0)$	∞	∞	0	0
$F^3(A_0)$	∞	3	0	0
$F^4(A_0)$	0	3	0	0
$F^5(A_0)$	0	3	0	0

(a) A symbolic dependency graph   (b) Minimum pre fixed-point computation

Fig. 4. Computation of minimum pre fixed-point assignment of a SDG

The difference from dependency graphs explained earlier is that for each hyper-edge of a SDG a weight is added to all of its target configurations and a new type of edge called a cover-edge is introduced. Let $G = (V, H, C)$ be a symbolic dependency graph. The size of G is $|G| = |V| + |H| + |C|$ where $|V|$, $|H|$ and $|C|$ is the size the of these components in a binary representation (note that the size of a hyper-edge depends on the number of nodes it connects to). For a hyper-edge $e = (v, T) \in H$ we call v the source configuration and T the target set of e. We also say that $(w, u) \in T$ is a hyper-edge branch with weight w pointing to the target configuration u. The successor set $succ(v) = \{(v, T) \in H\} \cup \{(v, k, u) \in C\}$ is the set of hyper-edges and cover-edges with v as the source configuration.

Figure 4(a) shows an example of a SDG. Hyper-edges are denoted by solid lines and hyper-edge branches have weight 0 unless they are annotated with another weight. Cover-edges are drawn as dashed lines annotated with a cover-condition. We shall now describe a global algorithm for the computation of the minimum pre fixed-point. The main difference is that symbolic dependency graphs operate over the complete lattice $\mathbb{N}_0 \cup \{\infty\}$, contrary to standard dependency graphs that use only boolean values.

An assignment $A : V \to \mathbb{N}_0 \cup \{\infty\}$ in an SDG $G = (V, H, C)$ is a mapping from configurations to values. We denote the set of all assignments by *Assign*. A *pre fixed-point assignment* is an assignment $A \in Assign$ such that $A = F(A)$ where $F : Assign \to Assign$ is defined as

$$F(A)(v) = \begin{cases} 0 & \text{if } \exists(v, k, v') \in C \text{ s.t. } A(v') \le k < \infty, \text{ or } A(v') < k = \infty \\ \min_{(v,T)\in H} \left(\max\{w + A(v') \mid (w, v') \in T\} \right) & \text{otherwise.} \end{cases}$$

$$(1)$$

If we consider the partial order $\sqsubseteq$ over assignments of a symbolic dependency graph G such that $A \sqsubseteq A'$ if and only if $A(v) \ge A'(v)$ for all $v \in V$, then the function F is clearly monotonic on the complete lattice of all assignments ordered by $\sqsubseteq$. It follows by Knaster-Tarski fixed-point theorem that there exists a unique minimum pre fixed-point assignment of G, denoted A_{min}.

Notice that we write $A \sqsubseteq A'$ if for all configurations v we have $A(v) \geq A'(v)$ in the opposite order. Hence, $A_0(v) = \infty$ for all $v \in V$ is the smallest element in the lattice.

As the lattice is finite and there are no infinite decreasing sequences of weights (nonnegative integers), the minimum pre fixed-point assignment A_{min} of G can be computed by a finite number of applications of the function F on the smallest assignment A_0, where all configurations have the initial value ∞. So there exists an $m \in \mathbb{N}_0$ such that $F^m(A_0) = F^{m+1}(A_0)$, implying that $F^m(A_0) = A_{min}$ is the minimum pre fixed-point assignment of G. Figure 4(b) shows a computation of the minimum pre fixed-point assignment on our example.

The next theorem demonstrates that fixed-point computation via the global algorithm (repeated applications of the function F) on symbolic dependency graphs still runs in polynomial time.

Theorem 3. *The computation of the minimum post fixed-point assignment for an SDG $G = (V, H, C)$ by repeated application of the function F takes time $O(|V| \cdot |C| \cdot (|H| + |C|))$.*

We now propose a local algorithm for minimum pre fixed-point computation on symbolic dependency graphs, motivated by the fact that in model checking we are often interested in the value for a single given configuration only, hence we might be able (depending on the formula we want to verify) to explore only a part of the reachable state space.

Given a symbolic dependency graph $G = (V, H, C)$, Algorithm 2 computes the minimum pre fixed-point assignment $A_{min}(v_0)$ of a configuration $v_0 \in V$. The algorithm is an adaptation of Algorithm 1. We use the same data-structures as in Algorithm 1. However, the assignment $A(v)$ for each configuration v now ranges over $\mathbb{N}_0 \cup \{\bot, \infty\}$ where $\bot$ once again indicates that the value is unknown at the moment.

Table 1 lists the values of the assignment A, the set W (implemented as queue) and the dependency set D during the execution of Algorithm 2 on the SDG Figure 4(a). Each row displays the values before the i'th iteration of the while-loop. The value of the dependency set $D(a)$ for a is not shown in the table because it remains empty.

In order to prove the correctness of Algorithm 2, we extend the loop invariant for the local algorithm on dependency graphs [16] with weights.

Lemma 1. *The while-loop in Algorithm 2 satisfies the following loop-invariants (for all configurations $v \in V$):*

1) If $A(v) \neq \bot$ then $A(v) \geq A_{min}(v)$.
2) If $A(v) \neq \bot$ and $e = (v, T) \in H$, then either
   a) $e \in W$,
   b) $e \in D(u)$ and $A(v) \leq x$ for some $(w, u) \in T$ s.t. $x = A(u) + w$, where $x \geq A(u') + w'$ for all $(w', u') \in T$, or
   c) $A(v) = 0$.
3) If $A(v) \neq \bot$ and $e = (v, k, u) \in C$, then either

Algorithm 2. Symbolic Local Algorithm

Input: A SDG $G = (V, H, C)$ and a configuration $v_0 \in V$
Output: Minimum pre fixed-point assignment $A_{min}(v_0)$ for v_0

1   Let $A(v) = \bot$ for all $v \in V$
2   $A(v_0) = \infty$; $W = succ(v_0)$
3   **while** $W \neq \emptyset$ **do**
4   Pick $e \in W$
5      $W = W \setminus \{e\}$
6   **if** $e = (v, T)$ *is a hyper-edge* **then**
7   **if** $\exists (w, u) \in T$ *where* $A(u) = \infty$ **then**
8            $D(u) = D(u) \cup \{e\}$
9   **else if** $\exists (w, u) \in T$ *where* $A(u) = \bot$ **then**
10           $A(u) = \infty$; $D(u) = \{e\}$; $W = W \cup succ(u)$
11   **else**
12            $a = \max\{A(u) + w \mid (w, u) \in T\}$
13   **if** $a < A(v)$ **then**
14              $A(v) = a$; $W = W \cup D(v)$
15   let $(w, u) = \underset{(w,u) \in T}{\arg\max} A(u) + w$
16   **if** $A(u) > 0$ **then**
17              $D(u) = D(u) \cup \{e\}$
18   **else if** $e = (v, k, u)$ *is a cover-edge* **then**
19   **if** $A(u) = \bot$ **then**
20           $A(u) = \infty$; $D(u) = \{e\}$; $W = W \cup succ(u)$
21   **else if** $A(u) \leq k < \infty$ *or* $A(u) < k == \infty$ **then**
22           $A(v) = 0$
23   **if** $A(v)$ *was changed* **then**
24             $W = W \cup D(v)$
25   **else**
26           $D(u) = D(u) \cup \{e\}$

27 **return** $A(v_0)$

---

a) $e \in W$,
b) $e \in D(u)$ and $A(u) > k$, or
c) $A(v) = 0$.

These loop-invariants allow us to conclude the correctness of the local algorithm.

Theorem 4. *Algorithm 2 terminates and computes an assignment A such that $A(v) \neq \bot$ implies $A(v) = A_{min}(v)$ for all $v \in V$. In particular, the returned value $A(v_0)$ is the minimum pre fixed-point assignment of v_0.*

We note that the termination argument is not completely straightforward as there is not a guarantee that it terminates within a polynomial number of steps as depicted on the SDG in Figure 5 where for technical convenience, we named

Table 1. Execution of Algorithm 2 on SDG from Figure 4(a)

i	$A(a)$	$A(b)$	$A(c)$	$A(d)$	W	$D(b)$	$D(c)$	$D(d)$
1	∞	$\bot$	$\bot$	$\bot$	$(a,5,b)$			
2	∞	∞	$\bot$	$\bot$	$(b,\{(0,c),(3,d)\})$	$(a,5,b)$		
3	∞	∞	∞	$\bot$	$(c,\{(0,d)\})$	$(a,5,b)$	$(b,\{(0,c),(3,d)\})$	
4	∞	∞	∞	∞	$(d,\emptyset)$	$(a,5,b)$	$(b,\{(0,c),(3,d)\})$	$(c,\{(0,d)\})$
5	∞	∞	∞	0	$(c,\{(0,d)\})$	$(a,5,b)$	$(b,\{(0,c),(3,d)\})$	$(c,\{(0,d)\})$
6	∞	∞	0	0	$(b,\{(0,c),(3,d)\})$	$(a,5,b)$	$(b,\{(0,c),(3,d)\})$	$(c,\{(0,d)\})$
7	∞	3	0	0	$(a,5,b)$	$(a,5,b)$	$(b,\{(0,c),(3,d)\})$	$(c,\{(0,d)\})$
8	0	3	0	0		$(a,5,b)$	$(b,\{(0,c),(3,d)\})$	$(c,\{(0,d)\})$

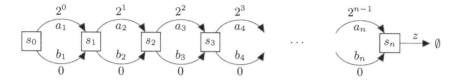

Fig. 5. A SDG where the local algorithm can take exponential running time

the hyper-edges $a_1,\ldots,a_n$, $b_1,\ldots,b_n$ and z. Consider now an execution of Algorithm 2 starting from the configuration s_0. Let us pick the edges from W at line 4 according to the strategy:

- if $z \in W$ then pick z, else
- if $a_i \in W$ for some i then pick a_i (there will be at most one such a_i), else
- pick $b_i \in W$ with the smallest index i.

Then the initial assignment of $A(s_0) = \infty$ is gradually improved to 2^n-1, 2^n-2, $2^n - 3$, $\ldots 1$, 0. Hence, in the worst case, the local algorithm can perform exponentially many steps before it terminates, whereas the global algorithm always terminates in polynomial time. However, as we will see in Section 7, the local algorithm is in practice performing significantly better despite its high (theoretical) complexity.

6 Model Checking with Symbolic Dependency Graphs

We are now ready to present an encoding of a WKS and a WCTL formula as a symbolic dependency graph and hence decide the model checking problem via the computation of the minimum pre fixed-point assignment.

Given a WKS $\mathcal{K}$, a state s of $\mathcal{K}$ and a WCTL formula φ, we construct the corresponding symbolic dependency graph as before with the exception that the existential and universal "until" operators are encoded by the rules given in Figure 6.

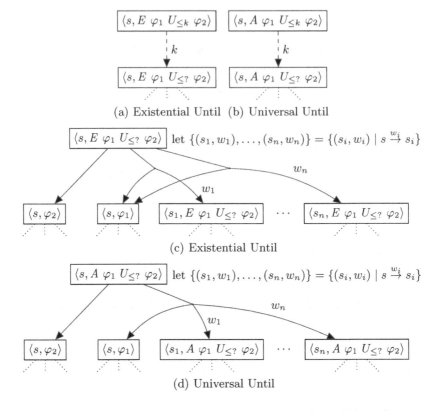

(a) Existential Until (b) Universal Until

(c) Existential Until

(d) Universal Until

Fig. 6. SDG encoding of existential and universal 'until' formulas

Theorem 5 (Encoding Correctness). *Let $\mathcal{K} = (S, \mathcal{AP}, L, \rightarrow)$ be a WKS, $s \in S$ a state, and φ a WCTL formula. Let G be the constructed symbolic dependency graph rooted with $\langle s, \varphi \rangle$. Then $s \models \varphi$ if and only if $A_{min}(\langle s, \varphi \rangle) = 0$.*

Proof. By structural induction on φ. □

In Figure 7 we depict the symbolic dependency graph encoding of $E \ a \ U_{\leq 1000} \ b$ for the configuration s in the single-state WKS from Figure 3. This clearly illustrates the succinctness of SDG compared to standard dependency graphs. The minimum pre fixed-point assignment of this symbolic dependency graph is now reached in two iterations of the function F defined in Equation (1).

We note that for a given WKS $\mathcal{K} = (S, \mathcal{AP}, L, \rightarrow)$ and a formula φ, the size of the constructed symbolic dependency graph $G = (V, H, C)$ can be bounded as follows: $|V| = O(|S| \cdot |\varphi|)$, $|H| = O(|\rightarrow| \cdot |\varphi|)$ and $|C| = O(|\varphi|)$. In combination with Theorem 3 and the fact that $|C| \leq |H|$ (due to the rules for construction of G), we conclude with a theorem stating a polynomial time complexity of the global model checking algorithm for WCTL.

Theorem 6. *Given a WKS $\mathcal{K} = (S, \mathcal{AP}, L, \rightarrow)$, a state $s \in S$ and a WCTL formula φ, the model checking problem $s \models \varphi$ is decidable in time $O(|S| \cdot |\rightarrow| \cdot |\varphi|^3)$.*

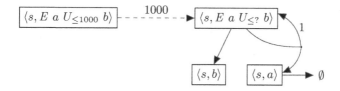

Fig. 7. SDG for the formula $s \models E\ a\ U_{\leq 1000}\ b$ and the WKS from Figure 3

As we already explained, the local model checking approach in Algorithm 2 may exhibit exponential running time. Nevertheless, the experiments in the section to follow show that this unlikely to happen in practice.

7 Experiments

In order to compare the performance of the algorithms for model checking WCTL, we developed a prototype tool implementation. There is a web-based front-end written in CoffeeScript available at

http://wktool-spin2013.jonasfj.dk

and the tool is entirely browser-based, requiring no installation. The model checking algorithms run with limited memory resources but the tool allows a fair comparison of the performance for the different algorithms. All experiments were conducted on a standard laptop (Intel Core i7) running Ubuntu Linux.

In order to experiment with larger, scalable models consisting of parallel components, we extend the process algebra CCS [17] with weight prefixing as well as proposition annotations and carry out experiments with weighted models of Leader Election [12], Alternating Bit Protocol [5], and Task Graph Scheduling problems for two processors [13]. The weight (communication cost) is associated with sending messages in the first two models while in the task graph scheduling the weight represents clock ticks of the processors.

7.1 Dependency Graphs vs. Symbolic Dependency Graphs

In Table 2 we compare the direct (standard dependency graph) algorithms with the symbolic ones. The execution times are in seconds and OOM indicates that verification runs out of memory. For a fixed size of the problems, we scale the bound k in the WCTL formulae. In the leader election protocol with eight processes, we verified a satisfiable formula $E\ \mathbf{true}\ U_{\leq k}\ leader$, asking if a leader can be determined within k message exchanges, and an unsatisfiable formula $E\ \mathbf{true}\ U_{\leq k}\ leader > 1$, asking if there can be more than one leader selected within k message exchanges. For the alternating bit protocol with a communication buffer of size four, we verified a satisfied formula $E\ \mathbf{true}\ U_{\leq k}\ delivered = 1$, asking if a message can be delivered within k communication steps, and an unsatisfied formula $E\ \mathbf{true}\ U_{\leq k}\ (s_0 \wedge d_1) \vee (s_1 \wedge d_0)$, asking whether the sender and receiver can get out of synchrony withing the first k communication steps.

Table 2. Scaling of bounds in WCTL formula (time in seconds)

	Leader Election						Alternating Bit Protocol				
	Direct		Symbolic				Direct		Symbolic		
k	Global	Local	Global	Local		k	Global	Local	Global	Local	
200	3.88	0.23	0.26	0.02	Satisfied	100	3.87	0.05	0.23	0.03	Satisfied
400	8.33	0.25	0.26	0.02		200	8.32	0.06	0.23	0.03	
600	OOM	0.24	0.26	0.02		300	OOM	0.10	0.28	0.04	
800	OOM	0.25	0.26	0.02		400	OOM	0.11	0.23	0.03	
1000	OOM	0.26	0.27	0.02		500	OOM	0.13	0.23	0.03	
200	7.76	8.58	0.26	0.26	Unsatisfied	100	3.39	3.75	0.27	0.23	Unsatisfied
400	17.05	20.23	0.26	0.26		200	6.98	8.62	0.30	0.25	
600	OOM	OOM	0.26	0.26		300	OOM	15.37	0.28	0.24	
800	OOM	OOM	0.26	0.26		400	OOM	OOM	0.27	0.24	
1000	OOM	OOM	0.26	0.26		500	OOM	OOM	0.27	0.22	

For the satisfied formula, the direct global algorithm (global fixed-point computation on dependency graphs) runs out of memory as the bound k in the formulae is scaled. The advantage of Liu and Smolka [16] local algorithm is obvious as on positive instances it performs (using DFS search strategy) about as well as the global symbolic algorithm. The local symbolic algorithm clearly performs best. We observed a similar behaviour also for other examples we tested and the symbolic algorithms were regularly performing better than the ones using the direct translation of WCTL formulae into dependency graphs. Hence we shall now focus on a more detailed comparison of the local vs. global symbolic algorithms.

7.2 Local vs. Global Model Checking on SDG

We shall now take a closer look at comparing the local and global symbolic algorithms. In Table 3 we return to the leader election and alternating bit protocol but we scale the sizes (number of processes and buffer capacity, resp.) of these models rather than the bounds in formulae. The satisfiable and unsatisfiable formulae are as before. In the leader election the verification of a satisfiable formula using the local symbolic algorithm is consistently faster as the instance size is incremented, while for unsatisfiable formulae the verification times are essentially the same. For the alternating bit protocol we present the results for the bound k equal to 10, 20 and ∞. While the results for unsatisfiable formulae do not change significantly, for the positive formula the bound 10 is very tight in the sense that there are only a few executions or "witnesses" that satisfy the formula. As the bound is relaxed, more solutions can be found which is reflected by the improved performance of the local algorithm, in particular in the situation where the upper-bound is ∞.

We also tested the algorithms on a larger benchmark of task graph scheduling problems [4]. The task graph scheduling problem asks about schedulability of a number of parallel tasks with given precedence constraints and processing times that are executed on a fixed number of homogeneous processors [13].

Table 3. Scaling the model size for the symbolic algorithms (time in seconds)

Leader Election				Alternating Bit Protocol						
	$k = 200$				$k = 10$		$k = 20$		$k = \infty$	
n	Global	Local		n	Global	Local	Global	Local	Global	Local
7	0.08	0.01	Satisfied	5	0.33	0.10	0.33	0.07	0.33	0.04
8	0.26	0.02		6	0.78	0.18	0.77	0.17	0.80	0.06
9	1.06	0.03		7	1.88	0.34	1.92	0.14	1.96	0.05
10	5.18	0.03		8	4.82	0.82	4.71	0.72	4.78	0.09
11	23.60	0.03		9	13.91	10.60	12.41	1.67	12.92	0.20
12	Timeout	0.04		10	OOM	OOM	OOM	6.29	OOM	0.23
7	0.08	0.08	Unsatisfied	4	0.27	0.24	0.27	0.23	0.29	0.24
8	0.26	0.26		5	0.54	0.43	0.51	0.37	0.57	0.40
9	1.05	1.06		6	1.42	0.98	1.21	0.93	1.31	1.02
10	4.97	4.96		7	2.70	2.05	2.93	2.06	3.14	2.21
11	23.57	24.07		8	6.15	4.98	7.08	5.57	6.86	5.34
12	Timeout	Timeout		9	OOM	OOM	OOM	OOM	OOM	OOM

Table 4. Scaling task graphs by the number of initial tasks (time is seconds)

	T0		T1		T2		
n	Global	Local	Global	Local	Global	Local	
2	0.24	0.04	0.06	0.01	0.07	0.01	Satisfied
3	3.11	0.01	0.15	0.08	0.19	0.01	
4	4.57	1.13	0.18	0.08	0.88	0.19	
5	6.09	0.03	2.73	0.01	7.05	0.02	
6	OOM	OOM	5.27	1.08	OOM	1.44	
7	OOM	0.02	OOM	0.02	OOM	0.01	
8	OOM	0.03	OOM	OOM	OOM	2.75	
9	OOM	OOM	OOM	OOM	OOM	1.86	
10	OOM	0.03	OOM	OOM	OOM	OOM	
2	0.22	0.20	0.05	0.05	0.08	0.01	Unsatisfied
3	2.91	2.55	0.14	0.13	0.20	0.01	
4	6.35	4.45	0.16	0.14	0.91	0.20	
5	7.45	5.00	2.31	1.69	7.48	0.03	
6	OOM	OOM	4.67	4.40	OOM	1.40	
7	OOM	OOM	OOM	OOM	OOM	OOM	

We automatically generate models for two processors from the benchmark containing in total 180 models and scaled them by the number of initial tasks that we include from each case into schedulability analysis.

The first three task graphs (T0, T1 and T2) are presented in Table 4. We model check nested formulae and the satisfiable one is E **true** $U_{\leq 90}$ $(t_{n-2}^{ready} \wedge A$ **true** $U_{\leq 80}$ $done)$ asking whether there is within 500 clock ticks a configuration where the task t_{n-2} can be scheduled such that then we have a guarantee that the whole schedule terminates within 500 ticks. When the upper-bounds are decreased to 5 and 10 the formula becomes unsatisfiable for all task graphs in the benchmark.

Table 5. Summary of task graphs verification (180 cases in total)

180 task graphs for	$k = 30$		$k = 60$		$k = 90$	
Algorithm	global	local	global	local	global	local
Number of finished tasks	32	85	32	158	32	178
Accumulated time (seconds)	50.4	12.9	47.6	2.30	47.32	0.44

Finally, we verify the formula E **true** $U_{\leq k}$ *done* asking whether the task graph can be scheduled within k clock ticks. We run the whole benchmark through the test (180 cases) for values of k equal to 30, 60 and 90, measuring the number of finished verification tasks (without running out of resources) and the total accumulated time it took to verify the whole benchmark for those cases where both the global and local algorithms provided an answer. The results are listed in Table 5. This provides again an evidence for the claim that the local algorithm profits from the situation where there are more possible schedules as the bound k is being relaxed.

8   Conclusion

We suggested a symbolic extension of dependency graphs in order to verify negation-free weighted CTL properties where temporal operators are annotated with upper-bound constraints on the accumulated weight. Then we introduced global and local algorithms for the computation of fixed-points in order to answer the model checking problems for the logic. The algorithms were implemented and experimented with, coming to the conclusion that the local symbol algorithm is the preferred one, providing order of magnitude speedup in the cases where the bounds in the logical formula allow for a larger number of possible witnesses of satisfiability of the formula.

In the future work we will study a weighted CTL logic with negation that combines lower- and upper-bounds. (The model checking problem for a logic containing weight intervals as the constraints is already NP-hard; showing this is easy.) From the practical point of view it would be worth designing good heuristics that can guide the search in the local algorithm in order to find faster the witnesses of satisfiability of a formula. Another challenging problem is to adapt our technique to support alternating fixed points.

References

1. Alur, R., Dill, D.: Automata for modeling real-time systems. In: Paterson, M. (ed.) ICALP 1990. LNCS, vol. 443, pp. 322–335. Springer, Heidelberg (1990)
2. Alur, R., La Torre, S., Pappas, G.J.: Optimal paths in weighted timed automata. In: Benedetto, Sangiovanni-Vincentelli (eds.) [7], pp. 49–62
3. Andersen, H.R.: Model checking and boolean graphs. Theoretical Computer Science 126(1), 3–30 (1994)

4. Kasahara Laboratory at Waseda University. Standard task graph set, http://www.kasahara.elec.waseda.ac.jp/schedule/
5. Bartlett, K.A., Scantlebury, R.A., Wilkinson, P.T.: A note on reliable full-duplex transmission over half-duplex links. Communications of the ACM 12(5), 260–261 (1969)
6. Behrmann, G., Fehnker, A., Hune, T., Larsen, K.G., Pettersson, P., Romijn, J., Vaandrager, F.W.: Minimum-cost reachability for priced timed automata. In: Benedetto, Sangiovanni-Vincentelli (eds.) [7], pp. 147–161
7. Di Benedetto, M.D., Sangiovanni-Vincentelli, A.L. (eds.): HSCC 2001. LNCS, vol. 2034. Springer, Heidelberg (2001)
8. Bouyer, P., Larsen, K.G., Markey, N.: Model checking one-clock priced timed automata. Logical Methods in Computer Science 4(2) (2008)
9. Brihaye, T., Bruyère, V., Raskin, J.-F.: Model-checking for weighted timed automata. In: Lakhnech, Y., Yovine, S. (eds.) FORMATS/FTRTFT 2004. LNCS, vol. 3253, pp. 277–292. Springer, Heidelberg (2004)
10. Buchholz, P., Kemper, P.: Model checking for a class of weighted automata. Discrete Event Dynamic Systems 20, 103–137 (2010)
11. Cassez, F., David, A., Fleury, E., Larsen, K.G., Lime, D.: Efficient on-the-fly algorithms for the analysis of timed games. In: Abadi, M., de Alfaro, L. (eds.) CONCUR 2005. LNCS, vol. 3653, pp. 66–80. Springer, Heidelberg (2005)
12. Chang, E., Roberts, R.: An improved algorithm for decentralized extrema-finding in circular configurations of processes. Commun. of ACM 22(5), 281–283 (1979)
13. Kwok, Y.-K., Ahmad, I.: Benchmarking and comparison of the task graph scheduling algorithms. Journal of Parallel and Distributed Computing 59(3), 381–422 (1999)
14. Laroussinie, F., Markey, N., Oreiby, G.: Model-checking timed ATL for durational concurrent game structures. In: Asarin, E., Bouyer, P. (eds.) FORMATS 2006. LNCS, vol. 4202, pp. 245–259. Springer, Heidelberg (2006)
15. Liu, X., Ramakrishnan, C.R., Smolka, S.A.: Fully local and efficient evaluation of alternating fixed points (Extended abstract). In: Steffen, B. (ed.) TACAS 1998. LNCS, vol. 1384, pp. 5–19. Springer, Heidelberg (1998)
16. Liu, X., Smolka, S.A.: Simple linear-time algorithms for minimal fixed points (extended abstract). In: Larsen, K.G., Skyum, S., Winskel, G. (eds.) ICALP 1998. LNCS, vol. 1443, pp. 53–66. Springer, Heidelberg (1998)
17. Milner, R.: A Calculus of Communication Systems. LNCS, vol. 92. Springer, Heidelberg (1980)

COMPL$_e$T$_e$—
A COMmunication Protocol vaLidation Toolchain

Sven Gröning, Christopher Rosas, and Christian Wietfeld

Communication Networks Institute (CNI), TU Dortmund University,
Dortmund 44227, Germany
{sven.groening,christopher.rosas,christian.wietfeld}@tu-dortmund.de
www.cni.tu-dortmund.de

Abstract. Because of shorter software development cycles for communication protocol stacks, the risk of design failures rises. Therefore, even within the protocol specification phase, appropriate validation should be performed in order to detect failures as early as possible. In the light of electric vehicle integration in a smart grid environment, the complexity of charging processes increases e.g. for demand management, and thus also complexity of requirements for associated communication protocols increases. Accordingly, it lends to describe the behavior of communication protocols by abstraction in form of models. The use of model checking processes can validate properties of future behavior, hence failures may be detected earlier. COMPL$_e$T$_e$ is a toolchain for validation of communication protocols, represented in an adapted version of UML-Statecharts. The toolchain uses the SPIN model checker and its composition is based on techniques of Model-Driven Software Development (MDSD).

Keywords: Communication Protocol Validation, COMPL$_e$T$_e$, SPIN, UML-Statecharts, Electric Mobility.

1 Introduction

Communication protocols in general, define the way of information exchange between devices or other entities on a network. To reach an agreement by involved parties about the way of information flow, the protocol description should be developed as a technical standard. Some standards already include a formal description, however only in rare cases. Furthermore, the description of the protocol behavior may also have a high level of complexity.

Especially in the context of electric mobility, a future widespread use of electric vehicles requires the deployment of reliable, uniform and comprehensive battery charging infrastructures. Therefore, the communication between all systems becomes an important factor for future acceptance.

By use of model checking techniques, the behavior of new communication protocol standards can be validated within the specification process. For this purpose, it is required to describe the behavior in a formal description language, which can be used by state-of-the-art model checking tools like SPIN[5].

E. Bartocci and C.R. Ramakrishnan (Eds.): SPIN 2013, LNCS 7976, pp. 196–208, 2013.

COMPL$_e$T$_e$ combines the possibility of an abstract behavior description represented as Unified Modeling Language (UML)-Statechart models, with a formal representation in PROMELA, which is used by SPIN as input language. Accordingly, COMPL$_e$T$_e$ facilitates the formal description process.

The remainder of this paper is structured as follows. In Section 2 the concept and design of the toolchain is described and their functionality is illustrated. Section 3 closes with a conclusion and an outlook including future work.

2   Concept and Design of COMPL$_e$T$_e$

COMPL$_e$T$_e$ realizes a COMmunication Protocol vaLidation Toolchain, by using formal and model-based specifications and descriptions. The concept takes the following requirements into account.

First, the support for creation and modification of graphical models which represent the behavior of communication protocols. This is realized by the front-end component, which is depicted at the left part of Figure 1. Moreover, an automatic transformation of the constructed graphical models to the input language of a corresponding model checker is realized. This transformation builds the link between the front-end and the back-end component in Figure 1. The back-end component integrates a model checker tool. Furthermore, editing the transformed models, based on the input language of the model checker is supported for evaluation purposes. In addition, properties can be defined with which models are checked against.

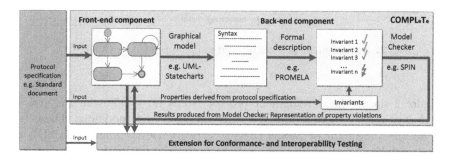

Fig. 1. Architecture of COMPL$_e$T$_e$

Secondly, beside the more functional requirements the toolchain is used within the Eclipse Integrated Development Environment (IDE). This ensures that components within the toolchain can easily be exchanged or modified (modularity and extensibility) and new components can be integrated in a simple way. Furthermore, open-source or free available existing tools are used in order to consider reusability.

2.1   Realization of Front-End Component

The front-end component realization of $COMPL_eT_e$ utilizes a combination of approaches described in [2] and [8] to use UML-Statecharts for modeling communication protocols and SPIN as model checker for verification purposes. The central question for a formal verification of UML-Statecharts is mostly the informal semantics of UML. Several approaches have been developed on this research topic. In [3] an overview of approaches for formal verification of UML-Statecharts is given. One representative approach which handles the transformation of UML-Statecharts to PROMELA is described in [7]. $COMPL_eT_e$ uses an similar approach described in [2] which uses a transformation from UML-Statecharts based on the domain-specific UML-Statecharts Description Language (UDL) to PROMELA. Typical UDL models are created in a textual description, so that an appropriate graphical editor needs to be created for $COMPL_eT_e$. In [8] a concept for meta-models for UDL and PROMELA is constructed in order to define a Model-to-Model (M2M) transformation, which represents a homomorphic mapping between meta-model elements. Because of an already existing UDL meta-model in [2], only a PROMELA meta-model is required.

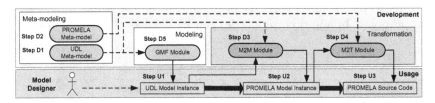

Fig. 2. Development process of front-end component in $COMPL_eT_e$

Figure 2 shows the development process (steps D1 - D5) which is grouped into the categories meta-modeling, transformation and modeling. These conform to the paradigm of Model-Driven Software Development (MDSD) and ensure modularity and extensibility of the toolchain. For this reason, the combination of the two approaches was chosen. The generation of meta-models for UDL and PROMELA is realized by use of Xtext and the Eclipse Modeling Framework (EMF) giving an Extended Backus-Naur Form (EBNF) grammar for UDL and PROMELA. The Model-to-Model (M2M) transformation from UDL to PROMELA model instances is provided by mapping rules between elements of the generated meta-models in the Atlas Transformation Language (ATL). Therefore the rules described in [2] are used as a basis for the appropriate mapping. The Model-to-Text (M2T) transformation from PROMELA model instances into PROMELA source code is achieved by the Xpand template language. The graphical editor for UDL respectively UML-Statecharts is built by use of the Graphical Modeling Framework (GMF).

(a) Statechart editing   (b) Generated PROMELA code

Fig. 3. Front-end component in COMPL$_e$T$_e$

With the COMPL$_e$T$_e$ front-end component, a model designer is able to create abstractions of communication protocols in form of UML-Statechart models which can be transformed into PROMELA models and subsequently into PROMELA source code. This is indicated in Figure 2 by the steps U1-U3, whereas Figure 3 gives an exemplary impression of the realized front-end component by showing a communication setup behavior model for electric vehicle charging in (a) and the resulting PROMELA code in (b).

2.2   Realization of Back-End Component

The development of a back-end component comprises the invocation of SPIN model checker as an Eclipse Plugin. Figure 4 summarizes the implemented functionality of COMPL$_e$T$_e$. The bottom layer shows the prerequisites and basic functions for the usage of SPIN. These are also partly described and supported by similar approaches in [4] and [6]. The basic invocation calls are also found in the *Tcl/Tk* based *iSpin/xSpin* graphical user interface, which is already shipped within the SPIN distribution.

In addition, several extensions are implemented in COMPL$_e$T$_e$ which build on top of these basic functions. As an example the invocation of an interactive and interactive-random simulation can be conducted enabling user-interaction. Furthermore, a *MSC-View* is included to allow visualization of the communication flow between PROMELA processes during simulations. This view is complemented with a *SimData-View* which shows variable values and queues of the PROMELA model. For verification purposes a specific *LTLProperty-View* is built to simplify the user interface. In addition it provides support of a so called *Multi-verification*. Thereby, for a given PROMELA model it can be invoked on

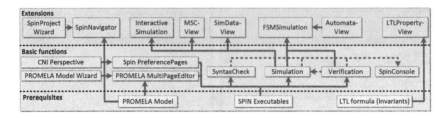

Fig. 4. Functions of back-end component of $COMPL_eT_e$

a number of selected invariants. In case of a violation the *Multi-verification* is terminated. Another extension is the *Automata-View*, in which the finite state machines of a corresponding PROMELA model are displayed by use of the Zest/- DOT tooling. The *FSMSimulation* represents a combination of the *Automata-*

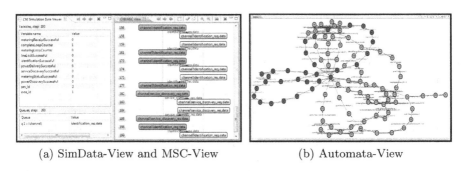

(a) SimData-View and MSC-View   (b) Automata-View

Fig. 5. Back-end component of $COMPL_eT_e$

View and a simulation. This allows to display a complete simulation-path by highlighting the visited states, from the beginning up to the occurrence of the invariant violation. Figure 5 depicts these extensions realized in $COMPL_eT_e$.

3   Conclusion and Future Work

In this paper the concept and realization of $COMPL_eT_e$ was introduced, which enables validation of communication protocols. The toolchain can be applied in the context of electric mobility as well as in further domains of interest. The communication protocol behavior described in UDL can be represented in a graphical statechart form by use of the UDL Editor. A conversion into an equivalent PROMELA code is accomplished via a M2M and a M2T transformation. For verification purposes, $COMPL_eT_e$ integrates the SPIN model checker and allows simplified usage by enabling mechanisms to specify invariant properties as LTL formulas and additional analysis extensions. Since $COMPL_eT_e$ is still under development to integrate extensions for conformance testing in the context of electric mobility, it has not yet a public release. However, a future open source version is intended.

For future work, the construction of a "complete" model for the upcoming ISO/IEC 15118 [1] standard is planned, in order to validate its related protocol behavior. Furthermore interoperability and conformance testing capabilities of COMPL$_e$T$_e$ shall be considered.

Acknowledgment. The work in this paper was funded by the *NRW Ziel 2* Program 2007-2013 (EFRE) of the European Union, the MBWSV and the MKULNV of NRW as part of the TIE-IN project with reference number 64.65.69-EM-1022A.

References

1. ISO/IEC DIS 15118, Road vehicles - Vehicle to grid Communication Interface (2012)
2. Ammann, C.: Verifikation von UML-Statecharts unter besonderer Berücksichtigung von Speicherverbrauch und Laufzeit des Model Checkers [Verification of UML-Statecharts with particular attention of memory usage and runtime of the model checker]. Softwaretechnik-Trends 31(3) (2011)
3. Bhaduri, P., Ramesh, S.: Model Checking of Statechart Models: Survey and Research Directions. CoRR cs.SE/0407038 (July 2004)
4. de Vos, B., Kats, L.C.L., Pronk, C.: EpiSpin: An Eclipse Plug-in for Promela/SPIN using Spoofax. In: Groce, A., Musuvathi, M. (eds.) SPIN Workshops 2011. LNCS, vol. 6823, pp. 177–182. Springer, Heidelberg (2011)
5. Holzmann, G.J.: The model checker SPIN. IEEE Transactions on Software Engineering 23(5), 279–295 (1997)
6. Kovše, T., Vlaovič, B., Vreže, A., Brezočnik, Z.: Eclipse Plug-In for SPIN and st2msc Tools-Tool Presentation. In: Păsăreanu, C.S. (ed.) Model Checking Software. LNCS, vol. 5578, pp. 143–147. Springer, Heidelberg (2009)
7. Latella, D., Majzik, I., Massink, M.: Automatic Verification of a Behavioural Subset of UML Statechart Diagrams Using the SPIN Model-checker. Formal Aspects of Computing 11(6), 637–664 (1999)
8. Mcumber, W.E., Cheng, B.H.: A general framework for formalizing UML with formal languages. In: Proceedings of the 23rd International Conference on Software Engineering, ICSE 2001, pp. 433–442 (2001)

A   Oral Tool Presentation

A.1   Structure of the Presentation

This section gives a structure of the demonstration of $COMPL_eT_e$ and is divided into the following three parts.

1. Motivation for designing $COMPL_eT_e$
   - $COMPL_eT_e$ in the electric mobility context
   - Protocol validation including verification (SPIN/PROMELA) and testing
2. Detailed development of $COMPL_eT_e$
   - Front-end: Model design and transformation
   - Back-end: SPIN integration and extensions
3. Case study: Application of a binding process for EV charging in $COMPL_eT_e$
   - Description of the binding process
   - Front-end component: Presenting UDL model and invoke automatic transformation into PROMELA source code
   - Back-end component: Demonstrate several functions of back-end component → *PromelaEditor, MSC-View, SimData-View, FSMSimulation, Automata-View, LTLProperty-View, SyntaxCheck*, Various simulation runs (random, guided, interactive simulation runs), Verification and *Multi-Verification* runs, Definition of invariants with regard to the generated PROMELA source code of the binding process and at last show analysis capabilities of $COMPL_eT_e$ by explaining the failed verification

A.2   Front-End: Model Design and Transformation

In the meta-modeling steps D1 and D2 (see Figure 2) appropriate meta-models on basis of an EBNF grammar, Xtext and EMF for both UDL and PROMELA are generated. The Listing 1.1 offers an excerpt of UDL grammar rules for creation of a corresponding UDL meta-model. Listing 1.2 shows an excerpt of the PROMELA grammar representing a rule for a PROMELA *proctype*.

Step D3 indicates the M2M transformation from UDL to PROMELA model instances via ATL. Listing 1.3 gives an exemplary M2M mapping rule in ATL describing the translation of UDL Enumerations into PROMELA *mtypes*.

```
 1  Model:
 2    (imports+=UDLInclude)*
 3    (variable+=UDLData)*
 4    (behaviour=UDLBehaviour)? ;
 5
 6  //State Rules
 7  UDLState:
 8    UDLSimpleState |
 9    UDLCompositeState |
10    UDLFinalState |
11    UDLInitialState ;
12
13  UDLSimpleState:
14    "simplestate" name=ID
15    "{"
16    (entry=UDLEntryAction)?
17    (exit=UDLExitAction)?
18    (out+=UDLTransition)+
19    "}";
```

Listing 1.1. Excerpt of UDL grammar

The M2T transformation from PROMELA model instances to PROMELA source code via Xpand templates is conducted in step D4. Listing 1.4 offers an excerpt of a Xpand template rule which shows the transformation of a PROMELA *proctype* element into its corresponding code fragment.

```
1  spec: // PARSER RULES
2    (specname=ID)?
3    (modules += module+);
4
5  module:
6      proctype    /* proctype declaration */
7    | init        /* init process      - max 1 per model */
8    | never       /* never claim       - max 1 per model */
9    | trace       /* event trace       - max 1 per model */
10   | utype       /* user defined types */
11   | mtype       /* mtype declaration  */
12   | decl_lst    /* global vars, chans */
13   | inline
14   | preprocess ;
15
16 proctype:
17   (active=active)?
18   PROCTYPELABEL name=ID PARENOPEN
19   (dlist=decl_lst)?
20   PARENCLOSE
21   (priority=priority)?
22   (enabler=enabler)?
23   BLOCKBEGIN
24   seq=sequence
25   BLOCKEND
26   (SEMICOLON)* ;
```

Listing 1.2. Excerpt of PROMELA grammar

```
1  -- @path UDLMM=/com.statechartverification/src-gen/com/statechartverification/UDL.ecore
2  -- @path PMLMM=/org.xtext.draft.promela/src-gen/org/xtext/draft/promela/PromelaDSL.ecore
3
4  module UDL2PML;
5  create OUT: PMLMM from IN: UDLMM;
6
7  -- Transform UDLEnumDeclare into Promela mtype declaration
8  rule UDLEnumDeclare2Promela {
9      from
10         udl_enum_declare_in: UDLMM!UDLEnumDeclare
11     to
12     pml_out: PMLMM!mtype (
13         name <- udl_enum_declare_in.getFirstEnumElementName(),
14         name <- udl_enum_declare_in.next
15             -> collect(e |
16             udl_enum_declare_in.getEnumDeclareNamePrefix() + e.name)
17     )
18 }
```

Listing 1.3. Excerpt of ATL transformation file

```
1  «IMPORT promelaDSL»
2
3  «DEFINE generateSpec FOR spec»
4    «IF this.specname != null»
5      «FILE this.specname+".promela"»
6        «EXPAND generateModules FOR this-»
7      «ENDFILE»
8    «ELSE»
9      «FILE "Test.promela"»
10       «EXPAND generateModules FOR this»
11     «ENDFILE»
12   «ENDIF»
13 «ENDDEFINE»
14
15 «DEFINE generateModule FOR proctype»
16   //Proctype ModuleDeclaration
17   «IF this.active != null»
18     «EXPAND generateActive FOR this.active»
19   «ENDIF-»proctype «this.name-»(
20     «IF this.dlist != null»
21       «EXPAND generateDeclarationList FOR this.dlist-»
22     «ENDIF»)
23     «IF this.priority != null»
24       «EXPAND generatePriority FOR this.priority»
25     «ENDIF-»
26     «IF this.enabler != null»
27       «EXPAND generateEnabler FOR this.enabler»
28     «ENDIF-» {
29       «IF this.seq != null»
30         «EXPAND generateSequence FOR this.seq»
31       «ENDIF»
32 }
33 «ENDDEFINE»
```

Listing 1.4. Excerpt of Xpand template file representing the M2T transformation

Step D5 describes the development of a graphical UDL Editor in Eclipse via GMF. Figure 6 shows the constructed graphical UDL Editor and the corresponding textual UDL Editor from [2].

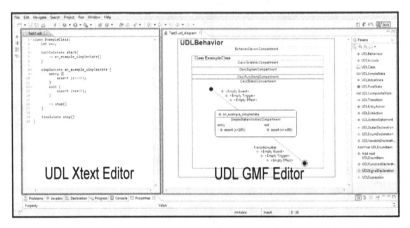

Fig. 6. Comparison textual UDL Editor and generated graphical UDL GMF Editor

A.3   Back-End: SPIN Integration and Extensions

The result of SPIN integration in COMPL$_e$T$_e$ as Eclipse Plugin is shown in Figure 7. With regard to simulation and verification capabilities Figure 5 shows the *MSC-View*, *SimData-View* and *Automata-View*.

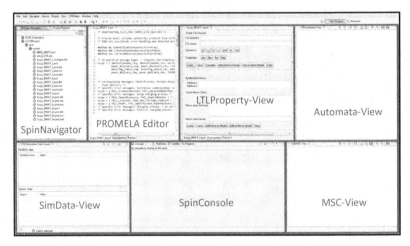

Fig. 7. Overview of the Spin Eclipse Plugin within COMPL$_e$T$_e$

A.4   Case Study: Application of a Binding Process for EV Charging in COMPL$_e$T$_e$

The applicability of COMPL$_e$T$_e$ is demonstrated by modeling an exemplary communication setup for electric vehicle charging. In general the binding process ensures a successful setup of a point-to-point connection between a Charge Point (CP) and an Electric Vehicle (EV) on IP-Level. The sequence of the binding process between a Charge Point and an EV is explained in Figure 8. At first the front-end component is used in order to model the binding process and to transform the models into executable PROMELA source code. Afterwards the source code is applied to SPIN model checker via the back-end component of COMPL$_e$T$_e$.

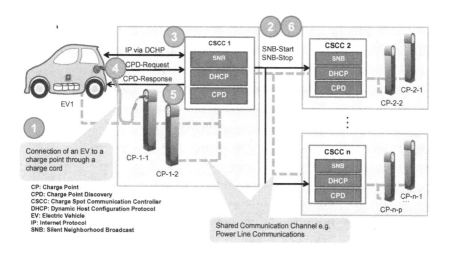

Fig. 8. Binding process for EV charging

Front-end Component: Presenting UDL Model and invoke Automatic Transformation into PROMELA Source Code. The front-end component of COMPL$_e$T$_e$ is used to model a simplified binding process resulting in UDL models respectively in UML-Statecharts for the Charge Point and the EV. The EV model is illustrated in Figure 9. Afterwards an automatic M2M and M2T transformation takes place, which produces corresponding PROMELA source code from the constructed UDL models. Listing 1.5 shows an excerpt of the generated PROMELA source code for the binding process for EV charging.

Back-end Component: Demonstrate Several Functions of Back-end Component. The generated PROMELA source code of the binding process is taken as input for SPIN. Therefore the invocation of a *Syntax Check* as well as several simulation runs are presented. For verification purposes the following example properties are defined in the *LTLProperty-View*:

```
 1  //Mtype ModuleDeclaration
 2  mtype = {ChargePoint_plug_detect_signal_cp, ChargePoint_timout_plc_guard_timer,
          ChargePoint_snb_start_request_received, ChargePoint_control_pilot_stateB, ChargePoint_binding_timout,
          ChargePoint_valid_cpd_request_received, ChargePoint_snb_stop_request_received,
          ChargePoint_timout_wait_binding_timer, ChargePoint_timout, ChargePoint_pilot_off_timout,
          Pev_plug_detect_signal_pev, Pev_control_pilot_switched_on_stateA, Pev_control_pilot_five_percent,
          Pev_dhcp_fails, Pev_ip_address_assigned, Pev_cpd_response_timout, Pev_cpd_response_ok,
          Environment_env_signal }
 3  //Decl_1st ModuleDeclaration
 4  bool oldSessionParametersAvailable;
 5  bool moreThanOneRetry;
 6  bool binding_complete_cp;
 7  bool binding_complete_pev;
 8  bool connected_cp;
 9  bool connected_pev;
10  chan ChargePoint_queue[1] = [2] of {mtype, bool};
11  chan Pev_queue[1] = [2] of {mtype, bool};
12  chan Environment_queue[1] = [2] of {mtype, bool};
13  //MacroDeclaration
14  #define ChargePoint_queue_access(x)(x-1)
15  //MacroDeclaration
16  #define Pev_queue_access(x)(x-2)
17  //MacroDeclaration
18  #define Environment_queue_access(x)(x-3)
19
20  //Proctype ModuleDeclaration
21  proctype ChargePoint(){
22  goto start;
23  //STMNT Labeled Statement
24  start:
25  if
26  ::
27  empty(ChargePoint_queue[ChargePoint_queue_access(_pid)]);
28  goto disconnected
29  ::
30  ChargePoint_queue[ChargePoint_queue_access(_pid)]?ChargePoint_plug_detect_signal_cp, _ ;
31  goto start
32  ::
33  ChargePoint_queue[ChargePoint_queue_access(_pid)]?ChargePoint_timout_plc_guard_timer, _ ;
34  goto start
35  ::
36  ChargePoint_queue[ChargePoint_queue_access(_pid)]?ChargePoint_snb_start_request_received, _ ;
37  goto start
38  ::
39  ChargePoint_queue[ChargePoint_queue_access(_pid)]?ChargePoint_control_pilot_stateB, _ ;
40  goto start
41  ::
42  ChargePoint_queue[ChargePoint_queue_access(_pid)]?ChargePoint_binding_timout, _ ;
43  goto start
44  ::
45  ChargePoint_queue[ChargePoint_queue_access(_pid)]?ChargePoint_valid_cpd_request_received, _ ;
46  goto start
47  ::
48  ChargePoint_queue[ChargePoint_queue_access(_pid)]?ChargePoint_snb_stop_request_received, _ ;
49  goto start
50  ::
51  ChargePoint_queue[ChargePoint_queue_access(_pid)]?ChargePoint_timout_wait_binding_timer, _ ;
52  goto start
53  ::
54  ChargePoint_queue[ChargePoint_queue_access(_pid)]?ChargePoint_timout, _ ;
55  goto start
56  ::
57  ChargePoint_queue[ChargePoint_queue_access(_pid)]?ChargePoint_pilot_off_timout, _ ;
58  goto start
59  fi;
60  }
61
62  //Proctype ModuleDeclaration
63  proctype Pev(){
64  goto start;
65  //STMNT Labeled Statement
66  start:
67  if
68  ::
69  empty(Pev_queue[Pev_queue_access(_pid)]) ;
70  goto disconnected
71  ::
72  Pev_queue[Pev_queue_access(_pid)]?Pev_plug_detect_signal_pev, _ ;
73  goto start
74  ::
75  Pev_queue[Pev_queue_access(_pid)]?Pev_control_pilot_switched_on_stateA, _ ;
76  goto start
77  ::
78  Pev_queue[Pev_queue_access(_pid)]?Pev_control_pilot_five_percent, _ ;
79  goto start
80  ::
81  Pev_queue[Pev_queue_access(_pid)]?Pev_dhcp_fails, _ ;
82  goto start
83  ::
84  Pev_queue[Pev_queue_access(_pid)]?Pev_ip_address_assigned, _ ;
85  goto start
86  ::
87  Pev_queue[Pev_queue_access(_pid)]?Pev_cpd_response_timout, _ ;
88  goto start
89  ::
90  Pev_queue[Pev_queue_access(_pid)]?Pev_cpd_response_ok, _ ;
91  goto start
92  fi;
93  }
```

Listing 1.5. Generated PROMELA source code of the binding process for EV charging

- Eventually the binding process will be completed. $\diamond$ *bindingComplete*
- The connection of EV and CP always implies the completion of the binding process (invariant property). $\square$ (*instancesConnected* $\implies$ *bindingComplete*)

Especially the invocation of verifications is a crucial point in evaluation of COMPLₑTₑ's capabilities. The verification of the binding process in PROMELA is demonstrated by use of aforementioned LTL formulas. For illustration purposes Figure 9 depicts the statemachine of the EV in the *Automata-View*.

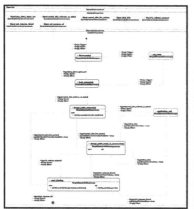 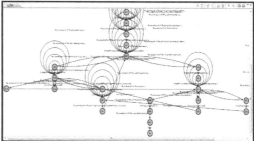

(a) UDL-Statechart of EV   (b) EV statemachine in Automata-View

Fig. 9. EV models

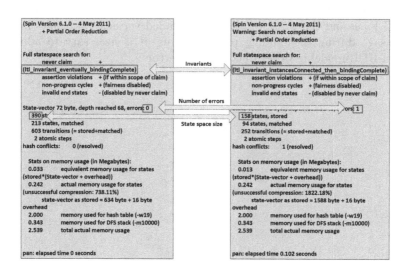

Fig. 10. Comparison of SPIN output for a successful and failed verification run

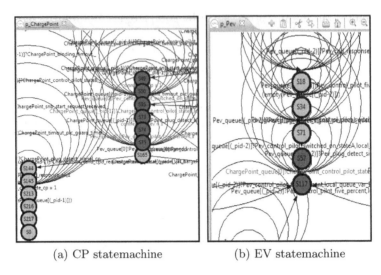

(a) CP statemachine   (b) EV statemachine

Fig. 11. Paths of EV and Charge Point statemachines for the error case

The verification of the first defined property succeeds without any errors but the second property fails. Figure 10 shows an contrasting comparison of the generated SPIN outputs. For analysis purposes, a guided simulation is conducted. Within COMPL$_e$T$_e$ the message flow is visualized in the *MSC-View*. In addition, the *FSMSimulation* shows the traversing of the states, which are iteratively highlighted in the *Automata-View*. An example of the *FSMSimulation* for the Charge Point and the EV is shown in Figure 11. By analyzing the model using the *MSC-View* and the *FSMSimulation*, the failed verification results in a loss of a message during the binding process. Thus, it is necessary to adapt the simplified UDL model in order to correct the error.

Towards Modeling and Model Checking Fault-Tolerant Distributed Algorithms*

Annu John, Igor Konnov, Ulrich Schmid, Helmut Veith, and Josef Widder

Vienna University of Technology (TU Wien)

Abstract. Fault-tolerant distributed algorithms are central for building reliable, spatially distributed systems. In order to ensure that these algorithms actually make systems more reliable, we must ensure that these algorithms are actually correct. Unfortunately, model checking state-of-the-art fault-tolerant distributed algorithms (such as Paxos) is currently out of reach except for very small systems.

In order to be eventually able to automatically verify such fault-tolerant distributed algorithms also for larger systems, several problems have to be addressed. In this paper, we consider modeling and verification of fault-tolerant algorithms that basically only contain threshold guards to control the flow of the algorithm. As threshold guards are widely used in fault-tolerant distributed algorithms (and also in Paxos), efficient methods to handle them bring us closer to the above mentioned goal.

As a case study we use the reliable broadcasting algorithm by Srikanth and Toueg that tolerates even Byzantine faults. We show how one can model this basic fault-tolerant distributed algorithm in PROMELA such that safety and liveness properties can be efficiently verified in SPIN. We provide experimental data also for other distributed algorithms.

1 Introduction

Even formally verified computer systems are subject to power outages, electrical wear-out, bit-flips in memory due to ionizing particle hits, etc., which may easily cause system failures. Replication is a classic approach to ensure that a computer system is fault-tolerant, i.e., continues to correctly perform its task even if some components fail. The basic idea is to have multiple computers instead of a single one (that would constitute a single point of failure), and ensure that the replicated computers coordinate, and for instance in the case of replicated databases, store the same information. Ensuring that all computers agree on the same information is non-trivial due to several sources of non-determinism, namely, faults, uncertain message delays, and asynchronous computation steps.

To address these issues, fault-tolerant distributed algorithms for state machine replication were introduced many years ago [33]. As they are designed to

---

* Supported by the Austrian National Research Network S11403 and S11405 (RiSE) of the Austrian Science Fund (FWF) and by the Vienna Science and Technology Fund (WWTF) through grants PROSEED, ICT12-059, and VRG11-005.

E. Bartocci and C.R. Ramakrishnan (Eds.): SPIN 2013, LNCS 7976, pp. 209–226, 2013.

increase the reliability of computing systems, it is crucial that these algorithms are indeed correct, i.e., satisfy their specifications. Due to the various sources of non-determinism, however, it is very easy to make mistakes in the correctness arguments for fault-tolerant distributed algorithms. As a consequence, they are very natural candidates for model checking. Still, model checking fault-tolerant distributed algorithms is particularly challenging due to the following reasons:

(i) Due to their inherent concurrency and the many sources of non-determinism, fault-tolerant distributed algorithms suffer from combinatorial explosion in the state-space, and in the number of behaviors. Moreover, distributed algorithms usually involve parameters such as the system size n and the maximum number of faulty components t.

(ii) Correctness and even solvability of problems like distributed agreement depend critically upon assumptions on the environment, in particular, degree of concurrency, message delays, and failure models; e.g., guaranteeing correct execution is impossible if there is no restriction on the number of faulty components in the system and/or the way how they may fail.

(iii) There is no commonly agreed-upon distributed computing model, but rather many variants, which differ in (sometimes subtle) details such as atomicity of a computing step. Moreover, distributed algorithms are usually described in pseudocode, typically using different (alas unspecified) pseudocode languages, which obfuscates the relation to the underlying computing model.

A central and important goal of our recent work is hence to initiate a systematic study of distributed algorithms from a verification point of view, in a way that does not betray the fundamentals of distributed algorithms. Experience tells that this has not always been observed in the past: The famous bakery algorithm [22] is probably the most striking example from the literature where wrong specifications have been verified or wrong semantics have been considered: Many papers in formal methods have verified the correctness of the bakery algorithm as an evidence for their practical applicability. Viewed from a distributed algorithms perspective, however, most of these papers missed the fact that the algorithm does not require atomic registers but rather safe registers only [23] — a subtle detail that is admittedly difficult to extract from the distributed algorithms literature for non-experts. Still, compared to state-of-the-art fault-tolerant distributed algorithms — and even the algorithms considered in this paper — the bakery algorithm rests on a quite simple computational model, which shows the need for a structured approach to handle distributed algorithms.

Contributions. In this paper, we present a structured approach for modeling an important family of fault-tolerant distributed algorithms, namely, threshold-guarded distributed algorithms discussed in Section 2. As threshold-guarded commands are omnipresent in this domain, our work is an important step towards the goal of verifying state-of-the-art fault-tolerant distributed algorithms. In Section 3, we obtain models of distributed algorithms expressed in slightly extended PROMELA [20] to capture the notions required to fully express fault-tolerant distributed algorithms and their environments, including resilience conditions involving parameters like n and t, fairness conditions, and atomicity assumptions. This formalization allows us to (i) instantiate system instances for different system sizes in order to perform explicit state model checking using SPIN as discussed in Section 4, and (ii) build a basis for our parameterized model checking technique based on parametric interval abstraction discussed in [21].

Using our approach, we can already formalize and model check several basic fault-tolerant distributed algorithms for fixed parameters, i.e., numbers of processes and faults. These algorithms include several variants of the classic asynchronous broadcasting algorithm from [34] under various fault assumptions, the broadcasting algorithm from [6] tolerating Byzantine faults, the classic broadcasting algorithm found, e.g., in [9], that tolerates crash faults, as well as a condition-based consensus algorithm [27] that also tolerates crash faults.

This captures the most interesting problems that are solvable [16] by distributed algorithms running in a purely asynchronous environment with faults. Our verification results build a corner stone for the verification of more advanced fault-tolerant distributed algorithms [13,9,26,37,10,18]. These algorithms use threshold-guarded commands as a building block, yet contain other features that call for additional model checking techniques.

2   Threshold-Guarded Distributed Algorithms

Processes, which constitute the distributed algorithms we consider, exchange messages, and change their state predominantly based on the received messages. In addition to the standard execution of actions, which are guarded by some predicate on the local state, most basic distributed algorithms (cf. [24,3]) add existentially or universally guarded commands involving received messages:

if received <m>	**if** received <m>
from some process	from all processes
then action (m);	**then** action (m);
(a) existential guard	(b) universal guard

Depending on the content of the message <m>, the function `action` performs a local computation, and possibly sends messages to one or more processes. Such constructs can be found, e.g., in (non-fault-tolerant) distributed algorithms for constructing spanning trees, flooding, mutual exclusion, or network synchronization [24]. Understanding and analyzing such distributed algorithms is already far from being trivial, which is due to the partial information on the global state present in the local state of a process. However, faults add another source of nondeterminism. In order to shed some light on the difficulties facing a distributed algorithm in the presence of faults, consider Byzantine faults [28], which allow a faulty process to behave arbitrarily: Faulty processes may fail to send messages, send messages with erroneous values, or even send conflicting information to different processes. In addition, faulty processes may even collaborate in order to increase their adverse power.

Fault-tolerant distributed algorithms work in the presence of such faults and provide some "higher level" service: In case of distributed agreement (or consensus), e.g., this service is that all non-faulty processes compute the same result even if some processes fail. Fault-tolerant distributed algorithms are hence used for increasing the system-level reliability of distributed systems [30].

If one tries to build such a fault-tolerant distributed algorithm using the construct of Example (a) in the presence of Byzantine faults, the (local state of the) receiver process would be corrupted if the received message <m> originates in a faulty process. A faulty process could hence contaminate a correct process. On the other hand, if one tried to use the construct of Example (b), a correct process would wait forever (starve) when a faulty process omits to send the required message. To overcome those problems, fault-tolerant distributed algorithms typically require assumptions on the maximum number of faults, and employ suitable thresholds for the number of messages which can be expected to be received by correct processes. Assuming that the system consists of n processes among which at most t may be faulty, *threshold-guarded commands* such as the following are typically used in fault-tolerant distributed algorithms:

> **if** received <m> from n−t distinct processes
> **then** action (m);

Assuming that thresholds are functions of the parameters n and t, threshold guards are a just generalization of quantified guards as given in Examples (a) and (b): In the above command, a process waits to receive $n - t$ messages from distinct processes. As there are at least $n - t$ correct processes, the guard cannot be blocked by faulty processes, which avoids the problems of Example (b). In the distributed algorithms literature, one finds a variety of different thresholds: Typical numbers are $\lceil n/2 + 1 \rceil$ (for majority [13,27]), $t + 1$ (to wait for a message from at least one correct process [34,13]), or $n - t$ (in the Byzantine case [34,2] to wait for at least $t + 1$ messages from correct processes, provided $n > 3t$).

In the setting of Byzantine fault tolerance, it is important to note that the use of threshold-guarded commands implicitly rests on the assumption that a receiver can distinguish messages from different senders. This can be achieved, e.g., by using point-to-point links between processes or by message authentication. What is important here is that Byzantine faulty processes are only allowed to exercise control on their own messages and computations, but not on the messages sent by other processes and the computation of other processes.

Reliable Broadcast and Related Specifications. The specifications considered in the area of fault tolerance differ from more classic areas, such as concurrent systems where dining philosophers and mutual exclusion are central problems. For the latter, one is typically interested in local properties, e.g., if a philosopher i is hungry, then i eventually eats. Intuitively, dining philosophers requires us to trace indexed processes along a computation, e.g., $\forall i.\ \mathbf{G}\,(\mathrm{hungry}_i \to (\mathbf{F}\,\mathrm{eating}_i))$, and thus to employ *indexed* temporal logics for specifications [7,11,12,14].

In contrast, fault-tolerant distributed algorithms are typically used to achieve *global* properties. Reliable broadcast is an ongoing "system service" with the following informal specification: Each process i may invoke a primitive called broadcast by calling $bcast(i, m)$, where m is a unique message content. Processes may deliver a message by invoking $accept(i, m)$ for different process and message pairs (i, m). The goal is that all correct processes invoke $accept(i, m)$ for the same set of (i, m) pairs, under some additional constraints: all messages broadcast by correct processes must be accepted by all correct processes, and $accept(i, m)$ may not be invoked, unless i is faulty or i invoked $bcast(i, m)$. Our case study is to verify that the algorithm from [34] implements these primitives on top of point-to-point channels, in the presence of Byzantine faults. In [34], the instances for different (i, m) pairs do not interfere. Therefore, we will not consider i and m. Rather, we distinguish the different kinds of invocations of $bcast(i, m)$ that may occur, e.g., the cases where the invoking process is faulty or correct. Depending on the initial state, we then have to check whether every/no correct process accepts. To capture this kind of properties, we have to trace only existentially or universally quantified properties, e.g., a part of the broadcast specification (relay) [34] states that if some correct process accepts a message, then all (correct) processes accept the message, that is, $\mathbf{G}\left((\exists i.\ accept_i) \rightarrow \mathbf{F}\left(\forall j.\ accept_j\right)\right)$.

We are therefore considering a temporal logic where the *quantification over processes is restricted to propositional formulas*. We will need two kinds of quantified propositional formulas that consider (i) the finite control state modeled as a single status variable sv, and (ii) the possible unbounded data. We introduce the set AP_{SV} that contains propositions that capture comparison against some status value Z from the set of all control states, i.e., $[\forall i.\ sv_i = Z]$ and $[\exists i.\ sv_i = Z]$.

This allows us to express specifications of distributed algorithms. To express the mentioned relay property, we identify the status values where a process has accepted the message. We may quantify over all processes as we only explicitly model those processes that follow their code, that is, correct or benign faulty processes. More severe faults that are unrestricted in their internal behavior (e.g., Byzantine faults) are modeled via non-determinism in message passing. For a detailed discussion see Section 3.

In order to express comparison of data variables, we add a set of atomic propositions AP_D that capture comparison of data variables (integers) x, y, and constant c; AP_D consists of propositions of the form $[\exists i.\ x_i + c < y_i]$.

The labeling function of a system instance is then defined naturally as disjunction or conjunction over all process indices; cf. [21] for complete definitions.

Given an $\mathsf{LTL} \setminus \mathsf{X}$ formula ψ over AP_D expressing justice [29], an $\mathsf{LTL} \setminus \mathsf{X}$ specification φ over AP_{SV}, a process description P in PROMELA, and the number of (correct) processes N, the problem is to verify whether

$$\underbrace{P \parallel P \parallel \cdots \parallel P}_{N\ times} \models \psi \rightarrow \varphi.$$

3   Threshold-Guarded Distributed Algorithms in Promela

Algorithm 1 is our case study for which we also provide a complete PROMELA implementation later in Figure 4. To explain how we obtain this implementation,

---

Algorithm 1. Core logic of the broadcasting algorithm from [34]

Code for processes i if it is correct:

Variables

1: $v_i \in \{\text{FALSE}, \text{TRUE}\}$
2: $\text{accept}_i \in \{\text{FALSE}, \text{TRUE}\} \leftarrow \text{FALSE}$

Rules

3: **if** v_i **and** not sent $\langle \text{echo} \rangle$ before **then**
4:    send $\langle \text{echo} \rangle$ to all;
5: **if** *received* $\langle \text{echo} \rangle$ from at least $t + 1$ *distinct* processes
        and not sent $\langle \text{echo} \rangle$ before **then**
6:    send $\langle \text{echo} \rangle$ to all;
7: **if** *received* $\langle \text{echo} \rangle$ from at least $n - t$ *distinct* processes **then**
8:    $\text{accept}_i \leftarrow \text{TRUE}$;

---

we proceed in three steps where we first discuss asynchronous distributed algorithms in general, then explain our encoding of message passing for threshold-guarded fault-tolerant distributed algorithms. Algorithm 1 belongs to this class, as it does not distinguish messages according to their senders, but just counts received messages, and performs state transitions depending on the number of received messages; e.g., line 7. Finally we encode the control flow of Algorithm 1. The rationale of the modeling decisions are that the resulting PROMELA model (i) captures the assumptions of distributed algorithms adequately, and (ii) allows for efficient verification either using explicit state enumeration (as discussed in this paper) or by abstraction as discussed in [21]. After discussing the modeling of distributed algorithms, we will provide the specifications in Section 3.4.

3.1 Computational Model for Asynchronous Distributed Algorithms

We recall the standard assumptions for asynchronous distributed algorithms. A system consists of n processes, out of which at most t may be faulty. When considering a fixed computation, we denote by f the actual number of faulty processes. Note that f is not "known" to the processes. It is assumed that $n > 3t \wedge f \leq t \wedge t > 0$. Correct processes follow the algorithm, in that they take steps that correspond to the algorithm. Between every pair of processes, there is a bidirectional link over which messages are exchanged. A link contains two message buffers, each being the receive buffer of one of the incident processes.

A step of a correct process is *atomic* and consists of the following three parts. (i) The process possibly receives a message. A process is not forced to receive a message even if there is one in its buffer [16]. (ii) Then, it performs a state transition depending on its current state and the (possibly) received message. (iii) Finally, a process may send at most one message to each process, that is, it puts a message in the buffers of the other processes.

Computations are asynchronous in that the steps can be arbitrarily interleaved, provided that each correct process takes an infinite number of steps.

(Algorithm 1 has runs that never accept and are infinite. Conceptually, the standard model requires that processes executing terminating algorithms loop forever in terminal states [24].) Moreover, if a message m is put into process p's buffer, and p is correct, then m is eventually received. This property is called *reliable communication*.

From the above discussion we observe that buffers are required to be unbounded, and thus sending is non-blocking. Further, receiving is non-blocking even if no message has been sent to the process. If we assume that for each message type, each correct process sends at most one message in each run (as in Algorithm 1), non-blocking send can in principle natively be encoded in PROMELA using message channels. In principle, non-blocking receive also can be implemented in PROMELA, but it is not a basic construct. We discuss the modeling of message passing in more detail in Section 3.2.

Fault Types. In our case study Algorithm 1 we consider *Byzantine* faults, that is, faulty processes are not restricted, except that they have no influence on the buffers of links to which they are not incident. Below we also consider restricted failure classes: *omission faults* follow the algorithm but may fail to send some messages, *crash faults* follow the algorithm but may prematurely stop running. Finally, *symmetric faults* need not follow the algorithm, but if they send messages, they send them to all processes. (The latter restriction does not apply to Byzantine faults which may send conflicting information to different processes).

Verification Goal. Recall that there is a condition on the parameters n, t, and f, namely, $n > 3t \wedge f \leq t \wedge t > 0$. As these parameters do not change during a run, they can be encoded as constants in PROMELA. The verification problem for a distributed algorithm with fixed n and t is then the composition of model checking problems that differ in the actual value of f (satisfying $f \leq t$).

3.2   Efficient Encoding of Message Passing

In threshold-guarded distributed algorithms, the processes (i) count how many messages of the same type they have received from *distinct* processes, and change their states depending on this number, (ii) always send to *all* processes (including the process itself), and (iii) send messages only for a fixed number of types (only messages of type ⟨echo⟩ are sent in Algorithm 1).

Fault-Free Communication. We discuss in the following that one can model such algorithms in a way that is more efficient in comparison to a straightforward implementation with PROMELA channels. In our final modeling we have an approach that captures both message passing and the influence of faults on correct processes. However, in order to not clutter the presentation, we start our discussion by considering communication between correct processes only (i.e., $f = 0$), and add faults later in this section.

In the following code examples we show a straightforward way to implement "received ⟨echo⟩ from at least x distinct processes" and "send ⟨echo⟩ to all" using PROMELA channels: We declare an array p2p of n^2 channels, one per pair of processes, and then we declare an array rx to record that at most one ⟨echo⟩ message from a process j is received by a process i:

```
mtype = { ECHO }; /* one message type */
chan p2p[NxN] = [1] of { mtype }; /* channels of capacity 1 */
bit   rx[NxN]; /* a bit map to implement "distinct" */
active[N] proctype STBcastChan() {
  int i, nrcvd = 0; /* nr. of echoes */
```

Then, the receive code iterates over n channels: for non-empty channels it receives an ⟨echo⟩ message or not, and empty channels are skipped; if a message is received, the channel is marked in rx:

```
i = 0; do
  :: (i < N) && nempty(p2p[i * N + _pid]) ->
     p2p[i * N + _pid]?ECHO; /* retrieve a message */
     if
       :: !rx[i * N + _pid] ->
          rx[i * N + _pid] = 1; /* mark the channel */
          nrcvd++; break; /* receive at most one message */
       :: rx[i * N + _pid];   /* ignore duplicates */
     fi; i++;
  :: (i < N) ->
     i++;   /* channel is empty or postpone reception */
  :: i == N -> break;
od
```

Finally, the sending code also iterates over n channels and sends on each:

```
for (i : 1 .. N) { p2p[_pid * N + i]!ECHO; }
```

Recall that threshold-guarded algorithms have specific constraints: messages from all processes are processed uniformly; every message is carrying only a message type without a process identifier; each process sends a message to all processes in no particular order. This suggests a simpler modeling solution. Instead of using message passing directly, we keep only the numbers of sent and received messages in integer variables:

```
int nsnt; /* one shared variable per a message type */
active[N] proctype STBcast() {
  int nrcvd = 0, next_nrcvd = 0; /* nr. of echoes */
  ...
step: atomic {
    if /* receive one more echo */
      :: (next_nrcvd < nsnt) ->
         next_nrcvd = nrcvd + 1;
      :: next_nrcvd = nrcvd; /* or nothing */
    fi;
    ...
    nsnt++; /* send echo to all */
  }
```

```
active[F] proctype Byz() {              active[F] proctype Symm() {
step: atomic {                          step: atomic {
  i = 0; do                              if
  :: i < N -> sendTo(i); i++;            :: /* send all */
  :: i < N -> i++; /* some */               for (i : 1 .. N)
  :: i == N -> break;                       { sendTo(i); }
  od                                     :: skip; /* or none */
}; goto step;                            fi
}                                       }; goto step;
                                        }


active[F] proctype Omit() {
step: atomic {
  /* receive as a correct */            active[F] proctype Clean() {
  /* compute as a correct */            step: atomic {
  if :: correctCodeSendsAll ->            /* receive as a correct */
  i = 0; do                               /* compute as a correct */
  :: i < N -> sendTo(i); i++;             /* send as a correct one */
  :: i < N -> i++; /* omit */             };
  :: i == N -> break;                     if
  od                                      :: goto step;
  :: skip;                                :: goto crash;
  fi                                      fi;
}; goto step;                             crash:
}                                       }
```

Fig. 1. Modeling faulty processes explicitly: Byzantine (Byz), symmetric (Symm), omission (Omit), and clean crashes (Clean)

As one process step is executed atomically (indivisibly), concurrent reads and updates of $nsnt$ are not a concern to us. Note that the presented code is based on the assumption that each correct process sends at most one message. We show how to enforce this assumption when discussing the control flow of our implementation of Algorithm 1 in Section 3.3.

Recall that in asynchronous distributed systems one assumes communication fairness, that is, every message sent is eventually received. The statement $\exists i.\ rcvd_i < nsnt_i$ describes a global state where messages are still in transit. It follows that a formula ψ defined by

$$\mathbf{G}\,\mathbf{F} \neg [\exists i.\ rcvd_i < nsnt_i] \qquad \text{(RelComm)}$$

states that the system periodically delivers all messages sent by (correct) processes. We are thus going to add such fairness requirements to our specifications.

Faulty Processes. In Figure 1 we show how one can model the different types of faults discussed above using channels. The implementations are direct consequences of the fault description given in Section 3.1. Figure 2 shows how the impact of faults on processes following the algorithm can be implemented in the shared memory implementation of message passing. Note that in contrast to

```
/* N > 3T ∧ T ≥ F ≥ 0 */
active[N-F] proctype ByzI() {
step: atomic {
  if
  :: (next_nrcvd < nsnt + F)
    -> next_nrcvd = nrcvd + 1;
  :: next_nrcvd = nrcvd;
  fi
  /* compute */
  /* send    */
  }; goto step;
}
```

```
/* N > 2T ∧ T ≥ Fp ≥ Fs ≥ 0 */
active[N-Fp] proctype SymmI() {
step: atomic {
  if
  :: (next_nrcvd < nsnt + Fs)
    -> next_nrcvd = nrcvd + 1;
  :: next_nrcvd = nrcvd;
  fi
  /* compute */
  /* send    */
  }; goto step;
}
```

```
/* N > 2T ∧ T ≥ F ≥ 0 */
active[N] proctype OmitI() {
step: atomic {
  if
  :: (next_nrcvd < nsnt) ->
    next_nrcvd = nrcvd + 1;
  :: next_nrcvd = nrcvd;
  fi
  /* compute */
  /* send    */
  }; goto step;
}
```

```
/* N ≥ T ∧ T ≥ Fc ≥ Fnc ≥ 0 */
active[N] proctype CleanI() {
step: atomic {
  if
  :: (next_nrcvd < nsnt - Fnc)
    -> next_nrcvd = nrcvd + 1;
  :: next_nrcvd = nrcvd;
  fi
  /* compute */
  /* send    */
  }; goto step;
}
```

Fig. 2. Modeling the effect of faults on correct processes: Byzantine (ByzI), symmetric (SymmI), omission (OmitI), and clean crashes (CleanI)

Figure 1, the processes in Figure 2 are *not* the faulty ones, but correct ones whose variable next_nrcvd is subject to non-deterministic updates that correspond to the impact of faulty process. For instance, in the Byzantine case, in addition to the messages sent by correct processes, a process can receive up to f messages more. This is expressed by the condition (next_nrcvd < nsnt + F).

For Byzantine and symmetric faults we only model correct processes explicitly. Thus, we specify that there are N-F copies of the process. Moreover, we can use Property (RelComm) to model reliable communication. Omission and crash faults, however, we model explicitly, so that we have N copies of processes. Without going into too much detail, the impact of faulty processes is modeled by relaxed fairness requirements: as some messages sent by these f faulty processes may not be received, this induces less strict communication fairness:

$$\mathbf{G}\,\mathbf{F}\,\neg\,[\exists i.\; rcvd_i + f < nsnt_i]$$

By similar adaptations one models, e.g., corrupted communication (e.g., due to faulty links) [31], or hybrid fault models [4] that contain different fault scenarios.

Figure 3 compares the number of states and memory consumption when modeling message passing using both solutions. We ran SPIN to perform exhaustive

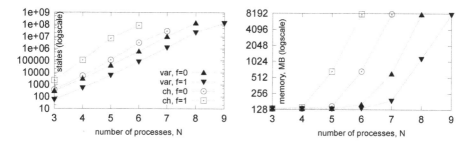

Fig. 3. Visited states (left) and memory usage (right) when modeling message passing with channels (ch) or shared variables (var). The faults are in effect only when $f > 0$. Ran with SAFETY, COLLAPSE, COMP, and 8GB of memory.

state enumeration on the encoding of Algorithm 1 (discussed in the next section). As one sees, the model with explicit channels and faulty processes ran out of memory on *six* processes, whereas the shared memory model did so only with *nine* processes. Moreover, the latter scales better in the presence of faults, while the former degrades with faults. This leads us to use the shared memory encoding based on *nsnt* variables.

3.3   Encoding the Control Flow

Recall Algorithm 1, which is written in typical pseudocode found in the distributed algorithms literature. The lines 3–8 describe one step of the algorithm. Receiving messages is implicit and performed before line 3, and the actual sending of messages is deferred to the end, and is performed after line 8.

We encoded the algorithm in Figure 4 using custom PROMELA extensions to express notions of fault-tolerant distributed algorithms. The extensions are required to express a parameterized model checking problem, and are used by our tool that implements the abstraction methods introduced in [21]. These extensions are only syntactic sugar when the parameters are fixed: symbolic is used to declare parameters, and assume is used to impose resilience conditions on them (but is ignored in explicit state model checking). Declarations atomic <var> = all (...) are a shorthand for declaring atomic propositions that are unfolded into conjunctions over all processes (similarly for some). Also we allow expressions over parameters in the argument of active.

In the encoding in Figure 4, the whole step is captured within an atomic block (lines 20–42). As usual for fault-tolerant algorithms, this block has three logical parts: the receive part (lines 21–24), the computation part (lines 25–32), and the sending part (lines 33–38). As we have already discussed the encoding of message passing above, it remains to discuss the control flow of the algorithm.

Control State of the Algorithm. Apart from receiving and sending messages, Algorithm 1 refers to several facts about the current control state of a process: "sent ⟨*echo*⟩ before", "if v_i", and "*accept$_i$* ← TRUE". We capture all possible

```
1   symbolic int N, T, F;  /* parameters */
2   /* the resilience condition */
3   assume(N > 3 * T && T >= 1 && 0 <= F && F <= T);
4   int nsnt;  /* number of echoes sent by correct processes */
5   /* quantified atomic propositions */
6   atomic prec_unforg = all(STBcast:sv == V0);
7   atomic prec_corr = all(STBcast:sv == V1);
8   atomic prec_init = all(STBcast@step);
9   atomic ex_acc = some(STBcast:sv == AC);
10  atomic all_acc = all(STBcast:sv == AC);
11  atomic in_transit = some(STBcast:nrcvd < nsnt);
12
13  active[N - F] proctype STBcast() {
14     byte sv, next_sv;              /* status of the algorithm */
15     int nrcvd = 0, next_nrcvd = 0; /* nr. of echoes received */
16     if  /* initialize */
17        :: sv = V0; /* v_i = FALSE */
18        :: sv = V1; /* v_i = TRUE */
19     fi;
20  step: atomic { /* an indivisible step */
21        if /* receive one more echo (up to nsnt + F) */
22           :: (next_nrcvd < nsnt + F) -> next_nrcvd = nrcvd + 1;
23           :: next_nrcvd = nrcvd; /* or nothing */
24        fi;
25        if /* compute */
26           :: (next_nrcvd >= N - T) ->
27             next_sv = AC; /* accept_i = TRUE */
28           :: (next_nrcvd < N - T && sv == V1
29              || next_nrcvd >= T + 1) ->
30             next_sv = SE; /* remember that <echo> is sent */
31           :: else -> next_sv = sv; /* keep the status */
32        fi;
33        if /* send */
34           :: (sv == V0 || sv == V1)
35              && (next_sv == SE || next_sv == AC) ->
36             nsnt++; /* send <echo> */
37           :: else; /* send nothing */
38        fi;
39        /* update local variables and reset scratch variables */
40        sv = next_sv; nrcvd = next_nrcvd;
41        next_sv = 0; next_nrcvd = 0;
42     } goto step;
43  }
44  /* LTL-X formulas */
45  ltl fairness { []<>(!in_transit) } /* added to other formulas */
46  ltl relay { [](ex_acc -> <>all_acc) }
47  ltl corr { []((prec_init && prec_corr) -> <>(ex_acc)) }
48  ltl unforg { []((prec_init && prec_unforg) -> []!ex_acc) }
```

Fig. 4. Encoding of Algorithm 1 in PROMELA with symbolic extensions

control states in a finite set SV. For instance, for Algorithm 1 one can collect the set $SV = \{\text{V0}, \text{V1}, \text{SE}, \text{AC}\}$, where:

- V0 corresponds to $v_i = \text{FALSE}$, $\text{accept}_i = \text{FALSE}$ and $\langle\text{echo}\rangle$ is not sent.
- V1 corresponds to $v_i = \text{TRUE}$, $\text{accept}_i = \text{FALSE}$ and $\langle\text{echo}\rangle$ is not sent.
- SE corresponds to the case $\text{accept}_i = \text{FALSE}$ and $\langle\text{echo}\rangle$ been sent. Observe that once a process has sent $\langle\text{echo}\rangle$, its value of v_i does not interfere anymore with the subsequent control flow.
- AC corresponds to the case $\text{accept}_i = \text{TRUE}$ and $\langle\text{echo}\rangle$ been sent. A process only sets accept to TRUE if it has sent a message (or is about to do so in the current step).

Thus, the control state is captured within a single *status variable* sv over SV with the set $SV_0 = \{\text{V0}, \text{V1}\}$ of initial control states.

3.4 Specifications

Specifications are an encoding of the broadcast properties [34], which contain a safety property called *unforgeability*, and two liveness properties called *correctness* and *relay*:

$$\mathbf{G}\left([\forall i.\ sv_i \neq \text{V1}] \rightarrow \mathbf{G}\ [\forall j.\ sv_j \neq \text{AC}]\right) \tag{U}$$

$$\mathbf{G}\left([\forall i.\ sv_i = \text{V1}] \rightarrow \mathbf{F}\ [\exists j.\ sv_j = \text{AC}]\right) \tag{C}$$

$$\mathbf{G}\left([\exists i.\ sv_i = \text{AC}] \rightarrow \mathbf{F}\ [\forall j.\ sv_j = \text{AC}]\right) \tag{R}$$

4 Experiments with SPIN

Figure 4 provides the central parts of the code of our case study. For the experiments we have implemented four distributed algorithms that use threshold-guarded commands, and differ in the fault model. We have one algorithm for each of the fault models discussed. In addition, the algorithms differ in the guarded commands. The following list is ordered from the most general fault model to the most restricted one. The given resilience conditions on n and t are the ones we expected from the literature, and their tightness was confirmed by our experiments:

BYZ. tolerates t Byzantine faults if $n > 3t$,
SYMM. tolerates t symmetric (identical Byzantine [3]) faults if $n > 2t$,
OMIT. tolerates t send omission faults if $n > 2t$,
CLEAN. tolerates t clean crash faults for $n > t$.

In addition, we verified a folklore reliable broadcasting algorithm that tolerates crash faults, which is given, e.g., in [9]. Further, we verified a Byzantine tolerant broadcasting algorithm from [6]. For the encoding of the algorithm from [6] we were required to use two message types — opposed to the one type of the $\langle\text{echo}\rangle$

Table 1. Summary of experiments related to [34]

#	parameter values	spec valid	Time	Mem.	Stored	Transitions	Depth
		BYZ					
B1 N=7,T=2,F=2	(U) ✓	3.13 sec.	74 MB	$193 \cdot 10^3$	$1 \cdot 10^6$	229	
B2 N=7,T=2,F=2	(C) ✓	3.43 sec.	75 MB	$207 \cdot 10^3$	$2 \cdot 10^6$	229	
B3 N=7,T=2,F=2	(R) ✓	6.3 sec.	77 MB	$290 \cdot 10^3$	$3 \cdot 10^6$	229	
B4 N=7,T=3,F=2	(U) ✓	4.38 sec.	77 MB	$265 \cdot 10^3$	$2 \cdot 10^6$	233	
B5 N=7,T=3,F=2	(C) ✓	4.5 sec.	77 MB	$271 \cdot 10^3$	$2 \cdot 10^6$	233	
B6 N=7,T=3,F=2	(R) ✗	0.02 sec.	68 MB	$1 \cdot 10^3$	$13 \cdot 10^3$	210	
		OMIT					
O1 N=5,To=2,Fo=2	(U) ✓	1.43 sec.	69 MB	$51 \cdot 10^3$	$878 \cdot 10^3$	175	
O2 N=5,To=2,Fo=2	(C) ✓	1.64 sec.	69 MB	$60 \cdot 10^3$	$1 \cdot 10^6$	183	
O3 N=5,To=2,Fo=2	(R) ✓	3.69 sec.	71 MB	$92 \cdot 10^3$	$2 \cdot 10^6$	183	
O4 N=5,To=2,Fo=3	(U) ✓	1.39 sec.	69 MB	$51 \cdot 10^3$	$878 \cdot 10^3$	175	
O5 N=5,To=2,Fo=3	(C) ✗	1.63 sec.	69 MB	$53 \cdot 10^3$	$1 \cdot 10^6$	183	
O6 N=5,To=2,Fo=3	(R) ✗	0.01 sec.	68 MB	17	135	53	
		SYMM					
S1 N=5,T=1,Fp=1,Fs=0	(U) ✓	0.04 sec.	68 MB	$3 \cdot 10^3$	$23 \cdot 10^3$	121	
S2 N=5,T=1,Fp=1,Fs=0	(C) ✓	0.03 sec.	68 MB	$3 \cdot 10^3$	$24 \cdot 10^3$	121	
S3 N=5,T=1,Fp=1,Fs=0	(R) ✓	0.08 sec.	68 MB	$5 \cdot 10^3$	$53 \cdot 10^3$	121	
S4 N=5,T=3,Fp=3,Fs=1	(U) ✓	0.01 sec.	68 MB	66	267	62	
S5 N=5,T=3,Fp=3,Fs=1	(C) ✗	0.01 sec.	68 MB	62	221	66	
S6 N=5,T=3,Fp=3,Fs=1	(R) ✓	0.01 sec.	68 MB	62	235	62	
		CLEAN					
C1 N=3,Tc=2,Fc=2,Fnc=0	(U) ✓	0.01 sec.	68 MB	668	$7 \cdot 10^3$	77	
C2 N=3,Tc=2,Fc=2,Fnc=0	(C) ✓	0.01 sec.	68 MB	892	$8 \cdot 10^3$	81	
C3 N=3,Tc=2,Fc=2,Fnc=0	(R) ✓	0.02 sec.	68 MB	$1 \cdot 10^3$	$17 \cdot 10^3$	81	

Fig. 5. SPIN memory usage (left) and running time (right) for BYZ

messages in Algorithm 1. Finally, we implemented the asynchronous condition-based consensus algorithm from [27]. We specialized it to binary consensus, which resulted in an encoding which requires four different message types.

The major goal of the experiments was to check the adequacy of our formalization. To this end, we first considered the four well-understood variants of [34], for each of which we systematically changed the parameter values. By doing so,

Table 2. Summary of experiments with algorithms from [9,6,27]

#	parameter values	spec	valid	Time	Mem.	Stored	Transitions	Depth
		FOLKLORE BROADCAST [9]						
F1 N=2		(U)	✓	0.01 sec.	98 MB	121	$7 \cdot 10^3$	77
F2 N=2		(R)	✓	0.01 sec.	98 MB	143	$8 \cdot 10^3$	48
F3 N=2		(F)	✓	0.01 sec.	98 MB	257	$2 \cdot 10^3$	76
F4 N=6		(U)	✓	386 sec.	670 MB	$15 \cdot 10^6$	$20 \cdot 10^6$	272
F5 N=6		(R)	✓	691 sec.	996 MB	$24 \cdot 10^6$	$370 \cdot 10^6$	272
F6 N=6		(F)	✓	1690 sec.	1819 MB	$39 \cdot 10^6$	$875 \cdot 10^6$	328
		ASYNCHRONOUS BYZANTINE AGREEMENT [6]						
T1 N=5,T=1,F=1		(R)	✓	131 sec.	239 MB	$4 \cdot 10^6$	$74 \cdot 10^6$	211
T2 N=5,T=1,F=2		(R)	✗	0.68 sec.	99 MB	$11 \cdot 10^3$	$465 \cdot 10^3$	187
T3 N=5,T=2,F=2		(R)	✗	0.02 sec.	99 MB	726	$9 \cdot 10^3$	264
		CONDITION-BASED CONSENSUS [27]						
S1 N=3,T=1,F=1		(V0)	✓	0.01 sec.	98 MB	$1.4 \cdot 10^3$	$7 \cdot 10^3$	115
S2 N=3,T=1,F=1		(V1)	✓	0.04 sec.	98 MB	$3 \cdot 10^3$	$18 \cdot 10^3$	128
S3 N=3,T=1,F=1		(A)	✓	0.09 sec.	98 MB	$8 \cdot 10^3$	$42 \cdot 10^3$	127
S4 N=3,T=1,F=1		(T)	✓	0.16 sec.	66 MB	$9 \cdot 10^3$	$83 \cdot 10^3$	133
S5 N=3,T=1,F=2		(V0)	✓	0.02 sec.	68 MB	1724	9835	123
S6 N=3,T=1,F=2		(V1)	✓	0.05 sec.	68 MB	3647	$23 \cdot 10^3$	136
S7 N=3,T=1,F=2		(A)	✓	0.12 sec.	68 MB	$10 \cdot 10^3$	$55 \cdot 10^3$	135
S8 N=3,T=1,F=2		(T)	✗	0.05 sec.	68 MB	$3 \cdot 10^3$	$17 \cdot 10^3$	135

we verify that under our modeling the different combination of parameters lead to the expected result. Table 1 and Figure 5 summarize the results of our experiments for broadcasting algorithms in the spirit of [34]. Lines B1−B3, O1−O3, S1−S3, and C1−C3 capture the cases that are within the resilience condition known for the respective algorithm, and the algorithms were verified by SPIN. In Lines B4−B6, the algorithm's parameters are chosen to achieve a goal that is known to be impossible [28], i.e., to tolerate that 3 out of 7 processes may fail. This violates the $n > 3t$ requirement. Our experiment shows that even if only 2 faults occur in this setting, the relay specification (R) is violated. In Lines O4−O6, the algorithm is designed properly, i.e., 2 out of 5 processes may fail ($n > 2t$ in the case of omission faults). Our experiments show that this algorithm fails in the presence of 3 faulty processes, i.e., (C) and (R) are violated.

Table 2 summarizes our experiments for the algorithms in [9], [6], and [27]. The specification (F) is related to agreement and was also used in [17]. Properties (V0) and (V1) are non-triviality, that is, if all processes propose 0 (1), then 0 (1) is the only possible decision value. Property (A) is agreement and similar to (R), while Property (T) is termination, and requires that every correct process eventually decides. In all experiments the validity of the specifications was as expected from the distributed algorithms literature.

For slightly bigger systems, that is, for $n = 11$ our experiments run out of memory. This shows the need for parameterized verification of these algorithms.

5 Related Work

As fault tolerance is required to increase the reliability of systems, the verification of fault tolerance mechanisms is an important challenge. There are two classes of approaches towards fault tolerance, namely *fault detection*, and *fault masking*.

Methods in the first class follow the fault detection, isolation, and recovery (FDIR) principles: at runtime one tries to detect faults and to automatically perform counter measures. In this area, in [32] SPIN was used to validate a design based on the well-known primary backup idea. Under the FDIR approach, validation techniques have also been introduced in [15,8,19].

However, it is well understood that it is not always possible to reliably detect faults; for instance, in asynchronous distributed systems it is not possible to distinguish a process that prematurely stopped from a slow process, and in synchronous systems there are cases where the border between correct and faulty behavior cannot be drawn sharply [1]. To address such issues, fault masking has been introduced. Here, one does not try to detect or isolate faults, but tries to keep those components operating consistently that are not directly hit by faults, cf. distributed agreement [28]. The fault-tolerant distributed algorithms that we consider in this paper belong to this approach.

Specific masking fault-tolerant distributed algorithms have been verified, e.g., a consensus algorithm in [36], and a clock synchronization algorithm in [35]. In [25], a bug has been found in a previously published clock synchronization algorithm that was supposed to tolerate Byzantine faults.

Formalization and verification of a class of fault-tolerant distributed algorithms have been addressed in [5]. Their formalization uses the fact that for many distributed algorithms it is relevant how many messages are received, but the order in which they are received is not important. They provide a framework for such algorithms and show that these algorithms can be efficiently verified using partial order reduction. While in this work we consider similar message counting ideas, our formalization targets at parameterized model checking [21] rather than partial order reductions for systems of small size.

6 Conclusions

In this paper we presented a way to efficiently encode fault-tolerant threshold-guarded distributed algorithms using shared variables. We showed that our encoding scales significantly better than a straightforward approach. With this encoding we were able to verify small system instances of a number of broadcasting algorithms [34,6,9] for diverse failure models. We could also find counter examples in cases where we knew from theory that the given number of faults cannot be tolerated. We also verified a condition-based consensus algorithm [27].

As our mid-term goal is to verify state-of-the-art fault-tolerant distributed algorithms, there are several follow-up steps we are taking. In [21] we show that the encoding we described in this paper is a basis for parameterized model checking techniques that allow us to verify distributed algorithms for any system size. We have already verified some of the algorithms mentioned above, while we are still working on techniques to verify the others. Also we are currently working on verification of the Paxos-like Byzantine consensus algorithm from [26], which is also threshold-guarded. The challenges of this algorithm are threefold. First, it consists of three different process types — proposers, accepters, learners — while the algorithms discussed in this paper are just compositions of processes of the same type. Second, to tolerate a single fault, the algorithm requires at least four proposers, six acceptors, and four learners. Our preliminary experiments show that 14 processes is a challenge for explicit state enumeration. Third, as the algorithm solves consensus, it cannot work in the asynchronous model [16], and we have to restrict the interleavings of steps, and the message delays.

References

1. Ademaj, A.: Slightly-off-specification failures in the time-triggered architecture. In: High-Level Design Validation and Test Workshop, pp. 7–12. IEEE (2002)
2. Aguilera, M.K., Delporte-Gallet, C., Fauconnier, H., Toueg, S.: Consensus with Byzantine failures and little system synchrony. In: DSN, pp. 147–155 (2006)
3. Attiya, H., Welch, J.: Distributed Computing, 2nd edn. John Wiley & Sons (2004)
4. Biely, M., Schmid, U., Weiss, B.: Synchronous consensus under hybrid process and link failures. Theoretical Computer Science 412(40), 5602–5630 (2011)
5. Bokor, P., Kinder, J., Serafini, M., Suri, N.: Efficient model checking of fault-tolerant distributed protocols. In: DSN, pp. 73–84 (2011)
6. Bracha, G., Toueg, S.: Asynchronous consensus and broadcast protocols. J. ACM 32(4), 824–840 (1985)
7. Browne, M.C., Clarke, E.M., Grumberg, O.: Reasoning about networks with many identical finite state processes. Inf. Comput. 81, 13–31 (1989)
8. Bucchiarone, A., Muccini, H., Pelliccione, P.: Architecting fault-tolerant component-based systems: from requirements to testing. Electr. Notes Theor. Comput. Sci. 168, 77–90 (2007)
9. Chandra, T.D., Toueg, S.: Unreliable failure detectors for reliable distributed systems. J. ACM 43(2), 225–267 (1996)
10. Charron-Bost, B., Schiper, A.: The heard-of model: computing in distributed systems with benign faults. Distributed Computing 22(1), 49–71 (2009)
11. Clarke, E., Talupur, M., Veith, H.: Proving Ptolemy right: the environment abstraction framework for model checking concurrent systems. In: Ramakrishnan, C.R., Rehof, J. (eds.) TACAS 2008. LNCS, vol. 4963, pp. 33–47. Springer, Heidelberg (2008)
12. Clarke, E., Talupur, M., Touili, T., Veith, H.: Verification by network decomposition. In: Gardner, P., Yoshida, N. (eds.) CONCUR 2004. LNCS, vol. 3170, pp. 276–291. Springer, Heidelberg (2004)
13. Dwork, C., Lynch, N., Stockmeyer, L.: Consensus in the presence of partial synchrony. J. ACM 35(2), 288–323 (1988)
14. Emerson, E., Namjoshi, K.: Reasoning about rings. In: POPL, pp. 85–94 (1995)
15. Feather, M.S., Fickas, S., Razermera-Mamy, N.A.: Model-checking for validation of a fault protection system. In: HASE, pp. 32–41 (2001)
16. Fischer, M.J., Lynch, N.A., Paterson, M.S.: Impossibility of distributed consensus with one faulty process. J. ACM 32(2), 374–382 (1985)

17. Fisman, D., Kupferman, O., Lustig, Y.: On verifying fault tolerance of distributed protocols. In: Ramakrishnan, C.R., Rehof, J. (eds.) TACAS 2008. LNCS, vol. 4963, pp. 315–331. Springer, Heidelberg (2008)

18. Függer, M., Schmid, U.: Reconciling fault-tolerant distributed computing and systems-on-chip. Distributed Computing 24(6), 323–355 (2012)

19. Gnesi, S., Latella, D., Lenzini, G., Abbaneo, C., Amendola, A., Marmo, P.: A formal specification and validation of a critical system in presence of Byzantine errors. In: Graf, S. (ed.) TACAS 2000. LNCS, vol. 1785, pp. 535–549. Springer, Heidelberg (2000)

20. Holzmann, G.: The SPIN Model Checker: Primer and Reference Manual. Addison-Wesley Professional (2003)

21. John, A., Konnov, I., Schmid, U., Veith, H., Widder, J.: Brief announcement: Parameterized model checking of fault-tolerant distributed algorithms by abstraction. In: ACM PODC (to appear, 2013) (long version at arXiv CoRR abs/1210.3846)

22. Lamport, L.: A new solution of Dijkstra's concurrent programming problem. Commun. ACM 17(8), 453–455 (1974)

23. Lamport, L.: On interprocess communication. Part I: Basic formalism. Distributed Computing 1(2), 77–85 (1986)

24. Lynch, N.: Distributed Algorithms. Morgan Kaufman, San Francisco (1996)

25. Malekpour, M.R., Siminiceanu, R.: Comments on the "Byzantine self-stabilizing pulse synchronization". protocol: Counterexamples. Tech. rep., NASA (February 2006)

26. Martin, J.P., Alvisi, L.: Fast Byzantine consensus. IEEE Trans. Dep. Sec. Comp. 3(3), 202–215 (2006)

27. Mostéfaoui, A., Mourgaya, E., Parvédy, P.R., Raynal, M.: Evaluating the condition-based approach to solve consensus. In: DSN, pp. 541–550 (2003)

28. Pease, M., Shostak, R., Lamport, L.: Reaching agreement in the presence of faults. J. ACM 27(2), 228–234 (1980)

29. Pnueli, A., Xu, J., Zuck, L.: Liveness with $(0,1,\infty)$- counter abstraction. In: Brinksma, E., Larsen, K.G. (eds.) CAV 2002. LNCS, vol. 2404, pp. 107–122. Springer, Heidelberg (2002)

30. Powell, D.: Failure mode assumptions and assumption coverage. In: FTCS-22, Boston, MA, USA, pp. 386–395 (1992)

31. Santoro, N., Widmayer, P.: Time is not a healer. In: Cori, R., Monien, B. (eds.) STACS 1989. LNCS, vol. 349, pp. 304–313. Springer, Heidelberg (1989)

32. Schneider, F., Easterbrook, S.M., Callahan, J.R., Holzmann, G.J.: Validating requirements for fault tolerant systems using model checking. In: ICRE, pp. 4–13 (1998)

33. Schneider, F.B.: Implementing fault-tolerant services using the state machine approach: A tutorial. ACM Comput. Surv. 22(4), 299–319 (1990)

34. Srikanth, T., Toueg, S.: Simulating authenticated broadcasts to derive simple fault-tolerant algorithms. Distributed Computing 2, 80–94 (1987)

35. Steiner, W., Rushby, J.M., Sorea, M., Pfeifer, H.: Model checking a fault-tolerant startup algorithm: From design exploration to exhaustive fault simulation. In: DSN, pp. 189–198 (2004)

36. Tsuchiya, T., Schiper, A.: Verification of consensus algorithms using satisfiability solving. Distributed Computing 23(5-6), 341–358 (2011)

37. Widder, J., Schmid, U.: Booting clock synchronization in partially synchronous systems with hybrid process and link failures. Distributed Computing 20(2), 115–140 (2007)

Guard-Based Partial-Order Reduction

Alfons Laarman, Elwin Pater, Jaco van de Pol, and Michael Weber

Formal Methods and Tools, University of Twente, The Netherlands
elwin.pater@gmail.com,
{laarman,vdpol,michaelw}@cs.utwente.nl

Abstract. This paper aims at making partial-order reduction independent of the modeling language. Our starting point is the stubborn set
algorithm of Valmari (see also Godefroid's thesis), which relies on necessary *enabling* sets. We generalise it to a guard-based algorithm, which
can be implemented on top of an abstract model checking interface.

We extend the generalised algorithm by introducing necessary *disabling* sets and adding a heuristics to improve state space reduction.
The effect of the changes to the algorithm are measured using an implementation in the LTSMIN model checking toolset. We experiment with
partial-order reduction on a number of PROMELA models, some with LTL
properties, and on benchmarks from the BEEM database in the DVE
language.

We compare our results to the SPIN model checker. While the reductions take longer, they are consistently better than SPIN's ample set and
even often surpass the ideal upper bound for the ample set, as established
empirically by Geldenhuys, Hansen and Valmari on BEEM models.

1 Introduction

Model checking is an automated method to verify the correctness of concurrent systems by examining all possible execution paths for incorrect behaviour.
The main difficulty is the *state space explosion*, which refers to the exponential
growth in the number of states obtained by interleaving executions of several
system components. Model checking has emerged since the 1980s [3] and several
advances have pushed its boundaries. Partial-order reduction is among those.

Partial-order reduction (POR) exploits independence and commutativity between transitions in concurrent systems. Exhaustive verification needs to consider
only a subset of all possible concurrent interleavings, without losing the global
behaviour of interest to the verified property. In practice, the state space is
pruned by considering a sufficient subset of successors in each state.

The idea to exploit commutativity between concurrent transitions has been
investigated by several researchers, leading to various algorithms for computing
a sufficient successor set. The challenge is to compute this subset during state
space generation (on-the-fly), based on the structure of the specification.

Already in 1981, Overman [20] suggested a method to avoid exploring all
interleavings, followed by Valmari's [28,31,30] *stubborn sets* in 1988, 1991 and
1992. Also from 1988 onwards, Peled [16] developed the *ample set* [23,24], later

E. Bartocci and C.R. Ramakrishnan (Eds.): SPIN 2013, LNCS 7976, pp. 227–245, 2013.

extended by Holzmann and Peled [14,25], Godefroid and Pirottin [8,10] the *persistent set* [9], and Godefroid and Wolper [11] *sleep sets*. These foundations have been extended and applied in numerous papers over the past 15 years.

Problem and Contributions. Previous work defines partial-order reduction in terms of either petri-nets [35] or parallel components with local program counters, called processes [14,9]. While this allows the exploitation of certain formalism-specific properties, like *fairness* [24] and token conditions [33], it also complicates the application to other formalisms, for instance, rule-based systems [12]. Moreover, current implementations are tightly coupled to a particular specification language in order to compute a good syntactic approximation of a sufficient successor set. In recognition of these problems, Valmari started early to generalise the stubborn set definition for "transition/variable systems" [29,31].

To address the same problem for model checking algorithms, we earlier proposed the PINS interface [2,19], separating language front-ends from verification algorithms. Through PINS (Partitioned Interface to the Next-State function), a user can use various high-performance model checking algorithms for his favourite specification language, cf. Figure 1. Providing POR as PINS2PINS wrapper once and for all benefits every combination of language and algorithm.

An important question is whether and how an abstract interface like PINS *can support partial-order reduction*. We propose a solution that is based on stubborn sets. This theory stipulates how to choose a subset of transitions, enabled and disabled, based on a careful analysis of their independence and commutativity relations. These relations have been described on the abstract level

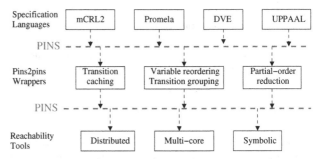

Fig. 1. Modular PINS architecture of LTSMIN

of transition systems before [31]. Additionally, within the context of petri-nets, the relations were refined to include multiple enabling conditions, a natural distinction in this formalism [33].

We generalise Valmari's work to a complete language-agnostic setting, by assuming that transitions consist of guard conditions and state variable assignments (Section 3). In Section 4, we extend PINS with the necessary information: a do-not-accord matrix and optional; necessary enabling matrix on guards. In addition, we introduce novel *necessary disabling sets* and a new heuristic-based selection criterion. As optimal stubborn sets are expensive to compute precisely [33], our heuristic finds reasonably effective stubborn sets fast, hopefully leading to smaller state spaces. In Section 5, we show how LTL can be supported.

Our implementation resides in the LTSMIN toolset [2], based on PINS. Any language module that connects to PINS now obtains POR without having to bother about its implementation details, it merely needs to export transition guards and their dependencies via PINS. We demonstrate this by extending LTSMIN's DVE and PROMELA [1] front-ends. This allows a direct comparison to SPIN [13] (Section 6), which shows that the new algorithm generally provides more reduction using less memory, but takes more time to do so. It also yields more reduction than the theoretically best reduction using ample sets, as reported by Geldenhuys et al. [7] on the DVE BEEM benchmarks [22].

Summarising, these are the main contributions presented in this work:

1. *Guard-based partial-order reduction*, which is a language-independent generalisation of the stubborn set method based on necessary enabling sets;
2. Some improvements to efficiently compute smaller stubborn sets:
   (a) A refinement based on *necessary disabling sets*;
   (b) A *heuristic selection criterion* for necessary enabling sets;
   (c) A more *dynamic* definition of *visibility*, yielding better reduction for LTL;
3. Two language module *implementations* exporting guards with dependencies;
4. An *empirical evaluation* of guard-based partial-order reduction in LTSMIN:
   (a) A comparison of resource consumption and effectiveness of POR between LTSMIN [2] and SPIN [13] on 18 PROMELA models/3 LTL formulas.
   (b) An impact analysis of necessary disabling sets and the heuristic selection.
   (c) A comparison with the ideal ample set from [7], on DVE BEEM models.

2   The Computational Model of Guarded Transitions

In the current section, we provide a model of computation comparable to [7], leaving out the notion of processes on purpose. It has three main components: states, guards and transitions. A state represents the global status of a system, guards are predicates over states, and a transition represents a guarded state change.

Definition 1 (state). *Let $S = E_1 \times \ldots \times E_n$ be a set of vectors of elements with some finite domain. A state $s = \langle e_1, \ldots, e_n \rangle \in S$ associates a value $e_i \in E_i$ to each element. We denote a projection to a single element in the state as $s[i] = e_i$.*

Definition 2 (guard). *A guard $g : S \to \mathbb{B}$ is a total function that maps each state to a boolean value, $\mathbb{B} = \{true, false\}$. We write $g(s)$ or $\neg g(s)$ to denote that guard g is true or false in state s. We also say that g is enabled/disabled.*

Definition 3 (structural transition). *A structural transition $t \in T$ is a tuple $(\mathcal{G}, a)$ such that a is an assignment $a : S \to S$ and $\mathcal{G}$ is a set of guards, also denoted as $\mathcal{G}_t$. We denote the set of enabled transitions by $en(s) := \{t \in T \mid \bigwedge_{g \in \mathcal{G}_t} g(s)\}$. We write $s \xrightarrow{t}$ when $t \in en(s)$, $s \xrightarrow{t} s'$ when $s \xrightarrow{t}$ and $s' = a(s)$, and we write $s \xrightarrow{t_1 t_2 \ldots t_k} s_k$, when $\exists s_1, \ldots, s_k \in S : s \xrightarrow{t_1} s_1 \xrightarrow{t_2} s_2 \ldots \xrightarrow{t_k} s_k$.*

Definition 4 (state space). *Let $s_0 \in S$ and let T be the set of transitions. The state space from s_0 induced by T is $M_T = (S_T, s_0, \Delta)$, where $s_0 \in S$ is the initial state, and $S_T \subseteq S$ is the set of reachable states, and $\Delta \subseteq S_T \times T \times S_T$ is the set of semantic transitions. These are defined to be the smallest sets such that $s_0 \in S_T$, and if $t \in T$, $s \in S_T$ and $s \xrightarrow{t} s'$, then $s' \in S_T$ and $(s, t, s') \in \Delta$.*

Valmari and Hansen [33, Def. 6] also define guards (conditions), which take the role of enabling conditions for disabled transitions. We later generalise this role to enabled transitions as well for our necessary disabling sets (Section 4.2).

In the rest of the paper, we fix an arbitrary set of vectors $S = E_1 \times \ldots \times E_n$, initial state $s_0 \in S$, and set of transitions T, with induced reachable state space $M_T = (S_T, s_0, \Delta)$. We often just write "transition" for elements of T.

It is easy to see that our model generalises the setting including processes (as in [7]). One can view the program counter of each process as a normal state variable, check for its current value in a separate guard, and update it in the transitions. But our definition is more general, since it can also be applied to models without a natural notion of a fixed set of processes, for instance rule-based systems, such as the linear process equations in mCRL [12].

Besides guarded transitions, structural information is required on the exact involvement of state variables in a transition.

Definition 5 (disagree sets). *Given states $s, s' \in S$, for $1 \leq i \leq n$, we define the set of indices on which s and s' disagree as $\delta(s, s') := \{i \mid s[i] \neq s'[i]\}$.*

Definition 6 (affect sets). *For $t = (\mathcal{G}, a) \in T$ and $g \in \mathcal{G}$, we define*

1. *the test set of g is $Ts(g) \supseteq \{i \mid \exists s, s' \in S : \delta(s, s') = \{i\} \land g(s) \neq g(s')\}$,*
2. *the test set of t is $Ts(t) := \bigcup_{g \in \mathcal{G}} Ts(g)$,*
3. *the write set of t is $Ws(t) \supseteq \bigcup_{s \in S_T} \delta(s, s')$ with $s \xrightarrow{t} s'$,*
4. *the read set of t is $Rs(t) \supseteq \{i \mid \exists s, s' \in S : \delta(s, s') = \{i\} \land s \xrightarrow{t} \land s' \xrightarrow{t} \land Ws(t) \cap \delta(a(s), a(s')) \neq \emptyset\}$ (notice the difference between S and S_T), and*
5. *the variable set of t is $Vs(t) := Ts(t) \cup Rs(t) \cup Ws(t)$.*

Although these sets are defined in the context of the complete state space, they may be statically over-approximated ($\supseteq$) by the language front-end.

Example 1. Suppose $s \in S = \mathbb{N}^3$, consider the transition: $t := IF\ (s[1] = 0 \land s[2] < 10)\ THEN\ s[3] := s[1] + 1$. It has two guards, $g_1 = (s[1] = 0)$ and $g_2 = (s[2] < 10)$, with test sets $Ts(g_1) = \{1\}$, $Ts(g_2) = \{2\}$, hence: $Ts(t) = \{1, 2\}$. The write set $Ws(t) = \{3\}$, so $Vs(t) = \{1, 2, 3\}$. The minimal read set $Rs(t) = \emptyset$ (since $s[1] = 0$), but simple static analysis may over-approximate it as $\{1\}$.

3   Partial-Order Reduction with Stubborn Sets

We now rephrase the stubborn set POR definitions. We follow the definitions from Valmari [30] and Godefroid's thesis [9], but avoid the notion of processes.

An important property of a stubborn set $\mathcal{T}_s \subseteq T$ is that it commutes with all paths of non-stubborn transitions $t_1, \ldots, t_n \in T \setminus \mathcal{T}_s$. If there is a path $s \xrightarrow{t_1, \ldots, t_n} s_n$ and a stubborn transition $t \in \mathcal{T}_s$ such that $s \xrightarrow{t} s'$, then there exists a state s'_n such that: $s' \xrightarrow{t_1, \ldots, t_n} s'_n$ and $s_n \xrightarrow{t} s'_n$. Or illustrated graphically:

$$
\begin{array}{ccccccc}
s \xrightarrow{t_1} s_1 & \cdots & s_{n-1} \xrightarrow{t_n} s_n & & & & s_n \\
\downarrow t & & & \Rightarrow & & & \downarrow t \\
s' & & & & s' \xrightarrow{t_1} s'_1 & \cdots & s'_{n-1} \xrightarrow{t_n} s'_n
\end{array}
$$

Moreover a stubborn set $\mathcal{T}_s$ at s is still a stubborn set at a state s_1 reached via the non-stubborn transition t_1. Since t_1 is still enabled after taking a stubborn transition, we can delay the execution of non-stubborn transitions without losing the reachability of any deadlock states. Figure 2 illustrates this; since s is not a deadlock state, s_d is still reachable after executing a transition from $\mathcal{T}_s$. The benefit is that, for the moment, we avoid exploring (and storing) states such as $s_1, \ldots, s_n$. "For the moment", because these states may still be reachable via other stubborn paths, therefore smaller stubborn sets are only a heuristic for obtaining smaller state spaces.

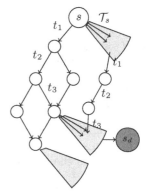

Fig. 2. Stubborn set

This theoretical notion of stubborn sets is a semantic definition. Therefore, we now present the notion of a *(static) stubborn set*, as developed by Valmari. While this definition is stronger, it efficiently (algorithmically) describes *how* to compute these sets (without referring to the entire state space). While researchers have attempted to identify even weaker notions that include more stubborn sets, increasing the chance to find one which yields a larger reduction [32, Sec. 7.4], we rely on the *strong* notion, which is still compatible for extension to LTL model checking [31] (cf. Section 5).

Definition 7 (Do not accord [30]). *First, we define* according with *as:*
$$A \subseteq \{(t,t') \in T \times T \mid \forall s, s', s_1 \in S : s \xrightarrow{t} s' \wedge s \xrightarrow{t'} s_1 \Rightarrow \exists s_1' : s' \xrightarrow{t'} s_1' \wedge s_1 \xrightarrow{t} s_1'\},$$
or illustrated graphically:

$$
\begin{array}{ccc}
s \xrightarrow{t'} s_1 & & s \xrightarrow{t'} s_1 \\
\downarrow^{t} & \Rightarrow & \downarrow^{t} \quad \downarrow^{t} \\
s' & & s' \xrightarrow{t'} s_1'
\end{array}
$$

And for do not-accord: $\mathcal{DNA} = T^2 \setminus A$. *We denote* $\mathcal{DNA}_t = \{t' \mid (t,t') \in \mathcal{DNA}\}$.

Each of the following criteria on $t, t' \in T$ is sufficient to conclude accordance:

1. shared variables $Vs(t) \cap Vs(t')$ are disjoint from the write sets $Ws(t) \cup Ws(t')$,
2. t and t' are never co-enabled, e.g. have different program counter guards, or
3. t and t' do not disable each other, and their actions commute, e.g. write and read to a FIFO buffer or performing atomic increments/decrements.

Definition 8 (necessary enabling set [9]). *Let* $t \in T$ *be a disabled transition in state* $s \in S_T$, $t \notin en(s)$. *A necessary enabling set for* t *in* s *is a set of transitions* $\mathcal{N}_t$, *such that for all sequences of the form* $s \xrightarrow{t_1, \ldots, t_n} s' \xrightarrow{t}$, *there is at least one transition* $t_i \in \mathcal{N}_t$ *(for some* $1 \le i \le n$*).*

Again, both relations can be safely over-approximated.

We used Valmari's definition for the do-not-accord relation instead of relying on a definition of "dependent", since it allows that transitions modify the same variable, provided they are commuting. As the definition is equivalent to Godefroid's definition of do-not-accord for enabled transitions, we can safely reuse the latter's stubborn set definition:

Definition 9 (stubborn set [9]). *A set $\mathcal{T}_s$ of transitions is* stubborn *in a state s, if $\mathcal{T}_s \cap en(s) = \emptyset \iff en(s) = \emptyset$, and for all transitions $t \in \mathcal{T}_s$:*
 1. *If t is disabled in s, then $\exists \mathcal{N}_t \subseteq \mathcal{T}_s$ (multiple sets $\mathcal{N}_t$ can exist), and*
 2. *If t is enabled in s, then $\mathcal{DNA}_t \subseteq \mathcal{T}_s$.*

Theorem 1. *Let $\mathcal{T}_s$ be a stubborn at a state s. Then $\mathcal{T}_s$ is dynamically stubborn at s. A search over only stubborn enabled transitions finds all deadlocks in S_T.*

Algorithm 1 from [9] implements the closure method from [32, Sec. 7.4]. It builds a stubborn set incrementally by making sure that each new transition added to the set fulfills the stubborn set conditions (Definition 9).

Example 2. Suppose Figure 2 is a partial run of Algorithm 1 on state s, and transition t_3 does not accord with some transition $t \in \mathcal{T}_s$. The algorithm will proceed with processing t and add all transitions that do-not-accord, including t_3, to the work set. Since t_3 is disabled in state s, we add the necessary enabling set for t_3 to the work set. This could for instance be $\{t_2\}$, which is then added to the work set. Again, the transition is disabled and a necessary enabling set for t_2 is added, for instance, $\{t_1\}$. Since t_1 is enabled in s, and has no other dependent transitions in this example, the algorithm finishes. Note that in this example, t_1 now should be part of the stubborn set.

To find a necessary enabling set for a disabled transition t (i.e. *find_nes(t, s)*), Godefroid uses fine-grained analysis, which depends crucially on program counters. The analysis can be roughly described as follows:

 1. If t is not enabled in global state s, because some local program counter has the "wrong" value, then use the set of transitions that assign the "right" value to that program counter as necessary enabling set;
 2. Otherwise, if some guard g for transition t evaluates to *false* in s, take all transitions that write to the *test set* of that guard as necessary enabling set. (i.e. include those transitions that can possibly change g to *true*).

In the next section, we show how to avoid program counters with guard-based POR.

```
 1  function stubborn(s)
 2      𝒯_work = {t̂} such that t̂ ∈ en(s)
 3      𝒯_s = ∅
 4      while 𝒯_work ≠ ∅ do
 5          𝒯_work = 𝒯_work − t, 𝒯_s = 𝒯_s ∪ {t} for some t ∈ 𝒯_work
 6          if t ∈ en(s) then
 7            | 𝒯_work = 𝒯_work ∪ {t′ ∈ Σ | (t, t′) ∈ 𝒟𝒩𝒜} ∖ 𝒯_s
 8          else
 9            | 𝒯_work = 𝒯_work ∪ 𝒩 ∖ 𝒯_s where 𝒩 ∈ find_nes(t, s)
10      return 𝒯_s
```

Algorithm 1. The *closure* algorithm for finding stubborn sets

4 Computing Necessary Enabling Sets for Guards

The current section investigates how necessary enabling sets can be computed purely based on guards, without reference to program counters. We proceed by introducing necessary enabling and disabling sets on guards, and a heuristic selection function. Next, it is shown how the PINS interface can be extended to support guard-based partial-order reduction by exporting guards, test sets, and the do-not-accord relation. Finally, we devise an optional extension for language modules to provide fine-grained structural information. Providing this optional information further increases the reduction power.

4.1 Guard-Based Necessary Enabling Sets

We refer to all guards in the state space $M_T = (S_T, s_0, \Delta)$ as: $\mathcal{G}_T := \bigcup_{t \in T} \mathcal{G}_t$.

Definition 10 (necessary enabling set for guards). *Let $g \in \mathcal{G}_T$ be a guard that is disabled in some state $s \in S_T$, i.e. $\neg g(s)$. A set of transitions $\mathcal{N}_g$ is a necessary enabling set for g in s, if for all states s' with some sequence $s \xrightarrow{t_1,\ldots,t_n} s'$ and $g(s')$, for at least one transition t_i $(1 \le i \le n)$ we have $t_i \in \mathcal{N}_g$.*

Given $\mathcal{N}_g$, a concrete necessary enabling set on transitions in the sense of Definition 8 can be retrieved as follows (notice the non-determinism):

$$find\_nes(t, s) \in \{\mathcal{N}_g \mid g \in \mathcal{G}_t \wedge \neg g(s)\}$$

Proof. Let t be a transition that is disabled in state $s \in S_T$, $t \notin en(s)$. Let there be a path where t becomes enabled, $s \xrightarrow{t_1,\ldots,t_n} s' \xrightarrow{t}$, On this path, all of t's disabled guards, $g \in \mathcal{G}_t \wedge \neg g(s)$, need to be enabled, for t to become enabled (recall that $\mathcal{G}_t$ is a conjunction). Therefore, any $\mathcal{N}_g$ is a $\mathcal{N}_t$. $\square$

Example 3. Let ch be the variable for a *rendez-vous channel* in a PROMELA model. A channel read can be modeled as a PROMELA statement ch? in some process $P1$. A channel write can be modeled as a PROMELA statement ch! in some process $P2$. As the statements synchronise, they can be implemented as a single transition, guarded by process counters corresponding to the location of the statements in their processes, e.g.: $P1.pc = 1$ and $P2.pc = 10$. The set of all transitions that assign $P1.pc := 1$, is a valid necessary enabling set for this transition. So is the set of all transitions that assign $P2.pc := 10$.

Instead of computing the necessary enabling set on-the-fly, we statically assign each guard a necessary enabling set by default. Only transitions that write to state vector variables used by this guard need to be considered (as in [21]):

$$\mathcal{N}_g^{\min} := \{t \in T \mid Ts(g) \cap Ws(t) \ne \emptyset\}$$

4.2   Necessary Disabling Sets

Consider the computation of a stubborn set $\mathcal{T}_s$ in state s along the lines of Algorithm 1. If a disabled t gets in the stubborn set, a necessary enabling set is required. This typically contains a predecessor of t in the control flow. When that one is not yet enabled in s, its predecessor is added as well, until we find a transition enabled in s. So basically a whole path of transitions between s and t ends up in the stubborn set.

Example 4. Assume two parallel processes P_1 and P_2, with $\mathcal{DNA}(t_1, t_7)$ and $\mathcal{DNA}(t_6, t_7)$. Initially $en(s_0) = \{t_1, t_7\}$; both end up in the stubborn set, since they do-not-accord and may be co-enabled. Then t_7 in turn adds t_6, which is disabled. Now working backwards, the enabling set for t_6 is t_5, for t_5 it is t_4, etc, eventually resulting in the fat stubborn set $\{t_1, \ldots, t_7\}$.

How can this large stubborn set be avoided? The crucial insight is that to enable a disabled transition t, it is necessary to disable any enabled transition t' which cannot be co-enabled with t. Quite likely, t' could be a successor of the starting point s, leading to a slim stubborn set.

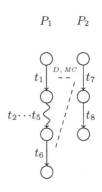

Example 5. Consider again the situation after adding $\{t_1, t_7, t_6\}$ to $\mathcal{T}_s$, in the previous example. Note that t_1 and t_6 cannot be co-enabled, and t_1 is enabled in s_0. So it must be disabled in order to enable t_6. Note that t_1 is disabled by itself. Hence t_1 is a necessary enabling set of t_6, and the algorithm can directly terminate with the stubborn set $\{t_1, t_7, t_6\}$. Clearly, using disabling information saves time and can lead to smaller stubborn sets.

Definition 11 (may be co-enabled for guards). *The* may be co-enabled *relation for guards, $MC_g \subseteq \mathcal{G}_T \times \mathcal{G}_T$ is a symmetric, reflexive relation. Two guards $g, g' \in \mathcal{G}_T$ may be co-enabled if there exists a state $s \in S_T$ where they both evaluate to true: $\exists s \in S_T : g(s) \wedge g'(s) \Rightarrow (g, g') \in MC_g$.*

Example 6. Two guards that can never be co-enabled are: $g_1 := v = 0$ and $g_2 := v \geq 5$. In e.g. PROMELA, these guards could implement the channel empty and full expressions, where the variable v holds the number of buffered messages. In e.g. mCRL2, the conditions of a *summand* can be implemented as guards.

Note that it is allowed to over-approximate the maybe co-enabled relation. Typically, transitions within a sequential system component can never be enabled at the same time. They never interfere with each other, even though their test and write sets share at least the program counter.

Definition 12 (necessary disabling set for guards). *Let $g \in \mathcal{G}_T$ be a guard that is enabled in some state $s \in S_T$, i.e. $g(s)$. A set of transitions $\overline{\mathcal{N}}_g$ is a necessary disabling set for g in s, if for all states s' with some sequence $s \xrightarrow{t_1, \ldots, t_n} s'$ and $\neg g(s')$, for at least one transition t_i $(1 \leq i \leq n)$ we have $t_i \in \overline{\mathcal{N}}_g$.*

The following disabling set can be assigned to each guard. Similar to enabling sets, only transitions that change the state indices used by g are considered.

$$\overline{\mathcal{N}}_g^{\min} := \{t \in T \mid Ts(g) \cap Ws(t) \neq \emptyset\}$$

Using disabling sets, we can find an enabling set for the current state s:

Theorem 2. *If $\overline{\mathcal{N}}_g$ is a necessary disabling set for guard g in state s with $g(s)$, and if g' is a guard that may not be co-enabled with g, i.e. $(g, g') \notin MC_g$, then $\overline{\mathcal{N}}_g$ is also a* necessary enabling set *for guard g' in state s.*

Proof. Guard g' is disabled in state s, since $g(s)$ holds and g' cannot be co-enabled with g. In any state reachable from s, g' cannot be enabled as long as g holds. Thus, to make g' true, some transition from the disabling set of g must be applied. Hence, a disabling set for g is an enabling set for g'. □

Given $\mathcal{N}_g$ and $\overline{\mathcal{N}}_g$, we can find a necessary enabling set for a particular transition $t = (\mathcal{G}, a) \in T$ in state s, by selecting one of its disabled guards. Subsequently, we can choose between its necessary enabling set, or the necessary disabling set of any guard that cannot be co-enabled with it. This spans the search space of our new *find_nes* algorithm, which is called by Algorithm 1:

$$\textit{find\_nes}(t, s) \in \{\mathcal{N}_g \mid \neg g(s)\} \cup \bigcup_{g' \in \mathcal{G}_T} \{\overline{\mathcal{N}}_{g'} \mid g'(s) \wedge (g, g') \notin MC_g\}$$

4.3   Heuristic Selection for Stubborn Sets

Even though the static stubborn set of Definition 9 is stronger than the dynamic stubborn set, its non-determinism still allows many different sets to be computed, as both the choice of an initial transition $\hat{t}$ at Line 2 and the *find_nes* function in Algorithm 1 are non-deterministic. In fact, it is well known that the resulting reductions depend strongly on a smart choice of the necessary enabling set [33]. A known approach to resolve this problem is to run an SCC algorithm on the complete search space for each enabled transition $\hat{t}$ [32] (but even more complicated means exist, like the *deletion algorithm* in [35]). The complexity of this solution can be somewhat reduced by choosing a 'scapegoat' for $\hat{t}$ [35].

We propose here a practical solution that does neither; using a heuristic, we explore all possible scapegoats, while limiting the search by guiding it towards a local optimum. (This makes the algorithm deterministic, which has other benefits, cf. Section 7). An effective heuristics for large partial-order reductions should select small stubborn sets [9]. To this end, we define a heuristic function h that associates some cost to adding a new transition to the stubborn set. Here enabled transitions weigh more than disabled transitions. Transitions that do not lead to additional work (already selected or going to be processed) do not contribute to the cost function at all. Below, $\mathcal{T}_s$ and $\mathcal{T}_{work}$ refer to Algorithm 1.

$$h(\mathcal{N}, s) = \sum_{t \in \mathcal{N}} cost(t, s), \text{ where } cost(t, s) = \begin{cases} 1 & \text{if } t \notin en(s) \text{ and } t \notin \mathcal{T}_s \cup \mathcal{T}_{work} \\ n & \text{if } t \in en(s) \text{ and } t \notin \mathcal{T}_s \cup \mathcal{T}_{work} \\ 0 & \text{otherwise} \end{cases}$$

Here n is the maximum number of outgoing transitions (degree) in any state, $n = \max_{s \in S}(|en(s)|)$, but it can be over-approximated (for instance by $|T|$).

We restrict the search to the cheapest necessary enabling sets:

$$find\_nes'(t, s) \in \{\mathcal{N} \in find\_nes(t, s) \mid \forall \mathcal{N}' \in find\_nes(t, s) : h(\mathcal{N}, s) \leq h(\mathcal{N}', s)\}$$

4.4   A Pins Extension to Support Guard-Based POR

In model checking, the state space graph of Definition 4 is constructed only implicitly by iteratively computing successor states. A generic next-state interface hides the details of the specification language, but exposes some internal structure to enable efficient state space storage or state space reduction.

The Partitioned Interface for the Next-State function, or PINS [2], provides such a mechanism. The interface assumes that the set of states S consists of vectors of fixed length N, and transitions are partitioned disjunctively in M partition groups T. PINS also supports K state predicates L for model checking. In order to exploit locality in symbolic reachability, state space storage, and incremental algorithms, PINS exposes a dependency matrix DM, relating transition groups to indices of the state vector. This yields orders of magnitude improvement in speed and compression [2,1]. The following functions of PINS are implemented by the language front-end and used by the exploration algorithms:

- INITSTATE: S
- NEXTSTATES: $S \rightarrow 2^{T \times S}$ and
- STATELABEL: $S \times L \rightarrow \mathbb{B}$
- DM: $\mathbb{B}_{M \times N}$

Extensions to PINS. POR works as a state space transformer, and therefore can be implemented as a PINS2PINS wrapper (cf. Figure 1), both using and providing the interface. This *POR layer* provides a new NEXTSTATES(s) function, which returns a subset of enabled transitions, namely: $stubborn(s) \cap en(s)$. It forwards the other PINS functions. To support the analysis for guard-based partial-order reduction in the POR layer, we introduced four essential extensions to PINS:

- STATELABEL additionally exports guards: $\mathcal{G}_T \subseteq L$,
- a $K \times N$ label dependency matrix is added for Ts,
- DM is split into a read and a write matrix representing Rs and Ws, and
- an $M \times M$ do-not-accord matrix is added.

Mainly, the language front-end must do some static analysis to estimate the do-not-accord relation on transitions based on the criteria listed below Definition 7 While Criterium 1 allows the POR layer to estimate the relation without help from the front-end (using Rs and Ws), this will probably lead to poor reductions.

Tailored Necessary Enabling/Disabling Sets. To support necessary disabling sets, we also extend the PINS interface with an optional maybe co-enabled matrix. Without this matrix, the POR layer can rely solely on necessary enabling sets.

Both $\mathcal{N}^{\mathrm{min}}$ and $\overline{\mathcal{N}}^{\mathrm{min}}$ can be derived via the refined PINS interface (using Ts and Ws). In order to obtain the maximal reduction performance, we extend the PINS interface with two more optional matrices, called $\mathcal{N}_g^{\mathrm{PINS}}$ and $\overline{\mathcal{N}}_g^{\mathrm{PINS}}$. The language front-end can now provide more fine-grained dependencies by inspecting the syntax as in Example 3. The POR layer actually uses the following intersections:

$$\mathcal{N}_g := \mathcal{N}_g^{\mathrm{min}} \cap \mathcal{N}_g^{\mathrm{PINS}} \qquad\qquad \overline{\mathcal{N}}_g := \overline{\mathcal{N}}_g^{\mathrm{min}} \cap \overline{\mathcal{N}}_g^{\mathrm{PINS}}$$

A simple insight shows that we can compute both $\mathcal{N}_g^{\mathrm{PINS}}$ and $\overline{\mathcal{N}}_g^{\mathrm{PINS}}$ using one algorithm. Namely, for a transition to be *necessarily disabling* for a guard g, means exactly the same as for it to be *necessarily enabling* for the inverse: $\neg g$. Or by example: to disable the guard $pc = 1$, is the same as to enable $pc \neq 1$.

5   Partial-Order Reduction for On-the-Fly LTL Checking

Liveness properties can be expressed in Linear Temporal Logic (LTL) [26]. An example LTL property is $\Box\Diamond p$, expressing that from any state in a trace ($\Box =$ generally), eventually ($\Diamond$) a state s can be reached s.t. $p(s)$ holds, where p is a predicate over a state $s \in S_T$, similar to our definition of guards in Definition 2.

In the automata-theoretic approach, an LTL property φ is transformed into a Büchi automaton $\mathbb{B}_\varphi$ whose ω-regular language $\mathcal{L}(\mathbb{B}_\varphi)$ represents the set of all infinite traces the system should adhere to. $\mathbb{B}_\varphi$ is an automaton $(M_\mathbb{B}, \Sigma, \mathcal{F})$ with additionally a set of transition labels Σ, made up of the predicates, and accepting states: $\mathcal{F} \subseteq S_\mathbb{B}$. Its language is formed by all infinite paths visiting an accepting state infinitely often. Since $\mathbb{B}_\varphi$ is finite, a lasso-formed trace exists, with an accepting state on the cycle. The system M_T is likewise interpreted as a set of infinite traces representing its possible executions: $\mathcal{L}(M_T)$. The model checking problem is now reduced to a *language inclusion* problem: $\mathcal{L}(M_T) \subseteq \mathcal{L}(\mathbb{B}_\varphi)$.

Since the number of cycles in M_T is exponential in its size, it is more efficient to invert the problem and look for error traces. The error traces are captured by the negation of the property: $\neg\varphi$. The new problem is a *language intersection and emptiness* problem: $\mathcal{L}(M_T) \cap \mathcal{L}(\mathbb{B}_{\neg\varphi}) = \emptyset$. The intersection can be solved by computing the synchronous cross product $M_T \otimes \mathbb{B}_{\neg\varphi}$ The states of $S_{M_T \otimes \mathbb{B}_{\neg\varphi}}$ are formed by tuples (s, s') with $s \in S_{M_T}$ and $s' \in S_{\neg\varphi}$, with $(s, s') \in \mathcal{F}$ iff $s' \in \mathcal{F}_{\neg\varphi}$. The transitions in $T_{M_T \otimes \mathbb{B}_{\neg\varphi}}$ are formed by synchronising the propositions Σ on the states $s \in S_{M_T}$. For an exact definition of $T_{M_T \otimes \mathbb{B}_{\neg\varphi}}$, we refer to [34]. The construction of the cross product can be done *on-the-fly*, without computing (*and storing!*) the full state space M_T. Therefore, the NDFS [4] algorithm is often used to find accepting cycles (= error traces) as it can do so on-the-fly as well. In the absence of accepting cycles, the original property holds.

Table 1. POR provisos for the LTL model checking of M_T with a property φ

C2	No $a \in stubborn(s)$ is *visible*, except when $stubborn(s) = en(s)$.
C3	$\nexists a \in stubborn(s)\colon a(s)$ is on the DFS stack, except when $stubborn(s) = en(s)$.

To combine partial-order reduction with LTL model checking, the reduced state space M_T^R is constructed on-the-fly, while the LTL cross product and emptiness check algorithm run on top of the reduced state space [25]. Figure 3 shows the PINS stack with POR and LTL as PINS2PINS wrappers.

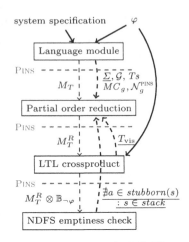

To preserve all traces that are captured by the LTL formula, POR needs to fulfill two additional constraints: the *visibility proviso* ensures that traces included in $\mathbb{B}_{\neg\varphi}$ are not pruned from M_T, the *cycle proviso* ensures the necessary fairness. The visible transitions T_{vis} are those that can enable or disable a proposition of φ ($p \in \Sigma$). Table 1 shows sufficient conditions to ensure both provisos (stubborn sets allow the use of the weaker conditions **V** and **L1/L2** [32]). These can easily be integrated in

Fig. 3. PINS w. LTL POR

Algorithm 1, which now also requires T_{vis} and access to the DFS stack.

We extend the NEXTSTATES function of PINS with a boolean, that can be set by the caller to pass the information needed for **C3**. For **C2**, we extend PINS with T_{vis}, to be set by the LTL wrapper based on the predicates Σ in φ:

$$T_{\mathrm{vis}}^{\min} := \{t \in T \mid Ws(t) \cap \bigcup_{p \in \Sigma} Ts(p) \neq \emptyset\}$$

Peled [23, Sec. 4.1] shows how to prove correctness. However, this is a coarse over-approximation, which we can improve by inputting φ to the language module, so it can export Σ as state labels, i.e. $\Sigma \subseteq \mathcal{G}$, and thereby obtain $\mathcal{N}/\overline{\mathcal{N}}$ for it:

$$T_{\mathrm{vis}}^{\mathrm{nes}} := \bigcup_{p \in \Sigma} \mathcal{N}(p) \cup \overline{\mathcal{N}}(p)$$

A novel idea is to make this definition dynamic:

$$T_{\mathrm{vis}}^{\mathrm{dyn}}(s) := \bigcup_{p \in \Sigma} \begin{cases} \overline{\mathcal{N}}(p) & \text{if } p(s) \\ \mathcal{N}(p) & \text{if } \neg p(s) \end{cases}$$

Finally, we can improve the heuristic (Section 4.3) to avoid visible transitions:

$$cost'(t, s) = \begin{cases} n^2 & \text{if } t \in en(s) \cap T_{\mathrm{vis}} \text{ and } t \notin \mathcal{T}_s \cup \mathcal{T}_{work} \\ cost(t, s) & \text{otherwise} \end{cases}$$

To summarise, we can combine guard-based partial-order reduction with on-the-fly LTL model checking with limited extensions to PINS: a modified NEXTSTATES function and a visibility matrix $T_{\mathrm{vis}} \colon T \to \mathbb{B}$. For better reduction, the language module needs only to extend the exported state labels from $\mathcal{G}$ to $\mathcal{G} \cup \Sigma$ and calculate the MC (and $\mathcal{N}^{\mathrm{PINS}}/\overline{\mathcal{N}}^{\mathrm{PINS}}$) for these labels as well.

6   Experimental Evaluation

Experimental Setup. The LTSMIN toolset implements Algorithm 1 as a language-independent PINS layer since version 1.6. We experimented with BEEM and PROMELA models. To this end, first the DIVINE front-end of LTSMIN was extended with the new PINS features in order to export the necessary static information. In particular, it supports guards, R/W-dependency matrices, the do-not-accord matrix, the co-enabled matrix, and disabling- and enabling sets. Later the PROMELA front-end SpinS [1] was extended, with relatively little effort.

We performed experiments and indicate performance measurements with LTSMIN 2.0[1] and SPIN version 6.2.1[2]. All experiments ran on a dual Intel E5335 CPU with 24GB RAM memory, restricted to use only one processor, 8GB of memory and 3 hours of runtime. None of the models exceeded these bounds.

We compared our guard-based stubborn method with the ample set method, both theoretically and experimentally. For the theoretical comparison the same BEEM models were used as in [7] to establish the best possible reduction with ample sets. For the experimental comparison, we used a rich set of PROMELA models[3], which were also run in SPIN with partial-order reduction.

BEEM Models. Table 2 shows the results obtained on those models from the BEEM database [22] that were selected by Geldenhuys, Hansen and Valmari [7]. The table is sorted by the best theoretical ample set reduction (best first). These numbers (column AMPLE) are taken from [7, column AMPLE2 Df/Rf]. They indicate the experimentally established best possible reduction that can be achieved with the deadlock-preserving ample set method (without **C2/C3**), while considering conditional dependencies based on full information on the state space.

The amount of reduction is expressed as the percentage of the reduced state space compared to the original state space (100% means no reduction). The next three columns show the reduction achieved by the guard-based stubborn approach, based on necessary enabling sets only (nes), the heuristic selection function (nes+h), and the result of including the necessary disabling sets (nes+h+d).

The results vary a lot. For instance, the best possible ample set reduction in `cyclic_scheduler.1` is far better than the actual reduction achieved with stubborn sets (nes). However, for `cyclic_scheduler.2` the situation is reversed. Other striking differences are `mcs.1` versus `leader_election`. Since we compare *best case* ample sets (using global information) with *actual* stubborn sets (using only static information), it is quite interesting to see that guard-based stubborn sets can provide more reduction than ample sets. One explanation is that the ample set algorithm with a dependency relation based on the full state space (Df/Rf, [7]) is still coarse. However, further comparison reveals that many models yield also better reductions than those using dynamic relations (Dd/Rd, [7]), e.g. `protocols.3` with 7% vs 70%. This prompted us to verify our generated

---

[1] `http://fmt.cs.utwente.nl/tools/ltsmin/`
[2] `http://spinroot.com`
[3] `http://www.albertolluch.com/research/promelamodels`

Table 2. Comparison of guard-based POR results with [7] (split in two columns)

Model	AMPLE	nes	nes +h	nes h+d	Model	AMPLE	nes	nes +h	nes h+d
cyclic_scheduler.1	1%	58%	1%	1%	driving_phils.1	69%	99%	68%	78%
mcs.4	4%	16%	16%	16%	protocols.3	71%	13%	7%	7%
firewire_tree.1	6%	8%	8%	8%	peterson.2	72%	82%	82%	82%
phils.3	11%	14%	16%	16%	driving_phils.2	72%	99%	45%	45%
mcs.1	18%	87%	85%	85%	collision.2	74%	75%	40%	39%
anderson.4	23%	58%	46%	46%	production_cell.1	74%	23%	19%	19%
iprotocol.2	26%	19%	17%	16%	telephony.1	75%	95%	95%	95%
mcs.2	34%	64%	64%	64%	lamport.3	75%	96%	95%	96%
phils.1	48%	60%	48%	48%	firewire_link.1	79%	42%	37%	33%
firewire_link.2	51%	24%	21%	19%	pgm_protocol.4	81%	93%	56%	55%
krebs.1	51%	94%	93%	93%	bopdp.2	85%	90%	73%	73%
leader_election.3	54%	13%	12%	6%	fischer.1	87%	87%	87%	87%
telephony.2	60%	95%	95%	95%	bakery.3	88%	99%	96%	96%
leader_election.1	61%	23%	22%	11%	exit.2	88%	94%	94%	94%
szymanski.1	63%	68%	65%	65%	brp2.1	88%	95%	80%	79%
production_cell.2	63%	26%	24%	24%	public_subscribe.1	89%	81%	79%	76%
at.1	65%	96%	95%	95%	firewire_tree.2	89%	84%	63%	47%
szymanski.2	66%	66%	64%	64%	pgm_protocol.2	89%	96%	72%	72%
leader_filters.2	66%	57%	53%	53%	brp.2	96%	76%	42%	42%
lamport.1	66%	95%	95%	95%	extinction.2	96%	25%	24%	21%
protocols.2	68%	18%	13%	13%	cyclic_scheduler.2	99%	46%	28%	27%
collision.1	68%	88%	59%	56%	synapse.2	100%	93%	93%	93%

stubborn sets, but we found no violations of the stubborn set definition. So we suspect that either the relations deduced in [7] are not entirely optimal or the POR heuristic of selecting the smallest ample set fails in these cases.

We also investigated the effects of the necessary disabling sets (Sec. 4.2) and heuristic selection (Sec. 4.3). Heuristic selection improves reductions (column nes+h). For instance, for `cyclic_scheduler.1` it achieves a similar reduction as the optimal ample set method. The reduction improves in nearly all cases, and it improves considerably in several cases. Using Necessary Disabling Sets (nes+nds) in itself did not yield an improvement compared to plain nes, hence we didn't include the results in the table. Combined with the heuristic selection, necessary disabling sets provide an improvement of the reduction in some cases (column nes+h+d). In particular, for `leader_election` the reduction doubles again. Also some other examples show a small improvement.

We can explain this as follows: Although nds allows smaller stubborn sets (cf. Example 5), there is no reason why the eager algorithm would find one. Only with the heuristic selection, the stubborn set algorithm tends to favour small stubborn sets, harvesting the potential gain of nds.

We conclude that, the heuristic selection is more important to improve reductions, than the necessary disabling sets. In terms of computation time the situation is reversed: the selection heuristics is costly, but the disabling sets lower the computation time. In the next section, we investigate computation times.

Table 3. Guard-based POR in LTSMIN vs ample set POR in SPIN (seconds and MB)

Model	States $|S_T|$	Trans $|\Delta|$	No PoR LTSMIN time	No PoR SPIN time	Guard-based POR $|S_T|$	Guard-based POR $|\Delta|$	Guard-based POR mem	Guard-based POR time	Ample-set POR $|S_T|$	Ample-set POR $|\Delta|$	Ample-set POR mem	Ample-set POR time
garp	48,363,145	247,135,869	166	267	4%	1%	21	68	18%	9%	932	25.2
i-protocol2	14,309,427	48,024,048	28	30	16%	10%	29	31	24%	16%	240	6.0
peterson4	12,645,068	47,576,805	23	17	3%	1%	6	3	5%	2%	37	0.5
i-protocol0	9,798,465	45,932,747	29	38	6%	2%	7	21	44%	29%	362	12.3
brp.prm	3,280,269	7,058,556	6.0	5.6	29%	15%	15	14	58%	39%	161	2.4
philo.pml	1,640,881	16,091,905	9.8	10	5%	2%	1.2	4.8	100%	100%	125	10.7
sort	659,683	3,454,988	2.8	3.8	182	181	0.0	0.3	182	182	0.3	0.0
i-protocol3	388,929	1,161,274	1.0	0.7	14%	7%	0.9	0.9	26%	16%	6.6	0.1
i-protocol4	95,756	204,405	0.5	0.1	28%	18%	0.5	0.6	38%	28%	2.5	0.0
snoopy	81,013	273,781	0.6	0.2	12%	4%	0.2	0.7	17%	7%	1.2	0.0
peterson3	45,915	128,653	0.4	0.0	8%	3%	0.1	0.4	10%	4%	0.5	0.0
SMALL1	36,970	163,058	0.5	0.0	18%	9%	0.1	0.4	48%	45%	0.9	0.0
SMALL2	7,496	32,276	0.4	0.0	19%	10%	0.0	0.4	48%	44%	0.4	0.0
X.509.prm	9,028	35,999	0.4	0.0	10%	4%	0.0	0.4	68%	34%	1.1	0.0
dbm.prm	5,112	20,476	0.4	0.0	100%	100%	0.1	0.5	100%	100%	0.7	0.0
smcs	5,066	19,470	0.4	0.1	17%	7%	0.0	0.4	25%	11%	0.7	0.0

PROMELA *Models.* Additionally, we compared our partial-order reduction results to the ample set algorithm as implemented in SPIN. Here we can also compare time resource usage. We ran LTSMIN with arguments `--strategy=dfs -s26 --por`, and we compiled SPIN with `-O2 -DNOFAIR -DNOBOUNDCHECK -DSAFETY`, which enables POR by default. We ran the `pan`-verifier with `-m10000000 -c0 -n -w26`. To obtain the same state counts in SPIN, we had to turn off control flow optimisations (`-o1`/`-o2`/`-o3`) for some models (see `ltsmin/spins/test/`).

Table 3 shows the results. Overall, we witness consistently better reductions by the guard-based algorithm (using nes+h+d). The reductions are significantly larger than the ample set approach in the cases of `garp`, dining philosophers (`philo.pml`) and `iprotocol`. As a consequence, guard-based POR in LTSMIN reduces memory usage considerably more than ample-based POR in SPIN (Though we included memory use for completeness, it only provides an indirect comparison, due to a different state representation and compression in LTSMIN [18]).

On the other hand, the additional computational overhead of our algorithm is clear from the runtimes. This was expected, as the stubborn-set algorithm considers all transitions whereas the ample-set algorithm only chooses amongst the less numerous process components of the system. Moreover, the heuristic search still considers all enabled transitions — we do not select a scapegoat — increasing the search space. Finally, the choice to store information on a guard basis requires our implementation to iterate over all guards of a transition at times. Unfortunately, this cannot be mitigated by combining this information on a transition basis, since enabled guards are treated differently from disabled guards. However, the runtimes never exceed the runtimes of benchmarks without partial-order reduction by a great margin.

Table 4. Reductions ($\%|S_T|$) and runtimes (sec) obtained for LTL model checking

| Model | States $|S_T|$ | LTSMIN ($\%|S_T|$) | | | | SPIN $\%|S_T|$ | LTSMIN (sec) | | | | | SPIN (sec) | |
		$T_{\text{vis}}^{\text{min}}$	$T_{\text{vis}}^{\text{nes}}$	$T_{\text{vis}}^{\text{dyn}}$	color		Full	$T_{\text{vis}}^{\text{min}}$	$T_{\text{vis}}^{\text{nes}}$	$T_{\text{vis}}^{\text{dyn}}$	color	Full	POR
garp	72,318,749	35%	32.6%	25.4%	3.6%	18.3%	1,162	1,156	1,069	843	135	2,040	127
i-prot.	20,052,267	100%	32.0%	29.3%	28.1%	41.4%	193	598	152	137	132	103	37
leader	89,771,572	94%	0.1%	0.1%	0.1%	1.2%	3,558	9,493	4	4	4	1,390	5

LTL Model Checking. To compare the reductions under LTL model checking with SPIN, we used 3 models that were verified for absence of livelocks, using an LTL property $\square\lozenge progress$. Table 4 shows the results of POR with **C2/C3**.

In LTSMIN, we used three implementations of the visibility matrix (see Section 5) and the color proviso [6] (`--proviso=color`). To obtain $T_{\text{vis}}^{\text{min}}$, we defined *progress* with a predicate on the program counter ($Proc.\_pc = 1$). For $T_{\text{vis}}^{\text{nes}}$, we exported an np_ label through pins and defined $\varphi := \square\lozenge\neg\text{np}\_$. SPIN also predefines this label, hence we used the same property (though negated [13]).

The results in Table 4 show that approximation $T_{\text{vis}}^{\text{min}}$ is indeed too coarse. Reductions with $T_{\text{vis}}^{\text{nes}}$ improve considerably; the novel dynamic visibility $T_{\text{vis}}^{\text{dyn}}$ and the color proviso provide the best results, also reducing more than SPIN.

7   Conclusions

We proposed guard-based partial-order reduction, as a language-agnostic stubborn set method. It extends Valmari's stubborn sets for transition systems [31] with an abstract interface (PINS) to language modules. It also generalises previous notions of guards [33], by considering them as disabling conditions as well. The main advantage is that a single implementation of POR can serve multiple specification languages front-ends and multiple high-performance model checking back-ends. This requires only that the front-end exports guards, guarded transitions, affect sets, and the do-not-accord matrix ($\mathcal{DNA}$). Optional extensions are matrices MC_g, $\mathcal{N}^{\text{PINS}}$ and $\overline{\mathcal{N}}^{\text{PINS}}$ (computing the latter merely requires negating the guards), which expose more static information to yield better reduction.

We implemented these functions for the DVE and PROMELA front-ends in LTSMIN. It should now be a trivial exercise to add partial-order reduction to the mCRL2 and UPPAAL language front-ends. Since the linear process of mCRL2 is rule-based and has no natural notion of processes, our generalisation is crucial.

We introduced two improvements to the basic stubborn set method. The first uses necessary disabling sets to identify necessary enabling sets of guards that cannot be co-enabled. This allows for the existence of smaller stubborn sets. Most of the reduction power of the algorithm is harvested by the heuristic selection function, which actively favours small stubborn sets.

Compared to the best possible ample set with conditional dependencies, the stubborn set can reduce the state space more effectively in a number of cases. Compared to SPIN's ample set, LTSMIN generally provides more reduction, but takes more time to do so, probably because of the additional complexity of the stubborn set method, but also due to overhead in the guard-based abstraction.

Comparing our stubborn set computation against earlier proposals, we see the following. While other stubborn set computation methods require $\mathcal{O}(c|T|)$ [32, Sec. 7.4] using scapegoat selection and resolving the dependencies of *find_nes* arbitrarily (where c depends on the modeling formalism used), our algorithm resolves non-deterministic choices heuristically potentially reducing the search space. It would therefore be interesting to compare our heuristic algorithm to other approaches like the deletion algorithm [35], selecting a scapegoat [35] and the strongly connected components method [32], or one of these combined with the heuristics. This would provide more insight in the trade-off between time spent on finding stubborn sets and state space reductions.

Challenges remain, as not all of LTSMIN's algorithmic backends can fulfill the POR layer's requirements. For example, the **C3** proviso relies on a DFS stack, and because DFS can probably not be parallelised efficiently, other methods have to be found. We partly solved this problem for a subset of LTL with the parallel DFS$_{\mathrm{FIFO}}$ algorithm [17, end of Sec. 5], but for other parallel algorithms, like CNDFS [5], this is still future work. One benefit for the parallel algorithms is that the heuristic selection algorithm can find small stubborn sets deterministically, which avoids well-known problems with possible re-explorations [15,27].

Acknowledgments. We are grateful to Antti Valmari, Patrice Godefroid and Dragan Bošnački for their useful feedback on this paper.

References

1. van der Berg, F.I., Laarman, A.W.: SpinS: Extending LTSmin with Promela through SpinJa. In: PDMC 2012, London, UK. ENTCS, Springer (September 2012)
2. Blom, S., van de Pol, J., Weber, M.: LTSMIN: Distributed and symbolic reachability. In: Touili, T., Cook, B., Jackson, P. (eds.) CAV 2010. LNCS, vol. 6174, pp. 354–359. Springer, Heidelberg (2010)
3. Clarke, E.M.: The birth of model checking. In: 25 Years of Model Checking, pp. 1–26. Springer, Heidelberg (2008)
4. Courcoubetis, C., Vardi, M., Wolper, P., Yannakakis, M.: Memory Efficient Algorithms for the Verification of Temporal Properties. In: Clarke, E., Kurshan, R.P. (eds.) CAV 1990. LNCS, vol. 531, pp. 233–242. Springer, Heidelberg (1991)
5. Evangelista, S., Laarman, A., Petrucci, L., van de Pol, J.: Improved Multi-core Nested Depth-First Search. In: Chakraborty, S., Mukund, M. (eds.) ATVA 2012. LNCS, vol. 7561, pp. 269–283. Springer, Heidelberg (2012)
6. Evangelista, S., Pajault, C.: Solving the Ignoring Problem for Partial Order Reduction. STTF 12, 155–170 (2010)
7. Geldenhuys, J., Hansen, H., Valmari, A.: Exploring the scope for partial order reduction. In: Liu, Z., Ravn, A.P. (eds.) ATVA 2009. LNCS, vol. 5799, pp. 39–53. Springer, Heidelberg (2009)
8. Godefroid, P.: Using Partial Orders to Improve Automatic Verification Methods. In: Clarke, E., Kurshan, R.P. (eds.) CAV 1990. LNCS, vol. 531, pp. 176–185. Springer, Heidelberg (1991)

9. Godefroid, P.: Partial-Order Methods for the Verification of Concurrent Systems: An Approach to the State-Explosion Problem. Springer, Secaucus (1996)
10. Godefroid, P., Pirottin, D.: Refining dependencies improves partial-order verification methods (extended abstract). In: Courcoubetis, C. (ed.) CAV 1993. LNCS, vol. 697, pp. 438–449. Springer, Heidelberg (1993)
11. Godefroid, P., Wolper, P.: Using partial orders for the efficient verification of deadlock freedom and safety properties. FMSD 2, 149–164 (1993)
12. Groote, J.F., Keiren, J., Mathijssen, A., Ploeger, B., Stappers, F., Tankink, C., Usenko, Y., van Weerdenburg, M., Wesselink, W., Willemse, T., van der Wulp, J.: The mCRL2 toolset. WASDeTT (2008)
13. Holzmann, G.J.: The model checker SPIN. IEEE TSE 23, 279–295 (1997)
14. Holzmann, G.J., Peled, D.: An Improvement in Formal Verification. In: IFIP WG6.1 ICFDT VII, pp. 197–211. Chapman & Hall, Ltd. (1995)
15. Holzmann, G.J., Peled, D., Yannakakis, M.: On Nested Depth First Search. In: SPIN, pp. 23–32. American Mathematical Society (1996)
16. Katz, S., Peled, D.: An efficient verification method for parallel and distributed programs. In: de Bakker, J.W., de Roever, W.-P., Rozenberg, G. (eds.) Linear Time, Branching Time and Partial Order in Logics and Models for Concurrency. LNCS, vol. 354, pp. 489–507. Springer, Heidelberg (1989)
17. Laarman, A., Faragó, D.: Improved On-The-Fly Livelock Detection. In: Brat, G., Rungta, N., Venet, A. (eds.) NFM 2013. LNCS, vol. 7871, pp. 32–47. Springer, Heidelberg (2013)
18. Laarman, A., van de Pol, J., Weber, M.: Parallel Recursive State Compression for Free. In: Groce, A., Musuvathi, M. (eds.) SPIN Workshops 2011. LNCS, vol. 6823, pp. 38–56. Springer, Heidelberg (2011)
19. Laarman, A., van de Pol, J., Weber, M.: Multi-Core LTSMIN: Marrying Modularity and Scalability. In: Bobaru, M., Havelund, K., Holzmann, G.J., Joshi, R. (eds.) NFM 2011. LNCS, vol. 6617, pp. 506–511. Springer, Heidelberg (2011)
20. Overman, W.T.: Verification of concurrent systems: function and timing. PhD thesis, University of California, Los Angeles (1981), AAI8121023
21. Pater, E.: Partial Order Reduction for PINS, Master's thesis (March 2011)
22. Pelánek, R.: BEEM: Benchmarks for explicit model checkers. In: Bošnački, D., Edelkamp, S. (eds.) SPIN 2007. LNCS, vol. 4595, pp. 263–267. Springer, Heidelberg (2007)
23. Peled, D.: All from One, One for All: on Model Checking Using Representatives. In: Courcoubetis, C. (ed.) CAV 1993. LNCS, vol. 697, pp. 409–423. Springer, Heidelberg (1993)
24. Peled, D.: Combining partial order reductions with on-the-fly model-checking. In: Dill, D.L. (ed.) CAV 1994. LNCS, vol. 818, pp. 377–390. Springer, Heidelberg (1994)
25. Peled, D.: Combining Partial Order Reductions with On-the-Fly Model-Checking. In: Dill, D.L. (ed.) CAV 1994. LNCS, vol. 818, pp. 377–390. Springer, Heidelberg (1994)
26. Pnueli, A.: The temporal logic of programs. In: FOCS, pp. 46–57. IEEE Computer Society (1977)
27. Schwoon, S., Esparza, J.: A Note on On-the-Fly Verification Algorithms. In: Halbwachs, N., Zuck, L.D. (eds.) TACAS 2005. LNCS, vol. 3440, pp. 174–190. Springer, Heidelberg (2005)
28. Valmari, A.: Error Detection by Reduced Reachability Graph Generation. In: APN, pp. 95–112 (1988)

29. Valmari, A.: Eliminating Redundant Interleavings During Concurrent Program Verification. In: Odijk, E., Rem, M., Syre, J.-C. (eds.) PARLE 1989. LNCS, vol. 366, pp. 89–103. Springer, Heidelberg (1989)
30. Valmari, A.: A Stubborn Attack On State Explosion. In: Larsen, K.G., Skou, A. (eds.) CAV 1991. LNCS, vol. 575, pp. 156–165. Springer, Heidelberg (1992)
31. Valmari, A.: Stubborn Sets for Reduced State Space Generation. In: Rozenberg, G. (ed.) APN 1990. LNCS, vol. 483, pp. 491–515. Springer, Heidelberg (1991)
32. Valmari, A.: The State Explosion Problem. In: Reisig, W., Rozenberg, G. (eds.) APN 1998. LNCS, vol. 1491, pp. 429–528. Springer, Heidelberg (1998)
33. Valmari, A., Hansen, H.: Can Stubborn Sets Be Optimal? In: Lilius, J., Penczek, W. (eds.) PETRI NETS 2010. LNCS, vol. 6128, pp. 43–62. Springer, Heidelberg (2010)
34. Vardi, M.Y., Wolper, P.: An Automata-Theoretic Approach to Automatic Program Verification. In: LICS, pp. 332–344. IEEE (1986)
35. Varpaaniemi, K.: On the Stubborn Set Method in Reduced State Space Generation. PhD thesis, Helsinki University of Technology (1998)

On the Synergy of Probabilistic Causality Computation and Causality Checking

Florian Leitner-Fischer and Stefan Leue

University of Konstanz, Germany

Abstract. In recent work on the safety analysis of systems we have shown how causal relationships amongst events can be algorithmically inferred from probabilistic counterexamples and subsequently be mapped to fault trees. The resulting fault trees were significantly smaller and hence easier to understand than the corresponding probabilistic counterexample, but still contain all information needed to discern the causes for the occurrence of a hazard. More recently we have developed an approach called Causality Checking which is integrated into the state-space exploration algorithms used for qualitative model checking and which is capable of computing causality relationships on-the-fly. The causality checking approach outperforms the probabilistic causality computation in terms of run-time and memory consumption, but can not provide a probabilistic measure. In this paper we combine the strengths of both approaches and propose an approach where the causal events are computed using causality checking and the probability computation can be limited to the causal events. We demonstrate the increase in performance of our approach using several case studies.

1 Introduction

Model Checking [11] is an established technique for the verification of systems. For a formal model of the system and a formalized requirement the model checker automatically checks whether the model satisfies the requirement. In case the requirement is not satisfied, a trace from the initial system state into a state violating the requirement is produced by the model checker. This error trace is called a counterexample. Counterexamples can be used to retrace the steps of the system that lead to a particular requirement violating state, but they do not provide any insight into which event did cause the requirement violation. Consequently, debugging a system using counterexamples is a difficult iterative and hence time-consuming process.

In the case of probabilistic model checking [6] the debugging of the system becomes even more difficult. While in qualitative model checking a single trace often provides valuable information for the debugging of the system, a single trace is most often not sufficient to form a probabilistic counterexample [4,17] since the violation of a probabilistic property with a probability-bound can hardly ever be traced back to a single error trace. In almost all cases a set of error traces is needed to provide an accumulated probability mass that violates the probability-bound of the specified probabilistic property. With an increasing number of error

E. Bartocci and C.R. Ramakrishnan (Eds.): SPIN 2013, LNCS 7976, pp. 246–263, 2013.

traces that are needed to form the probabilistic counterexample, an increasing number of different error traces need to be manually retraced and interpreted in order to get insight into why the property was violated.

In recent work [22,26] we have developed two approaches that help to debug complex systems:

1. The *probabilistic causality computation* approach described in [22], where causal relationships of events are algorithmically inferred from probabilistic counterexamples and subsequently mapped to fault trees [32]. Fault trees are a method widely used in industry to visualize causal relationships. The resulting fault trees were significantly smaller and hence easier to understand than the corresponding probabilistic counterexample, but still contain all information to discern the causes for the occurrence of a hazard.
2. The *Causality Checking* approach [26], where the causality computation algorithm is integrated into the state-space exploration algorithms used for qualitative model checking. This algorithm is capable of computing the causality relationships on the fly.

The obvious advantage of the probabilistic causality computation approach over the causality checking approach is that it computes a quantitative measure, namely a probability, for a combination of causal events and hazards to occur. The probability of an event combination causing a property violation to occur is an information that is needed for the reliability and safety analysis of safety-critical systems. An important shortcoming of the probabilistic causality computation approach compared to the causality checking approach is that the causality computation requires a complete probabilistic counterexample consisting of all traces that violate the property. The high amount of run-time and memory that is needed to compute the probabilities of all traces in the probabilistic counterexample limits the scalability of the probabilistic causality computation approach.

The goal of this paper is to leverage the causality checking approach in order to improve the scalability of the probabilistic causality computation approach. The key idea is to first compute the causal events using the causality checking approach and to then limit the probability computation to the causal event combinations that have first been computed. Our proposed combined approach can be summarized by identifying the following steps:

- The probabilistic PRISM model is mapped to a qualitative Promela model.
- The causality checking approach is applied to the qualitative model in order to compute the event combinations that are causal for the property violation.
- The information obtained through causality checking is mapped back via alternating automata to the probabilistic model. The probabilities for the different event combinations that are causal for the property violation to occur are computed using a probabilistic model checker.

Fig. 1. Overview of the approach

Figure 1 gives an overview of the approach.

The remainder of the paper is structured as follows: In Section 2 we briefly introduce probabilistic model checking, the PRISM language, and causality checking. We discuss the translation of probabilistic PRISM models to qualitative Promela models in Section 3. Section 4 is devoted to the translation of the information returned by the causality checker to the PRISM model and the probability computation of the causal events. In Section 5 we evaluate the usefulness of the proposed approach on several case studies. Related work is discussed throughout the paper and in Section 6. We conclude the paper and give an outlook on future research in Section 7.

2   Preliminaries

2.1   Probabilistic Model Checking

Probabilistic model checking [6] requires two inputs: a description of the system to be analyzed, typically given in some model checker specific modeling language, and a formal specification of quantitative properties of the system, related for example to its performance or reliability that are to be analyzed.

From the first of these inputs, a probabilistic model checker constructs the corresponding probabilistic model. The probabilistic models that we use in this paper are continuous-time Markov chains (CTMCs) [21] where transitions are assigned positive, real values that are interpreted as rates of negative exponential distributions.

The quantitative properties of the system that are to be analyzed are specified using a variant of temporal logic. The temporal logic we use is Continuous Stochastic Logic (CSL) [1,5].

2.2   The PRISM Language

We present an overview of the input language of the PRISM model checker [23], for a precise definition of the semantics we refer to [19]. A PRISM model is composed of a number of *modules* which can interact with each other. A *module* contains a number of local variables. The values of these variables at any given time constitute the state of the *module*. The global state of the whole model is determined by the local state of all *modules*. The behavior of each module is described by a set of commands. A command takes the form: "[*action_label*] *guard* → *rate*$_1$: *update*$_1$ &...& *update*$_n$;". The *guard* is a predicate over all variables in the model. The *update* commands describe a transition which the module can take if the *guard* is true. A transition is specified by giving the new values of the variables in the *module*, possibly as a function of other variables. A *rate* is assigned to each transition. The *action_label* is used for synchronizing transitions of different modules.

If two transitions are synchronized they can only be executed if the guards of both transitions evaluate to true. The rate of the resulting synchronized transition is the product of the two individual transitions. An example of a PRISM model is given in Listing 1.1. The module named *moduleA* contains two variables: *var1*, which is of type Boolean and is initially *false*, and *var2*, which is a numeric variable and has initially the value 0. If the guard (var2 < 4) evaluates to true, the update (var2' = var2 + 1) is executed with a rate of 0.8. If the guard (var2 = 2) evaluates to true, the update (var1' = *true*) is executed with a rate of 1.0.

```
module moduleA
    var1: bool init false;
    var2: [0..11] init 0;
    [Count] (var2 < 4) -> 0.8: ( var2'= var2 + 1);
    [End] (var2 = 4) -> 1.0: ( var1'= true);
endmodule
module moduleB
    var3: [0..2] init 0;
    [Count] (var3 < 2) -> 1.0: ( var3'= var3 + 1);
    [Count] (var3 = 2) -> 1.0: ( var3'= 0);
endmodule
```

Listing 1.1. A module in the PRISM language.

2.3   Railroad Crossing Example

In this paper we will use the example of a railroad crossing for illustrative purposes. In this example a train can approach the crossing (Ta), enter the crossing (Tc) and finally leave the crossing (Tl). Whenever a train is approaching, the gate should close (Gc) and open when the train has left the crossing (Go). It might also be the case that the gate fails (Gf). The car approaches the crossing (Ca) and enters the crossing (Cc) if the gate is open and finally leaves the crossing (Cl). We are interested in computing the causal events for the violation of the property "it is never the case that both the car and the train are in the crossing at the same time".

2.4   Causality Reasoning

The probabilistic causality computation approach and the causality checking approach are based on an adoption of the *structural equation model (SEM)* by Halpern and Pearl [16]. The SEM is an extension of the *counterfactual* reasoning approach and the *alternative world* semantics by Lewis [28,12]. The "naïve" counterfactual causality criterion according to Lewis is as follows: event A is causal for the occurrence of event B if and only if, were A not to happen, B would not occur. The testing of this condition hinges upon the availability of alternative worlds. In our setting possible system execution traces represent the alternative worlds. The SEM introduces the notion of causes being logical combinations of events as well as a distinction of relevant and irrelevant causes. In the SEM events are represented by variable values and the minimal number of causal variable valuation combinations is determined. In our precursory work [22,26], we extended the SEM by considering the order of the occurrences of events as possible causal factors. In order to be able to reason about event orderings we defined a temporal logic called *event order logic* (EOL).

We will now give a brief overview of the EOL as originally defined in [26]. The EOL allows one to connect variables representing the occurrence of events with the boolean connectives $\wedge$, $\vee$ and $\neg$. To express the ordering of events we introduced the ordered conjunction operator $\wedge$. The formula $a \wedge b$ with events a and b is satisfied if and only if events a and b occur in a trace and a occurs before b. In addition to the $\wedge$ operator we introduced the interval operators $\wedge_[$, $\wedge_]$, and $\wedge_< \phi \wedge_>$, which define an interval in which an event has to hold in all states. These interval operators are necessary to express the causal non-occurrence of events.

Definition 1. *Syntax of Event Order Logic (EOL). Simple EOL formulas over a set $\mathcal{A}$ of event variables are formed according to the following grammar:*

$$\phi ::= a \mid \phi_1 \wedge \phi_2 \mid \neg\phi \mid \phi_1 \vee \phi_2$$

where $a \in \mathcal{A}$ and ϕ, ϕ_1 and ϕ_2 are simple EOL formulas. Complex EOL formulas are formed according to the following grammar:

$$\psi ::= \phi \mid \psi_1 \wedge \psi_2 \mid \psi_1 \vee \psi_2 \mid \psi_1 \wedge \psi_2 \mid \psi \wedge_[\phi \mid \phi \wedge_] \psi \mid \psi_1 \wedge_< \phi \wedge_> \psi_2$$

where ϕ is a simple EOL formula and ψ_1 and ψ_2 are complex EOL formulas. Note that the $\neg$ operator binds more tightly than the $\wedge$, $\wedge_[$, $\wedge_]$, and $\wedge_< \phi \wedge_>$, operators and those bind more tightly than the $\vee$ and $\wedge$ operator.

The formal semantics of this logic is defined over execution traces. Notice that the $\wedge$, $\wedge_[$, $\wedge_]$, and $\wedge_< \phi \wedge_>$ operators are linear temporal logic operators and that the execution trace σ is akin to a linearly ordered Kripke structure.

Definition 2. *Semantics of Event Order Logic (EOL). Let $T = (S, \text{Act}, \rightarrow, I, AP, L)$ a transition system, let ϕ, ϕ_1, ϕ_2 simple EOL formulas, let ψ, ψ_1, ψ_2 complex EOL formulas, and let $\mathcal{A}$ a set of event variables, with $a_{\alpha_i} \in \mathcal{A}$, over which ϕ, ϕ_1, ϕ_2 are built. Let $\sigma = s_0, \alpha_1, s_1, \alpha_2, \ldots \alpha_n, s_n$ a finite execution trace of T and $\sigma[i..r] = s_i, \alpha_{i+1}, s_{i+1}, \alpha_{i+2}, \ldots \alpha_r, s_r$ a partial trace. We define that an execution trace σ satisfies a formula ψ, written as $\sigma \vDash_e \psi$, as follows:*

$$s_j \vDash_e a_{\alpha_i} \text{ iff } s_{j-1} \xrightarrow{\alpha_i} s_j$$

$$s_j \vDash_e \neg\phi \text{ iff not } s_j \vDash_e \phi$$

$$\sigma[i..r] \vDash_e \phi \text{ iff } \exists j : i \le j \le r . s_j \vDash_e \phi$$

$$\sigma \vDash_e \psi \text{ iff } \sigma[0..n] \vDash_e \psi, \text{ where } n \text{ is the length of } \sigma.$$

$$\sigma[i..r] \vDash_e \phi_1 \wedge \phi_2 \text{ iff } \sigma[i..r] \vDash_e \phi_1 \text{ and } \sigma[i..r] \vDash_e \phi_2$$

$$\sigma[i..r] \vDash_e \phi_1 \vee \phi_2 \text{ iff } \sigma[i..r] \vDash_e \phi_1 \text{ or } \sigma[i..r] \vDash_e \phi_2$$

$$\sigma[i..r] \vDash_e \psi_1 \wedge \psi_2 \text{ iff } \sigma[i..r] \vDash_e \psi_1 \text{ and } \sigma[i..r] \vDash_e \psi_2$$

$$\sigma[i..r] \vDash_e \psi_1 \vee \psi_2 \text{ iff } \sigma[i..r] \vDash_e \psi_1 \text{ or } \sigma[i..r] \vDash_e \psi_2$$

$$\sigma[i..r] \vDash_e \psi_1 \wedge \psi_2 \text{ iff } \exists j, k : i \le j < k \le r . \sigma[i..j] \vDash_e \psi_1 \text{ and } \sigma[k..r] \vDash_e \psi_2$$

$$\sigma[i..r] \vDash_e \psi \wedge_[\phi \text{ iff } (\exists j : i \le j \le r . \sigma[i..j] \vDash_e \psi \text{ and } (\forall k : j \le k \le r . \sigma[k..k] \vDash_e \phi))$$

$$\sigma[i..r] \vDash_e \phi \wedge_] \psi \text{ iff } (\exists j : i \le j \le r . \sigma[j..r] \vDash_e \psi \text{ and } (\forall k : 0 \le k \le j . \sigma[k..k] \vDash_e \phi))$$

$$\sigma[i..r] \vDash_e \psi_1 \wedge_< \phi \wedge_> \psi_2 \text{ iff } (\exists j, k : i \le j < k \le r . \sigma[i..j] \vDash_e \psi_1 \text{ and } \sigma[k..r] \vDash_e \psi_2$$
$$\text{and } (\forall l : j \le l \le k . \sigma[l..l] \vDash_e \phi))$$

We define that the transition system T satisfies the formula ψ, written as $T \vDash_e \psi$, iff $\exists \sigma \in T . \sigma \vDash_e \psi$.

A system execution trace $\sigma = s_0, \alpha_1, s_1, \alpha_2, \ldots \alpha_n, s_n$ induces an EOL formula $\psi_\sigma = a_{\alpha_1} \wedge \ldots \wedge a_{\alpha_n}$. For reasons of readability we omit the states in the execution traces from now on. For instance, the execution $\sigma = $ Ta, Ca, Cc, Gc, Tc of the railroad example induces the EOL formula $\psi_\sigma = $ Ta $\wedge$ Ca $\wedge$ Cc $\wedge$ Gc $\wedge$ Tc.

The adopted SEM defined in [22,26] can be used to decide whether the EOL formula ψ_σ, induced by an excution trace σ and which violates some target property φ actually represents a combination that is causal for the violation of φ. In the following the term property refers to the target property for which we want to compute the causal events that lead to its violation. The conditions imposed by the adopted SEM for some ψ to be causal can be summarized as follows:

- AC1: This condition is the positive side of the counterfactual test. It checks whether there exists an execution trace σ that violates the property and satisfies the EOL formula ψ.
- AC2(1): This condition resembles the counterfactual test, where it is checked whether there exists an execution trace σ' where the order and occurrence of the events is different from ψ and the property is not violated.
- AC2(2): This condition says that for a ψ to be causal it can not be possible to add an event so that causality is voided. This test serves to reveal causal non-occurrence.
- AC3: This condition ensures minimality of the causal event combinations and requires that no sub-formula of ψ satisfies AC1 and AC2.
- OC1: This condition checks for all events in ψ whether the order in which they occur is causal or not.

For all executions where the property is violated the conditions imposed by the adopted SEM are checked. For instance, the safety property for the railroad crossing example is violated on the execution trace $\sigma = $ Ta, Ca, Cc, Gc, Tc because the car is on the crossing when the gate closes and the train enters the crossing. Condition AC1 is fulfilled for $\psi_\sigma = $ Ta $\wedge$ Ca $\wedge$ Cc $\wedge$ Gc $\wedge$ Tc since σ exists and the property is violated. AC2(1) is fulfilled in this example since there exists the execution trace $\sigma' = $ Ta, Ca, Gc, Tc where the occurrence and order of the events is different from that specified by ψ_σ. For the AC2(2) test all good execution traces are needed to check whether there exists an event that can void the causality of ψ_σ. The condition AC2(2) reveals that there exists a good execution trace $\sigma'' = $ Ta, Ca, Cc, Cl, Gc, Tc where the property is not violated because the car leaves the crossing before the gate closes (Gc) and the train enters the crossing (Tc). In other words, the non-occurrence of the event Cl between the event Cc and the events $(Gc \wedge Tc)$ is causal and its occurrence can void the causality of ψ_σ.

According to the procedures defined in [26] the causal non-occurrence of Cl is reflected by adding $\neg Cl$ to ψ_σ. We then obtain a new formula $\psi_\sigma = $ Ta $\wedge$ Ca $\wedge$ Gf $\wedge$ Cc $\wedge_< \neg Cl \wedge_>$ Tc. AC3 is satisfied for ψ_σ because no subset of ψ_σ

satisfies AC1 and AC2. Finally, OC1 checks for all events whether their order is causal or not. If their order is not causal the ∧ operator is replaced by the ∧ operator. In our example, the order of the events Gf, Cc, ¬Cl, Tc is causal since only if the gate fails before the car and the train are entering the crossing, and the car does not leave the crossing before the train is entering the crossing an accident happens. Consequently after OC1 we obtain the EOL formula ψ_σ = (Ta ∧ (Ca ⩓ Cc)) ∧$_<$ ¬Cl ∧$_>$ (Gc ∧ Tc). The disjunction of all $\psi_{\sigma_1}, \psi_{\sigma_2}, ..., \psi_{\sigma_n}$ that satisfy the conditions AC1-AC3 and OC1 is the EOL formula describing all possible causes of the hazard. For the railroad crossing example the EOL formula returned by the causality checker is ψ = (Gf ∧ ((Ta ∧ (Ca ⩓ Cc)) ∧$_<$ ¬Cl ∧$_>$ Tc)) ∨ ((Ta ∧ (Ca ⩓ Cc)) ∧$_<$ ¬Cl ∧$_>$ (Gc ∧ Tc)).

Probabilistic Causality Computation. In order to apply the probabilistic causality computation described in [22] to a PRISM model all traces in the counterexample as well as all good execution traces first need to be computed. We use the DiPro tool [3] for this step. The causality computation is subsequently performed by checking conditions AC1-AC3 and OC1 for all bad traces. Once the causality computation is completed, the probabilities of the execution traces in the probabilistic counterexample are assigned to the disjuncts of the EOL formula generated by the causality computation. The resulting EOL formula is then mapped onto a Fault Tree.

Causality Checking [26]. The algorithms used for causality checking are integrated into the state-space exploration algorithms commonly used in explicit-state model checking. The state space of the model is traversed using breadth-first or depth-first search. Whenever a bad trace violating the property or a good trace not entailing a property violation is found, this trace is added to a data structure called sub-set graph. The conditions AC1-AC3 and OC1 are reduced to sub-execution test. Whether a combination of events is causal or not can be determined based on its position in the sub-set graph. This allows for an on the fly decision whether a good trace needs to be stored for later perusal by the AC2(2) test, or whether it can be discarded.

2.5   Alternating Automata

In this paper we translate EOL formulas generated by the causality checker into alternating automata on finite words [10,33]. Alternating automata are a generalization of nondeterministic automata in which choices along a path can be marked as either existential, which indicates that some branch has to reach an accepting state, or as universal, which means that all branches have to reach an accepting state. We use the definition of alternating automata from [15]. We note that this definition differs from the definitions in [10,33] in that the automata are not defined with input symbols labeling the edges, but with input symbols labeling the nodes instead.

Definition 3. *Alternating Automaton. An alternating automaton A is defined recursively as follows:*
$A ::= \epsilon_A \quad$ *(empty automaton)*
$\quad | \ \langle v, \delta, f \rangle \ $ *(single node)*
$\quad | \ A_1 \wedge A_2 $ *(conjunction of two automata)*
$\quad | \ A_1 \vee A_2 $ *(disjunction of two automata)*

where v is a state formula, δ is an alternating automaton expressing the next-state relation, and f indicates whether the node is accepting (denoted by $+$) or rejecting ($-$). We require the automaton be finite. The set of nodes of an automaton A, denoted by $\mathcal{N}(A)$ is formally defined as
$\mathcal{N}(\epsilon_A) \qquad = \varnothing$
$\mathcal{N}(\langle v, \delta, f \rangle) = \langle v, \delta, f \rangle \cup \mathcal{N}(\delta)$
$\mathcal{N}(A_1 \wedge A_2) = \mathcal{N}(A_1) \cup \mathcal{N}(A_2)$
$\mathcal{N}(A_1 \vee A_2) = \mathcal{N}(A_1) \cup \mathcal{N}(A_2)$

A path through a nondeterministic automaton is a sequence of nodes. A "path" through an alternating automaton is, in general, a tree.

Definition 4. *Tree. A tree is defined recursively as follows:*
$T ::= \epsilon_T \qquad$ *(empty tree)*
$\quad | \ T \cdot T \qquad$ *(composition)*
$\quad | \ \langle \langle v, \delta, f \rangle, T \rangle$ *(single node with child tree)*

Definition 5. *Run of an Alternating Automaton. Given a finite sequence of states $\sigma = s_0, ..., s_{n-1}$ and an automaton A, a tree T is called a run of σ in A if one of the following conditions holds:*
$A = \epsilon_A \qquad\qquad$ *and* $\quad T = \epsilon_T$
$A = \langle v, \delta, f \rangle \quad$ *and* $\quad n > 1, \ T = \langle \langle v, \delta, f \rangle, T' \rangle, \ s_0 \vDash v \ $ and T' is a run of $s_1, ..., s_{n-1}$
$\qquad\qquad\qquad\qquad$ in δ, or $n = 1$, $T = \langle \langle v, \delta, f \rangle, \epsilon_T \rangle$ and $s_0 \vDash v$
$A = A_1 \wedge A_2 \quad$ *and* $\quad T = T_1 \cdot T_2$, where T_1 is a run of A_1 and T_2 is a run of A_2
$A = A_1 \vee A_2 \quad$ *and* $\quad T$ is a run of A_1 or T is a run of A_2

Definition 6. *Accepting Run. A run is accepting if every path through the tree ends in an accepting node.*

For each alternating automaton A there exists a nondeterministic finite automaton A_n such that $L(A_n) = L(A)$, which was shown in [10,9,33].

3   Translating PRISM Models to Promela Models

Our goal is to compute causal events in a first step using the non-probabilistic causality checking approach. We then limit the probability computation in the second step to the causal events events computed in the first step. To achieve this goal we need to translate the model given by a continuous-time Markov chain (CTMC) [21] specified in the PRISM language to a labeled transition system in the Promela language [20]. The translation is necessary since the causality checking approach is based on the SpinJa toolset [13] which uses Promela as its input language.

The reachability property describing the hazard is specified in Continuous Stochastic Logic (CSL) [1,5]. This CSL formula needs to be translated into a formula in linear temporal logic [29]. This translation is straight forward: If the CSL formula is a state formula, then it is also an LTL formula. If the CSL formula is a path formula, then the path formula is an LTL formula if we replace a bounded-until operator included in the formula with an unbounded LTL until operator. For the time being we do not support CSL formulas containing nested path-operators.

We base our translation of PRISM models to Promela models on work described in [31]. Since no implementation of the described approach is available and the approach translates Markov Decision Processes specified in PRISM to a Promela model we need to provide an adopted translation method. In addition, the translation proposed in [31] maps synchronizing action labels to rendezvous channel chaining in Promela which is not consistent with the PRISM semantics specified in [19]. Our translation algorithm maps the CTMC to a labeled transition system.

Definition 7. *Labeled Continuous-time Markov Chain (CTMC) [21]. A labeled Continuous-time Markov Chain C is a tuple $(\mathcal{S}, s_0, \mathcal{R}, \mathcal{L})$, where $\mathcal{S}$ is a finite set of states, $s_0 \in \mathcal{S}$ is the initial state, $\mathcal{R} : \mathcal{S} \times \mathcal{S} \to \mathbb{R}_{\geq 0}$ is a transition rate matrix and $\mathcal{L} : \mathcal{S} \to 2^{AP}$ is a labeling function, which assigns to each state a subset of the set of atomic propositions AP.*

Definition 8. *Labeled Transition System [6]. A transition system TS is a tuple $(S, Act, \to, I, AP, L)$ where S is a finite set of states, Act is a finite set of actions, $\to \subseteq S \times Act \times S$ is a transition relation, $I \subseteq S$ is a set of initial states, AP is a set of atomic propositions, and $L : S \to 2^{AP}$ is a labeling function.*

Definition 9. *Transition System Induced by a CTMC. Let $C = (\mathcal{S}, s_0, \mathcal{R}, \mathcal{L})$ a CTMC then $T = (S, Act, \to, I, AP, L)$ is the transition system induced by C if: The set S of states in T is $S = \mathcal{S}$, the set I of initial states in T is $I = \{s_0\}$, and for all pairs $s, s' \in S$ we add a transition to $\to$ and a corresponding action to Act if $\mathcal{R}(s, s') > 0$.*

We translate the transition system induced by the CTMC into Promela. PRISM *modules* are translated to *active proctypes* in Promela consisting of a *do*-block which contains the transitions. Transitions that are synchronized are translated according to the parallel composition semantics of PRISM [19]. All variables in the PRISM model are translated to global variables of the corresponding type in the Promela model. This permits reading variables from other proctypes, as permitted in PRISM. Listing 1.2 shows the output of the PRISM to Promela translation of the PRISM code in Listing 1.1 from Section 2.2. The comments at the end of each transition are merely added to make the Promela model more readable but are not necessary for the translation.

Our approach requires that each command in the PRISM module is labeled with an action label representing the occurrence of an event. If a command of the PRISM model is not already labeled with an action label a unique action label is added to this command during the translation. This does not change the

```
bool var1 = false; byte var2 = 0; byte var3 = 0;
active proctype moduleA(){
  do
  :: atomic {((var3<2) && (var2<4)) -> var2=var2+1; var3=var3+1;}/*Count*/
  :: atomic {((var3==2) && (var2<4)) -> var2=var2+1; var3=0;}/*Count*/
  :: atomic {(var2==4) -> var1=true;}/*End*/
  od;}
active proctype moduleB(){
  do
  :: atomic {((var2<4) && (var3<2)) -> var3=var3+1; var2=var2+1;}/*Count*/
  :: atomic {((var2<4) && (var3==2)) -> var3=0; var2=var2+1;}/*Count*/
  od;}
```

Listing 1.2. Example Promela translation of the PRISM model from Section 2.2.

behavior of the PRISM model since the action label is unique and consequently is not synchronized with any other command.

After translating the PRISM model to Promela, qualitative causality checking can be performed. The results of this step can them be used to perform the probability computation, as described in Section 4.

4   Computing Probabilities for Causal Events

For the railroad crossing example from Section 2.3, the EOL formula returned by the causality checker is $\psi = (\mathrm{Gf} \wedge ((\mathrm{Ta} \wedge (\mathrm{Ca} \wedge \mathrm{Cc})) \wedge_< \neg \mathrm{Cl} \wedge_> \mathrm{Tc})) \vee ((\mathrm{Ta} \wedge (\mathrm{Ca} \wedge \mathrm{Cc})) \wedge_< \neg \mathrm{Cl} \wedge_> (\mathrm{Gc} \wedge \mathrm{Tc}))$. Intuitively, each disjunct of this formula represents a class of execution traces on which the events specified by the EOL formula cause the violation of the property.

In the rail road crossing example there are two classes of execution traces on which the hazard occurs.

1. If the gate fails (Gf) at some point of the execution and a train (Ta) and a car (Ca) are approaching, this results in a hazardous situation if the car is on the crossing (Cc) and does not leave the crossing (Cl) before the train (Tc) enters the crossing: $(\mathrm{Gf} \wedge ((\mathrm{Ta} \wedge (\mathrm{Ca} \wedge \mathrm{Cc})) \wedge_< \neg \mathrm{Cl} \wedge_> \mathrm{Tc}))$.
2. If a train (Ta) and a car (Ca) are approaching but the gate closes (Gc) when the car (Cc) is already on the railway crossing and is not able to leave (Cl) before the gate is closing and the train is crossing (Tc), this also corresponds to a hazardous situation: $((\mathrm{Ta} \wedge (\mathrm{Ca} \wedge \mathrm{Cc})) \wedge_< \neg \mathrm{Cl} \wedge_> (\mathrm{Gc} \wedge \mathrm{Tc}))$.

For instance, the execution traces $\sigma = \mathrm{Ca}, \mathrm{Ta}, \mathrm{Gf}, \mathrm{Cc}, \mathrm{Tc}$ and $\sigma' = \mathrm{Ca}, \mathrm{Ta}, \mathrm{Gc}, \mathrm{Tc}$, $\mathrm{Tl}, \mathrm{Go}, \mathrm{Ta}, \mathrm{Gf}, \mathrm{Cc}, \mathrm{Tc}$ are traces that belong to the first class of traces. The trace $\sigma'' = \mathrm{Ca}, \mathrm{Ta}, \mathrm{Cc}, \mathrm{Gc}, \mathrm{Tc}$ is an example for a trace in the second class.

We now formalize the observation that each disjunct of the EOL formula represents a class of traces by the notion of causality classes.

Definition 10. *Causality Class. Let* $T = (S, Act, \rightarrow, I, AP, L)$ *a transition system and* $\sigma = s_0, \alpha_1, s_1, \alpha_2, \dots \alpha_n, s_n$ *a finite execution trace of* T. *The set* Σ_B *is the set of traces for which some LTL property* φ *is violated. The causality classes* $CC_1, \dots, CC_n$ *defined by the disjuncts of the EOL formula* $\psi = \psi_1 \vee \dots \vee \psi_n$ *decompose the set* Σ_B *into sets* $\Sigma_{B_{\psi_1}}, \dots, \Sigma_{B_{\psi_n}}$ *with* $\Sigma_{B_{\psi_1}} \cup \dots \cup \Sigma_{B_{\psi_n}} = \Sigma_B$.

Note that it can be the case that $\sigma \in \Sigma_{B_{\psi_1}} \wedge \sigma \in \Sigma_{B_{\psi_2}}$ if $\sigma \vDash_e \psi_1 \wedge \sigma \vDash_e \psi_2$.

All causal information that is needed in order to debug the system is represented by the causality classes that we compute. We can leverage this fact and compute the probability sum of all traces represented by a causality class instead of computing the probability of all traces belonging to this class individually. This means that the number of probabilistic model checking runs is reduced to the number of causality classes instead of the number of traces in the counterexample.

We will now show how the probability sum of all traces represented by a causality class can be computed using the PRISM model checker [23]. In order to compute the probability of all traces represented by a causality class we translate the EOL formula representing the causality class to an automaton which accepts exactly those execution traces that are represented by the corresponding causality class. Subsequently we show how we can synchronize the execution of this automaton with a PRISM model, such that the probability of all sequences which are accepted by the automaton is the probability sum of all traces represented by the corresponding causality class.

Note that since causality checking is limited to reachability properties, a nondeterministic finite automaton (NFA) is sufficient to represent the finite execution traces represented by the causality class [6]. Since all orders of the events characterizing the causality class need to be considered, the size of the resulting NFA can be exponential in the size of the formula. To prevent this we use alternating automata on finite words [10,33] as defined in Section 2.5.

Given an EOL formula ψ we can construct an alternating automaton $A(\psi)$ such that $L(A(\psi)) = L(\psi)$. The construction of the automaton is by structural induction over the syntax of an EOL formula.

Definition 11. *Alternating Automaton for an EOL formula. Let ψ an EOL formula that is built over the set of event variables $a \in \mathcal{A}$. The automaton $A(\psi)$ for the EOL formula ψ can be constructed recursively following the structure of the formula as follows: For an event variable a: $A(a) = \langle a, \epsilon_A, + \rangle$, and for EOL formulas ψ_1, ψ_2 and ϕ_1:*

$$
\begin{aligned}
A(\psi_1 \wedge \psi_2) \quad &= A(\psi_1) \wedge A(\psi_2) \\
A(\psi_1 \vee \psi_2) \quad &= A(\psi_1) \vee A(\psi_2) \\
A(\psi_1 \wedge \psi_2) \quad &= \langle true, A(\psi_1 \wedge \psi_2), - \rangle \vee A_1 \quad where\ A_1 = A(\psi_1) \wedge A_2 \\
&\quad and\ A_2 = \langle true, A_2, - \rangle \vee A(\psi_2) \\
A(\phi_1 \wedge_] \psi_1) \quad &= A(\psi_1) \vee (\langle true, A(\phi_1 \wedge_] \psi_1), - \rangle \wedge A(\phi_1)) \\
A(\psi_1 \wedge_< \phi_1 \wedge_> \psi_2) &= \langle true, A(\psi_1 \wedge_< \phi_1 \wedge_> \psi_2), - \rangle \vee (A(\psi_1) \\
&\quad \wedge(\langle true, A(\psi_1 \wedge_< \phi_1 \wedge_> \psi_2), - \rangle \vee \langle true, A(\phi_1 \wedge_] \psi_2), - \rangle)))
\end{aligned}
$$

Note that since we consider only reachability properties, it can not be the case that an event voiding causality appears at the end of an execution trace. The EOL operator $\wedge_[$ can hence not be added to an EOL formula as a consequence of AC2(2) and consequently we do not specify a translation rule for this operator. Notice that the only way for a $\neg$ operator to be added to an EOL formula by the causality checking algorithm is when the non-occurrence of the negated event in the specified interval is causal. To illustrate the proposed translation consider that for the EOL formula $\psi = (\text{Ta} \wedge (\text{Ca} \wedge \text{Cc})) \wedge_< \neg\text{Cl} \wedge_> (\text{Gc} \wedge \text{Tc})$ of the railroad crossing example the first application of the recursive definition creates the following rewriting: $A(\psi) = \langle true, A((\text{Ta} \wedge (\text{Ca} \wedge \text{Cc})) \wedge_< \neg\text{Cl} \wedge_> (\text{Gc} \wedge \text{Tc})), -\rangle \vee (A((\text{Ta} \wedge (\text{Ca} \wedge \text{Cc}))) \wedge (\langle true, A((\text{Ta} \wedge (\text{Ca} \wedge \text{Cc})) \wedge_< \neg\text{Cl} \wedge_> (\text{Gc} \wedge \text{Tc})), -\rangle \vee \langle true, A(\neg\text{Cl} \wedge_] (\text{Gc} \wedge \text{Tc})), -\rangle))$.

In order to compute the probability of a causality class we need to translate the corresponding alternating automaton into the PRISM language and synchronize it with the PRISM model. Each action label in the PRISM model corresponds to an event variable in the set $\mathcal{A}$ over which the EOL formulas were built. As a consequence, each alternating automaton accepts a sequence of PRISM action labels.

We will now define translation rules from alternating automata to PRISM modules. We call a PRISM module that was generated from an alternating automaton a *causality class module*. The transitions of the causality class modules are synchronized with the corresponding transitions of the PRISM model. The transition rates of the causality class modules are set to 1.0, as a consequence, the transitions synchronizing with the causality class modules define the rate for the synchronized transition. In Listing 1.3 we present the pseudo-code of the algorithm that generates a causality class module from an alternating automaton representing an EOL formula.

The key idea is that for each event we add a boolean variable representing the occurrence of the event and a transition labeled with the action label of the event. The order constraints specified by the EOL formula are encoded by guards. Synchronized transitions can only be executed if for each other module containing transitions with the same action label the guard of at least one transition per module evaluates to true. It might hence be the case that the causality class module prevents the execution of transitions in the PRISM model with which the causality class module is synchronized. Since this would change the behavior of the PRISM model and affect the probability mass distribution, we add for each transition of the causality class module for which the guard is not always true a transition with the negated guard and without updates.

A PRISM *formula* acc_ψ, which is true whenever the corresponding sub-automaton is accepting the input word, is added for each sub-automaton. These formulas are used to construct a CSL formula of the form $P_{=?}[(true)U(\text{acc\_}\psi)]$ for each causality class. The CSL formulas can then be used to compute the probability of all possible sequences that are accepted by the causality class module, which is the probability sum of all traces that are represented by the causality class. Since it its possible that a trace belongs to more than one causality class, we add an additional CSL formula that computes the probability of all traces that are only in the causality class defined by ψ. This CSL formula has the form of $P_{=?}[(true)U(\text{acc\_}\psi)\&!(\text{acc\_}\psi_i|...|\text{acc\_}\psi_j))]$, where acc_$\psi_i$|...|acc_$\psi_j$ are the formulas of all causality classes except ψ.

```
global var var_def = "", trans = "", formulas = "";
function EOL_TO_PRISM(A(ψ)){
  PRISM_CODE(A(ψ),true)
  print "module ψ \n" + var_def +"\n"+ trans
      + " \n endmodule \n" + formulas; }
function PRISM_CODE(A(ψ), cond){
  IF A(ψ) = 'A(a)' THEN
    var_def += 's_ψ: bool init false;'
    IF cond = 'true' THEN
      trans += '[a] (cond) -> 1.0 : (s_ψ'=true);'
    ELSE
      trans += '[a] (cond) -> 1.0 : (s_ψ'=true);'
      trans += '[a] !(cond) -> 1.0 : true;'
    ENDIF
    formulas += 'formula acc_ψ = s_ψ;'
  ELSE IF A(ψ) = 'A(ψ1) ∧ A(ψ2)' THEN
    PRISM_CODE(A(ψ1), cond); PRISM_CODE(A(ψ2), cond);
    formulas += 'formula acc_ψ = acc_ψ1 & acc_ψ2;'
  ELSE IF A(ψ) = 'A(ψ1 ∧ ψ2)' THEN
    PRISM_CODE(A(ψ1), cond); PRISM_CODE(A(ψ2), cond);
    formulas += 'formula acc_ψ = acc_ψ1 & acc_ψ2;'
  ELSE IF A(ψ) = 'A(ψ1 ∨ ψ2)' THEN
    PRISM_CODE(A(ψ1), cond); PRISM_CODE(A(ψ2), cond)
    formulas += 'formula acc_ψ = acc_ψ1 | acc_ψ2;'
  ELSE IF A(ψ) = 'A(ψ1) ∨ A(ψ2)' THEN
    PRISM_CODE(A(ψ1), cond); PRISM_CODE(A(ψ2), cond);
    formulas += 'formula acc_ψ = acc_ψ1 | acc_ψ2;'
  ELSE IF A(ψ) = 'A(ψ1 ∧ ψ2)' THEN
    PRISM_CODE(A(ψ1), cond); PRISM_CODE(A(ψ2), acc_ψ1);
    formulas += formula acc_ψ = acc_ψ2;
  ELSE IF A(ψ) = 'A(φ1 ∧] ψ1)' THEN
    PRISM_CODE(A(¬φ1), cond); PRISM_CODE(A(ψ1), cond & !(acc_¬φ1));
    formulas += 'formula acc_ψ = acc_ψ1;'
  ELSE IF A(ψ) = 'A(ψ1 ∧< φ1 ∧> ψ2)' THEN
    PRISM_CODE(A(ψ1), cond); PRISM_CODE(A(¬φ1), acc_ψ1)
    PRISM_CODE(A(ψ2), (acc_ψ1 & !(acc_¬φ1))
    formulas += 'formula acc_ψ = acc_ψ2;'
  ENDIF }
```

Listing 1.3. Pseudo-code of the EOL to PRISM algorithm.

Due to space restrictions we can not show the causality class modules that are generated for the railroad crossing example here, they can be found in [27].

In the railroad example the total probability of a state where both the train and the car are on the crossing is p_total $= 2.312 \cdot 10^{-4}$. The proposed combined approach returns for the causality class characterized by $\psi_1 = \mathrm{Gf} \wedge ((\mathrm{Ta} \wedge (\mathrm{Ca} \wedge \mathrm{Cc})) \wedge_< \neg \mathrm{Cl} \wedge_> \mathrm{Tc})$ the total probability of $p_{\psi_1} = 4.386 \cdot 10^{-5}$ and the exclusive probability of $p_{\psi_1}\_\mathrm{excl} = 3.464 \cdot 10^{-5}$. For the causality class characterized by $\psi_2 = (\mathrm{Ta} \wedge (\mathrm{Ca} \wedge \mathrm{Cc})) \wedge_< \neg \mathrm{Cl} \wedge_> (\mathrm{Gc} \wedge \mathrm{Tc})$ the total probability is computed as $p_{\psi_2} = 1.970 \cdot 10^{-4}$, and the exclusive probability as $p_{\psi_2}\_\mathrm{excl} = 1.914 \cdot 10^{-4}$. We use the EOL to fault tree mapping proposed in [22] to visualize this results as a fault tree.

5   Experimental Evaluation

In order to evaluate the proposed *combined approach*, we have extended the SpinCause tool. SpinCause is based on the SpinJa toolset [13], a Java re-implementation of the explicit state model checker Spin [20]. The following experiments were performed on a PC with an Intel Xeon Processor (3.60 Ghz) and 144 GBs of RAM. We evaluate the combined approach on a case study from the PRISM benchmark suite [24] and two industrial case studies [2,7] for which the PRISM models where automatically generated by the QuantUM tool [25] from a higher-level architectural modeling language. The extended SpinCause tool and the PRISM models used in this paper can be obtained from http://se.uni-konstanz.de/research1/tools/spincause.

5.1   Case Studies

Embedded Control System [30]. The PRISM model of the embedded control system is part of the PRISM benchmark suite [24]. The system consists of a main processor, an input processor, an output processor, 3 sensors, and two actuators. Various failure modes can lead to a shutdown of the system. We are interested in computing the causal events for an event of the type "system shut down within one hour". Since one second is the basic time unit in our system one hour corresponds to a mission time of T=3,600 time units. The formalization of this property in CSL reads as $P_{=?}(true\ U^{\leq T}\ down)$. We set the constant MAX_COUNT, which represents the maximum number of processing failures that are tolerated by the main processor, to a value of 5.

Airbag System [2]. This case study models an industrial size airbag system. It contains a behavioral description of all system components that are involved in deciding whether a crash has occurred. It is a pivotal safety requirement that an airbag is never deployed if there is no crash situation. We are interested in computing the causal events for an inadvertent deployment of the airbag. In CSL, this property can be expressed using the formula $P_{=?}(noCrash\ U^{\leq T}\ AirbagIgnited)$. The causality checker returns 5 causality classes. The total probability for an inadvertent deployment of the airbag within T=100 computed by the combined approach is p_total = 0.228.

Train Odometer Controller [7]. The train odometer system consists of two independent sensors used to measure the speed and the position of a train. A monitor component continuously checks the status of both sensors. It reports failures of the sensors to other train components that have to disregard temporarily erroneous sensor data. If both sensors fail, the monitor initiates an emergency brake maneuver and the system is brought into a safe state. Only if the monitor fails, any subsequent faults in the sensors will no longer be detected. We are interested in computing the causal events for reaching an unsafe state of the system. This can be expressed by the CSL formula $P_{=?}[(true)U^{<=T}(unsafe)]$.

5.2   Discussion

As we would expect, for all case studies the total probability returned by the combined approach is equal to the probability returned for the respective probabilistic property by PRISM after a probabilistic model checking run. If we sum up the probabilities of the traces computed by DiPro for each causality class and only consider traces that belong to exactly one causality class, then the sum of the probability of each causality class is equal to the corresponding p_ψ_excl value of that causality class computed by the combined approach. If, on the other hand, we sum up the probabilities of of the traces computed by DiPro for each causality class and also consider the probability mass of traces that belong to more than one causality class, then the sum of each causality class is equal to the corresponding p_ψ value of that causality class computed by the combined

Table 1. This table shows the experiment results with the combined approach and the probabilistic causality computation approach

	Combined Approach		Probabilistic Causality Comp.	
	Run time (sec.)	Memory (MB)	Run time (sec.)	Memory (MB)
Embedded: States: 6,013 Transitions: 25,340				
T=10	3.06	19.27	2,003.00	409
T=3600	4.79	19.29	2,102.00	409
Airbag: States: 2,952 Transitions: 14,049				
T=10	10.88	52.44	682.00	154
T=1000	33.63	52.44	874.00	154
Train Odometer Controller: States: 117,222 Transitions: 66,262				
T=10	91.37	195.29	16,191.00	1,886
T=1000	2,572.74	195.29	44,356.00	1,886

approach. These observations make us confident that the combined approach computes correct probabilities.

Table 1 shows the run time and memory consumption of the combined approach and the probabilistic causality computation approach for each of the case studies. The runtime and memory values for the combined approach include the runtime and memory needed for all steps of the approach, namely translation from PRISM to Promela, causality checking, alternating automata derivation and mapping to PRISM, and the PRISM model checking. The combined approach consumes significantly less run time and memory than the probabilistic causality computation approach. This difference can be explained by the fact that for the probabilistic causality approach the probability of each traces in the counterexample needs to be computed individually, which requires a probabilistic model checking of a part of the model for each trace. The combined approach reduces the number of probabilistic model checking runs to the number of the computed causality classes. The run time of the combined approach increases with the mission time T because the time needed by the PRISM model checker to compute the probability for the different causality classes increases with an increasing T. The relatively low runtime that is needed by the combined approach for the embedded case study as compared to the other case studies can be explained by the relatively short length of the traces in the causality classes of the embedded case study.

6 Related Work

A translation from Markov decision processes (MDPs) into the PRISM language has been proposed in [31], but no implementation of the tool is publicly available. Furthermore, the proposed translation of synchronizing action labels to rendezvous channel chaining in Promela is not consistent with the PRISM semantics specified in [19].

In [8], a formalization of the semantics of dynamic fault trees (DFTs) [14] and a probabilistic analysis framework for DFTs based on interactive Markov chains [18] is presented. The approach in [8] takes the DFT as the only input. As a consequence, while this approach allows for a probabilistic analysis of the events in the DFT, there is no possibility to combine the analysis with a model containing the events of the DFT.

The approach of [7] computes minimal-cut sets, which are minimal combinations of events that are causal for a property violation, and their corresponding probabilities. Our approach extends and improves this approach by considering the event order as a causal factor. Work in [17] documents how probabilistic counterexamples for discrete-time Markov chains (DTMCs) can be represented by regular expressions. While the regular expressions define an equivalence class for some traces in the counterexample, it is possible that not all possible traces are represented by the regular expression and consequently not all causal event combinations are captured by the regular expression. In [4,34] probabilistic counterexamples are represented by identifying a portion of an analyzed Markov chain in which the probability to reach a safety-critical state exceeds the probability bound specified by an upper-bounded reachability property. The method proposed in this paper improves these approaches by identifying not only a portion of the Markov chain, but all event combinations and their corresponding order. Furthermore, the approach presented in [34] is applicable to DTMCs and MDPs, whereas our approach is applicable to CTMCs. In addition none of the approaches in [7,17,4,34] is able to reveal that the non-occurrence of an event is causal.

To the best of our knowledge there is no approach in the literature that combines qualitative causality reasoning with probabilistic causality computation.

7   Conclusion

We have discussed how the qualitative causality checking approach can be leveraged in order to improve the scalability of the probabilistic causality computation approach. Furthermore, we have proposed and implemented a mapping of CTMC models in the PRISM language to transition systems in the Promela language. In addition, we have shown how an EOL formula generated by the qualitative causality checking approach can be translated into an equivalent alternating automaton, and how the resulting alternating automaton can be translated to a causality class module in the PRISM language. The resulting causality class module can then be used to compute the probability sum of all traces represented by the causality class. We have demonstrated the performance increase of the proposed synergy approach compared to the probabilistic causality computation on several case studies from academia and industry.

In future work we plan to extend the combined approach to support DTMC and MDPs models and to implement a version of the causality checking approach that works directly on the probabilistic model.

References

1. Aziz, A., Sanwal, K., Singhal, V., Brayton, R.K.: Verifying Continuous-Time Markov Chains. In: Alur, R., Henzinger, T.A. (eds.) CAV 1996. LNCS, vol. 1102, pp. 269–276. Springer, Heidelberg (1996)
2. Aljazzar, H., Fischer, M., Grunske, L., Kuntz, M., Leitner-Fischer, F., Leue, S.: Safety Analysis of an Airbag System Using Probabilistic FMEA and Probabilistic Counterexamples. In: Proc. of QEST 2009. IEEE Computer Society (2009)
3. Aljazzar, H., Leitner-Fischer, F., Leue, S., Simeonov, D.: DiPro - A tool for probabilistic counterexample generation. In: Groce, A., Musuvathi, M. (eds.) SPIN Workshops 2011. LNCS, vol. 6823, pp. 183–187. Springer, Heidelberg (2011)
4. Aljazzar, H., Leue, S.: Directed explicit state-space search in the generation of counterexamples for stochastic model checking. IEEE Trans. Soft. Eng. (2009)
5. Baier, C., Haverkort, B., Hermanns, H., Katoen, J.-P.: Model-checking algorithms for continuous-time Markov chains. IEEE Trans. Soft. Eng. (2003)
6. Baier, C., Katoen, J.-P.: Principles of Model Checking. The MIT Press (2008)
7. Böde, E., Peikenkamp, T., Rakow, J., Wischmeyer, S.: Model Based Importance Analysis for Minimal Cut Sets. In: Cha, S(S.), Choi, J.-Y., Kim, M., Lee, I., Viswanathan, M. (eds.) ATVA 2008. LNCS, vol. 5311, pp. 303–317. Springer, Heidelberg (2008)
8. Boudali, H., Crouzen, P., Stoelinga, M.: A rigorous, compositional, and extensible framework for dynamic fault tree analysis. IEEE Transactions on Dependable and Secure Computing 7(2), 128–143 (2010)
9. Brzozowski, J.A., Leiss, E.: On equations for regular languages, finite automata, and sequential networks. Theoretical Computer Science 10(1), 19–35 (1980)
10. Chandra, A.K., Stockmeyer, L.J.: Alternation. In: 17th Annual Symposium on Foundations of Computer Science, pp. 98–108. IEEE (1976)
11. Clarke, E.M., Grumberg, O., Peled, D.A.: Model Checking, 3rd edn. The MIT Press (2001)
12. Collins, J. (ed.): Causation and Counterfactuals. MIT Press (2004)
13. de Jonge, M., Ruys, T.C.: The SPINJA model checker. In: van de Pol, J., Weber, M. (eds.) Model Checking Software. LNCS, vol. 6349, pp. 124–128. Springer, Heidelberg (2010)
14. Dugan, J., Bavuso, S., Boyd, M.: Dynamic Fault Tree Models for Fault Tolerant Computer Systems. IEEE Trans. Reliability (1992)
15. Finkbeiner, B., Sipma, H.: Checking finite traces using alternating automata. Formal Methods in System Design 24(2), 101–127 (2004)
16. Halpern, J., Pearl, J.: Causes and explanations: A structural-model approach. Part I: Causes. The British Journal for the Phil. of Science (2005)
17. Han, T., Katoen, J.-P., Damman, B.: Counterexample generation in probabilistic model checking. IEEE Trans. Softw. Eng. (2009)
18. Hermanns, H. (ed.): Interactive Markov Chains. LNCS, vol. 2428. Springer, Heidelberg (2002)
19. Hinton, A., Kwiatkowska, M., Norman, G., Parker, D.: The prism language - semantics, http://www.prismmodelchecker.org/doc/semantics.pdf
20. Holzmann, G.J.: The SPIN Model Checker: Primer and Reference Manual. Addison–Wesley (2003)
21. Kulkarni, V.: Modeling and analysis of stochastic systems. Chapman & Hall/CRC (1995)

22. Kuntz, M., Leitner-Fischer, F., Leue, S.: From probabilistic counterexamples via causality to fault trees. In: Flammini, F., Bologna, S., Vittorini, V. (eds.) SAFECOMP 2011. LNCS, vol. 6894, pp. 71–84. Springer, Heidelberg (2011)
23. Kwiatkowska, M., Norman, G., Parker, D.: PRISM 4.0: Verification of probabilistic real-time systems. In: Gopalakrishnan, G., Qadeer, S. (eds.) CAV 2011. LNCS, vol. 6806, pp. 585–591. Springer, Heidelberg (2011)
24. Kwiatkowska, M., Norman, G., Parker, D.: The PRISM benchmark suite. In: Proc. 9th International Conference on Quantitative Evaluation of SysTems (QEST 2012), pp. 203–204. IEEE CS Press (2012)
25. Leitner-Fischer, F., Leue, S.: QuantUM: Quantitative safety analysis of UML models. In: Proc. of the 9th Workshop on Quantitative Aspects of Programming Languages (QAPL 2011) (2011)
26. Leitner-Fischer, F., Leue, S.: Causality checking for complex system models. In: Giacobazzi, R., Berdine, J., Mastroeni, I. (eds.) VMCAI 2013. LNCS, vol. 7737, pp. 248–267. Springer, Heidelberg (2013)
27. Leitner-Fischer, F., Leue, S.: On the synergy of probabilistic causality computation and causality checking. Technical Report soft-13-01, Chair for Software Engineering, University of Konstanz (2013), http://www.inf.uni-konstanz.de/soft/research/publications/pdf/soft-13-01.pdf
28. Lewis, D.: Counterfactuals. Wiley-Blackwell (2001)
29. Manna, Z., Pnueli, A.: The temporal logic of reactive and concurrent systems. Springer-Verlag New York, Inc. (1992)
30. Muppala, J., Ciardo, G., Trivedi, K.: Stochastic reward nets for reliability prediction. Communications in Reliability, Maintainability and Serviceability 1(2), 9–20 (1994)
31. Power, C., Miller, A.: Prism2promela. In: Fifth International Conference on Quantitative Evaluation of Systems, QEST 2008, pp. 79–80. IEEE (2008)
32. U.S. Nuclear Regulatory Commission. Fault Tree Handbook (1981)
33. Vardi, M.Y.: An automata-theoretic approach to linear temporal logic. In: Moller, F., Birtwistle, G. (eds.) Logics for Concurrency. LNCS, vol. 1043, pp. 238–266. Springer, Heidelberg (1996)
34. Wimmer, R., Jansen, N., Ábrahám, E., Becker, B., Katoen, J.-P.: Minimal critical subsystems for discrete-time markov models. In: Flanagan, C., König, B. (eds.) TACAS 2012. LNCS, vol. 7214, pp. 299–314. Springer, Heidelberg (2012)

Mining Sequential Patterns to Explain Concurrent Counterexamples*

Stefan Leue[1] and Mitra Tabaei Befrouei[2]

[1] University of Konstanz
Stefan.Leue@uni-konstanz.de
[2] Vienna University of Technology
Tabaei@forsyte.at

Abstract. Concurrent systems are often modeled using an interleaving semantics. Since system designers tend to think sequentially, it is highly probable that they do not foresee some interleavings that their model encompasses. As a consequence, one of the main sources of failure in concurrent systems is unforeseen interleavings. In this paper, we devise an automated method for revealing unforeseen interleavings in the form of sequences of actions derived from counterexamples obtained by explicit state model checking. In order to extract such sequences we use a data mining technique called *sequential pattern mining*. Our method is based on contrasting the patterns of a set of counterexamples with the patterns of a set of correct traces that do not violate a desired property. We first argue that mining sequential patterns from the dataset of counterexamples fails due to the inherent complexity of the problem. We then propose a reduction technique designed to reduce the length of the execution traces in order to make the problem more tractable. We finally demonstrate the effectiveness of our approach by applying it to a number of sample case studies.

Keywords: concurrency bugs, counterexample explanation, sequential pattern mining, model checking.

1 Introduction

Concurrency bugs are among the most difficult software bugs to detect and diagnose. This is mainly due to the inherent inability of humans to comprehend concurrently executing computations and to foresee the possible interleavings that they can entail. The interleaving semantics commonly used to interpret the computation of concurrent systems imposes a total order on the execution of concurrent actions in a system. Concurrency is then interpreted as non-deterministic choices between different interleavings. System designers are used to thinking

---

* Supported by the Austrian National Research Network S11403-N23 (RiSE) of the Austrian Science Fund (FWF), by Deutsche Forschungsgemeinschaft (DFG) through the grants "DiRePro" and "IMCOS" and by the Vienna Science and Technology Fund (WWTF) through grants VRG11-005, PROSEED, and ICT12-059.

E. Bartocci and C.R. Ramakrishnan (Eds.): SPIN 2013, LNCS 7976, pp. 264–281, 2013.

sequentially when designing the model of a system. In concurrent systems it is therefore highly probable that they do not foresee some interleavings that their model encompasses. It is therefore a widely held view that one of the main sources of failure in concurrent systems is unforeseen interleavings resulting in undesired system behavior.

Model checkers are particularly well-suited for detecting concurrency bugs due to the exhaustive exploration of all possible interleavings of the concurrent actions that they perform. They can therefore reveal bugs which are impossible or difficult to find by testing methods. However, counterexamples generated by model checking tools only indicate symptoms of faults in a model, they do not offer aid in locating faults in the code of the model. In order to locate a root cause for a counterexample in the code of a model a significant amount of manual analysis is required. Since the manual inspection of lengthy counterexamples of sometimes up to thousands of events is time consuming and error prone, an automatic method for explaining counterexamples that assists model designers in localizing faults in their models is highly desirable.

In this paper we aim at developing an automated method for explaining counterexamples indicating the violation of a desired property in concurrent systems. Our method benefits from the analysis of a large number of counterexamples that can be generated by a model checking tool such as SPIN [9]. We refer to the set of counterexamples that show how the model violates a given property as the *bad* dataset. With the aid of SPIN, it is also possible to produce a set of execution traces that do not violate the desired property. We refer to this set of non-violating traces as the *good* dataset.

For explaining counterexamples, we examine the differences in the traces of the good and bad datasets, which is the foundation of a large number of approaches for locating faults in program code (see, for instance, [27]). Lewis' theory of causality and counterfactual reasoning provides justification for this type of fault localization approaches [13].

To reveal unforeseen interleavings in the form of sequences of actions, we use a data mining technique called *sequential pattern mining* or *frequent subsequence mining* [1,4]. This data mining technique has diverse applications in areas such as the analysis of customer purchase behavior, the mining of web access patterns and the mining of motifs in DNA sequences. Frequent subsequence mining is an active area of research and a number of algorithms for mining frequent subsequences have been developed which have been proven to be efficient in practice with respect to various test datasets [26,25,20].

By contrasting the sequential patterns of the good and bad datasets, we extract a set of sequences of actions that are only common in the bad dataset but not common in the good dataset. We refer to this approach as *contrast mining* and to the resulting patterns as *anomalies*. We assume that these anomalies can reveal to the model designer unforeseen interleavings or unexpected sequences of actions that cause the violation of a desired property.

The contributions of this work are as follows:

1. We propose an automated method based on contrast mining for explaining concurrency bugs.
2. We propose a length reduction technique to make the mining problem more tractable.
3. We show how concurrency bugs can be explained in general by only analyzing the good and the bad traces and without exploiting the characteristics of specific bugs such as data races or atomicity violations.

In our precursory work on explaining counterexamples [12] we extract ordered sequences of events consisting of contiguous events inside counterexamples. In this work, we improve our explanation by extracting sequences of events which do not necessarily occur contiguously inside counterexamples.

Structure of the Paper. Section 2 gives the definition of the problem and also motivates the problem by introducing a running example. Section 3 describes in detail our proposed method for explaining counterexamples. We then present experimental results in Section 4. Section 5 discusses closely related work from different domains. Section 6 concludes with a note on future work.

2   Problem Definition

2.1   Basic Concepts

Our goal is to identify ordered sequences of non-contiguous events that explain the violation of a safety property in a concurrent system. Such a violation represents that there exist undesired or unsafe states which are reachable by system executions. We use the explicit state model checker SPIN [9] in order to compute system executions represented as sequences of events that lead from an initial state of the system into a property violating state, often referred to as counterexamples. We use linear temporal logic (LTL) [2] to specify properties and we use $\sigma \not\models \varphi$ to express that a counterexample σ violates an LTL property φ.

Definition 1. *Let* Act *denote the finite set of actions in a concurrent system. If counterexample σ violates the safety property φ, then σ will be a finite sequence of events denoted as $\langle e_1, e_2, ..., e_n \rangle$ where each e_i corresponds to the execution of an action in the system.*

In fact, the finite set of actions, *Act*, corresponds to the Promela statements [9] of the concurrent system models verified by the SPIN model checker. According to Def. 1, we may use the terms *occurrence of an event* and *execution of an action* interchangeably since both refer to the same concept. When we refer to an *execution trace* or a *trace*, we mean a finite sequence of events according to Def. 1.

Although counterexamples are typically lengthy sequences of events, only a small number of events inside them are relevant to a property violation. In a concurrent system, the order of the events inside a counterexample can also be causal for the occurrence of a failure and can hence point to a bug. As we argue above, system failures are often due to an unexpected order of the occurrence of events in concurrent systems.

In this paper we explain concurrent counterexamples by identifying *explanatory* or *anomalous* sequences inside the counterexamples. Such sequences reveal specific orders between some events inside a counterexample which are presumed to be causal for the property violation.

Definition 2. $\psi = \langle e_0, e_1, e_2, ..., e_m \rangle$ *is a* subsequence *of* $\sigma = \langle E_0, E_1, E_2, ..., E_n \rangle$ *denoted as* $\psi \sqsubseteq \sigma$, *if and only if there exist integers* $0 \le i_0 < i_1 < i_2 < i_3... < i_m \le n$ *such that* $e_0 = E_{i_0}, e_1 = E_{i_1}, ..., e_m = E_{i_m}$. *We also call* σ *a super-sequence of* ψ.

Notice that a subsequence is not necessarily contiguous in the super-sequence. To capture the notion of a contiguous subsequence we introduce the concept of a *substring*.

Definition 3. ψ *is a* substring *of* σ, *if and only if there exist consecutive integers from* $0 \le i_0$ *to* $(i_0 + m) \le n$ *such that* $e_0 = E_{i_0}, e_1 = E_{i_0+1}, ..., e_m = E_{i_0+m}$.

Definition 4. *The sequence* $\psi = \langle e_0, e_1, e_2, ..., e_m \rangle$ *is an* explanatory sequence, *if for all execution traces* σ, *it holds that* $\psi \sqsubseteq \sigma \Rightarrow \sigma \not\models \varphi$.

In the following subsection we will use a motivating example to illustrate that in concurrent systems such explanatory sequences occur in general as the *subsequences* of counterexamples. In our previous work, the sequences isolated for explaining counterexamples are the *substrings* of counterexamples containing contiguous events inside the counterexamples.

2.2   A Motivating Example

Using an example case study we now illustrate how a deadlock can occur due to the temporal order of execution of a set of actions in the model of a concurrent system. Referring to this example we then argue that contrasting sequential patterns of the bad and good datasets can reveal the anomalous sequences of actions that can help to explain the violation of a property, such as a deadlock in a concurrent system. We use the model of a preliminary design of a plain old telephony system (POTS)[1] as an example. This model was generated with the visual modeling tool VIP [10] and contains a number of deadlock problems. It comprises four concurrently executing processes corresponding to two users and two phone handlers. Each user in this model talks to a phone handler for making calls. The phone handlers are communicating with each other in order to switch and route user calls.

---

[1] The Promela code of the POTS case study is available at
`http://www.inf.uni-konstanz.de/soft/tools/CEMiner/`
`POTS7-mod-07-dldetect-never.prm`

A portion of a counterexample indicating the occurrence of a deadlock in the POTS model is given in Fig. 1. The events in this figure are displayed along with the name of the proctypes[2] to which they belong. The events are, in fact, Promela statements [9] that are separated by a "." from the name of the proctypes to which they belong. The events highlighted by the arrows on the left hand side of the trace reveal a problematic sequence of actions which can be interpreted as giving an explanation for the occurrence of a deadlock. This identified sequence for explaining the deadlock is, in fact, an example of an unforeseen interleaving of concurrent events. The presumed assumption of the model designer is that the *User1* and *PhoneHandler1* proctypes are synchronized so that when the *Phone-Handler1* proctype sends a *dialtone* message, the *User1* proctype subsequently receives it before taking any other action. However, as Fig. 1 indicates the model contains faults so that the events 6 and 15, which correspond to the sending of a "dialtone" message by the *PhoneHandler1* proctype, are not followed by a receiving event of the *User1* proctype. The statements executed by the User1 proctype after events 6 and 15 are *!onhook* and *phone_number = 0*, respectively, which causes an unread message to remain in the channel between the *User1* and *PhoneHandler1* proctypes. While the unread message of the event 6 is received by event 14, there is no corresponding receive event for the message of the event 15. Since the channels have a capacity of one message, the unread message of the event 15 causes the *PhoneHandler1* proctype to block after event 22 when it tries to send a "busytone" message to the *User1* proctype. Because of the blocking of the *PhoneHandler1* proctype, the *User1* proctype also blocks after the event 23. Due to the symmetry in the model, a similar interaction can occur between the *User2* and *PhoneHandler2* proctypes, which finally leads the system to a deadlock state.

Fig. 1. Part of a counterexample in POTS model

---

[2] *proctype* is the keyword used in Promela for defining a process.

One interesting characteristic of the explanatory sequence in Fig. 1 is that the events belonging to this sequence do not occur adjacently inside the counterexample. Instead they are interspersed with unrelated events belonging to the interaction of the *User2* and *Phonehandler2* proctypes. In general, events belonging to an explanatory sequence can occur at an arbitrary distance from each other due to the non-deterministic scheduling of concurrent events implemented in SPIN. From this observation, it can be inferred that the explanatory sequences are, in fact, subsequences of the counterexamples. In conclusion, we maintain that sequential pattern mining algorithms, which extract the frequent subsequences from a dataset of sequences without limitations on the relative distance of events belonging to the subsequences, are an adequate and obvious choice to extract explanatory sequences from large sets of counterexamples.

3 Counterexample Explanation

3.1 Generation of the Good and the Bad Datasets

In order to use sequential pattern mining and perform the contrast mining for explaining counterexamples we use the SPIN model checker to generate two sets of counterexamples, namely the "good" and the "bad" datasets. With the aid of the option "-c0 -e", which instructs SPIN to continue the state space search even when a counterexample has been found, we generate a set of counterexamples violating a given property φ, called the *bad dataset*, denoted by Σ_B: $\Sigma_B = \{\sigma \mid \sigma \not\models \varphi\}$. The *good* dataset includes the traces that satisfy φ. Such traces can be generated by producing counterexamples to $\neg\varphi$. This is justified by the following lemma:

Lemma 1. *For an execution σ, if σ satisfies φ, which is denoted as $\sigma \models \varphi$, then it holds that $\sigma \models \varphi \Leftrightarrow \sigma \not\models \neg\varphi$ [2].*

If φ is a safety property, the negation of this property yields a liveness property. The counterexamples violating a liveness property are infinite lasso shaped traces.

Definition 5. *Let $\hat{\phi}$ and (ϕ') denote finite traces. We call $\phi = \hat{\phi}.(\phi')^\omega$ an infinite lasso shaped trace where $\hat{\phi}$ is the finite prefix of ϕ and ω denotes that ϕ' is repeated infinitely.*

For the purpose of our analysis we produce finite traces from the infinite good traces by concatenating $\hat{\phi}$ with one occurrence of ϕ'. We use Σ_G to denote a good dataset: $\Sigma_G = \{\phi \mid \phi \models \varphi \wedge \phi \text{ is finite}\}$

3.2 Sequential Pattern Mining

We now give a brief overview of terminology used in sequential pattern mining, for a more detailed treatment we refer the interested reader to the cited literature and in particular to [4].

A sequence dataset S, $\{s_1, s_2, ..., s_n\}$, is a set of sequences. The *support* of a sequence α is the number of the sequences in S that α is a subsequence of: $support_S(\alpha) = |\{s \mid s \in S \wedge \alpha \sqsubseteq s\}|$. Given a minimum support threshold, min_sup, the sequence α is considered a sequential pattern or a frequent subsequence if its support is no less than min_sup: $support_S(\alpha) \geq min\_sup$. We denote the set of all sequential patterns mined from S with the given support threshold min_sup by FS_{S,min_sup}, i.e., $FS_{S,min\_sup} = \{\alpha \mid support_S(\alpha) \geq min\_sup\}$.

Since mining all sequential patterns will typically result in a combinatorial number of patterns, some algorithms, such as [26,25] only mine *closed* sequential patterns. When a sequential pattern does not have any super sequence with the same support, it is considered as a closed pattern. The set of all closed sequential patterns mined from S with the given support threshold min_sup, denoted by CS_{S,min_sup}, is defined as follows:

Definition 6. $CS_{S,min\_sup} = \{\alpha \mid \alpha \in FS_{S,min\_sup} \wedge \nexists\beta \in FS_{S,min\_sup}$ *such that* $\alpha \sqsubset \beta \wedge support_S(\alpha) = support_S(\beta)\}$.

In fact, the support of a closed sequential pattern is different from that of its super-sequences. Since every frequent pattern is represented by a closed pattern, mining closed patterns leads to a more compact yet complete result set. In other words, closed patterns are the lossless compression of all the sequential patterns.

As an example, consider a sequence dataset S that has five sequences, $S = \{abced, abecf, agbch, abijc, aklc\}$. If the min_sup is specified as 4, $FS_{S,4} = \{a : 5, b : 4, c : 5, ab : 4, ac : 5, bc : 4, abc : 4\}$ where the numbers denote the respective supports of the patterns. However, $CS_{S,4}$ contains only two patterns, $\{abc : 4, ac : 5\}$.

For explaining counterexamples, we first mine closed sequential patterns from the bad and the good datasets with the given support thresholds T_B and T_G, respectively. We call the sets of closed patterns mined from the bad and the good datasets, CS_{Σ_B, T_B} and CS_{Σ_G, T_G}, respectively. Contrasting the sequential patterns of the good and the bad datasets results in the patterns which are only frequent in the bad dataset. We call these patterns *anomalies*.

Definition 7. *We call* $AS_{T_B, T_G} = \{\alpha \mid \alpha \in CS_{\Sigma_B, T_B} \wedge \alpha \notin CS_{\Sigma_G, T_G}\} = CS_{\Sigma_B, T_B} - CS_{\Sigma_G, T_G}$ *the set of all anomalies.*

The anomalies computed according to Def. 7 are, in fact, a set of ordered sequences of events which give an explanation for the property violation. We maintain that the extracted set of anomalies is indicative of one or several faults inside the model. These anomalies can hence be used as the clues to the exact location of the faults inside the model and thereby greatly facilitate the manual fault localization process.

3.3   Complexity Issues

One of the major challenges in applying sequential pattern mining algorithms for explaining counterexamples is the scalability of these algorithms. In our precursory work [12] we discuss that mining sequential patterns from the datasets of counterexamples generated from typical concurrent system models is intractable. As we argue, this observation is due to inherent characteristics of those datasets, in particular the average length of the sequences that they include as well as their denseness. We conclude that we need some technique for reducing the length of the counterexamples in order to make the use of sequential pattern mining in this application domain tractable. We will propose a length reduction technique in the subsequent subsection.

Reducing the Length of the Traces. We are mainly analyzing the behavior of non-terminating communication protocols. By inspecting the structure of the finite traces of these protocols in Σ_B and Σ_G it becomes obvious that events belonging to particular processes, for instance some event a, may occur repeatedly. For example, inside a trace of the POTS model in Fig. 3 we can observe multiple executions of the actions *User1.!offhook* and *User1.!onhook*. In order to reduce the length of the execution traces in the good and the bad datasets, we exploit repetitions of the execution of actions inside the traces. Instead of analyzing the temporal order between all the events of a trace, we decompose each trace into a number of *subtraces* and examine the temporal order of the events that they contain in isolation. A possible choice for decomposing a trace into *subtraces* is via breaking the traces at the execution of a repeating action a. Thus, the obtained subtraces contain the events occurring between each two subsequent executions of a. We define the notion of a subtrace as follows:

Definition 8. *Let ϕ denote a finite trace and action a executed n times inside ϕ. By breaking ϕ at the executions of a, n subtraces will be generated. The $(i+1)^{th}$ subtrace is defined as $\phi_{i+1,a} = \langle a_i, b_{i,0}, ..., b_{i,m} \rangle$ where a_i is the ith execution of the action a in ϕ and $b_{i,j}$ is j^{th} event between the occurrence of a_i and a_{i+1}. The event that occurs next to $b_{i,m}$ is a_{i+1}.*

The subtraces $\phi_{i,a}$ reveal the temporal order between the events that are preceded by the execution of a in the traces, and hence by analyzing these subtraces we can only extract the anomalous sequences of events that precede the execution of a to explain counterexamples. Hence, the extracted anomalous sequences for explaining counterexamples will only contain one execution of the action a. Notice that as a consequence of this abstraction we lose access to the causes of failures that spread over multiple cycles, for instance the repeated occurrence of event a itself without the occurrence of some other event in between.

Instead of mining patterns from the datasets Σ_B and Σ_G, we mine patterns from the datasets Σ_{BR_a} and Σ_{GR_a} containing the subtraces of the traces in Σ_B and Σ_G, respectively: $\Sigma_{BR_a} = \{\sigma_a \mid \sigma_a$ is a subtrace of σ and $\sigma \in \Sigma_B\}$ and $\Sigma_{GR_a} = \{\phi_a \mid \phi_a$ is a subtrace of ϕ and $\phi \in \Sigma_G\}$. In fact, for producing Σ_{BR_a}, we break up each trace in Σ_B and accumulate the resulting subtraces in Σ_{BR_a}. We do the same for Σ_{GR_a}. In analogy with Def. 7, anomalies are then computed by

$$\mathrm{AS}_{T_B, T_G, a} = \mathrm{CS}_{\Sigma_{BR_a}, T_B} - \mathrm{CS}_{\Sigma_{GR_a}, T_G}. \tag{1}$$

For instance, the identified sequence in the example of Sect. 2.2 for explaining the deadlock in the POTS model has portions $\langle 1, 2, 6, 7, 8 \rangle$ and $\langle 12, 13, 14, 15,$

19, 20, 21, 22, 23⟩ which can be mined from the subtraces achieved by breaking the traces at the execution of *User1.!offhook*. As we have seen in Sect. 2.2, each of these portions reveals a problematic sequence of actions that gives clues about the location of the fault in the model.

As we will see in the experimental results section, this reduction technique can reduce the average sequence length of the datasets significantly, and hence can make mining sequential patterns from them feasible. Table 1 shows the amount of the length reduction for the bad and good datasets of the POTS model obtained by applying this length reduction technique.

Table 1. Average sequence length before and after reduction, POTS model datasets

Model	Datasets	#seq. before reduction	#seq. after reduction	avg. seq. len. before reduction	avg. seq. len. after reduction
POTS	bad	4109	497595	1677	13
	good	107029	43668	3079	21

Determining an action *a* at which to break up the traces is a heuristic decision. In principle, any action whose execution is recurrent inside the execution traces can be used for breaking up the traces. However, considering the functionality of the model some actions may seem to be more interesting to be analyzed with respect to their ordering relationships with other actions. Such actions of interest can correspond, for instance, to the start of interactions between different concurrent processes in a communication protocol. For example, in the POTS model many interactions start with the execution of *User1.!offhook*. It initiates a sequence of events handling a telephone call and is hence a candidate for the event *a*. Apparently, we lose some ordering relationships between the actions of a model by shortening the traces via breaking them at the execution of some specific action. However, if we use the actions corresponding to the start of interactions between concurrent processes for breaking the traces, we may lose less important temporal orders from the user perspective. Currently, in our case studies we detect the first action that is taken by one of the processes in the system and use it for breaking up the traces. An alternative strategy for determining the action to break up the traces is by calculating how much reduction can be gained on the average from each individual action, and then to choose the one with the highest reduction ratio. Another heuristic is choosing those actions which divide the traces evenly or result in subtraces with similar length. For example, Table 2 shows different amount of length reduction gained from different actions in the POTS model. In the experimental results section, we report on the results achieved by breaking the traces at actions *U1.!offhook (117)* and *P1.?offhook* which give us the most length reduction.

Threats to Validity. It should be noted that this reduction technique is mainly applicable to execution traces that include repeating patterns of execution of actions, such as non-terminating communication protocols. For some large models

Table 2. Length reduction for different actions in the bad dataset of POTS model, U1 and P1 refer to User1 and PhoneHandler1 processes, respectively.

Action	U1.!offhook	U1.?ringtone	U1.!offhook	U1.!onhook	U1.!onhook	P1.?offhook
line no.	117	101	146	351	294	464
avg. seq. len.	14	343	1442	548	47	13

the proposed reduction technique may still not sufficiently reduce the length of the execution traces. As we have seen the produced anomalies for explaining counterexamples only contain one execution of the action a. If however for understanding the cause of the property violation inside the counterexample, the isolation of an ordered sequence of events containing more than one execution of a is required, then the analysis of the subtraces would not be sufficient. In other words, since we lose some temporal order by analyzing only the subtraces, we may not be able to explain some concurrency bugs.

3.4 Contrasting Sequential Patterns

For mining closed sequential patterns we use an algorithm called CloSpan [26]. The flowchart of our method is given in Fig. 2.

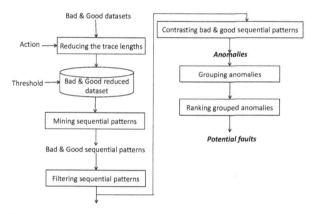

Fig. 2. Flowchart of explaining counterexamples method

The final result set of the method contains the distinguishing patterns representing the set of sequences of actions that are only frequent or typical in the bad dataset. This set is generated by equation (1). The user defined threshold values, T_B and T_G in equation (1) are, in fact, the parameters of our method. By decreasing the value of the support threshold, the number of the generated sequential patterns from a dataset of traces increases. In order to reduce the number of the mined patterns, we remove the patterns which are *substrings* of some other generated pattern. This is because the ordering relationship that can be inferred from these patterns can also be inferred from the longer patterns that these patterns are substrings of.

In order to facilitate the interpretation of the result set obtained by equation (1) we divide the anomalies into a number of groups so that each group contains patterns which are all subsequences of the longest pattern in that group. Fig. 4 shows an example of such a group of patterns. One temporal order that can be inferred from the longest pattern in Fig. 4 is $\langle 334, 1426, 444 \rangle$. From the subsequences of the longest pattern, it can be inferred that not always "1426" occurs between "334" and "444" because $\langle 334, 444 \rangle$ is also frequent, and not always "1426" is preceded by "334" because $\langle 1406, 1426, 444 \rangle$ is also frequent.

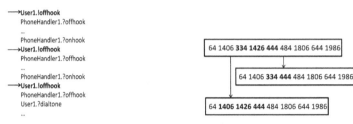

Fig. 3. Multiple occurrence of events inside an execution trace

Fig. 4. Patterns inside one group

The groups of patterns are then ordered based on the length of the longest pattern inside them. Groups with the shorter length of the longest pattern will be ranked higher because the analysis of these patterns by the user requires less effort.

4   Experimental Evaluation

The experiments that we report on in this section were performed on a 2.67 GHz PC with 8 GB RAM and Windows 7 64-bit operating system. The prototype implementation of our method was realized using the programming language C#.Net 2010. We discuss the results obtained by applying our method to a number of case studies.

Case Study 1: POTS Model. We first applied our method to the POTS model (see Sect. 2.2) in order to obtain explanations for the occurrence of deadlocks. The execution traces were shortened in length by breaking the original traces at the execution of the action *User1.!offhook* as it has been explained in Sect. 3.3. In order to study the effect of the threshold value on the number of the generated patterns in the result set we applied different threshold values, starting with a comparatively high threshold value of 90%. Fig. 5 shows how the number of the generated patterns is reduced after our filtering step. The reduction is by a factor of approximately 0.5. It also illustrates how the number of the closed sequential patterns increases when decreasing the threshold. Mining closed sequential patterns from the good dataset of POTS with the min_sup of 10% takes 359.651 sec. and consumes 31.327 MB of main memory while with the min_sup of 90% it takes only 0.074 sec. and consumes only 3.69 MB of main memory.

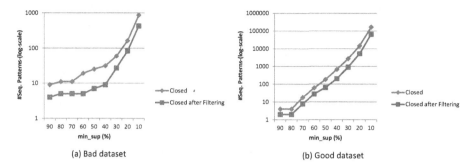

Fig. 5. Number of the closed sequential patterns in the bad and good datasets before and after filtering

In Fig. 6, the number of the anomalies obtained by equation (1) along with the number of the groups that these anomalies are divided into are given. From the figures 5 and 6, it can be inferred that although the number of the generated closed sequential patterns from the bad and good datasets can be quite high, the number of the anomalies that the user needs to inspect to understand the root cause of the deadlock is mostly less than 10, at least for thresholds of not less than 20. In Fig. 6, the precision of the method shows the number of the sequences in the result set which actually reveal some anomalous behavior. As this figure shows, only for the thresholds of 30%, 20% and 10% the precision is less than 100%. Considering the way that we generate the good and the bad datasets, these datasets may not include all the possible good and bad traces that can be produced by the execution of the model. In the final result set of the method, therefore, we may get some false positives that do not reveal any problematic behaviors in the model. The computed precision measure for each case study shows the number of the true anomalous sequences among all the sequences of the result set. This precision was calculated manually.

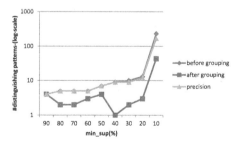

Fig. 6. Number of the anomalies, number of the groups of anomalies and the precision

The manual inspection of the anomalous sequences in the result set of the method reveals some faults in the model. In fact, two faults can be detected from the result sets generated by the thresholds 20% and 10%. Other result sets which are generated by higher threshold values only reveal one fault. For example, one

of the anomalous sequences for the support threshold of 90% is *User1.!offhook,
PhoneHandler1.?offhook, User1.?dialtone*, while according to the behavior of the
model the expected sequence from the user perspective is *User1.!offhook, Phone-
Handler1.?offhook, PhoneHandler1.!dialtone, User1.?dialtone*. Considering the
expected sequence a receiving *dialtone* message should always be preceded by a
sending *dialtone* message. The anomalous sequence reveals a deviation from the
expected sequence because in this sequence the receiving *dialtone* messages is not
preceded by a corresponding sending *dialtone* message. This implicitly reveals
the presence of an unread message in the channel. Finally, it can be inferred
that there is a lack of synchronization between the user and the phone handler
proctypes so that when the phone handler sends a *dialtone* message, the user
instead of receiving that message takes another action.

By breaking the traces at *PhoneHandler1.?offhook* instead of *User1.!offhook*,
by the support threshold of 90% a result set containing of 5 anomalies will be
generated. In fact, these anomalies also reveal the same fault as explained above.

It must be noted that our method is not supposed to be complete, and we
use the method as part of an iterative debugging process. After each run of the
method, aided by the revealed anomalous sequences the user will try to remove
as many causes of property violation as possible. In case the model still contains
faults after being modified, the user will apply the method again. This procedure
can be iterated until all the causes of property violation in the model have been
removed. For example, we tried to remedy the problem in POTS by adding some
code in the user proctype which removes a message *dialtone* from the channel
between the user and the phone handler proctypes, if it is present, when sending
an *onhook* message. After this modification, we again applied our method on
the resulting model, this time the number of the generated counterexamples
decreased from 4109 to 2229. The produced result set reveals that there is still
a lack of synchronization between the user and the phone handler proctypes.

Case Study 2: Rether Model. The second model is a Real-time Ethernet protocol named Rether. It was obtained from [21]. In order to reduce the size and
complexity of the original model from [21] we have reduced the values of its
parameters. A detailed description of this model can be found in [12]. We applied our method to this model in order to explain the occurrence of a deadlock.
The statement "i=0" of the Token proctype was used for breaking the execution
traces because the interaction between the processes in this model starts with
the execution of this statement. Table 3 shows the extent of the length reduction
of the traces for this case study.

Table 3. Results of length reduction in the Rether model datasets

datasets	#seq. before reduction	#seq. after reduction	avg. seq. len. before reduction	avg. seq. len. after reduction
bad	8	92	322	28
good	78	812	298	29

A threshold value of 2% was applied to the reduced length bad and good datasets for generating the sequential patterns. In Table 4 the number of the generated sequential patterns before and after filtering along with the number of the anomalies obtained by equation (1) and the number of the faults detected by the user inspection are given.

Table 4. Rether model results

datasets	#seq. patterns	#seq. patterns after filtering	#anomalies	#groups of anomalies	precision	#detected faults
bad	182	170	23	11	7	1
good	466	244				

Even though appr. 65% of the extracted groups reveal some problematic behavior in the system, the inspection of only 2 of them, corresponding to the first and the 8th groups in the ranked result set, is required for localizing an atomicity violation in one of the proctypes of the model. Due to space limitations we refer the interested reader to our previous work [12] for an extensive discussion of which specific sequence of actions reveals an atomicity violation in this model.

Comparison with Our Previous Work. The fault localization method that we proposed in a precursory paper [12] aids the user in locating unforeseen interleavings inside the counterexamples of concurrent systems by extracting a set of short substrings of mainly length two that only occur in the bad dataset. These short substrings along with the corresponding counterexamples are given to the user for further analysis. For example, for this case study, this method generates 3 short distinguishing substrings of length two which are given to the user along with the corresponding counterexamples. With the aid of these substrings, the user needs to inspect on the average 30 events inside the corresponding counterexamples in order to identify the anomalous sequences pointing to an atomicity violation bug in the model. However, the anomalous sequences detected with the aid of the method proposed in this paper are in themselves indicative of the atomicity violation bug in the model. In other words, as opposed to our precursory work an inspection of counterexamples is not required at all. Specifically, in order to detect an atomicity violation in this case study, an anomalous sequence of at least length 30 needs to be isolated inside a counterexample. With the aid of the short substrings of length 2 extracted by our previous method, the user still needs to inspect the counterexample in order to isolate an anomalous sequence of length 30, even though these substrings facilitate the user inspection greatly. However, the groups of anomalies generated by the method of this paper contain the anomalous sequence of length 30 required for locating the atomicity violation in the model. In fact, the last 7 events of this sequence appear in the first group of the ranked result set and the rest of the events are included in the 8th group. We contend that the current method imposes less inspection effort on the user for locating the faults in the model.

Table 5. Railway model results

datasets	#seq.	avg. len.	seq. #seq. patterns	#seq. patterns after filtering	#anomalies	#detected faults
bad	28	15	1	1	1	1
good	85	15	6	2		

Case Study 3: Railway Model. We finally applied our method to explain counterexamples indicating the violation of a safety property in the small railroad crossing example which is also used as a sample case study in [11]. The desired safety property is that the car and the train should never be in the crossing simultaneously, which is considered a hazardous state of the system. In this small model, the length reduction step was not necessary.

Table 5 summarizes all the figures related to this model and the achieved results by applying the high support threshold value of 90%. The detected anomalous sequence reveals a sequence of actions that leads the system to an undesired state in which the variables *"carcrossing"* and *"traincrossing"* have both the value "1". This indicates that both a car and a train are in the crossing at the same time, which is equivalent to a hazard state. This sequence, in fact, guides the user to the location of an atomicity violation bug in the *"Gate"* proctype. The presumed intention of the model designer is that the transmission of the signal "1" through the *gateCtrl* channel would be performed atomically with the changing of the global variable *"gatestatus"* to "1". However, due to the fault in the model, the execution of these two statements is interleaved with some other concurrent actions and leads the system to a hazard state.

Dataset Generation. As it has been explained in Sect. 3, we use the option *"-c0 -e"* in SPIN, for generating the good and the bad datasets which can be time-consuming for some case studies. For example, for the POTS model SPIN generates 303,589 good traces which takes around 14 hours. However, the dataset generation for the other two case studies takes less than a minute. If the generated datasets have fewer numbers of traces than the ones generated with the option *"-c0 -e"*, our method is still applicable to them since the method is not guaranteed to be complete. However, when the datasets offer a higher coverage of the good and the bad behaviors, the output of the method is more precise and the number of the false positives among the explanations is reduced.

5   Related Work

In this section, we briefly discuss closely related work that has not yet been addressed in earlier sections.

Pattern Mining in Software Analysis. Data mining techniques have proven to be useful in the analysis of very large amounts of data produced in the course of different activities during various states of the software system development cycle. Frequent pattern mining techniques which find commonly occurring patterns in a dataset are broadly used for mining specifications and localizing faults in program code [15,14,19,5,22]. The work documented in [15] adapts sequential pattern mining techniques in order to mine specifications from recorded traces of software system executions. It seems that the patterns generated by this method can also be used for counterexample explanation. However, we faced scalability issues when applying this method to the POTS model case study that we introduce in Section 2.2. The longest distinguishing patterns between the bad and the good datasets that could be generated by this method were only 2 events long and did not carry any interesting information with respect to ordering relationships amongst events. CHRONICLER [22] is a static analysis tool which infers function precedence protocols defining ordering relationships among function calls in program code. For extracting these protocols a sequence mining algorithm is used. The methods in [14,19,5] use graph and tree mining algorithms for localizing faults in sequential program code. A commonality of these methods is that they first construct behavior graphs such as function call graphs from execution traces. They then apply a frequent graph or tree mining algorithm on the passing and failing datasets of constructed graphs in order to determine the suspicious portions of the sequential program code. As opposed to this approach, our goal is to identify sequences of interleaved actions in concurrent systems, which the above cited works are unable to provide.

Concurrency Bug Detection Methods. AVIO [16] only detects atomicity violations and, as opposed to our method, is tailored to only identify single variable bugs. Examples of tools which only focus on detecting data races are lockset bug detection tools [23] and happens-before bug detection tools [18]. In contrast to these approaches, which lack generality and rely on heuristics that are specific to a class of bugs, the output of our method in the form of anomalous sequences can be indicative to any type of concurrency bugs in the program design that can be characterized by a reachability property.

The work described in [17] proposes a more general approach for finding concurrency bugs based on constructing context-aware communication graphs from execution traces. Context-aware communication graphs use communication context to encode access ordering information. A key challenge of this method is, however, that if the relevant ordering information is not encoded, bugs may not lead to graph anomalies and therefore remain undetected. Our method does not rely on such an encoding but directly analyzes the temporal ordering of the event. It therefore appears to be more general than the approach in [17].

Counterexample Explanation Methods. In [12], we provide a detailed comparison of our method with a closely related work by Groce and Visser [7]. For that comparison, the arguments given in [12] are also valid for our current work, because, in fact, the current method is the enhancement of our precursory work. The *causality checking* method proposed in [11] computes automatically the causalities in system models by adapting the counterfactual reasoning based on the *structural equation model (SEM)* by Halpern and Perl [8]. This method identifies sequences of events that cause a system to reach a certain undesired state by extending depth-first search and breadth-first search algorithms used for a complete state space exploration in explicit-state model checking. It seems that the main superiority of our method is less computational cost in terms of memory and running time for detecting at least one fault in the model. The *causality checking* method considers all the possible finite good and bad execution traces for identifying the combination of events which are causal for the violation of a safety property. Since we do not seek completeness, our mining method is still applicable even if the datasets do not include all the possible good and bad execution traces, which can be an impediment in practice.

Some other automated counterexample explanation techniques such as [3,24,6] only take the values of program or model variables into account when computing which variable values along a counterexample trace cause a violation of some desired property. In contrast, the method we propose here considers the order of execution of actions and can hence explain property violations which are due to a specific order of execution of actions.

6   Conclusion

We have presented an automated method for the explanation of model checking counterexamples for concurrent system models. From a dataset of counterexamples we extract a number of anomalous sequences of actions that prove to point to the location of the fault in the model by leveraging a frequent pattern mining technique called sequential pattern mining. An experimental analysis showed the effectiveness of our method for a number of indicative deadlock checking case studies.

In future work we plan to reduce the computational effort that our method entails by imposing a limit on the number of context switches in generation of the good and the bad traces.

Acknowledgements. We wish to gratefully acknowledge a careful review of this work by Georg Weissenbacher.

References

1. Agrawal, R., Srikant, R.: Mining sequential patterns. In: ICDE (1995)
2. Baier, C., Katoen, J.-P.: Principles of Model Checking. The MIT Press, Massachusetts (2008)
3. Beer, I., Ben-David, S., Chockler, H., Orni, A., Trefler, R.: Explaining counterexamples using causality. In: Bouajjani, A., Maler, O. (eds.) CAV 2009. LNCS, vol. 5643, pp. 94–108. Springer, Heidelberg (2009)
4. Dong, G., Pei, J.: Sequence Data Mining. Springer (2007)
5. Fatta, G.D., Leue, S., Stegantova, E.: Discriminative pattern mining in software fault detection. In: Proceedings of the 3rd International Workshop on Software Quality Assurance (2006)
6. Groce, A., Chaki, S., Kroening, D., Strichman, O.: Error explanation with distance metrics. In: International Journal on Software Tools for Technology Transfer (STTT) (2006)
7. Groce, A., Visser, W.: What went wrong: Explaining counterexamples. In: Ball, T., Rajamani, S.K. (eds.) SPIN 2003. LNCS, vol. 2648, pp. 121–135. Springer, Heidelberg (2003)

8. Halpern, J., Pearl, J.: Causes and explanations: A structural-model approach. part I: Causes. The British Journal for the Philosophy of Science (2005)
9. Holzmann, G.J.: The SPIN Model Checker: Primer and Reference Manual. Addision-Wesley (2003)
10. Kamel, M., Leue, S.: VIP: A visual editor and compiler for v-promela. In: Graf, S., Schwartzbach, M. (eds.) TACAS/ETAPS 2000. LNCS, vol. 1785, pp. 471–486. Springer, Heidelberg (2000)
11. Leitner-Fischer, F., Leue, S.: Causality checking for complex system models. In: Giacobazzi, R., Berdine, J., Mastroeni, I. (eds.) VMCAI 2013. LNCS, vol. 7737, pp. 248–267. Springer, Heidelberg (2013)
12. Leue, S., Tabaei Befrouei, M.: Counterexample explanation by anomaly detection. In: Donaldson, A., Parker, D. (eds.) SPIN 2012. LNCS, vol. 7385, pp. 24–42. Springer, Heidelberg (2012)
13. Lewis, D.: Counterfactuals. Wiley-Blackwell (2001)
14. Liu, C., Yan, X., Yu, H., Han, J., Yu, P.S.: Mining behavior graphs for backtrace of noncrashing bugs. In: Proceedings of the Fifth SIAM International Conference on Data Mining (2005)
15. Lo, D., Khoo, S., Liu, C.: Efficient mining of iterative patterns for software specification discovery. In: KDD (2007)
16. Lu, S., Tucek, J., Qin, F., Zhou, Y.: Avio: Detecting atomicity violations via access interleaving invariants. In: ASPLOS (2006)
17. Lucia, B., Ceze, L.: Finding concurrency bugs with context-aware communication graphs. In: Proceedings of the 42nd Annual IEEE/ACM International Symposium on Microarchitecture (2009)
18. Netzer, R., Miller, B.: Improving the accuracy of data race detection. In: Proceedings of the 3rd ACM Symposium on Principles and Practice of Parallel Programming. ACM Press (1991)
19. Parsa, S., Naree, S.A., Koopaei, N.E.: Software fault localization via mining execution graphs. In: Murgante, B., Gervasi, O., Iglesias, A., Taniar, D., Apduhan, B.O. (eds.) ICCSA 2011, Part II. LNCS, vol. 6783, pp. 610–623. Springer, Heidelberg (2011)
20. Pei, J., Han, J., Mortazavi-Asl, B., Pinto, H., Chen, Q., Dayal, U., Hsu, M.: Prefixspan: Mining sequential patterns efficiently by prefix-projected pattern growth. In: 17th International Conference on Data Engineering (ICDE 2001) (2001)
21. Pelanek, R.: Benchmarks for explicit model checkers (2006), http://anna.fi.muni.cz/models
22. Ramanathan, M.K., Grama, A., Jagannathan, S.: Path-sensitive inference of function precedence protocols. In: Proceedings of the 29th International Conference on Software Engineering (ICSE) (2007)
23. Savage, S., Burrows, M., Nelson, G., Sobalvarro, P., Anderson, T.: Eraser: a dynamic data race detector for multithreaded programs. ACM Transactions on Computer Systems (TOCS) 15(4) (1997)
24. Wang, C., Yang, Z., Ivančić, F., Gupta, A.: Whodunit? causal analysis for counterexamples. In: Graf, S., Zhang, W. (eds.) ATVA 2006. LNCS, vol. 4218, pp. 82–95. Springer, Heidelberg (2006)
25. Wang, J., Han, J.: Bide: Efficient mining of frequent closed sequences. In: ICDE (2004)
26. Yan, X., Han, J., Afshar, R.: Clospan: Mining closed sequential patterns in large datasets. In: Proceedings of 2003 SIAM International Conference on Data Mining (SDM 2003) (2003)
27. Zeller, A.: Why Programs Fail: A Guide to Systematic Debugging. Morgan Kaufmann, Burlington (2009)

Automatic Equivalence Checking of UF+IA Programs

Nuno P. Lopes and José Monteiro

INESC-ID / IST - TU Lisbon

Abstract. Proving the equivalence of programs has several important applications, including algorithm recognition, regression checking, compiler optimization verification, and information flow checking.

Despite being a topic with so many important applications, program equivalence checking has seen little advances over the past decades due to its inherent (high) complexity.

In this paper, we propose, to the best of our knowledge, the first algorithm for the automatic verification of partial equivalence of two programs over the combined theory of uninterpreted function symbols and integer arithmetic (UF+IA). The proposed algorithm supports, in particular, programs with nested loops.

The crux of the technique is a transformation of uninterpreted functions (UFs) applications into integer polynomials, which enables the summarization of loops with UF applications using recurrences. The equivalence checking algorithm then proceeds on loop-free, integer only programs.

We implemented the proposed technique in CORK, a tool that automatically verifies the correctness of compiler optimizations, and we show that it can prove more optimizations correct than state-of-the-art techniques.

1 Introduction

Proving the equivalence of programs has several important applications, including, but not limited to, algorithm recognition [2], regression checking [11,13,24], compiler optimization verification [18,23] and validation [30,32,40,43,46,47], and information flow proofs [5,42].

The objective of algorithm recognition is to identify known algorithms (such as a sorting algorithm, or even a specific algorithm like quicksort) out of large and complex programs. This can be useful, for example, to improve code comprehension and for automatic documentation generation. Algorithm recognition can be accomplished by searching for an equivalent algorithm in a database.

Regression verification aims at tracking the functional differences in a program in each code change. The idea is that a tool that performs regression verification can pinpoint the parts of the program where the semantics were changed since the previous code revision, so that the developer can manually confirm if those were the intended changes. Additionally, these tools can help the developer confirm if some code refactoring or manual optimization preserved the semantics or not.

E. Bartocci and C.R. Ramakrishnan (Eds.): SPIN 2013, LNCS 7976, pp. 282–300, 2013.

Compiler optimization verification consists in verifying that a given optimization is semantic preserving for all allowed code inputs, i.e., that the original and optimized code templates are equivalent. Optimization validation verifies that an optimization ran correctly by checking the original and optimized pieces of code for equivalence (after the optimization was run).

In the domain of information flow, proofs for the non-existence of information leaks can be accomplished by establishing the equivalence of the program with itself (self-composition). Since the programs have some non-determinism associated (the private information), a program will not be equivalent to itself if some of the non-determinism may be observable (meaning that it may leak secure information).

Uninterpreted function symbols (UFs) are frequently used in software verification tasks, including in the applications mentioned above. UFs are quite appealing because they allow certain details of the programs to be abstracted out by replacing with UFs the parts whose specifics are irrelevant to the proof being done.

Despite being an important area with several applications, state-of-the-art software verification tools, such as ARMC [33], BLAST [20,21], CPACHECKER [9], FSOFT [22], HSF [15], IMPACT [27], and SLAM [3], are unable to prove equivalence of most programs containing loops. These tools are usually not able to automatically derive sufficiently strong loop invariants to complete equivalence proofs of looping programs, even if just considering the theory of integer arithmetic, let alone the combined theory of uninterpreted function symbols and integer arithmetic (UF+IA).

In this paper, we present, to the best of our knowledge, the first algorithm to automatically prove the equivalence of programs consisting of integer arithmetic operations and applications of UFs. The proposed algorithm is applicable, in particular, to programs containing zero or more (nested) loops.

Applications of UFs are first rewritten to integer arithmetic expressions (polynomials over the inputs of the applications), and then our equivalence checking algorithm works on purely integer manipulating programs. Loops are summarized as recurrences, for which we compute the closed-form solution. The provably correct conversion of UF applications to integer expressions makes possible the representation of loops with UF applications using recurrences.

We have implemented the proposed algorithm in CORK, a tool that verifies the correctness of compiler optimizations, and we show that CORK can prove more optimizations correct than state-of-the-art techniques.

The rest of the paper is organized as follows. Section 2 gives an intuition of how our algorithm proves the equivalence of programs with a simple example. Section 3 presents the program model that we consider and gives preliminary definitions. Section 4 describes our algorithm for automatic partial equivalence checking of programs over the UF+IA theory. Section 5 presents CORK, a tool that verifies the correctness of compiler optimizations automatically, and provides an evaluation on how CORK compares with PEC [23], a state-of-the-art tool for compiler optimization verification. Section 6 presents the related work.

$$i := N$$
$$\textbf{while } i \geq 1 \textbf{ do}$$
$$\quad k := \mathsf{UF}(k, \ N - i)$$
$$\quad i := i - 1$$

$$i := 0$$
$$\textbf{while } i < N \textbf{ do}$$
$$\quad k := \mathsf{UF}(k, \ i)$$
$$\quad i := i + 1$$

$$\textbf{if } N \leq 0 \textbf{ then}$$
$$\quad i := 0$$
$$\textbf{else}$$
$$\quad i := N$$

Fig. 1. Example of two equivalent programs

2   Illustrative Example

We illustrate our algorithm for program equivalence checking on a simple example. Figure 1 shows two equivalent example programs. Our objective is to prove that these two programs are indeed equivalent.

The first step of the algorithm is to replace the applications of uninterpreted functions (UFs) with expressions over integers. In the left program, we replace the UF application with the following expression (a polynomial of degree one):

$$a \times k + b \times i + c$$

where a, b, and c are free variables not occurring in the input programs, and are associated with this specific UF symbol. Other UF symbols occurring in the program would have different sets of free variables associated with each input parameter. Similarly, for the UF application of the right program we obtain:

$$a \times k + b \times (N - i) + c$$

These expressions (polynomials) have a unique value for each set of UF symbol and input parameters, which is not reproducible through any other sequence of operations. This is because free variables are universally quantified, and therefore there always exists an assignment to the variables a, b, and c that leads to different results for different UF applications.

As we shall see later, the degree of the polynomials that replace UF applications is not always one. We give a lower bound for this degree in Section 4.2.

The second step that the algorithm performs is removing the loops. This is accomplished by replacing each loop with a set of assignments to the variables modified in the loop. The expressions assigned to each variable are expressed over the closed-form solution of a system of recurrences that summarizes the loop.

For the left program, we obtain the following system of recurrences:

$$R_i(n) = R_i(n - 1) + 1$$
$$R_i(0) = 0$$
$$R_k(n) = a \times R_k(n - 1) + b \times R_i(n - 1) + c$$
$$R_k(0) = k_0$$

$i := 0$
if $i < N$ then
    assume $R_i(n-1) < N \wedge R_i(n) \geq N$
    $k := R_k(n)$
    $i := R_i(n)$

$i := N$
if $i \geq 1$ then
    assume $V_i(n-1) \geq 1 \wedge V_i(n) < 1$
    $k := V_k(n)$
    $i := V_i(n)$

if $N \leq 0$ then
    $i := 0$
else
    $i := N$

Fig. 2. Programs of Figure 1 with loops and UF applications removed

where n represents the loop iteration number, and k_0 is the (arbitrary) value of k when the program starts (required since k is not initialized before its first usage). A recurrence for N is not needed, since it is not modified in the loop.

The recurrence $R_x(y)$ represents the value of variable x at iteration number y. For example, the recurrence $R_i(n)$ defined previously means that the value of i in any given iteration is equal to the value of i in the previous iteration plus one. Moreover, before the loop starts, i has the value zero.

Similarly, for the right program we obtain the following system of recurrences:

$$V_i(n) = V_i(n-1) - 1$$
$$V_i(0) = N$$
$$V_k(n) = a \times V_k(n-1) + b \times (N - V_i(n-1)) + c$$
$$V_k(0) = k_0$$

Figure 2 shows the programs of Figure 1 after both transformations (elimination of loops and UF applications) have been applied.

The **assume** command ensures that its input boolean expression is satisfiable, or the program execution is blocked otherwise. We use this command to implicitly compute the trip count of loops.

Intuitively, if m is the number of iterations performed by a loop, in the iterations numbered $0 \ldots (m-1)$ the loop guard is true, and it is false in the following iteration (m). Therefore, m is the first iteration when the loop guard becomes false.

After the **assume** command in the example is evaluated, the value of n is the number of times that the corresponding loop would have been executed and therefore $R_x(n)$ represents the value of the variable x after the loop terminates.

We can now compute the closed-form solution of the previously given systems of recurrences. For the left program we obtain the following solution (computed by Wolfram Mathematica 8):

$$R_i(n) = n$$
$$R_k(n) = \frac{b\left(a^n - an + n - 1\right) + (a-1)\left(a^n((a-1)k_0 + c) - c\right)}{(a-1)^2}$$

assume $i = \bar{i} \wedge k = \bar{k} \wedge N = \bar{N}$

$i := 0$
if $i < N$ **then**
    assume $R_i(n-1) < N \wedge R_i(n) \geq N$
    $k := R_k(n)$
    $i := R_i(n)$

$\bar{i} := \bar{N}$
if $\bar{i} \geq 1$ **then**
    assume $V_i(\bar{n}-1) \geq 1 \wedge V_i(\bar{n}) < 1$
    $\bar{k} := V_k(\bar{n})$
    $\bar{i} := V_i(\bar{n})$

if $\bar{N} \leq 0$ **then**
    $\bar{i} := 0$
else
    $\bar{i} := \bar{N}$

assert $i = \bar{i} \wedge k = \bar{k} \wedge N = \bar{N}$

Fig. 3. Sequential composition of the programs of Figure 2. The right program is renamed, so that each variable v becomes $\bar{v}$.

For the right program, the solution for $V_k(n)$ is equal to $R_k(n)$ of the left program, and for V_i is:

$$V_i(n) = N - n$$

The final step of the algorithm is to prove equivalent the transformed programs (that are now only over integer arithmetic and loop-free). To accomplish this, we first do the sequential composition of the two programs, where the second is renamed to operate over a distinct set of variables from the first program. We then add an assertion at the end of the composed program to verify that the value of the corresponding variables of the two programs are equal when the programs terminate.

The sequential composition of the programs of Figure 2 is shown in Figure 3. The references to recurrences were not replaced by their closed-form solutions to avoid cluttering the example.

If we prove that the composed program is safe, i.e., that the condition of the **assert** command is true for all inputs, then we have proved that the two input programs are equivalent.

To prove program safety, and since the number of symbolic paths of the composed programs is always finite (as we remove the loops), we can use a simple algorithm that enumerates all paths and checks if the assertion is violated in any of them.

$$e ::= n \mid v \mid e_1 \oplus e_2 \mid \mathsf{UF}(e_1, \ldots, e_n)$$
$$b ::= e \leq 0 \mid b_1 \otimes b_2$$
$$c ::= \mathbf{skip} \mid v := e \mid c_1 ; c_2 \mid \mathbf{if}\ b\ \mathbf{then}\ c_1\ \mathbf{else}\ c_2 \mid \mathbf{while}\ b\ \mathbf{do}\ c_1 \mid \mathbf{assume}\ b$$
$$\mid \mathbf{assert}\ b$$

Fig. 4. WHILE language syntax. n is an integer number, v is a variable name, UF is an uninterpreted function symbol, $\oplus$ is a binary operator over integer expressions (e.g., $+$, $-$), and $\otimes$ is a binary operator over boolean expressions (e.g., $\wedge$, $\vee$).

3 Program Model

We assume that programs are specified in the WHILE language, whose syntax is given in Figure 4, and with customary semantics. The expressions are over the combined theory of uninterpreted function symbols and integer arithmetic (UF+IA). The evaluation of expressions is parameterized on an interpretation for each UF symbol.

For the sake of ease of reading, in the examples given throughout the paper, we relax the syntax of expressions (e.g., to accept more operators than $\leq$), but those examples can be trivially converted to the WHILE language we present.

Let σ be a program state, which is a valuation of the program variables. Let $\sigma(v)$ be the value of the variable v in the program state σ. This notation is extended for expressions, such that $\sigma(e)$ is the expression e with each variable replaced with its value in state σ. Let $\sigma[v \mapsto n]$ be a program state that is identical to state σ, except for the value of variable v, which is n. Let σ_0 be the initial state of an execution of a program. We have that $\sigma_0(v) = v_0$ for each variable v used in the program, with variable v_0 being fresh.

A configuration $\langle c, \sigma \rangle$ is a pair where c is a command and σ is a state. Let $\langle c, \sigma \rangle \rightarrow \langle c', \sigma' \rangle$ be the reduction of the configuration $\langle c, \sigma \rangle$ to the configuration $\langle c', \sigma' \rangle$ in one step. Let $\langle c, \sigma \rangle \rightarrow \sigma'$ be the reduction in one step of the configuration $\langle c, \sigma \rangle$ to the state σ' when there are no further commands left to execute. Finally, let $\langle c, \sigma \rangle \rightarrow^* \sigma'$ be the reduction in one or more steps of the configuration $\langle c, \sigma \rangle$ to the state σ'.

Let $\mathsf{Vars}(P)$ be the set of variables of program P (a command). A variable v is fresh in program P if $v \notin \mathsf{Vars}(P)$. Let $\mathsf{Out}(P) \subseteq \mathsf{Vars}(P)$ be the set of output observable variables of a program P. Let $\sigma \downarrow V$ be the projection of the state σ over the set of variables V and let $\sigma \downarrow \mathsf{Out}(P)$ be the observable state of σ of program P.

Two programs are considered partially equivalent iff starting in the same arbitrary state, they terminate in the same observable state for all possible UF interpretations, i.e., P_1 and P_2 are partially equivalent iff the following holds:

$$\langle P_1, \sigma_0 \rangle \rightarrow^* \sigma_1 \wedge \langle P_2, \sigma_0 \rangle \rightarrow^* \sigma_2 \implies \sigma_1 \downarrow \mathsf{Out}(P_1) = \sigma_2 \downarrow \mathsf{Out}(P_2)$$

with $\mathsf{Out}(P_1) = \mathsf{Out}(P_2)$.

4   Program Equivalence Checking

In this section, we present the new algorithm to check if two programs over the UF+IA theory are partially equivalent.

4.1   Restrictions

We impose the following restrictions on the programs that our equivalence checking algorithm can handle:

1. UFs must have exactly one output parameter.
2. There can be no branching (i.e., **if** statements) inside loops. Nested loops, however, are allowed.
3. The trip count of inner loops may not depend on the outer loops, i.e., the number of times that inner loops iterate is constant relative to outer loops.
4. Loop conditions cannot involve UF applications.

Restriction 1 can be lifted by splitting UFs with more than one output into newly created UFs (one per output). Restriction 2 can be relaxed by allowing branching conditions that always evaluate to the same value in all loop iterations. In that case, the program can be rewritten to move the branches out of the loop.

4.2   Algorithm

The algorithm runs in three steps:

1. Eliminate UF applications.
2. Replace loops with recurrences.
3. Check resulting programs for equivalence.

Applications of UFs are abstracted using polynomials, in order to obtain programs with integer operations only. This allows us to compute the closed-form of loops using recurrences.

Although our algorithm is sound and complete (under the stated restrictions), computing the closed-form solution of recurrences is undecidable, and therefore the overall method is incomplete.

In the following sections, we describe each step of the algorithm separately.

Eliminate UF Applications. The first step of the algorithm is to eliminate UF applications. This is accomplished by replacing each UF application with a polynomial over its inputs, as defined by the transformation T:

$$T(e) = \sum_{i=1}^{n} \sum_{j=0}^{u(\mathsf{UF},i)} \mathsf{UF}_{i,j} \times (T(e_i))^j, \qquad \text{if } e = \mathsf{UF}(e_1, \ldots, e_n)$$

The other trivial (do nothing) cases are omitted for brevity.

The function $u(f, i)$ used by transformation T defines the degree of the polynomial that replaces an UF application. The value of $u(f, i)$ is the maximum number of times that the given UF f is applied with distinct values in the ith parameter in each and every program path minus one. Only function applications whose value is possibly used in a boolean expression need to be considered.

Intuitively, two programs with UF applications are equivalent iff, for each possible input and for each observable output, the number of times the UFs are applied is equal in both programs, and the values of the input parameters of each application are equal as well.

Transformation T captures this information precisely by replacing each UF application with a polynomial over the inputs of the application. Each UF symbol is assigned a set of fresh variables $UF_{i,j}$ that is used only by applications of that symbol. Therefore, the value of an UF application cannot be reproduced by any sequence of commands that does not include exactly the same UF application.

For example, the following boolean expression

$$f(x) = 0 \wedge f(y) = 1 \wedge f(z) = 2 \wedge g(x) \leq 0 \wedge y < z \wedge z < x$$

is translated to (assuming no more applications of f nor g in the rest of the program):

$$f_{1,2} \times x^2 + f_{1,1} \times x + f_{1,0} = 0 \wedge f_{1,2} \times y^2 + f_{1,1} \times y + f_{1,0} = 1 \wedge$$
$$f_{1,2} \times z^2 + f_{1,1} \times z + f_{1,0} = 2 \wedge g_{1,0} \leq 0 \wedge y < z \wedge z < x$$

where $f_{1,2}$, $f_{1,1}$, $f_{1,0}$, and $g_{1,0}$ are fresh variables. These variables are never written by the program, and are only read by transformed expressions that originally contained the same UF symbols (f and/or g).

The applications of the uninterpreted function f were transformed into polynomials of degree two, since we have three applications of f with (possibly) different input parameters.

A polynomial with a lower degree would not be sufficient to represent this boolean expression without imposing constraints on the input parameters that did not exist in the original expression with UFs. For example, if we use a polynomial of degree one for the applications of f, we obtain (excluding the constraint with g):

$$f_{1,1} \times x + f_{1,0} = 0 \wedge f_{1,1} \times y + f_{1,0} = 1 \wedge f_{1,1} \times z + f_{1,0} = 2 \wedge y < z \wedge z < x$$

This formula is not satisfiable, while its original UF form is. A polynomial of degree two (as shown above) or of higher degree, however, is guaranteed to yield a satisfiable formula for all distinct x, y, and z (by the Unisolvence Theorem [41]).

Computing the value of $u(f, i)$ as defined is hard, and may require prior static analysis. This value can, however, be safely over-approximated by the number of applications of f in the whole program, at the expense of generating more complex expressions.

For example, the optimal values for u in the following program excerpt are $u(f, 1) = 1$ and $u(f, 2) = 0$ (assuming no other UF applications in the rest of

while $i < n$ **do**
   $k := 2 \times k$
   $j := 0$
   while $j < m$ **do**
      $k := k + j$
      $j := j + 1$
    $i := i + 1$

$$R_j(x) = R_j(x - 1) + 1$$
$$R_j(0) = 0$$
$$R_k(x) = R_k(x - 1) + R_j(x - 1)$$
$$R_k(0) = 2 \cdot V_k(y - 1)$$
$$V_i(y) = V_i(y - 1) + 1$$
$$V_i(0) = i_0$$
$$V_k(y) = R_k(x)$$
$$V_k(0) = k_0$$

Fig. 5. An example program and the corresponding system of recurrences that summarizes the two loops, where R_j and R_k represent the behavior of the inner loop on the variables j and k, respectively, and V_i and V_k represent the outer loop

the program). Although there are three applications of f with a different first parameter, only two applications are ever encountered and used in a boolean expression in a single path.

if ... **then**
   $j := f(y, 3)$
else
   $k := f(z, 3)$

if $f(x, 3) \leq 0 \wedge j \leq 0 \wedge k \leq 0$ **then**
   ...

The value of $u(f, i)$ must be computed over the composed program (and not over each of the two input programs independently), including the **assert** command that is added at the end of it (Section 4.2).

Replace Loops with Recurrences. The second step of the algorithm is to eliminate loops, by replacing each loop with a system of recurrences. The transformation is carried out as follows. Each variable that is assigned in the loop gets a recurrence over a newly introduced variable that represents the loop trip count. For nested loops, the initial value of a recurrence in an inner loop is the value of the previous iteration of the outer loop.

An example program and its system of recurrences is shown in Figure 5. The recurrence $R_v(n)$ represents the value of the variable v at the inner loop iteration n, and $V_v(n)$ in the outer loop. For example, the value of variable k in the iteration x of the inner loop, $R_k(x)$, is equal to the sum of the values of variables k and j of the previous (inner loop) iteration. The value of k in the beginning of the first inner loop iteration, $R_k(0)$, is equal to twice the value of k in the previous outer loop iteration.

The closed-form solution for the system of recurrences is the following:

$$R_j(x) = x \qquad\qquad R_k(x) = \frac{4 \cdot V_k(y-1) + x^2 - x}{2}$$

$$V_i(y) = i_0 + y \qquad\qquad V_k(y) = \frac{k_0 \cdot 2^{y+1} + (x-1) \cdot x \cdot (2^y - 1)}{2}$$

We note that while the solution of $R_k(x)$ still includes a reference to a recurrence — $V_k(y-1)$ — it is only used to compute the solution of $V_k(y)$ and it is never used directly by the next steps of the algorithm. We only need the value of k after the outer loop terminates, which is represented by $V_k(y)$.

After computing the closed-form solution for the system of recurrences, each loop of the form "while b do c" is replaced with the following code:

if b **then**
    assume $\sigma_{n-1}(b) \wedge \sigma_n(\neg b)$
    $v_i := \sigma_n(v_i)$
else
    assume $n = 0$

The fresh variable n represents the number of iterations performed by the loop. σ_n is a state where each variable maps to the closed-form solution of its corresponding recurrence at point n, or to itself if the variable is not modified in the loop body c. Variable v_i ranges over all variables that are possibly modified in the loop body. For the previous example, we have for the inner loop, e.g., $\sigma_x(j) = R_j(x) = x$ and $\sigma_x(n) = n$.

Intuitively, a loop executes n times if the loop guard is true for the first n iterations (iterations $0 \ldots (n-1)$) and false in the following iteration (iteration n). The number of iterations is implicitly computed when the **assume** command is evaluated. Its expression states that the loop guard of iteration $n-1$ should be true, and that at iteration n the guard should be false instead.

We note that there can be multiple solutions for the expression given to the **assume** command if the loop guard is non-linear. In this case, the number of loop iterations is the smallest positive n that makes the formula satisfiable. Computing the smallest n can be achieved, for example, by using an optimizing solver or by doing multiple calls to an SMT solver.

For the example in Figure 5, the program after removing the loops is shown in Figure 6. The command "**assume** $y = 0$" at the end can be removed as an optimization, since there are no further uses of y afterward.

Equivalence Checking. The third and final step of the algorithm is to prove the equivalence between the two programs after they undergo the transformations previously described.

We do this by sequentially composing the first program with a renamed version of the second. The second program is renamed so that it operates over a different set of variables from the first.

if $i < n$ **then**
   assume $V_i(y-1) < n \land V_i(y) \geq n$
   $j := 0$
   if $j < m$ **then**
      assume $R_j(x-1) < m \land R_j(x) \geq m$
      $j := R_j(x)$
   else
      assume $x = 0$
   $k := V_k(y)$
   $i := V_i(y)$
else
   assume $y = 0$

Fig. 6. Program of Figure 5 after replacing the loops with a set of assignments over the system of recurrences including $V_i(n)$, $V_k(n)$, and $R_j(n)$

Let P_1' and P_2' be, respectively, the programs P_1 and P_2 after removing the UF applications and the loops. The composed program is as follows.

assume $\forall v \in \mathsf{Vars}(P_1') \cap \mathsf{Vars}(P_2') : v = \bar{v}$
P_1'
$\bar{P}_2'$
assert $\forall v \in \mathsf{Out}(P_1') : v = \bar{v}$

Program $\bar{P}_2'$ is the same as the program P_2', but where each variable v was renamed to $\bar{v}$. Moreover, $\mathsf{Out}(P_1') = \mathsf{Out}(P_2')$.

If the composed program is safe, i.e., if the condition of the **assert** command is true for all inputs, then the two original programs are partially equivalent.

To prove program safety, and since the number of symbolic paths is finite, we can use an algorithm that enumerates all paths and tests if any of those makes the condition of the **assert** command false.

Note that the value of $\mathsf{u}(f, i)$ defined in Section 4.2 for the composed program above must take into account the paths that pass through programs P_1 *and* P_2, as well as the **assert** command (which takes a boolean expression by itself).

5   Verification of Compiler Optimizations

To evaluate the proposed algorithm, we implemented a prototype to prove the correctness of compiler optimizations. This is an important topic, since all mainstream compilers were shown recently to have several bugs in the optimization passes [45]. Moreover, if the compiler is not proved correct, properties verified on the source-code level of a program are not carried to the binary code, since the compiler may introduce bugs during the translation process.

while $I < N$ do
   S
   $I := I + 1$

$\Rightarrow$

while $(I + 1) < N$ do
   S
   $I := I + 1$
   S
   $I := I + 1$
if $I < N$ then
   S
   $I := I + 1$

Fig. 7. Loop unrolling: the source template is on the left, and the transformed template on the right. Template statement S cannot modify template variables I and N.

5.1 From Compiler Optimizations to Program Equivalence

We specify a compiler optimization as a transformation function from a *source* template program to a *target* template program. These template programs can be modeled as UF+IA programs, where UFs represent arbitrary statements, or expressions that should be matched within a program under optimization.

We show an example optimization (loop unrolling) in Figure 7. This optimization transforms a loop into a new loop that performs only half of the iterations of the original loop, but where each iteration of the new loop performs twice the work of an iteration of the original loop.

The template statement S is a placeholder for an arbitrary statement (e.g., variable assignments, function calls, or other loops) that may be present in a loop under optimization. Template variables I and N are placeholders for arbitrary program variables. The transformation function states how each template statement/expression is transformed (e.g., moved, duplicated, eliminated) to produce the optimized program.

As an example, we apply loop unrolling to the following program.

while $i < n$ do
   $x := i + 2$
   $i := i + 1$

Running the optimization with S instantiated to "$x := i + 2$", I to "i", and N to "n" yields the following program:

while $i < n$ do
   $x := i + 2$
   $i := i + 1$
   $x := i + 2$
   $i := i + 1$
if $i < n$ then
   $x := i + 2$
   $i := i + 1$

To verify a compiler optimization correct, we split the transformation function into two programs (the source and target templates), and then we convert the template programs into UF+IA programs. Finally, we use the proposed equivalence checking algorithm to prove that the source and target templates are equivalent, which implies that the optimization is correct.

Preconditions of optimizations are specified as read and write sets of the template statements/expressions, which contain the variables that the template statements/expressions *may* read and write, respectively. For example, the read set of S in loop unrolling is $R(S) = \{c_1, I, N\}$, and the write set is $W(S) = \{c_1\}$, since the precondition is that S cannot modify variables I and N.

The conversion of a template program to an UF+IA program is done by replacing each template statement S with a set of assignments of the following form:

$$v_i := S_i(r_1, \ldots, r_n)$$

where $v_i \in W(S)$ and $R(S) = \{r_1, \ldots, r_n\}$. The transformation of template expressions is done similarly.

In the loop unrolling example, S is replaced with a single assignment (with S_1 being a fresh UF symbol):

$$c_1 := S_1(c_1, I, N)$$

Variable c_1 is what we call a context variable. These fresh variables c_i represent the variables that are possibly in scope where a template may be instantiated (possibly none) and that do not appear in the template function.

In our example, c_1 represents the effects of S in x. While variable x does not appear explicitly in the transformation function, S does indeed modify x in the example instantiation.

The values computed for the function u are the following: $u(S_1, 1) = 1$ and $u(S_1, 2) = 1$, since there are two applications of S_1 with possibly different values that are used in a boolean expression (the **assert** command); and $u(S_1, 3) = 0$, since N is constant.

At least one context variable is added to each program. Moreover, the read and write sets of each template statement must include at least one context variable, unless the precondition of the optimization states that, e.g., a given statement does not read any other variable than x. Similarly, template expressions may read a variable that is not present in the transformation function (again, unless stated otherwise in the precondition), and therefore their read set must include a context variable.

We may add more than one context variable to a program to express certain preconditions over template statements. For example, if a statement S is idempotent, we have that $R(S) \cap W(S) = \emptyset$. Therefore, we have to have at least two distinct context variables c_1 and c_2 to have, e.g., $R(S) = \{c_1\}$ and $W(S) = \{c_2\}$ to state that S cannot read a variable that it writes to, nor vice versa.

Similarly, to state that template statements S and T commute, we have $W(S) \cap R(T) = W(T) \cap R(S) = W(S) \cap W(T) = \emptyset$. In this case, we also need at least two distinct context variables.

5.2 Evaluation

We implemented a prototype named CORK[1], which stands for Compiler Optimization coRrectness checKer. CORK is implemented in OCaml ($\sim$ 1,100 LoC), and uses Wolfram Mathematica 8.0.4 for both constraint and recurrence solving.

CORK takes as input a transformation function in the format of the example in Figure 7. CORK then derives two programs over the UF+IA theory as described in the previous section, and subsequently checks if they are equivalent. The equivalence check is done by enumerating each path of the composed program, since the number of paths is finite and small. If the equivalence check fails, CORK prints a counterexample path.

CORK performs three optimizations to improve the performance. First, CORK discharges by itself equality tests of syntactically equal expressions. Second, CORK performs equality propagation on the satisfiability queries sent to Mathematica. Finally, CORK checks the equality of program variables (arising from the **assert** command at the end of the composed program) one-by-one, instead of just one satisfiability query per path. CORK then uses the established equalities in the following queries. Moreover, variable equality checks are ordered so that first are checked the induction variables, and the remaining variables are ordered by the length of their value expressions. Establishing first the equality of expressions involving induction variables improves the performance significantly.

We ran CORK over a set of optimizations (mostly loop-manipulating). The experiments were run on a machine running Linux 3.6.2 with an Intel Core 2 Duo 3.00 GHz CPU, and 4 GB of RAM. The results are shown in Table 1.

We first note that the number of recurrence solving queries is higher than expected (more than one per loop), since we compute the recurrences per path and we do not cache any information across paths. Optimizations that do not manipulate loops explicitly do not generate any recurrence.

We compare the results of CORK with the state-of-the-art tool PEC [23]. Since PEC is not publicly available, we compare only with the published results.

The table is divided in four sets of optimizations (described in, e.g., [1]). The first part is a set of optimizations that do not manipulate loops explicitly, which are trivially proven correct by both CORK and PEC. The second part is a set of optimizations that PEC can prove correct without the help of heuristics. The third part is a set of optimizations that PEC can only prove correct by using the permute heuristic [14, 47], since otherwise it could not find a bisimulation relation automatically. The fourth and last part of the table contains a set of optimizations that PEC cannot prove correct, since it cannot find a bisimulation automatically, even with the permute heuristic. CORK, on the other hand, is able to prove correct the loop strength reduction and loop tiling optimizations. CORK fails to prove correct the loop flattening optimization, since Mathematica is unable to compute the closed-form solution of recurrences with integer division.

---

[1] Prototype and benchmarks available from
`http://web.ist.utl.pt/nuno.lopes/cork/`.

Table 1. List of compiler optimizations [1], how PEC performs ($\checkmark_p$ means PEC needs the permute heuristic), the number of satisfiability and recurrence solving queries issued to Mathematica, and the time that CORK took to prove each optimization correct

Optimization	PEC	# Sat. queries	# Recurrences	Time
Code hoisting	$\checkmark$	2	0	0.32s
Constant propagation	$\checkmark$	0	0	0.33s
Copy propagation	$\checkmark$	0	0	0.33s
If-conversion	$\checkmark$	2	0	0.34s
Partial redundancy elimin.	$\checkmark$	2	0	0.34s
Loop invariant code motion	$\checkmark$	7	5	3.48s
Loop peeling	$\checkmark$	9	5	3.26s
Loop unrolling	$\checkmark$	13	8	12.17s
Loop unswitching	$\checkmark$	14	14	8.19s
Software pipelining	$\checkmark$	9	5	8.02s
Loop fission	$\checkmark_p$	10	12	23.45s
Loop fusion	$\checkmark_p$	10	12	23.34s
Loop interchange	$\checkmark_p$	15	24	29.30s
Loop reversal	$\checkmark_p$	7	5	8.41s
Loop skewing	$\checkmark_p$	16	24	8.50s
Loop flattening	$\times$	—	—	FAIL
Loop strength reduction	$\times$	6	4	5.63s
Loop tiling	$\times$	7	9	10.94s

The execution time of PEC and CORK is within the same order of magnitude, but CORK advances the state-of-the-art by being able to prove correct more optimizations than PEC.

6   Related Work

Proving the equivalence of programs is undecidable. However, there has been advances over the last decades to solve the problem under certain assumptions.

Several alternative approaches exist to prove the equivalence of programs, namely manual or semi-automated (with the help of an iterative theorem prover) approaches, bisimulation relation synthesis, symbolic execution, recurrence equivalence, and software model checking based techniques.

Manual and Semi-automated Proofs. Relational Hoare logic [7] is a proof system that enables the verification of equivalence between two programs. The system only supports the verification of structurally equivalent programs (yet, for example, many compiler optimizations do not obey this constraint). Barthe et al. [4] lift some of the restrictions of this work through the usage of product programs. The set of structural differences that the programs under equivalence checking may exhibit is still dependent on the set of built-in proof rules. Liang et al. [25] adapted relational Hoare logic to the setting of concurrent programs.

Bisimulation. Parameterized equivalence checking (PEC [23]) is a technique to verify the correctness of compiler optimizations automatically. It works by automatically finding a bisimulation relation [37] between the original and the optimized template programs. For structurally different loops, PEC relies on a set of heuristics inspired in [14, 47].

Recurrence Equivalence. Barthou et al. [6] and Shashidhar et al. [39] present different algorithms to prove the equivalence of systems of affine recurrence equations that are structurally similar. Verdoolaege et al. [44] propose an algorithm to prove the equivalence of integer affine programs where loops are described as recurrences. The algorithm does not compute the closed-form solution for the recurrences, but instead uses widening to reach a fixed point. The algorithm handles commutative operators by trying all possible permutations.

Symbolic Execution. Matsumoto et al. [26] and Person et al. [31] present different techniques to detect differences between two programs that are mostly equal. Ramos and Engler [34] present an algorithm to check for program equivalence automatically up to a bounded number of loop unrollings.

Software Verification and Invariant Synthesis. State-of-the-art software verification tools are unable to prove equivalence of most programs containing loops, since they are usually unable to automatically derive sufficiently strong loop invariants to complete the proof, even if just considering the theory of integer arithmetic, let alone the UF+LIA theory.

Beyer et al. [8] present an algorithm to synthesize loop invariants over the UF+LIA theory, and Rybalchenko and Stokkermans [36] present an algorithm to synthesize interpolants over the same theory. McMillan [28] introduced an algorithm to generate interpolants from the unsatisfiability proofs of Z3 [12]. However, the language of interpolants/invariants supported by these algorithms is not able to express an unbounded number of UF applications, which is often required to prove equivalence of programs that have UF applications inside loops.

Polynomial loop invariant generation techniques (e.g., [29, 35, 38]) can only generate invariants with bounded exponents, which is not sufficient for the verification of the integer programs we generate (after removing the UF applications), since these programs often require loop invariants with unbounded exponents.

Gupta et al. [19] present an algorithm to solve recursion-free Horn clauses in the theory of UF+LIA. Grebenshchikov et al. [15] extend this work to recursive Horn clauses in order to support the verification of recursive programs. The interpolation algorithm used suffers from the same limitations as the others.

Gulwani and Tiwari [17] present an algorithm for the verification of programs over the UF+LIA theory. However, only equalities over UF applications are supported, and conditional branches are abstracted non-deterministically, which is too weak for the application of equivalence checking.

Blanc et al. [10] and Gulwani et al. [16] present algorithms to compute symbolic bounds of loop trip counts. However, the computed trip counts may not be sufficiently precise for equivalence checking proofs.

7   Conclusion

In this paper we presented, as far as we know, the first algorithm for the equivalence checking of looping programs over the combined theory of uninterpreted function symbols and integer arithmetic (UF+IA).

For evaluation purposes, we developed CORK, a tool that proves the correctness of compiler optimizations, which is based on the proposed equivalence checking algorithm. CORK proves correct more optimizations than other tools known as state-of-the-art.

Acknowledgments. The authors thank João Pedro Afonso, Ruslán Ledesma-Garza, and the anonymous reviewers for their comments and suggestions on earlier drafts of this paper.

This work was partially supported by the FCT grants SFRH/BD/63609/2009 and INESC-ID multiannual funding PEst-OE/EEI/LA0021/2011.

References

[1] Aho, A.V., Lam, M.S., Sethi, R., Ullman, J.D.: Compilers: Principles, Techniques, and Tools, 2nd edn. Addison-Wesley (2006)

[2] Alias, C., Barthou, D.: On the recognition of algorithm templates. In: COCV (2003)

[3] Ball, T., Rajamani, S.K.: The SLAM project: debugging system software via static analysis. In: POPL (2002)

[4] Barthe, G., Crespo, J.M., Kunz, C.: Relational verification using product programs. In: Butler, M., Schulte, W. (eds.) FM 2011. LNCS, vol. 6664, pp. 200–214. Springer, Heidelberg (2011)

[5] Barthe, G., D'Argenio, P.R., Rezk, T.: Secure information flow by self-composition. In: CSFW (2004)

[6] Barthou, D., Feautrier, P., Redon, X.: On the equivalence of two systems of affine recurrence equations. In: Monien, B., Feldmann, R.L. (eds.) Euro-Par 2002. LNCS, vol. 2400, pp. 309–313. Springer, Heidelberg (2002)

[7] Benton, N.: Simple relational correctness proofs for static analyses and program transformations. In: POPL (2004)

[8] Beyer, D., Henzinger, T.A., Majumdar, R., Rybalchenko, A.: Invariant synthesis for combined theories. In: Cook, B., Podelski, A. (eds.) VMCAI 2007. LNCS, vol. 4349, pp. 378–394. Springer, Heidelberg (2007)

[9] Beyer, D., Keremoglu, M.E.: CPACHECKER: A tool for configurable software verification. In: Gopalakrishnan, G., Qadeer, S. (eds.) CAV 2011. LNCS, vol. 6806, pp. 184–190. Springer, Heidelberg (2011)

[10] Blanc, R., Henzinger, T.A., Hottelier, T., Kovács, L.: ABC: Algebraic bound computation for loops. In: Clarke, E.M., Voronkov, A. (eds.) LPAR-16 2010. LNCS, vol. 6355, pp. 103–118. Springer, Heidelberg (2010)

[11] Chaki, S., Gurfinkel, A., Strichman, O.: Regression verification for multi-threaded programs. In: Kuncak, V., Rybalchenko, A. (eds.) VMCAI 2012. LNCS, vol. 7148, pp. 119–135. Springer, Heidelberg (2012)

[12] de Moura, L., Bjørner, N.: Z3: An efficient SMT solver. In: Ramakrishnan, C.R., Rehof, J. (eds.) TACAS 2008. LNCS, vol. 4963, pp. 337–340. Springer, Heidelberg (2008)

[13] Godlin, B., Strichman, O.: Regression verification. In: DAC (2009)
[14] Goldberg, B., Zuck, L., Barrett, C.: Into the loops: Practical issues in translation validation for optimizing compilers. Electron. Notes Theor. Comp. Sci. 132 (2005)
[15] Grebenshchikov, S., Lopes, N.P., Popeea, C., Rybalchenko, A.: Synthesizing software verifiers from proof rules. In: PLDI (2012)
[16] Gulwani, S., Mehra, K.K., Chilimbi, T.: SPEED: precise and efficient static estimation of program computational complexity. In: POPL (2009)
[17] Gulwani, S., Tiwari, A.: Assertion checking over combined abstraction of linear arithmetic and uninterpreted functions. In: Sestoft, P. (ed.) ESOP 2006. LNCS, vol. 3924, pp. 279–293. Springer, Heidelberg (2006)
[18] Guo, S.-Y., Palsberg, J.: The essence of compiling with traces. In: POPL (2011)
[19] Gupta, A., Popeea, C., Rybalchenko, A.: Solving recursion-free horn clauses over LI+UIF. In: Yang, H. (ed.) APLAS 2011. LNCS, vol. 7078, pp. 188–203. Springer, Heidelberg (2011)
[20] Henzinger, T.A., Jhala, R., Majumdar, R., McMillan, K.L.: Abstractions from proofs. In: POPL (2004)
[21] Henzinger, T.A., Jhala, R., Majumdar, R., Sutre, G.: Lazy abstraction. In: POPL (2002)
[22] Ivančić, F., Yang, Z., Ganai, M.K., Gupta, A., Shlyakhter, I., Ashar, P.: F-SOFT: Software verification platform. In: Etessami, K., Rajamani, S.K. (eds.) CAV 2005. LNCS, vol. 3576, pp. 301–306. Springer, Heidelberg (2005)
[23] Kundu, S., Tatlock, Z., Lerner, S.: Proving optimizations correct using parameterized program equivalence. In: PLDI (2009)
[24] Lahiri, S.K., Hawblitzel, C., Kawaguchi, M., Rebêlo, H.: SymDiff: A language-agnostic semantic diff tool for imperative programs. In: Madhusudan, P., Seshia, S.A. (eds.) CAV 2012. LNCS, vol. 7358, pp. 712–717. Springer, Heidelberg (2012)
[25] Liang, H., Feng, X., Fu, M.: A rely-guarantee-based simulation for verifying concurrent program transformations. In: POPL (2012)
[26] Matsumoto, T., Saito, H., Fujita, M.: Equivalence checking of C programs by locally performing symbolic simulation on dependence graphs. In: ISQED (2006)
[27] McMillan, K.L.: Lazy abstraction with interpolants. In: Ball, T., Jones, R.B. (eds.) CAV 2006. LNCS, vol. 4144, pp. 123–136. Springer, Heidelberg (2006)
[28] McMillan, K.L.: Interpolants from Z3 proofs. In: FMCAD (2011)
[29] Müller-Olm, M., Seidl, H.: Computing polynomial program invariants. Inf. Process. Lett. 91, 233–244 (2004)
[30] Necula, G.C.: Translation validation for an optimizing compiler. In: PLDI (2000)
[31] Person, S., Dwyer, M.B., Elbaum, S., Păsăreanu, C.S.: Differential symbolic execution. In: SIGSOFT (2008)
[32] Pnueli, A., Siegel, M., Singerman, E.: Translation validation. In: Steffen, B. (ed.) TACAS 1998. LNCS, vol. 1384, pp. 151–166. Springer, Heidelberg (1998)
[33] Podelski, A., Rybalchenko, A.: ARMC: The logical choice for software model checking with abstraction refinement. In: Hanus, M. (ed.) PADL 2007. LNCS, vol. 4354, pp. 245–259. Springer, Heidelberg (2007)
[34] Ramos, D.A., Engler, D.R.: Practical, low-effort equivalence verification of real code. In: Gopalakrishnan, G., Qadeer, S. (eds.) CAV 2011. LNCS, vol. 6806, pp. 669–685. Springer, Heidelberg (2011)
[35] Rodríguez-Carbonell, E., Kapur, D.: Generating all polynomial invariants in simple loops. J. Symb. Comput. 42, 443–476 (2007)
[36] Rybalchenko, A., Sofronie-Stokkermans, V.: Constraint solving for interpolation. In: Cook, B., Podelski, A. (eds.) VMCAI 2007. LNCS, vol. 4349, pp. 346–362. Springer, Heidelberg (2007)

[37] Sangiorgi, D.: On the origins of bisimulation and coinduction. ACM Trans. Program. Lang. Syst. 31(4), 15:1–15:41 (2009)
[38] Sankaranarayanan, S., Sipma, H.B., Manna, Z.: Non-linear loop invariant generation using Gröbner bases. In: POPL (2004)
[39] Shashidhar, K.C., Bruynooghe, M., Catthoor, F., Janssens, G.: Verification of source code transformations by program equivalence checking. In: Bodik, R. (ed.) CC 2005. LNCS, vol. 3443, pp. 221–236. Springer, Heidelberg (2005)
[40] Stepp, M., Tate, R., Lerner, S.: Equality-based translation validator for LLVM. In: Gopalakrishnan, G., Qadeer, S. (eds.) CAV 2011. LNCS, vol. 6806, pp. 737–742. Springer, Heidelberg (2011)
[41] Strang, G.: Linear Algebra and Its Applications, 2nd edn. Academic Press (1980)
[42] Terauchi, T., Aiken, A.: Secure information flow as a safety problem. In: Hankin, C., Siveroni, I. (eds.) SAS 2005. LNCS, vol. 3672, pp. 352–367. Springer, Heidelberg (2005)
[43] Tristan, J.-B., Govereau, P., Morrisett, G.: Evaluating value-graph translation validation for LLVM. In: PLDI (2011)
[44] Verdoolaege, S., Janssens, G., Bruynooghe, M.: Equivalence checking of static affine programs using widening to handle recurrences. In: Bouajjani, A., Maler, O. (eds.) CAV 2009. LNCS, vol. 5643, pp. 599–613. Springer, Heidelberg (2009)
[45] Yang, X., Chen, Y., Eide, E., Regehr, J.: Finding and understanding bugs in C compilers. In: PLDI (2011)
[46] Zaks, A., Pnueli, A.: CoVaC: Compiler validation by program analysis of the cross-product. In: Cuellar, J., Sere, K. (eds.) FM 2008. LNCS, vol. 5014, pp. 35–51. Springer, Heidelberg (2008)
[47] Zuck, L., Pnueli, A., Goldberg, B., Barrett, C., Fang, Y., Hu, Y.: Translation and run-time validation of loop transformations. Form. Methods Syst. Des. 27 (2005)

Expression Reduction from Programs in a Symbolic Binary Executor

Anthony Romano and Dawson Engler

Stanford University
{ajromano,engler}@cs.stanford.edu

Abstract. Symbolic binary execution is a dynamic analysis method which explores program paths to generate test cases for compiled code. Throughout execution, a program is evaluated with a bit-vector theorem prover and a runtime interpreter as a mix of symbolic expressions and concrete values. Left untended, these symbolic expressions grow to negatively impact interpretation performance.

We describe an expression reduction system which recovers sound, context-insensitive expression reduction rules at run time from programs during symbolic evaluation. These rules are further refined offline into general rules which match larger classes of expressions. We demonstrate that our optimizer significantly reduces the number of theorem solver queries and solver time on hundreds of commodity programs compared to a default ad-hoc optimizer from a popular symbolic interpreter.

1 Introduction

The importance of program reliability, robustness, and correctness, has fueled interest for automated, unassisted program analysis and bug detection. As bug finding systems improve, they report deep bugs which are hard to explain and expensive to discover. It is often difficult or impractical to confirm these error reports by hand; instead, test cases establish logical soundness by serving as certificates against false positives. Likewise, amortizing the cost of the analysis process, so bugs are found in the first place, is subject to considerable study.

Symbolic execution is a popular technique [18] for automated test-case generation. These test cases are created with a goal of finding paths to bugs or interesting program properties in complicated or unfamiliar software. Conceptually, variant data (e.g., file contents) in a program is marked as symbolic and evaluated abstractly. When the program state reaches a control decision based on a symbolic condition, a satisfiability query is submitted to a theorem prover backed solver. If the symbolic condition is contingent the state is forked into two states, and a corresponding predicate is made into a *path constraint* which is added to each state's *constraint set*. Solving for the state's constraint set creates an assignment, or test case, which follows the state's path.

The convenience of applying dynamic analysis to unmodified program binaries led to the development of symbolic binary execution. Under symbolic binary execution, compiled executables are symbolically evaluated as-is; there is no

E. Bartocci and C.R. Ramakrishnan (Eds.): SPIN 2013, LNCS 7976, pp. 301–319, 2013.

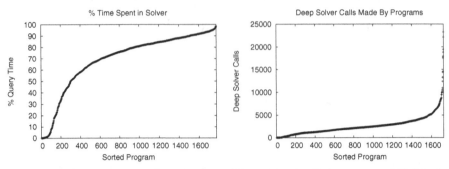

Fig. 1. Query time out of total time   **Fig. 2.** Total calls into external SMT solver

need for recompilation, annotations, special linking, or limited languages. This contrasts with older systems [4,12,19,20] which were built to process source code or a metadata-rich byte code. A typical system pairs a symbolic interpreter with a dynamic binary translation front-end [5,10,14,16,21]; the binary translator converts a program's machine code into instructions for the symbolic interpreter.

Shifting from specialized symbolic interpretation to general binary translation imposes a performance challenge. First, compilers target machine architectures. Fast code on hardware may be slow to interpret due to expensive solver queries. Next, resource mismatches from translation incur some overhead. For instance, register access may be translated into an intermediate value access plus an access into a region of memory representing a register file. Furthermore, type information, control structures, and other metadata from the source code, which is useful for inferring execution traits, is often unavailable at the binary level. Finally, simple ad-hoc tuning fails to scale to the variety of programs, compilers, and optimization configurations in the wild.

In practice, solver requests dominate symbolic execution running time. Figure 1 illustrates query overhead; of several hundred programs after running five minutes, 80% spend more time solving for satisfiability than dispatching instructions. Hence, reducing or eliminating queries can be expected to yield gains.

There is ample opportunity to optimize queries. Based on Figure 2, the total number of external calls made to the solver for the same programs, a typical symbolic execution session may submit thousands of queries to the solver. These solver calls primarily determine branch satisfiability for symbolic conditionals (e.g., whether a state should fork) and are inhrent to symbolic execution.

The expressions which define queries are redundant and suitable for optimization. As an example, a loop that increments an expression x every iteration might produce the bulky expression $(+ \ ... \ (+ \ (+ \ x \ 1) \ 1) \ ... \ 1)$ which should fold into a svelte $(+ \ x \ c)$. Binary code worsens the problem because translation overhead leads to more operations and hence larger expressions.

We propose an expression optimizer which learns reduction rules from symbolic evaluation of programs. During the learning phase, expressions produced at run time are keyed by a hash of samples and stored to a global database. Candidate rules are constructed by matching the sample hash against the hashes of shorter expressions in the database. Each candidate rule is validated using the theorem prover, applied in the interpreter, and saved for future use. Rules are further processed into generalized rules suitable for larger classes of expressions.

We implement and evaluate the expression optimizer in a symbolic binary executor, KLEE-MC. The optimizer is evaluated at scale with over two thousand commodity programs from a stock desktop Linux system. Rules are collected during a brief learning period and are shown to lessen the total number of queries dispatched during symbolic execution. Furthermore, rules improve running and solver time by at least 10% on average over the baseline interpreter.

2   Symbolic Execution and Expressions

Symbolic expressions are a byproduct of symbolic execution. A program is symbolically executed by marking its inputs as symbolic and evaluating abstractly. This evaluation emits *expressions* to represent operations on symbolic data.

The symbolic executor, KLEE-MC, is a machine code extension of the KLEE [4] symbolic LLVM interpreter. KLEE-MC simulates a program from the host machine by dynamically translating a snapshot's machine code into LLVM for the KLEE interpreter. First, a process snapshot is built from a running program binary through data gleaned from the operating system's debugging facilities (e.g., ptrace). KLEE-MC loads the snapshot where it is on-demand translated into LLVM operations. Machine code is translated by VEX [17] into VEX-IR super blocks (i.e., multiple exit basic blocks) which model the target machine architecture as operations on memory, registers, and control flow. Each super block is rendered into unary LLVM functions of the form $f : RegisterFileAddress \rightarrow JumpAddress$. Finally, KLEE-MC loops, translates code on-the-fly, interprets the LLVM bitcode, and models a symbolic Linux system call interface.

A mix of concrete values and symbolic expression data are manipulated by evaluating LLVM operations. LLVM operations are those defined by the LLVM IR, such as arithmetic, logical, and memory operations, as well as a handful of specialized LLVM intrinsics. Expressions are a subset of the SMTLIB [3] language, but operators will be written in shorthand notation when convenient. For instance, the expression to add two bit-vector expressions a and b is $(+ \ a \ b)$.

Large, redundant expressions are expensive. A large expression slows query serialization to the solver and is costly to evaluate into a constant on variable assignment. Expanded tautologies (e.g., $(x \lor \neg x)$), or expressions that evaluate to one value for all interpretations, pollute solver caches and incur unnecessary calls to the theorem prover. Worse, a large expression may linger as a path constraint, slowing future queries that must use the constraint set.

There are two strategies for shedding expression bloat: expression optimization and concretization. Expression optimization applies sound identities to reduce an expression to fewer terms. For instance, the bit-wise **or** expression $(or \ 0 \ x)$ is identical to x. The drawback is vital identities are program-dependent; it is infeasible to encode all useful reductions by hand. Alternatively, concretization of symbolic terms reduces expressions to constants but at the cost of completeness; x becomes $\{c\}$ instead of $x \subset \mathbb{N}$.

The original KLEE interpreter used both expression optimization and concretization. A hand-written optimizer folds constants and reduces excess terms from dozens of common redundancies. For concretization, path constraints are inspected through implied value concretization (IVC) to find and concretize variables which are constant for all valid interpretations. For instance, under IVC the constraint $(= x\ 1)$ replaces x with 1 in the program state.

We consider the problem of expression node minimization. Given an expression, we wish to find a semantically equivalent expression with the fewest possible terms. Formally, we define expression node minimization as follows: given an expression e the minimized expression e' is such that for all tautological expressions $(= e\ e_i)$, the number of nodes in e', $|e'|$, satisfies $|e'| \leq |e_i|$. It is worth noting e' is not unique under this definition. To solve this, first define an ordering operator on expressions $\leq$ where $e_i \leq e_j$ when there are fewer nodes, $|e_i| < |e_j|$, or by lexical comparison, $|e_i| = |e_j| \ \wedge \ \text{lex}(e_i) \leq \text{lex}(e_j)$. Uniqueness is given by the expression minimization problem of finding e' where $e' \leq e_i$.

A node minimizing optimizer has several advantages. Theoretically, it is bounded when greedy; optimization stops once the expression stops shrinking. If a conditional expression reduces to a constant, a solver call may be avoided. Contingent conditionals also benefit, such as through better independence analysis. Furthermore, smaller expressions improve the likelihood that IVC will discover concretizing implications. On the other hand, smaller expressions may lead to slower queries because some operations (e.g., divide) are slow; however, we observe performance improvements from our implementation in Section 7.

3   Rules from Programs

Expression minimizations form a *reduction relation*, $\rightarrow$. The theory of contractions is a classic formalization for converting terms in lambda calculus [6]. This theory was developed further in abstract rewriting systems as reduction relations under the notion of confluence [11]. We use reduction relations as a theoretical framework for reasoning about properties of the expression rewriting system.

The problem of discovering elements of $\rightarrow$ is handled with a database of reducts. The database, referred to as the EquivDB, is globally populated by expressions made during symbolic execution of binary programs. As expressions are created, they are matched against the EquivDB with assistance from a theorem prover to find smaller, but semantically equivalent, expressions. If equivalent, the expression reduces to the smaller expression and is related under $\rightarrow$.

Information about $\rightarrow$ is maintained as a set of rewrite rules. Each rule has a *from-pattern* and a *to-pattern* which describe classes of elements in $\rightarrow$ through expression templates. Once shown to be sound by the theorem prover, rules are used as the expression optimization directive format in the symbolic interpreter.

3.1   Reductions on Expressions

A reduction from one expression to another is cast in terms of reduction relations. A reduction relation is used to convert one λ-term to another λ-term. We omit the trivial proof of the existence of the correspondence from expressions to λ-terms, $\Lambda_E : Expr \rightarrow \Lambda$, but note all expressions for our purposes are in the set of closed sentences Λ^0. All variables are bound; arguments to $\Lambda_E(e)$ are De Bruijn indexes of 8-bit symbolic array read operations (`select` in SMTLIB) from e.

The reduction relation $\rightarrow$ is defined as the binary relation

$$\rightarrow = \{(\Lambda_E(e), \Lambda_E(e')) \mid (e, e') \in Expr^2, \ e' \leq e \wedge (= e' \ e)\}$$

The immediate reduction relation $\twoheadrightarrow$ is defined as

$$\twoheadrightarrow = \{(e, \ e') \in \rightarrow \ \mid \forall (e, e'') \in \rightarrow . \ \Lambda_E^{-1}(e') \leq \Lambda_E^{-1}(e'')\}$$

An expression is reduced by $\rightarrow$ through β-reduction. The reduction $a \rightarrow b$ is said to reduce the expression e when there exists an index assignment σ for $\Lambda_E(e)$ where $\Lambda_E(e)_\sigma$ is syntactically equal to a. β-reducing b with the terms in e substituted by σ on matching variable indices yields the shorter expression $[a \rightarrow b][e]$. The new $[a \rightarrow b][e]$ is guaranteed by referential transparency to be semantically equivalent to e and can safely substitute occurrences of e.

For instance, consider the following 8-bit expressions e and e'.

$$e = (\text{bvand bv128}[8] \ (\text{sign\_extend}[7] \ (= \ \text{bv0}[8] \ (\text{select} \ a \ \text{bv0}[32]))))$$

$$e' = (\text{concat} \ (= \ \text{bv0}[8] \ (\text{select} \ b \ \text{bv0}[32])) \ \text{bv0}[7])$$

Expressions e and e' are (nearly) semantically equivalent; both return the value 127 when index 0 of a symbolic array is zero. Applying Λ_E yields λ-terms,

$$\Lambda_E(e) = (\lambda x_1.(\text{and } 128 \ (\text{sgnext7} \ (= \ 0 \ x_1))))$$

$$\Lambda_E(e') = (\lambda x_1.(\text{concat} \ (= \ 0 \ x_1) \ 0_7))$$

Any expression syntactically equivalent to e up to the variable `select` term is reducible by $\Lambda_E(e) \rightarrow \Lambda_E(e')$. For instance, suppose the variable term were replaced with $(* \ 3 \ (\text{select} \ c \ 1))$. Applying the reduction rule with a β-reduction replaces the variable with the new term,

$$\Lambda_E(e')(* \ 3 \ (\text{select} \ c \ 1)) \rightarrow_\beta (\text{concat} \ (= \ 0 \ (* \ 3 \ (\text{select} \ c \ 1))) \ 0_7)$$

Finally, the new λ-term becomes an expression for symbolic interpretation,

$$(\text{concat} \ (= \ \text{bv0}[8] \ (\text{bvmul bv3}[8] \ (\text{select} \ c \ \text{bv1}[32]))) \ \text{bv0}[7])$$

3.2 EquivDB

Elements of $\rightarrow$ are discovered by observing expressions made during symbolic execution. Each expression is stored to a file in a directory tree, the EquivDB, to facilitate a fast semantic lookup of expression history across programs. The stored expressions are shorter candidate *reducts*. The expression and reduct are checked for semantic equivalence, then saved as a legal reduction rule.

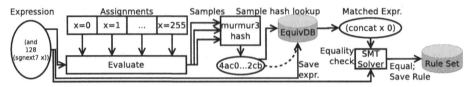

Fig. 3. Storing and checking an expression against the EquivDB

Generating Candidate Reducts. The expressions generated by programs are clues for reduction candidates. The intuition is several programs may share local behavior once a constant specialization triggers a compiler optimization. A path in symbolic execution reintroduces specializations on general code; expressions from the constrained path match the specialized code's semantics.

In the rule learning phase, candidate reducts are collected by the interpreter's expression builder, which are submitted to the EquivDB. Only top-level expressions are considered to avoid excess overhead from intermediate expressions which are generated by optimization rewrites during construction. To store an expression into the EquivDB, it is sampled, the values are hashed, and is written to the file path <bit-width>/<number of nodes>/<sample hash>. Entries are capped at 64 nodes maximum to avoid excessive space utilization.

Samples from expressions are found by assigning constant values to all array select accesses. The set of array assignments include all 8-bit values (e.g., for 1, all symbolic bytes are set to 1), non-zero values strided by up to 17 bytes (i.e., > 2× the 64-bit architecture word width to reduce aliasing), and zero strings strided by up to 17 bytes. The expression is evaluated for each array assignment and the sequence of samples is combined with a fast hashing algorithm [1]. It is worth noting this has obviously poor collision properties; for instance, the 32-bit comparisons (= x 12345678) and (= x 12345679) would have the same sample hashes because neither constant appears in the assignment set. Presumably, more samples would improve hash hit rates at the expense of additional computation.

The EquivDB storage and lookup facility is illustrated by Figure 3. At the top of the diagram, an expression from the interpreter is sampled with a set of assignments and the values are hashed. The expression is looked up by the sample hash in the EquivDB and saved for future reference. A lookup match is found and checked against the starting expression for semantic equality. Finally, the equality is found valid and the corresponding rule is stored into the rule set.

Reduction by Candidates. Before an expression e is stored in the EquivDB, the learning phase attempts to construct a reduction rule. Based on e's sample hash, the EquivDB is scanned for matching hashes with the same bit-width and fewer terms. Expression equivalence is checked using the theorem prover and, if valid and contracting, a rule is saved and applied to the running program.

A smaller expression is loaded from the EquivDB based on matching sample hash and bit-width. The candidate reduct e^* is parsed from an SMT file in the EquivDB to an expression and assigned temporary arrays for each symbolic read. The temporary arrays in e^* are replaced by index in $\Lambda_E(e^*)$ with the matching index terms from $\Lambda_E(e)$ to get e'. If the reduct is contracting, $e' < e$, and $(= e\ e')$ is valid by the solver, then $(e, e') \in\rightarrow$ and $e \rightarrow e'$ is saved as a rule for future reference. If $e \rightarrow e'$ is valid, the shorter e' is produced instead of e.

```
:extrafuns ((x Array[32:8]))
:formula
(= (ite (= bv0xffffffff00[40] (extract[63:24]
        (bvadd bv0xffffffff00000001[64]
        (zero_extend[56] (select x bv0[32])))))
    bv1[1] bv0[1]) bv0[1])
```

Fig. 4. A translation check query. The to-expression $\texttt{0xffffffff00}_{40}$ is compared with the from-expression $extract(63, 24, \texttt{0xffffffff00000001}_{64} + x_8)_{40}$. Negation of the translation equality is unsatisfiable, hence the translation is valid.

An example query for a candidate rule validity check is given in Figure 4. The equality expression on an arithmetic expression (e) and a constant value (e') is sent to the solver and a "sat" or "unsat" string is returned. To determine soundness of the rule $e \rightarrow e'$ with one query, the equality is negated so that validity is given by unsatisfiability.

Care is taken to handle several edge cases. Expressions e are often equivalent to a constant, but storing and accessing constant values from the EquivDB is needless overhead. Instead, the sample hash predicts e is constant by observing unchanging sample values c; the constant c serves as a candidate reduct $e \twoheadrightarrow c$ before falling back to the EquivDB. To avoid infinite recursion, if an expression is built by solver code, then it is queued for rule checking until the interpreter builds an expression directly through an LLVM operation. For reliability, if the solver fails or takes too long to check a rule's validity, then the query is aborted and e is returned for symbolic interpretation.

3.3   Rewrite Rules

Reductions in $\rightarrow$ are represented through rewrite rules. Every rewrite rule traces back to a sound primordial expression equality originating from the EquivDB. Each rewrite rule covers a *class* of reductions with expression template *patterns* that match and materialize classes of expressions. These rules direct expression optimization and are managed through persistent storage.

Every candidate rule taken from the EquivDB is verified by the solver. The equivalent expressions e, from the interpreter, and e', from the EquivDB, are converted into a from-pattern a and to-pattern b which are combined to make a rule $a \rightarrow b$. Once $a \rightarrow b$ is verified, all future applications of the rule $a \rightarrow b$ are conducted without invoking the interpreter.

Patterns in rules are flattened expressions with extra support for labeling replacement slots. Symbolic array reads are labeled as 8-bit slots which correspond to the variables from the expression transform Λ_E. These slots are used in pattern matching which is described in Section 4 and are important for correspondence between the from-pattern and to-pattern. Dummy variables, which are only matched on expression width and ignore structure, replace useless subexpressions through rule generalization (Section 6). Likewise, there are constrained slots for constants, also introduced through generalization, which match when a constant is a satisfying assignment for an expression bundled with the rule.

Rules are sent to persistent storage with a binary format and may be serialized into files and read in by the interpreter. Serialization flattens expressions into patterns by a pre-order traversal of all nodes. On disk, each rule is given a header which lets the rule loader gracefully recover from corrupted rules, specify version features, and overlook deactivated tombstone rules.

Manipulating rules, such as for generalization or other analysis, often requires *materialization* of patterns. A pattern, which represents a class of expressions, is materialized by building an expression from the class. Rules can be materialized into a validity check or by individual pattern into expressions. The validity check is a query which may be sent to the solver to verify that the relation $a \to b$ holds. Each materialized expression is assigned independent temporary arrays for symbolic data to avoid assuming properties from state constraint sets.

4   Rule-Directed Optimizer

The optimizer applies rules to a target expression to produce smaller, equivalent expressions. A set of reduction rules is loaded from persistent storage at interpreter initialization for the rule-directed expression builder. There are two phases for applying reduction rules when building a target expression. First, efficient pattern matching finds the arguments for a β-reduction from a rule's from-pattern to a target expression. When a rule match is found, the β-reduction applies the arguments to the rule's to-pattern to make a smaller expression.

4.1   Pattern Matching

Over the length of a program path, a collection of rules is applied to every expression. The optimizer analyzes every expression seen by the interpreter, so finding a rule must be fast and never call to the solver. Furthermore, thousands of rules may be active at any time, so matching rules must be efficient.

The optimizer has three ways to find a rule r which reduces an expression e. The simplest, linear scan, matches e against one rule at a time until reaching r. The next method hashes e ignoring constants and `select`s (skeletal hashing) then matches some r with the same hash for its from-expression. Flexible matching on the entire rule set, which includes subexpression replacement, is handled with a backtracking trie that is traversed in step with e. Both skeletal hashing and the trie are used by default to mitigate unintended rule shadowing.

Linear Scan. The expression and from-pattern are scanned and pre-order traversed with tokens checked for equality. Every pattern variable token assigns its label to the current subexpression and skips its children. If a label has already been assigned, the present subexpression is checked for syntactic equivalence to the labeled subexpression. If distinct, the variable assignment is inconsistent and the rule is rejected. All rules must match through linear scan; it is always applied after rule lookup to double-check the result.

Skeletal Hashing. Expressions and from-patterns are skeletal hashed [8] by ignoring `selects` and constants. A rule is chosen from the set by the target expression's skeletal hash. The hash is invariant with respect to array indexes and is imprecise; a hash matched rule will not necessarily reduce the expression. Lookup is made sound by checking a potential match by linear scanning.

Backtracking Trie. The tokenization for every from-pattern is stored in a trie. The expression is scanned and the trie matches on traversal. As nodes are matched to pattern tokens, subexpressions are collected to label the symbolic read slots. Choosing between labeling or following subexpressions is tracked with a stack and is backtracked on match failure. On average, an expression is scanned about 1.1 times, so the cost of backtracking is negligible.

Many expressions never match a rule because they are optimal or there is no known optimization. Since few expressions match on the rule set, rejected expressions are fast-pathed to avoid unnecessary lookups. Constants are the most common type expression and are already optimal; they are ignored by the optimizer. Misses are memoized; each non-constant expression is hashed and only processed if no expression with that hash failed to match a rule.

4.2 β-Reduction

Given a rule $a \rightarrow b$ which reduces expression e, a β-reduction contracts e to the b pattern structure. Subexpressions labeled by a on the linear scan of e serve as the variable index and term for substitution in b. There may be more labels in a than variables in b; superfluous labels are useless terms. On the other hand, more variables in b than labels in a indicates an inconsistent rule. To get the β-reduced, contracted expression, the b pattern is materialized and its `selects` on temporary arrays are substituted by label with subexpressions in e.

5 Building Rule Sets

Rules are organized by program into rule set files for offline refinement. Rule set files are processed by `kopt`, an independent program which uses expression and solver infrastructure from the interpreter. The `kopt` program checks rules for integrity and builds new rules by reapplying the rule set to materializations.

A rule set is checked for integrity at several points. Without integrity, the expression optimizer could be directed by a faulty rule to corrupt the symbolic computation. Worse, if a bogus rule is used to make more rules, such as by transitive closure, the error propagates, poisoning the entire rule set.

Additional processing refines a rule set's translations when building expressions. When rules are applied in aggregate, rather than in isolation, one rule may cause another rule's materialization to disagree its pattern; this introduces new structures unrecognized by the rule set. These new structures are recognized by creating new rules to transitively close the rule set. Further, to-patterns are normalized to improve rule set matching by canonicalizing production templates.

5.1 Integrity

Rules are only applied to a program when they are verified to be correct by the solver. Output from the learning phase is marked as pending and is verified by the solver independently. Rules are further refined past the pending stage into new rules which are checked as well. At program run time the rule set translations can be cross-checked against the baseline builder for testing composition.

Rule sets are processed for correctness. A rule set is loaded into kopt and each rule is materialized into an equivalence query. The external theorem prover verifies the equivalence is valid. Syntactic tests follow; components of the rule are constructed and analyzed. If the rule was not effective when materialized through the optimizer, it is thrown out.

A rule must be contracting to make forward progress. When expressions making up a rule are heavily processed, such as serialization to and from SMT or rebuilding with several rule sets, the to-expression may have more nodes than the from-expression. In this case, although the rule is valid, it is non-contracting and therefore removed. The rule can be recovered by swapping the patterns and checking validity, which is similar to the Knuth-Bendix algorithm [13].

As an end-to-end check, rule integrity is optionally verified at run time for a program under the symbolic interpreter. The rule directed expression builder is *cross-checked* against the default expression builder. Whenever a new expression is created from an operator $\circ$ and arguments $\bar{x}$, the expression $(\circ \ \bar{x})$ is built under both builders for e and e' respectively. If $(= \ e \ e')$ is not valid according to the solver, then one builder is wrong and the symbolic state is terminated with an error and expression debugging information. Cross-checking also works with a fuzzer to build random expressions which trigger broken translations.

5.2 Transitive Closure

Rules for large expressions may be masked by rules from smaller expressions. Once rules are applied to a program's expressions, updated rules may be necessary to optimize the new term arrangement. Fortunately, rules are contracting, and therefore expression size monotonically decreases; generating more rules through transitivity converges to a minima.

An example of how bottom-up building masks rules: consider the rules $r_1 = [(+ \ a \ b) \to 1]$ and $r_2 = [a \to c]$. Expressions are built bottom-up, so a in $(+a \ b)$ reduces to c by r_2, yielding $(+ \ c \ b)$. Rule r_1 no longer applies since r_2 eagerly rewrote a subexpression. However, all rules are contracting, so $|(+ \ c \ b)| < |(+ \ a \ b)|$. Hence, new rules may be generated by applying known rules, then added to the system with the expectation of convergence to a fixed point.

New rules *inline* new patterns as they are observed. For every instance of pattern materialization not matching the pattern itself (as above), a new rule is created from the new from-pattern materialization. Following the example, the rule r_1 must now match $(+ \ c \ b)$, so define a new rule $r_3 = [(+ \ c \ b) \to 1]$.

The convergence rate is influenced by the EquivDB. The database may hold inferior translations which bubble up into learned rules. However, since smaller expressions are stored to the database as the rules improve, the database improves along with the rules. Hence, a database of rule derived expressions continues to have good reductions even after discarding the initial rule set.

5.3   Normal Form Canonicalization

Expressions of same size may take different forms. Consider, $(= 0\ a)$ and $(= 0\ b)$ where $a = a_1 \ldots a_n$ and $b = a_n \ldots a_1$. Both are equivalent and have the same number of nodes but will not be reducible under the same rule because of syntactic mismatch. Instead, a *normal form* condition is imposed by selecting for the minimum of the expression ordering operator $\leq$ on semantic partitions on to-patterns. With normal forms, fewer rules are necessary because semantically equivalent to-patterns must materialize to one minimal syntactic representation.

The to-pattern materializations are collected from the rule set and partitioned by sample hashes. Each partition P of to-expressions is further divided by semantic equivalence by choosing the minimum expression $e_\perp \in P$, querying for valid equality over every pair $(e_\perp, e)$ where $e \in P$. If the pair is equivalent, the expression e is added to the semantic partition $P(e_\perp)$. Once $P(e_\perp)$ is built, a new $e'_\perp$ is chosen from $P \backslash P(e_\perp)$ and the process is repeated until P is exhausted.

Rules are replaced by their normal forms. Once the to-expressions are partitioned, the rule set is scanned for rules with to-expressions e where there is some $P(e_\perp)$ with $e \in P(e_\perp)$ where $e_\perp \neq e$. The rule's to-pattern is replaced with the to-pattern for $e_\perp$ and the old rule is removed from the rule set file.

6   Rule Generalizations

The class of expressions a rule matches may be extended by selectively relaxing terms in the from-pattern. The process of generalization goes beyond transitive closure by inserting new variables into expressions. Useless subterms are relaxed with dummy variables by subtree elimination. Constants with a set of equisatisfiable values are relaxed by assigning constraints to a constant label.

6.1   Subtree Elimination

Useless terms in from-expressions are marked as dummy variables in the from-pattern through subtree elimination. A rule's from-expression e has its subexpressions post-order replaced with dummy, unconstrained variables. For each new expression e', the solver finds for the validity of $(= e\ e')$. If e' is equivalent, the rule's from-pattern is rewritten with e' so that it has the dummy variable.

As an example, let $e = (= 0\ (\text{or } 1023\ (\texttt{concat}\ (\texttt{select } 0\ x)\ (\texttt{select } 1\ x))))$. The or term is always non-zero, so $e \twoheadrightarrow 0$. Traversal will first mark the 0, or, and 1023 terms as dummy variables but the solver rejects equivalence. The concat term, however, may take any value so it is marked as a 16-bit dummy variable v16, yielding the pattern $(= 0\ (\text{or } 1023\ \text{v16}))$, which matches *any* 16-bit term.

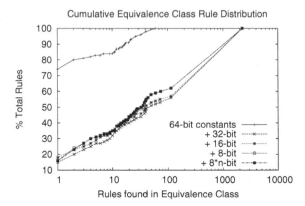

Fig. 5. Acceptance of constant widths on expression equivalence class hits

6.2   Constant Relaxation

A large class of expressions generalize from a single expression by perturbing the constants. In a rule, constant slots serve as constraints on the expression. Consider the 16-bit expression e, (and 0x8000 (or 0x7ffe (ite (x) 0 1)). The values of the ite if-then-else term never set the 15th bit, so $e \twoheadrightarrow 0$. By marking 0x8000 as a labeled constant c, this reduction generalizes to the rule (and 0x8000 (or c (ite (x) 0 1)) where $c < $ 0x8000 is the *constant constraint*, which expands the rule's reach from one to thousands of elements in $\twoheadrightarrow$.

To find candidates for constant relaxation, rules are partitioned by from-pattern expression materialization into constant-free equivalence classes. The constant-free syntactic equivalence between expressions e and e' is written as $e \equiv_c e'$. Let the function $\alpha_c : Expr \to Expr$ α-substitute all constants with a fixed sequence of distinct free variables. When the syntactic equivalence $\alpha_c(e) \equiv \alpha_c(e')$ holds, then constant-free equivalence $e \equiv_c e'$ follows.

A cumulative distribution of equivalence class sizes in $\equiv_c$ from hundreds of rules is given in Figure 5. Constants in rules are α-substituted with a dummy variable by bit-width from 64-bit only to all byte multiples. Singleton equivalence classes hold rules that are syntactically unique. In contrast, rules in large classes are syntactically common modulo constants. Aside from admitting more rules total, the distribution is insensitive to constant width past 64-bits; few rules are distinct in $\equiv_c$ and one large class holds nearly a majority of rules.

Constants are selected from a rule one at a time. The constant term t is replaced by a unique variable c. The variable c is subjected to various constraints to find a new rule which matches a *set* of constants on c. This generalizes the base rule where the implicit constraint is $(= c\ t)$.

Constant Disjunction. The simplest way to relax a constant is to constrain the constant by all values seen for its position in a class of rules in $\equiv_c$. A constant is labeled and the constraint is defined as the disjunction of a set of observed values for all similar rules. The resulting rule is a union of observed rules with similar parse trees pivoted on a certain constant slot.

The disjunction is built by greedily augmenting a constant set. The first in the set of values S is the constant c from the base rule. A new constant value v is taken from the next rule and a query is sent to the solver to check if v can be substituted into the base rule over c. If the validity check fails, v is thrown away as a candidate. If v is a valid substitution, it is added to S. When all candidate values from the rule equivalence class are exhausted, the constraint on the labeled constant slot c is $\bigvee_{s \in S}(= c\ s)$

Ranges. Range constraints restrict a constant to a contiguous region of values. The values for the range $[a, b]$ on the constant substitution x are computed through binary search in the solver. The constant from the base rule c is used as the initial pivot for the search so $c \in [a, b]$ to match the base rule. Starting from c, one binary search finds a from $[0, c]$ and another finds b from $[c, 2^n - 1]$. The constraint $a \leq x \leq b$ is placed on the new rule and the solver verifies equivalence to the from-expression from the base rule.

Bit masks. A constant in a rule may only depend on a few bits being set or zeroed, leaving all other bits unconstrained. Ranges on constants only support contiguous ranges, so it is necessary to introduce additional constraint analysis. Constant constraints on a constant x's bits are found by creating a mask m and value c which is valid for a predicate of the form $x\ \&\ m\ =\ c$.

The solver is used to find the mask m bit by bit. Since the base rule is valid, the rule's constant value a must satisfy $a\ \&\ m\ =\ c$. Bit k of the mask is computed by solving for the validity of $(=\ x\ (a\ \&\ 2^k))$ when x is constrained by the base rule. Each set bit k implies bit k of x must match bit k of a.

7 Evaluation

The expression optimizer is evaluated in terms of performance, effects on queries, and system characteristics on two thousand programs. Foremost, rules improve running time and solver performance on average. Total queries are reduced on average from baseline by the optimizer. The space overhead and expression distribution of the EquivDB illustrate properties of the learning phase. Rule effectiveness is measured by number of rules used and rate of sharing.

7.1 Implementation

The expression reduction system was written on top of a modern symbolic execution stack. The core symbolic binary executor is based on a heavily modified version of KLEE (KLEE-MC), LLVM-3.1, valgrind-3.8.1, and the latest SVN of STP [9]. To attain a degree of confidence in interpreter fidelity, intermediate interpreter results are tested through replay against intermediate LLVM JIT results. For stability, STP is invoked as a separate process.

Table 1. Lines of code for expression optimization

Component	Lines of Code
EquivDB/Learning	645
Rule Builder	1900
kopt	2519
Hand-written Builder	1315

Table 1 shows the lines of C++ code for major components of the expression handling system. Qualitatively, the code for the new optimizer represents a modest effort compared to the ad-hoc version. The largest component is kopt, the offline rule analysis program, where the cost of complexity is low. The rule builder, which applies the vetted rules as expressions are built inside the interpreter, is primarily focused on the fast matching trie. The EquivDB learning builder uses the least code since creating candidate rules is relatively simple.

7.2 Test System

Programs. All experiments are performed over a set of approximately 2300 programs. The programs are from the system binary directories /{usr/,}{sbin,bin} of an up-to-date x86-64 Gentoo Linux system. Each program is breakpointed at its entry point and snapshotted. All future accesses to the program reuse the snapshot for reproducibility purposes; every snapshot contains the full process memory image, including linked shared libraries, such as the C library glibc.

Programs are set to run under the symbolic interpreter for at most five minutes. Each program is allocated five minutes on one core of an 8-core desktop chip with 16GB of memory. There is minor additional processing and book keeping; overall, one symbolic run of the program set takes slightly more than a day.

Path Replay. Two sets of runs are taken for basis of comparison: one with only the ad-hoc optimizer and the other with the rule-directed optimizer as well. The same paths must be followed to give an accurate comparison between the baseline symbolic interpreter and the optimizer. Since paths are known a priori, persistent query caches are disabled to avoid distorted times.

KLEE-MC supports two kinds of path replay: concrete tests and branch paths. A concrete test is a solution to path constraints which replaces symbolic values with constants to duplicate the path. A branch path is a list of branch decisions.

Each branch path is a log of taken branch indexes (e.g., true, false) for some completed state. Branch replay reads an entry from the log for every branch decision and directs the replaying state toward the desired path. As an optimization, if a branch replay forks off a state with a branch log which is a prefix for another branch path, the branch path replay begins at the forked state.

Branch path equivalence is not guaranteed between paths with different rules, despite all rules being sound. Mismatched branch paths arise between distinct rule sets when the interpreter syntactically checks for constant expressions to avoid extra work; a decision is elided on a constant for one rule set, but recorded

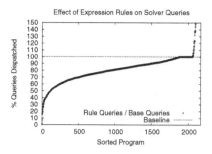
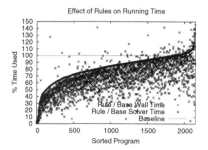

Fig. 6. Percentage of queries submitted when using rule sets over baseline

Fig. 7. Percentage run time for expression optimization over baseline

for a non-constant on another set, so the logs are no longer synchronized. A concrete test, on the other hand, is a semantic interpretation, and therefore insensitive to expression structure. Concrete tests preserve paths across rule sets so they are used to rebuild branch paths.

7.3 Performance

The effect of rules on running time and solver time is given sorted in Figure 7. Overall, there are significant performance gains made on average with the rule directed optimizer. Additionally, the correlation between run and solver time is evident by solver improvements closely following run time gains.

On average, the optimizer improves performance of the symbolic interpreter on a wide variety of programs. The optimizer improved times by producing shorter expressions and syntactic structures favorable to solver optimizations. The fastest 50th percentile decreases running time by at least 10%. Limited to the fastest 25th percentile, programs see decreased running time of at least 27%.

A few programs do not benefit from the optimizer. Either no improvement or a performance loss were observed in slightly fewer than 13% of all programs. Only five programs (0.2%) took more than 2× of baseline execution time. There is no requirement, however, to run the optimizer, so applications which exhibit a performance penalty with rules can simply go without and retain baseline speed.

Ultimately, less time is spent in the solver. A 94% majority of the programs spent less time in the solver by using the optimizer. A sizeable 36% of all programs are at least twice as fast in the solver. The 6% minority of programs, like for running time, incurred additional solver overhead. Solver time improvement and running time improvement appear related; only 5% of faster programs had running time decrease more than solver time.

The percent change in queries submitted to the solver is shown ordered in Figure 6. On average, the total number of solver queries dispatched for consideration is lower with the optimizer than without. Within the best 50th percentile, at least 17% of queries submitted to the solver were eliminated. In total, fewer queries were dispatched for 87% of the programs. The query histogram in Figure 8 illustrates a shift toward faster queries from slower queries.

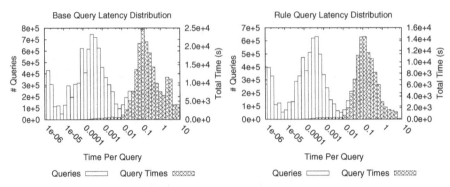

Fig. 8. Query time distribution for baseline and rule test cases

7.4 EquivDB

The EquivDB reduct distribution is given in Figure 9. Data for the EquivDB was collected from a single run of all programs with a five minute learning period. On the file system, the EquivDB uses approximately 4GB of storage and contains 1.2 million expressions, a modest overhead. Ridges appear at 8 bit multiples, indicating expressions are often byte aligned; possibly because symbolic arrays have byte granularity and most machine instructions are byte-oriented. Some ridges appear to extend past the node limit, suggesting the cut-off could be raised. Blank areas, such as those between 32 and 40 bits indicate no entries. As an outlier, there are 63485 expressions with seven nodes at 64 bits.

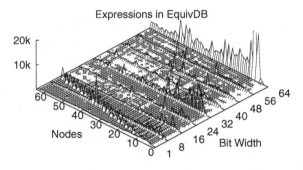

Fig. 9. Distribution of expressions by number of nodes and bitwidth in EquivDB

7.5 Rules

A large number of rules is indicative of poor rule efficiency. If rules are applied as one-off translations, then it is unlikely a fixed rule set will be effective in general. However, as illustrated in Figure 11, most programs have fewer than a few thousand rules and fewer than a hundred generalized rules. Rule explosion is from only a few programs interacting poorly with the optimizer.

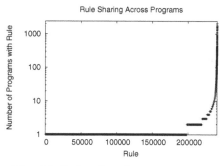

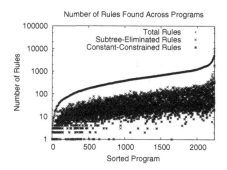

Fig. 10. Rules shared among programs   **Fig. 11.** Rules for measured programs

Code sharing is common through shared libraries, so it is reasonable to expect rules to be shared as well. Figure 10 counts the frequency of rules found across programs and confirms sharing. There are 41795 shared rules out of a total of 240052 rules; 17% of rules are shared. The most common rule, with 2035 programs, is an equality lifting rule: $(= -1_{32} (\texttt{concat} -1_{24} x_8)) \rightarrow (= -1_8 x_8)$.

8 Related Work

Peephole optimizers using a SAT solver to find optimal short instruction sequences on machine code is a well-known technique [2,15]. Our expression optimization is similar because it seeks minimal operations. The benefit of applying optimization at the expression level over the instruction level is rules can path-specialize expressions regardless of the underlying code.

For compilers, HOP [8] automatically generated peephole rules by using a formal specification of the target machine. PO simulates runs of register transfers symbolically, using primitive abstract interpretation. It speculatively translates the combined effects back into assembly code. If successful, it replaces the original with the shorter code segment. HOP improved PO by demonstrating skeletal hashes to memoize the rewrite rules for a faster peephole optimizer.

Prior work on symbolic execution uses rule based term rewriting for optimizing solver queries. F-Soft [20] applies a term writing system [7] to expressions generated through symbolic interpretation of C sources. The term rewrite system is seeded with a hundreds of handwritten rules from formal systems (e.g., Presburger arithmetic, equational axiomatization), was applied to a handful of programs, and found improved solver times. However, from the total rules observed in our system and poor performance of hand-written rules in KLEE, we believe manual rule entry alone is best suited to carefully selected workloads.

Acknowledgements. This work was supported in part by the US Air Force through contract AFRL-FA8650-10-C-7024 and by DARPA award HR0011-12-2-009. Any opinions, findings, conclusions, or recommendations expressed herein are those of the authors, and do not necessarily reflect those of the US Government or the Air Force.

References

1. Appleby, A.: murmurhash3 (November 2012),
   http://sites.google.com/site/murmurhash
2. Bansal, S., Aiken, A.: Binary translation using peephole superoptimizers. In: OSDI 2008, pp. 177–192 (2008)
3. Barrett, C., de Moura, L., Stump, A.: Design and results of the first satisfiability modulo theories competition (SMT-COMP 2005). Journal of Automated Reasoning 35(4), 373–390 (2005)
4. Cadar, C., Dunbar, D., Engler, D.: Klee: unassisted and automatic generation of high-coverage tests for complex systems programs. In: OSDI 2008, pp. 209–224 (2008)
5. Chipounov, V., Kuznetsov, V., Candea, G.: S2E: A Platform for In-vivo Multi-Path Analysis of Software Systems. In: ASPLOS 2011, pp. 265–278 (2011)
6. Church, A., Rosser, J.B.: Some Properties of Conversion. Transactions of the American Mathematical Society 39(3), 472–482 (1936)
7. Clavel, M., Durán, F., Eker, S., Lincoln, P., Martí-Oliet, N., Meseguer, J., Talcott, C.: The Maude 2.0 System. In: Nieuwenhuis, R. (ed.) RTA 2003. LNCS, vol. 2706, pp. 76–87. Springer, Heidelberg (2003)
8. Davidson, J.W., Fraser, C.W.: Automatic generation of peephole optimizations. In: SIGPLAN Symposium on Compiler Construction, pp. 111–116 (1984)
9. Ganesh, V., Dill, D.L.: A decision procedure for bit-vectors and arrays. In: Damm, W., Hermanns, H. (eds.) CAV 2007. LNCS, vol. 4590, pp. 519–531. Springer, Heidelberg (2007)
10. Godefroid, P., Levin, M.Y., Molnar, D.: Automated whitebox fuzz testing. In: Proceedings of the Network and Distributed System Security Symposium, NDSS 2008. The Internet Society (2008)
11. Huet, G.: Confluent reductions: Abstract properties and applications to term rewriting systems. J. ACM 27(4), 797–821 (1980)
12. Khurshid, S., Păsăreanu, C.S., Visser, W.: Generalized symbolic execution for model checking and testing. In: Garavel, H., Hatcliff, J. (eds.) TACAS 2003. LNCS, vol. 2619, pp. 553–568. Springer, Heidelberg (2003)
13. Knuth, D., Bendix, P.: Simple word problems in universal algebras. In: Siekmann, J., Wrightson, G. (eds.) Automation of Reasoning. Symbolic Computation, pp. 342–376. Springer, Heidelberg (1983)
14. Martignoni, L., McCamant, S., Poosankam, P., Song, D., Maniatis, P.: Path-exploration lifting: hi-fi tests for lo-fi emulators. In: ASPLOS 2012, pp. 337–348 (2012)
15. Massalin, H.: Superoptimizer: A look at the smallest program. In: ASPLOS-II, pp. 122–126 (1987)
16. Molnar, D., Li, X.C., Wagner, D.A.: Dynamic test generation to find integer bugs in x86 binary linux programs. In: Proceedings of the 18th Conference on USENIX Security Symposium, SSYM 2009, pp. 67–82 (2009)
17. Nethercote, N., Seward, J.: Valgrind: a framework for heavyweight dynamic binary instrumentation. In: PLDI 2007, pp. 89–100 (2007)
18. Păsăreanu, C., Visser, W.: A survey of new trends in symbolic execution for software testing and analysis. STTT, 339–353 (2009)

19. Sen, K., Marinov, D., Agha, G.: CUTE: A concolic unit testing engine for C. In: ESEC/FSE-13, pp. 263–272 (September 2005)
20. Sinha, N.: Symbolic program analysis using term rewriting and generalization. In: FMCAD 2008, pp. 19:1–19:9. IEEE Press, Piscataway (2008)
21. Song, D., Brumley, D., Yin, H., Caballero, J., Jager, I., Kang, M.G., Liang, Z., Newsome, J., Poosankam, P., Saxena, P.: BitBlaze: A New Approach to Computer Security via Binary Analysis. In: Sekar, R., Pujari, A.K. (eds.) ICISS 2008. LNCS, vol. 5352, pp. 1–25. Springer, Heidelberg (2008)

Model Checking Unbounded Concurrent Lists

Divjyot Sethi[1], Muralidhar Talupur[2], and Sharad Malik[1]

[1] Princeton University
[2] Strategic CAD Labs,
Intel Corporation

Abstract. We present a model checking based method for verifying list-based concurrent data structures. Concurrent data structures are notorious for being hard to get right and thus, their verification has received significant attention from the verification community. These data structures are unbounded in two dimensions: the list size is unbounded and an unbounded number of threads access them. Thus, their model checking requires abstraction to a model bounded in both the dimensions.

In previous work, we showed how the unbounded number of threads can be model checked by reduction to a finite model. In that work, we used the CMP (CoMPositional) method which abstracts the unbounded threads by keeping one thread as is (concrete) and abstracting all the other threads to a single environment thread. Next, this abstraction was iteratively refined by the user in order to prove correctness. However, in that work we assumed that the number of list elements was bounded by a fixed value. In practice this fixed value was small; model checking could only complete for small sized lists.

In this work, we overcome this limitation and model check the unbounded list as well. While it is possible to show correctness for unbounded threads by keeping one concrete thread and abstracting others, this is not directly possible in the list dimension as the nodes pointed to by the threads change during list traversal. Our method addresses this challenge by constructing an abstraction for which the concrete nodes can change with program execution and allowing for refinement of this abstraction to prove invariants. We show the soundness of our method and establish its utility by model checking challenging concurrent list-based data structure examples.

1 Introduction

We present a method for model checking list-based concurrent data structures. These data structures are highly efficient concurrent list-based implementations of popular data structures such as sets, queues etc. and are increasingly available in libraries such as Intel Thread Building Blocks and Java.util.concurrent. These list-based implementations utilize sophisticated synchronization techniques, such as fine-grained locking or lock free synchronization, to achieve high efficiency. Due to the complex synchronization used, these data structures are notorious for being highly error prone, as exemplified by bugs in published algorithms [15]. Consequently, verification of these data structures has been of interest to the verification community [1–4, 6, 7, 11, 23, 25, 26, 28, 29].

E. Bartocci and C.R. Ramakrishnan (Eds.): SPIN 2013, LNCS 7976, pp. 320–340, 2013.

Linearizability [10] is the widely accepted correctness criterion for concurrent data structures. Intuitively, Linearizability implies that the execution of every access method of the concurrent data structure appears to occur atomically at some point – the *linearization point* – between the invocation and the response of the method.

In previous work [21], we showed how to model check Linearizability for concurrent data structures. Concurrent list-based data structures are unbounded in two dimensions – they have an unbounded number of list nodes and an unbounded number of threads accessing the list items. In our work, we verified these data structures for an unbounded number of threads. This was accomplished by using the CMP (CoMPositional) method [5]. The CMP method is used to verify symmetric parameterized systems of the form $P(N)$, with N identical threads $1..N$. The properties verified are candidate invariants of the form $\forall i \in [1..N].\Phi(i)$, where $\Phi(i)$ is a propositional logic formula on the variables of thread i and shared variables.

The CMP method exploits symmetry and locality; i.e., it assumes that the violation occurs at a particular thread, say thread 1. Consequently, the CMP method constructs an abstract model which consists of one thread from the original system (say thread 1 since the system is symmetric) and an environment thread (named *Other*) that over-approximates the remaining threads. Then, if the property $\Phi(1)$ holds on thread 1 in the abstract model, $\forall i \in [1..N].\Phi(i)$ holds for $P(N)$ by symmetry. The verification of the abstract model is done by using a model checker. The refinement of the abstract model is done in a loop, referred to as the CMP loop. In the loop, if the abstract model is falsified by the model checker, the model is refined by the user by supplying non-interference lemmas, in order to constrain the *Other* thread [21].

The key advantage of using the CMP method is that the user-added lemmas also get verified. Thus, the CMP method is sound in the sense that if the CMP loop converges and the property is verified, all user-added lemmas along with the property under check hold. Another advantage of the CMP method is that it uses a model checker as a proof assistant. Thus, the added lemmas together with the property under check need not add up to be inductive, unlike most theorem proving based approaches [22]. These features in practice have been instrumental in making the CMP method useful in verifying complex cache coherence protocols [17, 22].

Since the CMP method does not handle unbounded list size, in our initial work [21], we had assumed the list size to be bounded. Further, in practice, we were only able to scale to a small number of list nodes. This, we believe was primarily due to the large number of interleavings in the execution of concurrent data structures and is consistent with the limited success of other model checking based efforts for concurrent data structures [4, 26, 28, 29]. The limited scalability in bounding the number of list nodes motivated us to study possible extensions of the CMP method approach in order to model check Linearizability for data structures with an unbounded list size as well.

1.1 Challenges in Extending the CMP Method to the List Dimension

The list dimension has some key differences from the thread dimension which make the extension of the CMP method to the list dimension challenging. First, unlike the thread dimension, the list dimension lacks symmetry: the heap elements are connected asymmetrically depending on the heap shape. Second, in the list dimension, while checking the correctness can be localized to the few nodes that are being updated (additions and deletions), these localized nodes will change as the list is traversed. This dynamic nature of the nodes of interest precludes consideration of one or a small set of fixed nodes for the abstract model.

1.2   Extending the CMP Method to List Dimension

In this work we extend the CMP method to the list dimension and show how abstraction and refinement can be done in this dimension.

Abstraction Intuition: The abstraction in the list dimension has been used earlier [20] and is straightforward. It proceeds by retaining the nodes pointed to by the pointers in the program as is. These retained nodes are referred to as *concrete nodes*. Next, all nodes which are not pointed to by any pointers are abstracted. This is done by replacing all chains of nodes, such that no node in the chain is pointed to by any pointer, by *abstract nodes*. Fig 1a shows the intuition behind replacing a chain of concrete nodes by an abstract node. In the figure, nodes 2 and 3 are replaced by the abstract node (shown by a rectangle) on abstraction.

Observe that as the program state evolves, the pointers move. This moves the position of the concrete nodes as well. This movement of concrete nodes happens when the abstract nodes are accessed by pointers during transitions. Intuitively, access to an abstract node can be understood as a non-deterministic access to some concrete node which is a part of the chain of concrete nodes represented by the abstract node.

As an example in Fig 1b, when pointer p_3 accesses the abstract node, the abstract node is split into a concrete node with an abstract node on each side. The concrete node is assigned a non-deterministic value v. The pointer p_3 then points to this newly created concrete node. Since this newly created node v has a non-deterministic value, it may lead to a violation of the property under check. Thus, a refinement step may be required to constrain the value taken by v.

Refinement Intuition: Refinement is done by constraining the value v. This is done by specifying list lemmas (invariants on the heap) which v should not violate. As an

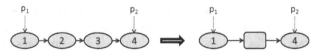

(a) Abstraction: nodes 2 and 3 are replaced by an abstract node (represented by a rectangle)

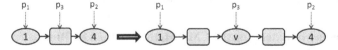

(b) Splitting: abstract node is split into multiple nodes.

Fig. 1. Abstract node creation and splitting: the concrete nodes are shown as circles with indicated values and the abstract nodes are represented as rectangles

example, a list lemma could state that the list elements are ordered (also referred to as *ordering* invariant). Then, the splitting may be done by assuming the invariant that the list nodes are ordered; and thus $v \in (1, 4)$.

1.3   Framework Description

Fig 2 shows the extended CMP method loop with the extensions circled. As shown in the figure, the loop proceeds by first abstracting the threads as in the prior CMP method approach. Next, the unbounded list is abstracted.[1] On abstraction, in case the model is falsified by the model checker, the user inspects the counter-example. If the counter-example is a valid counter-example, a real bug has been found and the loop terminates. On the other hand, if the counter-example is spurious, the user refines the model in either the thread or list dimension.

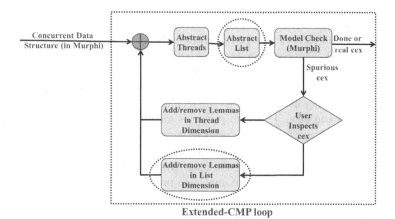

Fig. 2. Extended CMP Method: the circled steps indicate the key extensions in this work

1.4   Key Contributions

Our extension preserves the advantages of the CMP method: in case the extended CMP loop converges, both the property under check and the added invariants to constrain the list are proven to be correct. Thus the extended CMP loop is sound. Further, as in the CMP method, the added invariants need not add up to be inductive.

We make the following contributions in this work:

- We extend the CMP method to the list dimension and provide a syntactic abstraction of the unbounded list (Section 3) and mechanisms for refinement in the list dimension (Section 4).
- We show the soundness of the extended CMP method and show how the added list lemmas are also proven correct if the extended loop converges (Section 4).

---

[1] In general, the abstractions are commutative. But, we present them in the order of the thread abstraction first and then the list abstraction.

– We establish the utility of our method by model checking Linearizability of the *Fine-grained* [9] and *Optimistic* [9] data structures (Section 5).

Key Limitations: (1) The user has to manually come up with lemmas to refine the model. However due to the small length of concurrent data structure implementations (most implementations fit in one page [9]), this has not been a problem in practice. (2) The abstraction used for verifying certain key properties of the *Optimistic* algorithm did not scale well. This is because of a large number of interleavings.

1.5 Related Work

Concurrent data structures have been proposed as a promising approach to harness the power of multi-core processors [9]. Given their importance and the challenges associated with proving them right, verification of concurrent data structures is garnering much recent attention [1–4, 6, 23, 25, 26, 28, 29].

In [25], verification of concurrent data structures was done using a mechanical proof assistant and the interference between concurrent threads was specified using rely and guarantee conditions. These approaches allow both arbitrary number of accessing threads and elements but they are manual effort intensive.

Among model checking approaches, Vechev et al. [26] describe their experience with verifying Linearizability using the SPIN model checker. Similarly, the work by Zhang et al. [28, 29] and Liu et al. [13] also performs model checking to verify concurrent data structures. Both these approaches use a refinement based proof approach and scale to not more than a small number of threads and list nodes. A different approach is taken by Alur et al. [4]: they treat a list as a string and the thread as an automaton and then derive conditions on the automaton to prove decidability of Linearizability. The key focus of their work is on decidability instead of scalability; while they handle unbounded list size, they do not scale to more than 2-3 threads. Noll et al. [16] handle unbounded lists and unbounded number of threads. Their list abstraction is similar to ours. In the thread dimension, instead of fully throwing away threads 2..N, they do a counter abstraction which results in increased state. Further, their refinement approach in both list and thread dimensions results in more added state, thus limiting scalability (they only apply their method to a small example).

Verification of concurrent data structures has been of significant interest to the separation logic community [7, 11, 23, 24]. Among these, the RGSep based approach [23, 24] is closest to our work. It works by combining separation logic with rely-guarantee reasoning into a logic called RGSep. Their approach is automatic for a subset of RGSep. While automatic, the designer still needs to specify concurrent actions which model the interference, just like in rely-guarantee reasoning, for proving assertions. Further, the designer also has to have an understanding of RGSep. In contrast to separation logic based approaches, our method requires the user to refine the abstraction by specifying lemmas, which are standard Boolean formulas. Further, these lemmas are checked for correctness as well: any false lemmas will be weeded out. Next, shape analysis based approaches, like based on the tool TVLA [1] and thread modular analysis [8], are able to verify unbounded concurrent data structures. The primary focus of these approaches is to lift the heap abstractions for single threaded programs to concurrent programs.

In [27], multiple threads in the same local state are abstracted into one abstract configuration and mechanisms for refinement through addition of more predicates are provided. In contrast to these approaches, our method focusses on mechanisms for efficient abstraction and refinement without the addition of extra state, to enable efficient model checking. Further, the user-supplied lemmas for refinement are also checked.

Finally, while the CMP (CoMPositional) method [5] is a highly successful parameterized verification technique, numerous work has been done in the area of parameterized verification, for e.g. [12, 18, 19]. While some of these classical methods are potentially applicable to concurrent data structures as well, given the success of the CMP method in verifying industrial cache coherence protocols [17], we believe that our method, which has a similar flavor to the CMP method, provides a scalable and effective alternative approach.

2   Modelling Concurrent Data Structures

2.1   Preliminaries

We model a concurrent list-based data structure as a program P with M heap nodes and N *identical* threads with ids $1..N$, where M and N are arbitrary but fixed. The set of threads is denoted by $Threads$ and the set of heap nodes is denoted by $List$.

Each node n of the heap consists of the fields key, $next$, $lock$ and $\{l_1, l_2, \ldots\}$, a finite set of local fields with values from a finite domain. The key field is defined on a generic data domain D which has comparison $(<)$ and equality $(=)$ operations. The $next$ field is used to indicate the adjacent node. If $n_j = n_i.next$, we say that n_j is a *successor* of n_i (or next to n_i), and that n_i is the *predecessor* of n_j. Finally, the $lock$ field takes values from $0..N$, where 0 represents unlocked and value i represents locked by thread i.

The heap nodes are pointed to by *global pointers* and by threads. Each thread i consists of a finite number of local state variables (with finite domain) for program execution and a finite number of *pointer variables* which access the heap nodes. We assume that the local variables of all threads (both local state and pointer variables) are stored in arrays ranging over thread ids $[1..N]$. Thus, a local variable v of thread i is written as $v[i]$. Similarly, $p[i]$ represents a local pointer of thread i.

Verification of concurrent data structures is done by checking for refinement against a specification set [25]. The specification set, denoted by S, is a sequential specification of the set implemented by the concurrent data structure implementation. The set S consists of key values which are from the same domain D as the key fields of the heap nodes.

Transitions: Following the approach of [4], we model each statement of thread i as a transition of the form (l_i, G, Act, Ins, l_i'), where l_i and l_i' are initial and final states of thread i for the transition, G is the guard, Act is an action on the heap and Ins is the instrumented action on the set S. The guards G are Boolean expressions constructed on the global pointers, thread local state variables, and thread local pointer variables.

The thread actions are defined as follows:

Heap Traversal: $p_a[i] := p_b[i]$, $p_a[i] := p_b[i].next$,
Heap shape update: $p_a[i].next := p_b[i]$, and
Heap node update: $p[i].field = val$, where val is a value of appropriate type.[2]

Finally, the instrumented action Ins can either be (1) a nil action or, (2) an addition of $e \in D$ to S, denoted by $seqAdd(e)$ or, (3) a removal of an element $e \in D$ from S, denoted by $seqRemove(e)$ or, (4) a check for containment of an element $e \in D$ in S, denoted by $seqContains(e)$.

Definitions: We define predicate $\mathcal{R}_{p1}(p)$ to indicate that the node pointed to by p is reachable from that pointed to by $p1$. $\widehat{\mathcal{R}}_p$ refers to the set of all the nodes reachable from p. This definition extends in an obvious way to a set of pointers. Next, we call a node a *referred* node if it is pointed to by a thread pointer or a global pointer. We write $Ref_i(n)$ to indicate that some pointer in thread i points to node n. Further, we use $Ref(n)$ to indicate that the node n is pointed to by some pointer (thread local or global pointer) in the system. Finally, we define $isMuInt(n_i, n_j)$ to indicate that no node from the list segment n_i to n_j is referred to by any thread or global pointer in the program and further, the predecessor of n_i and successor of n_j are both referred nodes. Such a list segment is also referred to as a *maximally uninterrupted* list segment.

Property: In this paper we focus on verifying invariants specified on the above program. These invariants are of the form $\forall i : \phi(i)$, where $\phi(i)$ is an invariant involving the local variables of thread i and global variables quantified on the heap.

2.2   Running Example

We present the ideas in this paper through a *Fine-grained* list-based set ([9]) implementation. This implementation uses a linked list to implement a standard set. The methods in the implementation are the standard *Add*, *Remove* and *Contains* methods. The linked list consists of nodes with fields: 1) a *key* field holding values as integers, 2) a *next* pointer for accessing the next node in the list, and 3) a *lock* field representing whether that node is currently locked. In addition, there are two special (sentinel) nodes, the node *Head* and the node *Tail*, that can neither be added nor be removed. These nodes are pointed to by global pointers H and T respectively.

The concurrent implementation consists of potentially an unbounded number of threads. These threads are assumed to be symmetric.[3] Instead of locking the entire list, each method of the *Fine-grained* data structure traverses the list by using *hand-in-hand* locking. Fig 3a shows the implementation of the *Remove* function of the *Fine-grained* data structure. The *Remove* method uses hand-in-hand locking during traversal: $p_0[i]$ is unlocked (line 6), pointed to successor $p_1[i]$ (line 7), $p_1[i]$ is advanced (line 8) and locked again (line 9). This locking and unlocking is done by calling the lock() and unlock() methods for each node: these methods have standard semantics.

---

[2] This includes synchronization mechanisms; i.e., updates to the *lock* field.
[3] While the threads are symmetric, they can execute different methods (such as *Add* or *Remove* or *Contains*) by non-deterministically calling any of these methods.

The concurrent list-based implementation implements a sequential set specification, denoted by S. The methods of the specification set are denoted by $seqAdd$, $seqRemove$ and $seqContains$. These methods have standard sequential set semantics.

Murphi Encoding: We show the encoding of the *Remove* method in the Murphi language for model checking. Our choice of Murphi was based on the powerful model checker which comes along with Murphi, and the legacy implementation of both, our abstraction tool (Abster [22]) and *Fine-grained* and *Optimistic* data structures.

Murphi uses a standard guard-action based syntax: the applications are written as a collection of rules of the form $\rho \rightarrow a$, where ρ is the guard and a is the action. Fig 3b shows the guard-action based encoding of a few statements of the method.[4] Observe that the variable $pc[i]$ represents the program counter and is used to enforce a sequential execution of the rules. This is done in order to simulate the sequential execution of statements within a thread, since we assume a sequentially consistent memory model. This guard-action based encoding is useful in presenting the ideas in this paper.

```
Remove (key)
 1: p₀[i] := H;
 2: p₀[i].lock();
 3: p₁[i] := p₀[i].next;
 4: p₁[i].lock();
 5: while (p₁[i].key < key)
 6:        p₀[i].unlock();
 7:        p₀[i] := p₁[i];
 8:        p₁[i] := p₀[i].next;
 9:        p₁[i].lock();
10: if p₁[i].key = key then
11:        p₂[i] := p₁[i].next;
12:        p₀[i].next := p₂[i];
          [*SeqRemove(key)]
13:        result := true;
14: else
15:        result := false;
          [*SeqRemove(key)]
16: p₀[i].unlock();
17: p₁[i].unlock();
```

$$\forall i \in Threads : (pc[i] = 1) \rightarrow \{$$
$$p_0[i] := H;$$
$$pc[i] + +; \}$$

$$\forall i \in Threads : (pc[i] = 3) \rightarrow \{$$
$$p_1[i] := p_0[i].next;$$
$$pc[i] + +; \}$$

$$\forall i \in Threads : (pc[i] = 12) \rightarrow \{$$
$$p_0[i].next := p_2[i];$$
$$pc[i] + +;$$
$$[*SeqRemove(key)] \}$$

(b) Murphi based guard-action pairs for statements with line numbers 1,3 and 12

(a) Pseudo-code for linked list-based *Fine-grained* set algorithm. The linearization points are marked with a *.

Fig. 3. *Remove* function and Murphi encoding

Example State: Fig 4 shows an example of a state in the execution of the list-based implementation. In this state, the linked list is accessed by 3 threads, with ids 1, 2 and 3. Further, the value of the specification set S is also shown in the figure. Observe that

---

[4] The complete guard-action based encoding of the *Remove* method is provided in Appendix A.1.

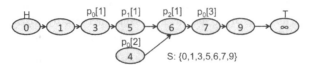

Fig. 4. Heap accessed by pointers of threads 1,2 and 3. $p_j[i]$ denotes the jth pointer of thread i.

$ConcSet$ and S match, where $ConcSet$ is the set of key values of all the nodes reachable from H. Thus, 4 is not in S since node 4 is note reachable from H. Next, observe that $Ref(1)$ is false but $Ref(0)$ is true. Further, $isMuInt(1,1)$, $isMuInt(9,9)$ are true and $isMuInt(n_i, n_j)$ is false for all other pairs of n_i and n_j, as all the other nodes are referred nodes.

Property under Verification. In this work, we verify *Linearizability* [10] by a refinement based approach, as described in [25]. The refinement is proven against the specification set S. This is done by matching the results of the call to S (inserted at linearization point) against the return value of the implementation method.

As an example, for the *Remove* method shown in Fig 3a, the linearization point for *Remove* in case the call is successful is marked with [*SeqRemove(key)*] on Line 12. Similarly, [*SeqRemove(key)*] on Line 15 denotes the linearization point in the failing case. If both, the concurrent methods and the embedded specification methods return the same value, the concurrent data structure is Linearizable. Formally, for each $Method \in \{Add, Remove, Contains\}$, we check that $Method(key) \Leftrightarrow SeqMethod(key)$.

Another key property of interest checks if the list nodes refine the specification set S. This invariant is referred to as the *refinement map*. The refinement map states that S matches with the set of values of nodes reachable from the head node, the $ConcSet$. Formally, the refinement map is then stated as: $\forall v.v \in S \Leftrightarrow v \in ConcSet$, where $ConcSet = \{\bigcup_{\forall n \in \widehat{\mathcal{R}}_H} : n.key\}$.

Finally, another key property is the *ordering* invariant. This states that if n_1 is the successor of n_2, then the key of n_1 is greater than the key of n_2.

3   Abstraction

In this section we show how the unbounded threads and list nodes can be abstracted to obtain a finite model.

3.1   Abstracting Unbounded Threads

We abstract the unbounded number of threads by using *data type reduction* [14]. This abstraction keeps thread 1 unchanged and creates an environment thread *Other* representing threads $[2..N]$. The abstraction operation involves throwing away all the state variables of threads $[2..N]$ and over-approximating expressions in the guards involving them. For instance $pc[i] = 12$ for $i \in [2..N]$ is thrown away and replaced by *true* or *false* (depending on which replacement leads to an over-abstraction). Next, the action in the transitions of thread *Other* may refer to the heap using local pointers. Since the thread *Other* is stateless, the local pointers do not have any stored value. Then, the local pointer values are non-deterministically chosen to complete the actions. This abstraction is completely syntactic in nature [21].

Example. Consider for example, the transition corresponding to line 12 in Fig 3a, the Murphi rule for which is shown in Fig 3b. In the constructed abstraction, the transition for thread 1 is obtained by substituting i with 1 in the rule . Next, for the *Other* thread, the transition is obtained by first over-abstracting the guard with $true$ and second, by replacing $p_0[i]$ and $p_2[i]$ by non-deterministic pointers Np_0 and Np_2. The obtained rule is as follows:

$$\forall Np_0, Np_2 \in List : (true) \rightarrow \{ Np_0.next := Np_2; \} .$$

3.2   Abstracting Unbounded List

Abstracting the State: The list abstraction consists of two components: first, the shape of the list, and second, the values (key values in particular) of the nodes.
Shape Abstraction Since the unbounded number of threads have been abstracted to only a single thread, certain nodes in the model may not be reachable from the pointer variables of thread 1 or the global pointers. These nodes are discarded and replaced by a representative node $\widehat{nd}$.[5] The shape abstraction of the remaining heap proceeds by replacing all maximally uninterrupted chains of nodes by *abstract* nodes. Thus, an abstract node in the abstraction represents a chain of one or more concrete nodes.

Value Abstraction: In order to prove the refinement map, the correspondence of $ConcSet$ and S must be checked. This requires defining key values for the abstract nodes also. This is done by replacing D with D^{abs}, where D^{abs} is an interval set induced on D and has a comparison operator. In D^{abs} $(a, b) < (c, d)$, if $b < c$ in D.

Specification set abstraction: Correspondingly, the specification set S is also abstracted to S^{abs} with values from D^{abs}. The sequential methods are also abstracted: as an example, $seqContains$ is abstracted to $seqContains^{abs}$. $seqContains^{abs}(e)$ is specified for e being a singleton set only. It returns $true$ if $e \in S^{abs}$ and $false$ if $\forall interval \in S^{abs} : e \notin interval$. Otherwise, it has a non-deterministic behavior. The methods of S^{abs} are straightforward and are provided in Appendix A.4.

Example: Fig 5 shows the state obtained after doing the list abstraction followed by thread abstraction of Fig 4. The node corresponding to node 4 is thrown away. Next, the node 1 and nodes 7-9 are replaced by abstract nodes. Finally, the key values as well as the values of the abstracted specification set S^{abs} are replaced by values from the interval set induced on $[0, \infty)$.

Abstracting the Transitions: A key requirement for abstracting the transitions is that they over-abstract the original transitions and they transition from one valid abstract state to another. The abstracted transitions proceed in 3 phases: (1) a setup phase where

---

[5] Nodes which become a part of $\widehat{nd}$ can, in practice, never become reachable from any thread pointer again. This is true for the list-based concurrent set data structures we have seen in [9] and is discussed in the Appendix A.2.

Fig. 5. Abstracting unbounded nodes: maximally uninterrupted nodes replaced by abstract nodes (rectangles)

the abstract nodes are split if required, (2) a transition phase, where the transition from the *original* program is executed, and (3) a cleanup phase, where after the transition the newly obtained state is lifted to a valid abstract state. We explain these in detail below.

Setup phase: interaction with abstract nodes Since the list abstraction is intuitively designed to have threads accessing only concrete nodes, any access to an abstract node is resolved by non-deterministically splitting the abstract node into a chain of concrete and abstract nodes. The accessing thread then accesses the created concrete node.

Accesses to an abstract node happen in two cases:

(a) *Access to next field of a node with an abstract node as successor.* This, is resolved by, intuitively, selecting the leftmost node in the chain of concrete nodes represented by the abstract node. This is implemented by the GETNEXT function shown in Fig 7a. The GETNEXT function returns the next value by splitting the next abstract node (pointed by $p.next$) non-deterministically in the following two cases: (1) it splits the abstract node into a concrete node followed by an abstract node, and (2) it assumes that the abstract node represents exactly one concrete node and so replaces it by a concrete node. This is accomplished by calling the SPLIT method. The SPLIT method also assigns non-deterministic field values to the newly created nodes by calling the ASSIGNKEYS function. Fig 6 shows how this works for our running example.

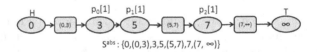

Fig. 6. List traversal by thread 1 by the operation: $p_2[1] := getNext(p_2[1])$. A new concrete node with key 7 and an abstract node with key $(7, \infty)$ are created. The node with key 6 becomes an abstract node.

(b) *Thread Other accesses an abstract node:* In this case the abstract node is split by calling the GETNODE function shown in Fig 7b. This function splits the abstract node non-deterministically in one of four ways: (1) it assumes that the concrete node to be returned on splitting is the leftmost node and so splits into a concrete node followed by an abstract node, (2) it assumes that the concrete node is the rightmost node and so splits into an abstract node followed by the concrete node, (3) it assumes that the concrete node is some central node and so splits into an abstract node followed by the concrete node followed by another abstract node, and (4) it assumes that abstract node represents exactly one concrete node and so replaces it by the concrete node. Non-deterministic values are assigned to the newly created nodes by the SPLIT function by calling ASSIGNKEYS. Fig 8 shows how this is done for our running example.

GETNEXT(p)
  if $p.next$ is concrete
    return $p.next$;
  else
    n, n_1 := new nodes;
    Switch(non-det value $v \in \{1, 2\}$)
    Case 1:
      SPLIT $(p.next, (n, n_1))$;
    Case 2:
      SPLIT $(p.next, (n))$;
    return n;
  END

(a)

GETNODE($p_i[o]$)
  if $p_i[o]$ is concrete
    return $p_i[o]$;
  else
    n, n_1, n_2, n_3 := new nodes;
    Switch(non-det value $v \in \{1, 2, 3, 4\}$)
    Case 1:
      SPLIT $(p_i[o], (n, n_1))$;
      return n;
    Case 2:
      SPLIT $(p_i[o], (n_2, n))$;
      return n;
    Case 3:
      SPLIT $(p_i[o], (n_2, n, n_1))$;
      return n;
    Case 4:
      SPLIT $(p_i[o], (n))$;
      return n;
  END

(b)

SPLIT $(absNode, n\_list)$
  pred, succ := predecessor, successor
    of $absNode$;
  replace $pred \to absNode$
    $\to succ$ by
  $pred \to n\_list_0 \to ...$
    $n\_list_k \to succ$;
  $S^{abs} := S^{abs} - absNode.key$;
  ASSIGNKEYS (n_list);
  END

(c)

ASSIGNKEYS $(node\_list)$
  for each node $n \in node\_list$
    assign non-det value to $n.key$;
  $S^{abs} := S^{abs} + n.key$;
  END

(d)

Fig. 7. The GETNEXT and GETNODE methods

Transition phase. Since all the pointers now refer to concrete nodes, and further, the reads of the next nodes of any pointers also are concrete nodes, the transitions can be executed as though they were executing on the original program with no list abstraction. This is essential in enabling syntactic construction of the list abstraction, as discussed in Section 4.2.

Cleanup phase: canonicalizing to a valid abstract state. Once the transition executes as described above, the new state may not be a valid abstract state; i.e., there may be nodes which are not pointed to by any thread pointer which need to be replaced by abstract nodes. Further, there may be nodes which are not reachable from any pointer in the system. The mapping of the new state to a valid abstract state is accomplished by calling the CANONICALIZE method at the end of the transition, as shown in Fig 9.

Example: As an example, consider the transition corresponding to line 3 in Fig 3a, the corresponding Murphi rule for which is shown in Fig 3b (rule with $pc[i] = 3$). For that transition, on doing the list abstraction to the rule for thread 1 (which is obtained by thread abstraction), the following rule is obtained:

$(pc[1] = 3) \to \{ p_1[1] := getNext(p_0[1]); pc[1] + +;$
CANONICALIZE (); }

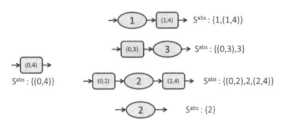

Fig. 8. Splitting of abstract node when a pointer of the *Other* thread non-deterministically accesses it. There are four possibilities: the concrete node (1) is the rightmost node (2) is the leftmost node (3) is some node in middle or (4) is the only node in the chain of nodes represented by the abstract node.

For the *Other* thread, the above rule becomes a no-op since no update to the heap is involved.

Next, for the rule corresponding to $pc[i] = 12$, the rule obtained by doing a list abstraction of the rule for thread *Other* (obtained after thread abstraction) is:

$\forall Np_0, Np_2 \in List : (true) \rightarrow \{ getNode(Np_0).next := getNode(Np_2);$
CANONICALIZE (); } .

CANONICALIZE:
  $\mathcal{P}$: Set of all thread local & global pointers
  Throw away nodes $n \notin \widehat{\mathcal{R}}_{\mathcal{P}}$;
  for each $n_i, n_j \in \widehat{\mathcal{R}}_{\mathcal{P}}$
    if (ISMUINT (n_i, n_j))
      JOIN (n_i, n_j);

JOIN (n_i, n_j):
  $pn_i := $ predecessor of n_i;
  $sn_j := $ successor of n_j;
  $pn_i.next := n_{ij}^A$;
  $n_{ij}^A.next := sn_j$;
  for each node n in $n_i \rightarrow ... \rightarrow n_j$
    $S^{abs} = S^{abs} - n.key$;
  ASSIGNKEYS (n_{ij}^A);

ISMUINT (n_i, n_j):
  $pn_i := $ predecessor of n_i;
  $sn_j := $ successor of n_j;
  if $(Ref(pn_i) \wedge Ref(sn_j))$
    node $n := pn_i$;
    while$(n.next! = sn_j)$ do
      $n := n.next$;
      if$(Ref(n))$ then
        return false;
    return true;
  else
    return false;

Fig. 9. CANONICALIZE Method

Syntactic construction of the abstraction: The thread and list abstractions can be constructed syntactically. The syntactic construction of the thread abstraction is discussed in our previous work [21]. The syntactic construction of the list abstraction can be done in the following 3 steps: (1) replace accesses to all nodes by pointer Np of the *Other* thread with GETNODE (Np). (2) Next, replace all reads to the next field of any node, say of the form $p.next$, with GETNEXT (p). (3) Finally, at the end of each transition, insert a call to CANONICALIZE () function.

While the syntactic construction of the thread abstraction has been implemented in a tool called Abster [22], extension to the list dimension is part of our ongoing work.

4   Refining the Abstraction: Extended CMP Method

The above defined abstraction may be too coarse to prove the property. This may be due to two reasons: (1) the environment thread, *Other*, may non-deterministically execute transitions which spuriously violate the property, and (2) the method ASSIGNKEYS called by SPLIT and JOIN may non-deterministically assign key values to the newly created nodes which violate the property. Thus, to prove the property, the above abstraction may have to be refined either in the thread dimension (refining *Other*) or in the list dimension (by constraining values assigned by ASSIGNKEYS).

The abstraction and refinement is then done in a loop which is shown in Fig 2. The loop proceeds by iteratively model checking the system model. If the system model at any stage in the refinement loop passes the model checker, the property is proven. If, on the other hand, there is a counterexample for the system model, the user must examine the counterexample. In case the counterexample is valid, a bug has been found. On the other hand, if the counterexample is invalid, the user needs to distinguish between two possible cases. 1) The spurious counterexample is caused due to a spurious transition non-deterministically executed by the *Other* thread. 2) The spurious counterexample is due to a new node introduced by the ASSIGNKEYS method.

4.1   Refinement in Thread Dimension

Since the environment thread *Other* non-deterministically selects nodes and executes transitions, it may exhibit spurious behaviors. In order to constrain the *Other* thread, the user adds candidate lemmas which are conjoined with the guards of the rules. Formally, suppose that the candidate lemma L is used. Now consider a rule r of the program P defined as: $\rho \rightarrow a$, where ρ is the guard and a is an action. Then, refining P with L involves strengthening the guard by L to obtain the strengthened rule $\rho \wedge L \Rightarrow a$ and strengthening the property under check, say Φ, to $\Phi \wedge L$. The new program is then re-abstracted to obtain the refined abstraction. Observe that in this refinement approach, no extra state gets added to the abstract model. This is important for efficiency.

Example: Consider our example for rule with $pc = 12$, for which the abstracted rule for thread *Other* is discussed in Section 3.2. Since that rule is highly unconstrained and may lead to a spurious counterexample, the user may add the lemma that $p_2[i]$ is the successor of $p_1[i]$ which is the successor of $p_0[i]$. This lemma can be expressed as $p_0[i].next = p_1[i] \wedge p_1[i].next = p_2[i]$. Thus, the *strengthened* rule is now:

$(pc[i] = 12 \wedge p_0[i].next = p_1[i] \wedge p_1[i].next = p_2[i]) \rightarrow \{ p_0[i].next := p_2[i]; pc[i] + +; \}$

Re-abstraction leads to a more constrained abstract rule for the *Other* thread.

$\forall Np_0, Np_1, Np_2 \in Nodes : (true \wedge Np_0.next = Np_1 \wedge Np_1.next = Np_2) \rightarrow \{ getNode(Np_0).next := getNode(Np_2);$
    CANONICALIZE $(); \}$

Further, the above lemma is also added to the property under verification and thus is also verified when the model checking is done on the refined model.

4.2 Refinement in List Dimension

In order to prevent property violations due to non-deterministic values assigned by AS-SIGNKEYS method, the user strengthens the model by adding list lemmas (i.e., candidate invariants on list variables). These lemmas are then used to constrain the values assigned to the newly created node.

This list lemma based strengthening is implemented in the GETNODE and GET-NEXT functions by modifying the ASSIGNKEYS function to ASSIGNKEYS', as shown in Fig 10. The ASSIGNKEYS' method checks the added list lemmas before assigning the key values and exits the while loop when such values are found. Note that the list lemmas checked by ASSIGNKEYS' are also added to the property under check. Thus these lemmas also get verified during model checking. Finally, observe that refinement in the list dimension also does not add extra state to the abstract model.

```
ASSIGNKEYS' (node_list)
  while(true)
    for (node n ∈ node_list)
      assign non-det value to n.key and update S;
    if (list lemmas satisfied)
      break;
  END
```

Fig. 10. The ASSIGNKEYS' method

Example: As an example, the keys of the nodes are assumed to be sorted (ordering invariant). Thus, in case the new node is assigned a value such that the ordering invariant is violated, it will lead to a violation of properties like Linearizability as well. The user then adds the ordering lemma during the refinement process.

We show how the strengthening in the list dimension with the ordering lemma affects the following operations: (1) list traversal by thread 1 through call to GETNEXT and (2) list updates by thread *Other* by call to GETNODE.

Fig 6 shows how after list traversal ($p_2[1] := p_2[1].next$) from the original state shown in Fig 5, the key value of the newly created nodes respect the ordering lemma.

Next, Fig 8 shows that when the *Other* thread accesses an abstract node, the node is split non-deterministically in one of four ways. Observe that after splitting, the values to the newly created nodes are assigned such that the ordering lemma holds.

Proof of Correctness: The correctness of the refinement in the list dimension can be established by the following theorem, the proof for which is provided in Appendix A.3.[6]

Theorem. *Let P be the original program, let P^{abs} be the abstracted program and let P_g^{abs} be the program obtained by strengthening the list with list lemmas $g1, g2, ...$ Then, if the strengthened program P_g^{abs} satisfies $\phi \wedge g$, where g is $g1 \wedge g2 \wedge g3 ...$ and ϕ is any invariant, the original program P also satisfies $\phi \wedge g$.*

Note that the above theorem implies that if P_g^{abs} satisfies $\phi \wedge g$, the added list lemmas, g, hold for P as well.

---

[6] For the proof of correctness of the refinement in the thread dimension, we refer the interested reader to [22].

5 Experiments

We verified properties of the *Fine-grained* and *Optimistic* algorithms presented in [9] using our method. The *Optimistic* algorithm differs from the *Fine-grained* algorithm in the sense that it reduces contention by traversing the list without locking.

We modeled the two concurrent data structures and their access methods in the Murphi language (CMurphi 5.4.6). The abstraction was implemented by hand. This step is fully automatable but the abstraction tool we used in our earlier work [21] does not yet handle lists (this extension is part of our ongoing work). The strengthening was carried out manually as well. All the experiments were run on a 2.40 GHz, Intel Core 2 Quad processor, with 3.74 GB RAM.

Verifying Linearizability. As discussed in Section 2.2, we verify Linearizability by a refinement based approach.

Added Lemmas: The list lemmas which had to be added to verify Linearizability were: (1) the ordering lemma, which states that the ordering invariant holds, and (2) the refinement lemma [7], which states that the refinement map holds.

Next, in order to refine the thread dimension, the following (classes of) thread lemmas were added. (1) Lemmas specifying relationships between thread pointers while the thread makes updates. For example, for line 12 of the *Remove* method, a lemma stating that the node pointed to by $p_1[i]$ is next to that pointed to by $p_0[i]$ was added. And (2), synchronization lemmas for stating that certain updates be made only when the node pointed to by the pointer is locked by that thread. As an example, in lines 11 and 12 of *Remove* method, the pointers $p_0[i]$, $p_1[i]$ and $p_2[i]$ should have the nodes they point to locked. In all, we had to add 5 thread lemmas for *Fine-grained* algorithm and 6 for the *Optimistic* algorithm.

Runtime: The model checking of the *Fine-grained* algorithm took about 0.97 hours to finish, with 463385 states explored and 344365137 rules fired. The model checking of the *Optimistic* algorithm on the other hand took 24 hours with 6851860 states and 7591017821 rules.[8]

The increased model checking time is due to the large number of fired rules and state space explored. This is due to the large number of interleavings due to fine-grained synchronization and is consistent with similar scalability challenges faced by other model checking efforts in this domain [4, 26, 28, 29].

Verifying Ordering. Since just verifying the ordering invariant does not require checking refinement against S, there is no need to prove the refinement map. Then, the pointers H and T can be dropped thus reducing the abstraction size.

The runtime for checking ordering with above approach was about 79 secs for *Fine-grained* algorithm, with 19620 explored states and 2264535 fired rules. For the *Optimistic* algorithm the runtime was 35 min with 408834 states and 143706285 rules.

---

[7] The refinement lemma is not explicitly added to ASSIGNKEYS'; it is implicitly a part of SPLIT and JOIN. This special treatment is given to it because, strictly speaking, it is a lemma across both, the list and the specification set S.

[8] We did some manual optimizations for the *Optimistic* algorithm to reduce the maximum number of list nodes in the abstraction, in order to reduce the runtime.

While no list lemmas had to be added to verify ordering, 6 lemmas had to be added to constrain the *Other* thread for *Fine-grained* and 7 for *Optimistic* algorithms. Note that most of the non-interference lemmas added for proving Linearizability got reused for proving ordering as well.

6   Conclusion and Future Work

We have presented a powerful approach for verifying concurrent list-based data structures and have successfully applied it to verify challenging examples. The key advantage of our approach is that, though it involves some manual guidance, it is largely automatic and it scales to both unbounded number of threads and list nodes.

There are two natural directions in which our work can be extended. Firstly, we can minimize the number of user supplied lemmas by automatically discovering useful lemmas similar to the approach we take in [21]. Secondly, the model checking time for verifying Linearizability can be reduced by designing more efficient abstractions. These abstractions can be used as a part of our overall abstraction-refinement based extended CMP method approach. We plan to take this up next.

In conclusion, our approach opens up a new way for verifying list-based concurrent data structures, which thus far have been handled mainly by separation logic. The preliminary experimental results presented in this paper clearly establish our approach as an alternative model checking based method to verify such data structures.

References

1. Berdine, J., Lev-Ami, T., Manevich, R., Ramalingam, G., Sagiv, M.: Thread quantification for concurrent shape analysis. In: Gupta, A., Malik, S. (eds.) CAV 2008. LNCS, vol. 5123, pp. 399–413. Springer, Heidelberg (2008)
2. Burckhardt, S., Dern, C., Musuvathi, M., Tan, R.: Line-up: a complete and automatic linearizability checker. In: Proceedings of the 2010 ACM SIGPLAN Conference on Programming Language Design and Implementation, PLDI 2010, pp. 330–340. ACM, New York (2010)
3. Calcagno, C., Parkinson, M., Vafeiadis, V.: Modular safety checking for fine-grained concurrency. In: Riis Nielson, H., Filé, G. (eds.) SAS 2007. LNCS, vol. 4634, pp. 233–248. Springer, Heidelberg (2007)
4. Černý, P., Radhakrishna, A., Zufferey, D., Chaudhuri, S., Alur, R.: Model checking of linearizability of concurrent list implementations. In: Touili, T., Cook, B., Jackson, P. (eds.) CAV 2010. LNCS, vol. 6174, pp. 465–479. Springer, Heidelberg (2010)
5. Chou, C.-T., Mannava, P.K., Park, S.: A simple method for parameterized verification of cache coherence protocols. In: Hu, A.J., Martin, A.K. (eds.) FMCAD 2004. LNCS, vol. 3312, pp. 382–398. Springer, Heidelberg (2004)
6. Colvin, R., Groves, L., Luchangco, V., Moir, M.: Formal verification of a lazy concurrent list-based set algorithm. In: Ball, T., Jones, R.B. (eds.) CAV 2006. LNCS, vol. 4144, pp. 475–488. Springer, Heidelberg (2006)
7. Dinsdale-Young, T., Dodds, M., Gardner, P., Parkinson, M.J., Vafeiadis, V.: Concurrent abstract predicates. In: D'Hondt, T. (ed.) ECOOP 2010. LNCS, vol. 6183, pp. 504–528. Springer, Heidelberg (2010)
8. Gotsman, A., Berdine, J., Cook, B., Sagiv, M.: Thread-modular shape analysis. SIGPLAN Not. 42(6), 266–277 (2007)

9. Herlihy, M., Shavit, N.: The Art of Multiprocessor Programming. Morgan Kaufmann Publishers Inc., San Francisco (2008)
10. Herlihy, M.P., Wing, J.M.: Linearizability: a correctness condition for concurrent objects. ACM Trans. Program. Lang. Syst. 12, 463–492 (1990)
11. Jacobs, B., Piessens, F.: Expressive modular fine-grained concurrency specification. In: Proceedings of the 38th Annual ACM SIGPLAN-SIGACT Symposium on Principles of Programming Languages, POPL 2011, pp. 271–282. ACM, New York (2011)
12. Lahiri, S.K., Bryant, R.E.: Predicate abstraction with indexed predicates. ACM Trans. Comput. Logic 9 (December 2007)
13. Liu, Y., Chen, W., Liu, Y.A., Sun, J.: Model checking linearizability via refinement. In: Cavalcanti, A., Dams, D.R. (eds.) FM 2009. LNCS, vol. 5850, pp. 321–337. Springer, Heidelberg (2009)
14. McMillan, K.L.: Verification of infinite state systems by compositional model checking. In: Pierre, L., Kropf, T. (eds.) CHARME 1999. LNCS, vol. 1703, pp. 219–237. Springer, Heidelberg (1999)
15. Michael, M.M., Scott, M.L.: Correction of a memory management method for lock-free data structures. Tech. rep., Rochester, NY, USA (1995)
16. Noll, T., Rieger, S.: Verifying dynamic pointer-manipulating threads. In: Cuellar, J., Sere, K. (eds.) FM 2008. LNCS, vol. 5014, pp. 84–99. Springer, Heidelberg (2008)
17. O'Leary, J., Talupur, M., Tuttle, M.: Protocol verification using flows: An industrial experience. In: Formal Methods in Computer-Aided Design, FMCAD 2009, pp. 172–179 (November 2009)
18. Pnueli, A., Ruah, S., Zuck, L.D.: Automatic deductive verification with invisible invariants. In: Margaria, T., Yi, W. (eds.) TACAS 2001. LNCS, vol. 2031, pp. 82–97. Springer, Heidelberg (2001)
19. Pnueli, A., Xu, J., Zuck, L.D.: Liveness with $(0, 1, \infty)$-counter abstraction. In: Brinksma, E., Larsen, K.G. (eds.) CAV 2002. LNCS, vol. 2404, pp. 107–122. Springer, Heidelberg (2002)
20. Sagiv, M., Reps, T., Wilhelm, R.: Parametric shape analysis via 3-valued logic. In: Proceedings of the 26th ACM SIGPLAN-SIGACT Symposium on Principles of Programming Languages, POPL 1999, pp. 105–118. ACM, New York (1999)
21. Sethi, D., Talupur, M., Schwartz-Narbonne, D., Malik, S.: Parameterized model checking of fine grained concurrency. In: Donaldson, A., Parker, D. (eds.) SPIN 2012. LNCS, vol. 7385, pp. 208–226. Springer, Heidelberg (2012)
22. Talupur, M., Tuttle, M.: Going with the flow: Parameterized verification using message flows. In: Formal Methods in Computer-Aided Design, FMCAD 2008, pp. 1–8 (November 2008)
23. Vafeiadis, V.: Shape-value abstraction for verifying linearizability. In: Jones, N.D., Müller-Olm, M. (eds.) VMCAI 2009. LNCS, vol. 5403, pp. 335–348. Springer, Heidelberg (2009)
24. Vafeiadis, V.: Automatically proving linearizability. In: Touili, T., Cook, B., Jackson, P. (eds.) CAV 2010. LNCS, vol. 6174, pp. 450–464. Springer, Heidelberg (2010)
25. Vafeiadis, V., Herlihy, M., Hoare, T., Shapiro, M.: Proving correctness of highly-concurrent linearisable objects. In: PPoPP 2006, pp. 129–136. ACM, New York (2006)
26. Vechev, M., Yahav, E., Yorsh, G.: Experience with model checking linearizability. In: Păsăreanu, C.S. (ed.) SPIN 2009. LNCS, vol. 5578, pp. 261–278. Springer, Heidelberg (2009)
27. Yahav, E.: Verifying safety properties of concurrent java programs using 3-valued logic. In: Proceedings of the 28th ACM SIGPLAN-SIGACT Symposium on Principles of Programming Languages, POPL 2001, pp. 27–40. ACM, New York (2001)
28. Zhang, S.J.: Scalable automatic linearizability checking. In: Proceeding of the 33rd International Conference on Software Engineering, ICSE 2011, pp. 1185–1187. ACM, New York (2011)
29. Zhang, S.J., Liu, Y.: Model checking a lazy concurrent list-based set algorithm. In: Proceedings of the 2010 Fourth International Conference on Secure Software Integration and Reliability Improvement, SSIRI 2010, pp. 43–52. IEEE Computer Society, Washington, DC (2010)

A   Appendix

A.1   Murphi Encoding of the Complete *Remove* Method

The Murphi encoding of the complete *Remove* method is shown in Fig 11.

$\forall i \in Threads : (pc[i] = 1) \rightarrow \{$
  $p_0[i] := H;$
  $pc[i] + +; \}$

$\forall i \in Threads : (pc[i] = 2 \wedge$
$p_0[i].lock = 0) \rightarrow \{$
  $p_0[i].lock := i;$
  $pc[i] + +; \}$

$\forall i \in Threads : (pc[i] = 3) \rightarrow \{$
  $p_1[i] := p_0[i].next;$
  $pc[i] + +; \}$

$\forall i \in Threads : (pc[i] = 4 \wedge$
$p_1[i].lock = 0) \rightarrow \{$
  $p_1[i].lock := i;$
  $pc[i] + +; \}$

$\forall i \in Threads : (pc[i] = 5) \rightarrow \{$
  $if(p_1[i].key < Key);$
  $pc[i] + +;$
  $else\, pc[i] = 10;$
  $pc[i] + +; \}$

$\forall i \in Threads : (pc[i] = 6) \rightarrow \{$
  $p_0[i].lock := 0;$
  $pc[i] + +; \}$

$\forall i \in Threads : (pc[i] = 7) \rightarrow \{$
  $p_0[i] := p_1[i];$
  $pc[i] + +; \}$

$\forall i \in Threads : (pc[i] = 8) \rightarrow \{$
  $p_1[i] := p_0[i].next;$
  $pc[i] + +; \}$

$\forall i \in Threads : (pc[i] = 9 \wedge$
$p_0[i].lock = 0) \rightarrow \{$
  $p_1[i].lock := i;$
  $pc[i] := 5; \}$

$\forall i \in Threads : (pc[i] = 10) \rightarrow \{$
  if $(p_1[i].key = Key)$
  then $pc[i] + +;$
  else $pc[i] = 15; \}$

$\forall i \in Threads : (pc[i] = 11) \rightarrow \{$
  $p_2[i] := p_1[i].next; pc[i] + +; \}$

$\forall i \in Threads : (pc[i] = 12) \rightarrow \{$
  $p_0[i].next := p_2[i]; pc[i] + +; \}$

$\forall i \in Threads : (pc[i] = 13) \rightarrow \{$
  $result[i] := true;$
  $pc[i] := pc[i] + 3; \}$

$\forall i \in Threads : (pc[i] = 14) \rightarrow \{$
  [else] $pc[i] + +; \}$

$\forall i \in Threads : (pc[i] = 15) \rightarrow \{$
  $result[i] := false; pc[i] + +; \}$

$\forall i \in Threads : (pc[i] = 16) \rightarrow \{$
  $p_0[i].lock := 0; pc[i] + +; \}$

$\forall i \in Threads : (pc[i] = 17) \rightarrow \{$
  $p_1[i].lock := 0; \}$

Fig. 11. Murphi model for method *Remove* for thread i: each rule corresponds to a line in the *Remove* method shown in Fig 3a.

A.2   Nodes in $\widehat{nd}$

Nodes in $\widehat{nd}$ are those nodes which have been allocated but have become unreachable from any node in the system. In this section we explain why nodes in $\widehat{nd}$ can never become reachable in the system again and thus affect the abstraction state space.

Note that this condition gets automatically verified in the model checking because of the relationship lemma, discussed in Section 5.

We informally explain the reasoning for this as applied to the *Remove* method of the *Fine-grained* algorithm. For $\widehat{nd}$ to become reachable again, there must be a node n, such that n is reachable in the system and $n.next$ is assigned to $\widehat{nd}$. Since the relationship lemma holds, there must exist a node n_1, such that $n.next$ is n_1 and $n_1.next$ is $\widehat{nd}$. But, if this holds, $\widehat{nd}$ is reachable from n and thus reachable in the system. Since this is a contradiction, such a node n_1 does not exist.

A.3   Proof of Correctness

Theorem. *Let P be the original program, let P^{abs} be the abstracted program and let P_g^{abs} be the program obtained by strengthening the list with list invariants $g1, g2, \ldots$ Then, if the strengthened program P_g^{abs} satisfies $\phi \wedge g$, where g is $g1 \wedge g2 \wedge g3 \ldots$ and ϕ is any invariant, the original program P also satisfies $\phi \wedge g$.*

Proof. We show that any counter-example in the original program is also a counter-example in P_g^{abs}.

Suppose the original program does not satisfy $\phi \wedge g$ and let $s_0 \rightarrow^{t_0} s_1 \rightarrow^{t_1} \ldots s_{n-1} \rightarrow^{t_{n-1}} s_n$ be the counterexample, where t_i are transitions and s_i are states. Further, the counterexample is assumed to be of minimal length, i.e., s_n is the first state in which $\phi \wedge g$ is violated.

We prove this in two parts: first we show that the correct part of the counterexample can be simulated (part 1) and next, we show that the bug is also simulatable (part 2).

Part 1: We first show that $s_0 \rightarrow^{t_0} s_1 \rightarrow^{t_1} \ldots s_{n-1} \rightarrow^{t_{n-2}} s_{n-1}$ can be simulated in the program. We prove this by induction on the counterexample trace. Suppose $s_0 \rightarrow^{t_0} s_1 \rightarrow^{t_1} \ldots s_{i-1} \rightarrow^{t_{i-1}} s_i$ can be simulated in P_g^{abs}. We show that the transition t_i can also be simulated. Suppose t_i involves reading or writing to nodes $n_1, n_2 \ldots, n_k$ in the original program. Since $i < n$ and the counterexample is minimal, the list satisfies g. This includes the nodes $n_1, n_2 \ldots, n_k$.

For the corresponding execution in P_g^{abs}, some of the nodes from $n_1, n_2 \ldots, n_k$ might be created from splitting abstract nodes. In order to show that the transition t_i is possible in P_g^{abs}, we need to show that if any nodes are created from splitting the abstract nodes, they can still take the field values which are taken by these nodes in the original program. In other words, we need to show that constraining the nodes obtained by splitting abstract nodes to satisfy g by AssignKeys' does not constrain the nodes to take values taken by $n_1, n_2, \ldots$ in P. But, since $n_1, n_2, \ldots$ satisfy g in the original program, constraining by g in P_g^{abs} will not prevent the newly created nodes from taking these values. Thus, the transition will be simulated.

Part 2: Next we show that a violation of t_{n-1} will also be simulated, assuming the rest of the counterexample has been simulated thus far. Without loss of generality, by symmetry, we assume that t_{n-1} is a transition of thread 1. Now, if this happens, we have the following 2 cases:

Case 1: The property ϕ is violated. In this case, like in part 1, assumption of g by AS-SIGNKEYS' does not rule out any transitions. Thus, the error-prone transition violating ϕ will be simulated, leading to a violation of ϕ in P_g^{abs} as well.

Case 2: The list-lemma g is violated. In this case, we need to show that the violation occurs in P_g^{abs} and occurs at the transition phase. The violation occurs, due to the same reasoning as for case 1. We show that it occurs in the transition phase.

In case g is violated, the transition t_{n-1} in P can not be a transition with a heap traversal action (as defined in Section 2.1), since it lead to a violation of a list invariant. This is because list invariants depend only on heap values (and potentially on S for refinement map): none of these change in list traversal in P.

Thus t_{n-1} can only be a transition with a heap update action (either heap shape update or heap node update). Such transitions, for thread 1, are mapped to transitions in P_g^{abs} for which the following two conditions hold: (1) all actions by thread 1 occur on concrete nodes, and (2) the nodes which are referred nodes do not change. Consequently, the setup and cleanup phases of this mapped transition do not make any updates to the heap. Thus the violation of the property will occur exclusively at the transition phase. Then, this violation will be simulated in P_g^{abs} as well.

Thus we have shown that any counter-example in the original program P has a corresponding counter-example in P_g^{abs}. Then, our abstraction-refinement method is sound.   □

A.4   Methods of S^{abs}

$seqContains^{abs}(e) : \{$
if (e not singleton) unspecified;
else if ($\forall interval \in S^{abs} : e \not\subseteq interval$) then return false;
else if ($e \in S^{abs}$) then return true;
else return non-det;$\}$

$seqAdd^{abs}(e) : \{$
if (e not singleton) unspecified;
else if ($\forall interval \in S^{abs} : e \not\subseteq interval$) then $S^{abs} := S^{abs} + e$; return true;
else if ($e \in S^{abs}$) then return false;
else return non-det;$\}$

$seqRemove^{abs}(e) : \{$
if (e not singleton) unspecified;
else if ($\forall interval \in S^{abs} : e \not\subseteq interval$) then return false;
else if ($e \in S^{abs}$) then $S^{abs} := S^{abs} - \{e\}$; return true;
else return non-det;$\}$

Fig. 12. Methods of the sequential set S^{abs}

Property-Driven Benchmark Generation

Bernhard Steffen[1], Malte Isberner[1,2], Stefan Naujokat[1],
Tiziana Margaria[3], and Maren Geske[1]

[1] Dortmund University of Technology, Chair for Programming Systems
Dortmund, D-44227, Germany
{steffen,stefan.naujokat,maren.geske}@cs.tu-dortmund.de
[2] Carnegie Mellon University
Moffett Field, CA, USA
isberner@cmu.edu
[3] Universität Potsdam, Chair Service and Software Engineering,
Potsdam, D-14482, Germany
margaria@cs.uni-potsdam.de

Abstract. We present a systematic approach to the automatic generation of platform-independent benchmarks of tailored complexity for evaluating verification tools for reactive systems. Key to this approach is
a tool chain that essentially transforms a set of automatically generated LTL properties into source code for various formats, platforms, and
competition scenarios via a sequence of property-preserving steps. These
steps go through dedicated representations in terms of Büchi Automata,
Mealy machines, Decision Diagram Models, Code Models, and finally
the source code of the chosen scenario. The required transformations
comprise LTL synthesis, model checking, property-oriented expansion,
path condition extraction, theorem proving, SAT solving, and code motion. This combination allows us to address different communities via
a growing set of programming languages, tailored sets of programming
constructs, different notions of observation, and the full variety of LTL
properties – ranging from mere reachability over general safety properties to arbitrary liveness properties. The paper illustrates the whole
tool chain along accompanying examples, emphasizes the current state
of development, and sketches the envisioned potential and impact of our
approach.

Keywords: Benchmark generation, LTL synthesis, model checking,
property-oriented expansion, path condition extraction, theorem proving, SAT solving, code motion.

1 Motivation

Twenty years ago, at CAV 1993 in Elounda, Crete, the essence of the business
meeting could have been summarized as "We have developed numerous powerful
methods and tools, what we are missing are appropriate problems." Since then,
numerous impressive case studies have been presented, competitions and challenges have been organized, and industrial cooperations have been conducted,

E. Bartocci and C.R. Ramakrishnan (Eds.): SPIN 2013, LNCS 7976, pp. 341–357, 2013.
© Springer-Verlag Berlin Heidelberg 2013

but all these initiatives remained very partial: they focused on very specific scenarios, thus limiting their potential for the generalization of the results and fair comparison of technologies, let alone for establishing a clear application profile for the wealth of academic and industrial tools. What is needed for an unbiased evaluation of the tools' application profiles is an infinite source of benchmark problems of tailored size and complexity, with known properties of varying difficulty that are accessible to everybody.[1] Only this way one can fine-tune the experimental tool analysis, reproduce analysis results, and explore and compare the conceptual limitations of the proposed solutions. All these are preconditions for an in-depth and responsible, profile-based recommendation for a tool or a technology.

In short, what is missing is a systematic way to obtain classified benchmark suites that are expressive enough to reveal the individual tools'/technologies' strengths and weaknesses both at the conceptual and the pragmatic level.

In this paper, we present a systematic approach to the automatic generation of platform-independent benchmarks of tailored complexity for evaluating verification tools for reactive systems. In order to optimally clarify 1) the intuition behind our approach, 2) the three major challenges, and 3) its technical ingredients we explain each dimension in a separate subsection. The overall benchmark generation process has its own full section (cf. Sec. 2), followed by individual sections on its steps (cf. Secs. 3–9). The paper closes in Sec. 10 with our conclusions and directions to future work.

1.1   The Intuition

The intuition behind our approach is quite similar to that of the now popular outdoor game geocaching[2]: in geocaching, recognizing the points of interest once one is there is trivial. In our case we simply leave a mark that is easily recognizable by any tool. The point of the game is to reach the correct location despite dedicated hurdles. Our corresponding "riddles" are of course program analysis questions to be solved in the overall game. With this mindset, the intuition behind our automatic benchmark generation process is easy to explain:

– We randomly place "treasures" and connect them with an envisioned feasible path, i.e., a path that the player will have to follow. In our case, this results in a Mealy machine that we obtain as a result of a synthesis process from a more declarative specification in terms of LTL properties.
– We randomly insert "riddles" along the path. In our case, these are randomly generated program structures that need to be correctly analyzed to win the game. The point is that the insertion of these obstacles is property preserving. This is realized by applying a sequence of elementary, provably property-preserving insertion/transformation steps.

---

[1] Of course, dedicated real(-istic) problems are also extremely important, but because of their "singularity" and a priori unknown properties, they are not suitable for a careful, wide-range profile analysis.

[2] In particular "mystery" and "multi" caches. See http://www.geocaching.com/

Like in geocaching, even though recognizing the treasures is simple, it is possible to construct problems of almost arbitrary complexity simply by changing the riddles. This could mean moving from simple reachability problems to safety, liveness or even arbitrary LTL properties in program structures of increasing complexity that may comprise complex conditions, data structures, loops, or as new vision even polymorphism and virtual methods. The configurable scale and randomization of the generation process guarantees that each of the problems is entirely distinct from any other.

What is truly different from geocaching is the fact that once given the complexity profile, these problems are fully automatically generated without any human interaction. Consequently, the solution can be kept secret even from the organizers of a challenge/competition, enabling them to participate themselves without any advantage – provided that the profile and the code/specification of the benchmark generator is made public.

1.2   The Three Major Challenges

Three quite general questions need to be answered when aiming at quality benchmark problem generation:

- **Where and how to throw the dice:** In order to get balanced benchmarks of challenging size, one needs a fine granular concept of randomization. Our multi-step generation process (cf. Sec. 2) is explicitly designed for aspect-specific randomization, as will be illustrated in the main sections of the paper.
- **How to impose/guarantee the properties:** Obviously, this must be done by construction, as extracting the properties from the final benchmark is meant to be a challenging (open) problem. Central throughout the whole process is therefore the fact that maintaining language inclusion wrt. the ω-language of the Büchi automaton synthesized from the LTL formulas is sufficient to guarantee property preservation. This simple principle is strictly followed during the whole generation process depicted in Fig. 1, and it can be applied straightforwardly to further enhance the program structure with almost arbitrarily complex program elements.
- **How to avoid generator footprints (hints):** An important goal of benchmark generation must be that the generated problems are not biased (beyond their abstract profile), and that it does not make sense to exploit any knowledge about the generation process. Optimally, even the developers of the benchmark generator should have no (significant) advantage.

1.3   Summary of the Involved Technologies

Technical key to this approach is a tool chain that essentially transforms a set of automatically generated (or hand-selected) LTL properties via a series of property-preserving steps into source code for various formats, platforms, and competition scenarios. These steps pass various phases characterized by representations in terms of Büchi automata, Mealy machines, code models, and finally the source code of the chosen scenario. The required transformations are based on LTL synthesis [1, 2], model checking [3], property-oriented expansion [4], path condition extraction [5], theorem prover/SAT solver-based linking of pre and post conditions [6, 7], and (semantic) code motion [8–13].

In order to make the benchmarks accessible by most tools and interesting for different communities, we aim at supporting

- a growing set of programming languages (e.g. Java, Scala, C/C++, C#, Promela,...),
- a tailored use of programming constructs (loops, linear and non-linear arithmetics, methods calls, virtual methods...) and diverse data structures (integers, arrays, lists, floating-point numbers, ...),
- different notions of observation: reached program labels, exceptions being thrown, output written to the console, method invocations, ...
- the full variety of LTL properties, ranging from mere reachability over general safety properties to liveness properties and arbitrary mixtures thereof.

Section 2 sketches the process (cf. Fig. 1) connecting all these technologies to fully automatically generate randomized benchmark problems of guaranteed property profile (cf. Theorem 1).

The paper illustrates the whole tool chain along accompanying examples, emphasizes the current state of development, discusses our experience with our first version gained during the RERS Challenge 2012 [14], and sketches the envisioned potential and impact of our approach. We will use the corresponding tool to generate the problems for the RERS Challenge 2013, which will take place as a satellite event of ASE 2013 in Mountain View (USA) in November.

In the next section, we will summarize the tool chain (cf. Fig. 1) before we sketch its seven conceptual steps each in its own dedicated section. Subsequently, Sec. 10 discusses our conclusions and perspectives.

2   The Generation Process from a Bird's Eye View

Our solution is centered around a property-driven benchmark generation process (cf. Fig. 1). It starts with a randomized property selection that can be transformed to Büchi automata using standard techniques, and then it successively enriches/changes the representations via various property-preserving model and code transformations to provide problems of almost arbitrary complexity and size. Its characteristic conceptual steps, which will be discussed in more detail in the remainder of the paper, can be sketched as follows from a bird's eye view:

Pattern-Based LTL Generation: In this step we randomly choose and then instantiate LTL property specification patterns [15] that we partition into a small *defining set* used in the subsequent synthesis step, and a larger set of additional properties whose validity is later checked on the synthesized model via model

Organizer

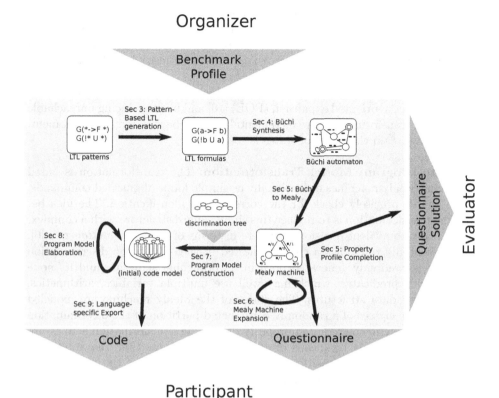

Fig. 1. Overview of property-preserving steps

checking. Typically, we generate around 100 properties, about ten of which can be defining, in order to still allow for automated synthesis.

LTL Synthesis: Here we can apply any of the standard algorithms that translate an LTL formula into a Büchi automaton representing all its models (satisfying paths). Our current implementation uses LTL2Buchi [2], but, e.g., LTL2BA [1] could have been chosen as well.

From Büchi to Mealy: Completing the Property Profile: The point of this step is the generation of a concrete reactive system model (e.g. a Mealy machine) from the Büchi automaton that represents *all* words/paths satisfying the defining properties. The construction of this Mealy machine is randomized and can be customized in various dimensions, e.g., the size of the model, the size of the input and output alphabets, the density of the transition graph etc.. Important is only that the construction obeys our language inclusion-based correctness principle which guarantees that all the defining properties remain valid.

The subsequent completion step for the property profile can straightforwardly be realized by model checking the additional (non-defining) properties on the generated Mealy machine. After this step the property profile for this benchmark is determined once and for all, as all remaining steps also obey our correctness principle. More concretely, the observable language of all the generated artifacts is guaranteed to be included in the language of the synthesized Büchi automaton.

Mealy Machine Expansion: These Mealy Machines are then enlarged via randomized property-oriented expansion (POE) [16] and by introducing unreachable states. Both transformations are incremental and can be stopped at any moment, e.g. when a certain threshold of states is reached.

Mealy-to-Program Model Transformation: The transformation is based on viewing Mealy machines operationally as simple loops of guarded commands, whose guards precisely check for the correct state identification. The idea behind the transformation is to replace this simple guard structure with a complex, semantically equivalent decision structure in terms of a *discrimination tree* [6], which essentially resembles a complex nested "if-then-else". The discrimination tree itself is randomly generated both in its branching structure and its node labeling with predicates, which may well use multiple variables, arithmetics, relations, and data structures. The states of the Mealy machine are modeled by equivalence classes of a randomly constructed partition of the discrimination tree's leaves. Key to the required property preserving transformation is to establish the correct wiring by means of adequate assignments that guarantee that the postcondition of a transition implies the precondition of the target state, and to extract corresponding complex guarded commands. Path condition generation and SAT solving/theorem proving provide a powerful basis for deriving non-trivial conditional structures (cf. Sec. 7).

Elaboration of the Program Model Structure: We employ data-flow analysis and transformation techniques to randomly elaborate the program model structure along both the logical and the control structure:

- *Overcoming the Simple Loop Structure:* Up to here, the programs are still reminiscent of Event Condition Action Systems [17, 18] or PLC programs [19], a structure the 2012 RERS Challenge focused on [14]. Using randomized property-oriented expansion [4], this structure can be generalized to obtain quite general "while"-program-like structures [20].
- *De-Localization of the Logical Reasoning:* Our approach for establishing postconditions that match the required preconditions characterizing the subsequent state is local, i.e., a Mealy machine can be reconstructed essentially by a pairwise check of the various preconditions and postconditions. We therefore employ code motion techniques [8–13, 21, 22] for de-localizing the information and therefore require a global analysis for reconstructing the transition relation.

Language Extraction: Currently we have implemented a simple template mechanism which works for Java and C/C++ and maintains the behavioral and structural properties of its argument code models. Currently, we are extending our template mechanism to capture many more target languages in order to approach our goal of serving the needs of as many tool developers as possible

As all steps of our benchmark generation process are designed to obey our correctness principle, it is guaranteed that the observable language of all the generated artifacts is included in the language of the synthesized Büchi automaton. This means that all LTL properties are maintained! Thus we have:

Theorem 1 (Correctness). *The language-specific code generated by our benchmark generation process is guaranteed to satisfy the property profile established during the profile completion (step 3).*

The idea of a language specific export is quite general and was in essence also used by the winning team of the RERS Challenge 2012 to generate Promela input for their tool landscape centering around the LTSmin model checker [23]. In order to support cross-community challenges, we currently aim at lowering the entry hurdle for participants by providing them with various language formats. It should be noted, however, that providing e.g. Promela code is not quite the same as providing code of the other mentioned programming languages as it requires non-trivial design decisions concerning the adequate abstraction. Thus we are considering to provide a Promela generator instead, which is parameterized in the abstraction.

3   Property Generation

The goal of fully automatically generating a large set of interesting benchmarks inevitably calls for the random generation not only of system models, but also of their underlying properties. While this could be achieved by randomly generating LTL syntax trees, the resulting formulae would most likely be very different from what real-life property specifications look like.

Instead of randomly generating whole formulae, we therefore randomly instantiate specification *patterns*, like for example those described in the seminal work of Matthew Dwyer et al. [15]. Additionally to producing more realistic properties, this approach also yields the benefit that an intuitive textual description can be provided for each LTL formula. Such properties might include, but are not limited to, the following:

- *Absence*, e.g. $\mathbf{G} \neg \mathsf{bad}$: "Action bad does never occur"
- *Existence*, $\mathbf{F}$ good: "Eventually, action good will be performed"
- *Response*, $\mathbf{G}(\mathsf{a} \Rightarrow \mathbf{F}\,\mathsf{b})$: "Whenever event a occurs, this will lead to action b being observed eventually"

In a challenge scenario, each of these properties (plus dozens of others) would have to be checked separately on the given system.

In the generation phase, however, a small subset of all properties is selected to constrain the randomized on-the-fly construction of the initial Mealy machine model [24].[3] This step is prepared by synthesizing a Büchi automaton from the selected properties, as the next section will detail.

4   Büchi Synthesis

Formally, from the set Φ of all generated properties we select two subsets Φ^+, Φ^- which should (resp. should not) hold *by construction*. A Büchi automaton A_ψ is created from the conjunct of the selected property sets

$$\psi = \bigwedge_{\phi \in \Phi^+} \phi \wedge \bigwedge_{\phi \in \Phi^-} \neg\phi,$$

Generating Büchi automata from LTL formulae is a very expensive task for larger formulae, thus the choice of the size of the sets Φ^+ and Φ^- crucially depends on how much computing power should be invested in this step. Usually, we obtain fairly good results already with very small sets: the problems of the RERS challenge 2012 were generated using between four and six defining properties.

In the example of the previous section, the conjunct of all non-negated specification formulae is

$$\psi = \mathbf{G} \, \neg\text{bad} \wedge \mathbf{F} \, \text{good} \wedge \mathbf{G}(\text{a} \Rightarrow \mathbf{F} \, \text{b}).$$

Figure 2 shows the corresponding Büchi automaton, which already contains a significant number of transitions given the rather small and simple specification formula. This Büchi automaton was generated using the LTL2BA algorithm [1], but other algorithms such as LTL2Buchi [2] could have been used as well. Note that this automaton, as it is, is not a valid model fulfilling the given properties: first, assuming a granularity of one action/observation per step, some of the transitions such as `!bad && good && b` can never be realized, as *either* action good *or* action b occurs. Similarly, transitions like `!bad && b` can be shortened to just b. The second aspect regards the set of allowed input symbols (events). The transition label `!bad` represents an otherwise unrestricted set of alphabet symbols, although generally we assume that the set of observable events is constrained in one way or the other.

Finally, there is no equivalent for accepting states in a Mealy machine: in each concrete instantiation of a system it has to be ensured that the reflexive transition labeled `(!bad && !a) || (!bad && b)` of state init cannot be taken infinitely often in a row.

In the next section, we will describe how to construct a Mealy machine whose infinite runs all satisfy the constraints imposed by this Büchi automaton.

---

[3] We chose Mealy machines as our intermediate model structure because of their input/output distinction. Of course also labeled transition systems [25] or IO automata [26] could have been chosen as well.

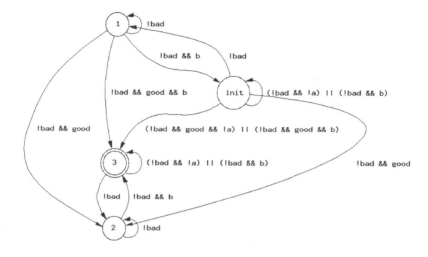

Fig. 2. Resulting Büchi automaton for set ψ

5   From Büchi to Mealy: Completing the Property Profile

The construction of a concrete Mealy machine from a constraining Büchi automaton is based on the idea of constructing on-the-fly a product automaton. Starting with the initial state of the Büchi automaton and a freshly created initial state of the Mealy machine, successor states are either newly generated or taken from the set of existing Mealy machine states. This has to be done consistently with the Büchi automaton, i.e., a transition between two states in the Mealy machine needs to match a transition between the associated Büchi states. When creating states in the Mealy machine, several Büchi states might be eligible for being associated with the new state due to non-determinism. In this case, one can be chosen at random. This selection might eliminate accepting runs during the model construction, but does not affect correctness.

Special care has to be taken when transitions to existing states in the Mealy machine are created: this introduces loops. The Büchi acceptance criterion requires every loop in the model includes at least one accepting state. At first, this can be easily achieved by creating back edges only to accepting states. As the model construction proceeds, a set of *safe states* gradually emerges: these are states where all the outgoing infinite paths are accepting. These safe states can be used as targets for cross edges. If no back or cross edge to a safe state can be created even if some given hard limit on the number of states is reached, the transition is completely discarded and we may need to backtrack in order to ensure that there are no states with zero outdegree (deadlocks). This is important to guarantee our correctness principle, which is based on the fact that diminishing the set of (infinite) traces preserves ω-language inclusion and therefore the validity of LTL properties.

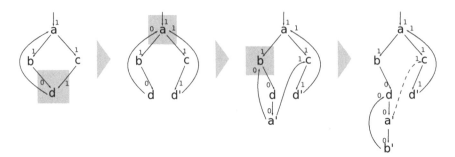

Fig. 3. Property-Oriented Expansion (POE) with random boolean property (0/1)

Obviously, each formula $\phi \in \Phi^+$ is satisfied on the resulting Mealy machine *by construction*, whereas each formula in Φ^- is unsatisfied. However, at this point it is unknown whether the remaining properties in $\Phi \setminus (\Phi^+ \cup \Phi^-)$ hold as well, and this cannot be deduced from the construction itself.

The property profile therefore has to be completed by model checking the remaining properties on the model. This is a comparatively quite easy task: whereas generating a Büchi automaton for the conjunct of all formulae in Φ is beyond tractability, an automaton $A_{\neg\phi}$ for each single $\phi \in \Phi$ can be synthesized quite efficiently. Using $A_{\neg\phi}$ to model check the generated Mealy machine is straightforward and can be achieved by standard techniques [3]. We currently use our own implementation, which performs a language emptiness test on the product automaton by analyzing reachability of strongly connected components with accepting states, but of course one could also resort to an external LTL model checker.

6   Mealy Machine Expansion

Once the Mealy machine is constructed from the LTL/Büchi specification, we increase its size (i.e. number of states) artificially while preserving the properties. This is done by iteratively applying the following steps:

– addition of unreachable nodes and model structures,
– splitting nodes with POE according to some randomly set property,
– pruning outgoing transitions.

Adding unreachable structures. The first operation simply adds nodes or even arbitrary new Mealy machines over the same alphabet into the original model. To increase the analysis complexity, the states of those newly added model fragments may have transitions into the original Mealy machine. As no transition leads from the original model into the newly added parts, the new nodes remain unreachable and therefore do not alter the original models' behavior.

Splitting under Property-Oriented Expansion. The second operation introduces
new reachable states by splitting existing ones. This is done by defining arbitrary new properties and assigning them randomly to every transition. Figure 3
illustrates the POE transformation pattern by expanding a four node directed
graph according to properties resembling a simple coin toss, i.e., a single boolean
property that randomly assumes the values 0 or 1 to each transition.[4] Whenever
a node is reached via incoming transitions that have different values for this
property, it is duplicated. Figure 3 shows the effects in detail: the highlighted
state d is reached from b with property value 0 and from c with property value
1, causing it to be split into states d and d', connected to the same successor
states of the original d (here a) via transitions that inherit the resp. property
value. Now a becomes reachable with property values 0 and 1 respectively, so it
must be split too. This introduces a new transition from a' to b with a different
property value, so finally also b is split. Already from this small example it becomes apparent that randomized property-oriented expansion is a flexible way
to significantly increase a model while preserving the set of its traces.

Pruning. These two steps affect only the structure of the model, but not its behavior: the set of traces remains unchanged, and hence a minimization operation
would result in the original Mealy machine. This trivially guarantees property
preservation, but on the other hand does not truly increase the state space.

A way to overcome this is to prune arbitrary transitions in the intermediate
model. Looking at the same example, pruning the dashed transition from a' to
c would truly distinguish a' from a, as only in one case there is a transition to c.
This transformation is legal (i.e., property preserving) as it only *reduces* the set
of all infinite traces in the model, hence it is impossible to introduce unsatisfying
paths by pruning outgoing transitions.

7   Mealy-to-Program Model Transformation

This transformation is based on viewing Mealy machines operationally as simple
loops of guarded commands, whose guards precisely check for the correct state
identification. Its aim is to replace this simple guard structure with a complex,
semantically equivalent decision structure in terms of a *discrimination tree* [6],
which essentially resembles a complex nested "if-then-else". This is achieved in
two steps.

In the first step, a discrimination tree is randomly generated both in its
branching structure and its node labeling with predicates. The idea is to represent the states of the Mealy machine by equivalence classes of a randomly
constructed partition of the discrimination tree's leaves. This step is illustrated
in Fig. 4 which shows a three state Mealy machine in part (a) and a corresponding discrimination tree in part (b). In this tree, $p_1 \dots p_n$ represent arbitrary
predicates, and, e.g., the state s is represented by by the leaves labeled s_1 to s_4.

---

[4] In order to emphasize the essence of the POE pattern, we decided to illustrate it on
a simple directed graph rather than on a deterministic Mealy machine.

(a)   (b)

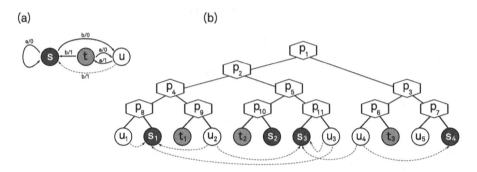

Fig. 4. Discrimination Tree over Mealy machine

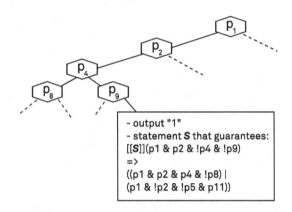

Fig. 5. Code model construction

The point of the second step is to maintain property preservation during the transformation step, which essentially requires to establish the correct' wiring' by means of adequate assignments that guarantee that the postcondition of a transition implies the precondition of the target state, and to extract corresponding complex guarded commands. This steps also leaves a lot of room for randomization:

- As there are multiple ways of using the members of the equivalences classes associated to the states, we can first randomly select adequate representations for each transition of the Mealy machine. The dotted lines at the bottom of Fig. 4(b) show the representation of just one such transition: the $b/1$ transition from u to s.
- Fig. 5 sketches an excerpt of a program model which may have been derived from the discrimination tree (including the dotted lines) shown in Fig. 4(b). The big box summarizes the condition required at leave u_2 to properly implement the $b/1$ transition from u to s: in response to b, the output 1 needs to be generated and either s_1 or s_3 needs to be reached. In our setting this means that the required reachability constraint must be realized by inserting

a statement S that make the correctness assertion (which can technically be regarded as a *Hoare triple*)

$$\{p_1 \wedge p_2 \wedge \neg p_4 \wedge \neg p_9\}\mathbf{S}\{(p_1 \wedge p_2 \wedge p_4 \wedge \neg p_8) \vee (p_1 \wedge \neg p_2 \wedge \neg p_5 \wedge p_{11})\}$$

valid [27, 28], or equivalently, that satisfies the following implication:

$$[\![S]\!](p_1 \wedge p_2 \wedge \neg p_4 \wedge \neg p_9) \;\Rightarrow\; (p_1 \wedge p_2 \wedge p_4 \wedge \neg p_8) \vee (p_1 \wedge \neg p_2 \wedge \neg p_5 \wedge p_{11})$$

The selection of S also leaves plenty of room for random choices.

A deeper discussion of this step, which involves SAT solving/theorem proving [6, 7] is beyond the scope of this paper. Of course, the deeper the analysis the more sophisticated conditional structures can be built. For the RERS Challenge 2012 we first considered a quite simple setting which only uses integers and no arithmetic. As this turned out to be too easy to be truly discriminating, we added arithmetic in the second round. This, from the generation point of view minor change, had a dramatical effect. E.g., it excluded exhaustive symbolic execution, which was still successful in round one. This shows the power of being able to fine-tune the benchmarks' profiles.

8   Elaboration of the Program Model Structure

Program models constructed from Mealy machines and discrimination trees are still quite cycle-oriented and may allow for a reconstruction of the defining Mealy machine, as introduced conditions are locally checkable leaving the transition "wiring" transparent. This can be overcome by applying known global program analysis and transformation techniques:

- Applying randomized POE [4, 29] together with some pruning heuristics allows one to almost arbitrarily "obfuscate" the original cycle orientation, and it provides room for
- a subsequent application of (global) code motion techniques, ranging from merely syntactical analyses reminiscent of partial redundancy elimination [8, 11, 13, 21, 30–33] to more semantic transformations in terms of semantic code motion [9, 10, 22, 34, 35], which shifts the original local reasoning problem to the global level.

9   Language-Specific Export

The last step in the benchmark generation process is the process of generating language-specific code. The basis for that is the fully developed abstract code representation that resulted from the previous step. Some of the supported languages are

- Java
- C/C++/C#
- Promela [36]

Ideally the abstract code representation does not contain any real code snippets yet, as this would immediately restrict the generation process to a specific set of programming languages. Even the semantics of simple operations like boolean operators may differ slightly from one language to another. However, as long as the operation semantics are well defined on an abstract level, it is possible to map these operations to concrete language constructs. Adding support for another programming language simply amounts to defining in a template file instantiating patterns for the abstract operations in the target language.

```
if(((((((((178 < a12) && (395 >= a12))  &&   ((95 < a23) && (264 >= a23)) )
     && a26) && (a1==2)) && (a19==11)) && a13)){
     throw new IllegalStateException( "error_48" );
}
```

Fig. 6. Java code fragment from problem 13 of RERS 2012

The benefits of template-based code generation were used in the course of the 2012 RERS challenge, where we were able to adapt the problems for the specific needs of some of the contestants' tools in order to attract a larger community. An example is the support of C code along with the specifics of the language. For example, considering the Java code in Figure 6, it makes use of boolean variables and exceptions, both of which are not part of the C language. However, by the C template those constructs are automatically translated to 0/1 integer variables and **assert** statements with corresponding labels, respectively. The resulting code fragment is shown in Figure 7.

```
if(((((((((178 < a12) && (395 >= a12))  &&   ((95 < a23) && (264 >= a23)) )
     && (a26==1)) && (a1==2)) && (a19==11)) && (a13==1)))){
     error_48: assert(0);
}
```

Fig. 7. C code using integers and **assert**

10   Conclusion and Perspectives

We have presented a systematic approach to automatically generating platform-independent benchmarks of tailored complexity. Key to this approach is a tool chain that essentially transforms a set of automatically generated LTL properties in property-preserving steps into source code for various formats, platforms, and competition scenarios. We have illustrated the whole tool chain, which allows us to address different communities via a growing set of programming languages, tailored sets of programming constructs, different notions of observation, and the full variety of LTL properties, along accompanying examples.

Central throughout the whole process is the fact that maintaining language inclusion wrt. the ω-language of the Büchi automaton synthesized from the LTL formulae is sufficient to guarantee property preservation. This simple preservation principle has been strictly followed during the whole generation process depicted in Fig. 1, which, in fact, generated very challenging problems for the RERS Challenge 2012, and which will be used with slight extensions for the RERS Challenge 2013. We plan to release our benchmark generation framework to the public in 2014 in order to support the wide range profile analysis of analysis tools. In particular, this will allow research groups across the world to generate benchmarks tailored to their specific needs and profile, and provide a constant source of problems for further development and improvement of their respective tools.

The preservation principle is not bound to the current "while program"-like structure. It can also be followed when introducing almost arbitrary language and data structure extensions. Those might include, but are not limited to, the procedural abstraction-based construction of methods, pattern-based generation of object structures, or the introduction of further (structured) data types like arrays, lists, structs, as well as object-oriented principles like polymorphism and virtual methods. Of course, each of these extensions needs its own reasoning for keeping up to our correctness principle, and therefore introduce their own line of research.

The situation changes when switching from linear time to branching time properties, as this requires to base the correctness principle on simulation rather than simply on language inclusion.[5] On the other hand, it would allow one to consider also structural properties like points of decision [37], and checking e.g. mu calculus formulae even for procedural models/programs is known for a long time [38, 39].

We are currently developing a service-oriented framework for graphically modeling tailored benchmark generators on the basis of a library for property preserving transformations, on top of our service-oriented process modeling framework jABC [40]. Based on this development we envisage to be able to provide an easy to use open version of our benchmark framework early next year. Its flexibility should allow us to address different communities via a growing set of programming languages, tailored sets of programming constructs, different notions of observation, and the full variety of LTL properties. In fact, we envisage people to develop their own benchmark generators that supply whole communities with an infinite source of tailored benchmarks.

References

1. Gastin, P., Oddoux, D.: Fast LTL to Büchi Automata Translation. In: Berry, G., Comon, H., Finkel, A. (eds.) CAV 2001. LNCS, vol. 2102, pp. 53–65. Springer, Heidelberg (2001)

---

[5] Even though checking simulation is computationally simpler than checking language inclusion, preserving simulation is inherently more complicated than preserving language inclusion.

2. Giannakopoulou, D., Lerda, F.: From States to Transitions: Improving Translation of LTL Formulae to Büchi Automata. In: Peled, D.A., Vardi, M.Y. (eds.) FORTE 2002. LNCS, vol. 2529, pp. 308–326. Springer, Heidelberg (2002)
3. Clarke, E., Grumberg, O., Peled, D.: Model Checking. MIT Press (2001)
4. Steffen, B.: Unifying models. In: Reischuk, R., Morvan, M. (eds.) STACS 1997. LNCS, vol. 1200, pp. 1–20. Springer, Heidelberg (1997)
5. Snelting, G., Robschink, T., Krinke, J.: Efficient path conditions in dependence graphs for software safety analysis. ACM Transactions on Software Engineering and Methodology (TOSEM) 15(4), 410–457 (2006)
6. Robinson, A., Voronkov, A. (eds.): Handbook of Automated Reasoning, vol. I & II. Elsevier (2001)
7. Biere, A., Heule, M.J.H., van Maaren, H., Walsh, T. (eds.): Handbook of Satisfiability. Frontiers in Artificial Intelligence and Applications, vol. 185. IOS Press (February 2009)
8. Morel, E., Renvoise, C.: Global optimization by suppression of partial redundancies. Comm. ACM 22(2), 96–103 (1979)
9. Steffen, B., Knoop, J.: Finite Constants: Characterizations of a New Decidable Set of Constants. In: Kreczmar, A., Mirkowska, G. (eds.) MFCS 1989. LNCS, vol. 379, pp. 481–491. Springer, Heidelberg (1989)
10. Rosen, B.K., Wegman, M.N., Zadeck, F.K.: Global Value Numbers and Redundant Computations. In: Conference Record of the Fifteenth Annual ACM Symposium on Principles of Programming Languages. ACM Press (1988)
11. Knoop, J., Rüthing, O., Steffen, B.: Lazy code motion. In: Proc. of the ACM SIGPLAN 1992 Conference on Programming Language Design and Implementation (PLDI), pp. 224–234. ACM (1992)
12. Knoop, J., Rüthing, O., Steffen, B.: Lazy Strength Reduction. Journal of Programming Languages 1, 71–91 (1993)
13. Briggs, P., Cooper, K.D.: Effective partial redundancy elimination. In: Proc. ACM SIGPLAN Conf. Prog. Lang. Design and Impl. (PLDI 1994), pp. 159–170 (1994)
14. Howar, F., Isberner, M., Merten, M., Steffen, B., Beyer, D.: The RERS Grey-Box Challenge 2012: Analysis of Event-Condition-Action Systems. In: Margaria, T., Steffen, B. (eds.) ISoLA 2012, Part I. LNCS, vol. 7609, pp. 608–614. Springer, Heidelberg (2012)
15. Dwyer, M.B., Avrunin, G.S., Corbett, J.C.: Patterns in property specifications for finite-state verification. In: Proc. of the 1999 Int. Conf. on Software Engineering, pp. 411–420. IEEE (1999)
16. Steffen, B.: Property-oriented expansion. In: Cousot, R., Schmidt, D.A. (eds.) SAS 1996. LNCS, vol. 1145, pp. 22–41. Springer, Heidelberg (1996)
17. Hayes-Roth, F.: Rule-Based Systems. Commun. ACM 28(9), 921–932 (1985)
18. McCarthy, D.R., Dayal, U.: The Architecture of An Active Data Base Management System. In: Proceedings of the 1989 ACM SIGMOD International Conference on Management of Data, pp. 215–224. ACM Press (1989)
19. Almeida, E.E., Luntz, J.E., Tilbury, D.M.: Event-Condition-Action Systems for Reconfigurable Logic Control. IEEE T. Automation Science and Engineering 4(2), 167–181 (2007)
20. Apt, K.R., Olderog, E.R.: Verification of Sequential and Concurrent Programs. Texts and Monographs in Computer Science. Springer (1991)
21. Knoop, J., Rüthing, O., Steffen, B.: Partial Dead Code Elimination. In: Proceedings of the ACM SIGPLAN 1994 Conference on Programming Language Design and Implementation (PLDI), pp. 147–158. ACM (1994)

22. Knoop, J., Rüthing, O., Steffen, B.: Expansion-Based Removal of Semantic Partial Redundancies. In: Jähnichen, S. (ed.) CC 1999. LNCS, vol. 1575, pp. 91–107. Springer, Heidelberg (1999)
23. Blom, S., van de Pol, J., Weber, M.: LTSMIN: Distributed and symbolic reachability. In: Touili, T., Cook, B., Jackson, P. (eds.) CAV 2010. LNCS, vol. 6174, pp. 354–359. Springer, Heidelberg (2010)
24. Mealy, G.H.: A Method for Synthesizing Sequential Circuits. Bell System Technical Journal 34(5), 1045–1079 (1955)
25. Milner, R.: Communication and concurrency. PHI Series in computer science. Prentice-Hall, Inc., Upper Saddle River (1989)
26. Kaynar, D.K., Lynch, N.A., Segala, R., Vaandrager, F.W.: Timed I/O Automata: A Mathematical Framework for Modeling and Analyzing Real-Time Systems. In: Proceedings of the 24th IEEE Real-Time Systems Symposium (RTSS 2003), pp. 166–177. IEEE Computer Society (2003)
27. Floyd, R.W.: Assigning meaning to programs. In: Proc. of Symposium on Applied Mathematics. Mathematical aspects of computer science, vol. 19, pp. 19–32. American Mathematical Society (1967)
28. Hoare, C.A.R.: An axiomatic basis for computer programming. Communications of the ACM 12(10), 576–580 (1969)
29. Steffen, B., Rüthing, O.: Quality Engineering: Leveraging Heterogeneous Information - (Invited Talk). In: Jhala, R., Schmidt, D. (eds.) VMCAI 2011. LNCS, vol. 6538, pp. 23–37. Springer, Heidelberg (2011)
30. Dhamdhere, D.M.: A new algorithm for composite hoisting and strength reduction optimisation (+ Corrigendum). Int. J. Comp. Math. 27, 1–14 (1989)
31. Knoop, J., Rüthing, O., Steffen, B.: Optimal Code Motion: Theory and Practice. ACM Trans. Program. Lang. Syst. 16(4), 1117–1155 (1994)
32. Knoop, J., Rüthing, O., Steffen, B.: The Power of Assignment Motion. In: Proceedings of the ACM SIGPLAN 1995 Conference on Programming Language Design and Implementation (PLDI). ACM (1995)
33. Rüthing, O., Knoop, J., Steffen, B.: Sparse Code Motion. In: Proceedings of the 27th ACM SIGPLAN-SIGACT Symposium on Principles of Programming Languages (POPL 2000), pp. 170–183. ACM (2000)
34. Steffen, B., Knoop, J., Rüthing, O.: The Value Flow Graph: A Program Representation for Optimal Program Transformations. In: Jones, N.D. (ed.) ESOP 1990. LNCS, vol. 432, pp. 389–405. Springer, Heidelberg (1990)
35. Steffen, B., Knoop, J., Rüthing, O.: Efficient Code Motion and an Adaption to Strength Reduction. In: Abramsky, S. (ed.) TAPSOFT 1991. LNCS, vol. 494, pp. 394–415. Springer, Heidelberg (1991)
36. Holzmann, G.J.: The SPIN Model Checker - Primer and Reference Manual. Addison-Wesley (2004)
37. Steffen, B.: Characteristic Formulae. In: Ronchi Della Rocca, S., Ausiello, G., Dezani-Ciancaglini, M. (eds.) ICALP 1989. LNCS, vol. 372, pp. 723–732. Springer, Heidelberg (1989)
38. Steffen, B., Claßen, A., Klein, M., Knoop, J., Margaria, T.: The Fixpoint-Analysis Machine. In: Lee, I., Smolka, S.A. (eds.) CONCUR 1995. LNCS, vol. 962, pp. 72–87. Springer, Heidelberg (1995)
39. Burkart, O., Steffen, B.: Model Checking the Full Modal Mu-Calculus for Infinite Sequential Processes. In: Degano, P., Gorrieri, R., Marchetti-Spaccamela, A. (eds.) ICALP 1997. LNCS, vol. 1256, pp. 419–429. Springer, Heidelberg (1997)
40. Steffen, B., Margaria, T., Nagel, R., Jörges, S., Kubczak, C.: Model-Driven Development with the jABC. In: Bin, E., Ziv, A., Ur, S. (eds.) HVC 2006. LNCS, vol. 4383, pp. 92–108. Springer, Heidelberg (2007)

Error-Completion in Interface Theories*

Stavros Tripakis[1], Christos Stergiou[1], Manfred Broy[2], and Edward A. Lee[1]

[1] University of California, Berkeley
[2] TU Munich

Abstract. Interface theories are compositional theories where components are represented as abstract, formal interfaces which describe the component's input/output behavior. A key characteristic of interface theories is that interfaces are non-input-complete, meaning that they allow specification of *illegal* inputs. As a result of non-input-completeness, interface theories use game-theoretic definitions of composition and refinement, which are both conceptually and computationally more complicated than standard notions of composition and refinement that work with input-complete models. In this paper we propose a lossless transformation, called error-completion, which allows to transform a non-input-complete interface into an input-complete interface while preserving and allowing to retrieve completely the information on illegal inputs. We show how to perform composition of relational interfaces on the error-complete domain. We also show that refinement of such interfaces is equivalent to standard implication of their error-completions.

1 Introduction

Interface theories such as the theory of *interface automata* are compositional theories proposed by Alfaro and Henzinger in the early 2000s [9,10], and since then studied extensively (e.g., see [7,11,20,22,12]). Generally speaking, an interface theory provides the following:

- A notion of *interface* which is an abstract, formal description of a component's interface behavior. Different notions of interfaces exist in the literature, e.g., in [9] interfaces are automata, while in [22] they are static or dynamic logical formulas.
- One or more *composition operators* which allow to compose interfaces and form new interfaces. Different notions of composition are available depending on the theory, e.g., asynchronous composition in [9], synchronous composition in [22].
- A *refinement relation* which is a binary relation between interfaces.

---

* This work was supported in part by the iCyPhy Center (supported by IBM and United Technologies), the CHESS Center (supported by awards NSF #0720882 (CSR-EHS: PRET) and #0931843 (ActionWebs), NRL #N0013-12-1-G015, Bosch, National Instruments, and Toyota), and by the NSF Expeditions in Computing project *ExCAPE: Expeditions in Computer Augmented Program Engineering*.

E. Bartocci and C.R. Ramakrishnan (Eds.): SPIN 2013, LNCS 7976, pp. 358–375, 2013.
© Springer-Verlag Berlin Heidelberg 2013

- A set of theorems, typically including:

  - *Preservation of refinement by composition*, e.g., if A' refines A and B' refines B, then the composition of A' and B' refines the composition of A and B.
  - *Preservation of certain properties by refinement*, e.g., if A' refines A and A satisfies, say, a safety property p, then A' also satisfies p.

Theorems such as the above support incremental design methodologies and reconfigurability. For instance, if we have shown that a certain system consisting of the composition of A and B satisfies p, and later A needs to be replaced by A', proving that A' refines A is sufficient to ensure that p will not be compromised by such a replacement, i.e., it will continue to hold on the new system composed of A' and B.

A key characteristic of interface theories such as interface automata [9] and relational interfaces [22] is that interfaces in these theories are generally *non-input-complete*, that is, they may specify that certain inputs are *illegal*.[1] This is in contrast with other compositional theories such as I/O automata [16], FOCUS [5,6], and reactive modules [2], where specifications are assumed to be input-complete. As argued in [22], non-input-completeness is essential to obtain a theory which allows a lightweight verification methodology, akin to type-checking. In particular, non-input-completeness allows to define semantic or *behavioral* notions of interface compatibility. These go beyond syntactic compatibility notions like correct port matching.

As a result of non-input-completeness, and the fact that components are generally non-deterministic (meaning that for a given input they may produce different outputs) the definitions of composition and refinement in interface theories are *game-theoretic* in nature.

Although game-theoretic notions such as demonic composition and alternating refinement are relatively well-understood, they are more complex than the corresponding standard notions, and generally involve computing strategies in a two-player game [3,10,8,22]. It makes sense, then, to ask whether there exists a transformation from non-input-complete to input-complete interfaces, which allows to reduce the above operations into standard composition and refinement.

In this paper we answer the above question in the affirmative for the setting of relational interfaces of [22]. In particular, we propose a *lossless* transformation called *error-completion*. Given a (generally non-input-complete) interface ϕ, error-completion returns an input-complete interface $\mathsf{EC}(\phi)$, with an additional boolean output variable which captures illegal inputs. The main results of the paper are:

- We show that $\mathsf{EC}(\phi)$ does not lose any information contained in ϕ, by providing an inverse transformation EC^{-1} and showing that $\mathsf{EC}^{-1}(\mathsf{EC}(\phi)) \equiv \phi$ for all ϕ.

---

[1] We use the term *input-complete* following [22]. Other terms used in the literature are *input-enabled, receptive,* or *total*.

– We show that serial and parallel composition of relational interfaces can be performed in the error-complete domain, and the result can be transformed backwards using EC^{-1} to obtain the equivalent composition in the original domain.
– We show that the (alternating) refinement relation $\phi_1 \sqsubseteq \phi_2$ is equivalent to the standard implication $\mathsf{EC}(\phi_1) \rightarrow \mathsf{EC}(\phi_2)$.

We point out that error-completion is discussed in [22]. However, the definition of error-completion given in [22] is not satisfactory because, as already observed in [22], it does not allow to reduce refinement checking of general relational interfaces to checking standard implication on their error-completed versions. In this paper we propose a new definition of error-completion which achieves this, among other properties. We also provide an in-depth discussion of error-completion and possible alternatives.

The rest of the paper is organized as follows. Section 2 summarizes the theory of [22]. Section 3 describes error-completion. Section 4 discusses possible extensions. Section 5 presents related work. Section 6 concludes the paper.

2 Preliminaries

In this section we summarize the relational interface framework developed in [22].

2.1 Relational Interfaces

Let V be a finite set of variables. A property over V is a first-order logic formula ϕ such that any free variable of ϕ is in V. We write $\mathcal{F}(V)$ for the set of all properties over V. Assuming that every variable is associated with a certain domain, an assignment over V is a function mapping every variable in V to a certain value in the domain of that variable. The set of all assignments over V is denoted by $\mathcal{A}(V)$.

Assume a component with inputs X and outputs Y. We identify states with observational histories, i.e., a state of the component is an element of $\mathcal{A}(X \cup Y)^*$.

Definition 1 (Relational interface). *A relational interface (RI) is a tuple (X, Y, f) where X and Y are two finite and disjoint sets of input and output variables, respectively, and f is a function from states to contracts, i.e., for every $s \in \mathcal{A}(X \cup Y)^*$, $f(s) \in \mathcal{F}(X \cup Y)$.*

Note that we allow X or Y to be empty. If $X = \emptyset$ then the interface is a *source*. If $Y = \emptyset$ then the interface is a *sink*.

In order to simplify the presentation we will restrict the definitions and the rest of the formalization to the case of stateless interfaces, i.e. interfaces that specify the same contract for each state or input-output history. We also often omit the term relational and speak simply of interfaces, for the sake of brevity.

Definition 2 (Stateless interface). *An interface $I = (X, Y, f)$ is stateless iff for all $s, s' \in \mathcal{A}(X \cup Y)^*$, $f(s) = f(s')$.*

For the sake of simplicity, we will specify a stateless interface as a triple (X, Y, ϕ), where $\phi \in \mathcal{F}(X \cup Y)$.

An example of a stateless relational interface is shown in Figure 1. This interface, called Div, is the interface of a component that is supposed to perform division. The component has two inputs x_1 and x_2 and produces the result $y = \frac{x_1}{x_2}$ on its output. There are different properties of this component that one might want to capture in its interface Div. Two possible contracts for Div, ϕ_1 and ϕ_2, are shown in Figure 1. Both specify that input x_2 has to be different than 0. Note that the first contract ϕ_1 completely determines the behavior of the component; it is an example of a *deterministic* contract: given legal inputs, outputs are unique. Contract ϕ_2, on the other hand, only provides guarantees about the sign of the output.

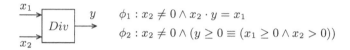

$$\phi_1 : x_2 \neq 0 \wedge x_2 \cdot y = x_1$$
$$\phi_2 : x_2 \neq 0 \wedge (y \geq 0 \equiv (x_1 \geq 0 \wedge x_2 > 0))$$

Fig. 1. Component Div outputs at y the division of its inputs x_1/x_2

The theory does not separate requirements on inputs from guarantees on the outputs. A single formula on input and output variables captures the behavioral specification of a stateless interface. We can however extract the requirements a contract makes on the inputs by existentially quantifying over the output variables.

Definition 3 (Input requirement). *Given a contract $\phi \in \mathcal{F}(X \cup Y)$, the input requirement of ϕ is the formula* $\mathrm{in}(\phi) := \exists Y : \phi$.

A note on notation: if ϕ is a formula over a set of variables V, and $U \subseteq V$, with $U = \{u_1, u_2, ..., u_k\}$, then $\exists U : \phi$ is shorthand notation for $\exists u_1, u_2, ..., u_n : \phi$. Note that U is allowed to be empty. If $U = \emptyset$, then $(\exists U : \phi) \equiv \phi$.

$\mathrm{in}(\phi)$ is a property over X only, and represents the requirements that the contract places on the component inputs. For example, for the division component with contract $\phi \equiv (x_2 \neq 0 \wedge x_2 \cdot y = x_1)$, the input requirement is $\mathrm{in}(\phi) \equiv (\exists y : x_2 \neq 0 \wedge x_2 \cdot y = x_1) \equiv x_2 \neq 0$. Note that if ϕ belongs to a source (that is, if $X = \emptyset$), and ϕ is satisfiable, then $\mathrm{in}(\phi) \equiv \mathrm{true}$. If ϕ belongs to a sink (i.e., if $Y = \emptyset$), then $\mathrm{in}(\phi) \equiv \phi$. In all cases, $\phi \rightarrow \mathrm{in}(\phi)$.

Definition 4 (Input-completeness). *An interface $I = (X, Y, \phi)$ is input-complete iff* $\mathrm{in}(\phi)$ *is valid.*

Going back to the examples of Figure 1, note that $\mathrm{in}(\phi_1) \equiv \mathrm{in}(\phi_2) \equiv x_2 \neq 0$. Therefore, both ϕ_1 and ϕ_2 are not input-complete. If, however, the contract was specified as $\phi_3 \equiv (x_2 \neq 0 \rightarrow x_2 \cdot y = x_1)$, then $\mathrm{in}(\phi_3)$ would be true. ϕ_3 is thus an example of an input-complete contract.

Definition 5 (Well-formedness). *An interface* $I = (X, Y, \phi)$ *is* well-formed *iff* ϕ *is satisfiable.*

At this point it is worth making the following remark. Syntactically, relational interfaces are represented by formulas. Semantically, they are relations between input and output assignments, that is, subsets of $\mathcal{A}(X \cup Y)$ (hence the term *relational*). Clearly, different formulas correspond to the same relation. For example, both $x \wedge \neg x$ and false represent the same relation (in this case the empty set). What we are mainly interested in is the semantics, not the syntax. For formulas ϕ_1 and ϕ_2, we can check whether they represent the same relation by checking whether they are equivalent, $\phi_1 \equiv \phi_2$.

Based on the above discussion, the canonical non-well-formed interface can be represented by false.

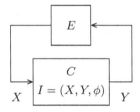

Fig. 2. Component C specified by interface I in feedback with environment E

A relational interface $I = (X, Y, \phi)$ can be seen as specifying a game between a component and its environment. In Figure 2, the component and the environment are represented by blocks C and E respectively. The game proceeds in a sequence of rounds. At the end of each round, an assignment $a \in \mathcal{A}(X \cup Y)$ is chosen. Typically, the environment plays first and chooses an assignment for the inputs X of the component, $a_X \in \mathcal{A}(X)$. If a_X does not satisfy in(ϕ) then this is not a legal input and the environment loses. Otherwise, the component plays by choosing an assignment for the outputs Y, $a_Y \in \mathcal{A}(Y)$. If (a_X, a_Y) does not satisfy ϕ then this is not a legal output for this input, and the component loses the game. Otherwise, the round is complete, and the game moves to the next round.

2.2   Composition

We can compose two interfaces I_1 and I_2 in series by connecting some of the output variables of I_1 to some of the input variables of I_2. Variables that have the same name are implicitly connected. As it was argued in [22], composition by conjunction of the interface contracts is not sufficient, and instead a "demonic" definition of serial composition needs to be used.

Definition 6 (Serial composition). *Let* $I_1 = (X_1, Y_1, \phi_1)$ *and* $I_2 = (X_2, Y_2, \phi_2)$ *be two interfaces.* I_1 *and* I_2 *are said to be* composable *if* $X_1 \cap X_2 = X_1 \cap Y_2 =$

$Y_1 \cap Y_2 = \emptyset$. *If I_1 and I_2 are composable, then we can define the serial composition of I_1 and I_2, denoted $I_1 \rightsquigarrow I_2$, as the interface $I = (X, Y, \phi_1 \rightsquigarrow \phi_2)$ where $X = X_1 \cup (X_2 \setminus Y_1)$, $Y = Y_2 \cup Y_1$ and*

$$\phi_1 \rightsquigarrow \phi_2 := \phi_1 \wedge \phi_2 \wedge \forall Y_1 : (\phi_1 \rightarrow in(\phi_2)) \tag{1}$$

It is often convenient to automatically hide the connected outputs $Y_1 \cap X_2$ right after the composition. For that purpose, we introduce the additional operator of serial composition with hiding, denoted $I_1 \rightsquigarrow^* I_2$, which defines interface $I' = (X, Y', \phi_1 \rightsquigarrow^* \phi_2)$, where X is as above, $Y' = Y_2 \cup (Y_1 \setminus X_2)$, and

$$\phi_1 \rightsquigarrow^* \phi_2 := \exists (Y_1 \cap X_2) : (\phi_1 \rightsquigarrow \phi_2) \tag{2}$$

Note that in the definition above, Y_1 and X_2 could also be disjoint, which means that no connections exist between I_1 and I_2. This can be used to model the *parallel composition* of I_1 and I_2, which then becomes a special case of serial composition.

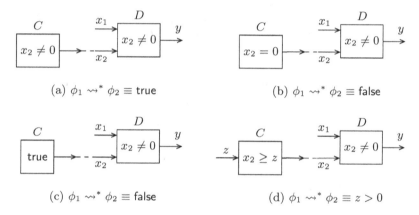

(a) $\phi_1 \rightsquigarrow^* \phi_2 \equiv$ true

(b) $\phi_1 \rightsquigarrow^* \phi_2 \equiv$ false

(c) $\phi_1 \rightsquigarrow^* \phi_2 \equiv$ false

(d) $\phi_1 \rightsquigarrow^* \phi_2 \equiv z > 0$

Fig. 3. Four examples of serial composition of relational interfaces

Four serial composition examples are shown in Figure 3. In all of them, a component C with different guarantees is connected to a component D that is expecting its second input, x_2, to be different than zero.

In case (a), the contract of C guarantees that its output x_2 will be non-zero, and indeed, the composite interface contract is equal to true and thus well-formed.

In cases (b) and (c), where the contracts of C are $x_2 = 0$ and true, the resulting contract of the composition is false, i.e., $C \rightsquigarrow D$ is not well-formed in these two cases. In case (b) this is not surprising since we know that $x_2 = 0$ is an illegal input for D. In case (c), the contract of C is too weak, therefore it cannot be guaranteed that the input to D will be legal.

Case (d) presents a more interesting example. In this case the interface of C is $(\{z\}, \{x_2\}, x_2 \geq z)$. The requirement that $x_2 \neq 0$ induces a new requirement in the resulting contract, namely, that input z be strictly positive. This is the weakest requirement on z that allows to ensure $x_2 \neq 0$.

Definition 7 (Compatibility). *Let $I_1 = (X_1, Y_1, \phi_1)$ and $I_2 = (X_2, Y_2, \phi_2)$ be two composable interfaces. We say that I_1 and I_2 are* compatible *if $I_1 \rightsquigarrow I_2$ is well-formed.*

In Figure 3, in examples (a) and (d), the interfaces of C and D are compatible, whereas in examples (b) and (c) they are not.

We remark that we view compatibility as a key differentiating aspect of input-complete theories and interface theories. Compatibility is a local correctness property, akin to type checking. As the examples of Figure 3 illustrate, we can speak of compatibility between components without proving any property about the entire system. We view this as more lightweight than full system verification. In addition, example (d) illustrates how composition can be used to induce new input constraints, which is akin to type inference.

The difference between $\rightsquigarrow$ and standard composition, i.e., conjunction, lies in the last conjunct of Formula (1), namely $\forall Y_1 : (\phi_1 \rightarrow \mathsf{in}(\phi_2))$. The latter is a condition on the free inputs of the composite interface (because $\phi_1 \rightarrow \mathsf{in}(\phi_2)$ is a formula on $X_1 \cup Y_1 \cup X_2$). This conjunct states that, for a given input to the composite interface, any outputs that satisfy ϕ_1 will be legal inputs for ϕ_2. It can be easily seen that if ϕ_2 is input-complete, then this conjunct evaluates to true, so $\phi_1 \rightsquigarrow \phi_2$ becomes equivalent to $\phi_1 \wedge \phi_2$. The same holds when ϕ_1 is deterministic, so standard composition is a special case of $\rightsquigarrow$.

Theorem 1 (Special cases of composition [22]). *Let $I_1 = (X_1, Y_1, \phi_1)$ and $I_2 = (X_2, Y_2, \phi_2)$ be two composable interfaces. If I_2 is input-complete or I_1 is deterministic, then $\phi_1 \rightsquigarrow \phi_2 \equiv \phi_1 \wedge \phi_2$.*

2.3   Refinement

Definition 8 (Refinement). *We say that an interface $I' = (X', Y', \phi')$ refines an interface $I = (X, Y, \phi)$, written $I' \sqsubseteq I$, iff $X' \subseteq X$, $Y' \supseteq Y$, and the following formula is valid:*

$$\mathsf{in}(\phi) \rightarrow \big(\mathsf{in}(\phi') \wedge (\phi' \rightarrow \phi)\big) \tag{3}$$

The condition can be written as the conjunction of two conditions:

$$\mathsf{in}(\phi) \rightarrow \mathsf{in}(\phi') \tag{4}$$
$$(\mathsf{in}(\phi) \wedge \phi') \rightarrow \phi \tag{5}$$

The first condition guarantees that any input assignment that is legal in I will also be legal in I'. The second states that for every input assignment that is legal in I, all output assignments that can be possibly computed by I' from that input, can also be produced by I.

Theorem 2 (Refinement preserves well-formedness [22]). *Let I, I' be stateless interfaces such that $I' \sqsubseteq I$. If I is well-formed, then I' is well-formed.*

Theorem 3 (Composition preserves refinement [22]). *Let I_1, I_2, I_1', and I_2' be interfaces such that $I_1' \sqsubseteq I_1$ and $I_2' \sqsubseteq I_2$. Then $I_1' \rightsquigarrow I_2' \sqsubseteq I_1 \rightsquigarrow I_2$.*

We can conclude from Theorems 2 and 3 that refinement preserves compatibility:

Corollary 1 (Refinement preserves compatibility [22]). *Let I_1, I_2 be compatible interfaces. Let I_1', and I_2' be interfaces such that $I_1' \sqsubseteq I_1$, $I_2' \sqsubseteq I_2$. Then I_1' and I_2' are also compatible.*

3 Error-Completion

Error-completion is a lossless transformation from (possibly non-input-complete) relational interfaces to input-complete relational interfaces. The idea is to capture illegal inputs using an extra boolean output variable. This has already been proposed in [22]. However, the way in which error-completion is defined in [22] is too strict, and does not allow us to reduce checking refinement of RIs to checking implication of their error-completed versions. We explain this further below.

In this paper we provide a less restrictive version of error-completion:

Definition 9 (Error-completion). *Let $I = (X, Y, \phi)$ be an interface. Let e be a new output variable, such that $e \notin X \cup Y$. The error-completion of ϕ is the formula $\mathsf{EC}(\phi)$ over $X \cup Y \cup \{e\}$, defined as follows:*

$$\mathsf{EC}(\phi) := \mathsf{in}(\phi) \rightarrow (\phi \wedge \neg e) \tag{6}$$

It is easy to verify that $\mathsf{EC}(\phi)$ is input-complete, for any ϕ. Also note that if ϕ is input complete, then $\mathsf{EC}(\phi) \equiv (\phi \wedge \neg e)$.

In the example of the division component in Figure 1 where $\phi \equiv (x_2 \neq 0 \wedge x_1 = y \cdot x_2)$, the error-completion of ϕ is:

$$\mathsf{EC}(\phi) \equiv x_2 \neq 0 \rightarrow (x_1 = y \cdot x_2 \wedge \neg e)$$

Definition 10 (Inverse transformation). *Let $I = (X, Y, \phi)$ be an interface and let $\phi_e = \mathsf{EC}(\phi)$ be the error-completion of ϕ. We can retrieve ϕ from ϕ_e using the following transformation:*

$$\mathsf{EC}^{-1}(\phi_e) := (\exists e : \phi_e) \wedge (\forall Y \cup \{e\} : \phi_e \rightarrow \neg e) \tag{7}$$

It can be shown that the two conjuncts of the definition of EC^{-1} correspond to $\phi \vee \neg \mathsf{in}(\phi)$ and $\mathsf{in}(\phi)$, respectively. Intuitively $\exists e : \phi_e$ adds all illegal inputs to the domain of ϕ and $\forall Y \cup \{e\} : \phi_e \rightarrow \neg e$ removes them. Formally, EC^{-1} is a left inverse of EC:

Lemma 1. *Any formula ϕ over $X \cup Y$ is equivalent to $\mathsf{EC}^{-1}(\mathsf{EC}(\phi))$, i.e.:*

$$\phi \equiv \mathsf{EC}^{-1}(\mathsf{EC}(\phi)) \tag{8}$$

Proof. If we expand the definitions of EC and EC^{-1}, $EC(EC^{-1}(\phi))$ is equal to:

$$EC(EC^{-1}(\phi)) \equiv (\exists e : (in(\phi) \rightarrow (\phi \wedge \neg e))) \wedge (\forall Y \cup \{e\} : (in(\phi) \rightarrow (\phi \wedge \neg e)) \rightarrow \neg e).$$

We examine the two conjuncts separately. The first conjunct is:

$$\exists e : (in(\phi) \rightarrow (\phi \wedge \neg e)) = in(\phi) \rightarrow (\phi \wedge \exists e : \neg e)$$
$$= in(\phi) \rightarrow \phi.$$

Let Φ be the formula $(in(\phi) \rightarrow (\phi \wedge \neg e)) \rightarrow \neg e$.

For $e = $ true, Φ is equal to $(in(\phi) \rightarrow$ false$) \rightarrow$ false $\equiv in(\phi)$.

For $e = $ false, Φ is equal to $(in(\phi) \rightarrow \phi) \rightarrow$ true $\equiv$ true.

Therefore the second conjunct is equivalent to $\forall Y : in(\phi)$ or $in(\phi)$ since the latter does not depend on Y variables.

Going back to $EC^{-1}(EC(\phi))$, we get:

$$EC^{-1}(EC(\phi)) \equiv (in(\phi) \rightarrow \phi) \wedge in(\phi) \equiv \phi \wedge in(\phi) \equiv \phi.$$

$\square$

It can be easily shown that any function that has a left inverse is injective. Therefore, $\phi_1 \not\equiv \phi_2$ implies $EC(\phi_1) \not\equiv EC(\phi_2)$.

Lemma 1 is an important result, as it proves that the transformations EC, EC^{-1} are *lossless*. In addition, as we shall show next, Lemma 1 allows to prove that EC forms a bijection between relational interfaces and an appropriate subclass of error-complete interfaces.

3.1   Meaningful ECI

We have seen that EC^{-1} is a left inverse of EC. Note, however, that it is not the case that EC^{-1} is a right inverse of EC, that is, $EC(EC^{-1}(\phi_e))$ is *not* always equivalent to ϕ_e. For example, if $\phi_e := (y = e)$ where y is an output, then:

$$EC^{-1}(\phi_e) \equiv (\exists e : y = e) \wedge (\forall Y \cup \{e\} : (y = e) \rightarrow \neg e) \equiv \text{true} \wedge \text{false} \equiv \text{false}$$

while

$$EC(EC^{-1}(\phi_e)) \equiv EC(\text{false}) \equiv in(\text{false}) \rightarrow (\text{false} \wedge \neg e) \equiv \text{false} \rightarrow \text{false} \equiv \text{true}.$$

The same can be shown for less elementary contracts. For instance, if $\phi_e := (x = 0 \rightarrow \neg e) \wedge (x = 1 \rightarrow e)$, then $EC^{-1}(\phi_e) = (x = 0)$ but $EC(x = 0) \neq \phi_e$.

In fact we can prove that ϕ_e is generally stronger than $EC(EC^{-1}(\phi_e))$.

Lemma 2. *Any formula ϕ_e over $X \cup Y \cup \{e\}$ is equivalent or stronger than $EC(EC^{-1}(\phi_e))$:*

$$\phi_e \rightarrow EC(EC^{-1}(\phi_e)) \tag{9}$$

As the above results show, even though, by Lemma 1, EC is injective, it is not surjective. This means that there are error-complete interfaces which do not correspond to any meaningful relational interfaces. However, note that it was never our intention to handle arbitrary error-complete interfaces, that is, arbitrary formulas over $X \cup Y \cup \{e\}$. Instead, what we are interested in is a transformation from contracts over $X \cup Y$ to input-complete contracts over $X \cup Y \cup \{e\}$. We are thus only interested in the subclass of error-complete interfaces which are obtained from relational interfaces via EC. That is, we are only interested in the image of EC. We call this subclass the class of *meaningful error-complete interfaces* (MECI). MECI is a strict subset of the set of all input-complete interfaces over $X \cup Y \cup \{e\}$, which we denote by ECI.

Definition 11 (Meaningful error-complete interfaces). *Let ϕ_e be a formula over $X \cup Y \cup \{e\}$. ϕ_e is said to be* meaningful *iff there exists a formula ϕ over $X \cup Y$ such that $EC(\phi) \equiv \phi_e$.*

Theorem 4. *Let ϕ_e be a formula over $X \cup Y \cup \{e\}$. ϕ_e is meaningful iff $EC(EC^{-1}(\phi_e)) \equiv \phi_e$.*

Proof. Suppose $EC(EC^{-1}(\phi_e)) \equiv \phi_e$. By definition of EC^{-1}, $EC^{-1}(\phi_e)$ is a formula over $X \cup Y$. Therefore, setting $\phi := EC^{-1}(\phi_e)$, we have $EC(\phi) \equiv \phi_e$, thus ϕ_e is meaningful.

In the other direction, suppose ϕ_e is meaningful. Then there is a formula ϕ over $X \cup Y$ such that $EC(\phi) \equiv \phi_e$. $EC(\phi) \equiv \phi_e$ implies $EC^{-1}(EC(\phi)) \equiv EC^{-1}(\phi_e)$. By Lemma 1, $EC^{-1}(EC(\phi)) \equiv \phi$, therefore, $\phi \equiv EC^{-1}(\phi_e)$. This implies $EC(\phi) \equiv EC(EC^{-1}(\phi_e))$. Since $EC(\phi) \equiv \phi_e$, we get $\phi_e \equiv EC(EC^{-1}(\phi_e))$. $\qquad\square$

Theorem 4 is an important result which shows that EC, restricted to the class MECI, is a bijection. This is illustrated in Figure 4. Note that we interpret the spaces RI, ECI, MECI, and so on, as containing *semantic* rather than syntactic objects, that is, relations rather than formulas. Alternatively, and equivalently, a point in each of these spaces represents the equivalence class of all equivalent formulas.

3.2   Composition in the ECI Domain

Beyond merely having a lossless transformation from relational interfaces to error-complete interfaces and back, we are interested in using the error-completion to perform operations on relational interfaces more efficiently. In this section we show how error-completion can be used to compute serial composition of relational interfaces by avoiding the universal quantification formula $\forall Y_1 : (\phi_1 \rightarrow \text{in}(\phi_2))$ used in the definition of $\rightsquigarrow$. The idea is to *delay* computing the game-theoretic demonic composition as much as possible. In that sense, we can perform serial composition on the error-complete domain, and use the inverse transformation EC^{-1} (which introduces the universal quantification) to return to the non-input-complete domain whenever necessary. To achieve this, we define a serial composition operator $\overset{e}{\rightsquigarrow}$ on error-completions:

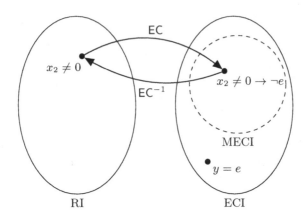

Fig. 4. Meaningful error-complete interfaces

Definition 12. *Let $I_1 = (X_1, Y_1, \phi_1)$, $I_2 = (X_2, Y_2, \phi_2)$ be two composable interfaces. Let e_1, e_2 be two fresh variables, i.e., $e_1, e_2 \notin X_1 \cup Y_1 \cup X_2 \cup Y_2$. Let ψ_1, ψ_2 be two predicates over $X_1 \cup Y_1 \cup \{e_1\}$ and $X_2 \cup Y_2 \cup \{e_2\}$ respectively, such that $\psi_1 = \mathsf{EC}(\phi_1)[e/e_1]$ and $\psi_2 = \mathsf{EC}(\phi_2)[e/e_2]$ where $\xi[e/e_i]$ denotes the formula ξ' obtained by ξ by replacing e with e_i. We define the composition of ψ_1 and ψ_2 as:*

$$\psi_1 \overset{e}{\rightsquigarrow} \psi_2 := \exists e_1, e_2 : \big(\psi_1 \wedge \psi_2 \wedge e = (e_1 \vee e_2)\big) \tag{10}$$

The operator $\overset{e}{\rightsquigarrow}$ is illustrated in Figure 5 for the simple case of single-input/single-output components.

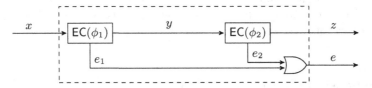

Fig. 5. Illustration of serial composition in the error-complete domain

We can now state a main result which allows to compute serial composition losslessly on the error-complete domain:

Theorem 5. *Let $I_1 = (X_1, Y_1, \phi_1)$, $I_2 = (X_2, Y_2, \phi_2)$ be two composable interfaces. Then the following is true:*

$$\mathsf{EC}^{-1}\big(\mathsf{EC}(\phi_1) \overset{e}{\rightsquigarrow} \mathsf{EC}(\phi_2)\big) \equiv \phi_1 \rightsquigarrow \phi_2 \tag{11}$$

Examples. Let us look at the composition examples of Figure 3 and see how serial composition is performed in the error-complete domain. We first look at example (c) and compute the error-completion of the contracts of the two components:

$$\psi_1 := \mathsf{EC}(\mathsf{true})[e/e_1] \equiv \mathsf{true} \to (\mathsf{true} \land \neg e_1) = \neg e_1$$

$$\begin{aligned}
\psi_2 := \mathsf{EC}(x_2 \neq 0)[e/e_2] &\equiv \mathsf{in}(x_2 \neq 0) \to (x_2 \neq 0 \land \neg e_2) \\
&\equiv x_2 \neq 0 \to (x_2 \neq 0 \land \neg e_2) \\
&\equiv x_2 \neq 0 \to \neg e_2
\end{aligned}$$

The serial composition contract in the error-complete domain is:

$$\begin{aligned}
\psi_1 \overset{e}{\leadsto} \psi_2 &\equiv \exists e_1, e_2 : \mathsf{true} \land (x_2 \neq 0 \to \neg e_2) \land (e = e_1 \lor e_2) \\
&\equiv \exists e_1, e_2 : (x_2 \neq 0 \to \neg e_2) \land (e = e_1 \lor e_2) \\
&\equiv \mathsf{true}
\end{aligned}$$

If we apply the EC^{-1} operator, we indeed get back the serial composition contract we had computed before:

$$\begin{aligned}
\mathsf{EC}^{-1}(\mathsf{true}) &\equiv (\exists e : \mathsf{true}) \land (\forall x_2 \forall e : \mathsf{true} \to \neg e) \\
&\equiv (\forall x_2 \forall e : \neg e) \\
&\equiv \mathsf{false}
\end{aligned}$$

In case (d) of Figure 3, the error-completion of the contract of the division component, ψ_2, is the same as before, and for component C we get:

$$\begin{aligned}
\psi_1 := \mathsf{EC}(x_2 \geq z)[e/e_1] &\equiv \mathsf{in}(x_2 \geq z) \to (x_2 \geq z \land \neg e_1) \\
&\equiv (\exists x_2 : x_2 \geq z) \to (x_2 \geq z \land \neg e_1) \\
&\equiv x_2 \geq z \land \neg e_1
\end{aligned}$$

The serial composition contract in the error-complete domain is:

$$\begin{aligned}
\psi := \psi_1 \overset{e}{\leadsto} \psi_2 &\equiv \exists e_1, e_2 : (x_2 \geq z \land \neg e_1) \land (x_2 \neq 0 \to \neg e_2) \land (e = e_1 \lor e_2) \\
&\equiv (x_2 \geq z \land \neg e) \lor (x_2 \geq z \land x_2 = 0 \land e) \\
&\equiv x_2 \geq z \land (\neg e \lor (x_2 = 0 \land e))
\end{aligned}$$

We examine the two conjuncts of EC^{-1} separately:

$$\begin{aligned}
\exists e : \psi &\equiv \exists e : (x_2 \geq z \land (\neg e \lor (x_2 = 0 \land e))) \\
&\equiv x_2 \geq z \land \exists e : (\neg e \lor (x_2 = 0 \land e)) \equiv x_2 \geq z
\end{aligned}$$

$$\begin{aligned}
\forall x_2 \forall e : \psi \to \neg e &\equiv \forall x_2 \forall e : (x_2 \geq z \land (\neg e \lor (x_2 = 0 \land e))) \to \neg e \\
&\equiv \forall x_2 : (x_2 \geq z \land (\mathsf{false} \lor (x_2 = 0 \land \mathsf{true}))) \to \mathsf{false} \\
&\equiv \forall x_2 : \neg(x_2 \geq z \land x_2 = 0) \\
&\equiv \neg \exists x_2 : (x_2 \geq z \land x_2 = 0) \\
&\equiv z > 0
\end{aligned}$$

Thus $\mathsf{EC}^{-1}(\psi_1 \overset{e}{\leadsto} \psi_2) \equiv x_2 \geq z \land z > 0$, and if we hide the connected input x_2 we get $\exists x_2 : (x_2 \geq z \land z > 0) \equiv z > 0$ which is equal to $\phi_1 \leadsto^* \phi_2$.

3.3 Refinement in the ECI Domain

In the previous section we showed how to perform composition on the error-complete domain. In this section we show that checking refinement of relational interfaces can be reduced to checking standard implication on their error-completions.

Theorem 6. *Let* $I_1 = (X_1, Y_1, \phi_1)$, $I_2 = (X_2, Y_2, \phi_2)$ *be two interfaces such that* $X_1 \subseteq X_2$ *and* $Y_1 \supseteq Y_2$. *Then* $I_1 \sqsubseteq I_2$ *iff* $\mathsf{EC}(\phi_1) \to \mathsf{EC}(\phi_2)$ *is valid.*

Proof. (only if) We repeat Formula (3) for convenience:

$$\mathsf{in}(\phi_2) \to \big(\mathsf{in}(\phi_1) \wedge (\phi_1 \to \phi_2)\big)$$

We need to show that if Formula (3) is valid then

$$\big(\mathsf{in}(\phi_1) \to (\phi_1 \wedge \neg e)\big) \to \big(\mathsf{in}(\phi_2) \to (\phi_2 \wedge \neg e)\big) \tag{12}$$

is also valid. To show that Formula (12) is valid, consider a valuation a that satisfies $\big(\mathsf{in}(\phi_1) \to (\phi_1 \wedge \neg e)\big) \wedge \mathsf{in}(\phi_2)$. We need to show that a also satisfies $\phi_2 \wedge \neg e$. Because a satisfies $\mathsf{in}(\phi_2)$ and Formula (3) is valid, a also satisfies $\mathsf{in}(\phi_1) \wedge (\phi_1 \to \phi_2)$. Because a satisfies $\mathsf{in}(\phi_1)$ and also $\big(\mathsf{in}(\phi_1) \to (\phi_1 \wedge \neg e)\big)$, it also satisfies $\phi_1 \wedge \neg e$. And because it satisfies ϕ_1 and $\phi_1 \to \phi_2$ it also satisfies ϕ_2. Thus, it satisfies $\phi_2 \wedge \neg e$.

(if) We need to show that if Formula (12) is valid then Formula (3) is also valid. It suffices to show that if the negation of Formula (3) is satisfiable then the negation of Formula (12) is also satisfiable.

The negation of Formula (3) is

$$\mathsf{in}(\phi_2) \wedge \big(\neg\mathsf{in}(\phi_1) \vee (\phi_1 \wedge \neg\phi_2)\big) \tag{13}$$

The negation of Formula (12) is

$$\big(\mathsf{in}(\phi_1) \to (\phi_1 \wedge \neg e)\big) \wedge \mathsf{in}(\phi_2) \wedge (\neg\phi_2 \vee e) \tag{14}$$

Suppose a satisfies Formula (13). Notice that a is an assignment over variables in $X_2 \cup Y_1$. In particular, a does not assign a value to e. There are two cases:

1. a satisfies $\mathsf{in}(\phi_2) \wedge \neg\mathsf{in}(\phi_1)$: We extend assignment a to assignment a' over $X_2 \cup Y_1 \cup \{e\}$, such that a' sets e to true and keeps the values of a for all other variables. Clearly, a' satisfies the last conjunct $\neg\phi_2 \vee e$ of Formula (14). Also, because a satisfies the first two conjuncts of Formula (14) and because these conjuncts do not refer to e, a' satisfies them as well. Therefore, a' satisfies Formula (14).
2. a satisfies $\mathsf{in}(\phi_2) \wedge \phi_1 \wedge \neg\phi_2$: As before we extend a to a' but now a' sets e to false. It can be seen that this a' satisfies the consequent of the first conjunct and the last two conjuncts of Formula (14) and thus satisfies Formula (14).

Thus, in both cases Formula (14) is satisfiable.   □

We can now fulfill our promise to explain why the error-completion transformation defined in [22] is not satisfactory. The definition given in [22] is:

$$EC_{strict}(\phi) := (\neg in(\phi) \wedge e) \vee (\phi \wedge \neg e) \tag{15}$$

Unfortunately, Theorem 6 does not hold if we replace EC by EC_{strict}. Intuitively, this is because EC_{strict} is too strict. It requires that the error variable is true when an input is given that does not satisfy $in(\phi)$. This demand goes against the contravariant definition of refinement: a refinement of ϕ can accept more inputs than ϕ. To give a concrete example, consider two interfaces I, I' with contracts $\phi \equiv x > 0$ and $\phi' = true$ respectively. true accepts more inputs than $x > 0$, therefore we have $I' \sqsubseteq I$. Indeed if we consider the error-completions $\psi := EC(\phi)$ and $\psi' := EC(\phi')$ we get:

$$\psi \equiv x > 0 \to \neg e \quad \text{and} \quad \psi' \equiv \neg e$$

and it is true that $\psi' \to \psi$.

However, if we consider the strict error-completions we get:

$$\psi_{strict} := EC_{strict}(\phi) \equiv (x > 0 \wedge \neg e) \vee (x \leq 0 \wedge e)$$
$$\psi'_{strict} := EC_{strict}(\phi') \equiv \neg e$$

and it is not the case that $\psi'_{strict} \to \psi_{strict}$.

4 Discussion

4.1 Extension to Stateful

We first discuss how the ideas of error-complete interfaces can be applied in the case of stateful interfaces. For the sake of brevity, we do this by means of an example. Nonetheless, we are confident that the results in the paper extend without problem to the general case of stateful interfaces.

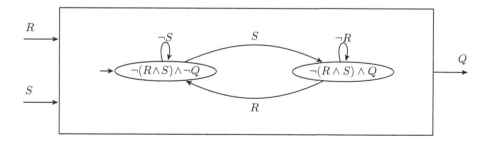

Fig. 6. Stateful interface example

Stateful interfaces can be represented as extended automata whose states are annotated with contracts. Figure 6 shows the stateful interface of an SR flip-flop. An SR flip-flop has two inputs, S for set, R for reset, and an output Q which is equal to the current flip-flop state. When neither S nor R are present, the flip-flop maintains its state. When S is present and R is not, the output Q is set to true. When R is present and S is not, the output Q is set to false. The combination of both S and R being present is illegal; in that case, in real implementations, the output depends on gate propagation delays, and hence it is considered an error state. In the game interpretation of interfaces, after the environment decides on the values of R and S, the interface will move to the correct state and produce an output Q that satisfies the contract of that state.

Performing error-completion on stateful interfaces is straightforward: it amounts to perform error-completion on the contract of every state. In the case of the SR flip-flop interface shown above, it amounts to adding a new boolean output variable e and modifying its two contracts as follows:

$$\begin{aligned} \mathsf{EC}(\neg(R \wedge S) \wedge \neg Q) &\equiv \mathsf{in}(\neg(R \wedge S) \wedge \neg Q) \rightarrow (\neg(R \wedge S) \wedge \neg Q \wedge \neg e) \\ &\equiv \neg(R \wedge S) \rightarrow (\neg(R \wedge S) \wedge \neg Q \wedge \neg e) \\ &\equiv \neg(R \wedge S) \rightarrow (\neg Q \wedge \neg e) \end{aligned}$$

$$\mathsf{EC}(\neg(R \wedge S) \wedge Q) \equiv \neg(R \wedge S) \rightarrow (Q \wedge \neg e)$$

4.2   Value-Completion

An alternative way to achieve a notion of error-completion is to introduce error *values* in the domains of the original output variables, without adding new error variables. Let us discuss this alternative.

Let ϕ be a formula over input and output variables $X \cup Y$. In this subsection, we assume that Y is non-empty. For each variable v, let D_v denote the domain of v, i.e., the set of all possible values that v can take. Let $\perp$ be a new value, not in D_v, for any v. Let $D_v^{\perp} := D_v \cup \{\perp\}$. The *value-completion* of ϕ is a formula $\mathsf{VC}(\phi)$ over $X \cup Y$, where every output variable y is assumed to range over domain $D_y^{\perp}$. $\mathsf{VC}(\phi)$ is defined as follows:

$$\mathsf{VC}(\phi) := \mathsf{in}(\phi) \rightarrow (\phi \wedge \bigwedge_{y \in Y} y \neq \perp) \tag{16}$$

As with $\mathsf{EC}(\phi)$, it is easy to verify that $\mathsf{VC}(\phi)$ is input-complete, for any ϕ.

For example, the contract $\phi \equiv (x_2 \neq 0 \wedge x_2 \cdot y = x_1)$ has the following value-completion:

$$\mathsf{VC}(\phi) \equiv x_2 \neq 0 \rightarrow (x_2 \cdot y = x_1 \wedge y \neq \perp)$$

Consider a value-complete formula ϕ_b. Interpreting ϕ_b as a relation, we can define the inverse operation VC^{-1} which yields a formula over $X \cup Y$, where each output variable y ranges over D_y. $\mathsf{VC}^{-1}(\phi_b)$ will contain all valuations

(a_X, a_Y) over $\mathcal{A}(X \cup Y)$, such that $(a_X, a_Y) \in \phi_b$ and if there exists a'_Y such that $(a_X, a'_Y) \in \phi_b$, then for all $y \in Y$, $a'_Y(y) \neq \perp$. Formally:

$$VC^{-1}(\phi_b) := \{(a_X, a_Y) \in \mathcal{A}(X \cup Y) \mid (a_X, a_Y) \in \phi_b \land$$
$$\forall a'_Y : (a_X, a'_Y) \in \phi_b \to \forall y \in Y : a'_Y(y) \neq \perp \}$$

We can show that VC^{-1} is a left inverse of VC:

$$VC^{-1}(VC(\phi)) \equiv \phi$$

In a similar way that we used to define MECI, we can now define a space of meaningful value-complete interfaces, or MVCI, which is a subclass of VCI, the set of all value-complete interfaces. Doing so, we obtain a bijection, VC, between RI and MVCI. We also have the bijection EC between RI and MECI. Therefore, there exists a bijection between MECI and MVCI, which means that MECI and MVCI are isomorphic. This is illustrated in Figure 7, which expands our previous Figure 4.

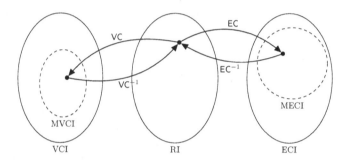

Fig. 7. Meaningful value-complete and error-complete interfaces

5   Related Work

Component-based design is one of the holy grails of computer science, and as a result, a large number of compositional specification and design frameworks exist in the literature. See, for instance, [21,1,15,17,4], and the related work discussion in [22]. As mentioned in the introduction, our work follows the approach of interface theories [9,10], where specifications can be non-input-complete. This is in contrast with other compositional theories such as I/O automata [16], FO-CUS [5,6], and reactive modules [2], where specifications are assumed to be input-complete.

Input-completion of finite automata is a folklore technique. Given a finite automaton with a partial transition function, input-completion consists in adding one extra, non-accepting, state to the automaton, and directing all missing transitions to that state. This results in an equivalent automaton which accepts the same language as the original one. Moreover, the resulting automaton has a total transition function, thus can be seen as being "input-complete". Input-completion can be adapted to interface automata [10] in a straightforward way: add an error state, direct all missing inputs to that state, and add a self-loop for any possible (input or output, and assuming no internal) action to the error state. This transformation appears to correctly reduce the alternating refinement relation between interface automata to a standard simulation relation, however, we were unable to find a reference in the literature to corroborate this.

In the context of viewing programs as predicates or relations [19,14], the question arises whether these relations should be total or partial. This question naturally arises in sequential programs that contain "while" loops, and where modeling program (non-)termination is a concern. The question has received a lot of attention in the literature (see [18] for a survey) and has also generated some controversy [13]. In this paper we accept as a fact that partial relations (i.e., non-input-complete interfaces) are useful, so non-input-completeness is our starting point. An extensive argument on the usefulness of non-input-completeness can be found in [22], which also introduces the framework of relational interfaces used in this paper.

Finally, as already mentioned in the introduction, the error-completion operator introduced in [22] is different from the one defined in this paper, which we believe is the right one.

6 Conclusions and Future Work

We presented a set of transformations EC, EC^{-1}, which allow to transform non-input-complete relational interfaces into input-complete ones, so that composition and refinement can be computed using standard methods on the error-complete domain. We emphasize that we do not propose error-complete interfaces as a new interface theory. We merely suggest them as convenient lossless representations of non-input-complete relational interfaces, which can make computation of composition and refinement easier.

Regarding future work, a number of algorithmic issues need to be resolved to make the relational interface theory (with or without error-completion) practical, including effective procedures for formula simplification and quantifier elimination. Another interesting question is raised in [22]: can feedback composition be defined for general interfaces, rather than for a subclass of stateful interfaces? This question remains open. Another issue is how to extend the relational interface theory to liveness properties. Finally, value-completion also deserves a more thorough study. In particular, it is not entirely obvious how to perform value-completion on sink components, that is, those with no outputs.

References

1. Abrial, J.-R.: The B-book: assigning programs to meanings. Cambridge University Press, New York (1996)
2. Alur, R., Henzinger, T.: Reactive modules. Formal Methods in System Design 15, 7–48 (1999)

3. Alur, R., Henzinger, T.A., Kupferman, O., Vardi, M.Y.: Alternating refinement relations. In: Sangiorgi, D., de Simone, R. (eds.) CONCUR 1998. LNCS, vol. 1466, pp. 163–178. Springer, Heidelberg (1998)
4. Back, R.-J., Wright, J.: Refinement Calculus. Springer (1998)
5. Broy, M.: Compositional refinement of interactive systems. J. ACM 44(6), 850–891 (1997)
6. Broy, M., Stølen, K.: Specification and development of interactive systems: focus on streams, interfaces, and refinement. Springer (2001)
7. Chakrabarti, A., de Alfaro, L., Henzinger, T.A., Mang, F.Y.C.: Synchronous and bidirectional component interfaces. In: Brinksma, E., Larsen, K.G. (eds.) CAV 2002. LNCS, vol. 2404, pp. 414–427. Springer, Heidelberg (2002)
8. de Alfaro, L.: Game models for open systems. In: Dershowitz, N. (ed.) Verification: Theory and Practice. LNCS, vol. 2772, pp. 269–289. Springer, Heidelberg (2004)
9. de Alfaro, L., Henzinger, T.: Interface automata. In: Foundations of Software Engineering, FSE. ACM Press (2001)
10. de Alfaro, L., Henzinger, T.A.: Interface theories for component-based design. In: Henzinger, T.A., Kirsch, C.M. (eds.) EMSOFT 2001. LNCS, vol. 2211, pp. 148–165. Springer, Heidelberg (2001)
11. Doyen, L., Henzinger, T., Jobstmann, B., Petrov, T.: Interface theories with component reuse. In: 8th ACM & IEEE International Conference on Embedded Software, EMSOFT, pp. 79–88 (2008)
12. Geilen, M., Tripakis, S., Wiggers, M.: The Earlier the Better: A Theory of Timed Actor Interfaces. In: 14th Intl. Conf. Hybrid Systems: Computation and Control, HSCC 2011. ACM (2011)
13. Hehner, E.C.R., Parnas, D.L.: Technical correspondence. Commun. ACM 28(5), 534–538 (1985)
14. Hoare, C.A.R.: Programs are predicates. In: Proc. of a Discussion Meeting of the Royal Society of London on Mathematical Logic and Programming Languages, pp. 141–155. Prentice-Hall, Inc., Upper Saddle River (1985)
15. Liskov, B.: Modular program construction using abstractions. In: Bjorner, D. (ed.) Abstract Software Specifications. LNCS, vol. 86, pp. 354–389. Springer, Heidelberg (1980)
16. Lynch, N.A., Tuttle, M.R.: An introduction to input/output automata. CWI Quarterly 2, 219–246 (1989)
17. Meyer, B.: Applying "design by contract". Computer 25(10), 40–51 (1992)
18. Nelson, G.: A generalization of dijkstra's calculus. ACM Trans. Program. Lang. Syst. 11(4), 517–561 (1989)
19. Parnas, D.L.: A generalized control structure and its formal definition. Commun. ACM 26(8), 572–581 (1983)
20. Raclet, J.-B., Badouel, E., Benveniste, A., Caillaud, B., Legay, A., Passerone, R.: A modal interface theory for component-based design. Fundam. Inf. 108(1-2), 119–149 (2011)
21. Spivey, J.M.: The Z notation: a reference manual. Prentice-Hall, Inc., Upper Saddle River (1989)
22. Tripakis, S., Lickly, B., Henzinger, T.A., Lee, E.A.: A theory of synchronous relational interfaces. ACM Transactions on Programming Languages and Systems (TOPLAS) 33(4) (July 2011)

Author Index